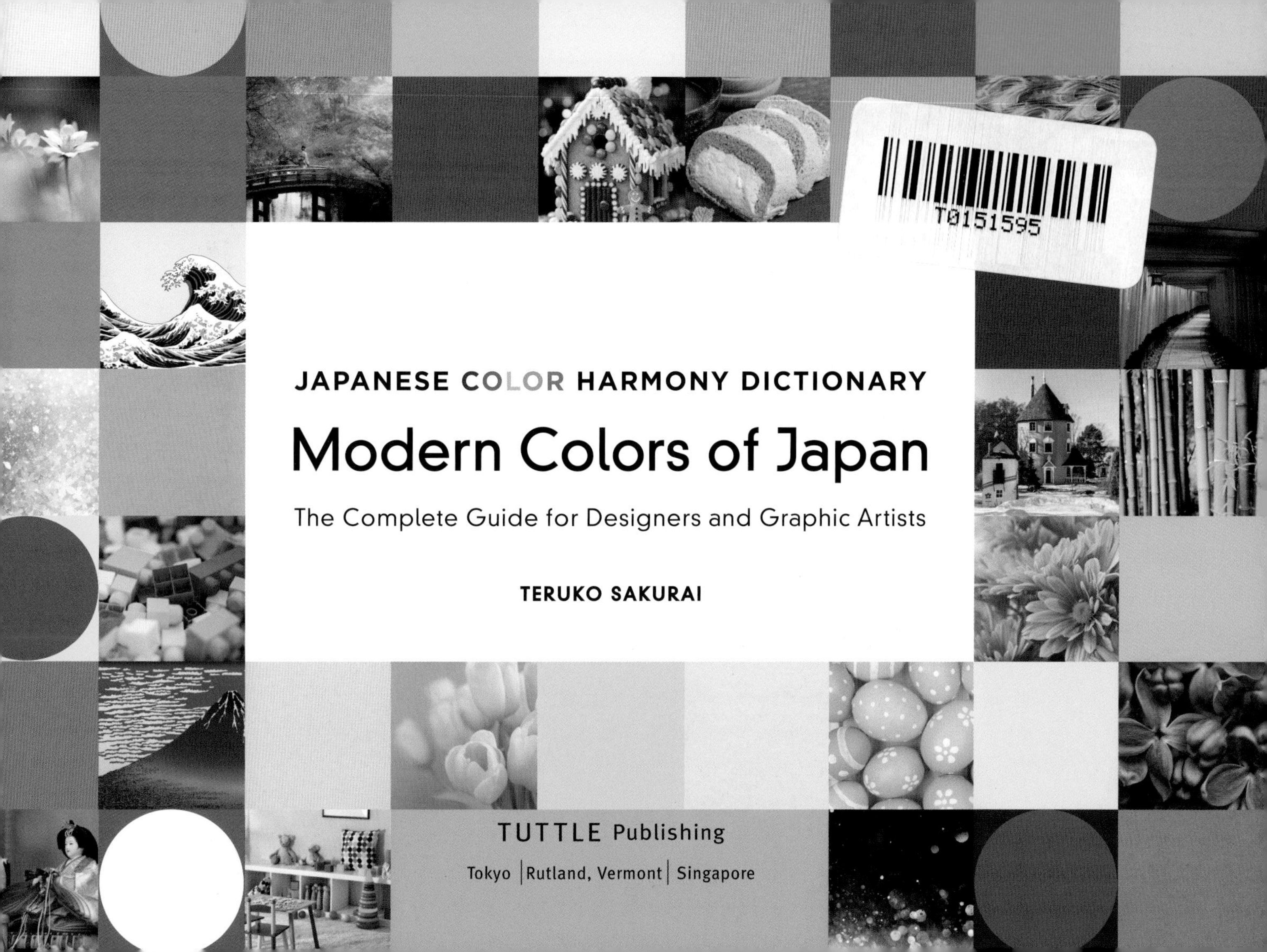

JAPANESE COLOR HARMONY DICTIONARY

Modern Colors of Japan

The Complete Guide for Designers and Graphic Artists

TERUKO SAKURAI

TUTTLE Publishing

Tokyo | Rutland, Vermont | Singapore

Contents

Part 01
Casual + Active + Pop

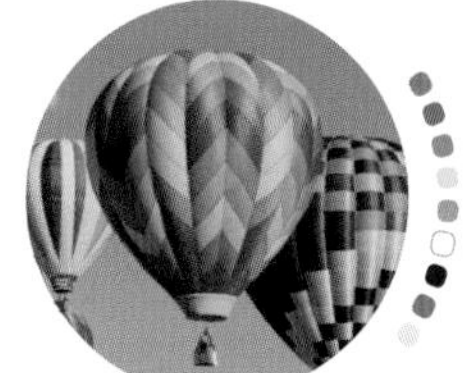

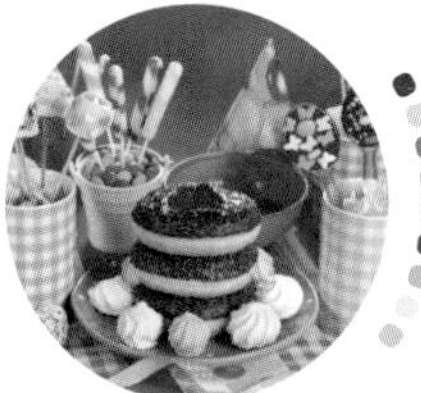

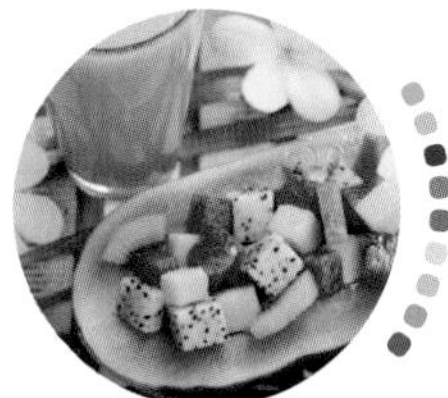

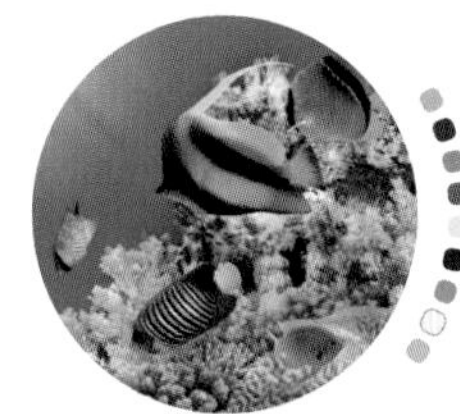

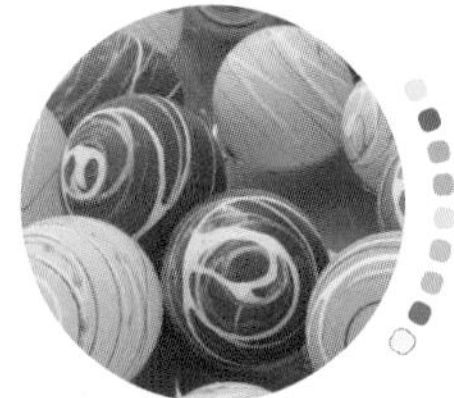

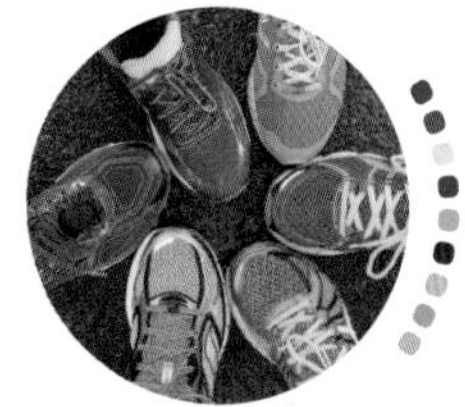

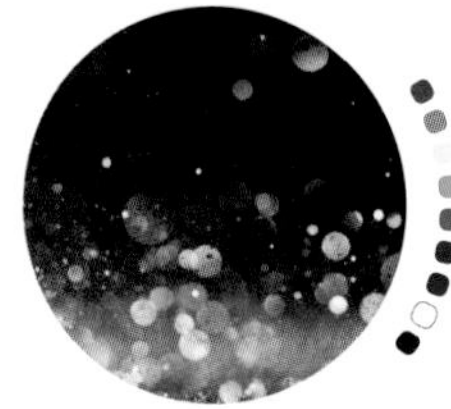

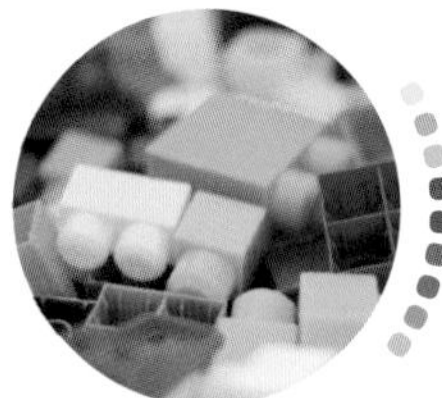

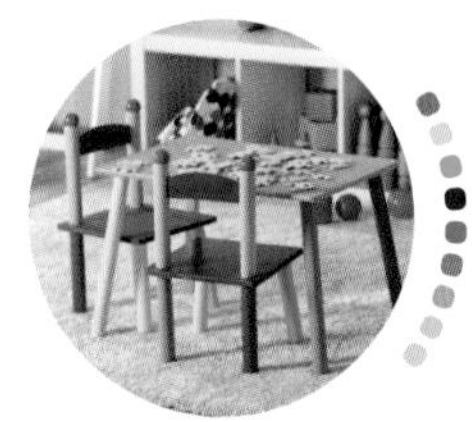

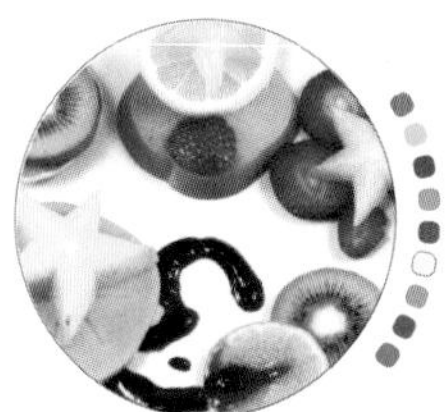

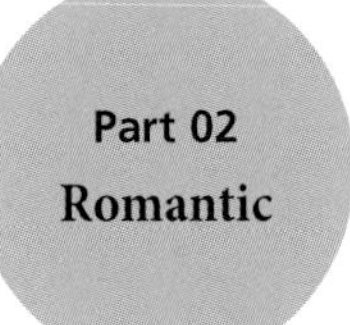

Part 02 Romantic

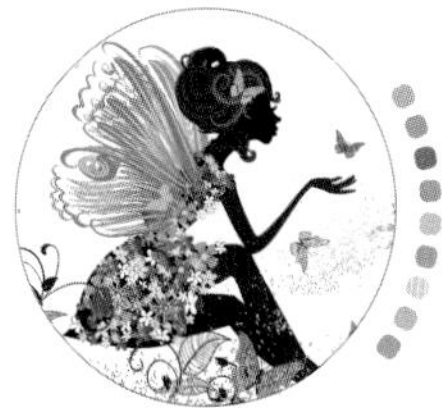

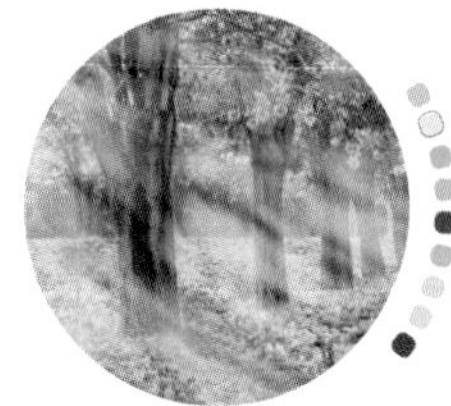

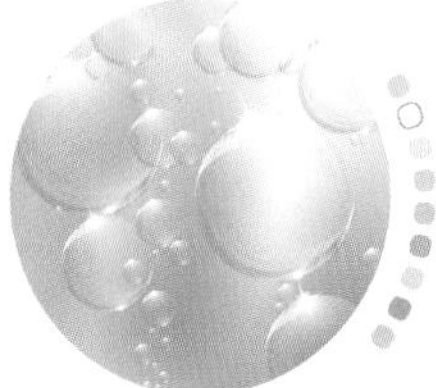

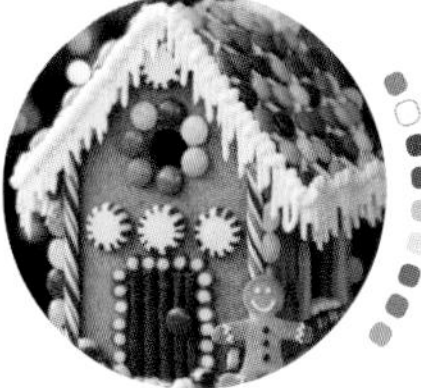

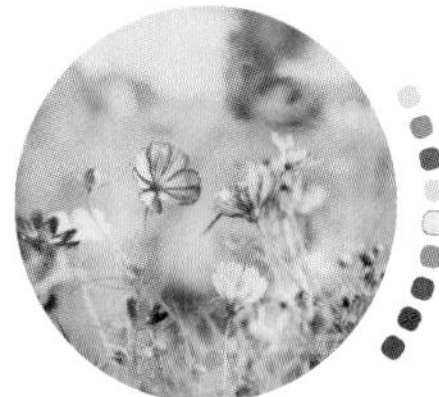

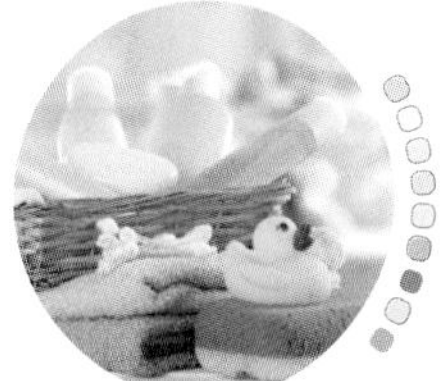

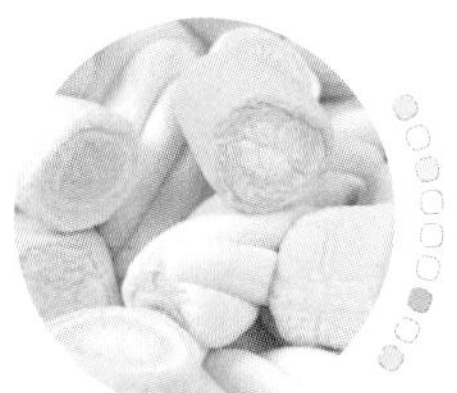

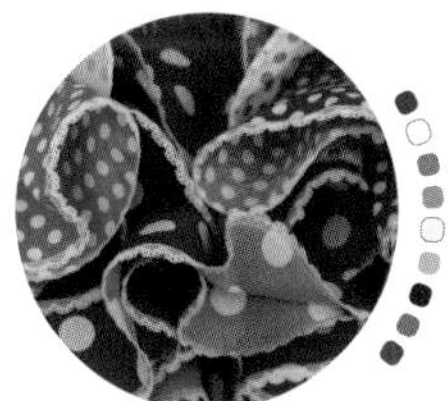

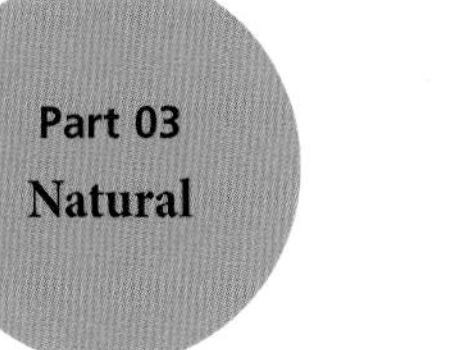

Part 03 Natural

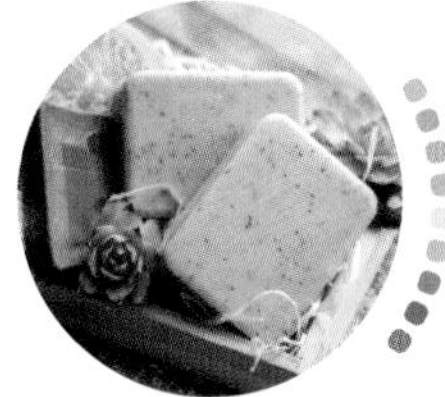

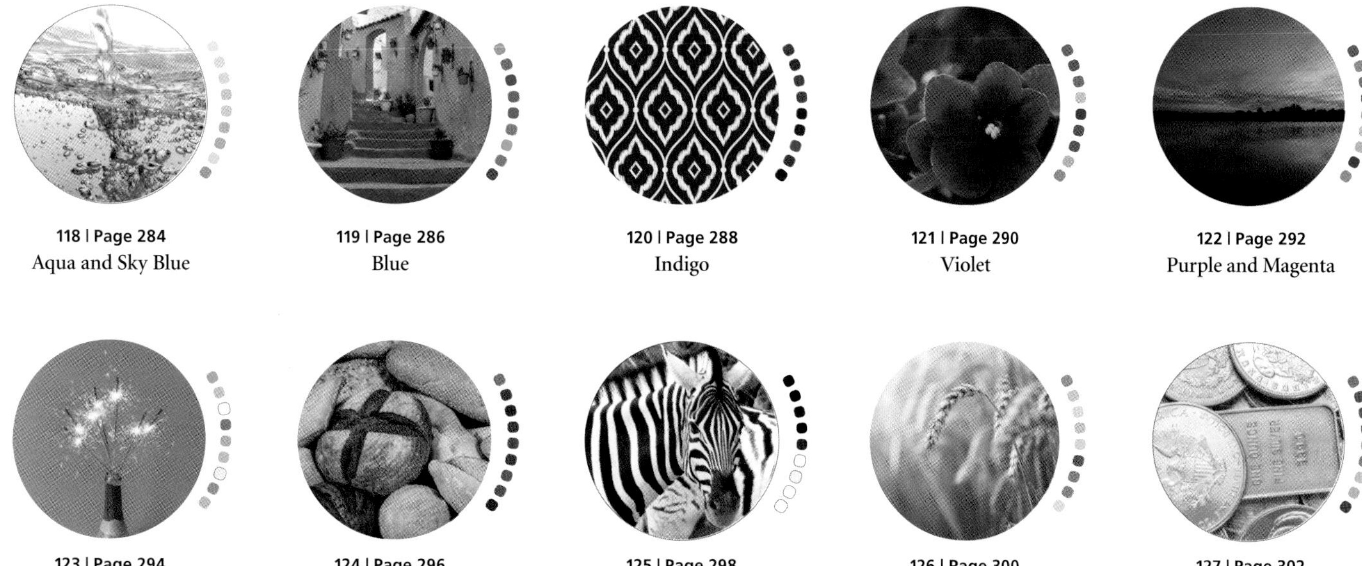

Notes on the names of colors

In this book, some colors have been independently named by the author according to various ideas and evocative images. Other colors use the names prescribed under Japanese Industrial Standards JIS Z 8102:2001, "names of non-luminous object colors." Color names that include JIS in their titles and colors from Part 13, "Rainbow Palettes," are colors recognized by the above Japanese Industrial Standards.

Notes on CMYK and RGB numerical values

Colors can appear different depending on the materials and methods of printing, computer screen displays and output device. Please treat the CMYK and RGB numerical values as references only.

How to Use This Book

The main sections of this book are divided broadly into four "steps." Step 1, the "theme and image evoked by the colors," is to enjoy the Japanese colors and stories behind them. Step 2 is "the color scheme palette and numerical values of the colors," which allows the colors to be incorporated into designs with Japanese influence. Step 3 involves "color scheme examples" using two-color and three-color combinations. Step 4 includes "examples of the

❶ **CHAPTER INDEX COLORS**
A different colored tab is used for each chapter.

❷ **THEME NUMBERS**
Each of the 127 color themes or "recipes" is numbered.

❸ **THEME NAMES**
Each of the color themes has a name.

❹ **LEAD PARAGRAPHS**
Topics and anecdotes to help describe the inspiration behind the colors are featured here.

❺ **KEY POINTS**
A list of important points to consider when using the themed color scheme.

❻ **PHOTOGRAPHS AND CAPTIONS**
The photograph (or illustration) on which the color theme is based, along with a brief description.

❼ **COLOR SCHEME PALETTES AND SWATCHES**
There are nine colors in each color scheme. The color swatch is gradated in order to create a sense of what the color looks like in solid form.

❽ **COLOR SCHEME NUMBERS**
The number of the colors within the color scheme and an explanation of the color's origins are given here.

❾ **NUMERICAL VALUES**
The numerical CMYK and RGB values corresponding to the color scheme numbers are given here. Values beginning with the hash symbol (#) in the third row of numerical values are the 16-bit RGB numbers.

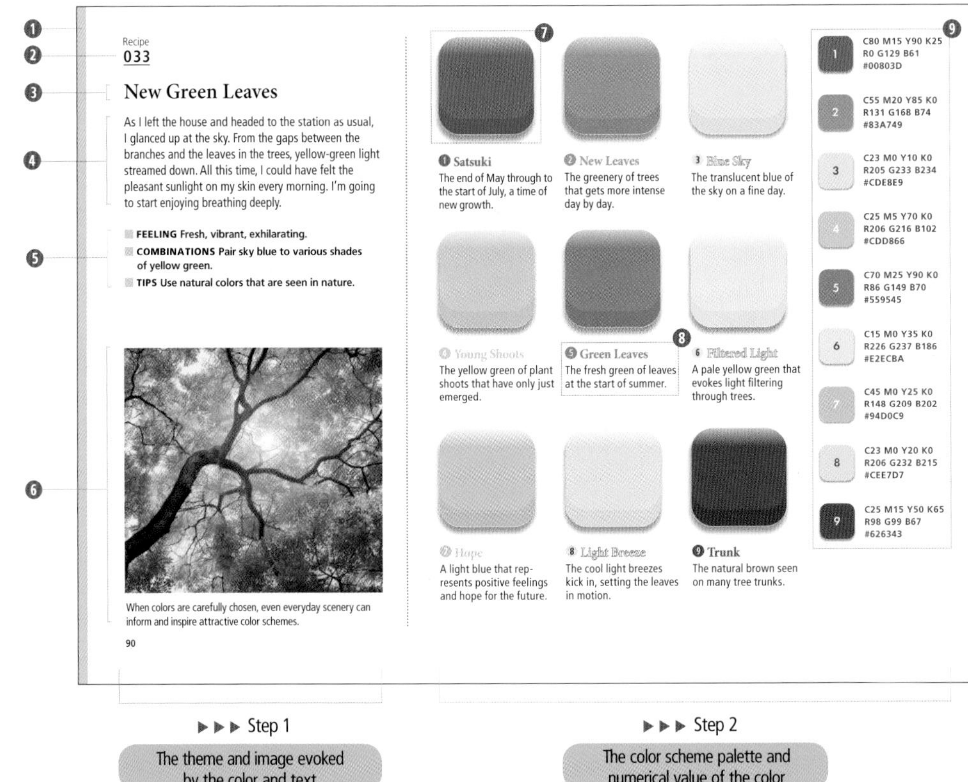

❶
❷ Recipe 033
❸ New Green Leaves

❹ As I left the house and headed to the station as usual, I glanced up at the sky. From the gaps between the branches and the leaves in the trees, yellow-green light streamed down. All this time, I could have felt the pleasant sunlight on my skin every morning. I'm going to start enjoying breathing deeply.

❺
FEELING Fresh, vibrant, exhilarating.
COMBINATIONS Pair sky blue to various shades of yellow green.
TIPS Use natural colors that are seen in nature.

❻ When colors are carefully chosen, even everyday scenery can inform and inspire attractive color schemes.

90

❼ ❽

1 Satsuki
The end of May through to the start of July, a time of new growth.

2 New Leaves
The greenery of trees that gets more intense day by day.

3 Blue Sky
The translucent blue of the sky on a fine day.

4 Young Shoots
The yellow green of plant shoots that have only just emerged.

5 Green Leaves
The fresh green of leaves at the start of summer.

6 Filtered Light
A pale yellow green that evokes light filtering through trees.

7 Hope
A light blue that represents positive feelings and hope for the future.

8 Light Breeze
The cool light breezes kick in, setting the leaves in motion.

9 Trunk
The natural brown seen on many tree trunks.

❾

1	C80 M15 Y90 K25 R0 G129 B61 #00803D
2	C55 M20 Y85 K0 R131 G168 B74 #83A749
3	C23 M0 Y10 K0 R205 G233 B234 #CDE8E9
4	C25 M5 Y70 K0 R206 G216 B102 #CDD866
5	C70 M25 Y90 K0 R86 G149 B70 #559545
6	C15 M0 Y35 K0 R226 G237 B186 #E2ECBA
7	C45 M0 Y25 K0 R148 G209 B202 #94D0C9
8	C23 M0 Y20 K0 R206 G232 B215 #CEE7D7
9	C25 M15 Y50 K65 R98 G99 B67 #626343

▶▶▶ Step 1
The theme and image evoked by the color and text

▶▶▶ Step 2
The color scheme palette and numerical value of the color

color scheme in designs and illustrations" and shows actual examples of the scheme in use. This book is designed to allow applications of the color schemes to become reality little by little from Steps 1 to 4, and can be used in various situations by anyone from beginners through to advanced level users of color. Flip through the book to find a theme you like and then refer to the colors to begin using the color schemes.

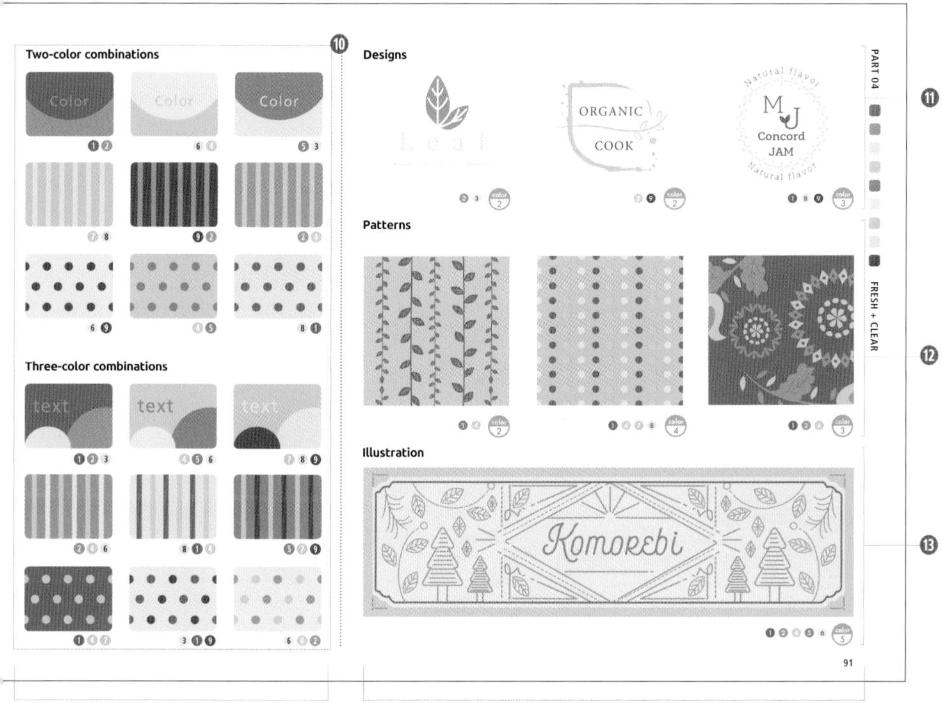

⑩ Two-color combinations

Three-color combinations

Designs ⑪

Patterns ⑫

Illustration ⑬

▶▶▶ Step 3

Simple color scheme examples

▶▶▶ Step 4

Examples of the color scheme used in designs and illustrations

⑩ COLOR COMBINATIONS WITH TWO/THREE COLORS

Simple, functional color schemes of two and three colors are provided here. The color numbers for both the two- and the three-color schemes run from the left, starting with the color taking up the greatest surface area.

⑪ DESIGN COLOR SCHEMES

Specific examples of color schemes matched to designs used for logos and patterns are provided here. The color icons at bottom right are the numbers of colors used.

⑫ PATTERN COLOR SCHEMES

Specific examples of color schemes matched to patterns and textures are provided here.

⑬ ILLUSTRATION COLOR SCHEMES

Specific examples of schemes matched to illustrations are included here. The color numbers for designs, patterns and illustrations are listed in numerical order.

The advantages of a book having long, wide pages and a short height

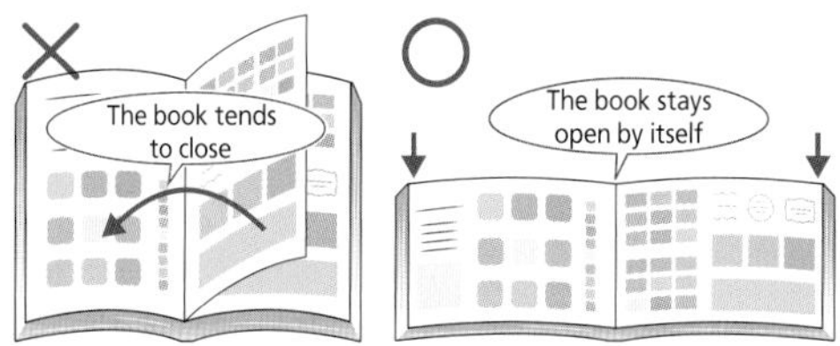

The horizontal length means the book's own weight stops it from closing and it can stand by itself.

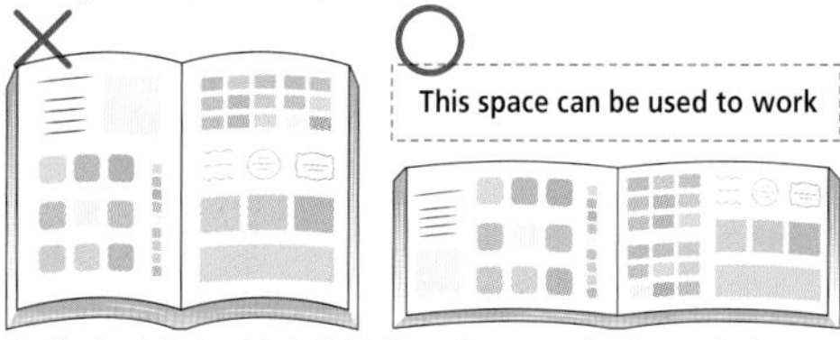

As the book is short in height, it can be opened out on a desk without interfering with your work space.

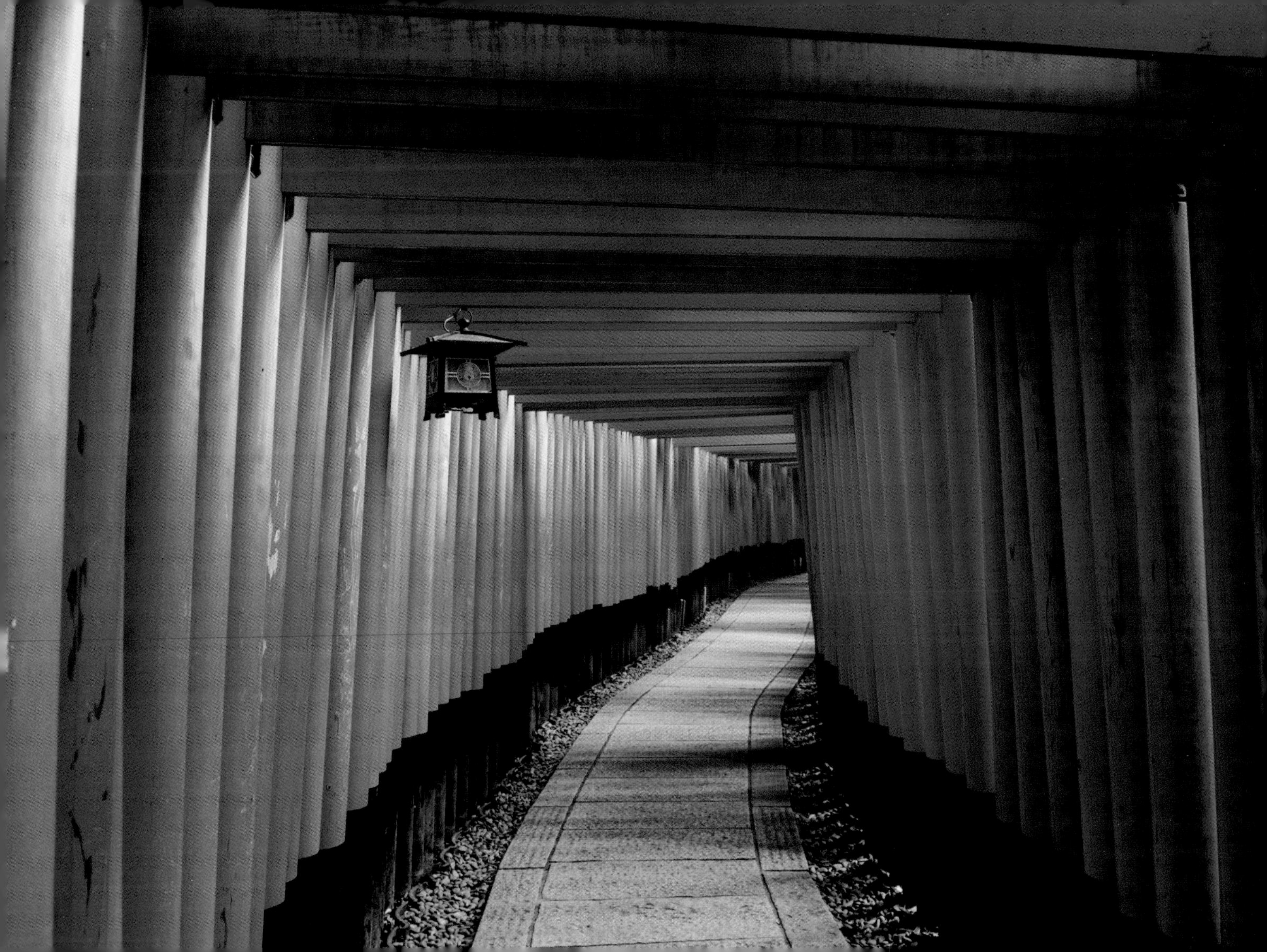

Why I Write This Book

My aim in assembling this modern take on Japanese design, imagery and inspiration was to create a color scheme reference unlike any other.

Each of the 127 color themes in the book is created using a nine-color palette, with photographs accompanied by anecdotes and observations about the colors to further extend the worlds suggested by the themes.

For each color, practical combinations with one or two other colors are listed along with designs, patterns and illustrations that apply the various colors.

This means that there are a total of 3,300 color scheme samples that can be used in a variety of situations from basic to more advanced. Make use of these images as a creative tool to enhance your designs and ideas in the same way as you might enjoy looking at a favorite magazine, coffee table book or any resource that captures your eye and excites your mind.

I hope this book fires your imagination and inspires you to color your world in boldly modern ways!

—***Teruko Sakurai***

Part

01

Casual + Active + Pop

Evoking scenes from parties and festivals along with rainbow motifs, these color schemes are created purely from vibrant tones such as the bright, bursting hues of tropical fruits. It's a fun color palette that seems to leap from the page.

Color Schemes That are Cheerful, Fun and Active.

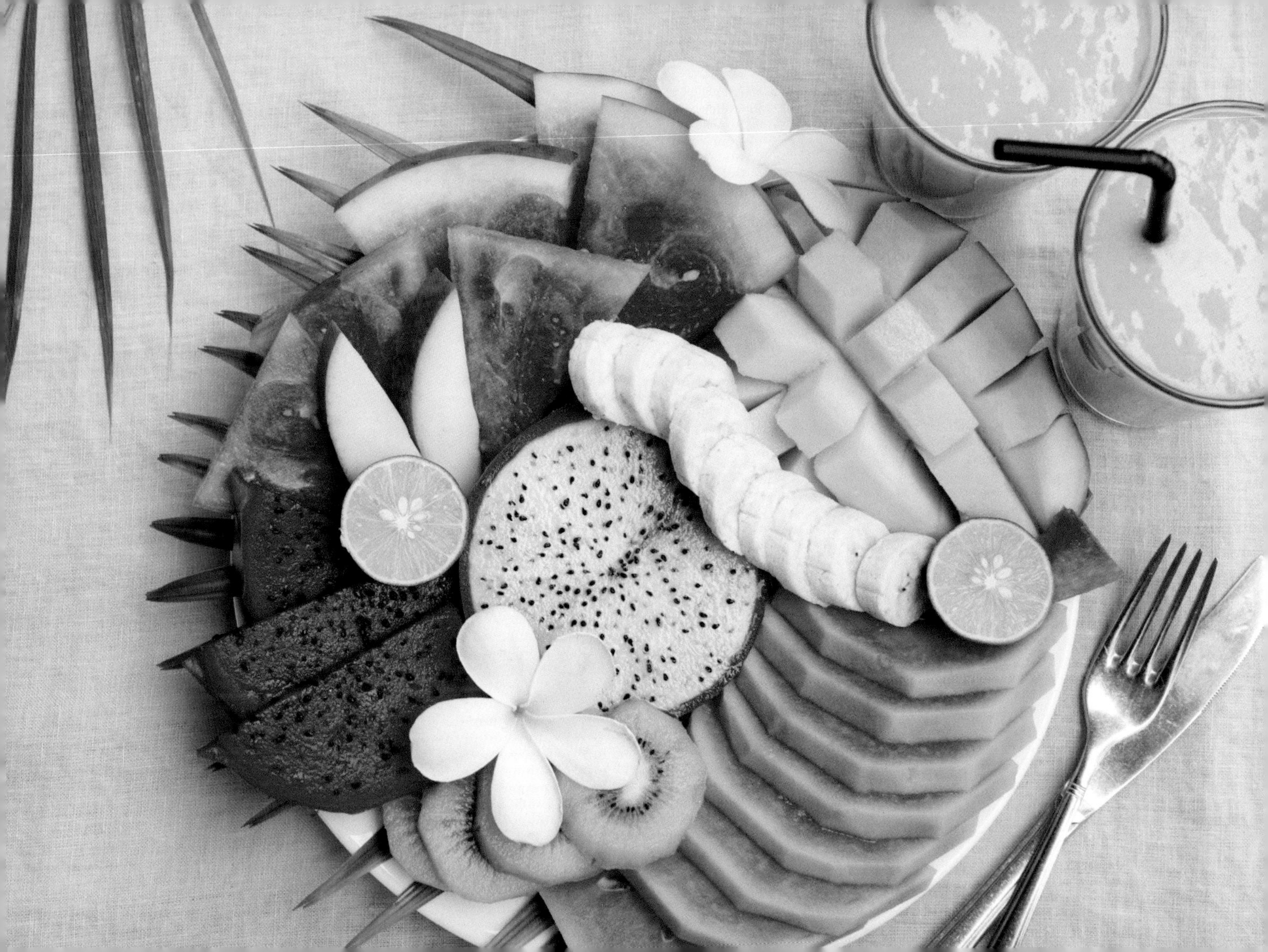

Recipe

001

Hot Air Balloon Festival

Floating in a hot air balloon is an experience that many want to try once in their life. The world's largest hot-air balloon festival is held every October in Albuquerque, New Mexico. It's an ideal location with its remarkable clear blue skies and pleasant weather year-round. This is a color scheme drawn from the sky, clouds and sun.

- **FEELING Energized, bold, fresh.**
- **COMBINATIONS Combine colorful shades in a polychromatic color scheme.***
- **TIPS Using mainly warm shades makes the color scheme even more eye-catching.**

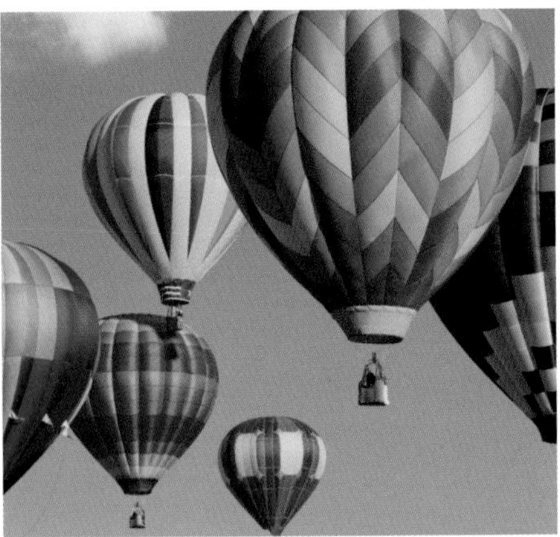

The highly saturated tones of the colorful balloons against the blue sky offer a study in contrasting patterns.

❶ Cerulean Blue
The brisk, refreshing blue of a perfectly clear sky.

❷ Rescue Orange
The highly visible, eye-catching orange of rescue teams' uniforms.

❸ Flame Orange
The passionate orange of blazing flames.

❹ Sunshine
A vibrant yellow evocative of the sun's rays.

❺ Sky High
A vivid blue like that of the sky on a fine day.

⑥ White Cloud
The white of clouds drifting across the sky before disappearing.

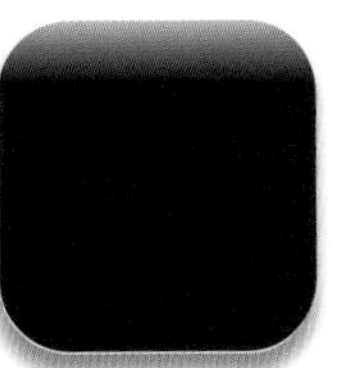

❼ Lapis Lazuli
A deep blue like that of lapis lazuli stone; also called azure.

❽ Forest Leaf
The green of forest trees emanating a sense a quiet power.

❾ Pale Sky Blue
The color of the sky at dusk—a bright, translucent blue.

1 C80 M0 Y5 K30
R0 G141 B183
#008DB7

2 C0 M80 Y100 K0
R234 G85 B4
#EA5404

3 C0 M65 Y100 K0
R238 G120 B0
#EE7700

4 C0 M13 Y100 K0
R255 G220 B0
#FFDC00

5 C65 M20 Y0 K0
R82 G165 B220
#51A5DC

6 C5 M0 Y0 K0
R245 G251 B254
#F5FAFE

7 C97 M100 Y0 K0
R38 G31 B135
#261F87

8 C100 M0 Y80 K23
R0 G133 B84
#008554

9 C27 M0 Y0 K0
R194 G230 B250
#C2E5F9

* Polychromatic color scheme is a color scheme that combines more than four different shades; also called multicolor.

Two-color combinations

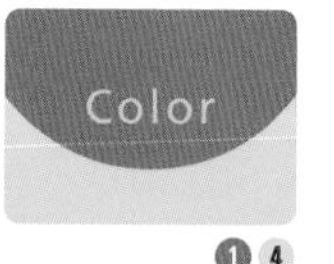

1 4

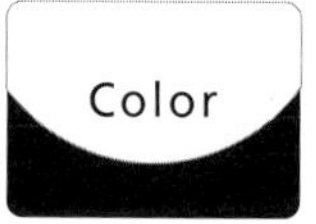

6 7

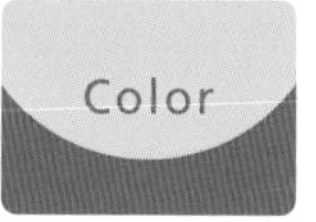
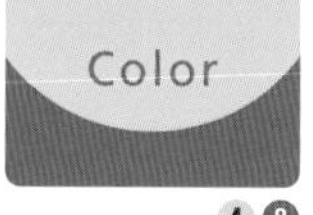

4 8

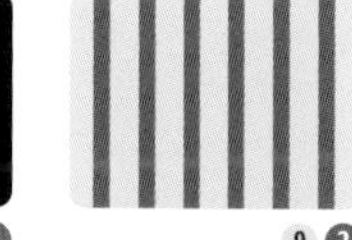

7 8

9 2

5 3

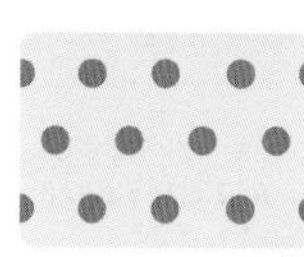

9 1

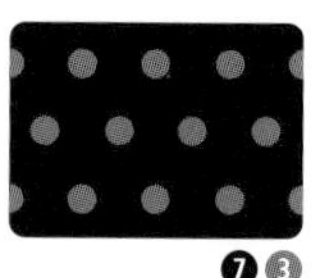

7 3

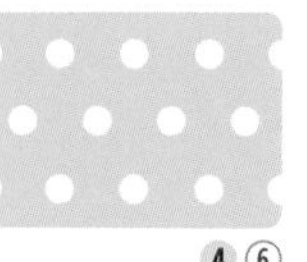

4 6

Three-color combinations

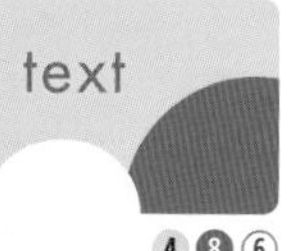

4 8 6

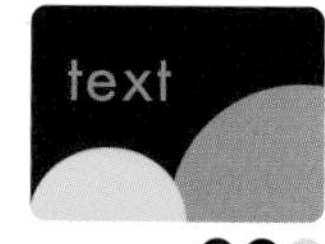

7 5 4

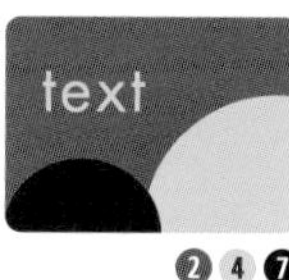

2 4 7

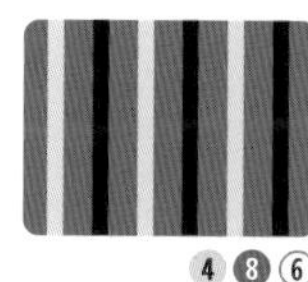

4 8 6

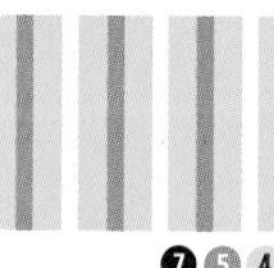

7 5 4

2 4 7

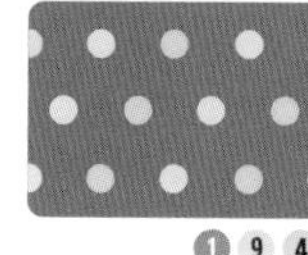

1 9 4

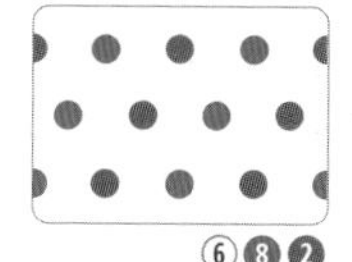

6 8 2

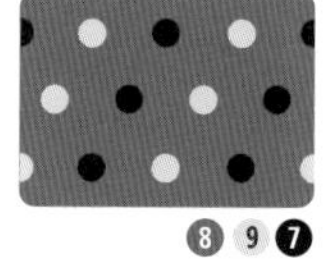

8 9 7

Designs

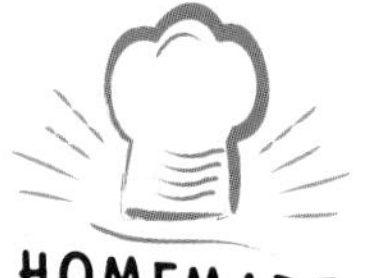

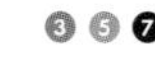
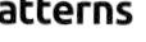

3 5 7 color 3

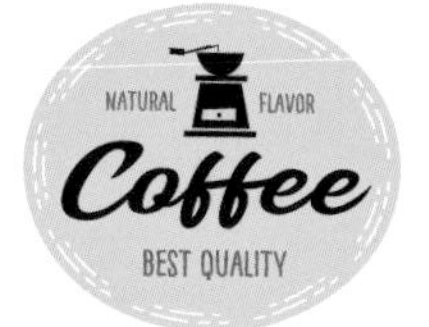

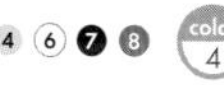

4 6 7 8 color 4

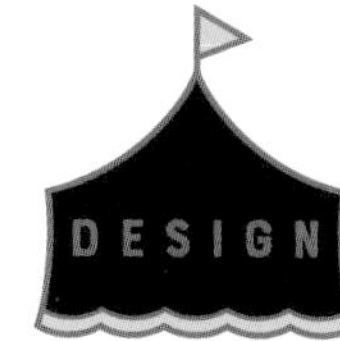

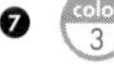

3 4 7 color 3

Patterns

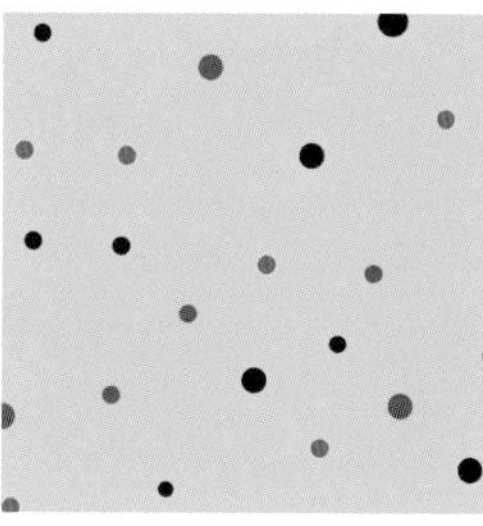

2 4 7 8 color 4

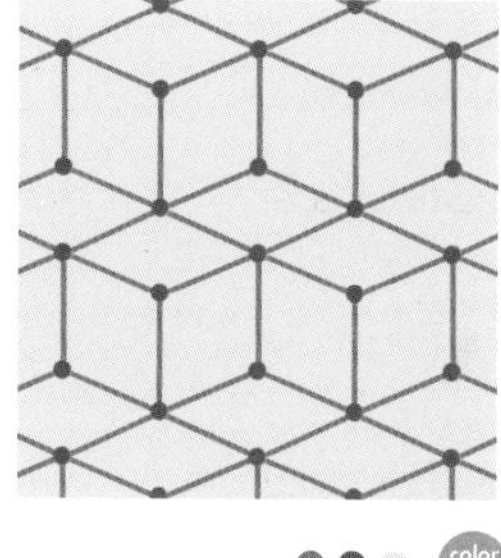

1 2 9 color 3

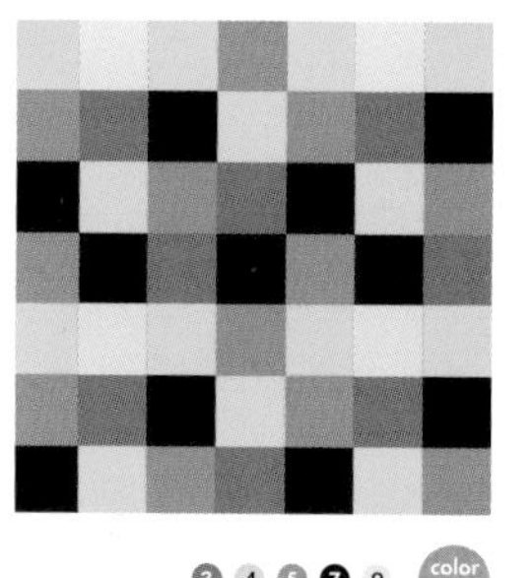

3 4 5 7 9 color 5

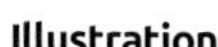

Illustration

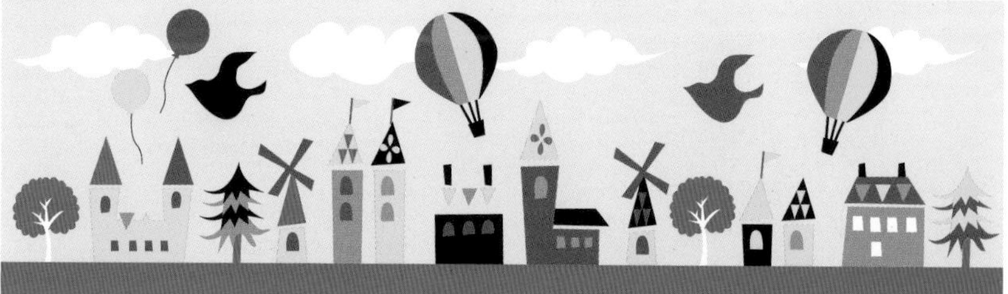

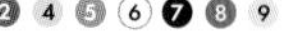

2 4 5 6 7 8 9 color 7

Recipe
002

Girls' Party

Bring some decadent desserts and we'll meet at the usual place! Just for today, we'll forget about our busy lives and chat as long as we like. Spending time with my best friends makes me come alive. With shocking pink as the main color, these colorful shades bring to mind a bright, energetic, positive woman.

- **FEELING** Gaudy, eye-catching, stimulating.
- **COMBINATIONS** Use highly saturated colors, focusing on pink shades.
- **TIPS** Using more than three colors at once is effective.

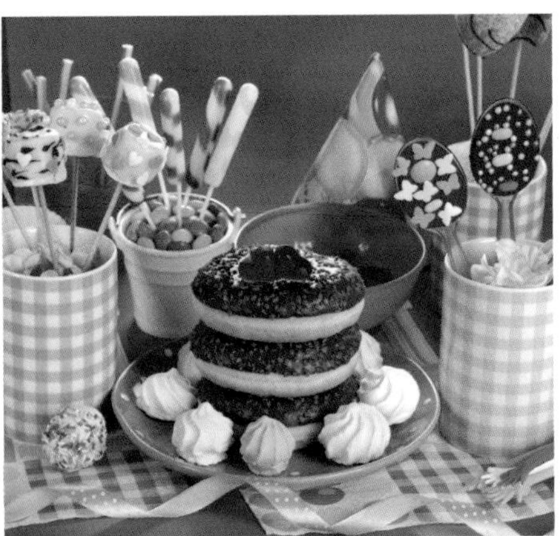

Gingham items also lend a girlish look.

❶ Magenta
One of the three primary colors for pigments, the name is derived from an area in Italy.

❷ Cherry-blossom
A pale, sweet pink like that of cherry blossoms.

❸ Shocking Pink
A vibrant, energetic pink that dazzles the eye.

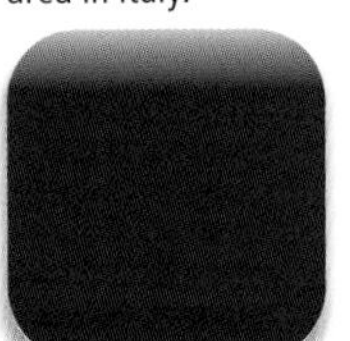

❹ Violet Bloom
An intense violet like that of the flower of the same name.

❺ Candy Pink
A pink associated with a sweet, soft flavor.

❻ Poppy Flower
The warm, vivid red of a poppy flower.

❼ Fresh Green
A green that evokes new shoots and fresh spring vegetables.

❽ Lemonade
A color like that of sweet-sour lemonade.

❾ Aqua
A translucent, refreshing blue.

1 C0 M100 Y0 K0 R228 G0 B127 #E4007E

2 C0 M25 Y0 K0 R249 G211 B227 #F8D2E3

3 C0 M75 Y0 K0 R234 G96 B158 #E9609E

4 C50 M100 Y0 K0 R146 G7 B131 #920683

5 C0 M43 Y20 K0 R244 G171 B175 #F3ABAE

6 C0 M97 Y70 K0 R230 G22 B58 #E61639

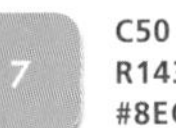

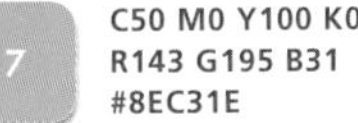

7 C50 M0 Y100 K0 R143 G195 B31 #8EC31E

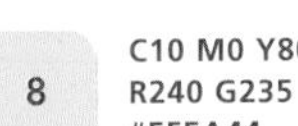

8 C10 M0 Y80 K0 R240 G235 B69 #EFEA44

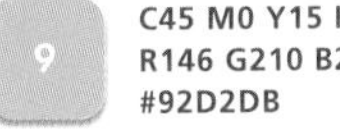

9 C45 M0 Y15 K0 R146 G210 B220 #92D2DB

Two-color combinations

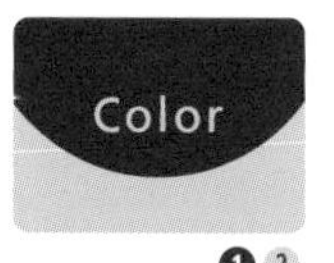

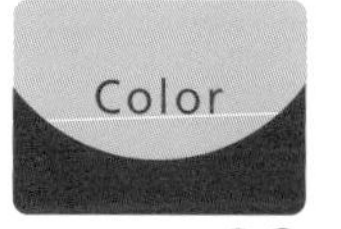

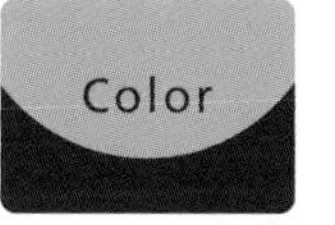

1 2   9 6   5 4

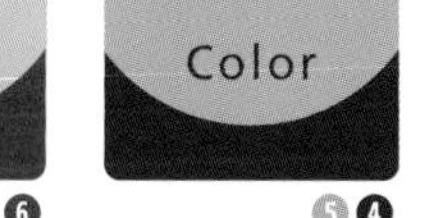

7 5   1 8   3 6

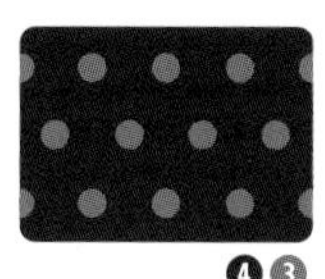

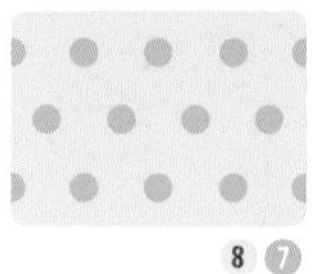

9 8   4 3   8 7

Three-color combinations

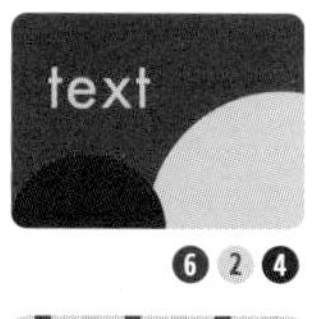

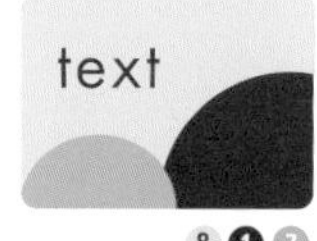

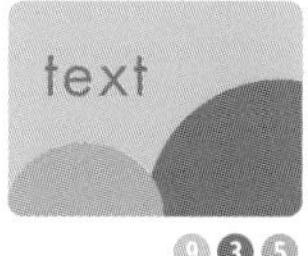

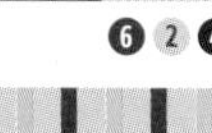

6 2 4   8 1 7   9 3 5

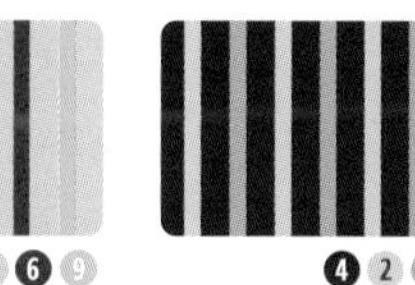

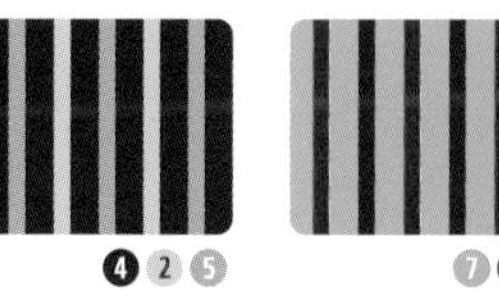

2 6 9   4 2 5   7 1 4

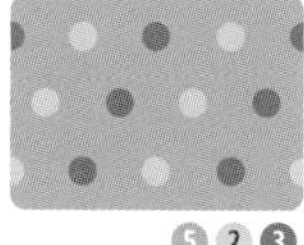

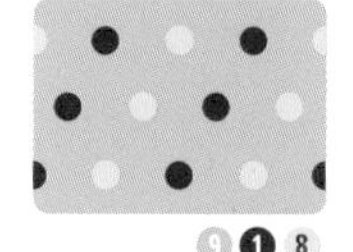

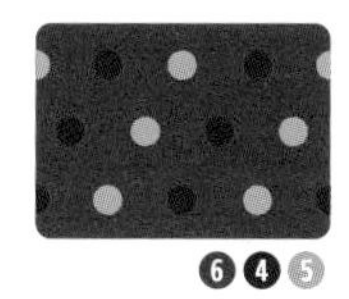

5 2 3   9 1 8   6 4 5

Designs

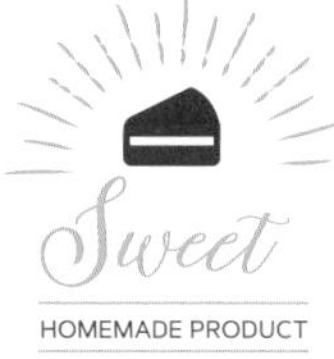

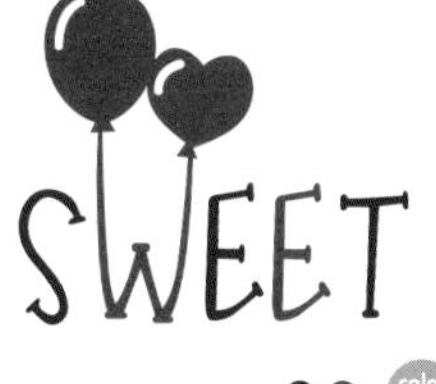

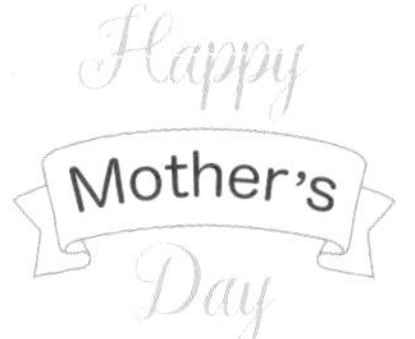

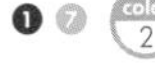

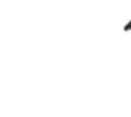

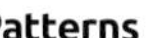

1 7 color 2   4 6 color 2   5 6 9 color 3

Patterns

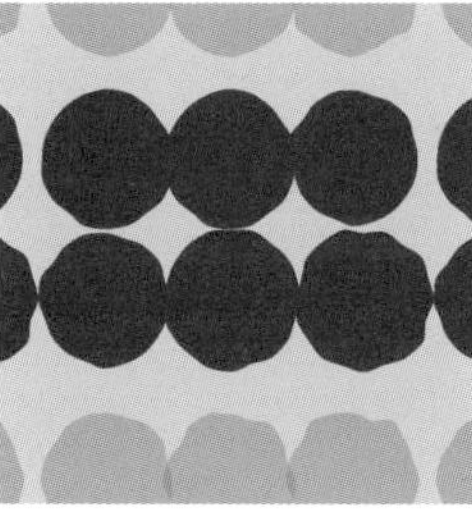

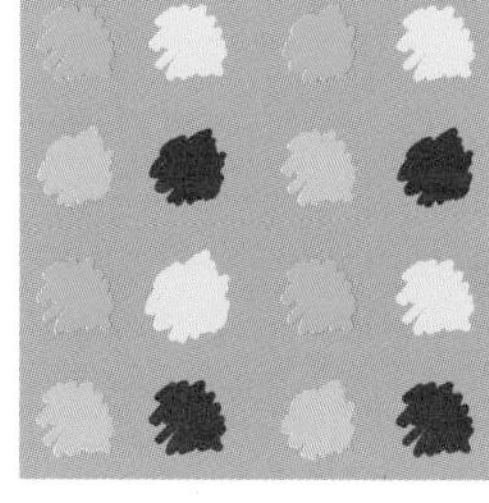

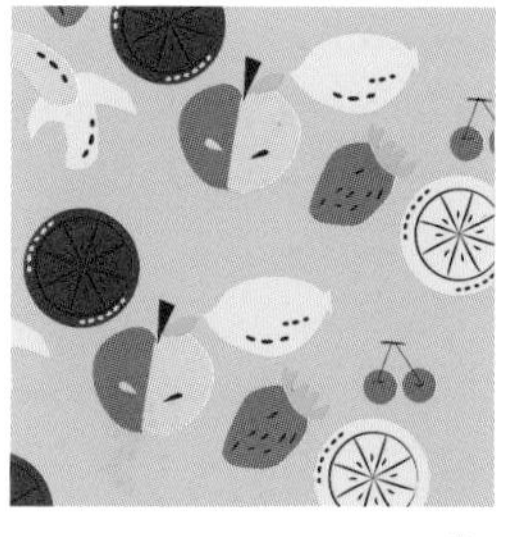

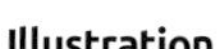

2 3 6 color 3   5 6 7 8 9 color 5   1 2 4 6 7 8 9 color 7

Illustration

1 2 3 4 5 6 7 8 9 color 9

Recipe

003

Tropical Fruits

Ripe and heavy on the tree from the strong rays of the sun, tropical fruits are exceptionally vibrant. The oranges and yellows often found in tropical fruits contrast with the emerald blue of Color 1, with each color complementing and highlighting the other. A combination of yellows and light greens like lemon and lime has been a popular pairing since the 1950s.

- **FEELING** Energetic, juicy, tropical.
- **COMBINATIONS** Boldly combine fruit colors.
- **TIPS** Make effective use of emerald blue.

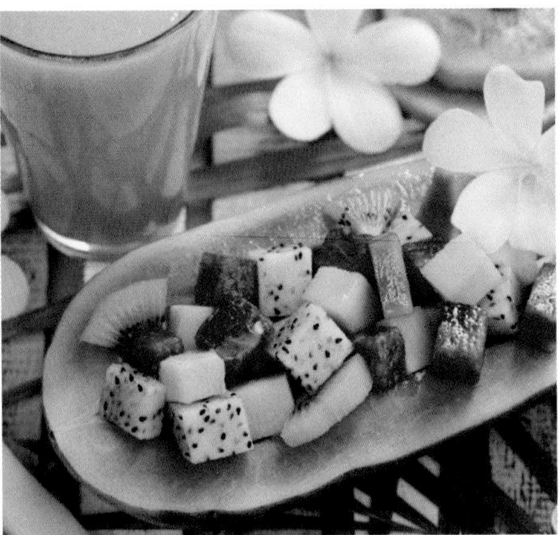

A tropical fruit salad highlights the role color plays in the foods we eat from the yellow of mango to papaya's distinctive orange.

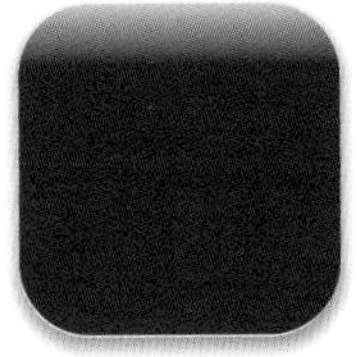

❶ Emerald Blue
A clear, intense blue like that of a tropical sea.

❷ Papaya
The color of papaya fruit, also called pawpaw.

❸ Dragonfruit
This tropical fruit has a red skin and white flesh.

❹ Juicy Orange
A juicy, freshly picked orange.

❺ Guava Juice
The color of sweetly sour guava juice.

❻ Banana
The yellow of the skin of a ripe banana.

❼ Golden Kiwi
The yellow color of kiwi fruit of this variety.

❽ Kiwi Fruit
The color of traditional kiwi fruit.

❾ Jungle Green
The green of lush vegetation on tropical islands.

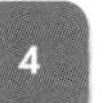

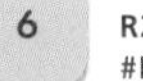

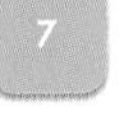

No.	CMYK	RGB	Hex
1	C73 M0 Y10 K0	R0 G181 B222	#00B5DE
2	C0 M35 Y90 K0	R248 G182 B22	#F8B516
3	C15 M100 Y90 K0	R208 G17 B38	#D01026
4	C0 M70 Y90 K0	R237 G109 B31	#EC6C1F
5	C0 M83 Y60 K0	R233 G76 B78	#E94C4D
6	C10 M10 Y90 K0	R238 G219 B21	#EDDA15
7	C30 M10 Y90 K0	R195 G202 B46	#C2CA2E
8	C60 M15 Y100 K0	R116 G169 B45	#73A82D
9	C85 M50 Y100 K0	R42 G110 B58	#2A6D39

Two-color combinations

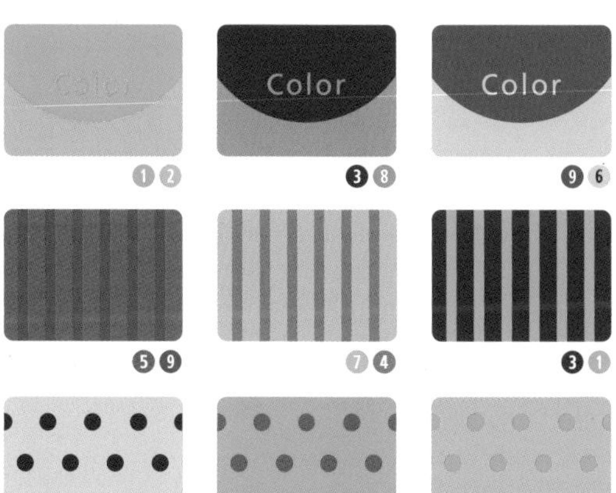

Three-color combinations

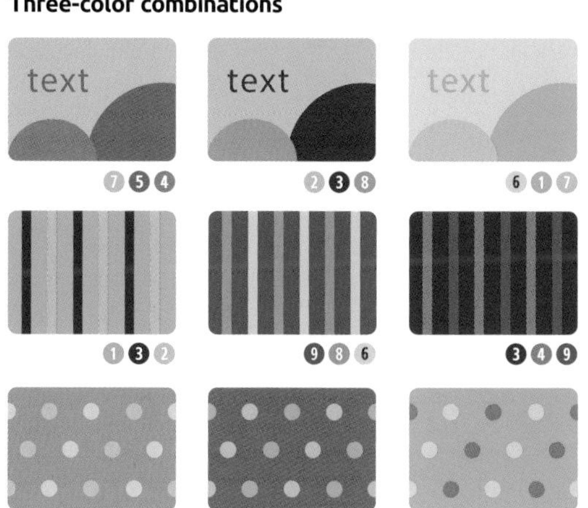

Designs

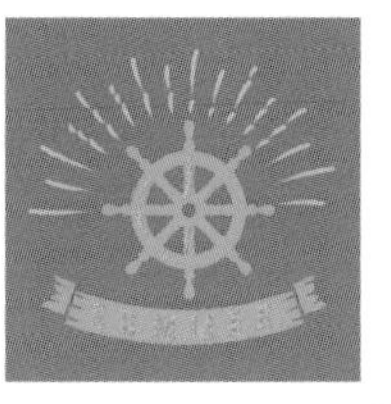
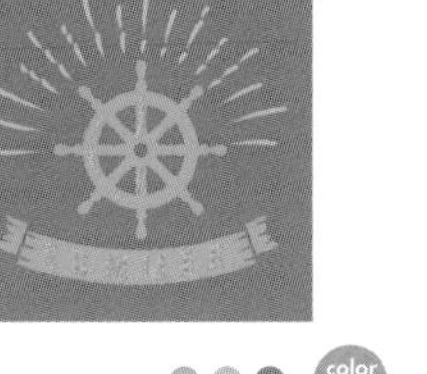
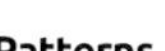
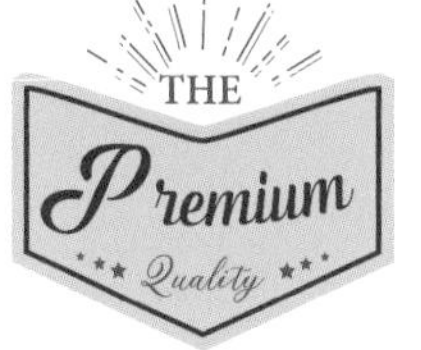

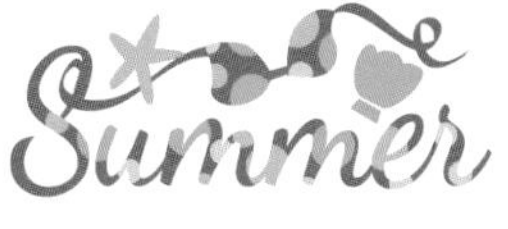

Patterns

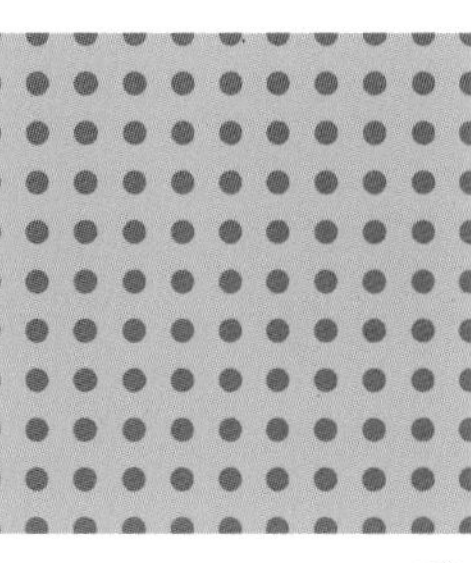
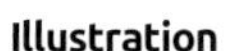
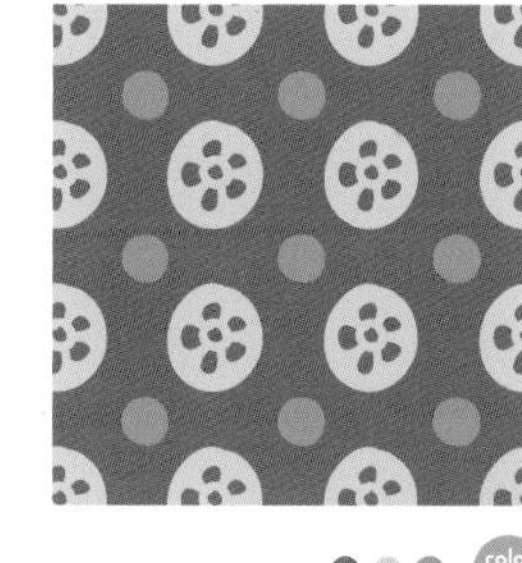
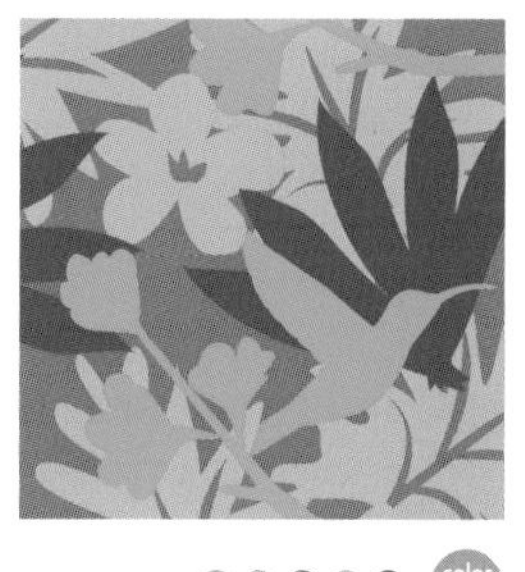

Illustration

Recipe
004

Tropical Paradise Fish

Seventy percent of the earth's surface is ocean, while 30 percent is land. The first time I went diving, viewing the endless expanse of the sea floor really allowed me to experience this fact for myself. In the coral reefs, colorful fish swim freely through the vast expanse. It's a whole other world of color.

- **FEELING** Colorful, lively, clear.
- **COMBINATIONS** Use different shades of blue as the base.
- **TIPS** Often the bodies of fish are covered in contrasting colors.*

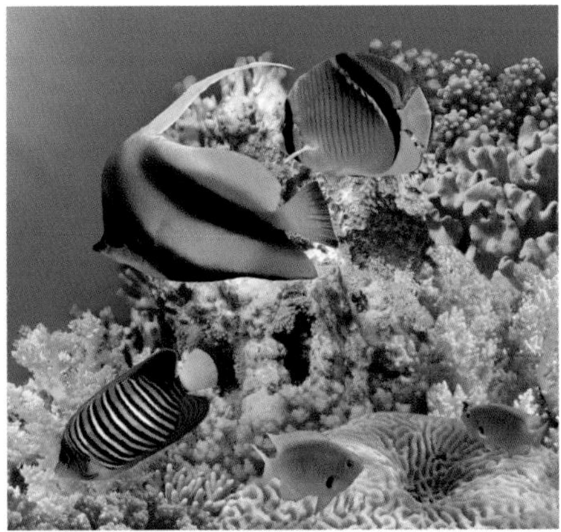

The clownfish is a familiar form, its bright stripes and garish colors make it a standout of the deep.

❶ Great Barrier Reef
The turquoise of the world's largest coral reef, located in Australia.

❷ Under the Sea
The blue of the ocean where fish dwell.

❸ Clownfish
A vivid orange like that on the body of the clownfish.

❹ Sea Anemone
A bright pink like that seen on a sea anemone.

5 Butterfly Fish
The yellow of a butterfly fish stands out for its vibrancy.

❻ Edge Black
Black appears primarily on the fins and tails of tropical fish.

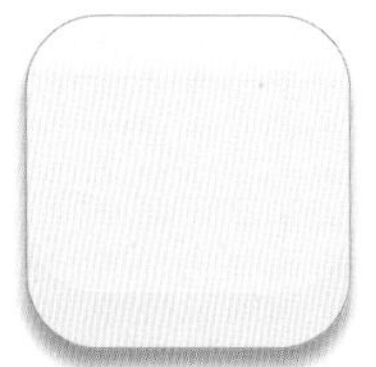

❼ Scale Gray
A gray like that of fish scales twinkling in the ocean.

⑧ White Coral
A warm white like that of white coral.

❾ Look Up
The blue that's visible when looking at the sea's surface from underwater.

1 — C50 M15 Y0 K0 / R132 G186 B229 / #84B9E5

2 — C90 M75 Y0 K20 / R32 G61 B138 / #1F3D89

3 — C0 M63 Y100 K0 / R239 G124 B0 / #EE7B00

4 — C25 M80 Y25 K0 / R194 G80 B126 / #C14F7E

5 — C0 M8 Y90 K0 / R255 G230 B0 / #FFE500

6 — C40 M40 Y40 K75 / R65 G56 B53 / #403734

7 — C2 M0 Y0 K45 / R168 G170 B171 / #A7A9AB

8 — C0 M0 Y15 K5 / R248 G246 B222 / #F8F5DE

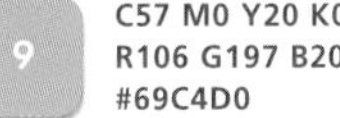

9 — C57 M0 Y20 K0 / R106 G197 B208 / #69C4D0

* Contrasting color schemes refer to color schemes where there is a significant difference in color or tone, creating a dynamic effect.

Two-color combinations

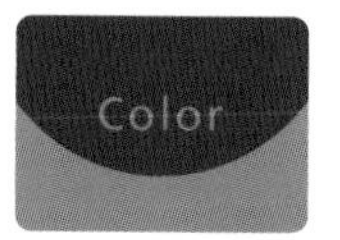

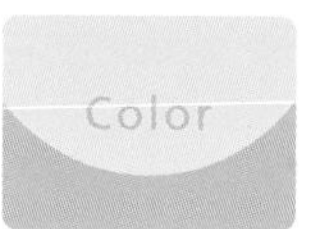

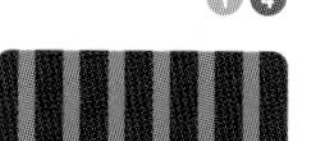

1 4 · 2 3 · 5 9

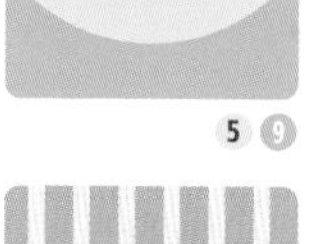
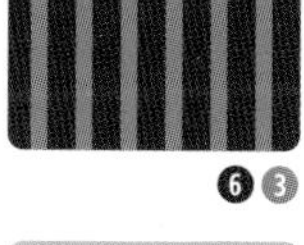
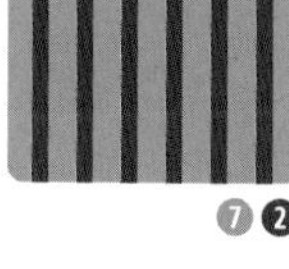
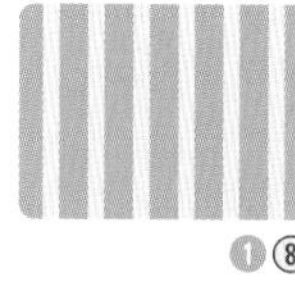

6 3 · 7 2 · 1 8

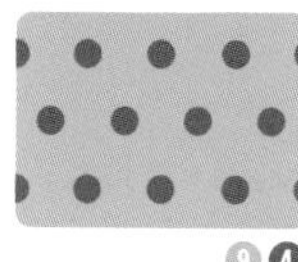
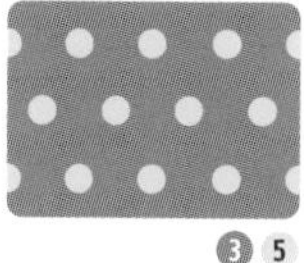
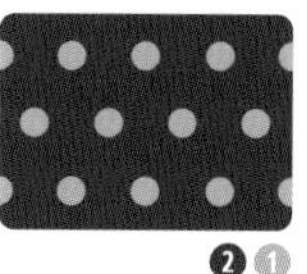

9 4 · 3 5 · 2 1

Three-color combinations

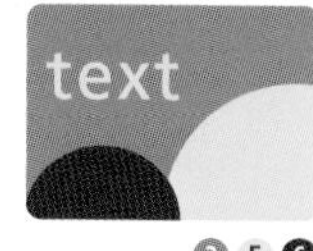

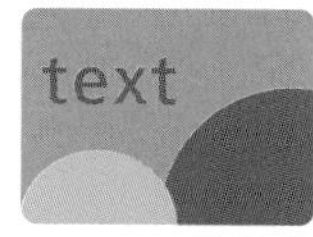

1 2 4 · 3 5 6 · 7 4 9

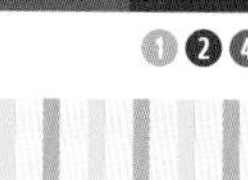
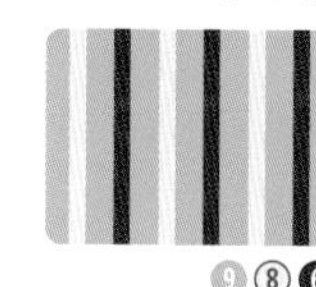
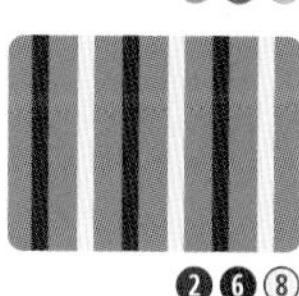

8 5 1 · 9 8 6 · 2 6 8

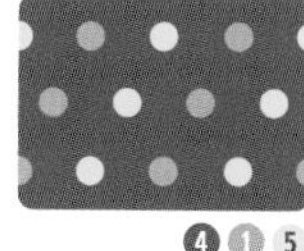
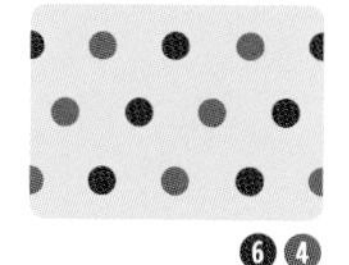
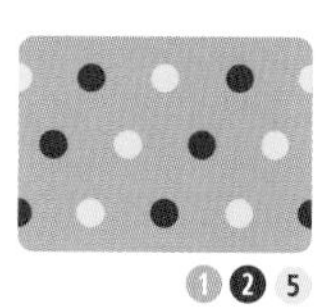

4 1 5 · 6 4 · 1 2 5

Designs

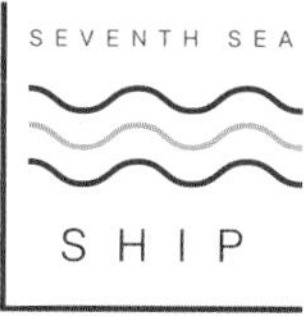

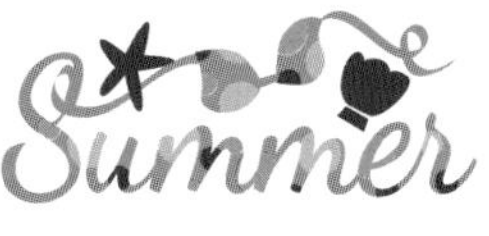

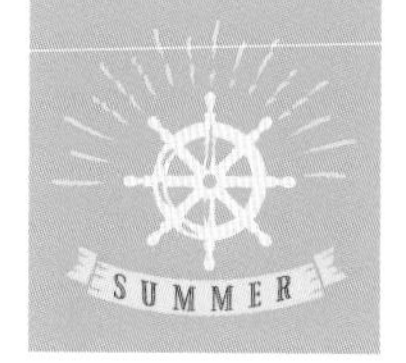

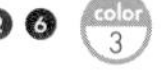
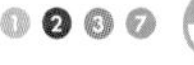
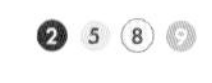
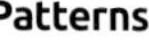

1 2 6 color 3 · 1 2 3 7 color 4 · 2 5 8 9 color 4

Patterns

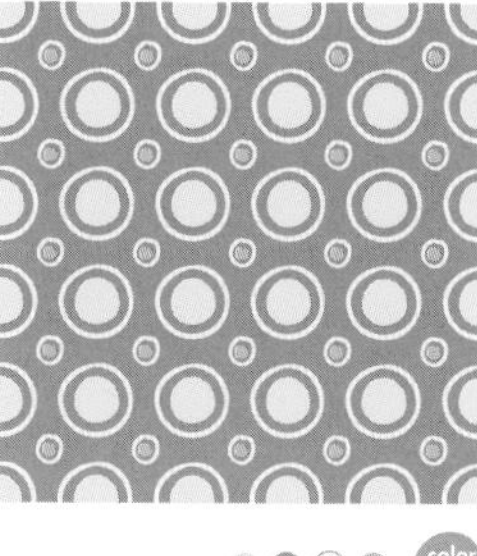
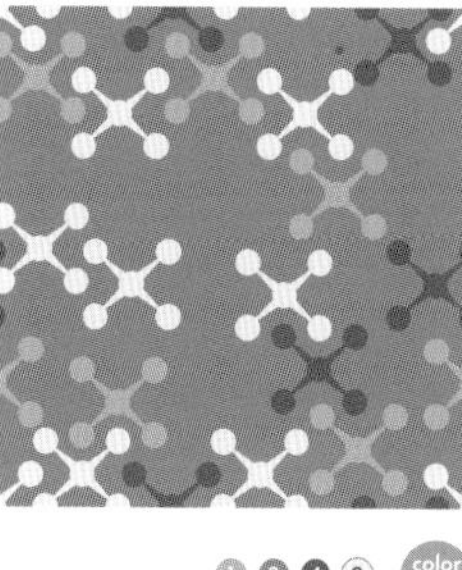
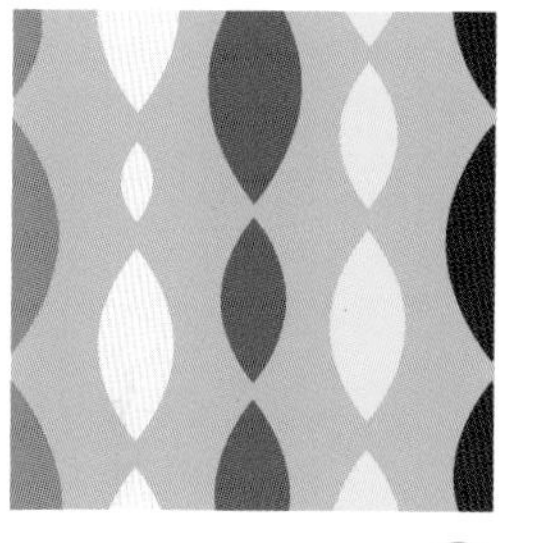

5 7 8 9 color 4 · 1 3 4 8 color 4 · 3 4 5 6 8 9 color 6

Illustration

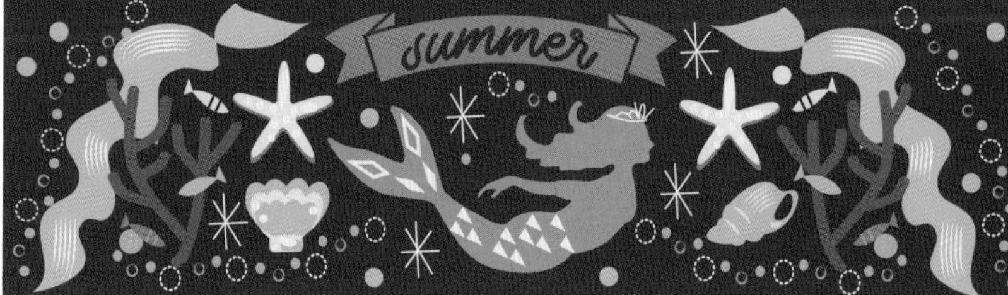

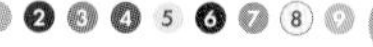

1 2 3 4 5 6 7 8 9 color 9

Recipe
005

Colorful Floating Balloons

Everyone watching people fishing for floating balloons at a Japanese festival shares the same emotions: They're all the same, or are they? You know the answer when you find the perfect one. In shades of red, orange and yellow, the balloons gently bob in the big blue tank of water. Maybe I'll try for an orange one first.

- **FEELING** Fun, pop, lively.
- **COMBINATIONS** Use a polychromatic color scheme focusing on red, orange and yellow.
- **TIPS** Use cool colors as accents, focusing on blue.

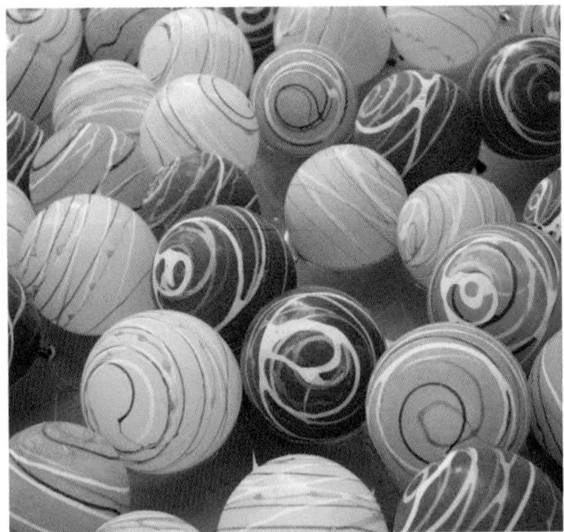

The swirling white patterns act as accent colors, adding movement and flow to the rounded forms.

1 Baby Chick
In olden times, chicks were sold at festivals.

2 Candied Apricot
Apricots dipped in translucent syrup are standard fare at festival stalls.

3 Goldfish Scooping
The orange of a nimble little goldfish.

4 Cotton Candy 1
Fluffy pink folds of the sugary carnival and street-fair treat.

5 Cotton Candy 2
The blue version tastes the same, so it's just a matter of preference.

6 Water Balloon Blue
A blue accented with yellow, purple and white.

7 Water Balloon Green
A slightly unusual green used for water balloons.

8 Water Tank
The blue of the tank that sets off the warm shades of the water balloons.

9 Swirls
The white used to create the swirling pattern on the water balloons.

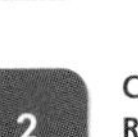

1 C5 M3 Y97 K0 R250 G233 B0 #F9E900

2 C0 M85 Y40 K0 R232 G69 B102 #E84566

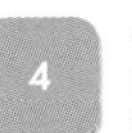

3 C0 M43 Y97 K0 R245 G166 B0 #F5A500

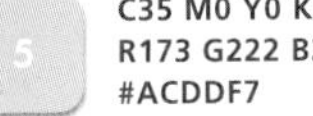

4 C0 M43 Y0 K0 R243 G174 B204 #F3ADCB

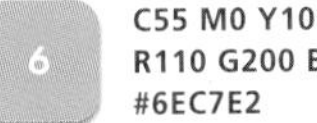

5 C35 M0 Y0 K0 R173 G222 B248 #ACDDF7

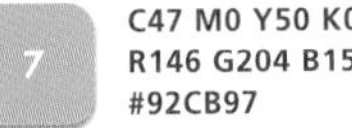

6 C55 M0 Y10 K0 R110 G200 B226 #6EC7E2

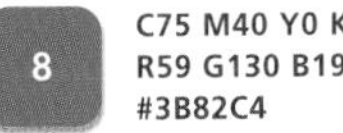

7 C47 M0 Y50 K0 R146 G204 B151 #92CB97

8 C75 M40 Y0 K0 R59 G130 B197 #3B82C4

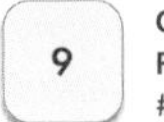

9 C5 M5 Y0 K0 R244 G243 B249 #F4F3F9

Two-color combinations

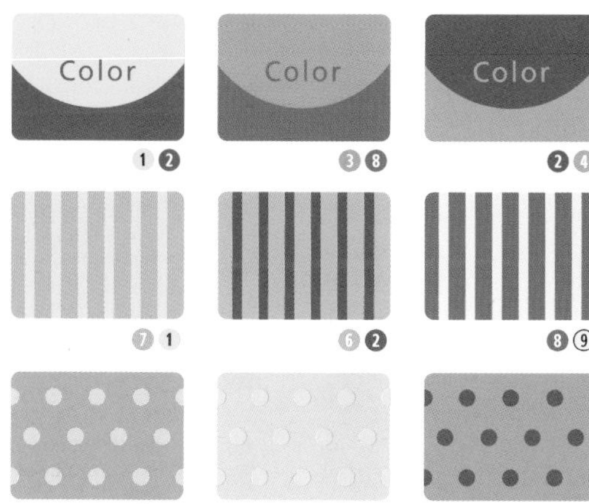

Three-color combinations

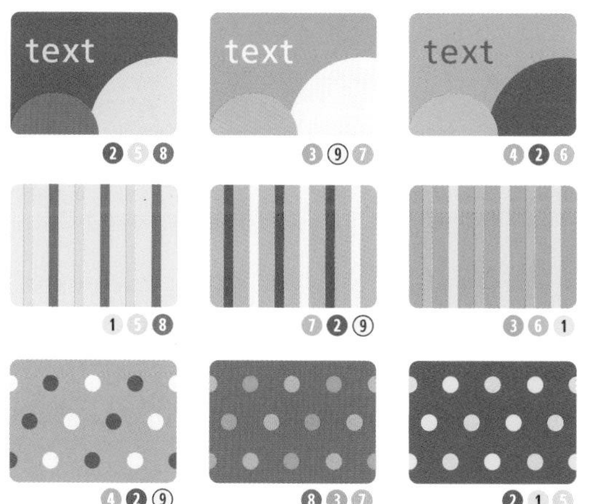

Designs

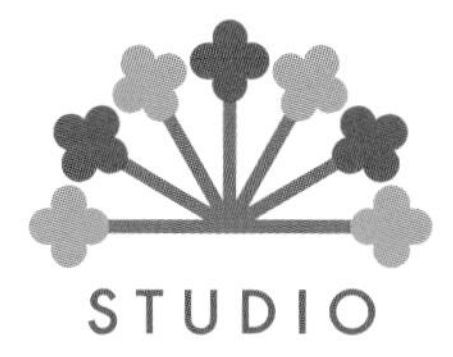

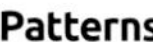
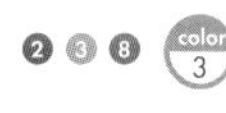
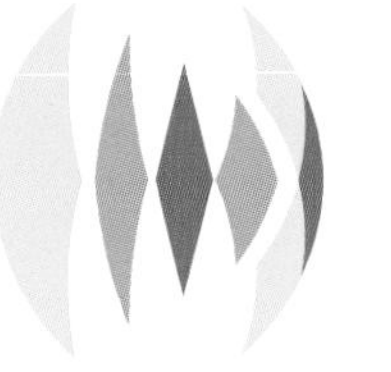

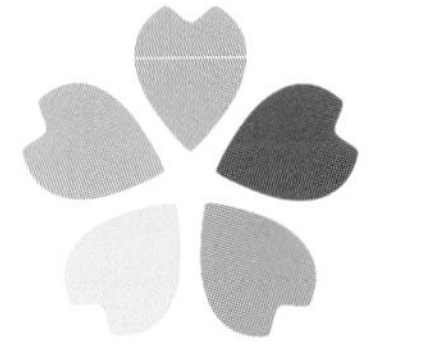
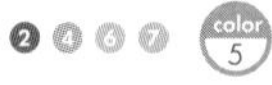

Patterns

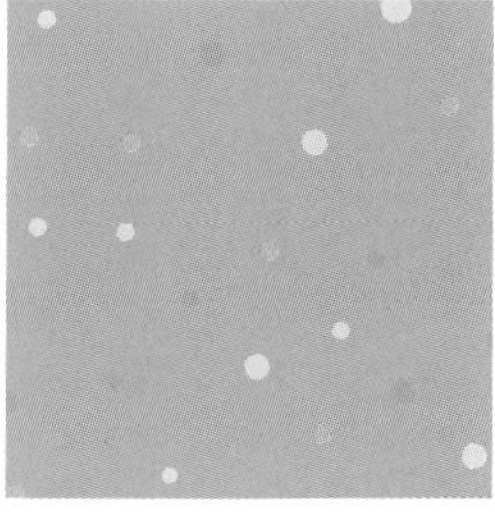

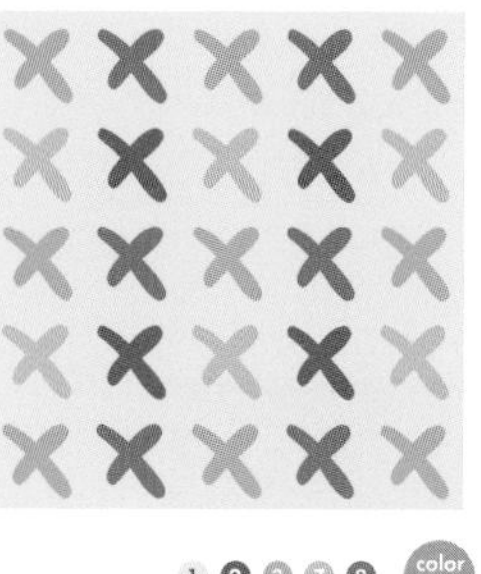
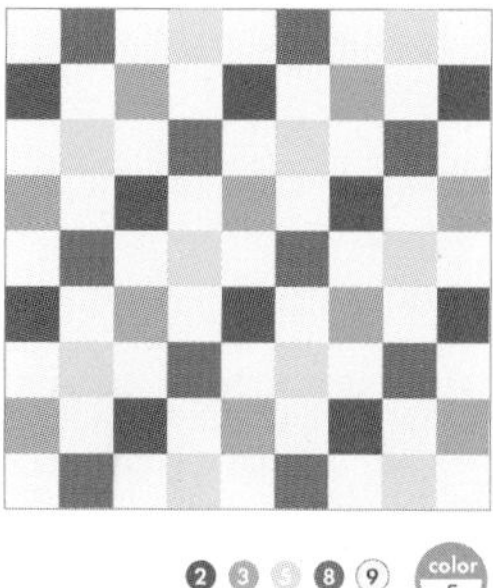

Illustration

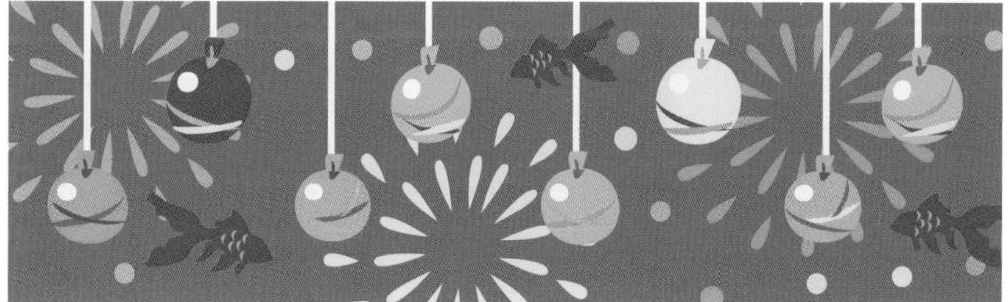
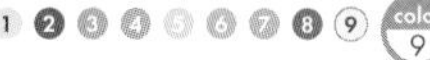

Recipe
006

Sneakers

I can't go without my daily morning run. I started running in order to lose weight, but now I'd like to take part in the Honolulu Marathon some day. I run every day toward this secret goal, but I haven't told anyone yet. Coordinating the colors of my sneakers that are bursting with vivid color helps get my feet moving.

- **FEELING** Vivid, punchy, springy.
- **COMBINATIONS** Combine similarly vibrant shades.
- **TIPS** Use fluorescent colors as effective accents.

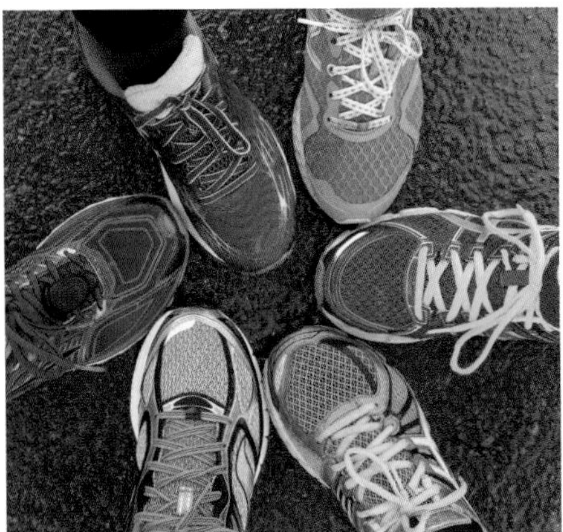

Shoelaces add yet another layer of accent color to the vivid palettes created by the sneakers.

❶ True Blue
The bluest of blues, this is a standard color for sportswear.

❷ Honolulu Sunset
The purple that appears at sundown on tropical islands.

③ Cheetah
The yellow of cheetahs, the world's fastest land animal.

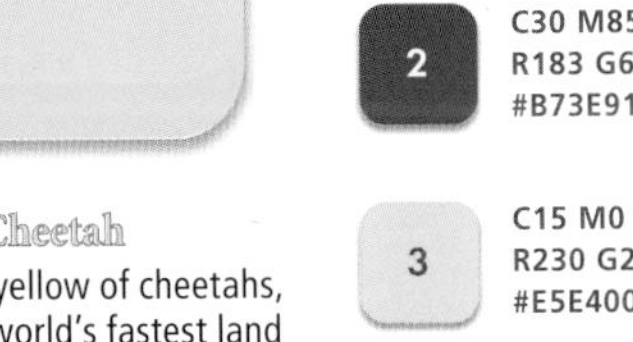

❹ Energy
A vibrant red full of energy and power.

❺ Future Green
A blue green that evokes the near future.

❻ Midnight Run
Black creates a deep, strong impression.

❼ Neo Green
A sporty yellow green.

❽ Asphalt
The color of a road covered in asphalt.

❾ Waikiki Beach
The color of the water at Waikiki Beach, a bright, clear blue.

	CMYK	RGB	Hex
1	C90 M75 Y0 K0	R38 G73 B157	#25489C
2	C30 M85 Y0 K0	R183 G63 B145	#B73E91
3	C15 M0 Y100 K0	R230 G228 B0	#E5E400
4	C0 M100 Y27 K0	R229 G0 B104	#E40067
5	C70 M0 Y50 K0	R53 G181 B151	#34B496
6	C7 M0 Y0 K90	R58 G57 B58	#3A3839
7	C20 M0 Y100 K15	R197 G202 B0	#C4CA00
8	C4 M0 Y0 K40	R175 G179 B181	#AFB3B5
9	C65 M0 Y10 K0	R63 G189 B224	#3EBDE0

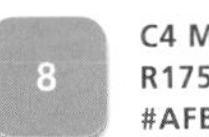
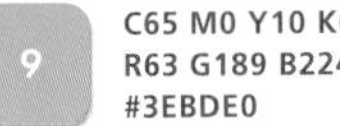

Two-color combinations

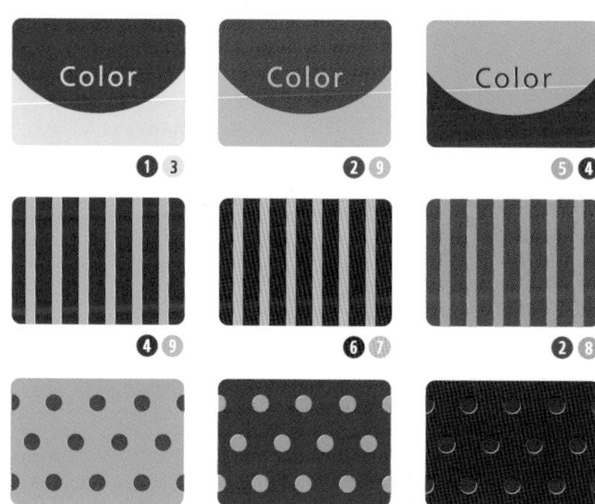

Three-color combinations

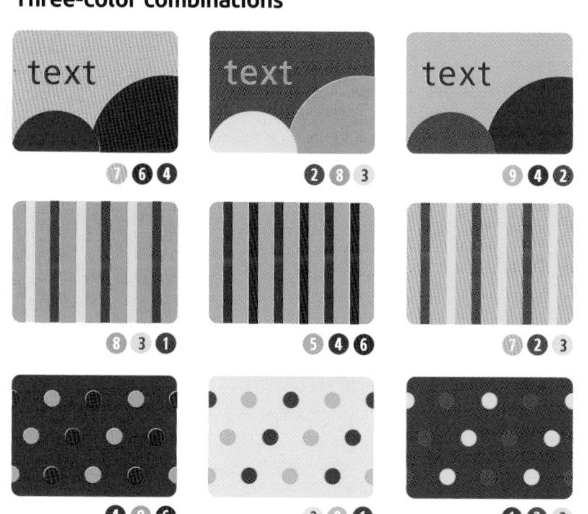

Designs

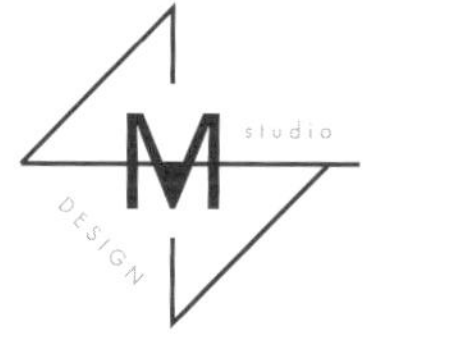

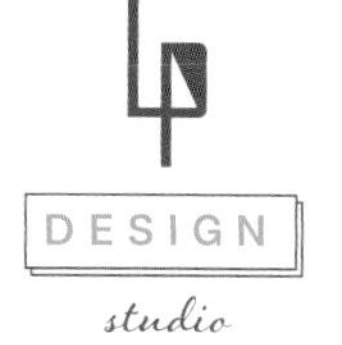

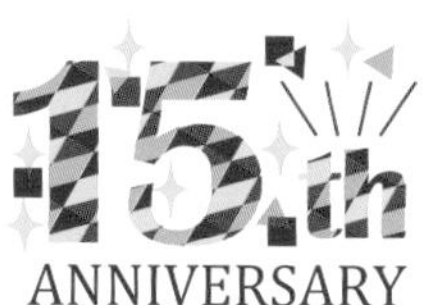

Patterns

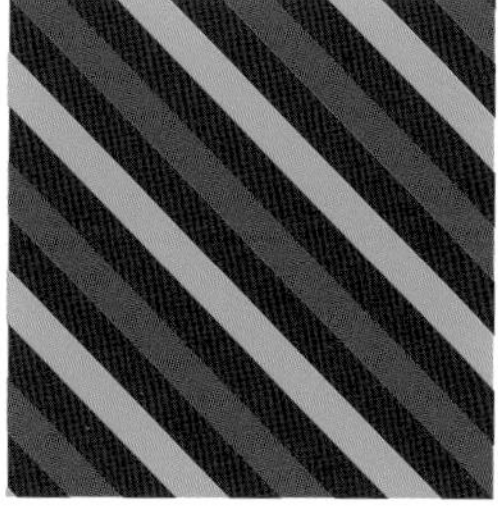

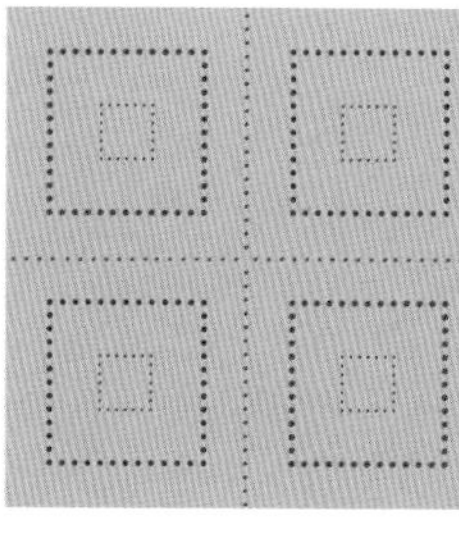

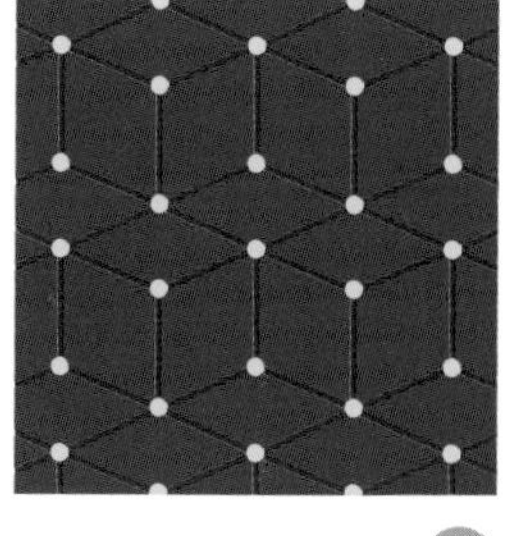

Illustration

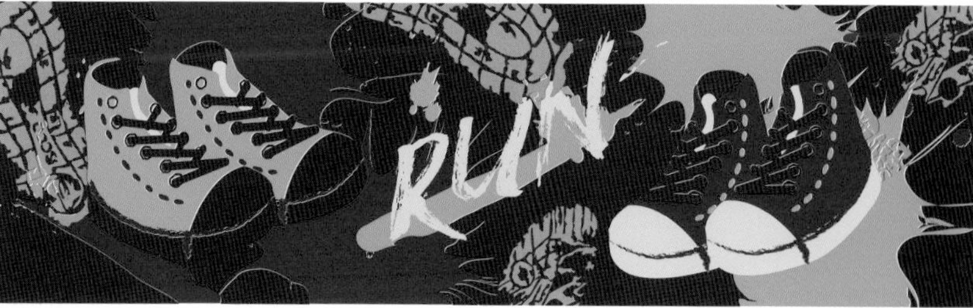

Recipe
007

Rainbow Bridge

A rainbow is seen as a symbol of good fortune all around the world. In ancient Greek mythology, the natural phenomenon was seen as the goddess Iris appearing in another form, while in ancient Scandinavia, a rainbow serves as the bridge the heroes who had died in battle crossed to enter the palace of the gods. It's easy to see how a striped pathway in the sky sparks imaginations.

- **FEELING** Lucky, well balanced, all-inclusive.
- **COMBINATIONS** Follow the sequence in a rainbow to create as polychromatic a color scheme as possible.
- **TIPS** Use vivid, highly saturated colors.

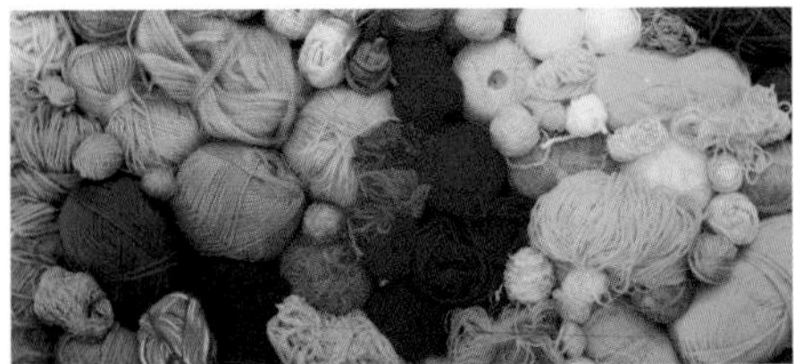

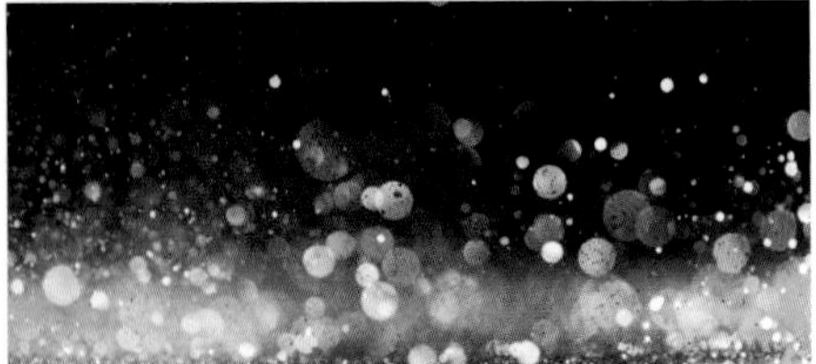

Black and white help to bring out the key colors comprising a rainbow.

❶ Spectrum Red

The red seen in a rainbow, this color has the longest wavelength.

② Spectrum Orange

The orange seen in a rainbow, a bridge to the hues beside it.

3 Spectrum Yellow

The yellow seen in a rainbow, the third of the rainbow's warm colors.

④ Spectrum Green

The green seen in a rainbow, the center of the rainbow's spectrum.

❺ Spectrum Blue

The blue seen in a rainbow, bringing a cooler shade to the effect.

❻ Spectrum Violet

The purple seen in a rainbow, this color has the shortest wavelength.

❼ Indigo

The indigo seen in a rainbow.

⑧ Pure White

A white with no impurities, the brightest of all the colors.

❾ Pure Black

Pure black is the darkest of all the colors.

No.	CMYK	RGB	Hex
1	C0 M100 Y100 K0	R230 G0 B18	#E50011
2	C0 M65 Y100 K0	R238 G120 B0	#EE7700
3	C0 M0 Y100 K0	R255 G241 B0	#FFF000
4	C80 M0 Y100 K0	R0 G167 B60	#00A73B
5	C100 M53 Y0 K0	R0 G100 B180	#0064B3
6	C75 M100 Y0 K0	R96 G25 B134	#5F1885
7	C95 M97 Y0 K0	R43 G36 B137	#2A2489
8	C0 M0 Y0 K0	R255 G255 B255	#FEFEFE
9	C0 M0 Y0 K100	R0 G0 B0	#000000

Two-color combinations

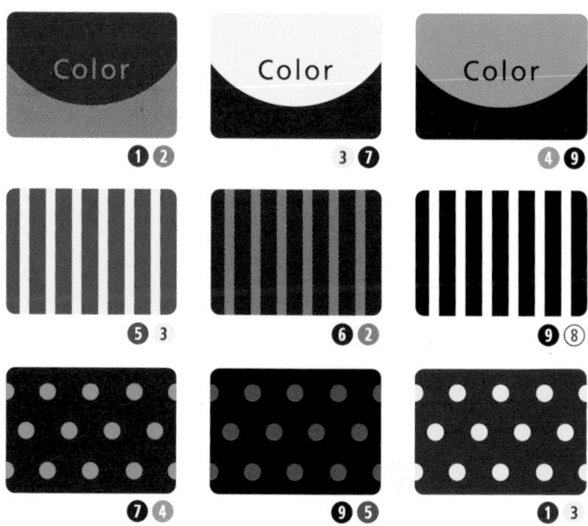

Three-color combinations

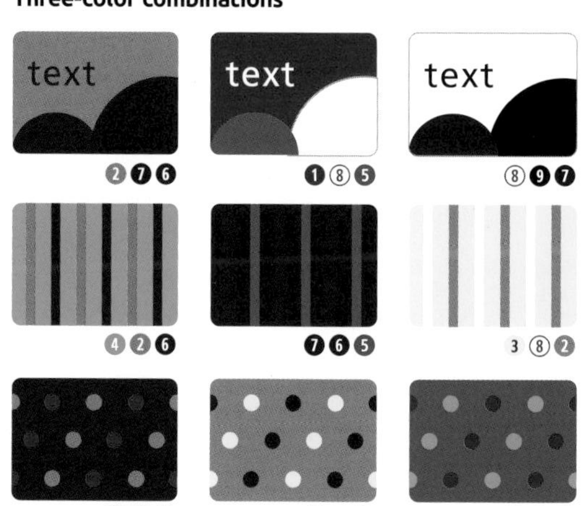

Designs

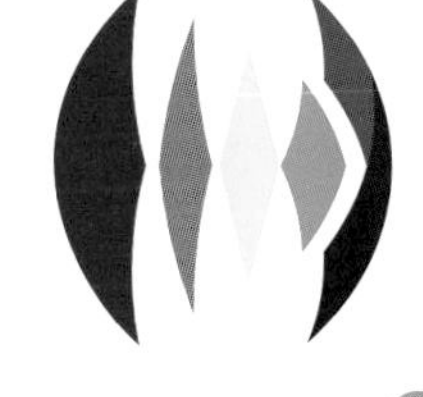

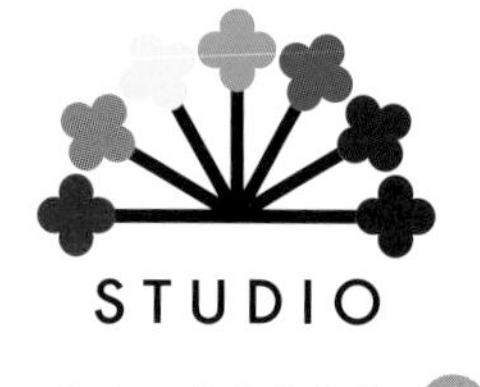

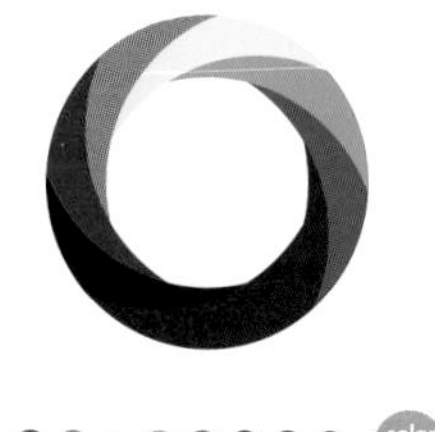

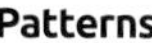

Patterns

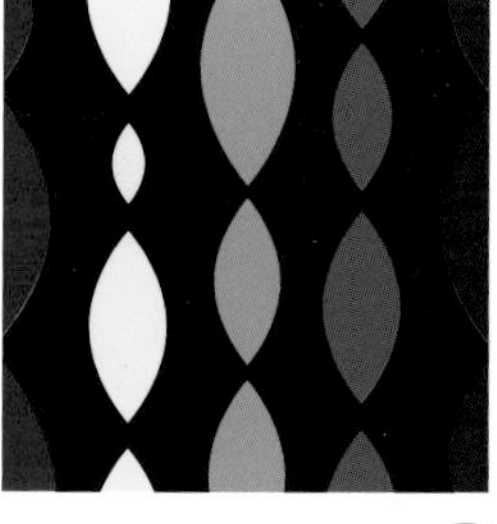

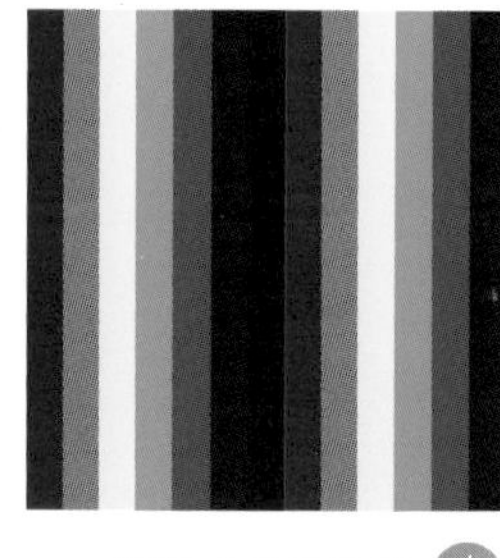

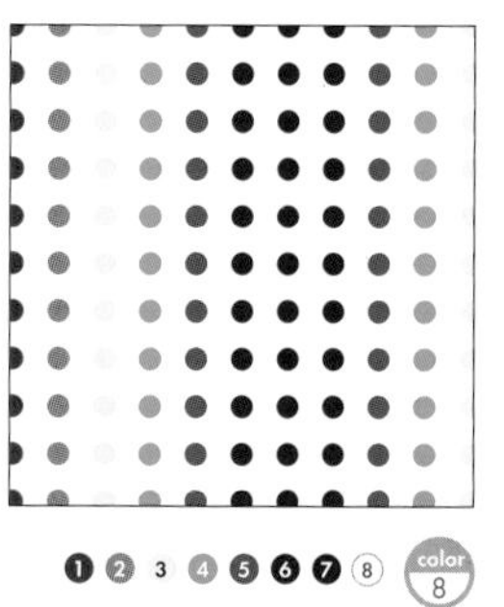

Illustration

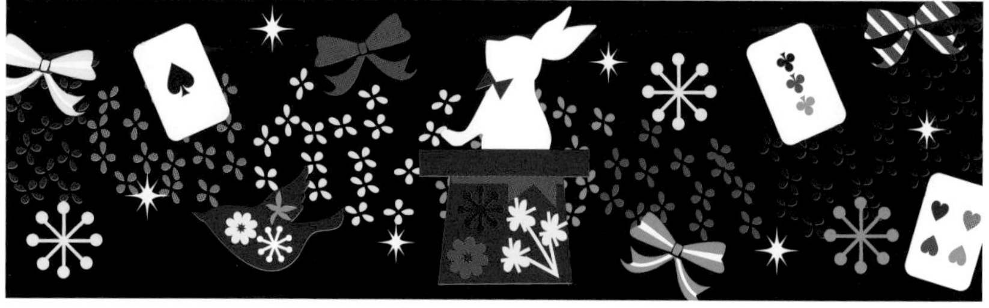

Recipe
008

Toy Blocks

It's not surprising that children's toys are made in bright colors, as studies have shown they appeal to the infant and toddler set. The standard colors for infants' toys are those known as the psychological primaries: red, yellow, green and blue. Working from a child's viewpoint, the vibrant, warm color schemes are taken from color palettes that foster children's creativity.

- **FEELING** Fun, active, vivid.
- **COMBINATIONS** Make sure to create distinct visual contrasts.
- **TIPS** Colors 1, 2 and 4 are similar to the three primary pigment colors.

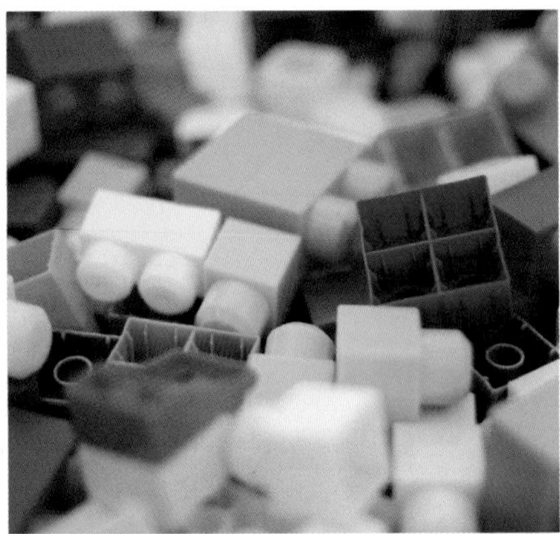

The main colors used are vibrant shades such as those used for crayons and origami paper.

1 Bright Yellow
A bright, vibrant yellow with a perky air.

2 Clear Turquoise
A bright turquoise blue full of vitality.

3 Spring Green
A yellow green that calls to mind the gentle warmth of spring.

4 Bright Pink
Vivid, purple-tinged pink. This color makes a strong impact.

5 Pure Blue
The exact shade of blue in a set of paints.

6 Brilliant Orange
A vivid, glowing orange.

7 Summer Green
The fresh, deep green of leaves on summer trees.

8 Light Orange
The orange of a mandarin skin.

9 Cheerful Yellow
A yellow that brightens and cheers.

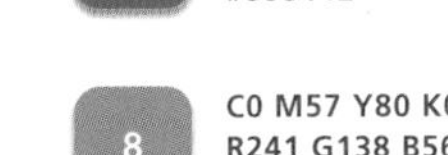

No.	CMYK	RGB	Hex
1	C0 M7 Y100 K0	R255 G230 B0	#FFE600
2	C70 M0 Y13 K0	R13 G184 B218	#0DB8D9
3	C43 M0 Y100 K0	R163 G202 B15	#A2CA0E
4	C20 M85 Y15 K0	R201 G66 B132	#C84283
5	C85 M60 Y0 K0	R38 G96 B173	#2660AC
6	C0 M80 Y93 K0	R234 G85 B25	#EA5419
7	C90 M25 Y95 K5	R0 G133 B67	#008442
8	C0 M57 Y80 K0	R241 G138 B56	#F08A37
9	C0 M33 Y100 K0	R249 G185 B0	#F8B800

Two-color combinations

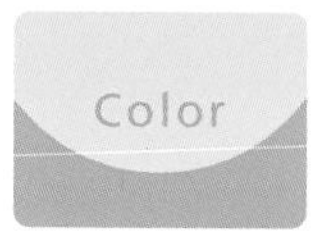

1 2

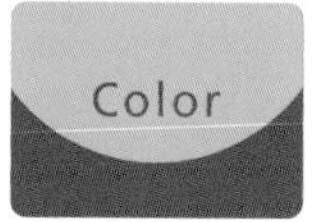

3 4

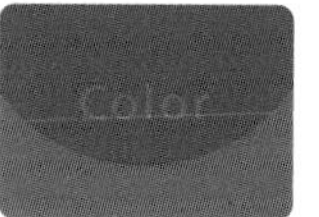
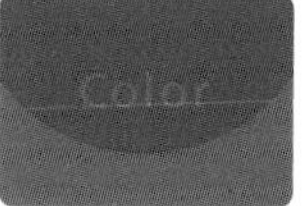

5 6

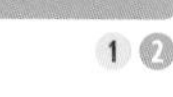

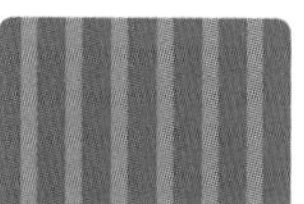
7 8

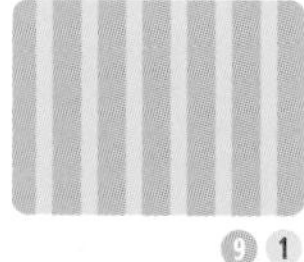
9 1

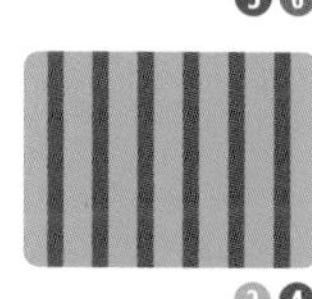
2 4

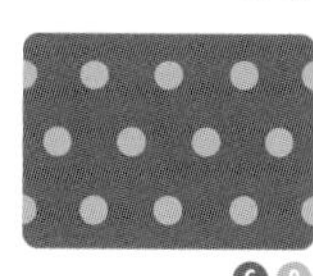
6 9

4 5

8 9

Three-color combinations

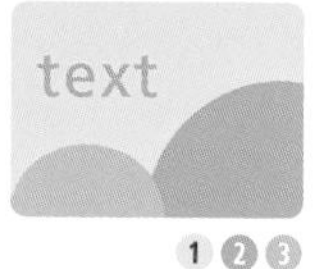

1 2 3

4 5 6

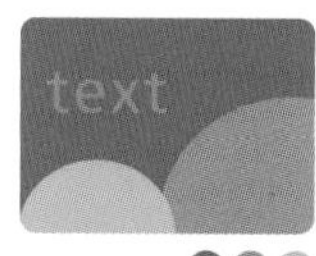

7 8 9

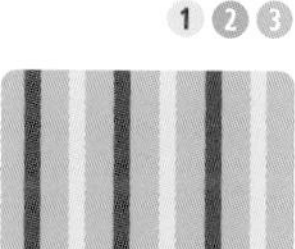
3 4 1

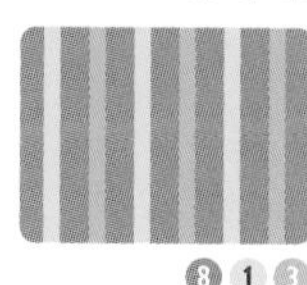
8 1 3

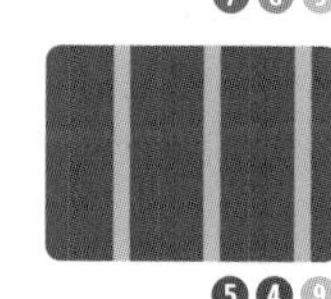
5 4 9

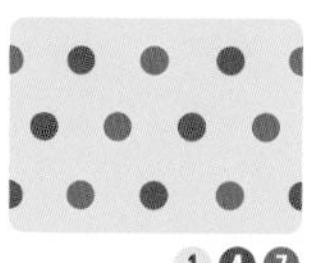
1 4 7

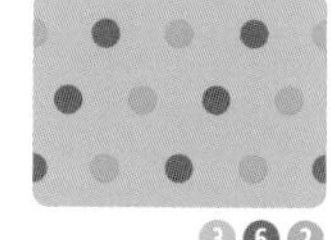
3 6 2

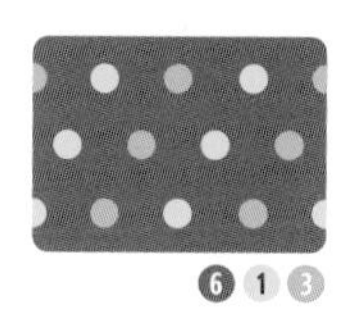
6 1 3

Designs

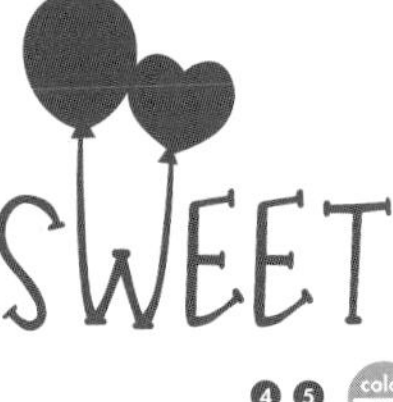

4 5 color 2

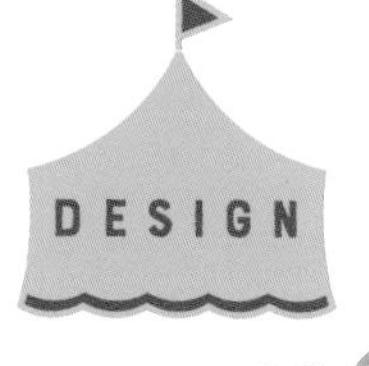

3 4 color 2

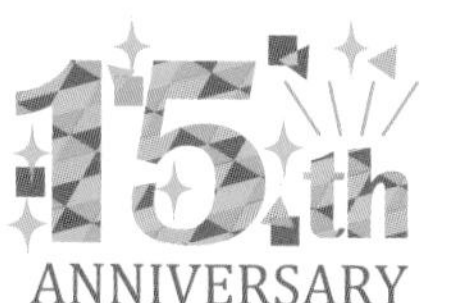

2 3 6 9 color 4

Patterns

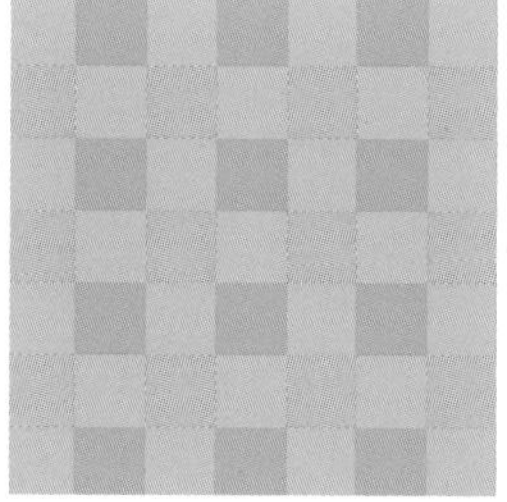
2 3 9 color 3

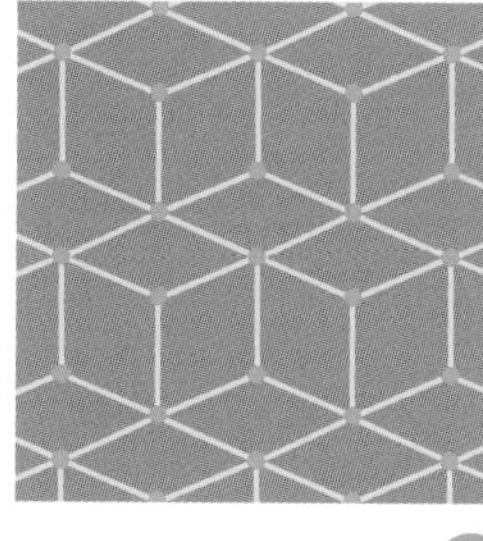
1 2 8 color 3

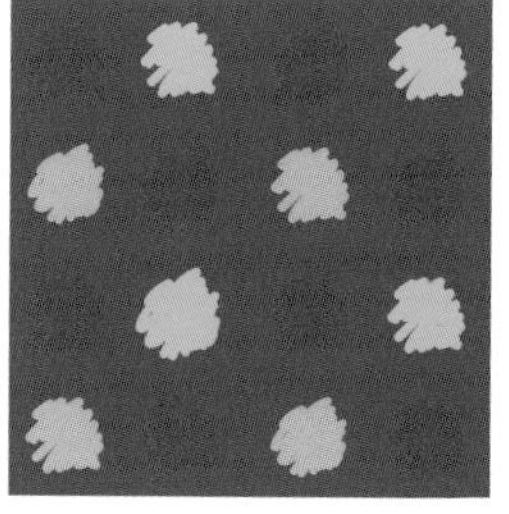
3 4 5 9 color 4

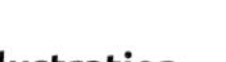

Illustration

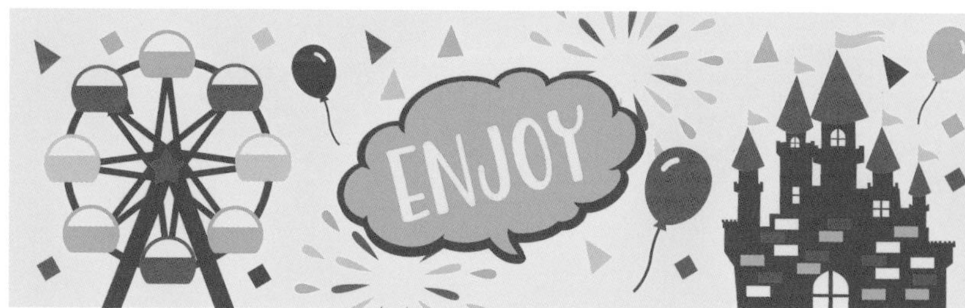

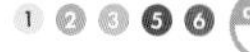
1 2 3 5 6 color 5

Recipe
009

Children's Play Room

Someone I look up to told me that mothers should always wear attractive colors for the sake of their children, as rich colors foster a rich emotional life. I'm a mother of two, and I'm thinking first of all I might try switching my regular apron for a more colorful one, then introducing colorful fabric to the children's room.

- **FEELING** Energetic, clear-cut, fun.
- **COMBINATIONS** Create bold combinations with a sense of playfulness.
- **TIPS** For large surface areas, use light, bright colors.

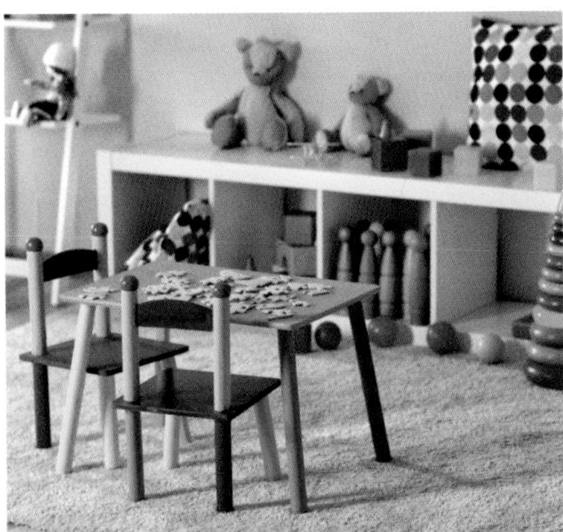

Infants tend to prefer vivid colors that encourage tactile interactions with the world around them.

❶ Carrot Orange
An intense orange like that of a carrot.

❷ Sunflower
The yellow of a sunflower that turns toward the sun to bloom.

❸ Cyan
A vivid blue with a green tinge, one of the three primary pigment colors.

❹ Madonna Blue
The color of benevolence and a symbol of the Virgin Mary.

❺ Evergreen
A deep green like that of evergreen leaves.

❻ Happy
A bright pink that symbolizes love and happiness.

❼ Orange Juice
The color of fresh orange juice.

❽ Little Boy Blue
A pale blue that is more highly saturated than baby blue (see page 52).

❾ Little Girl Pink
This pale pink tinged with purple traditionally symbolized girls.

1 — C0 M67 Y80 K10 / R223 G108 B49 / #DE6C31

2 — C0 M17 Y100 K0 / R254 G214 B0 / #FED500

3 — C100 M0 Y0 K0 / R0 G160 B233 / #00A0E8

4 — C97 M87 Y0 K0 / R21 G54 B146 / #153692

5 — C100 M23 Y100 K0 / R0 G133 B66 / #008542

6 — C0 M75 Y20 K0 / R234 G96 B136 / #EA6088

7 — C0 M40 Y85 K5 / R239 G167 B43 / #EFA72B

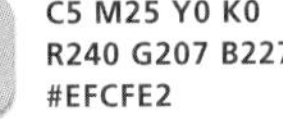

8 — C35 M10 Y0 K0 / R174 G208 B238 / #AECFED

9 — C5 M25 Y0 K0 / R240 G207 B227 / #EFCFE2

Two-color combinations

Color — 2 1

Color — 6 4

Color — 5 7

7 3

9 4

2 6

6 9

4 5

8 2

Three-color combinations

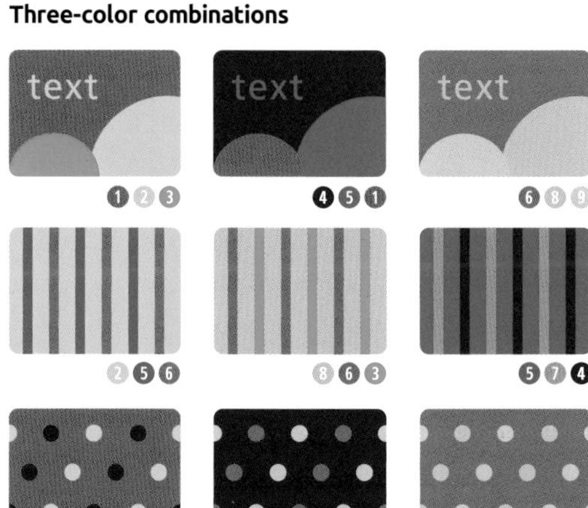

1 2 3

4 5 1

6 8 9

2 5 6

8 6 3

5 7 4

1 4 2

4 6 9

6 8 9

Designs

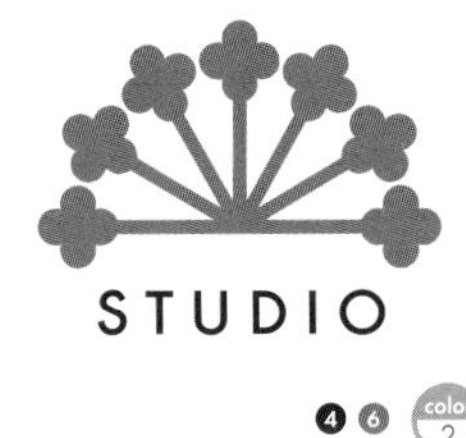

4 6 color 2

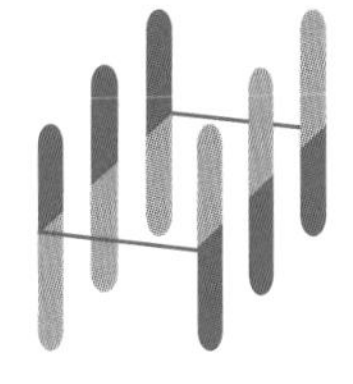

5 7 color 2

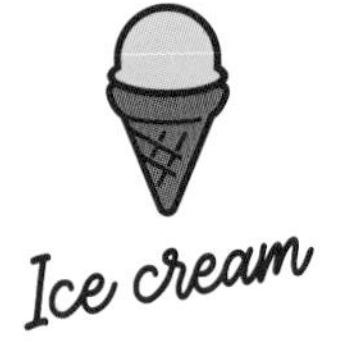

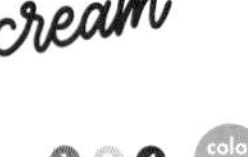

1 2 4 color 3

Patterns

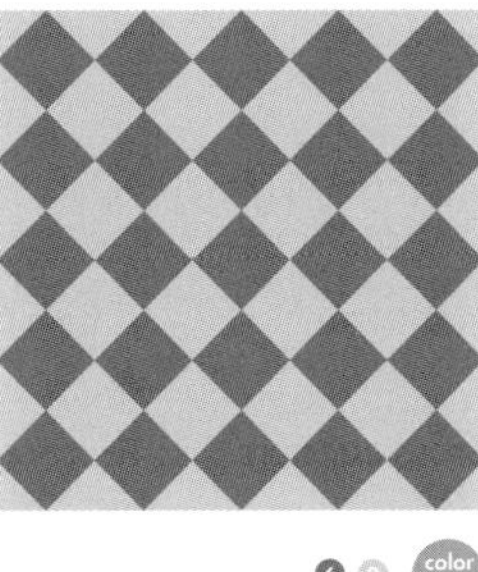

6 9 color 2

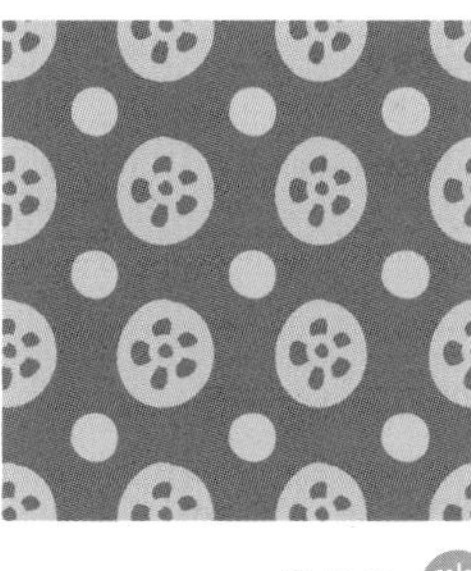

6 8 9 color 3

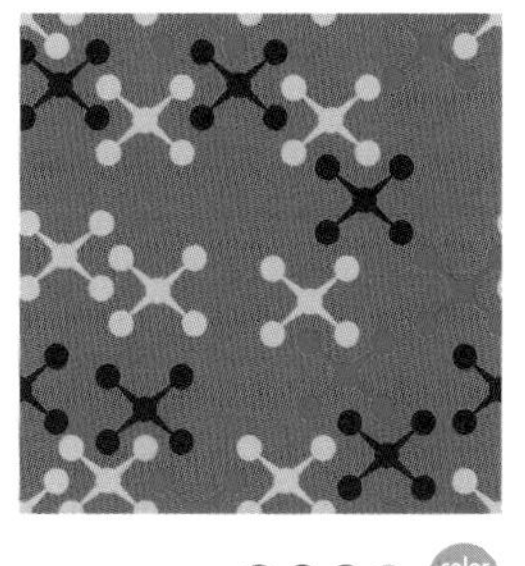

1 4 5 8 color 4

Illustration

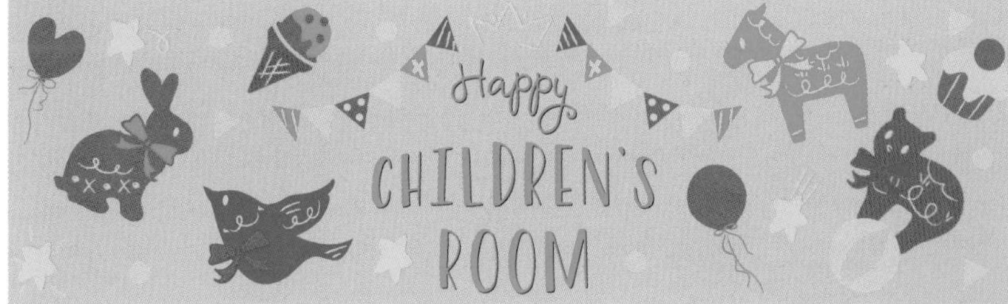

1 2 3 5 6 8 color 6

Recipe
010

Hot Cakes with Fruit

Fresh fruit and fluffy hot cakes are a winning combination for perking me up. At 10am on Saturday morning, I'm eating them with great gusto. Should I pour plenty of honey over them, or maybe chocolate sauce? Clearly there's no wrong answer! I get the feeling this is going to be a great weekend.

- **FEELING** Fun, exciting, full of vitality.
- **COMBINATIONS** Use warm colors with a yellow base.
- **TIPS** For the best result, use brown shades for the base color.

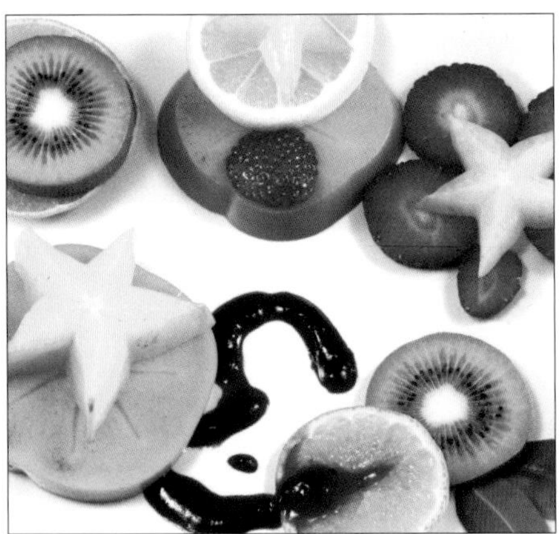

A pancake base supports the tempting layers of red, green and orange. Does it look too good to eat?

1 Golden Brown
In Japanese, this color is called "fox color."

2 Honey
The yellow of thick, sweet honey.

3 Strawberry
A red that evokes perfectly ripe strawberries.

4 Kiwi
The famous fruit from New Zealand.

5 Chocolate Sauce
The color of sweetly satisfying chocolate sauce.

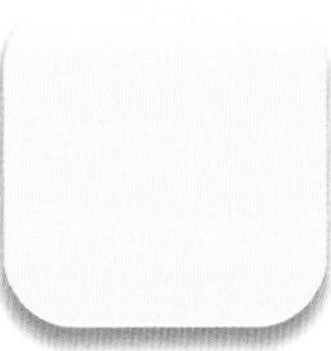

6 Star Fruit
The color of the skin of star fruit.

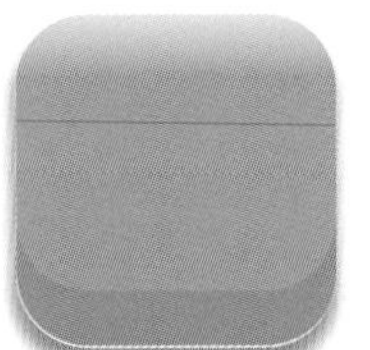

7 Persimmon
The deep orange of a ripe persimmon.

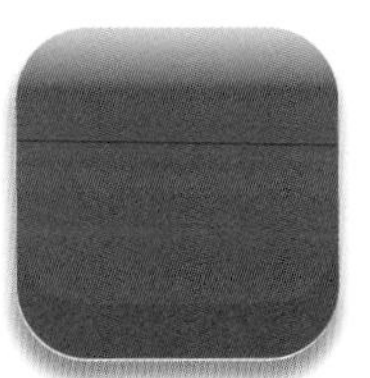

8 Sweet Cherry
A highly saturated pink that has a faint tinge of yellow to it.

9 Refresh
Green revitalizes and relieves fatigue.

1 C10 M55 Y90 K10 R211 G129 B33 #D38120

2 C0 M20 Y83 K0 R253 G210 B52 #FDD133

3 C0 M93 Y80 K0 R231 G45 B47 #E72C2E

4 C60 M10 Y90 K0 R114 G175 B67 #71AF43

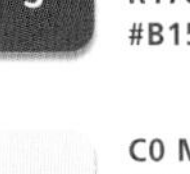

5 C25 M70 Y90 K15 R178 G92 B38 #B15B26

6 C0 M0 Y77 K0 R255 G243 B75 #FFF34A

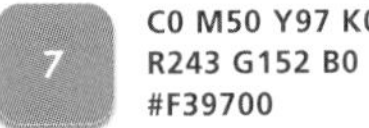

7 C0 M50 Y97 K0 R243 G152 B0 #F39700

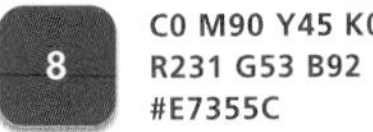

8 C0 M90 Y45 K0 R231 G53 B92 #E7355C

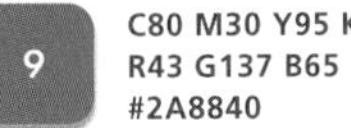

9 C80 M30 Y95 K0 R43 G137 B65 #2A8840

Two-color combinations

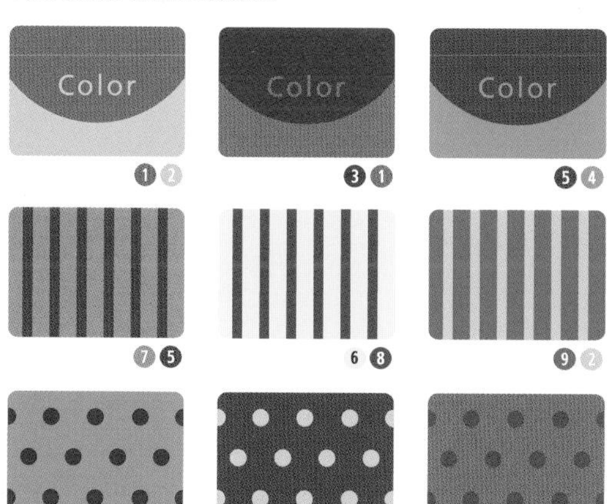

Three-color combinations

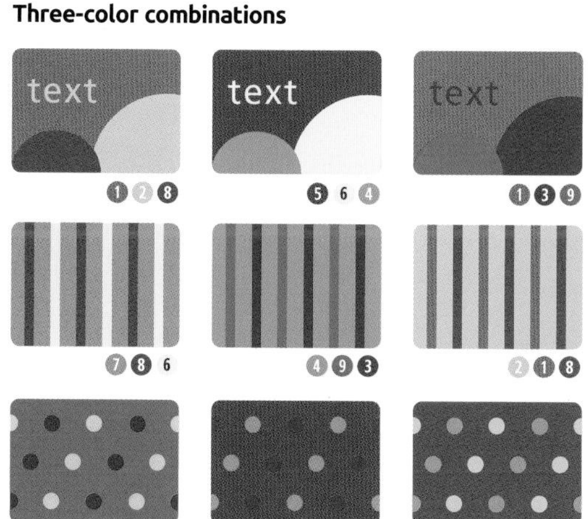

Designs

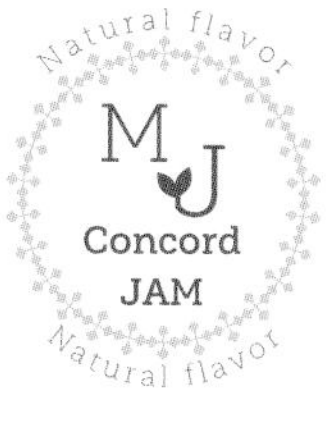

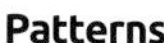

1 2 5 color 3

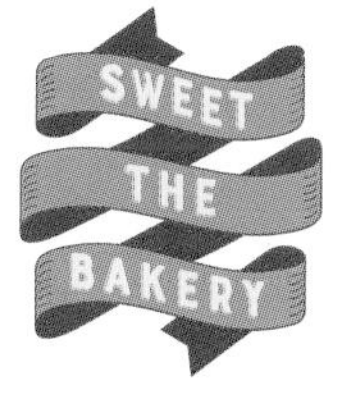

3 5 6 7 color 4

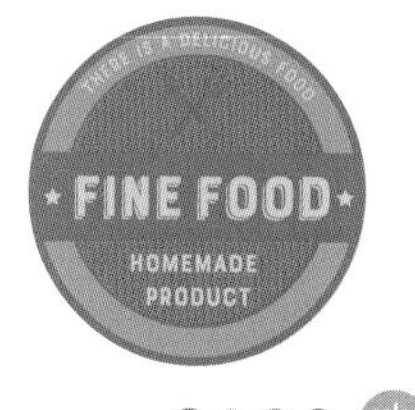

1 2 4 9 color 4

Patterns

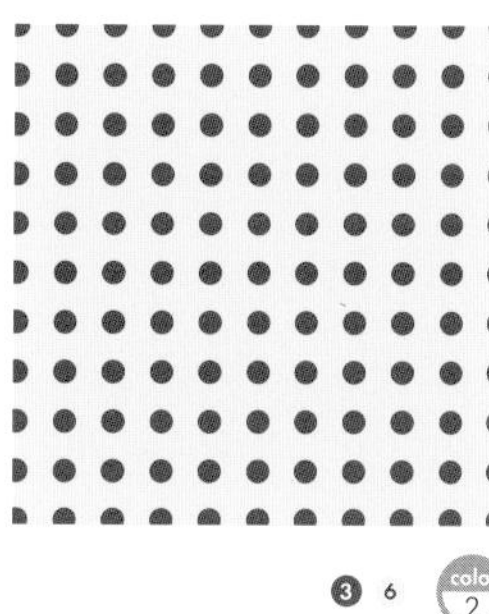

3 6 color 2

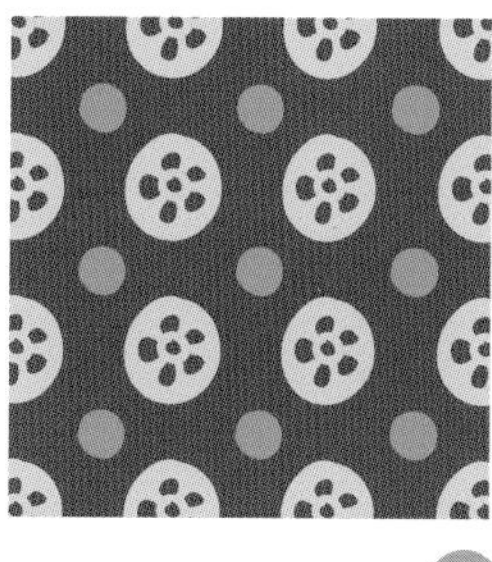

2 4 5 color 3

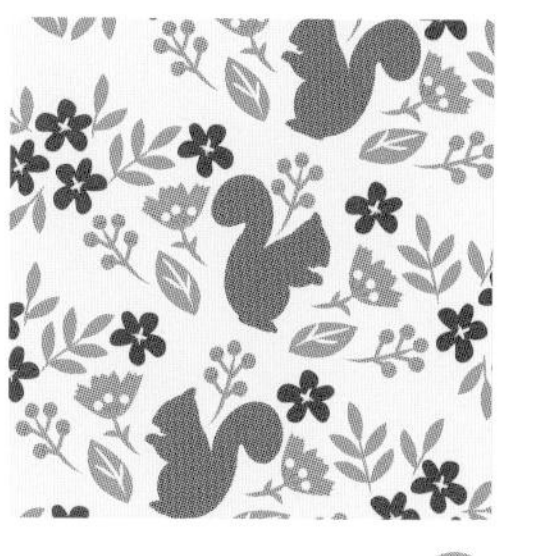

1 2 3 4 7 color 5

Illustration

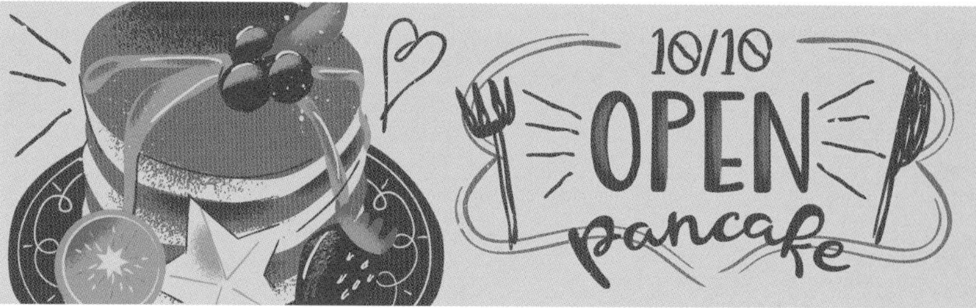

1 2 3 4 5 6 7 8 9 color 9

Part

02

Romantic

In this section, I've gathered inspiration from the softer side of the spectrum. You're sure to find the scheme you're looking for from these delicate, subtle palettes that focus on light pastel shades.

Color Schemes That are Sweet and Gentle

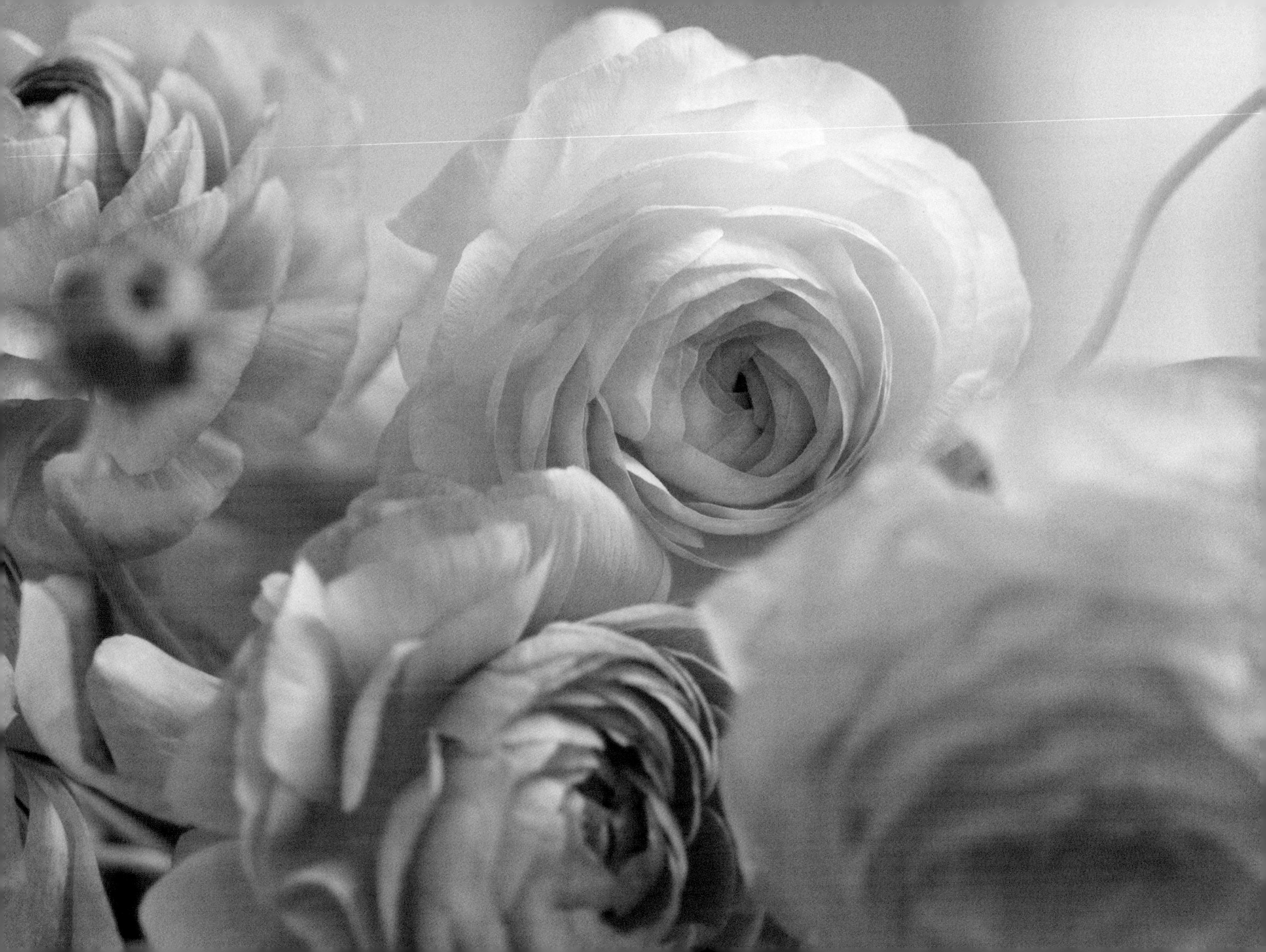

Recipe
011

Happy Easter

Easter eggs symbolize birth and renewal, while rabbits are a symbol of fertility and abundance. Easter falls on the Sunday after the first full moon following the spring equinox. The light, subdued color palette that the holiday suggests evokes the arrival of spring.

- **FEELING** The arrival of spring, light, soft.
- **COMBINATIONS** Focus on pastel shades for an airy feel.
- **TIPS** As much as possible, use colors with the same level of brightness.

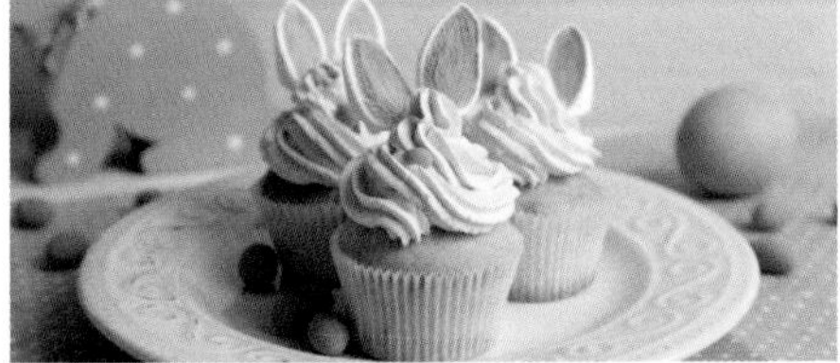

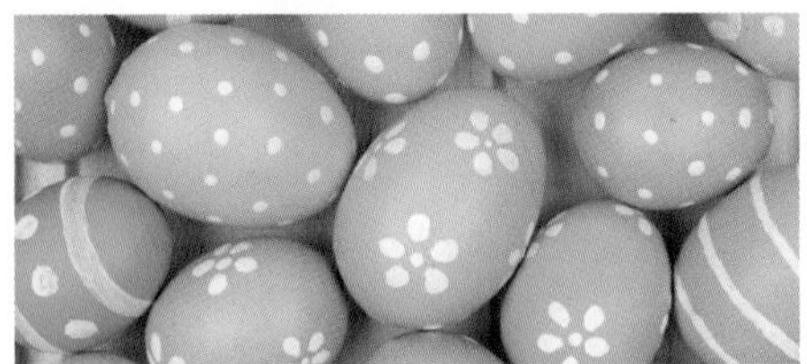

Confections and colorfully decorated eggs are common sights at Easter.

① Easter Egg
A warm yellow like that of an egg yolk.

② Light Emerald
A light emerald green.

③ Sweet Pink
A pink that calls to mind cotton candy.

④ Light Purple
There is an airy, gentle feel to this light purple shade.

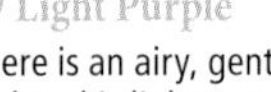

⑤ Milky White
A creamy, soft white like that of milk.

⑥ Sprout Green
A slightly whitish yellow green like that of a new bud.

⑦ Spring Blue
Light sky blue; a spring blue with a light translucency to it.

⑧ Warm Gray
A warm gray slightly tinged with yellow.

⑨ Light Coral
A light pink with a yellow tinge.

1
C0 M10 Y67 K0
R255 G229 B104
#FFE567

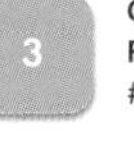

2
C45 M0 Y30 K0
R149 G208 B192
#94D0BF

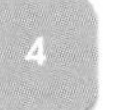

3
C0 M40 Y15 K0
R244 G178 B186
#F4B2BA

4
C10 M30 Y0 K0
R229 G194 B219
#E4C1DB

5
C0 M0 Y10 K0
R255 G254 B238
#FFFDED

6
C35 M0 Y55 K0
R180 G215 B141
#B4D78C

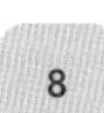

7
C25 M13 Y0 K0
R199 G212 B237
#C6D4EC

8
C0 M0 Y15 K17
R226 G225 B203
#E2E0CB

9
C0 M35 Y30 K0
R246 G187 B167
#F6BBA6

Two-color combinations

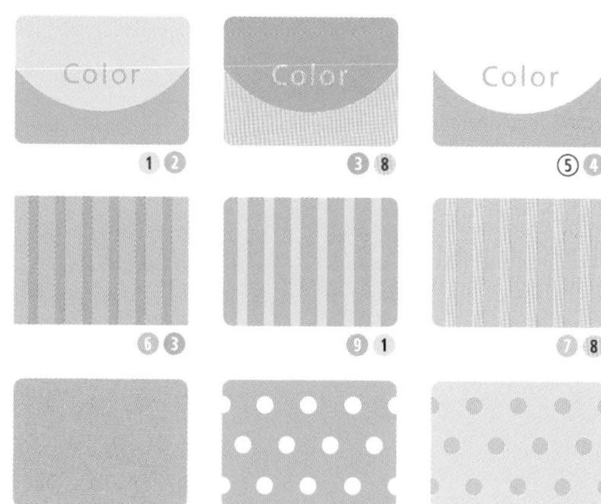

Three-color combinations

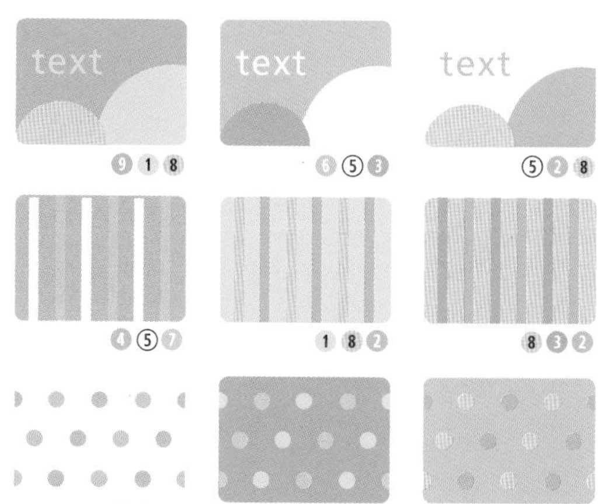

Designs

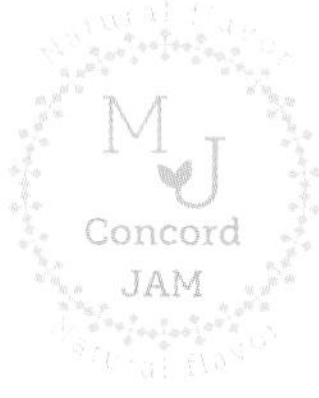

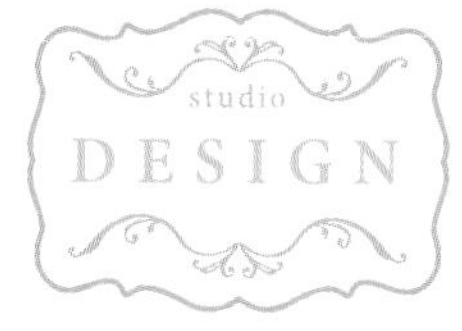

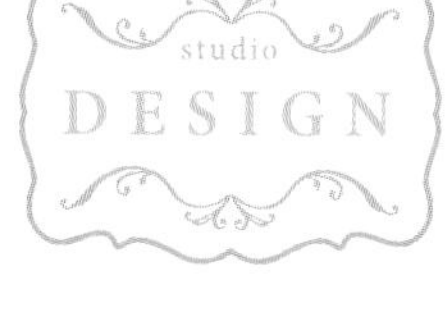

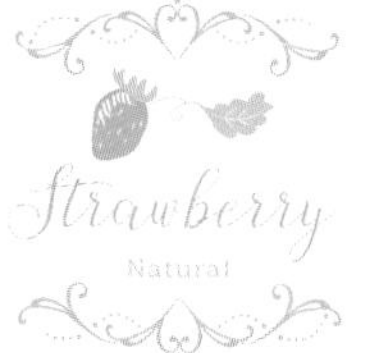

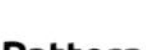

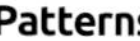

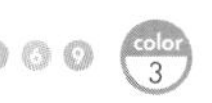

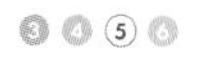

Patterns

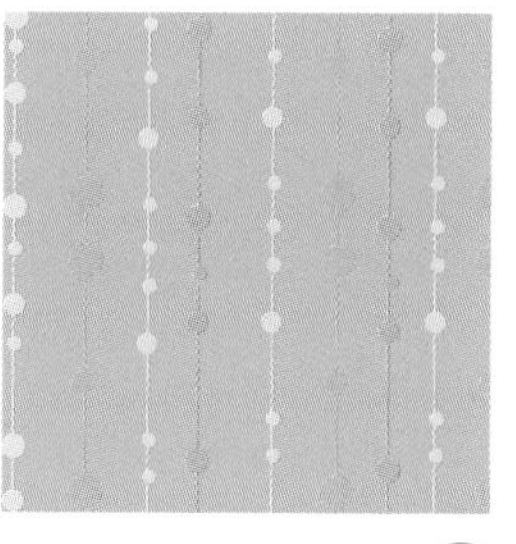

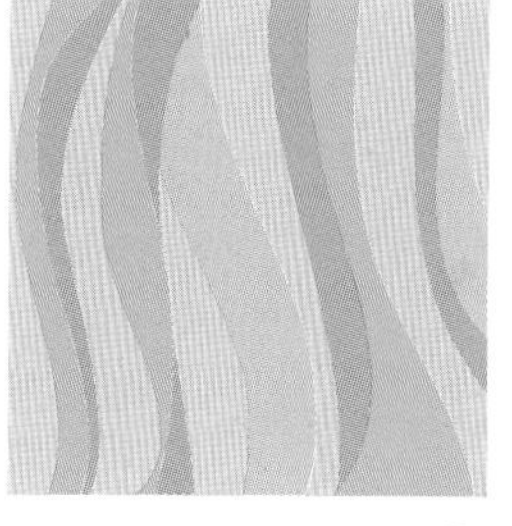

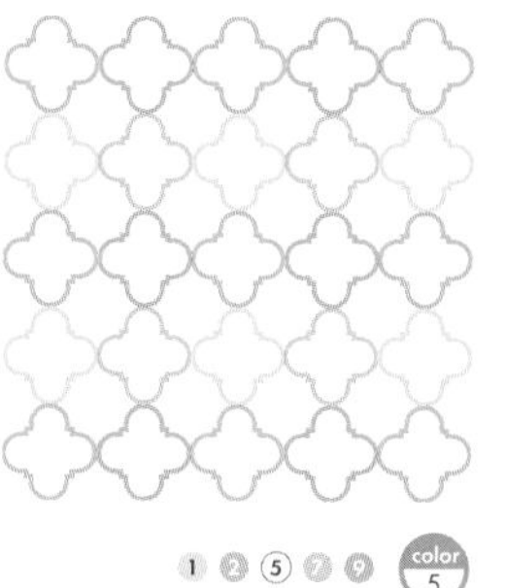

Illustration

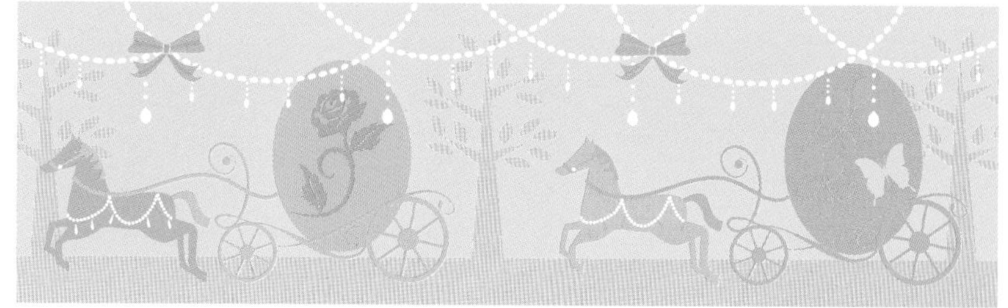

Recipe
012

The Flower Fairy

If you've been feeling irritated or gloomy lately, think of this fairy! The flower fairy's gifts are nine colors with gently enveloping auras to soothe and heal. In time, the gloominess is dispelled, the clouds part and a new direction emerges. These pastel colors make the mind supple and open to possibility.

- **FEELING** Delicate, lithe, airy.
- **COMBINATIONS** Make pink and purple shades the main colors.
- **TIPS** Use accent colors sparingly.

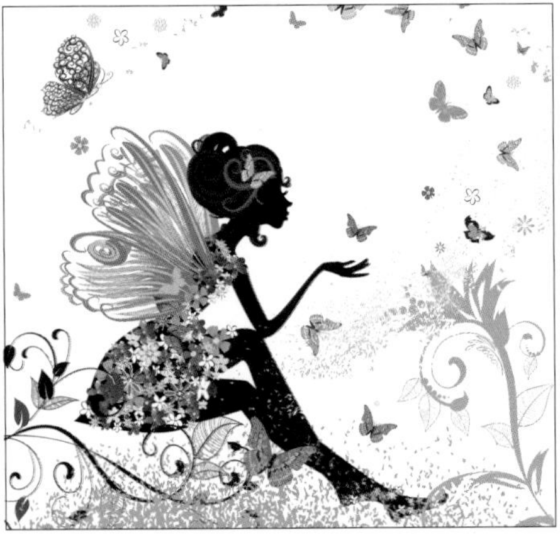

Pink and purple pair well with softly ethereal or otherwordly effects.

1 Lavender Mist
A color evoking the air of the highlands where lavender blooms.

2 Muse Pink
In Greek mythology, a muse inspired creative expression.

3 Fairy Orchid
An elegant, gorgeous purple like that of orchids.

4 Lilac
The color of lilacs, which are used as an ingredient in perfume.

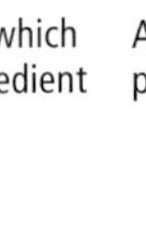

5 Fairy Pink
An airy, gentle, delicate pink.

6 Forget-me-not
The color of forget-me-not flowers, a symbol of true love.

7 Twinkle Star
A faint yellow like that of a twinkling star in the night sky.

8 Grayish Green
A calm green with just a touch of gray.

9 Leaf Green
A natural green like that seen on tree leaves.

1	C25 M30 Y0 K3 R195 G180 B213 #C2B3D5
2	C10 M50 Y5 K0 R224 G152 B187 #E098BA
3	C20 M65 Y15 K10 R191 G108 B145 #BF6B90
4	C25 M45 Y5 K0 R197 G154 B191 #C59ABF
5	C5 M35 Y5 K0 R237 G187 B207 #EDBBCF
6	C53 M30 Y0 K0 R129 G161 B212 #81A0D3
7	C5 M0 Y70 K10 R233 G225 B93 #E9E15D
8	C40 M10 Y50 K0 R168 G198 B146 #A7C592
9	C60 M15 Y65 K0 R112 G171 B115 #70AB72

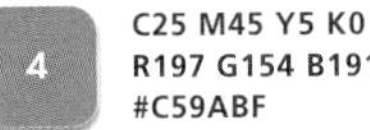
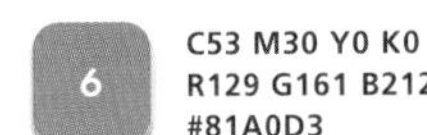
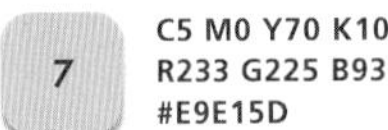

Two-color combinations

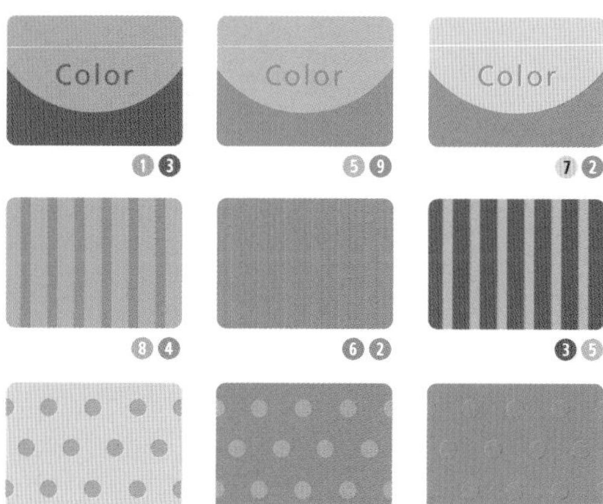

Three-color combinations

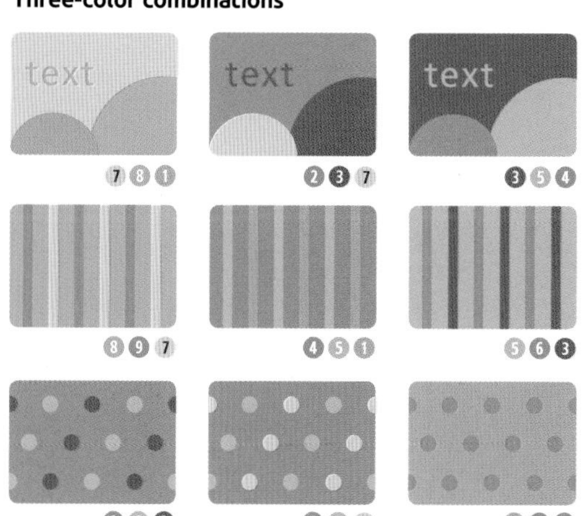

Designs

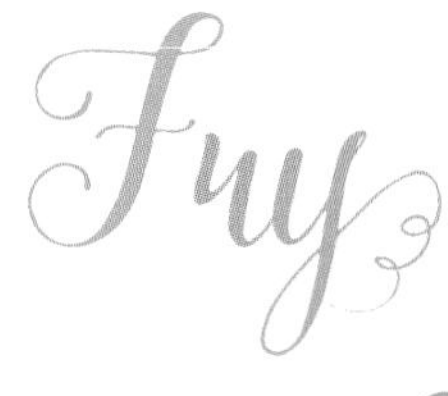

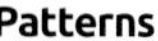

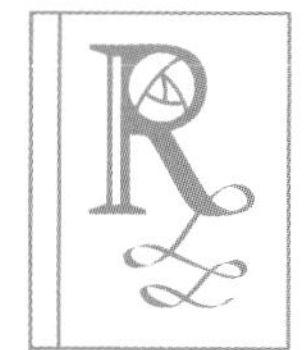

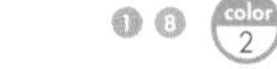

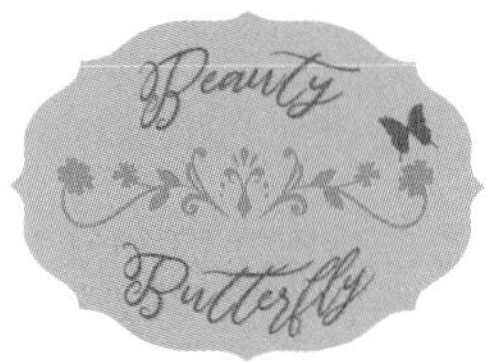

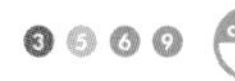

Patterns

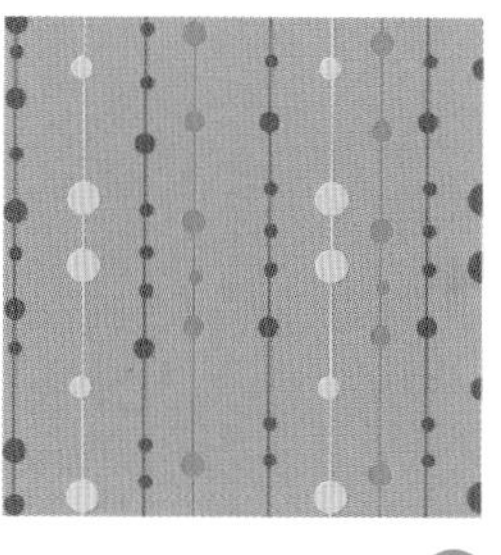

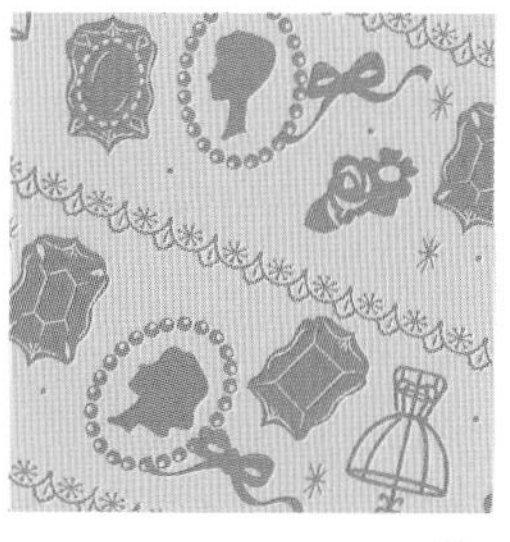

color 3 · color 4 · color 4

Illustration

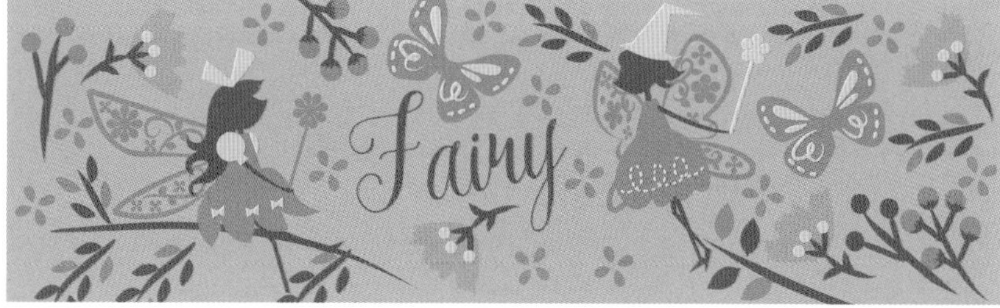

color 6

PART 02

ROMANTIC

Recipe
013

Cherry Blossom Trees

Cherry blossoms bloom for one brief week. It's easy to walk past cherry trees most of the year without even noticing them, but the pink color is in their bark. Textile artisan Fukumi Shimura creates the cherry blossom color by using the bark of the mountain cherry collected just before the flowers bloom. The pink color is full of the vitality of life.

- **FEELING** Happy, fulfilled, gentle.
- **COMBINATIONS** Pair pale pink with a little green or brown.
- **TIPS** Combine various pinks to bring out depth.

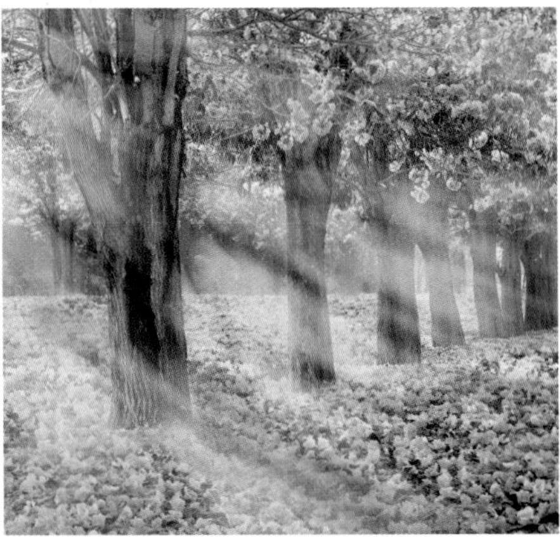

Cherry blossom pink is a special color that raises the spirit.

① Mountain Cherry
The long-living cherry referenced in Japanese tanka poetry.

② Somei Yoshino
The variety of cherry developed in Somei during the Edo period.

③ Double Cherry Blossom
A two-blossom variety comes in varied colors.

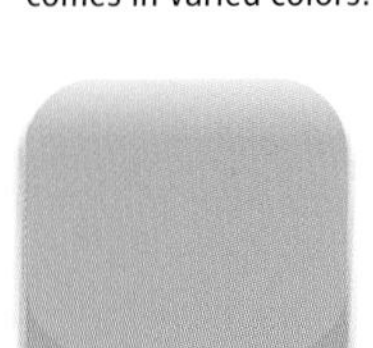

④ Cherry Blossom Tea
Cherry blossoms pickled in salt open in hot water. Used at auspicious events.

⑤ Cherry Tree
A dark brown tinged with red, this color matches well with pink.

⑥ Cherry Leaf
The leaves of cherry trees pickled in salt, wrapping mochi cakes.

⑦ Sunlight
A color that evokes the warm rays of the sun at the start of spring.

⑧ Eggshell
A pale yellow with a red tinge like that of eggshells.

⑨ Adzuki
A dark red like that of an adzuki bean, from the Edo period.

1 C0 M30 Y2 K0 R247 G201 B219 #F7C8DA

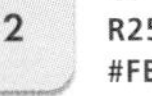

2 C0 M15 Y3 K0 R251 G229 B235 #FBE5EB

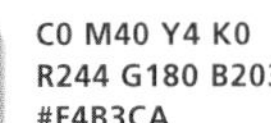

3 C0 M40 Y4 K0 R244 G180 B203 #F4B3CA

4 C0 M37 Y20 K0 R246 G184 B182 #F5B8B5

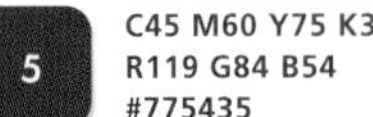

5 C45 M60 Y75 K35 R119 G84 B54 #775435

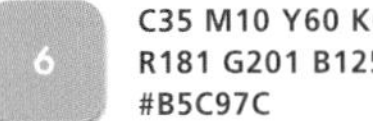

6 C35 M10 Y60 K0 R181 G201 B125 #B5C97C

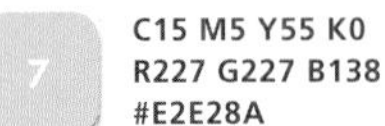

7 C15 M5 Y55 K0 R227 G227 B138 #E2E28A

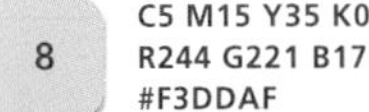

8 C5 M15 Y35 K0 R244 G221 B175 #F3DDAF

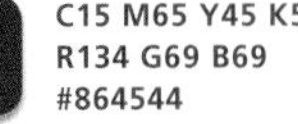

9 C15 M65 Y45 K50 R134 G69 B69 #864544

Two-color combinations

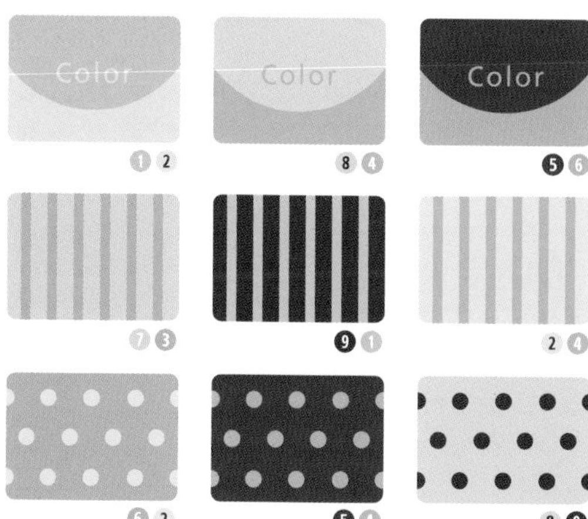

Three-color combinations

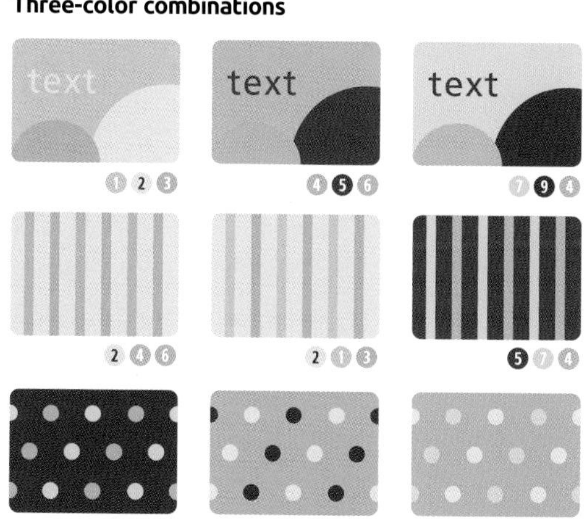

Designs

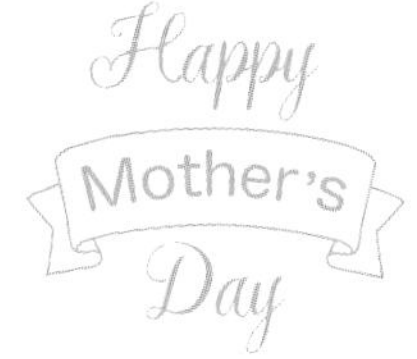

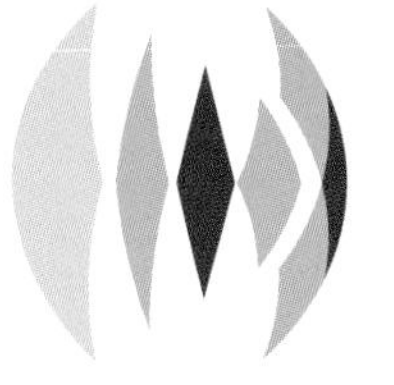

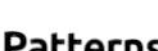

Patterns

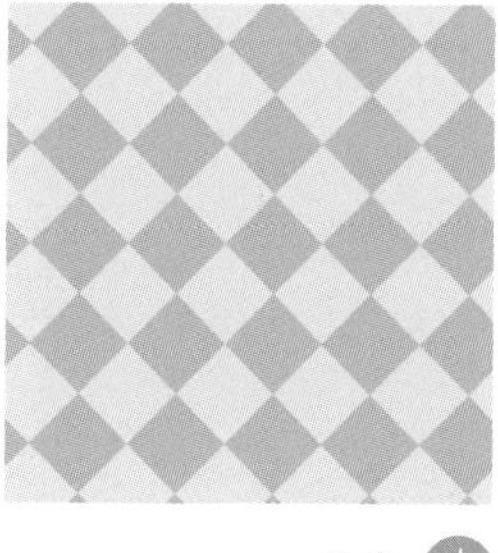

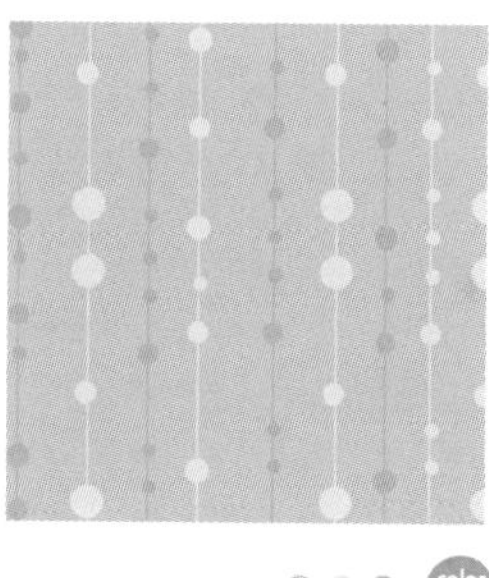

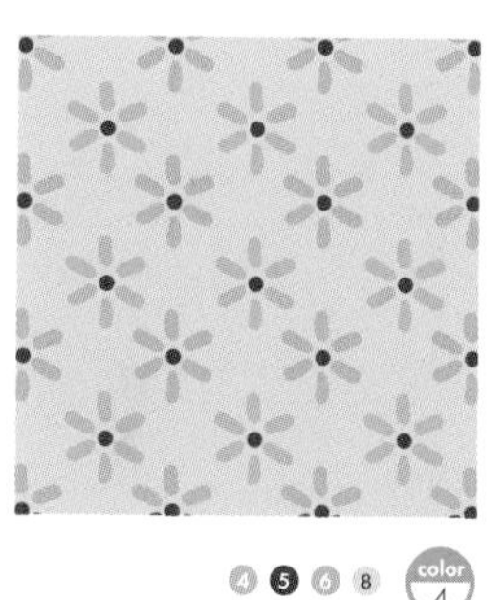

Illustration

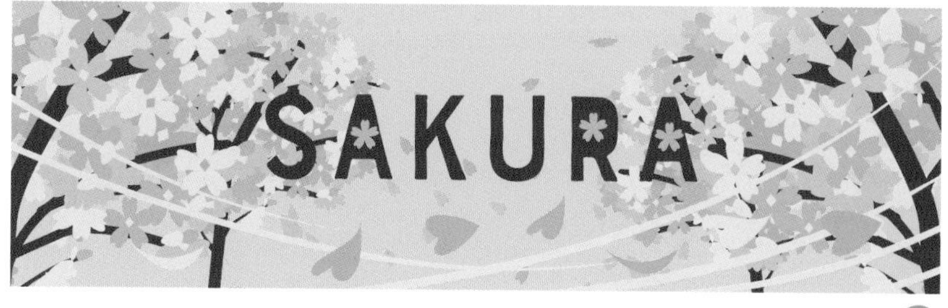

Recipe
014

Soap Bubble Rainbows

The reason that rainbow colors wind their way over the surface of soap bubbles is due to movement called the interference of light. When light passes through the bubble and is reflected back out, it overlaps with light that is also reflecting off the surface, resulting in the sparkling rainbow colors. The color schemes express the gentle rays of color seemingly floating through the air.

- **FEELING** Dreamy, whimsical, elusive.
- **COMBINATIONS** Focus on pale shades of blue and purple.
- **TIPS** Keep things gentle and don't add contrast.

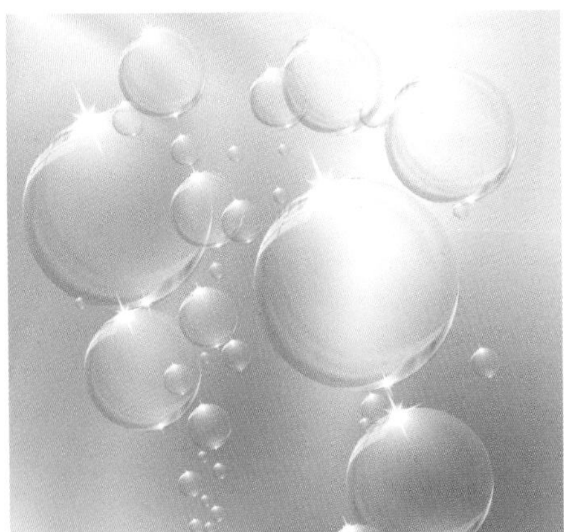

The diaphanous bubbles serve as prisms adding color and light to the scene.

1 Reflection Blue
A translucent blue that creates the sense of reflected light.

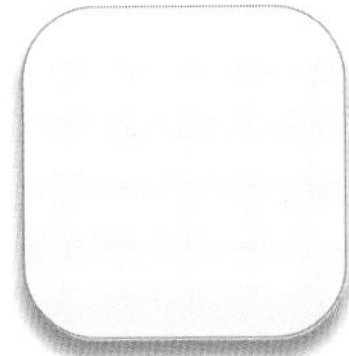

2 Bubble White
Clear white like that of the membrane on a soap bubble.

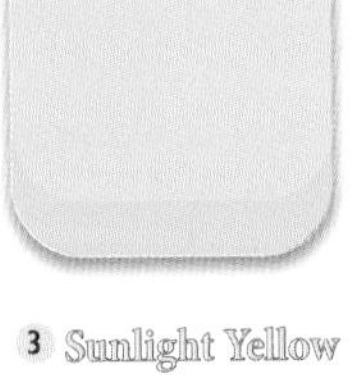

3 Sunlight Yellow
A yellow that calls to mind a warm ray of sunlight.

4 Air Blue
A blue with the translucence of air.

5 Shiny Pink
A mellow, glossy pink.

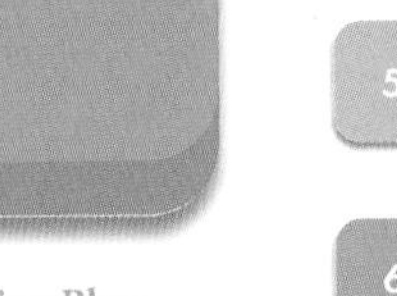

6 Shiny Blue
An elegant blue with an air of cleanliness.

7 Air Green
A pale green like that of a refreshing breeze blowing over grasslands.

8 Shiny Purple
The purple that appears on the surface of a soap bubble.

9 Shiny Rose
The pink that appears on the surface of a soap bubble.

No.	CMYK	RGB	Hex
1	C40 M0 Y5 K0	R160 G216 B239	#9FD8EE
2	C10 M0 Y0 K0	R234 G246 B253	#EAF6FD
3	C15 M0 Y45 K0	R227 G235 B164	#E2EBA3
4	C30 M10 Y0 K0	R187 G212 B239	#BAD4EE
5	C0 M30 Y20 K0	R248 G198 B189	#F7C6BD
6	C35 M25 Y5 K0	R176 G184 B214	#B0B7D6
7	C27 M0 Y30 K0	R198 G226 B195	#C5E2C2
8	C25 M40 Y0 K0	R197 G164 B204	#C5A3CB
9	C0 M30 Y5 K0	R247 G200 B214	#F7C8D6

Two-color combinations

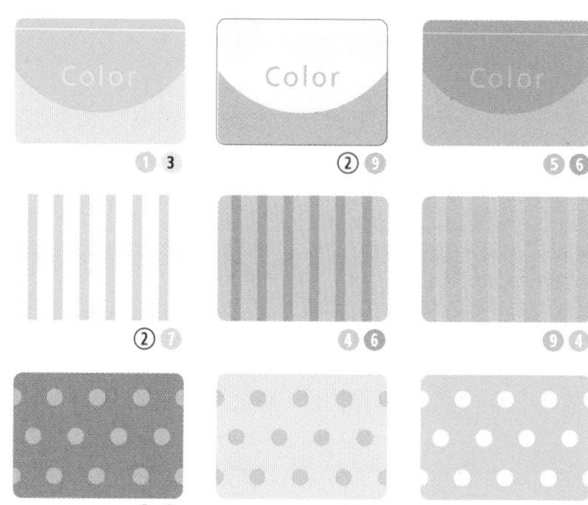

Three-color combinations

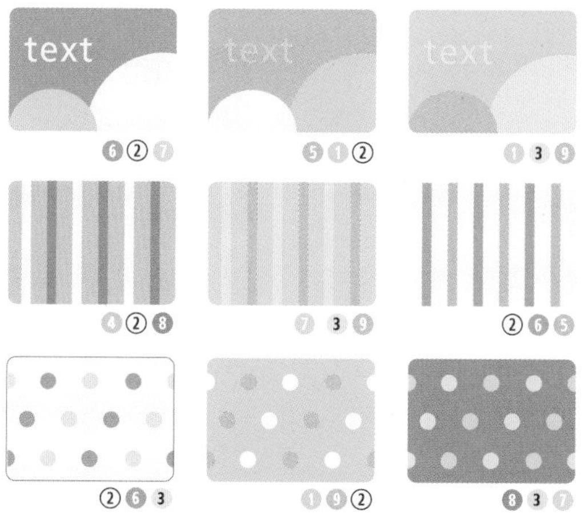

Designs

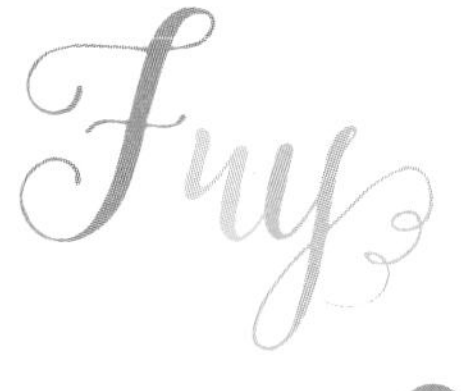

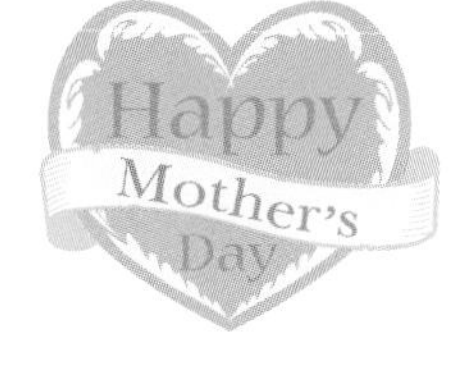

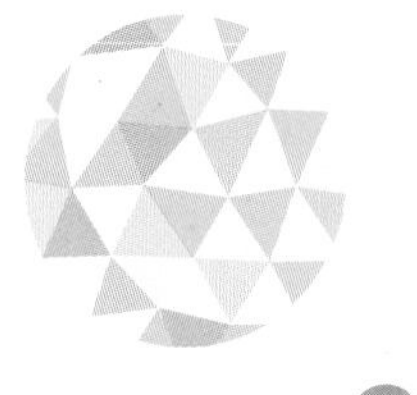

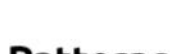

Patterns

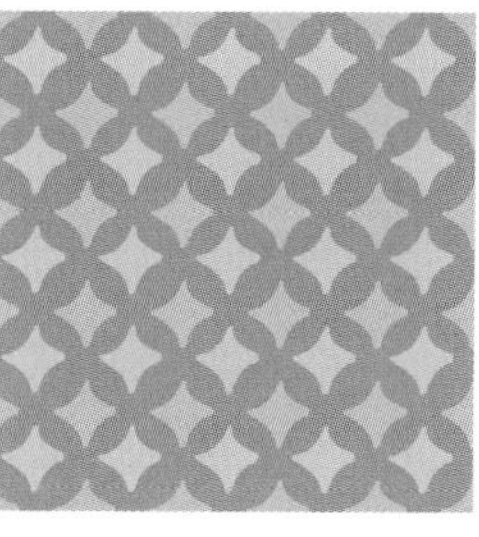

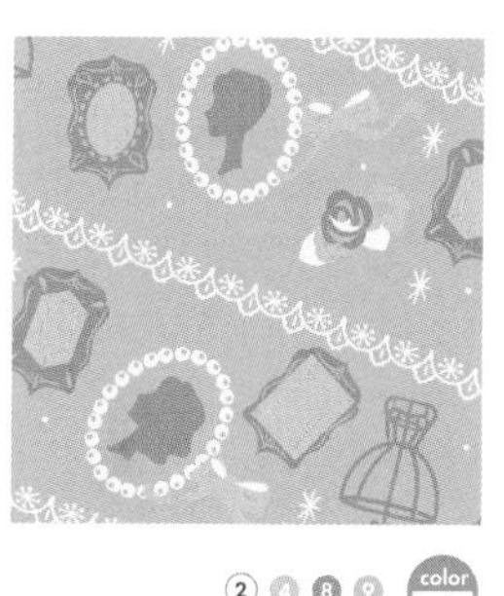

Illustration

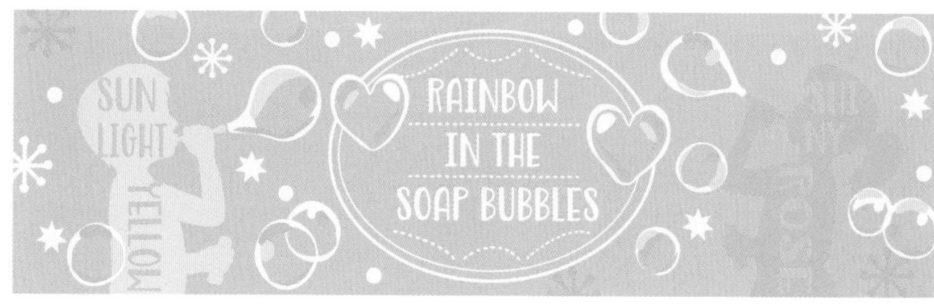

Recipe
015

Gingerbread House

The gingerbread house figures prominently in the fairy tale "Hansel & Gretel." The mismatch of a wicked witch living in a charmingly edible edifice remains etched in one's mind. In German families, gingerbread houses are made during the Christmas season, a tradition adopted elsewhere too. This color palette reflects a dream-like fairy land.

- **FEELING** Dream-like, magical, fabled.
- **COMBINATIONS** Use plenty of different shades of brown.
- **TIPS** If using multiple colors, keep the tones similar.

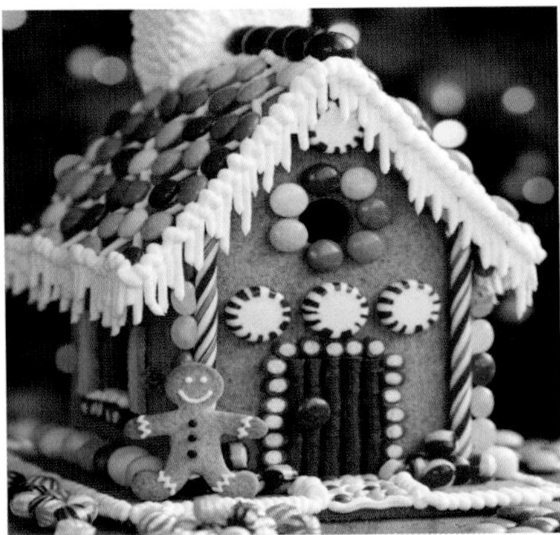

In German, this is called a hexenhaus, or witches' house.

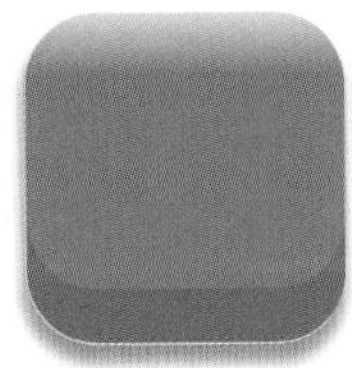

❶ Gingerbread
The color of the cookie used to make the walls of gingerbread houses.

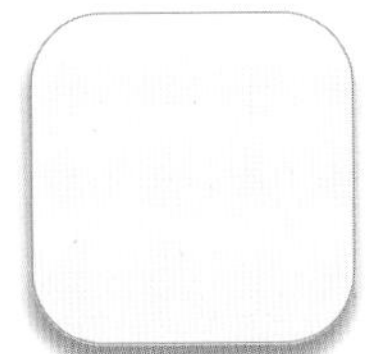

② Whipped Cream
The white of the sweet, light, cream that melts in the mouth.

❸ Milk Chocolate
The brown of milk chocolate.

❹ Cherry Bonbon
The red color of a cherry bonbon.

❺ Pistachio
The yellow green of a fragrant pistachio.

❻ Custard Cream
The yellow of custard cream made using plenty of egg yolks.

❼ Dreamy Pink
This color symbolizes the gingerbread house. It's the pink of dreams.

❽ Candied Violet
A sweet violet shade like that of candied violet flowers.

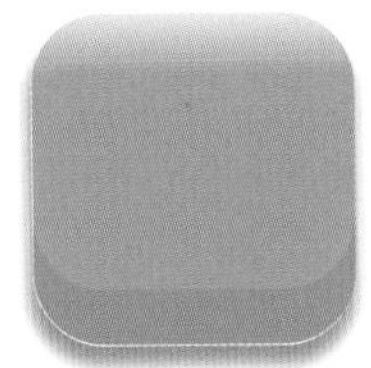

❾ Blue Sugar
The color of sugar dyed blue. Use it as an accent color.

No.	CMYK	RGB	Hex
1	C30 M50 Y70 K0	R190 G139 B85	#BD8A55
2	C0 M0 Y7 K3	R251 G250 B240	#FBFAEF
3	C55 M70 Y75 K15	R124 G84 B66	#7C5341
4	C3 M90 Y60 K0	R228 G55 B74	#E3364A
5	C45 M0 Y80 K0	R156 G202 B84	#9BCA54
6	C0 M10 Y75 K0	R255 G228 B80	#FFE350
7	C5 M80 Y0 K0	R225 G81 B151	#E15097
8	C37 M60 Y0 K0	R172 G118 B176	#AC75B0
9	C60 M15 Y0 K0	R98 G176 B227	#61B0E2

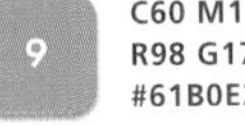

Two-color combinations

Color 1 3

Color 2 4

Color 7 5

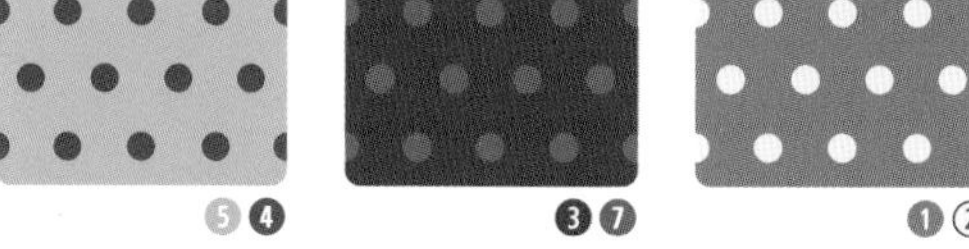

8 6

9 1

3 4

5 4

3 7

1 2

Three-color combinations

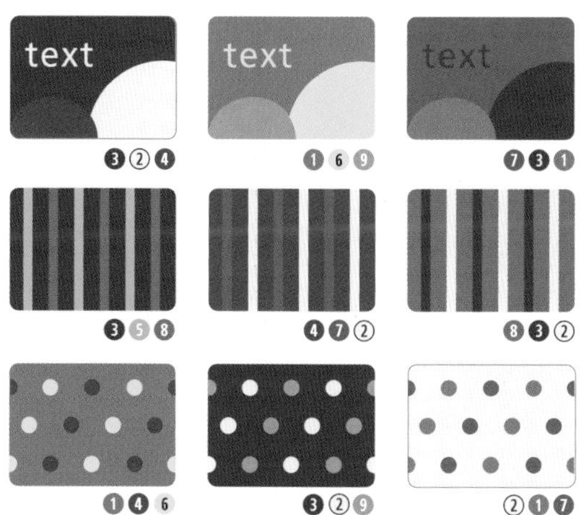

3 2 4

1 6 9

7 3 1

3 5 8

4 7 2

8 3 2

1 4 6

3 2 9

2 1 7

Designs

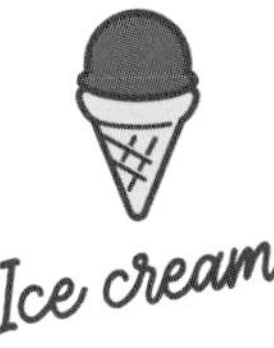

3 6 7 color 3

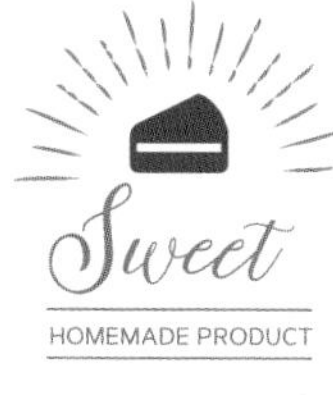

1 3 8 color 3

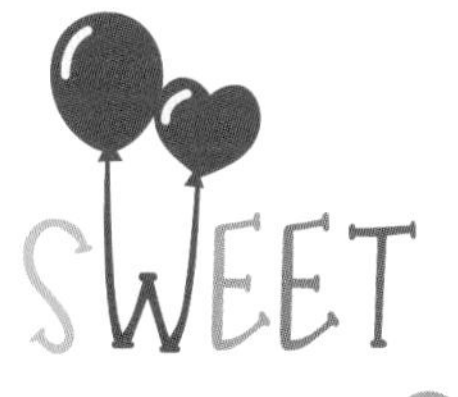

1 4 5 7 9 color 5

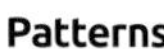

Patterns

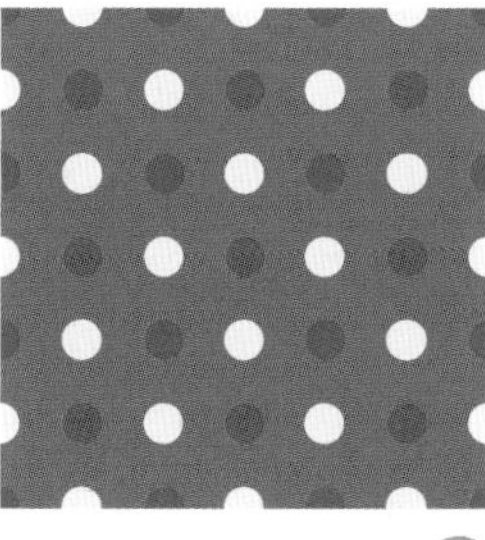

2 7 8 color 3

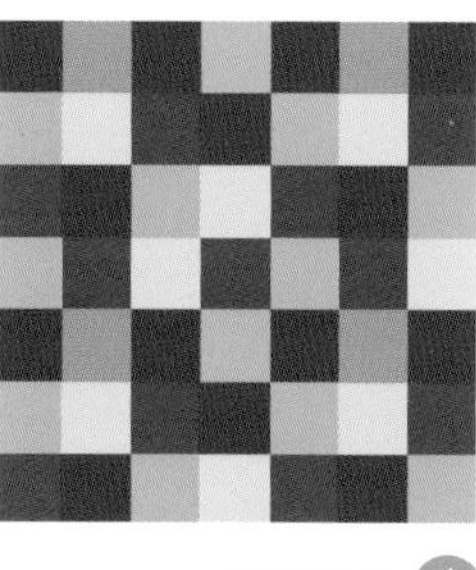

3 4 5 6 color 4

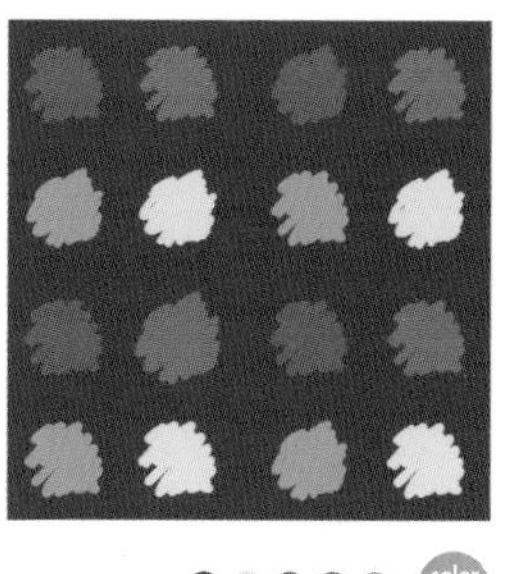

3 6 7 8 9 color 5

Illustration

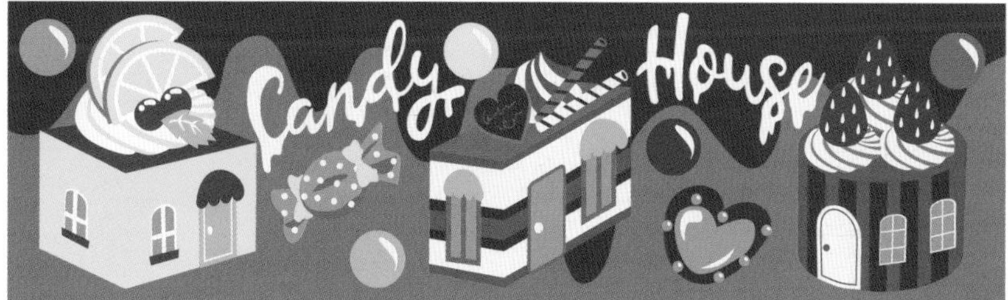

1 2 3 4 5 6 7 8 9 color 9

Recipe
016

Cosmos Flowers

Usually, cosmos come in different shades of purple, but one day my elementary-school-aged daughter came home with her eyes shining and said, "Mom, did you know there are chocolate cosmos flowers? They really look delicious! My teacher told us today!" I think I'll go to the florist and check out those novel brown cosmos.

- **FEELING** Calm, elegant, relaxed.
- **COMBINATIONS** Combine purples and yellow greens with low saturation levels.
- **TIPS** Use deep fall shades as accent colors.

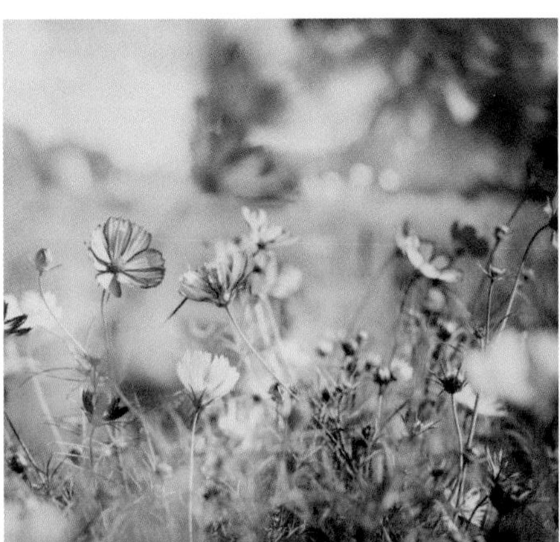

Cosmos takes their name from the Greek word "kosmos," which means harmony and universe.

① Grassland
The green of grasslands, lighter than the color of cosmos leaves.

② Maiden's True Heart
A pretty soft pink, reminiscent of a carnation.

③ Harmony
A color that balances red and blue.

④ Modesty
A word associated with cosmos in the language of flowers.

⑤ Fall Wind
A pale grayish green that evokes the wind in fall.

⑥ Dull Green
A dull tone of green with a lot of gray mixed in.

⑦ Dark Green
A relaxed green with a low degree of brightness.

⑧ Chocolate Cosmos
A cosmos flower that has a cocoa-colored tint.

⑨ Grape
The purple that is symbolic of grapes.

1 C25 M0 Y70 K0 R206 G222 B104 #CDDE67

2 C15 M50 Y20 K3 R213 G147 B163 #D492A3

3 C13 M80 Y0 K0 R213 G79 B151 #D44F97

4 C5 M20 Y10 K0 R241 G216 B217 #F1D7D8

5 C15 M0 Y20 K3 R221 G235 B213 #DDEBD5

6 C50 M27 Y70 K0 R145 G163 B99 #90A362

7 C80 M50 Y67 K10 R57 G106 B91 #38695A

8 C0 M75 Y50 K45 R158 G61 B62 #9D3C3E

9 C45 M85 Y13 K0 R157 G64 B135 #9C4087

Two-color combinations

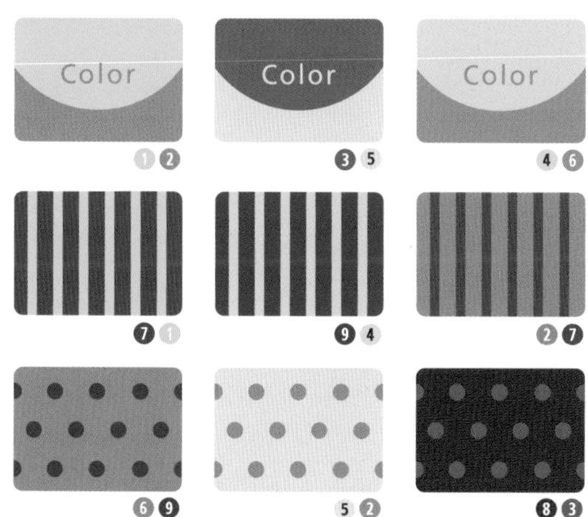

Three-color combinations

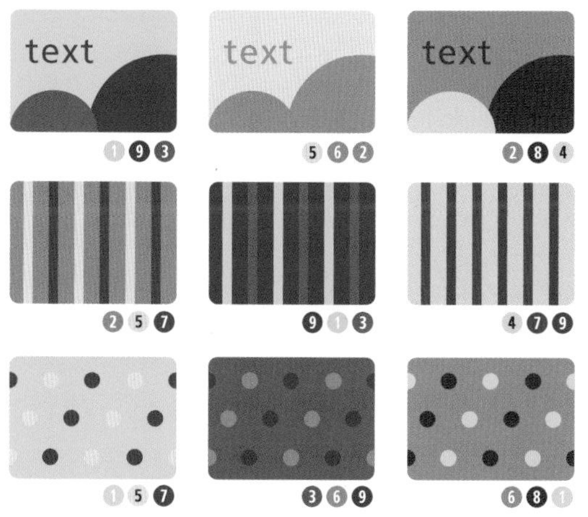

Designs

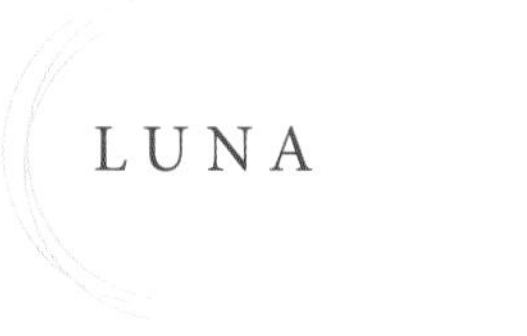

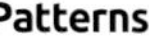
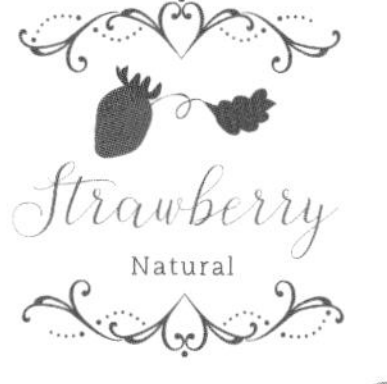

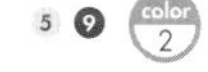

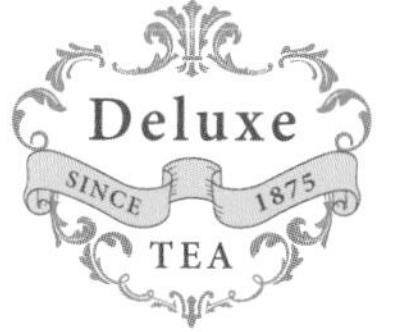

Patterns

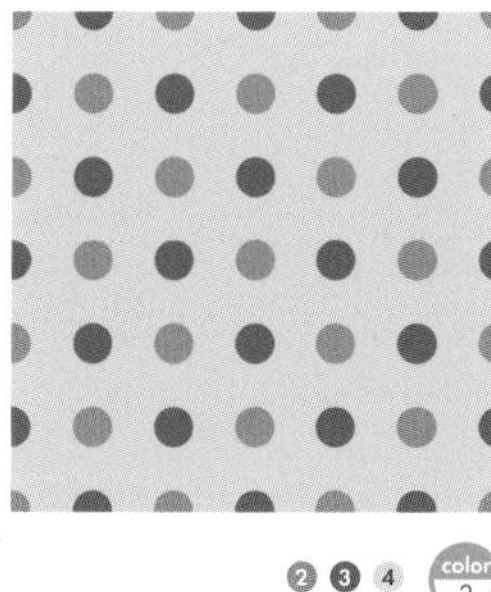
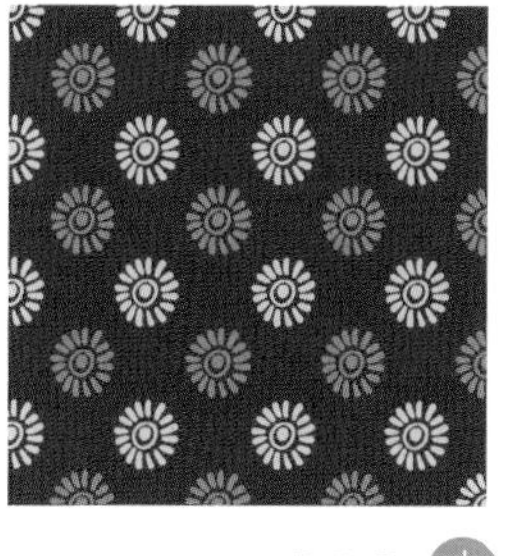
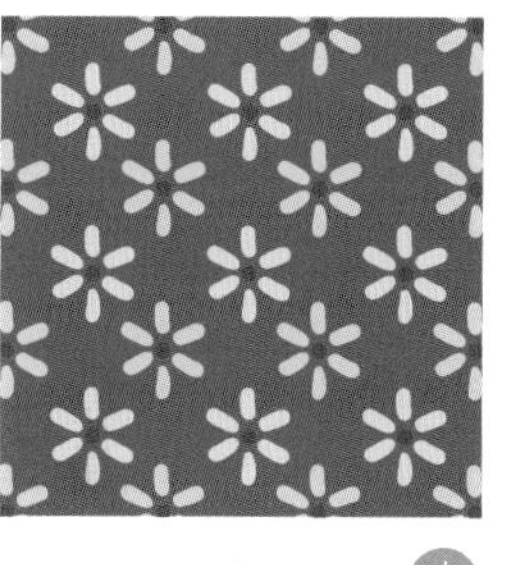

Illustration

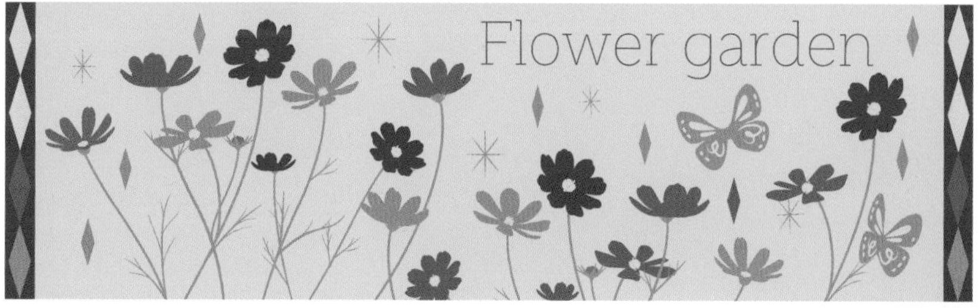

Recipe
017

Baby's Room

Light colors create an airy, light, soft image. In order to create them, in the case of paints, plenty of white needs to be be mixed in. All this white yields a pure, clear aura. Newborn babies have a similarly pure presence. These color schemes comprise shades commonly used for baby items.

- **FEELING** Gentle, soft, delicate.
- **COMBINATIONS** Use only light, pale colors.
- **TIPS** Create designs that incorporate and balance warm and cool shades.

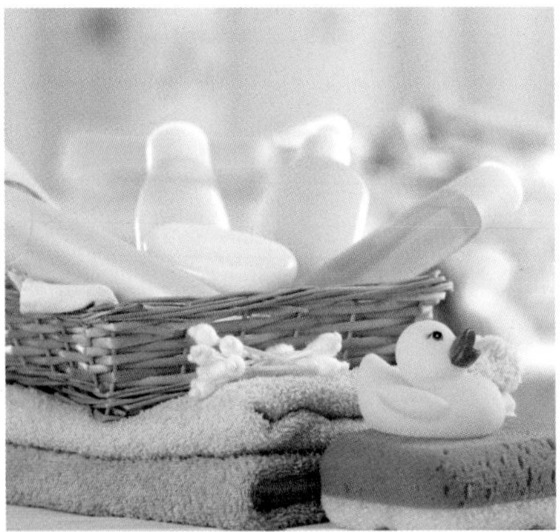

Baby items are designed in delicate colors that have a high level of brightness but a low level of saturation.

① Baby Pink
One of the traditional colors used for baby girls' clothing.

② Powder Yellow
This soft yellow can be used regardless of gender.

③ Baby Blue
One of the traditional colors used for baby boys' clothing.

④ Powder Orange
A shade of orange that is close to white and has a calm, secure air.

⑤ Powder Green
A delicate green with a pure, translucent feel.

⑥ Melty Pink
An airy, soft pink that seems as if it could melt.

⑦ Nursery Pink
The kind of pink that is used inside nursery schools.

⑧ Rubber Duck
The color of the floating rubber duck, the ideal bath toy.

⑨ Morning Breeze
A color that calls to mind the crisp air of the morning breeze.

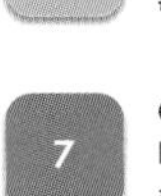
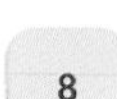

No.	CMYK	RGB	Hex
1	C0 M20 Y5 K0	R250 G220 B226	#FADBE1
2	C5 M0 Y25 K0	R247 G248 B208	#F6F7D0
3	C15 M5 Y0 K0	R223 G234 B248	#DEEAF7
4	C0 M15 Y20 K0	R252 G227 B205	#FCE2CC
5	C20 M0 Y15 K0	R213 G235 B225	#D4EBE1
6	C0 M35 Y10 K0	R246 G190 B200	#F5BDC8
7	C0 M65 Y30 K0	R237 G121 B135	#EC7986
8	C0 M8 Y63 K0	R255 G233 B115	#FFE873
9	C40 M23 Y0 K0	R163 G183 B222	#A3B6DE

Two-color combinations

①② 8 9 ⑤ 6

7 ⑤ 9 ① ②④

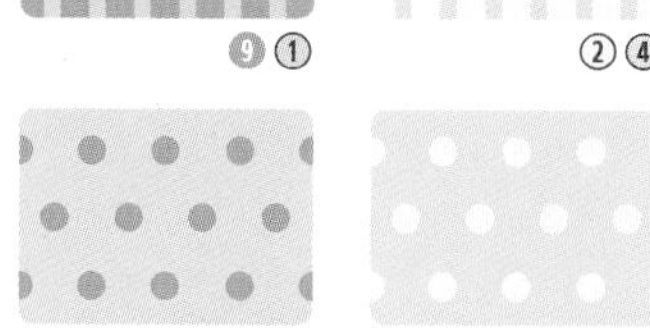

6 ① ④ 9 8 ②

Three-color combinations

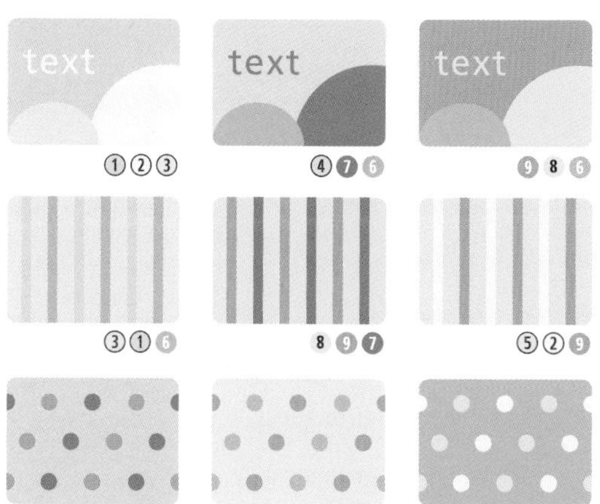

①②③ ④ 7 6 9 8 6

③① 6 8 9 7 ⑤② 9

① 9 7 ③ 6 9 6 8 ②

Designs

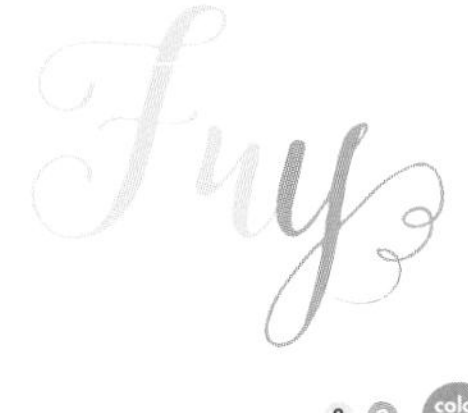

8 9 color 2

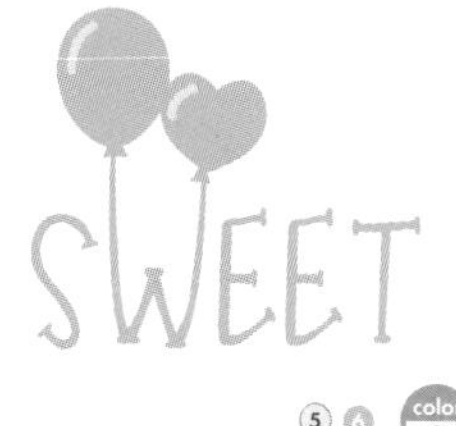

⑤ 6 color 2

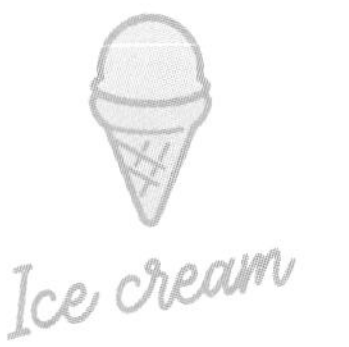

6 8 color 2

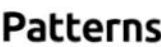

Patterns

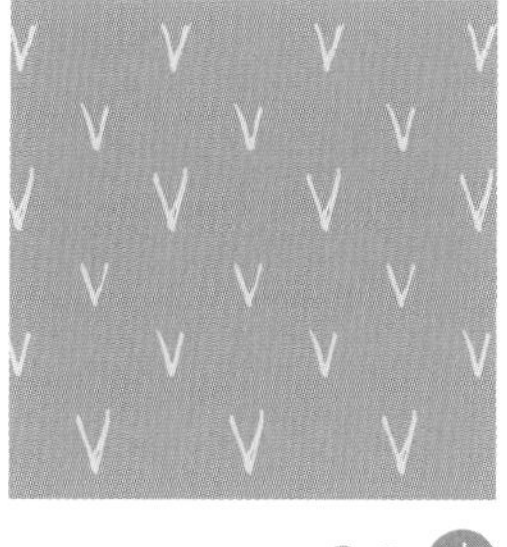

④ 9 color 2

② 9 ⑤ color 3

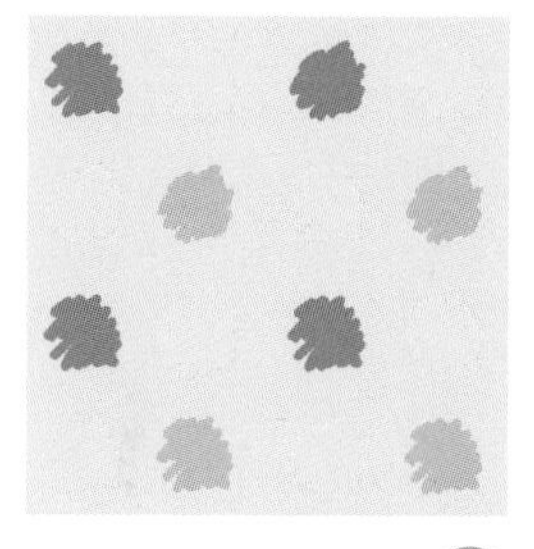

⑤ 6 7 8 color 4

Illustration

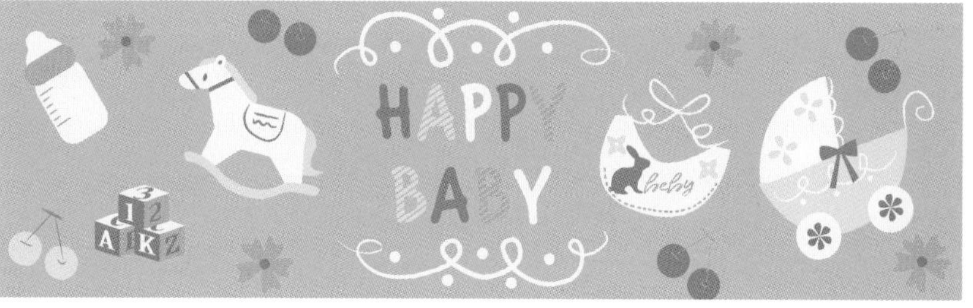

② 6 7 8 9 color 5

Recipe
018

A "Thank You" Bouquet

Expressing gratitude, love or thanks by sending a bouquet of blooms is a gesture that isn't extended often enough. When the sentiment is appropriate, send a parcel of posies that tap into the soothing natural tones of artfully arranged flowers.

- **FEELING** Warm, gentle, magnanimous.
- **COMBINATIONS** Create combinations focusing on warm, bright tones.
- **TIPS** Use dark colors sparingly as accents.

Give the gift of a bouquet in warm, soft shades to express gratitude.

① Thank You
Thank you is a magic phrase, offering warmth and gratitude.

② I Trust You
A color that expresses to the recipient that you trust them.

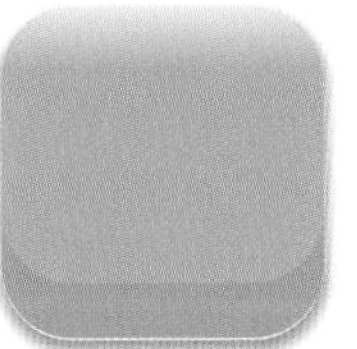

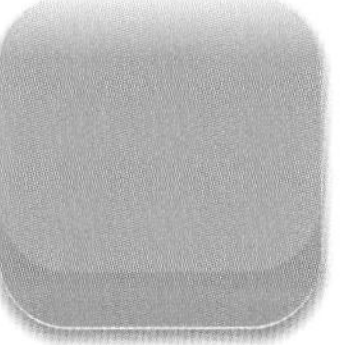

③ I Respect You
A color that expresses to the recipient that you respect them.

④ I Love You
A color that expresses to the beloved the feelings you have for them.

⑤ I Care for You
A color that expresses to the recipient that feel affection for them.

⑥ Peace of Mind
A color that expresses to the beloved the security you feel at their side.

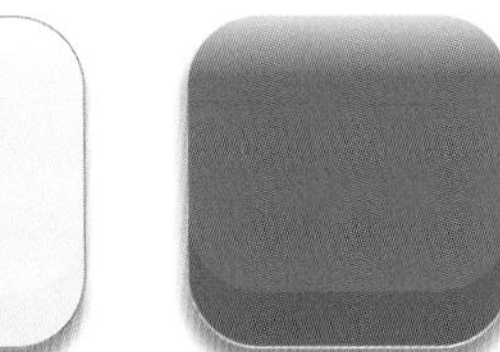

⑦ Be Honest
A color that evokes being honest with one's own emotions.

⑧ Love
A color that evokes feelings of high regard for the recipient.

⑨ Knot
The bond and connection between spouses and romantic partners.

1	C0 M40 Y37 K0 R245 G176 B150 #F4B095
2	C25 M5 Y70 K0 R206 G216 B102 #CDD866
3	C35 M15 Y45 K0 R180 G196 B153 #B3C399
4	C0 M30 Y5 K0 R247 G200 B214 #F7C8D6
5	C15 M30 Y0 K0 R219 G190 B218 #DABEDA
6	C5 M10 Y60 K0 R247 G226 B123 #F6E27A
7	C0 M5 Y20 K0 R255 G245 B215 #FFF4D6
8	C15 M70 Y10 K0 R212 G105 B154 #D36899
9	C60 M70 Y10 K0 R124 G90 B153 #7B5A99

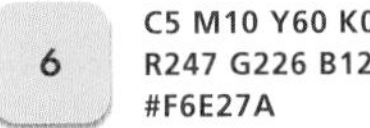

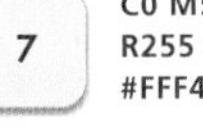
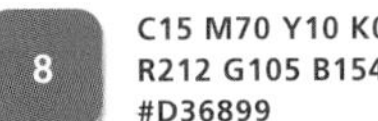
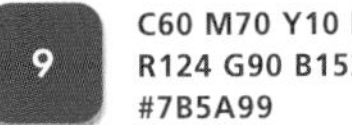
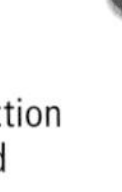

Two-color combinations

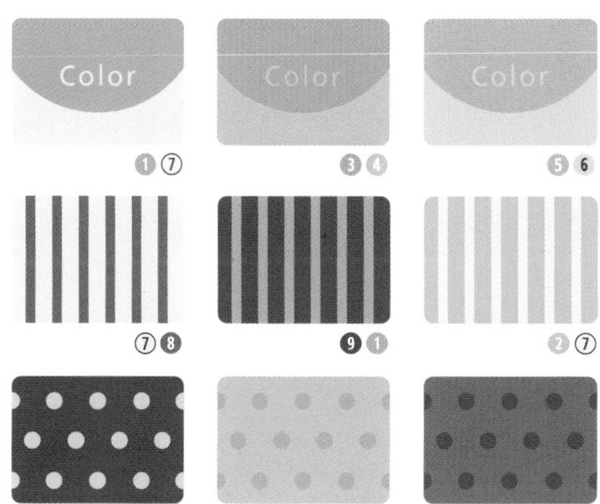

Three-color combinations

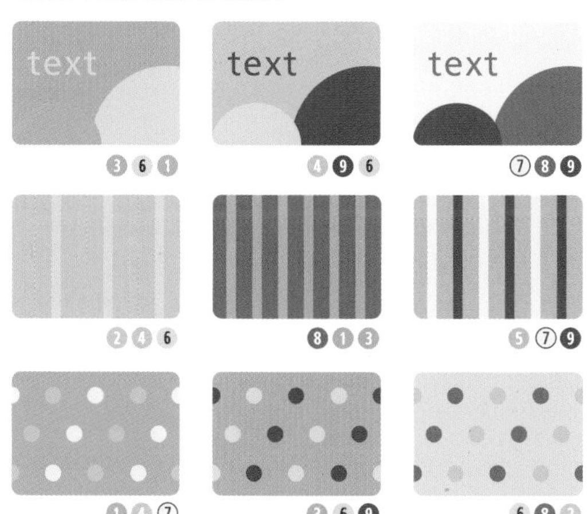

Designs

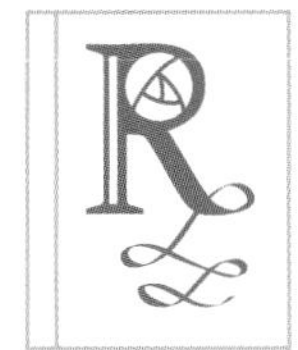

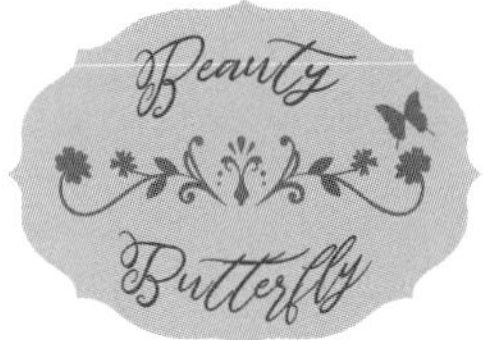

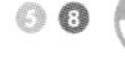

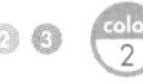

Patterns

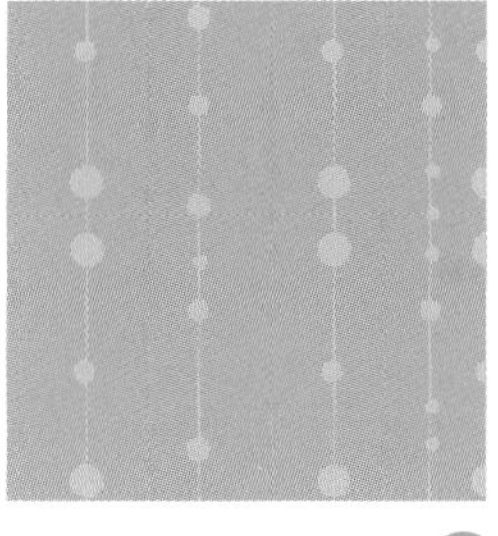

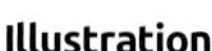

Illustration

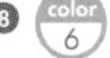

Recipe
019

Marshmallows

Fluffy, melt-in-the-mouth marshmallows embody the softer sweeter side of pastels. Color schemes using only marshmallow colors are gentle, sweet and soft. Here, colors lighter than pastels are referred to as "pale colors" and those even lighter are called "icy colors."

- **FEELING** Pale, soft, gentle.
- **COMBINATIONS** Combine similar colors.
- **TIPS** Make sure there are no strong contrasts.

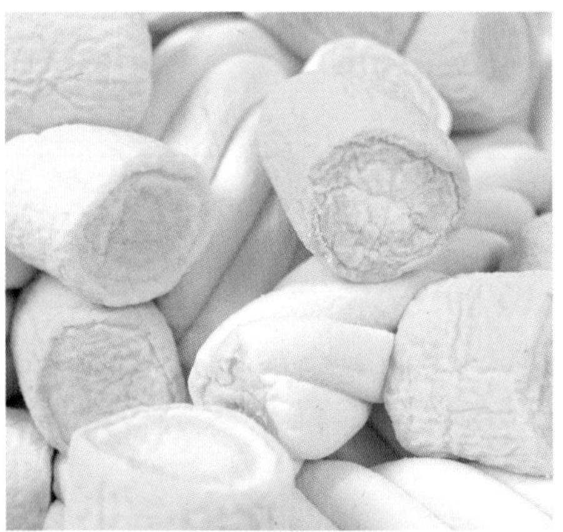

Guimauve are similar to marshmallows.

① Pale Pink
A pink with a high level of brightness but a low level of saturation.

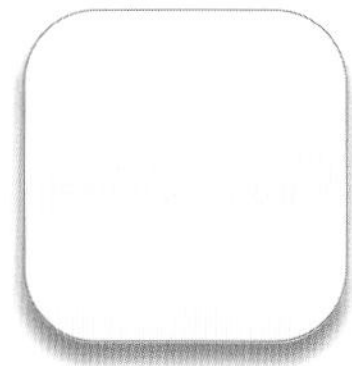

② Pale Yellow
A yellow with a faint tone to it, a thin wash of color.

③ Pale Aqua
This blue is often used for men's dress shirts.

④ Icy Pink
An extremely faint pink that is nearly white.

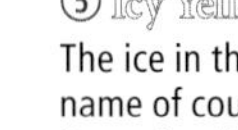

⑤ Icy Yellow
The ice in this color's name of course indicates its cooler side.

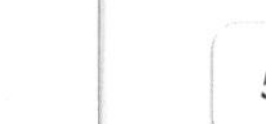

⑥ Icy Aqua
Only just blue, this color looks brighter than a regular white.

⑦ Pastel Pink
A pink with a high degree of brightness.

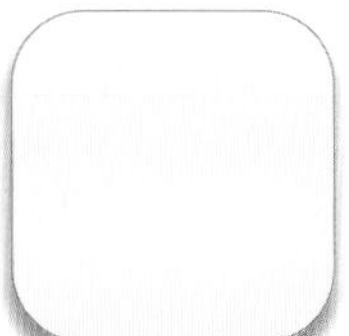

⑧ Pastel Yellow
Pastel suggests a faint or washed-out quality to the tone.

⑨ Pastel Aqua
A blue found everywhere: in nature, at home, at the store.

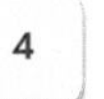
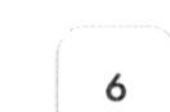

1	C0 M15 Y5 K0 R252 G229 B232 #FBE5E7
2	C0 M0 Y35 K0 R255 G250 B188 #FFFABB
3	C20 M0 Y5 K0 R212 G236 B243 #D3ECF3
4	C0 M6 Y0 K0 R254 G246 B249 #FDF5F9
5	C0 M0 Y8 K0 R255 G254 B242 #FFFEF1
6	C6 M0 Y0 K0 R243 G250 B254 #F3F9FD
7	C0 M35 Y5 K0 R246 G190 B208 #F5BECF
8	C0 M0 Y47 K0 R255 G248 B160 #FFF7A0
9	C30 M0 Y5 K0 R187 G226 B241 #BBE2F1

Two-color combinations

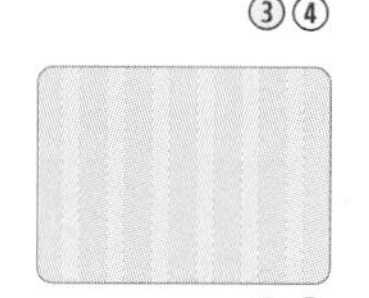

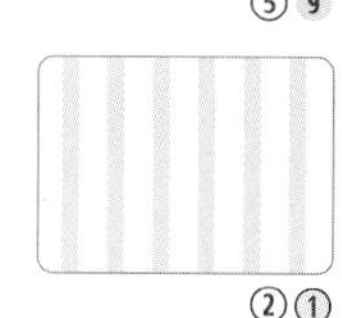

① ② ③ ④ ⑤ 9

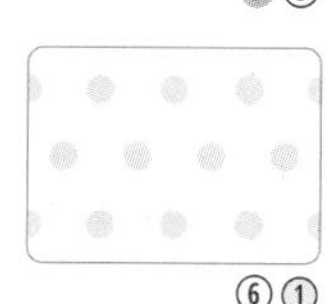

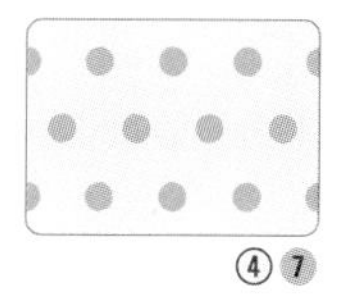

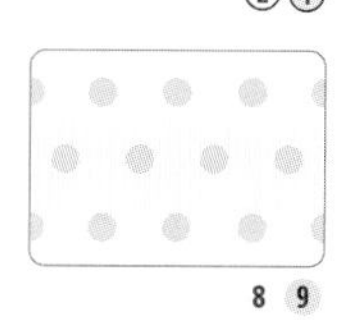

7 ⑤ 9 ① ② ①

⑥ ① ④ 7 8 9

Three-color combinations

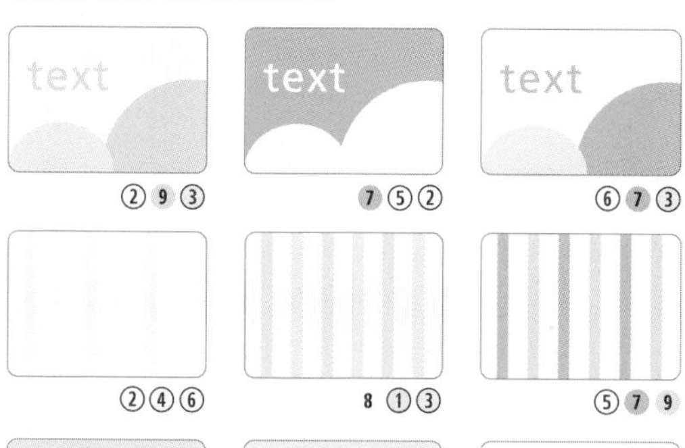

② 9 ③ 7 ⑤ ② ⑥ 7 ③

② ④ ⑥ 8 ① ③ ⑤ 7 9

① ④ 7 ③ ⑥ 9 ⑥ 8 ③

Designs

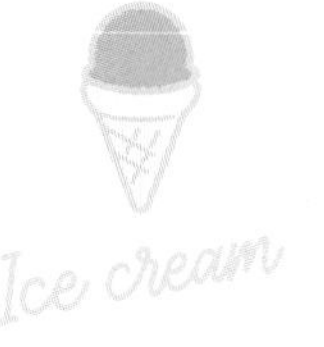

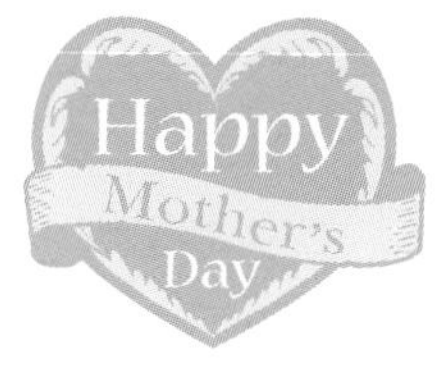

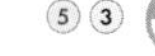

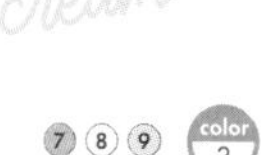

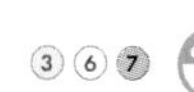

⑤ ③ color 2 7 ⑧ ⑨ color 3 ③ ⑥ 7 color 3

Patterns

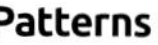

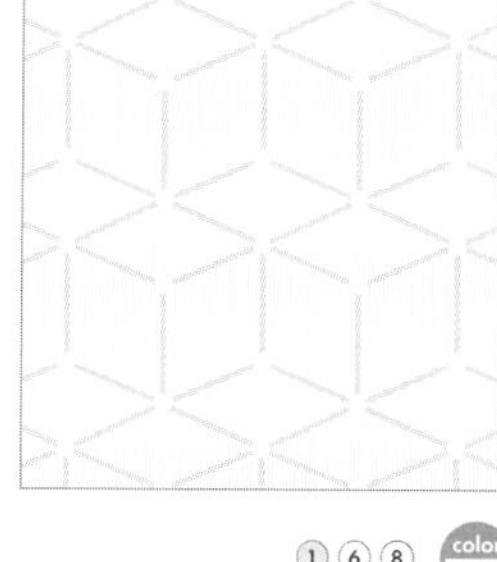

② ③ ④ color 3 ① ⑥ ⑧ color 3 ① ② ⑤ ⑥ color 4

Illustration

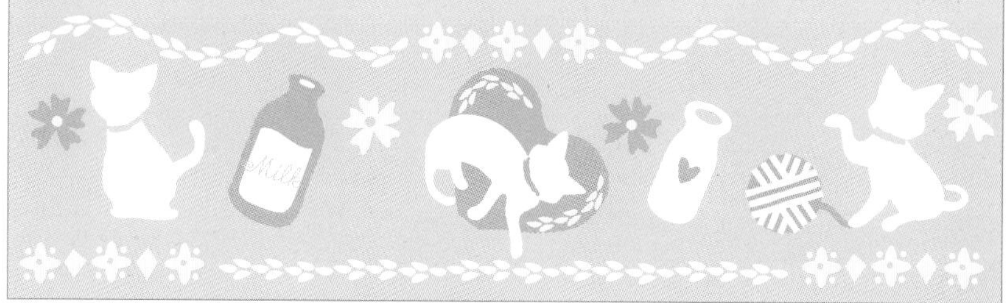

⑤ ⑥ 7 ⑧ ⑨ color 5

PART 02

ROMANTIC

Recipe
020

Frills and Lace

Frills and lace continue to come in and out of fashion. Add polka dots and the triple threat is complete. The particular scheme using blue, white and red is known simply as tricolor. On the French flag, each color has symbolic meaning: blue for liberty, white for equality and red for fraternity.

- **FEELING** Soft, adorable, retro.
- **COMBINATIONS** Use different shades of the colors in the tricolor.
- **TIPS** The greater the amount of white spread over an area, the cleaner the result.

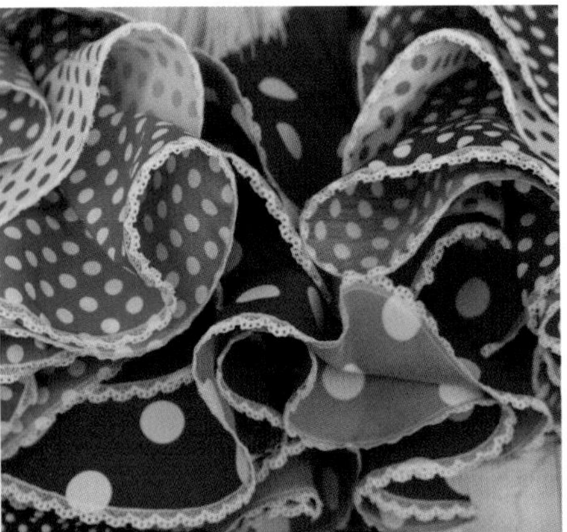

The tricolor effect, so commonly seen in flag design, offers a balanced yet vibrant scheme.

❶ French Red
An elegant, sophisticated red with a hint of purple to it.

② French White
A mild white with just a touch of yellow.

❸ French Blue
A blue slightly greener than Japan blue.

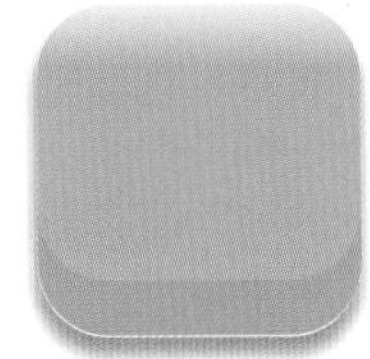

❹ Strawberry Milk
The harmony of sour-sweet strawberries with milk.

⑤ Meringue
A white like that of meringue, made by whipping egg whites.

❻ Lady Blue
A dignified blue that calls to mind a noblewoman.

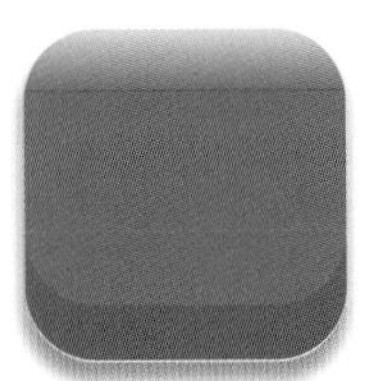

❼ Rose Red
A deep, purple-tinged red like that of rose petals.

❽ Strawberry Parfait
The color of strawberry sauce and whipped cream.

❾ Happy Bird
A beautiful blue that evokes the bluebird of happiness.

1	C20 M97 Y77 K0 R200 G33 B54 #C82136
2	C0 M0 Y7 K0 R255 G254 B243 #FFFEF3
3	C90 M30 Y10 K0 R0 G134 B193 #0086C0
4	C10 M55 Y30 K0 R224 G140 B146 #DF8C91
5	C0 M9 Y3 K0 R253 G240 B242 #FDF0F1
6	C45 M15 Y10 K0 R149 G190 B215 #95BED7
7	C40 M100 Y100 K20 R146 G24 B30 #91181D
8	C10 M75 Y50 K0 R220 G95 B98 #DB5F62
9	C100 M40 Y10 K30 R0 G93 B147 #005D92

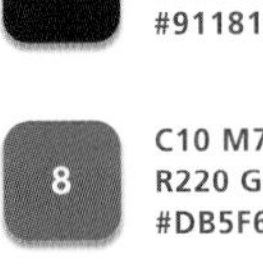

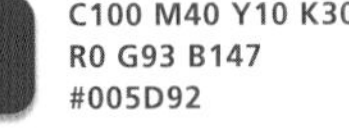

Two-color combinations

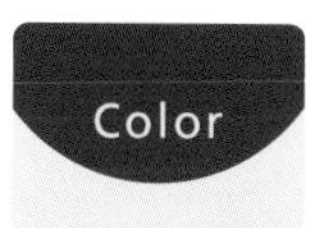

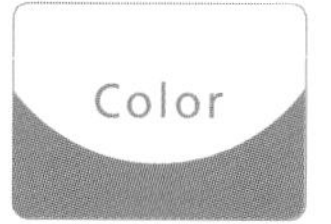

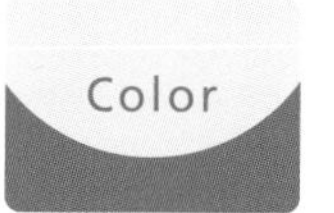

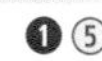

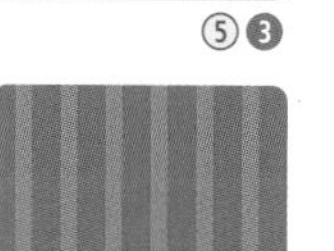
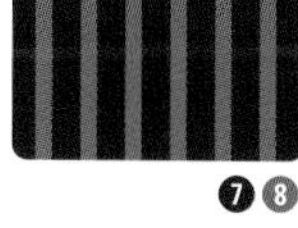
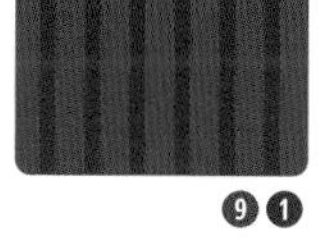

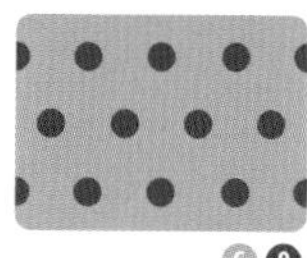
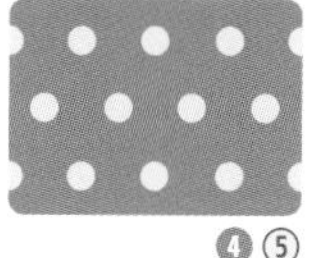
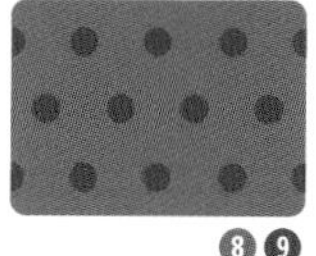

Three-color combinations

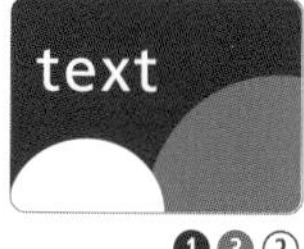

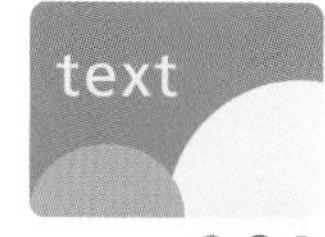

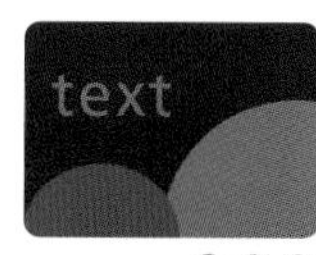

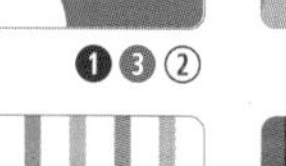
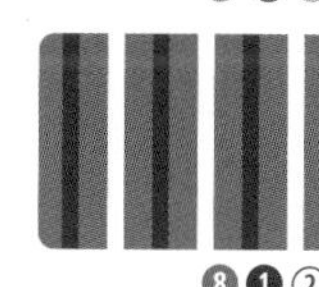
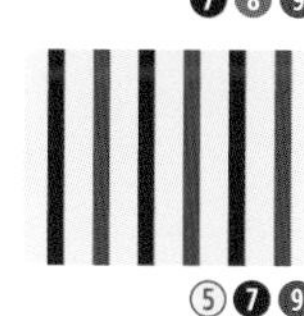
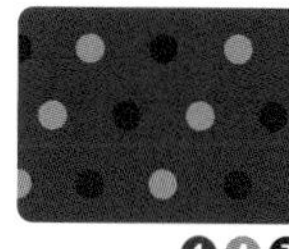
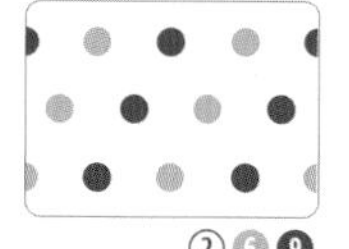
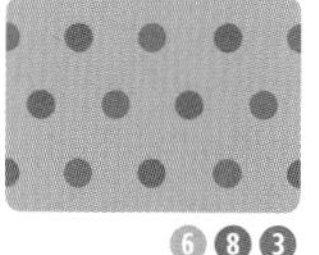

Designs

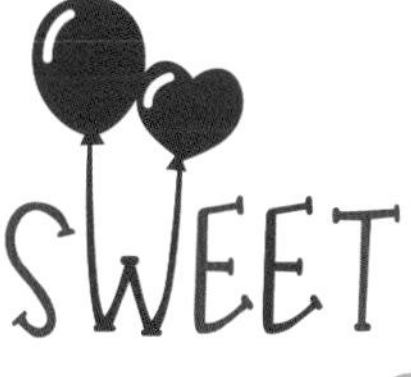

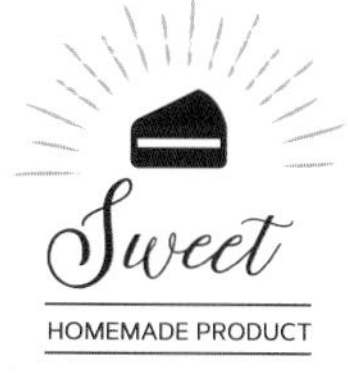

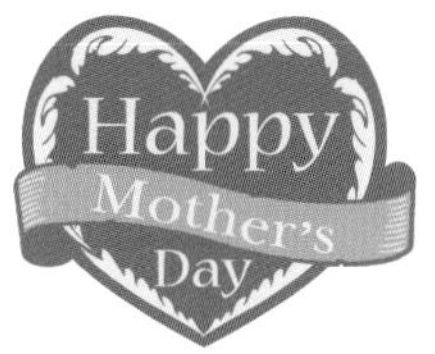

Patterns

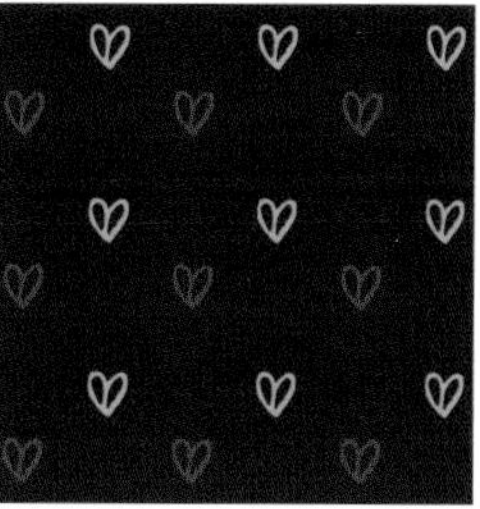

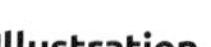

Illustration

Super Simple! The Basics of Color Schemes

Create Cohesion Using Similar Shades: Use Contrasting Colors to Draw Colors Out

Theories of color harmony originated with the ancient Greeks. Although even professional designers may sometimes find it difficult to pair colors together, the foundations of the theory are actually simple. In order to create successful color schemes, there are, broadly speaking, two courses of action—either to create a cohesive look by using similar shades, or using contrasting colors that set each other off.

If aiming for a cohesive feel, shades of the same color or type or those that border each other on the color wheel are used. In contrast to this, if a dynamic look is the goal, combinations are formed of opposing colors, complementary colors or tones that are far apart on the color wheel. Refer to the diagram on the right to explore which color scheme you'll use.

In addition to these two methods for creating color schemes is that of combining an accent color with a base color. The base color is a standard color that is used over a large surface area or used repeatedly. An accent color can be thought of in terms of cooking, in which case it is a spice that pulls the flavors together. To add variation to a color scheme, try using an assort color over the surface area that is largest in size, adding it after the base color.

A cohesive color scheme using similar colors

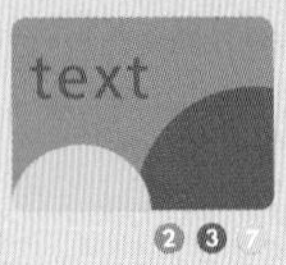

Use different shades of pink for ② and ③, with ⑦—a completely different color—as the accent color.

A color scheme with colors accenting a base

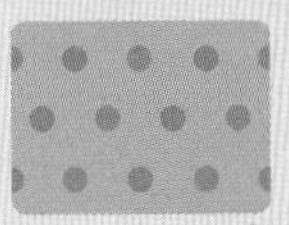

Use ① and ④ to create the overall feel, with polka dots in 9 as the accent color.

Flower fairy color palette (page 42)

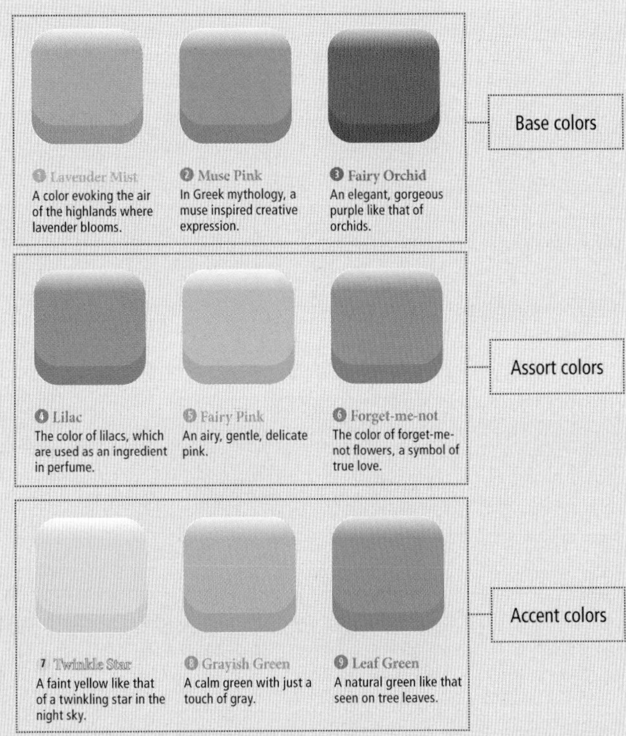

In this book, the color palettes are by and large laid out with the base colors in the top row, assort colors in the second row and accent colors in the third row.

Using the Color Wheel to Decide

When deciding on colors, it's usual to choose from cool or warm shades; in other words, by the property of the color called the hue. In the color wheel, colors close to one another are called analogous colors, while those distant from one another are called contrasting colors. Of the contrasting colors, those directly opposite one another are called complementary colors. They serve to powerfully draw each other out. The diagram below shows a two-color scheme, of which one is a vibrant yellow.

Consider Tone When Aiming for an Evocative Color Scheme

Used in color theory, the term "tone" indicates brightness, saturation or intensity. For example, if you're aiming for a lighter, softer look, go for pale tones (pl) and very pale tones (vp); if you want a deep, refined look, focusing on deep tones (dp) and dark tones (dk) will allow you to achieve the color scheme you have in mind. In the diagram below, differences in brightness are shown vertically while differences in saturation are reflected horizontally.

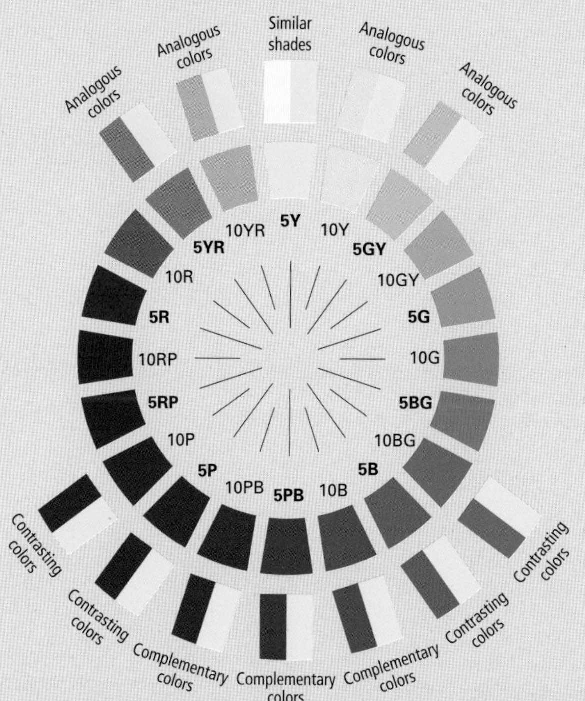

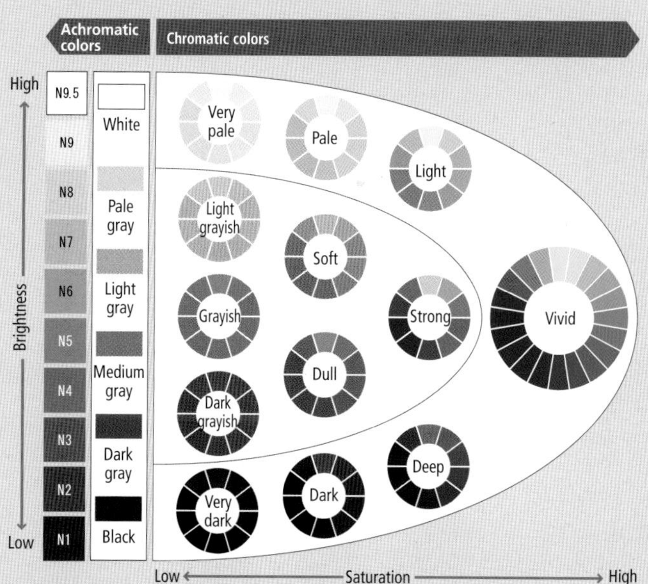

Use neighboring tones to create cohesive color schemes.
Combine distant tones for dynamic color schemes that create impact.
Diagram reproduced with the assistance of the Designers Skill Certification Organization for the International Color Design Association.

Part

03

Natural

Gathered here are color palettes are derived from natural landscapes and natural color schemes similar to those of herbal teas and Japanese sweets. Enjoy the cozy sense of calm and peace of mind.

Color Schemes That Have a Calm, Relaxing, Natural Feel.

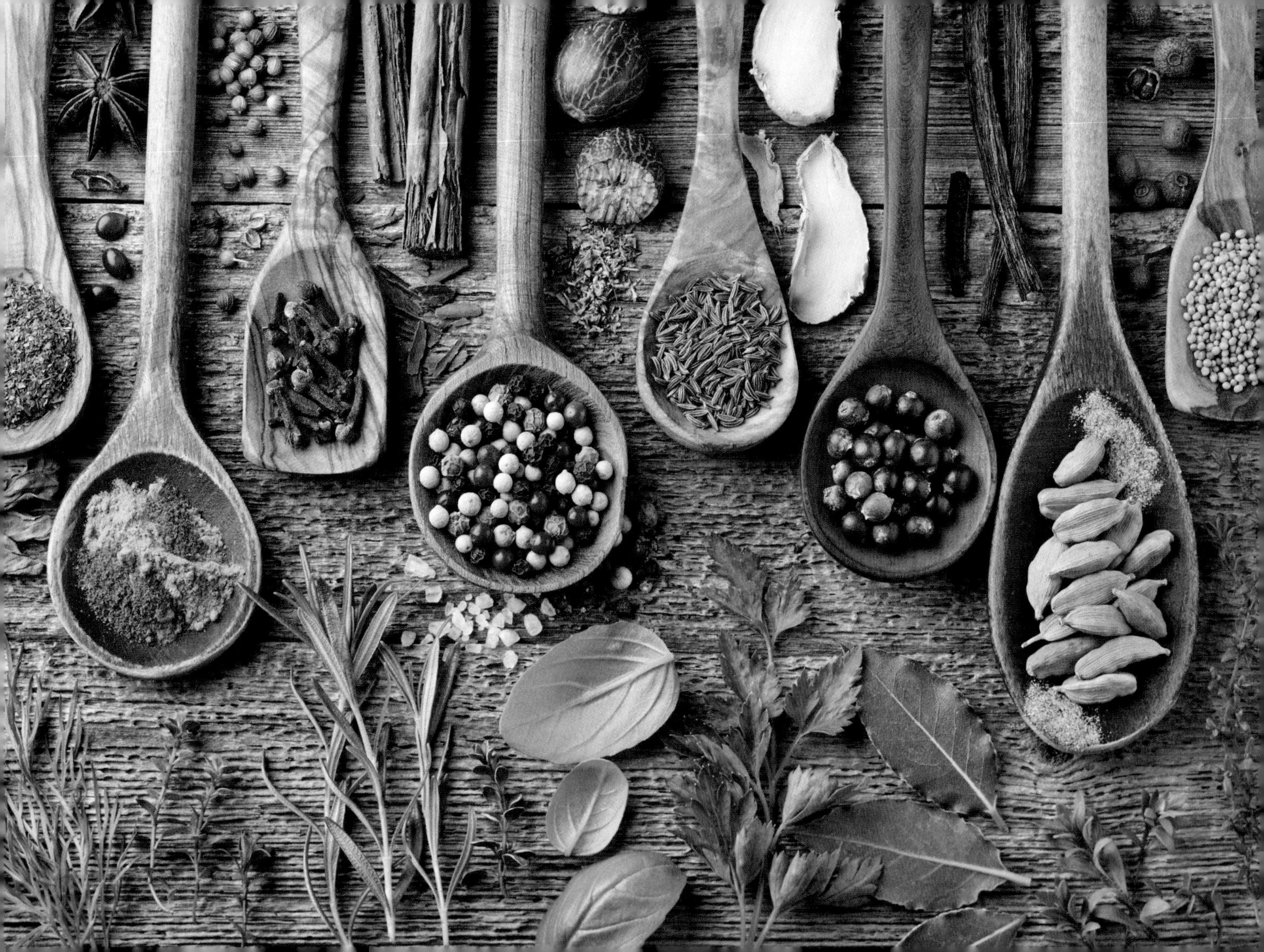

Recipe

021

Spring Has Arrived!

Every year at this particular time, the mountains around villages turn pink. A rosy glow seems to envelop some groves. The trees all put on a show of color at the same time. In the spring mist, the distant landscape becomes vaguely gradated. The cherry trees that went unnoticed during winter have transformed. They're energized: spring's here!

- **FEELING** Spring-like, cheerful, energetic.
- **COMBINATIONS** Use relaxed colors of medium intensity.
- **TIPS** Make pink the main color for a gorgeous look.

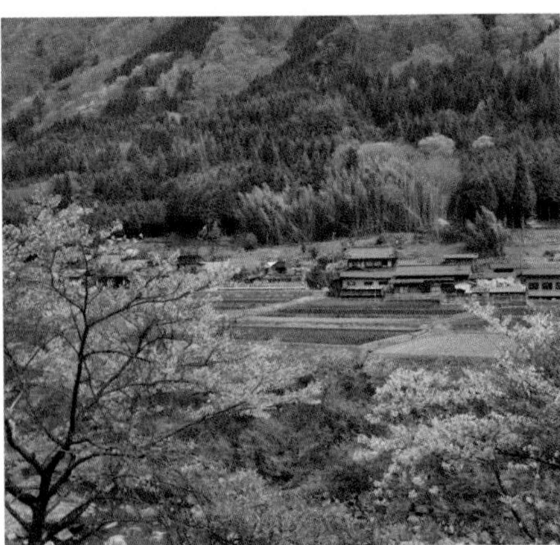

A color scheme drawing on a gentle Japanese palette.

❶ Cherry
The word for cherry (sakura) derives from a goddess's name.

❷ Willow
This is a whitish green like that of willow leaves.

❸ Kite
The color of a kite's feathers.

❹ Moss
A yellow green like that of moss growing on a cliff.

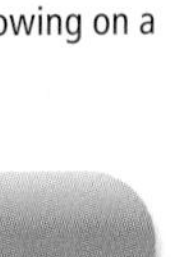

❺ Rose Plum
The color of plum blossoms, a term from the Heian period.

❻ Sawtooth Oak
A light brown achieved with the liquid from boiling acorns.

❼ Dovewing Gray
A color between brown and gray, the color of turtledove feathers.

❽ Peach Blossom
A color like that of peach blossoms or the fruit itself.

❾ Middle Purple
This refers appropriately to a color between dark and pale purple.

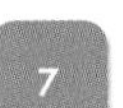

No.	CMYK	RGB	Hex
1	C5 M25 Y10 K0	R240 G206 B211	#F0CED3
2	C30 M10 Y63 K0	R193 G205 B118	#C1CD75
3	C55 M55 Y65 K0	R135 G118 B94	#87755E
4	C63 M30 Y80 K0	R110 G149 B83	#6E9452
5	C5 M40 Y15 K5	R229 G171 B181	#E5AAB4
6	C10 M35 Y40 K15	R207 G163 B134	#CEA286
7	C30 M37 Y35 K3	R187 G162 B153	#BAA298
8	C15 M70 Y30 K0	R212 G105 B130	#D46981
9	C30 M65 Y30 K40	R133 G77 B96	#854C60

Two-color combinations

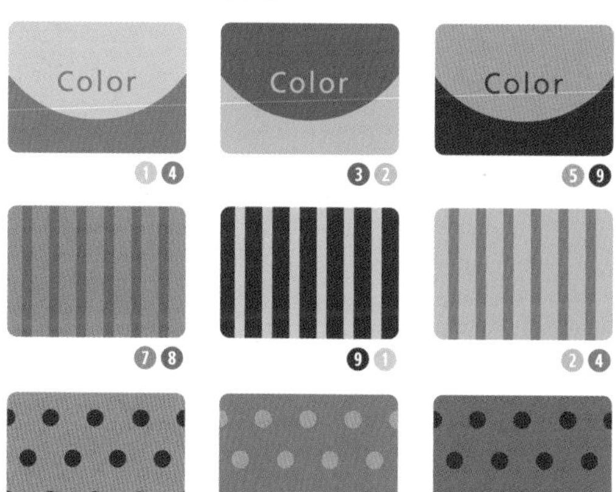

Three-color combinations

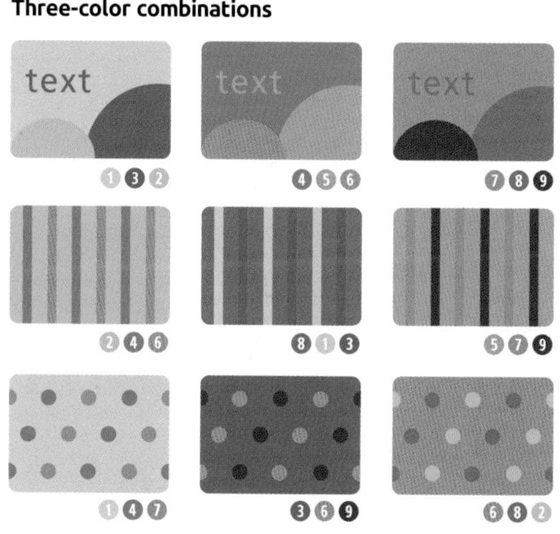

Designs

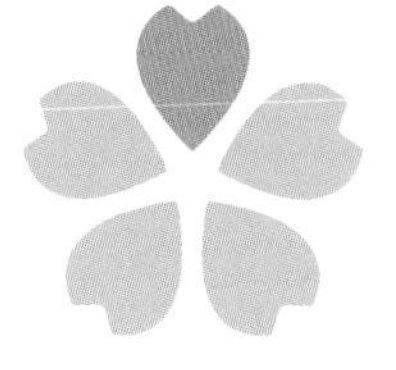

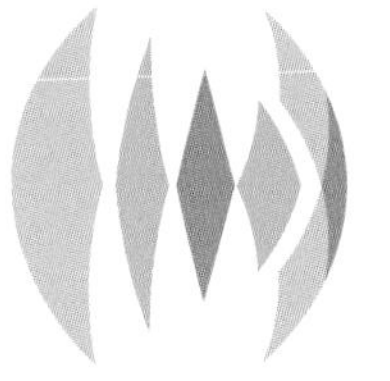
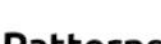

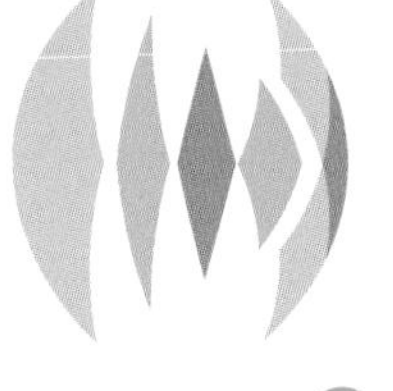

Patterns

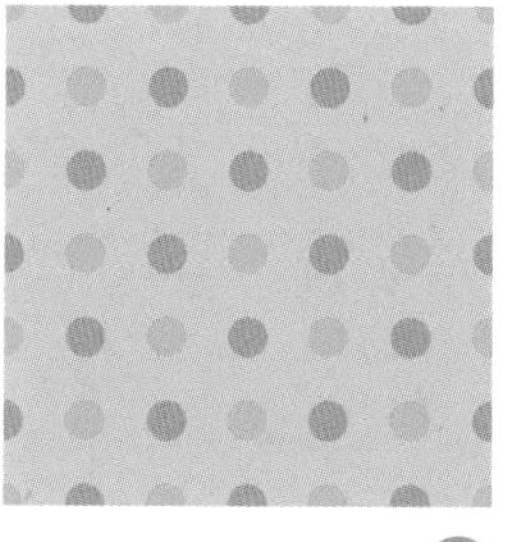
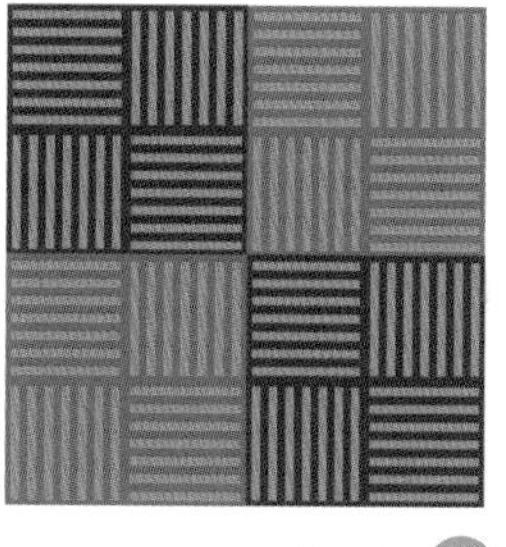
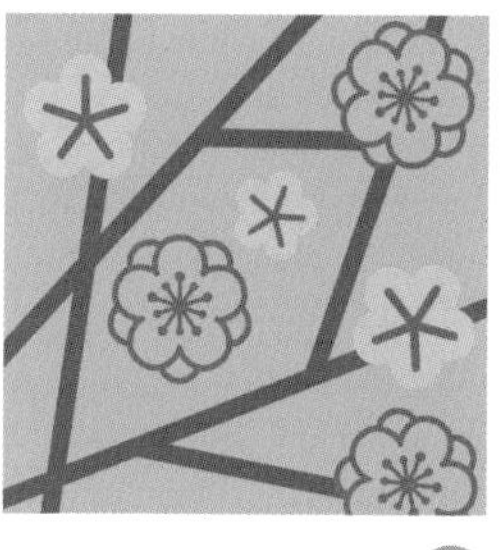

Illustration

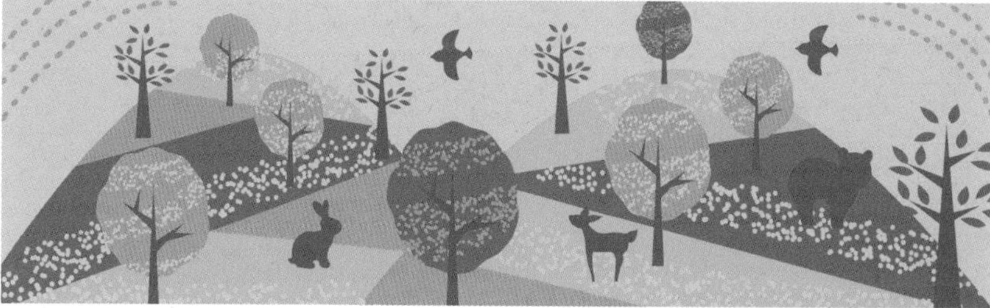

Recipe
022

Handmade Herbal Soaps

People have long sought out the uses and effects of herbs. As the sayings go, "plants are medicine" and "herbs are gifts from the gods." Herbs are used not only in cooking but in religious ceremonies too. Their calm, soft colors are said to be healing hues, and it's these salutary tones that make up this color scheme.

- **FEELING** Calm, gentle, natural.
- **COMBINATIONS** Combine calm colors with similarly moderate tones.
- **TIPS** Alter the brightness of the colors in the chart and the background colors for a good result.

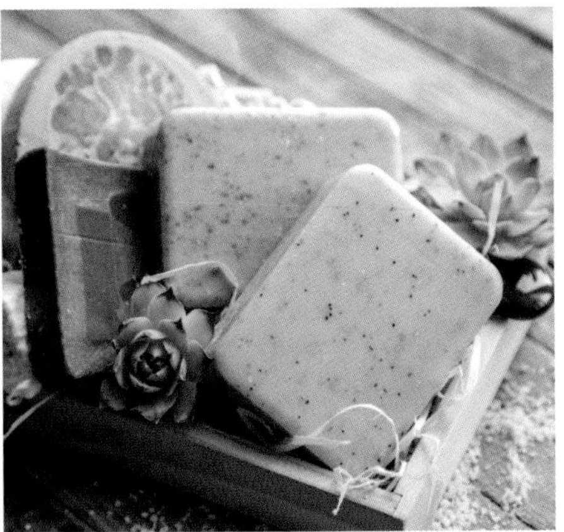

Herbs all have particular fragrances and medicinal uses.

1 Chamomile
A color like that of dried chamomile flowers.

2 Lemongrass
Dried lemongrass smells similar to lemon.

3 Rose Petal
A pale pink like that of rose petals.

4 Natural Brown
A gentle, pale brown like achieved with vegetable dye.

5 Soap White
A slightly yellowish white like that of soap.

6 Eucalyptus
The whitish green of eucalyptus leaves.

7 English Lavender
The word "lavender" is derived from the Latin meaning "to wash."

8 Chives
An attractive purple like that of chive flowers.

9 Cloves
Cloves are used as a spice.

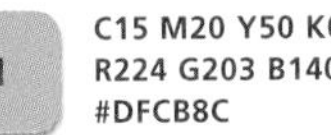

C15 M20 Y50 K0
R224 G203 B140
#DFCB8C

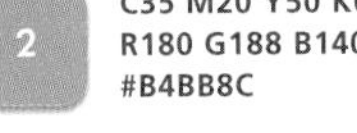

C35 M20 Y50 K0
R180 G188 B140
#B4BB8C

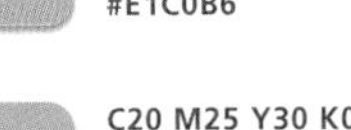

C5 M25 Y20 K10
R225 G192 B183
#E1C0B6

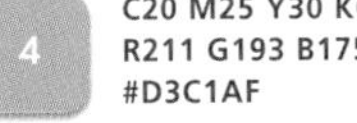

C20 M25 Y30 K0
R211 G193 B175
#D3C1AF

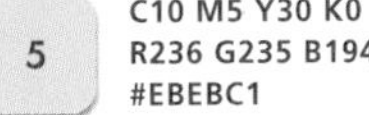

C10 M5 Y30 K0
R236 G235 B194
#EBEBC1

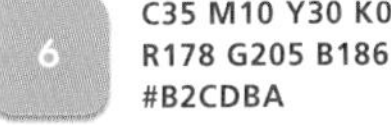

C35 M10 Y30 K0
R178 G205 B186
#B2CDBA

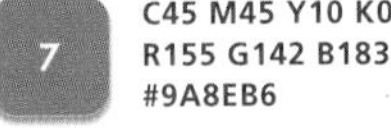

C45 M45 Y10 K0
R155 G142 B183
#9A8EB6

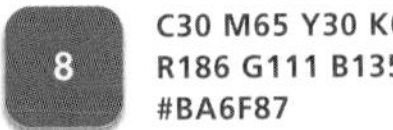

C30 M65 Y30 K0
R186 G111 B135
#BA6F87

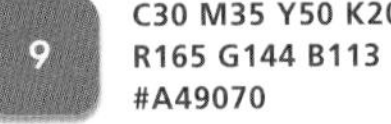

C30 M35 Y50 K20
R165 G144 B113
#A49070

Two-color combinations

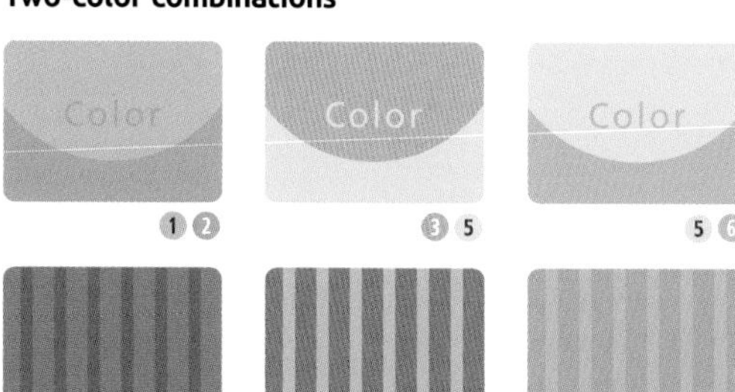

1 2 · 3 5 · 5 6

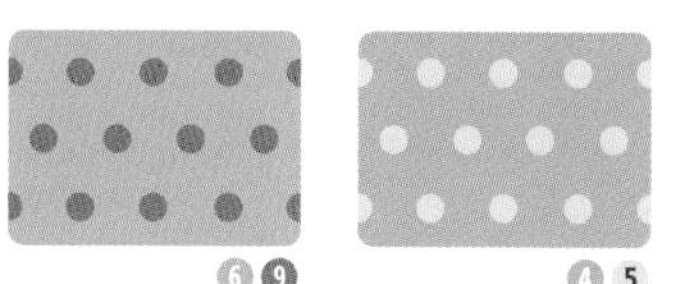

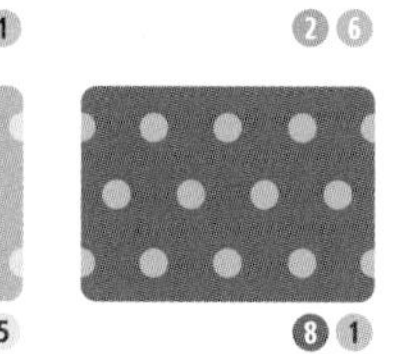

7 8 · 9 1 · 2 6

6 9 · 4 5 · 8 1

Three-color combinations

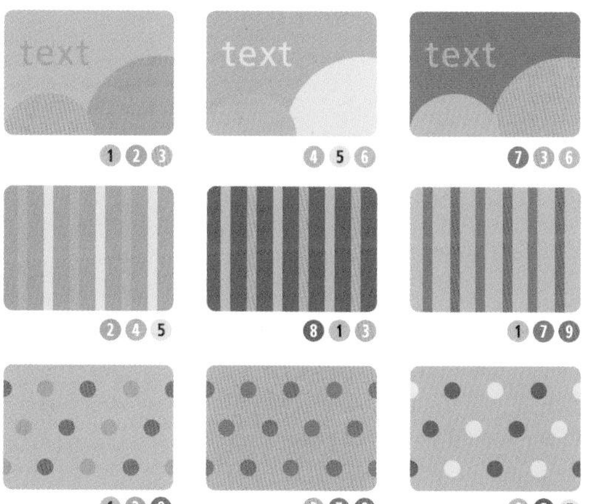

1 2 3 · 4 5 6 · 7 3 6

2 4 5 · 8 1 3 · 1 7 9

1 2 9 · 3 7 9 · 6 8 5

Designs

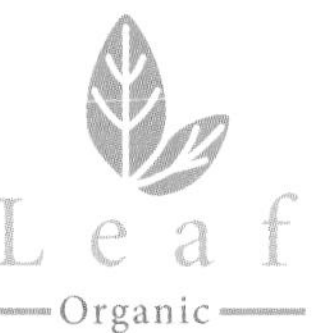

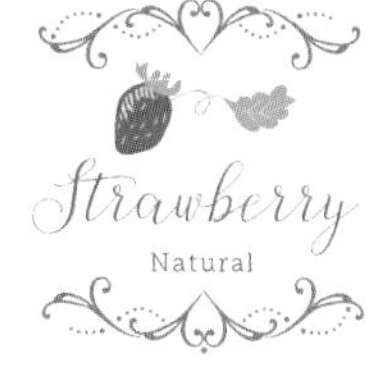

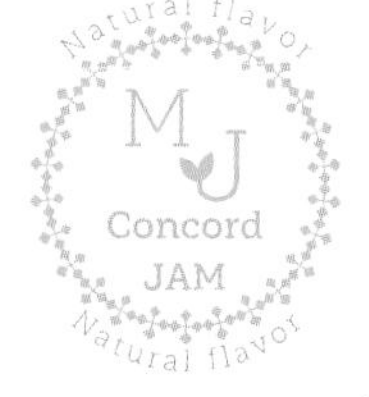

1 2 9 color 3

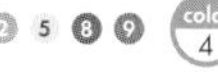

2 5 8 9 color 4

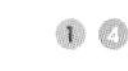
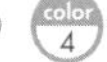

1 4 6 7 color 4

Patterns

4 5 9 color 3 · 1 2 5 6 color 4

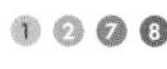

1 2 7 8 9 color 5

Illustration

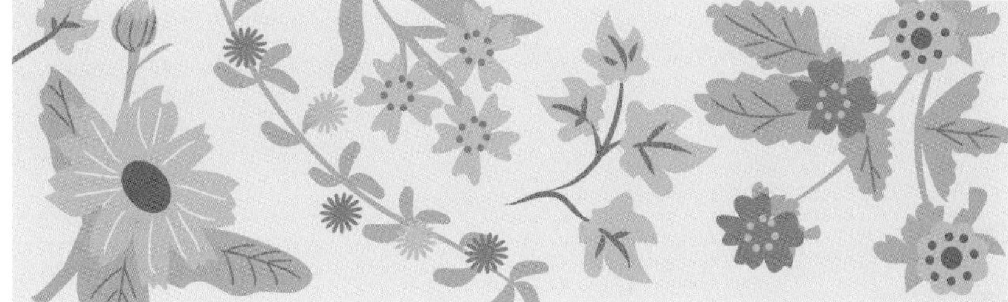

2 5 6 7 8 9 color 6

Recipe
023

Dish Cloths

Dish cloths are an everyday item most of us can't do without. I unwaveringly choose dish cloths in natural shades. The natural, calm colors that look achieved with vegetable dyes soothe me to my very soul. After dinner, I wash them and hang them in their usual spot; it's my routine chore.

- **FEELING** Natural, unembellished, quiet.
- **COMBINATIONS** Use only calm colors with low levels of intensity.
- **TIPS** Color schemes without accent colors are more cohesive.

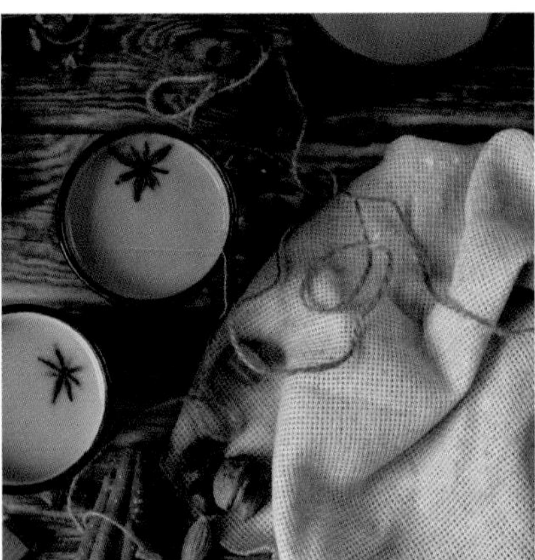

Use off-white as a base and add natural shades to develop the color scheme.

① Natural White
An unbleached white with a touch of color to it.

② Calm Brown
An extremely faint brown that creates a calm impression.

③ Milky Brown
A brown that is close to white.

④ Mild Pink
A gentle, mild pink with a yellow tinge.

⑤ Light Beige
Beige is derived from the word for the fabric made from undyed wool.

⑥ Milk Caramel
A color like that of sweet, milky caramel.

⑦ Sage
A grayish green that brings to mind the leaves of the sage plant.

⑧ Pecan Nuts
A reddish brown that suggests types of nuts.

⑨ Akebia
The purple reminiscent of steamed akebia fruits.

No.	CMYK	RGB	Hex
1	C5 M5 Y10 K10	R229 G227 B218	#E5E2DA
2	C0 M15 Y20 K30	R199 G179 B163	#C6B3A3
3	C5 M10 Y15 K10	R229 G218 B205	#E4DACD
4	C5 M25 Y25 K5	R234 G198 B180	#E9C6B4
5	C5 M10 Y30 K10	R229 G216 B178	#E5D8B2
6	C5 M25 Y50 K20	R209 G174 B119	#D0AE76
7	C40 M10 Y50 K30	R132 G157 B116	#839C74
8	C10 M25 Y35 K40	R164 G142 B119	#A48D76
9	C25 M45 Y30 K35	R149 G114 B117	#957275

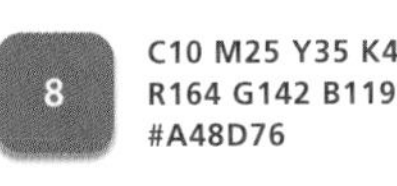
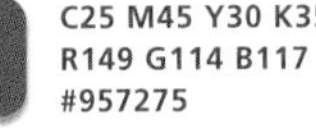

Two-color combinations

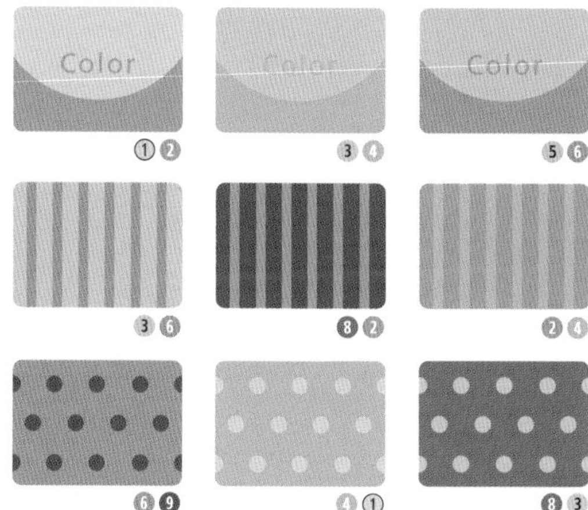

Three-color combinations

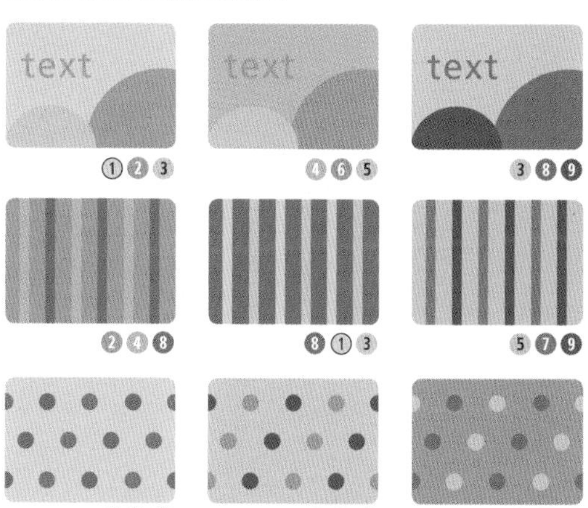

Designs

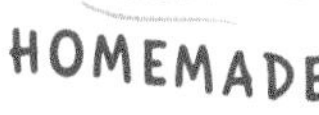

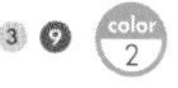
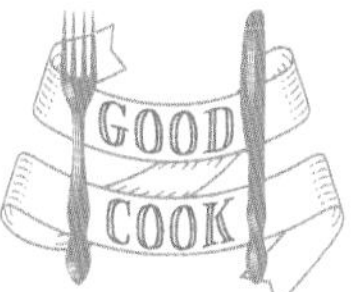

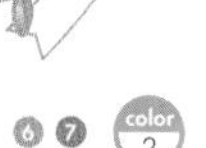
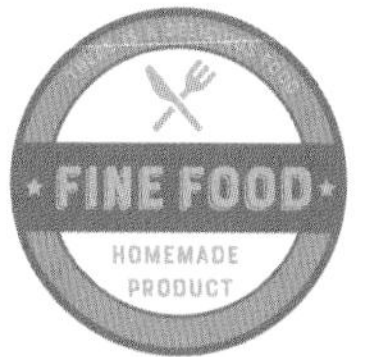

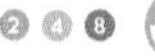
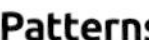

Patterns

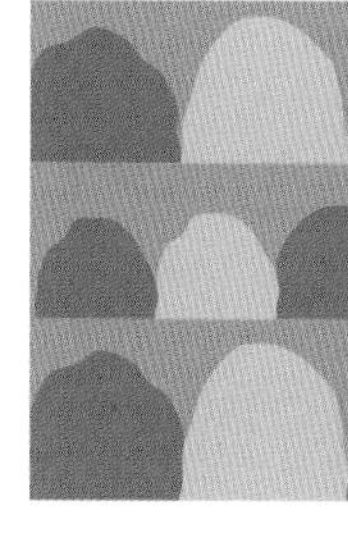
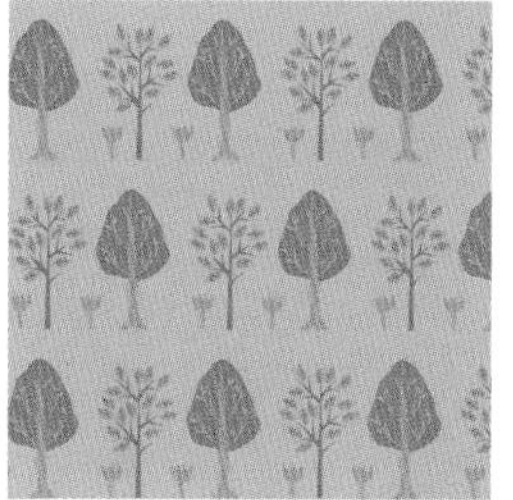
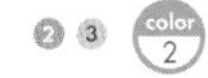
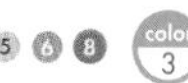
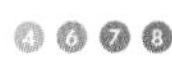

Illustration

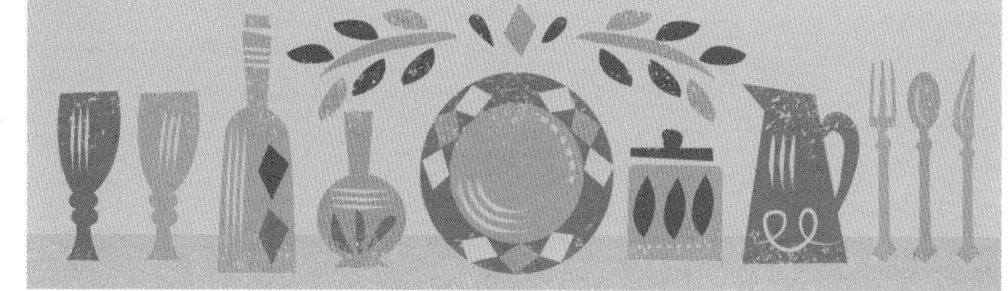

Recipe
024

Matcha Sweets

A long time ago, I was given a huge shock when an American girl told me "Japanese tea is green like a bog." Since then, time has passed, and these days matcha is used in sweets such as chocolate, soft serve ice cream and cheesecake. When I read that "to foreigners, the green of matcha is symbolic of Japan," I realize how far it's come. I remembered that girl.

- **FEELING** Traditional, having a sense of security, tranquil.
- **COMBINATIONS** Add brown to serene yellowish greens.
- **TIPS** Make low-intensity, refined yellowish greens the focus.

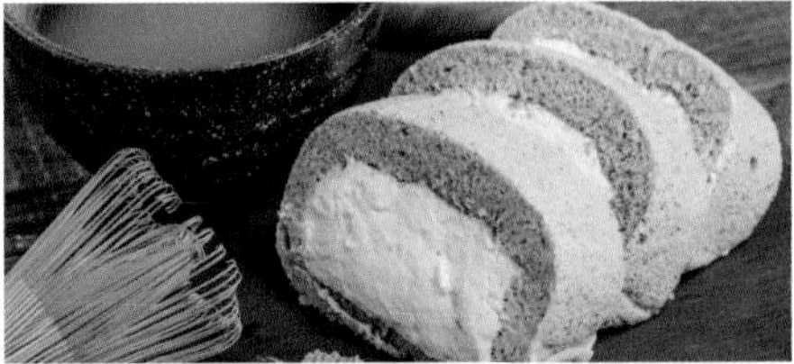

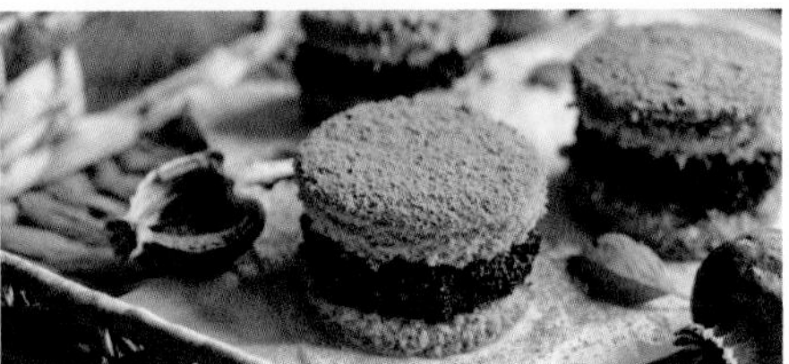

The depth of color in matcha varies depending on factors such as where it's grown and its brand.

❶ Matcha
Matcha is steamed green tea that is ground finely on a mortar.

❷ Weak Tea
Tea made with only a small amount of matcha.

❸ Strong Tea
Tea made with a large amount of matcha.

❹ Rikyu
A yellowish green of low intensity associated with tea master Senno Rikyu.

❺ Matcha Mouse
A gray tinged with green. In traditional color terms, mouse signified gray.

❻ Kinako
This is flour made from roasted soybeans.

❼ Walnut
The color resulting from a dye made of the bark and nut of the walnut tree.

❽ Yokan
The deep brown of sweet bean jelly or adzuki bean jam.

❾ Charcoal
Black but depending on the angle, it appears to be a deep gray.

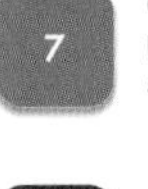

No.	CMYK	RGB	Hex
1	C45 M20 Y85 K10	R148 G165 B64	#94A540
2	C30 M15 Y60 K0	R193 G198 B122	#C0C67A
3	C60 M43 Y85 K0	R122 G132 B70	#7A8446
4	C23 M15 Y45 K20	R179 G178 B134	#B2B285
5	C28 M10 Y30 K15	R176 G191 B169	#AFBEA9
6	C5 M10 Y33 K5	R238 G224 B179	#EDDFB2
7	C40 M50 Y80 K0	R170 G133 B70	#A98546
8	C20 M50 Y65 K60	R112 G74 B43	#6F4A2A
9	C65 M50 Y50 K50	R65 G74 B75	#404A4A

Two-color combinations

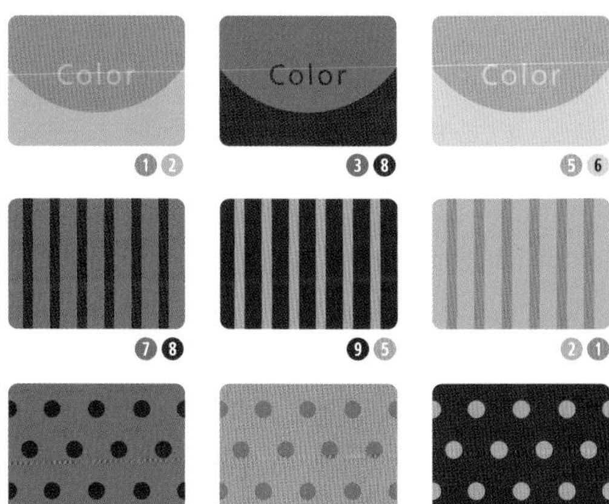

Three-color combinations

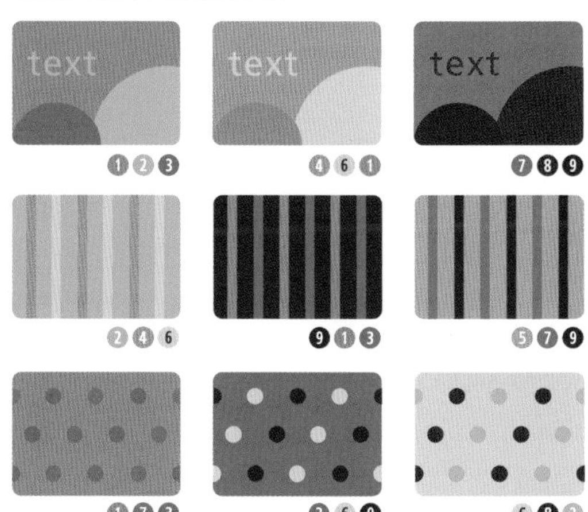

Designs

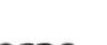

Patterns

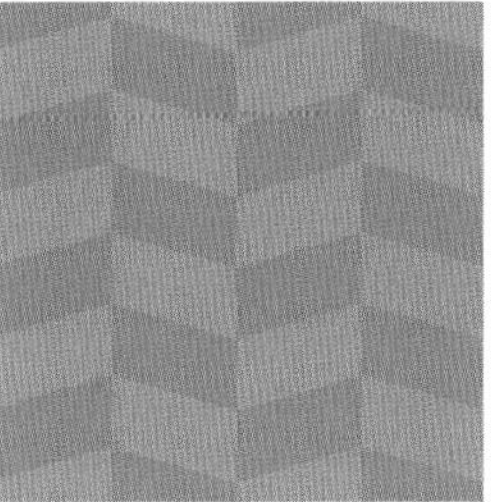

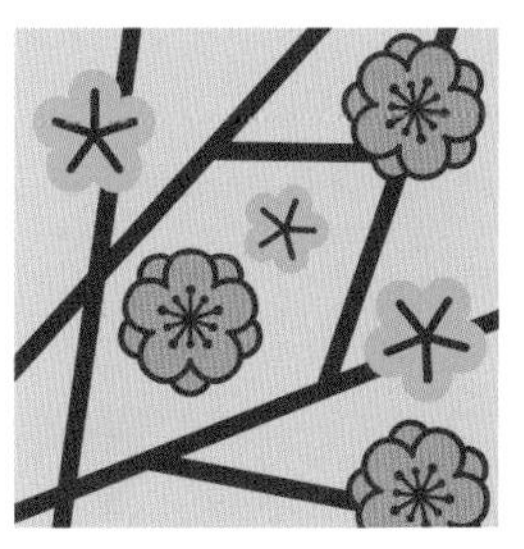

Illustration

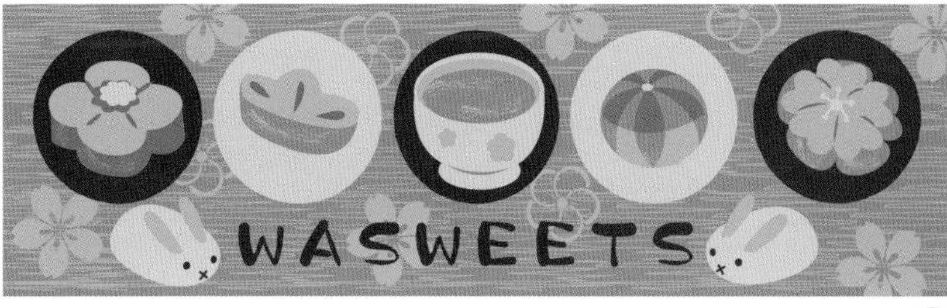

Recipe
025

Dandelions

When I was in elementary school, we used to use dandelions that we found along the roadside to tell fortunes, pulling out the seeds to find out whether "he loves me" or "he loves me not." A custom among American kids is to make a wish then blow on the dried-out head of seeds, dispersing them in the wind.

- **FEELING** Natural, peaceful, mature.
- **COMBINATIONS** Create natural combinations of gentle colors.
- **TIPS** Use each color over roughly the same amount of surface area.

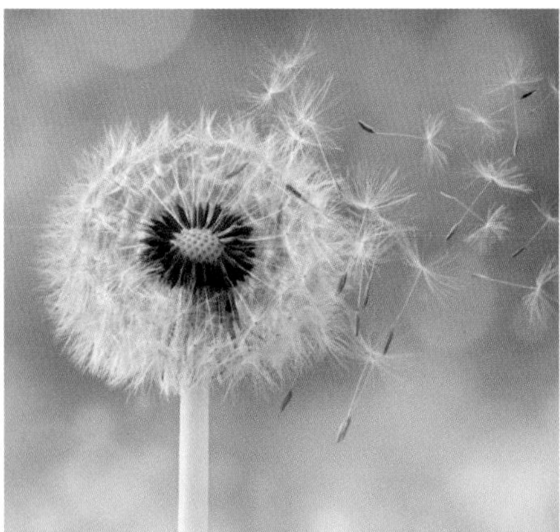

The palette captures the full life cycle of the flowering weed, from sprout to bushy-headed ball of seeds.

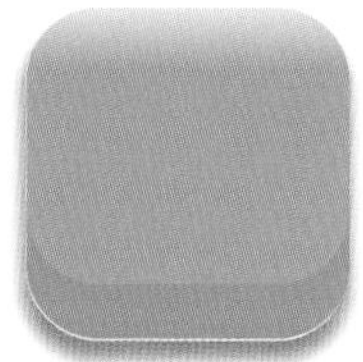

① **Future**
Hopes and slight unease about what the future holds.

② **Unrequited Love**
In part, one tries to remain cool and detached.

③ **Mutual Love**
That happy moment when two people's feelings are in sync.

④ **Cotton Wool**
The color of cotton wool, like clouds that shift shapes in the sky.

⑤ **Unbleached Cloth**
The color of unbleached cloth conveys a sense of reassurance.

⑥ **Confusion**
The state of wavering due to feelings of uncertainty.

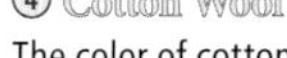
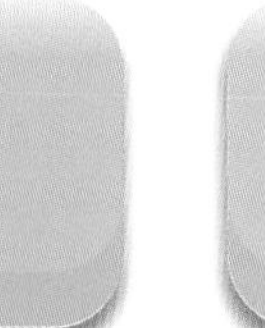

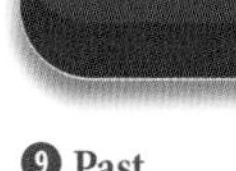

⑦ **New Buds**
The green of fresh new buds that are just beginning to emerge.

⑧ **Spring Stream**
The blue of water when temperatures rise at the start of spring.

⑨ **Past**
Old photographs are in sepia-colored monochrome.

	CMYK	RGB	Hex
1	C5 M5 Y2 K0	R244 G243 B247	#F4F3F6
2	C50 M10 Y25 K0	R136 G191 B193	#87BFC1
3	C10 M5 Y50 K0	R237 G232 B150	#EDE795
4	C5 M0 Y5 K5	R238 G243 B239	#EEF2EF
5	C5 M5 Y20 K0	R246 G241 B214	#F5F0D6
6	C30 M30 Y40 K0	R190 G176 B152	#BEB098
7	C35 M0 Y70 K0	R182 G213 B106	#B5D569
8	C35 M0 Y20 K0	R176 G220 B213	#B0DBD4
9	C60 M60 Y60 K10	R117 G101 B93	#74645C

Two-color combinations

Color ① ②

Color ③ ④

Color ⑤ ⑥

⑦ ⑧

⑨ ①

② ④

⑥ ⑨

② ③

⑧ ⑨

Three-color combinations

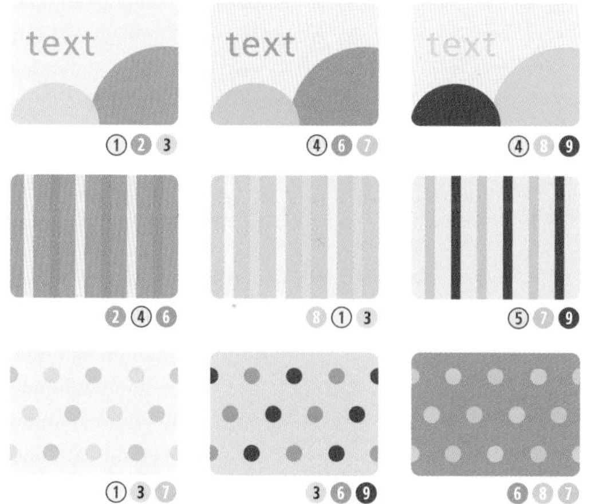

Designs

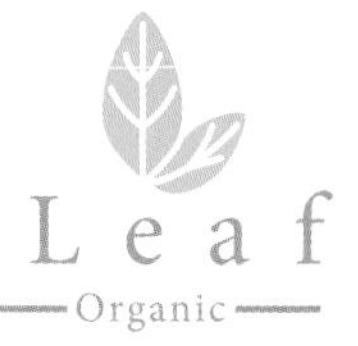

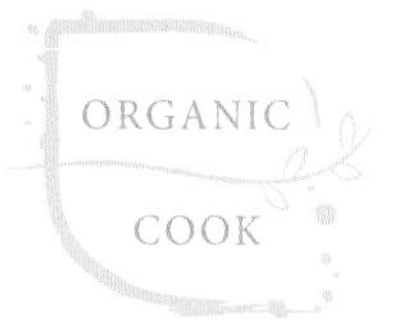

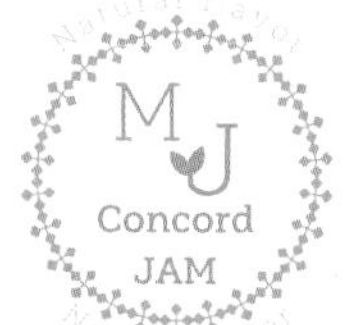

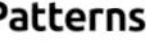

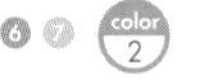

⑥ ⑦ color 2

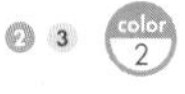

② ③ color 2

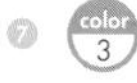

② ⑥ ⑦ color 3

Patterns

③ ⑤ color 2

③ ⑤ ⑦ color 3

③ ④ ⑤ ⑧ color 4

Illustration

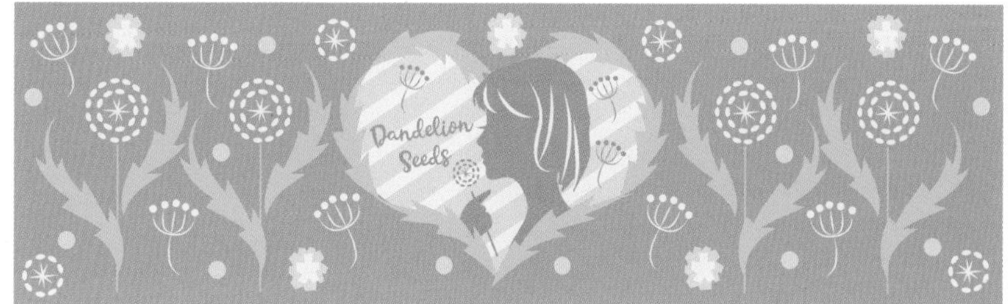

① ② ③ ⑥ ⑦ color 5

Recipe
026

Afternoon Tea

Blessings from plants and the sun dissolve in warm water to create the simple gift known as herbal tea. Close your eyes, take a deep breath and savor the aromas of the herbs. After a cup of tea, I somehow feel wonderfully calm and able to keep working a bit longer, a weekday afternoon respite.

- **FEELING** Tranquil, secure, comfortable.
- **COMBINATIONS** Focus on yellow, green and brown.
- **TIPS** Use similar colors for a cohesive result.

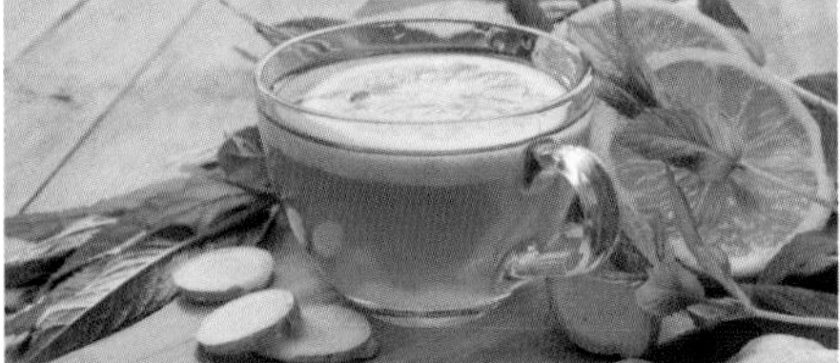

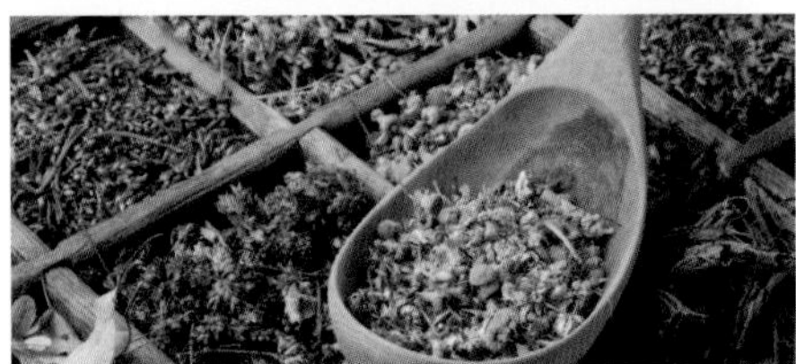

Consider whether you want to detox, improve your skin or increase circulation when choosing a tea blend.

❶ Ginger
A light brown with a touch of yellow like that of ginger skin.

❷ Olive Yellow
Yellow with just the faintest hint of green.

❸ Olive Green
The yellow green of an olive.

❹ Dry Brown
A brown like that of dried plants.

❺ Reddish Brown
A red-tinged brown that evokes abundance.

❻ Dry Green
A deep green like that of dried plants.

❼ Red Soil
A color like red earth; there are various colors of soil.

❽ Blue Mallow
Mallow tea changes from blue to purple to pink.

❾ Black Soil
The color of soil that is rich with nutrients; a thick brown.

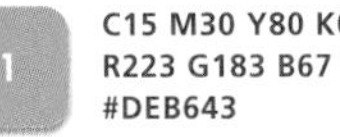

1 C15 M30 Y80 K0 R223 G183 B67 #DEB643

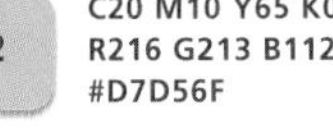

2 C20 M10 Y65 K0 R216 G213 B112 #D7D56F

3 C45 M15 Y90 K0 R158 G182 B58 #9EB639

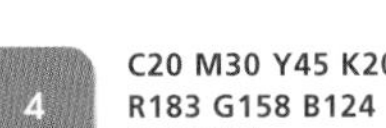

4 C20 M30 Y45 K20 R183 G158 B124 #B69E7C

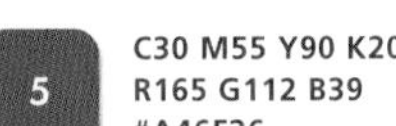

5 C30 M55 Y90 K20 R165 G112 B39 #A46F26

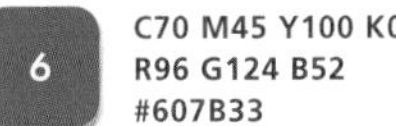

6 C70 M45 Y100 K0 R96 G124 B52 #607B33

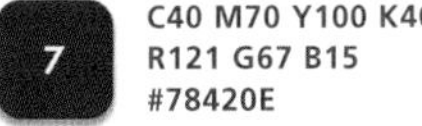

7 C40 M70 Y100 K40 R121 G67 B15 #78420E

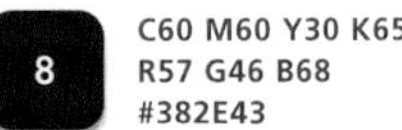

8 C60 M60 Y30 K65 R57 G46 B68 #382E43

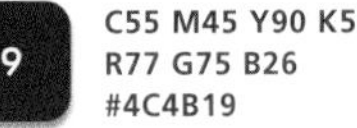

9 C55 M45 Y90 K55 R77 G75 B26 #4C4B19

Two-color combinations

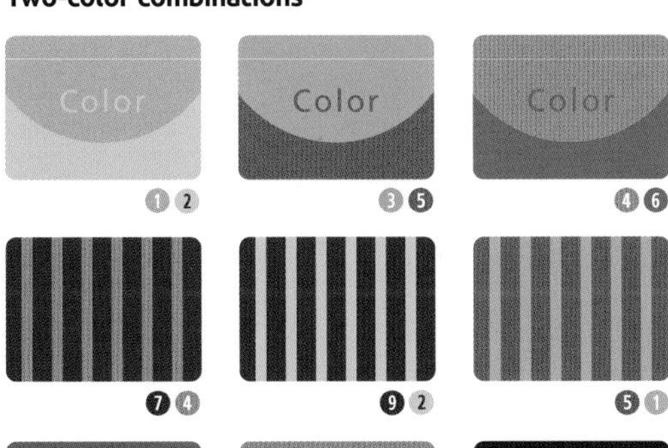

Three-color combinations

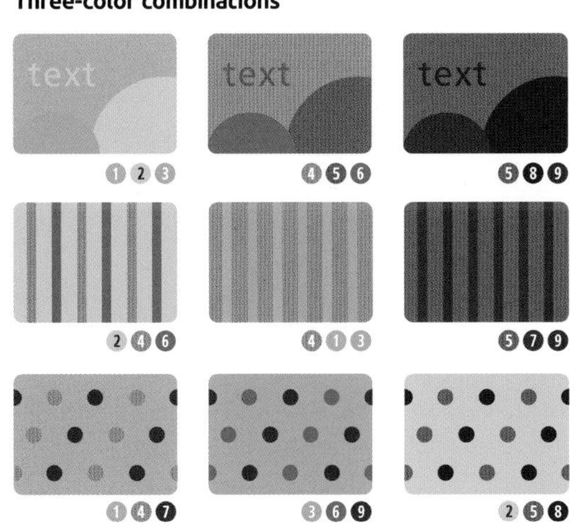

Designs

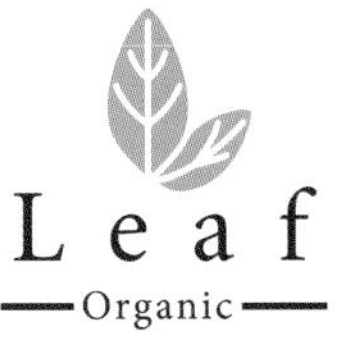

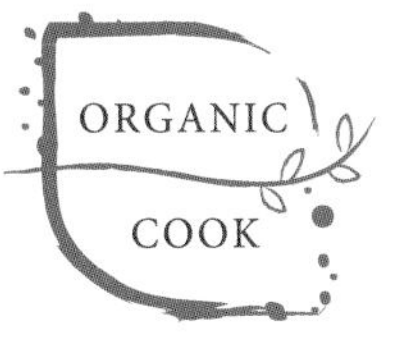

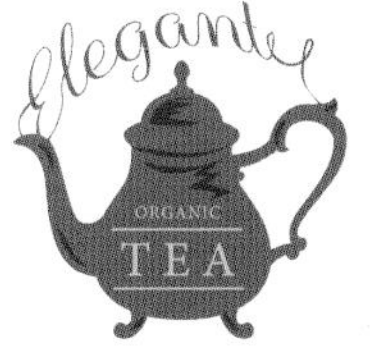

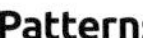

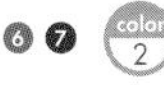
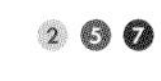

Patterns

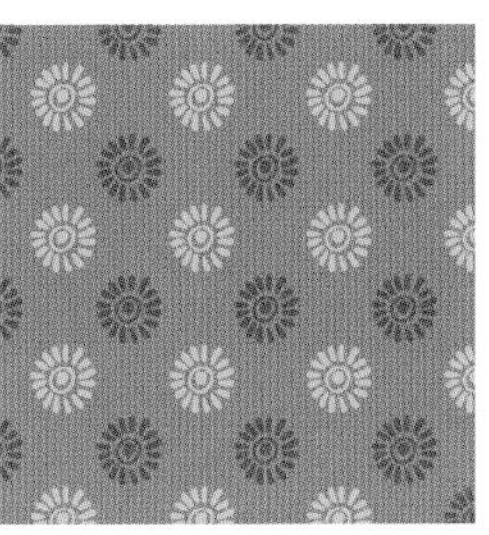
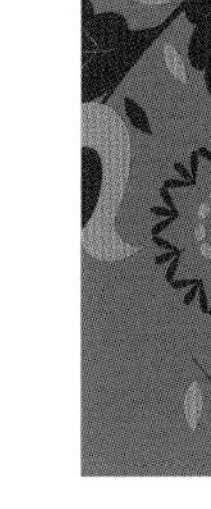
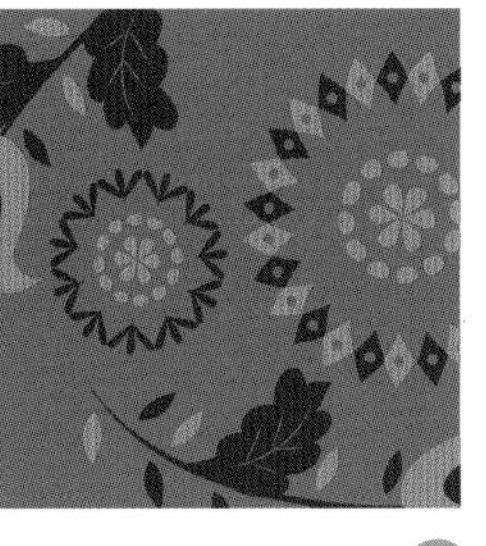

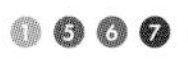

Illustration

PART 03

NATURAL

Recipe
027

Dusk

The color of the sky at sunset changes by the minute. Where blue and orange were fading into each other, a mysterious purple appears, creating swirling hues and blends never witnessed quite like that before. It's a light and color show I savor until the sun sinks beneath the horizon line.

- **FEELING** Vast, fantastical, shifting.
- **COMBINATIONS** Combine orange with purples and blues.
- **TIPS** Create a composition from the colors of the dusky sky that change every minute.

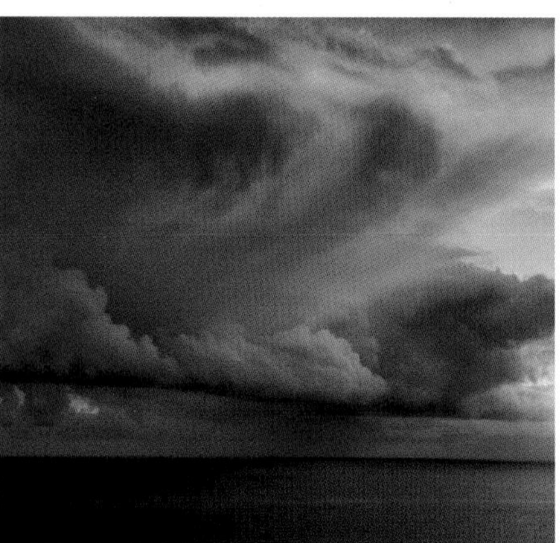

Use colors such as purple and blue over a large area to achieve a serene look.

❶ **Burnt Orange**
Strongly tinged with red, this orange appears to glow.

❷ **Sunset**
A light, vivid orange like that of the setting sun.

❸ **Purple Shadow**
A reddish purple that appears as the shadow of a cloud.

❹ **Golden Cloud**
The color of a cloud shining gold from the rays of the sun.

❺ **Evening Breeze**
A grayish blue like that of the evening breeze.

❻ **Grayish Sky**
The sky when it seems blue and gray have been equally mixed.

❼ **Evening Pink**
A dull-toned pink that appears between the sky and the sea.

❽ **Twilight Red**
The subtle red of the evening sun reflected on the surface of the ocean.

❾ **Sky Blue**
The regular color of the sky. This blue evokes a sense of magnanimity.

No.	CMYK	RGB	Hex
1	C0 M73 Y70 K0	R236 G102 B68	#EB6644
2	C0 M50 Y75 K0	R243 G153 B69	#F29944
3	C50 M70 Y25 K0	R147 G94 B137	#925E88
4	C0 M27 Y75 K10	R234 G186 B71	#EAB947
5	C35 M30 Y10 K20	R153 G152 B175	#9997AE
6	C60 M50 Y10 K30	R93 G98 B140	#5D618C
7 	C10 M70 Y50 K10	R207 G100 B96	#CF635F
8 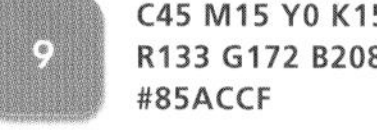	C25 M75 Y60 K30	R154 G70 B66	#9A4642
9	C45 M15 Y0 K15	R133 G172 B208	#85ACCF

Two-color combinations

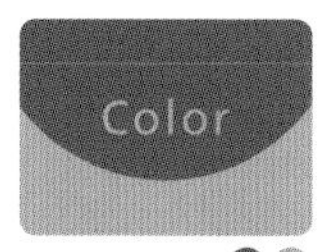

1 2

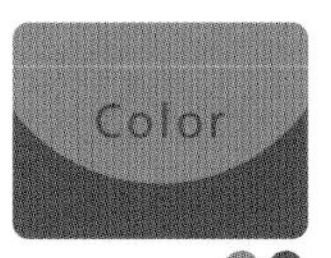

3 4

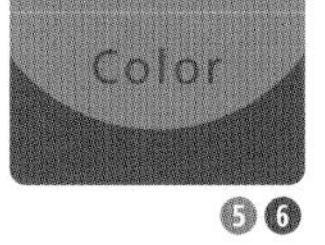

5 6

7 8

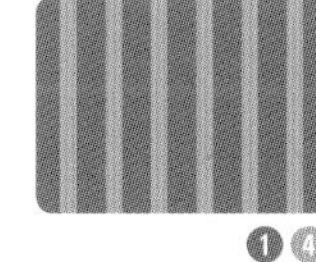

9 6

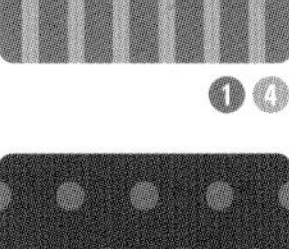

1 4

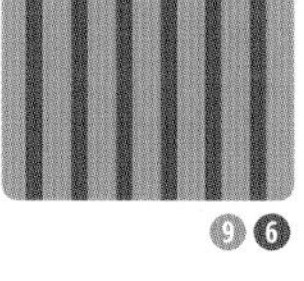

6 9

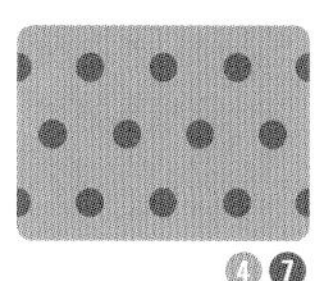

4 7

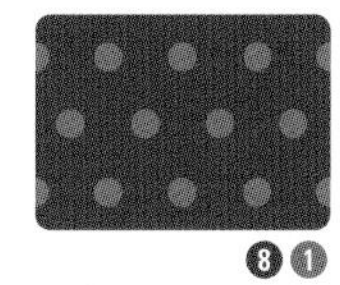

8 1

Three-color combinations

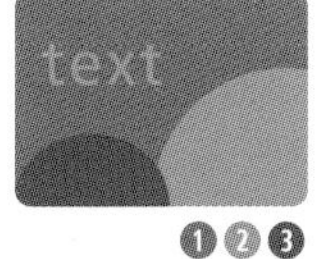

1 2 3

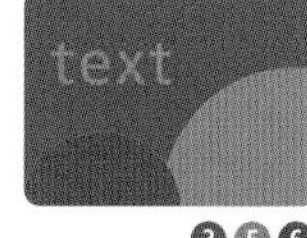

3 5 6

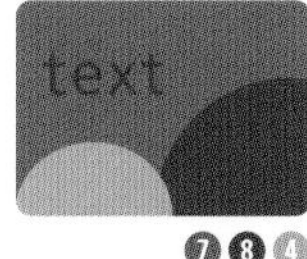

7 8 4

9 7 6

8 1 3

5 7 4

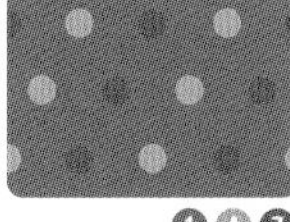

1 4 7

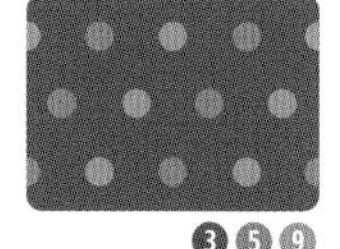

3 5 9

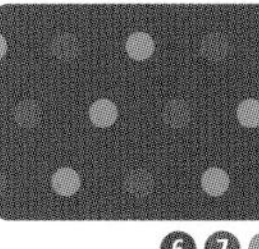

6 7 2

Designs

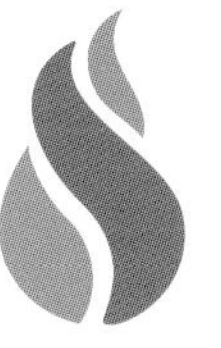

1 2 color 2

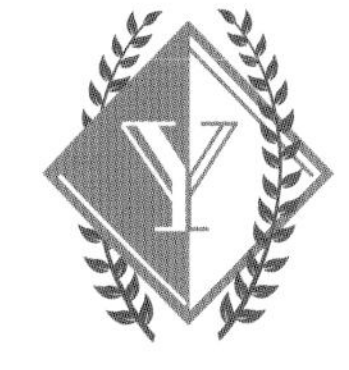

3 5 color 2

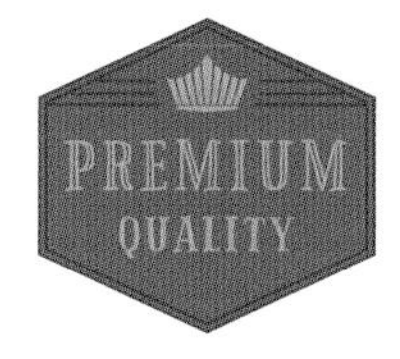

4 7 8 color 3

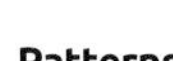

Patterns

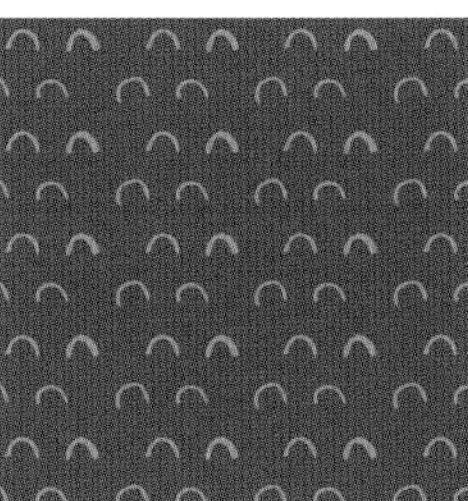

6 9 color 2

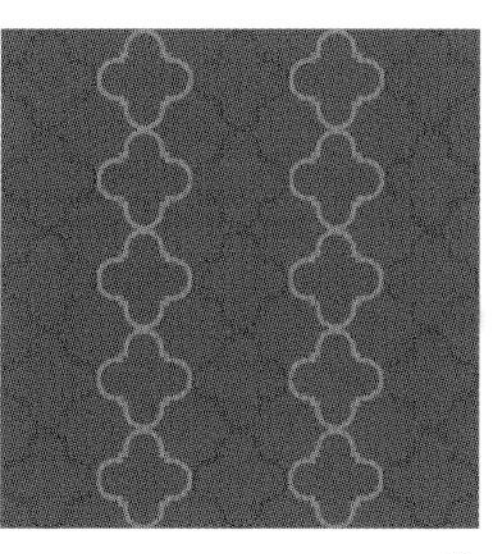

3 5 6 color 3

4 7 8 color 3

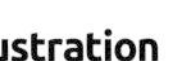

Illustration

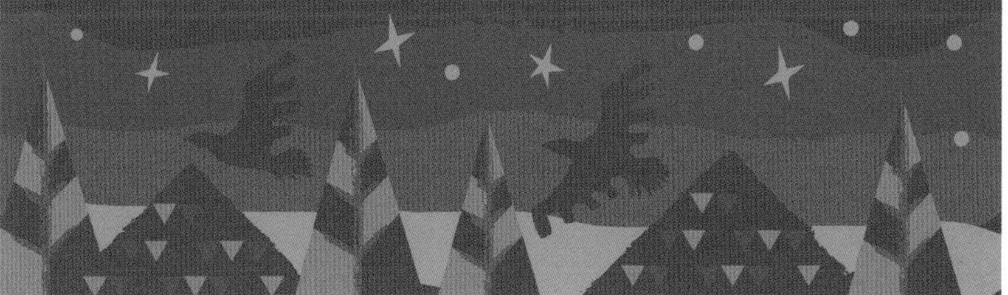

1 2 3 5 6 color 5

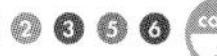

Recipe
028

Geological Strata

Over the earth's long history, soil and sand have been carried by water and wind to form multicolored layers of land. These look just like mille feuille but made out of stone. This palette brings with it not only a sense of magnanimity and security, but also the romance of adventure.

- **FEELING** Tranquil, stable, magnanimous.
- **COMBINATIONS** Use extremely similar colors to create a Faux Camaieu* effect.
- **TIPS** Enjoy the subtle color combinations and differences in texture.

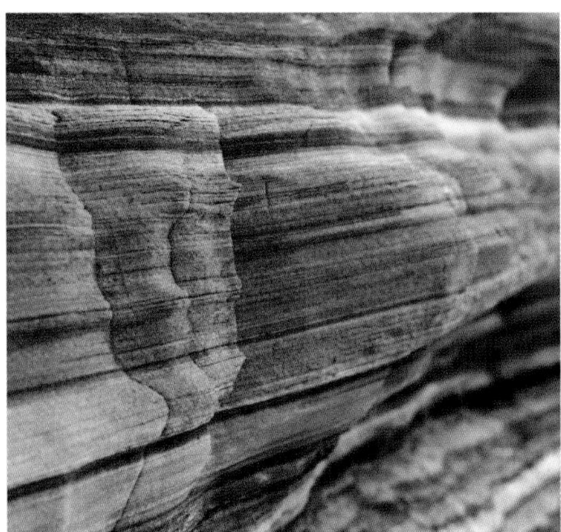

Alternating bands of brown and gray make up the composition.

❶ Basic Brown
This basic brown goes well with any other color.

❷ Red Clay
The color of red earth, used as pigment since ancient times.

❸ Light Gray
A neutral gray with a high level of brightness.

❹ Burnt Brown
A burnt, scorched brown.

❺ Sand Beige
The color of sand; a mixture of gray and beige.

❻ Medium Gray
A neutral gray of medium brightness.

❼ Jurassic Brown
A deep reddish brown that calls to mind the age of the dinosaurs.

❽ Blue Gray
A cool shade of gray that tends toward blue.

❾ Ancient Black
A mysterious black that evokes ancient times.

No.	CMYK	RGB	Hex
1	C40 M50 Y70 K10	R159 G125 B81	#9F7D50
2	C40 M75 Y90 K15	R153 G79 B43	#984F2B
3	C20 M10 Y10 K10	R198 G207 B211	#C6CED3
4	C60 M60 Y90 K30	R99 G84 B44	#63532B
5	C45 M35 Y50 K0	R157 G157 B130	#9C9C82
6	C20 M15 Y15 K50	R132 G132 B133	#838484
7	C40 M60 Y60 K65	R82 G52 B41	#523329
8	C60 M40 Y25 K10	R109 G131 B156	#6D839B
9	C75 M65 Y50 K40	R59 G65 B78	#3B404E

* Faux Camaieu color scheme: a scheme using colors that are similar in hue, brightness and intensity (see page 121).

Two-color combinations

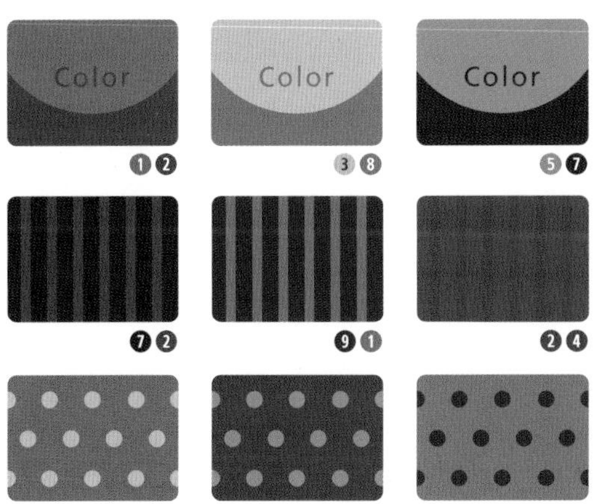

Three-color combinations

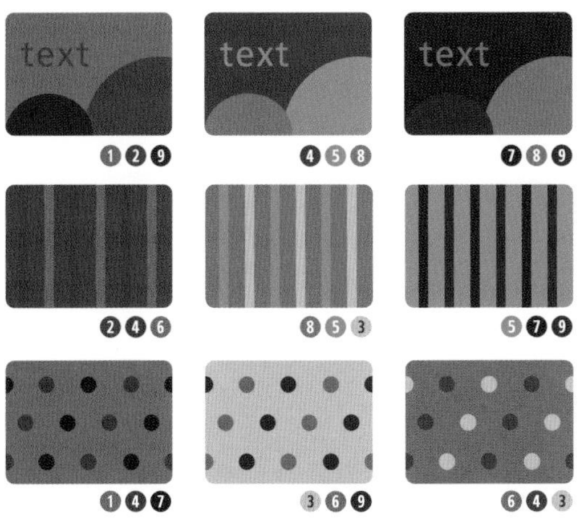

Designs

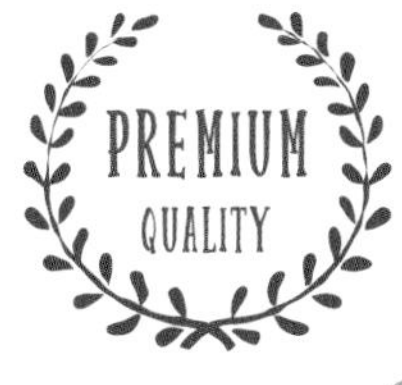

2 4 color 2

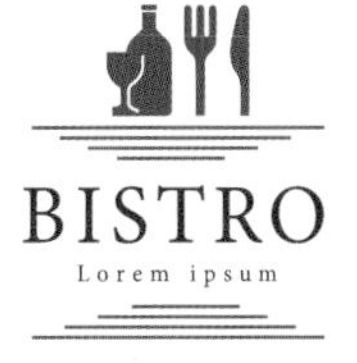

2 7 color 2

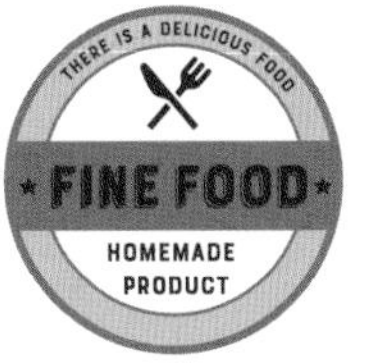

3 6 7 color 3

Patterns

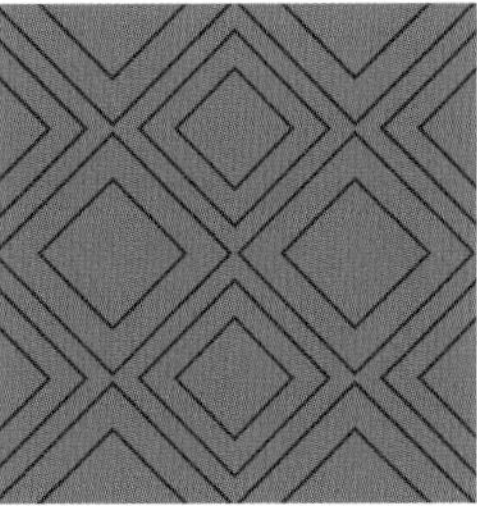

8 9 color 2

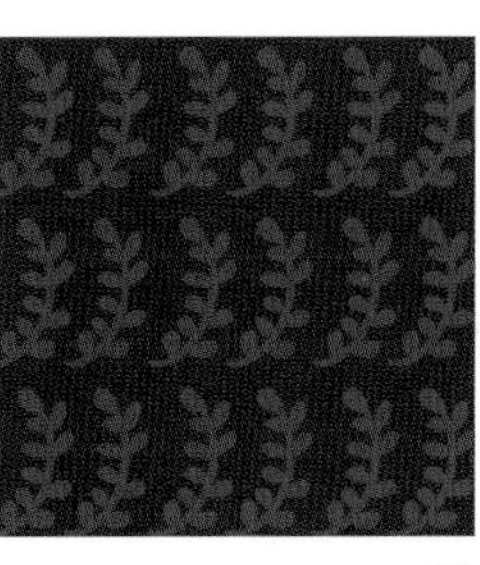

4 7 color 2

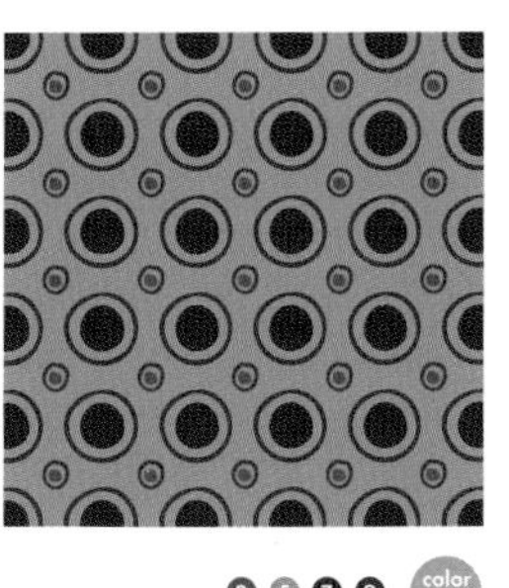

2 5 7 9 color 4

Illustration

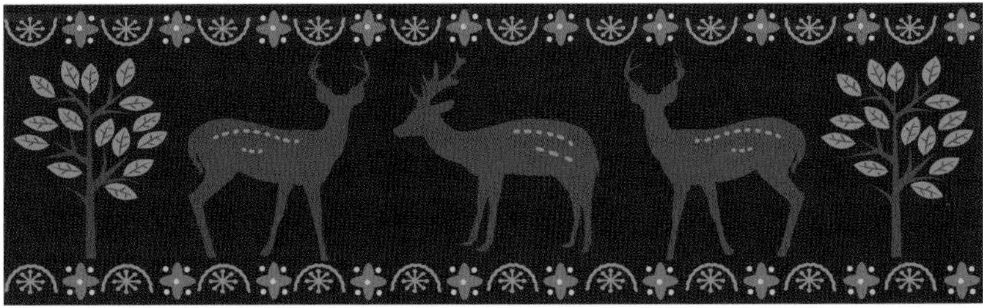

1 2 3 5 7 color 5

Part

04

Fresh + Clear

These refreshing, magnificent color palettes take their themes from the towering snow-peaked Alps, moss-covered forests, the Great Barrier Reef and other natural features that stand out on a massive scale. They're also helpful as prompts when a theme or scheme with a sense of translucency is required.

Color Schemes That Are Fresh and Bracing With a Sense of Translucency

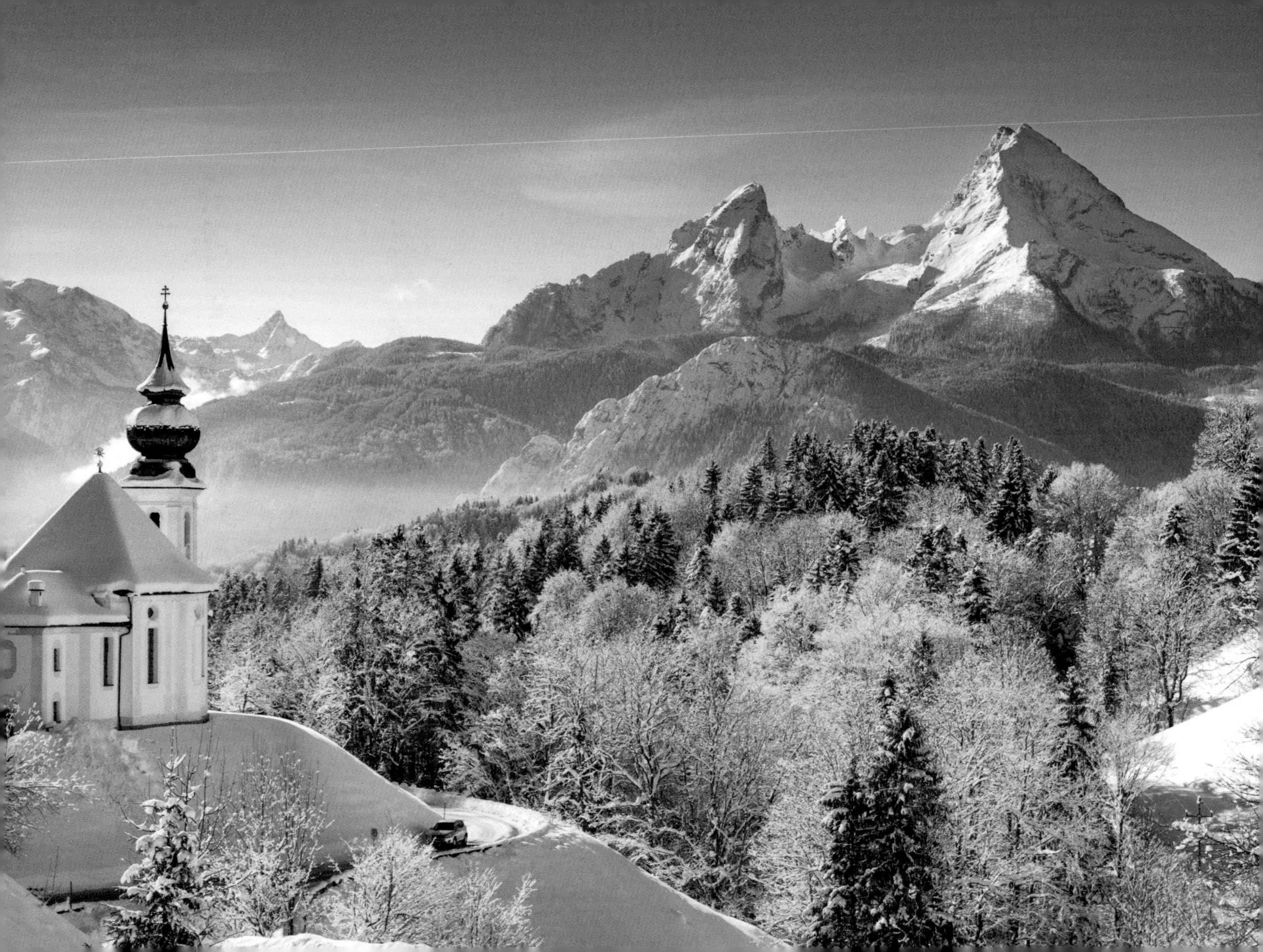

Recipe
029

Mont Blanc

Among the Alps, Mont Blanc stands the tallest. It calls to mind the cake made from chestnuts that takes its name from the mountain. The cake originated in the early 1900s when a long established cafe in Paris created a dessert made from cream piped onto a meringue base.

- **FEELING** Clear, awe-inspiring, bracing.
- **COMBINATIONS** Add brown and deep green to light blue.
- **TIPS** Use contrasting brightness between the back ground colors and those in the chart.

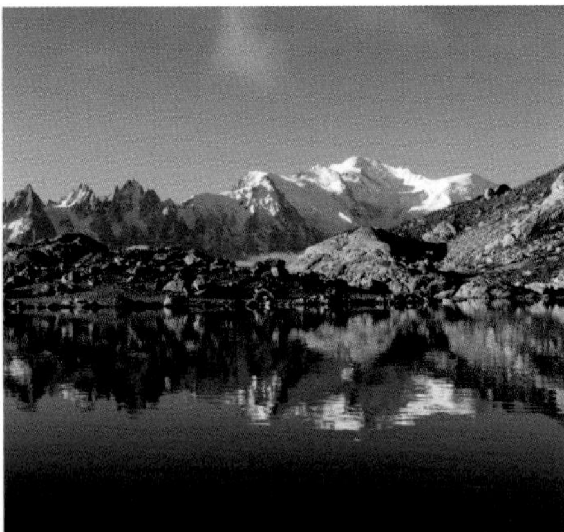

The brown of the rock face and earth against the deep blue serve as a reminder that nature's power is present.

❶ Alps Blue

A magnificent blue, a mountain reflected on the water's surface.

C100 M55 Y0 K5
R0 G95 B173
#005EAC

❷ Calm Blue

A calm, quiet grayish blue.

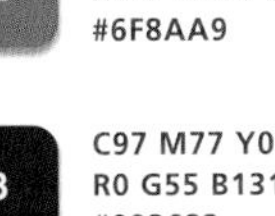

C45 M20 Y0 K35
R111 G138 B170
#6F8AA9

❸ Majestic Blue

A blue that is rich in tone and more deeply saturated.

C97 M77 Y0 K25
R0 G55 B131
#003682

❹ Clear Sky

The color of a clear sky on a fine day.

C50 M10 Y10 K0
R133 G192 B219
#84C0DA

❺ Mont Blanc White

The blue-tinged white of the snow that remains on Mont Blanc.

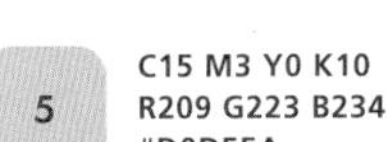

C15 M3 Y0 K10
R209 G223 B234
#D0DEEA

❻ Snow Shadow

A blue gray like that of snow in shadow.

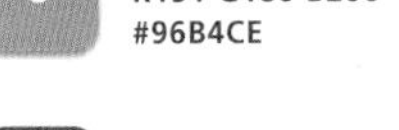

C35 M10 Y0 K20
R151 G180 B206
#96B4CE

❼ Forest Limit

The green seen at the point where a forest meets a rocky ridge.

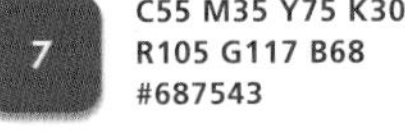

C55 M35 Y75 K30
R105 G117 B68
#687543

❽ Canyon

A crevasse in shadow, where the sun's rays don't reach.

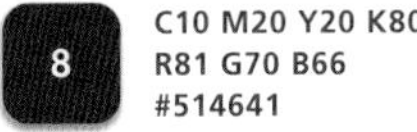

C10 M20 Y20 K80
R81 G70 B66
#514641

❾ Stone Brown

The grayish brown seen on rocky surfaces.

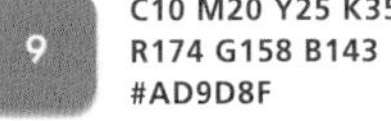

C10 M20 Y25 K35
R174 G158 B143
#AD9D8F

Two-color combinations

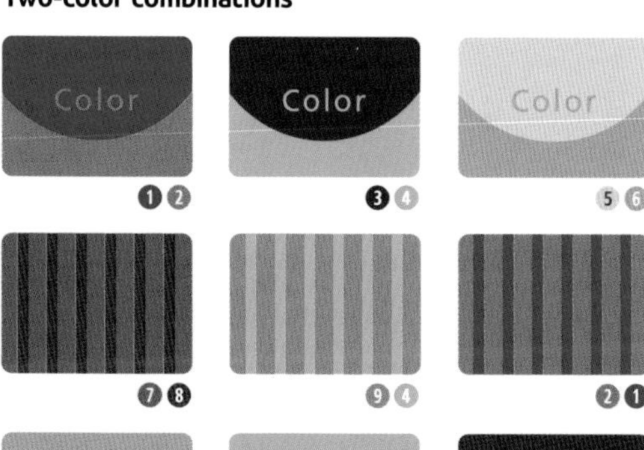

Three-color combinations

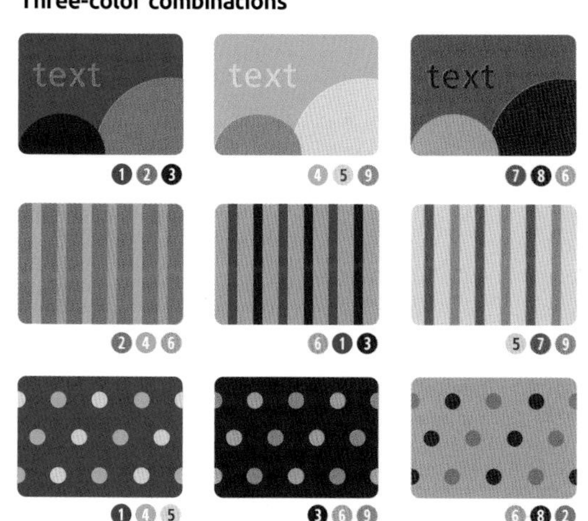

Designs

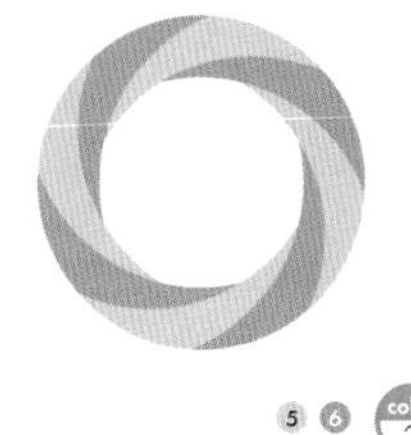

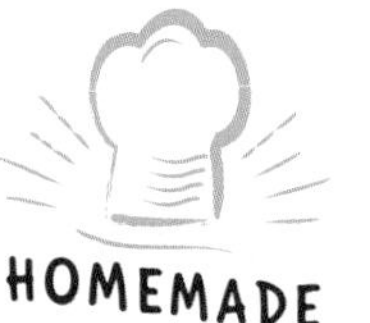

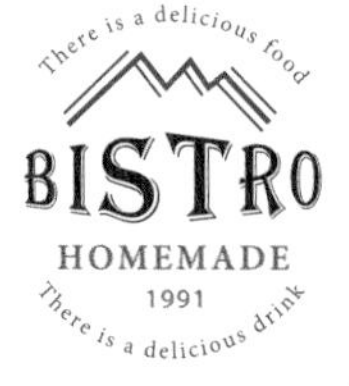

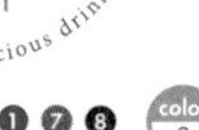

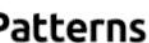

Patterns

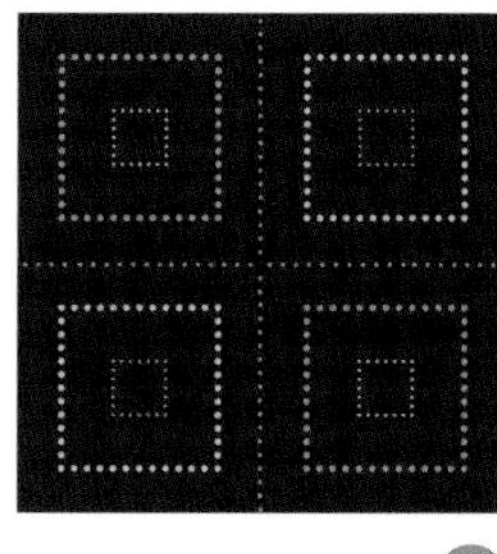

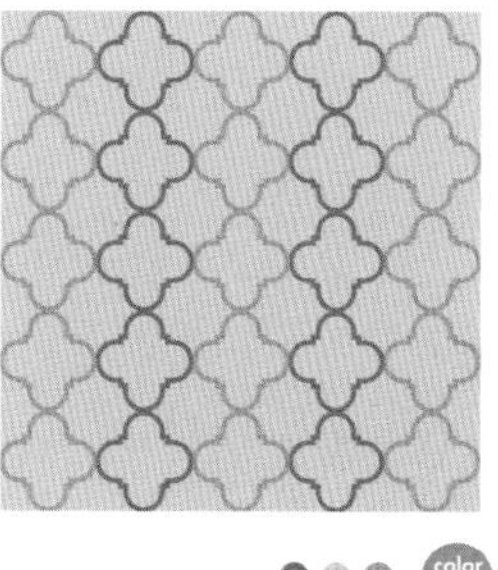

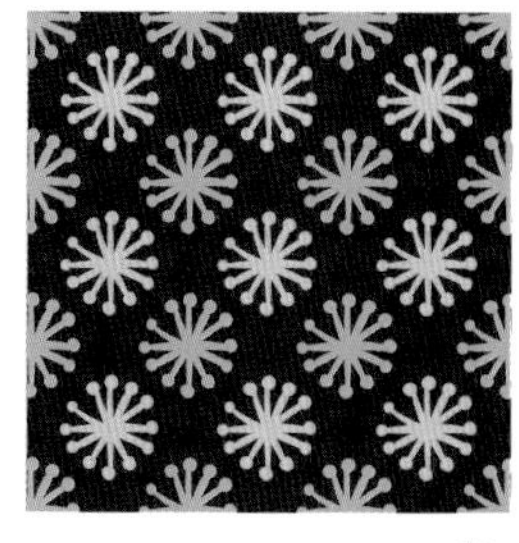

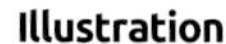

Illustration

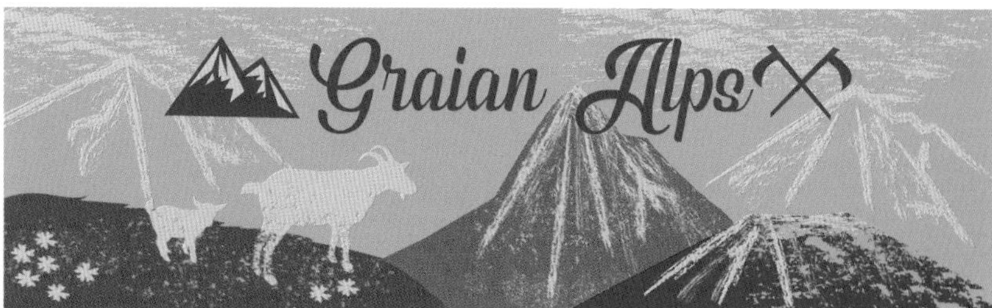

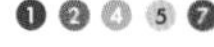

Recipe
030

Winter Wonderland

White snow glides down from a gray sky. People in their warm houses look outside and delightedly say "Look, it's snowing!" I remember this happening when I stayed in Stockholm, Sweden. The snow often creates its own problems, but everyone loves it. I imagine they enjoy strolling through their silvery white world on weekends.

- **FEELING** Brisk, clear, cool.
- **COMBINATIONS** Use natural colors of the sky and snow as they are.
- **TIPS** White is the brightest of all the colors.

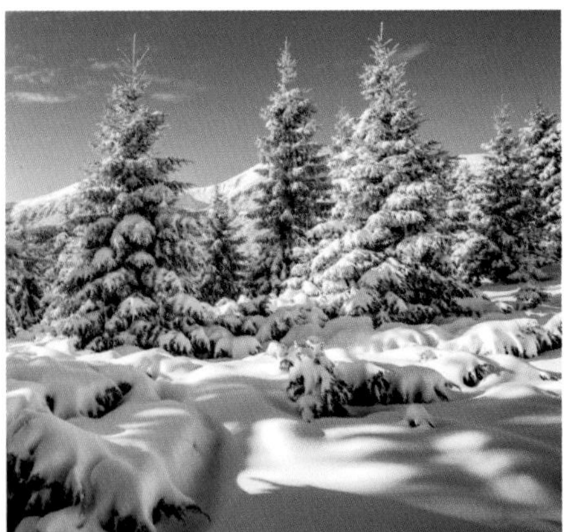

When the sun's rays hit the snow, the white is so dazzling that it's nearly blinding.

① **Powder Snow**
A white like that of snow with a hint of blue.

② **Winter Morning**
The bluish white of the sky in the moments just after dawn.

③ **Shadow Gray**
The gray of snow darkened by shadow.

④ **Brilliant Sky**
A sky blue that creates a vivid contrast with the white of the snow.

⑤ **Eternal Blue**
A sky that couldn't be bluer and makes one think of eternity.

⑥ **Pale Sky**
The pale, clear sky that can be seen near the horizon line.

⑦ **Winter White**
A pure white that calls to mind the quiet snow-covered landscape.

⑧ **Angora Rabbit**
A soft gray like that of angora rabbit fur.

⑨ **Fir Tree**
The deep green of fir tree leaves.

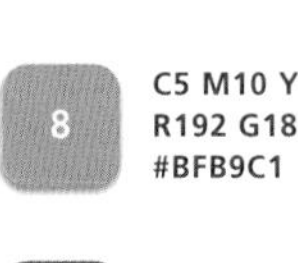

1	C10 M3 Y0 K0 R234 G242 B251 #EAF2FA
2	C25 M10 Y0 K5 R193 G211 B233 #C1D2E9
3	C25 M15 Y0 K30 R157 G165 B186 #9CA5B9
4	C70 M30 Y8 K0 R73 G148 B198 #4893C6
5	C80 M53 Y0 K0 R53 G109 B181 #346CB5
6	C45 M30 Y0 K0 R151 G168 B213 #97A7D5
7	C7 M0 Y10 K0 R242 G248 B237 #F1F7EC
8	C5 M10 Y0 K30 R192 G186 B193 #BFB9C1
9	C76 M35 Y65 K25 R52 G112 B89 #336F58

Two-color combinations

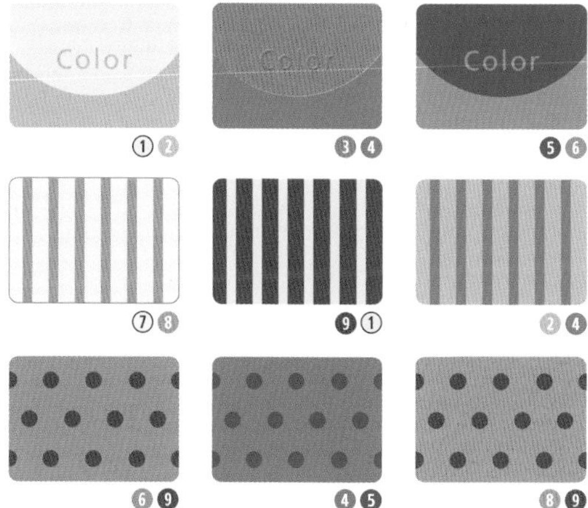

Three-color combinations

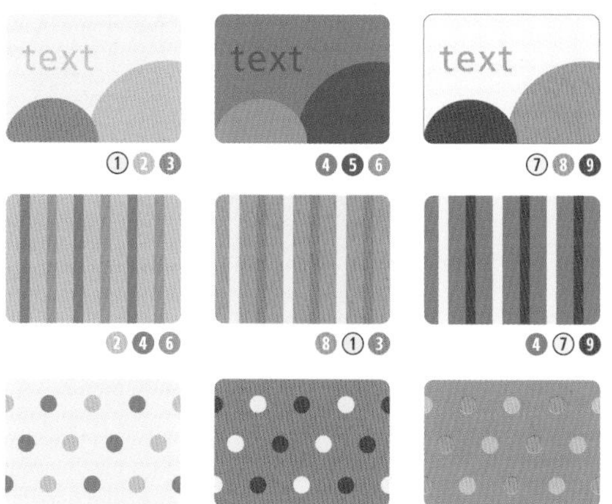

Designs

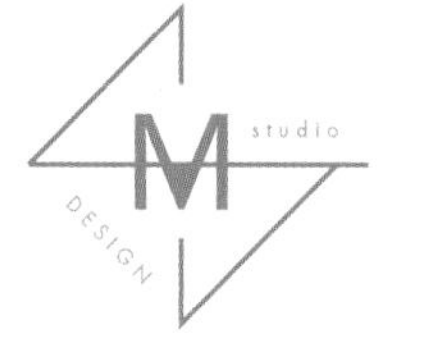

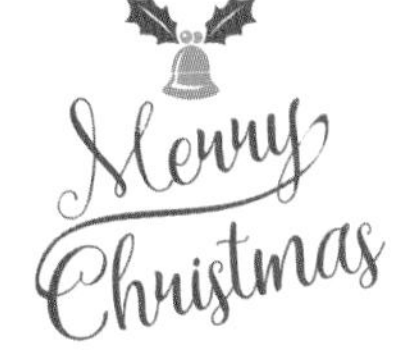

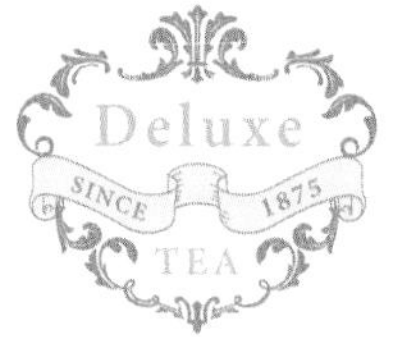

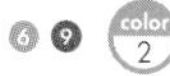

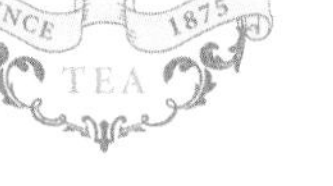

Patterns

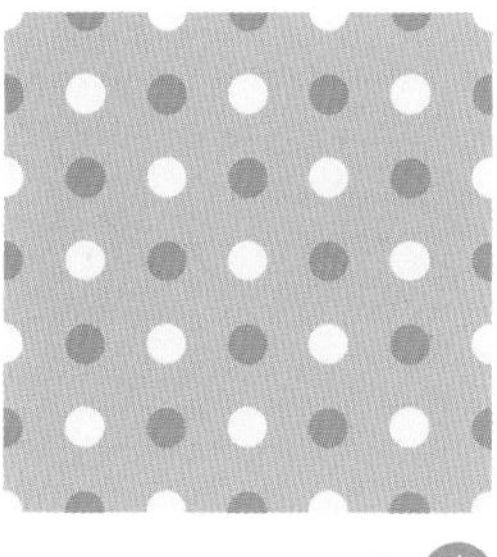

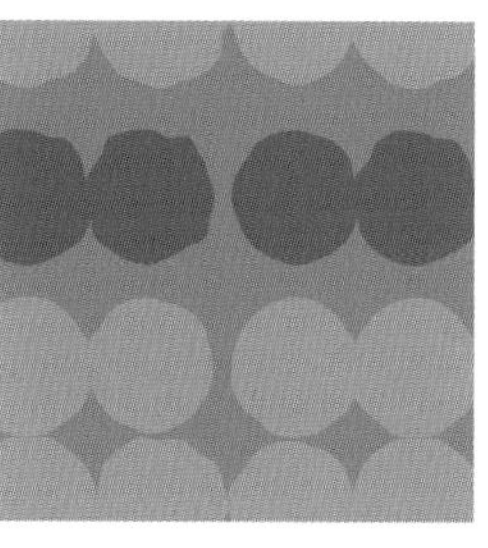

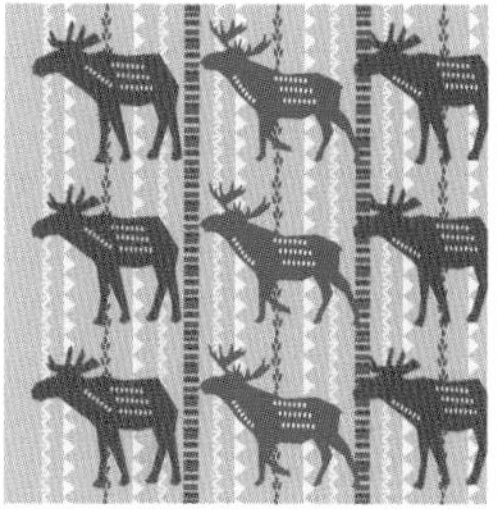

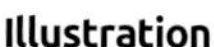

Illustration

PART 04

FRESH + CLEAR

Recipe
031

Mt. Fuji at Sunrise

The nursery song "Mount Fuji" begins "With its head above the clouds it looks over the mountains in all directions" and finishes with "Fuji is the best mountain in all Japan." Indeed. Mount Fuji symbolizes Japan, but this color palette is drawn from the shades in this photo of the mountain taken at an unusual angle and time.

- **FEELING** Bracing, beginning, mysterious.
- **COMBINATIONS** Match orange to different shades of blue gray.
- **TIPS** Blue and orange serve to draw each other out.

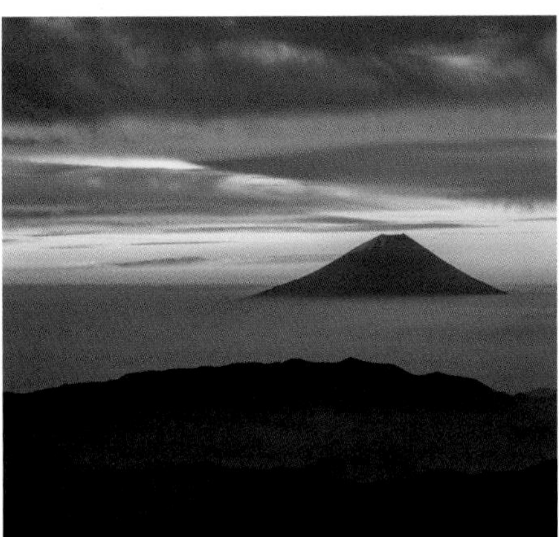

Depth, density and overlapping bands of color combine to inspire a one-of-a-kind palette.

❶ Dawn Orange
Also called salmon, this is the orange of dawn.

❷ Sunrise Glow
An orange like that of the glowing light that appears with the dawn.

❸ Ridge Gray
The blue gray of a mountain ridge.

❹ Heavenly Blue
In Japanese its name contains the characters "heaven" and "color."

❺ Early Morning
The color of the sky before the sun rises, a bluish white light.

❻ Blue Shadow
A deep navy, this is the color of shadows that appear to be blue.

❼ Cloud Sea
Clouds that resemble the sea, stretching as far as the eye can see.

❽ Warm White
The white tinged with orange that appears in the evening sky.

❾ Clear Blue
Blue that has a crisp translucency to it.

1 — C0 M75 Y77 K0 / R235 G97 B56 / #EB6137

2 — C0 M55 Y90 K0 / R241 G142 B29 / #F18D1D

3 — C50 M30 Y5 K15 / R125 G147 B186 / #7D93BA

4 — C80 M55 Y0 K10 / R52 G99 B168 / #3362A8

5 — C50 M40 Y5 K10 / R132 G138 B183 / #8489B6

6 — C60 M45 Y0 K55 / R64 G75 B115 / #404A72

7 — C20 M5 Y0 K5 / R205 G223 B239 / #CCDFEF

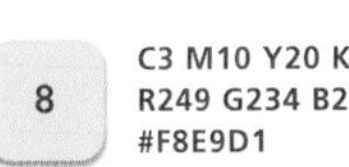

8 — C3 M10 Y20 K0 / R249 G234 B210 / #F8E9D1

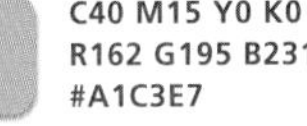

9 — C40 M15 Y0 K0 / R162 G195 B231 / #A1C3E7

Two-color combinations

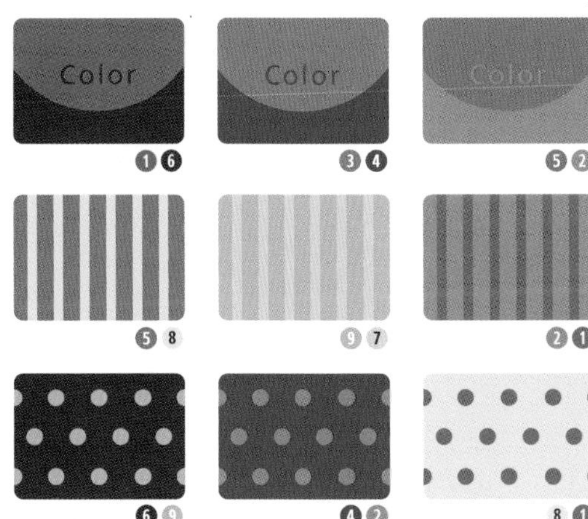

Three-color combinations

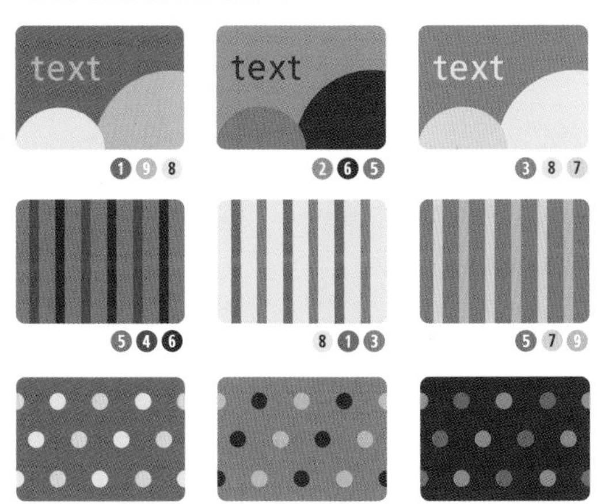

Designs

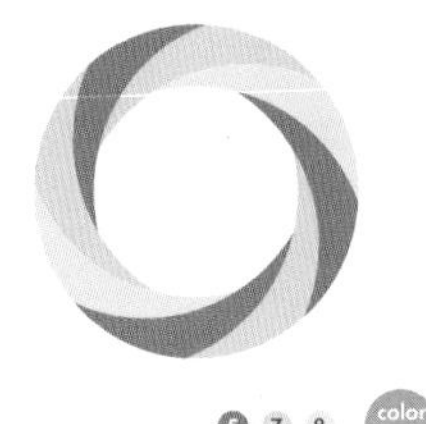

Patterns

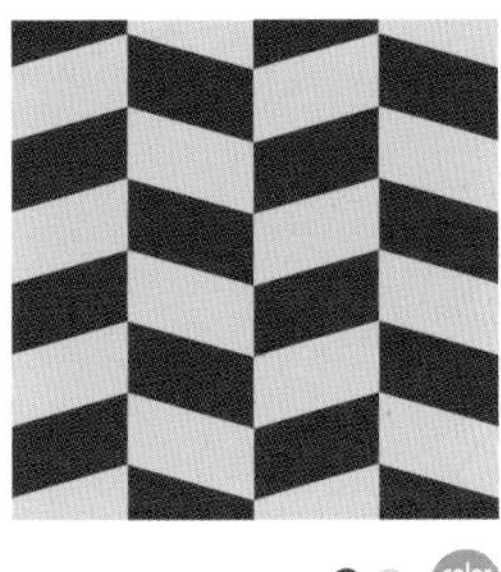

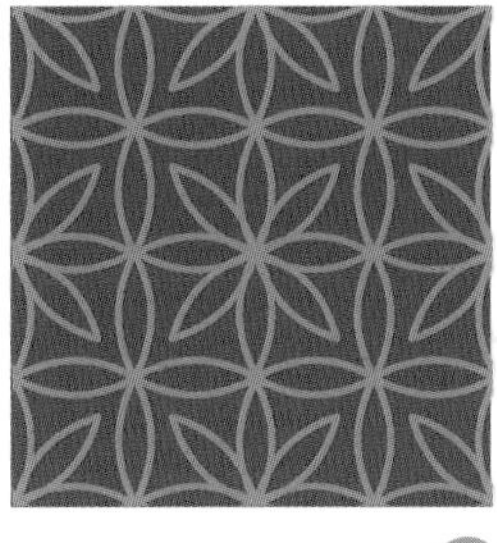

Illustration

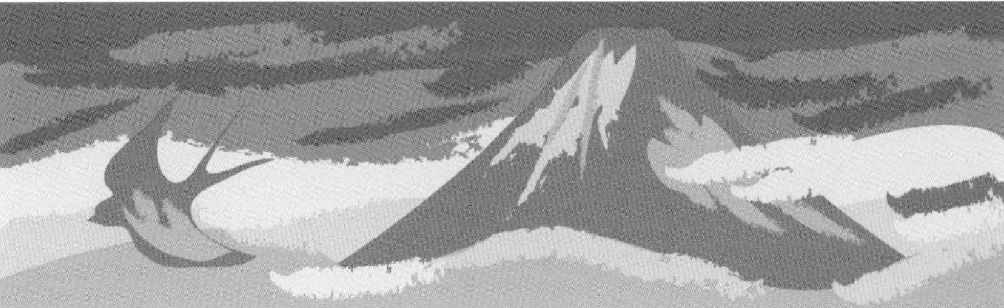

1 2 3 5 7 8 9 color 7

Recipe
032

A Sacred Forest

Kagoshima prefecture's Yakushima Island is a mysterious place where clear streams run deep in the heart of Yakushima cedar forests and moss covers the rocks. As the local saying goes: "20,000 people, 20,000 monkeys, 20,000 deer" and if you walk through the forests you'll encounter monkeys and deer. This color palette comprises shades of the deep forest, colors that coexist with nature.

- **FEELING** Natural, sacred, tranquil.
- **COMBINATIONS** Use various shades of green, with brown to pull them all together.
- **TIPS** Use yellow greens for light and dark blue greens for shadow.

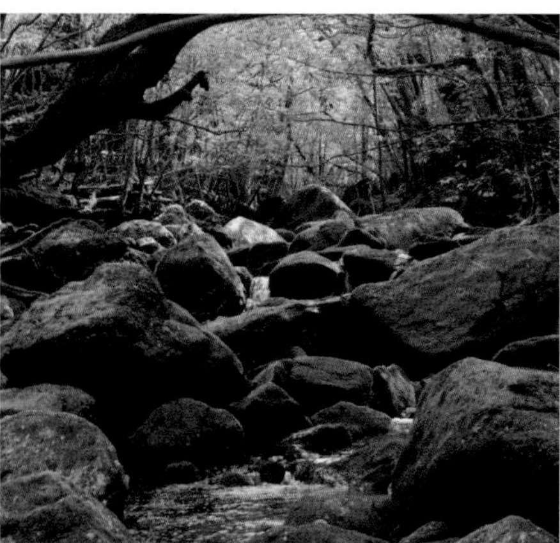

Only trees older than 1,000 are called Yakushima cedars.

❶ Dry Moss
Green with a white cast like that of dry moss.

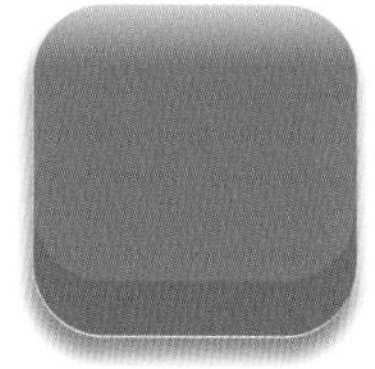

❷ Moss Green
A typical green the color of moss.

❸ Cedar Green
A deep green like that of Japanese cedar leaves.

❹ Sacred Green
A deep blue green with a sense of stillness to it.

❺ Wet Moss
A deep green like that of moss beside a mountain stream.

❻ Night Forest
Close to black, this green evokes a forest at night.

❼ Fawn Brown
A light brown that evokes a newborn fawn.

❽ Deer Brown
Monkeys and deer coexist on Yakushima Island.

❾ Monkey Brown
Monkeys ride the deer to get around, grooming them in return.

	CMYK	RGB	Hex
1	C35 M10 Y45 K0	R180 G203 B157	#B3CB9C
2	C60 M30 Y80 K3	R117 G148 B81	#759450
3	C70 M15 Y65 K10	R69 G153 B108	#45996C
4	C85 M10 Y60 K45	R0 G107 B86	#006B56
5	C65 M0 Y60 K45	R51 G126 B88	#327D58
6	C60 M0 Y60 K80	R22 G66 B40	#154228
7	C10 M15 Y40 K25	R193 G179 B137	#C1B389
8	C15 M40 Y70 K65	R108 G79 B33	#6C4E21
9	C15 M30 Y50 K40	R157 G131 B94	#9C835E

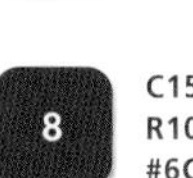
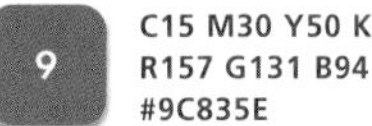

Two-color combinations

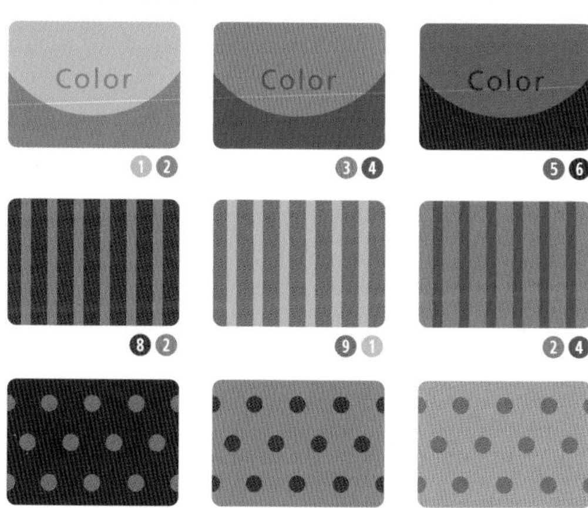

Three-color combinations

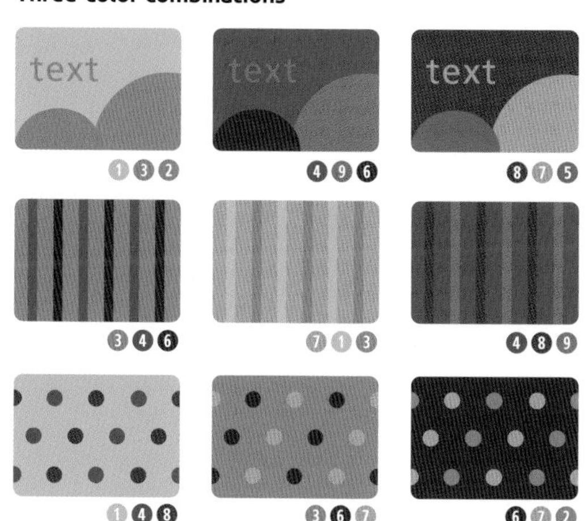

Designs

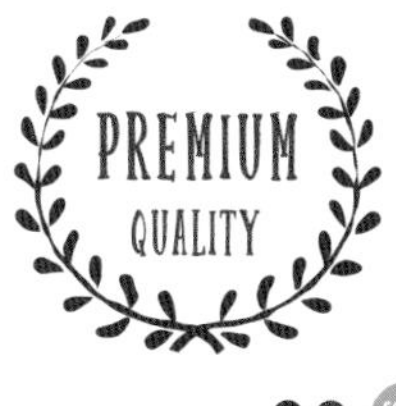

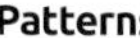

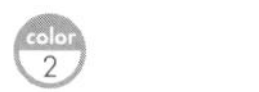

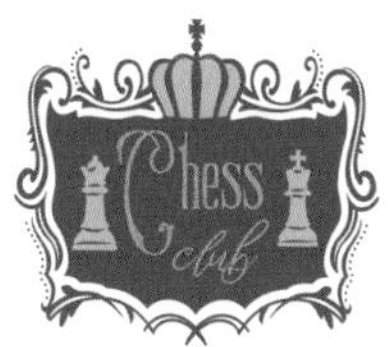

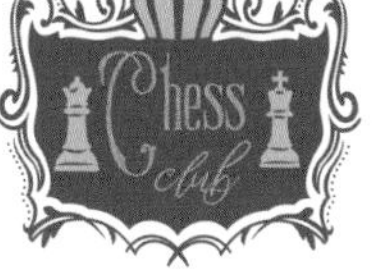

Patterns

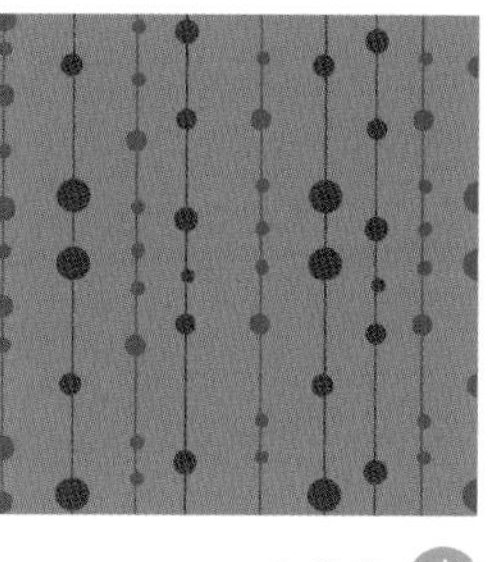

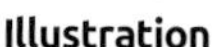

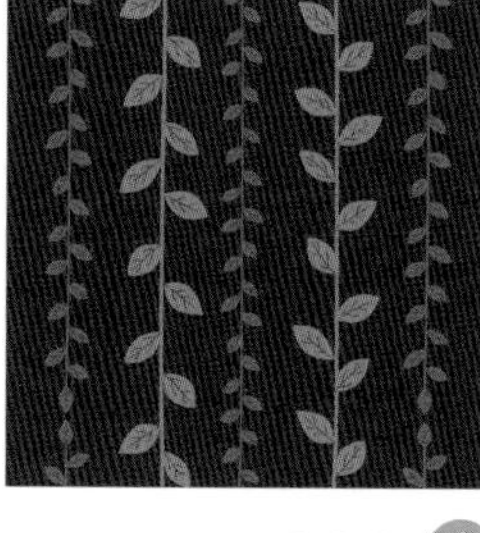

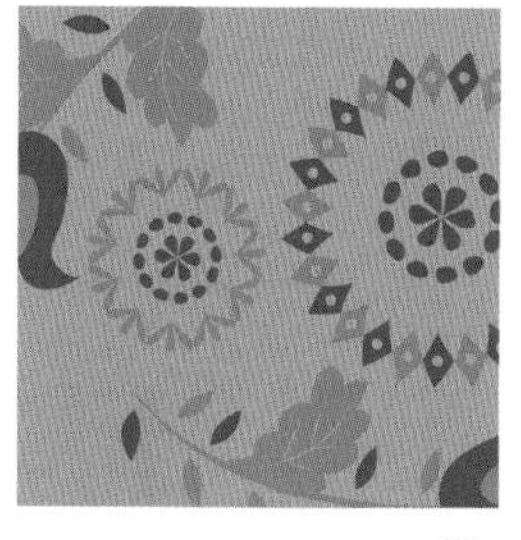

Illustration

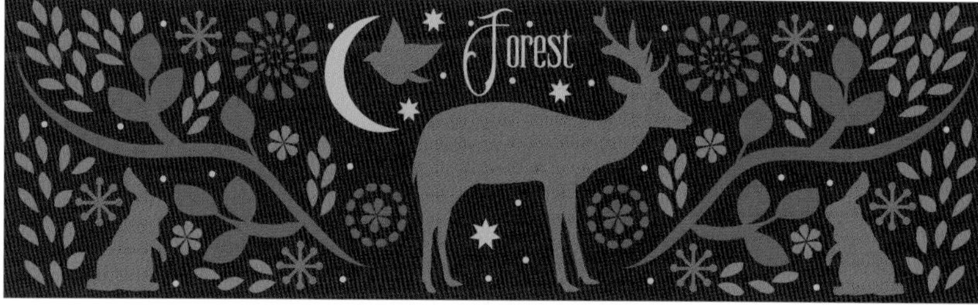

PART 04

FRESH + CLEAR

Recipe
033

New Green Leaves

As I left the house and headed to the station as usual, I glanced up at the sky. From the gaps between the branches and the leaves in the trees, yellow-green light streamed down. All this time, I could have felt the pleasant sunlight on my skin every morning. I'm going to start enjoying breathing deeply.

- **FEELING** Fresh, vibrant, exhilarating.
- **COMBINATIONS** Pair sky blue to various shades of yellow green.
- **TIPS** Use natural colors that are seen in nature.

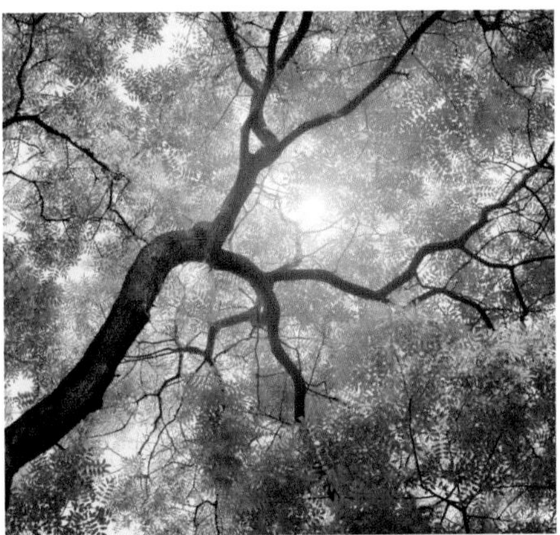

When colors are carefully chosen, even everyday scenery can inform and inspire attractive color schemes.

❶ Satsuki
The end of May through to the start of July, a time of new growth.

❷ New Leaves
The greenery of trees that gets more intense day by day.

❸ Blue Sky
The translucent blue of the sky on a fine day.

❹ Young Shoots
The yellow green of plant shoots that have only just emerged.

❺ Green Leaves
The fresh green of leaves at the start of summer.

❻ Filtered Light
A pale yellow green that evokes light filtering through trees.

❼ Hope
A light blue that represents positive feelings and hope for the future.

❽ Light Breeze
The cool light breezes kick in, setting the leaves in motion.

❾ Trunk
The natural brown seen on many tree trunks.

1 C80 M15 Y90 K25 / R0 G129 B61 / #00803D

2 C55 M20 Y85 K0 / R131 G168 B74 / #83A749

3 C23 M0 Y10 K0 / R205 G233 B234 / #CDE8E9

4 C25 M5 Y70 K0 / R206 G216 B102 / #CDD866

5 C70 M25 Y90 K0 / R86 G149 B70 / #559545

6 C15 M0 Y35 K0 / R226 G237 B186 / #E2ECBA

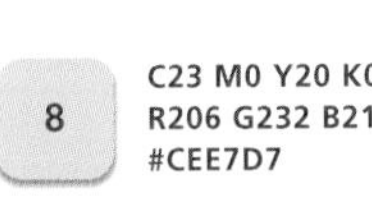

7 C45 M0 Y25 K0 / R148 G209 B202 / #94D0C9

8 C23 M0 Y20 K0 / R206 G232 B215 / #CEE7D7

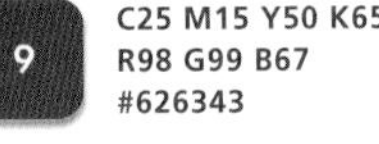

9 C25 M15 Y50 K65 / R98 G99 B67 / #626343

Two-color combinations

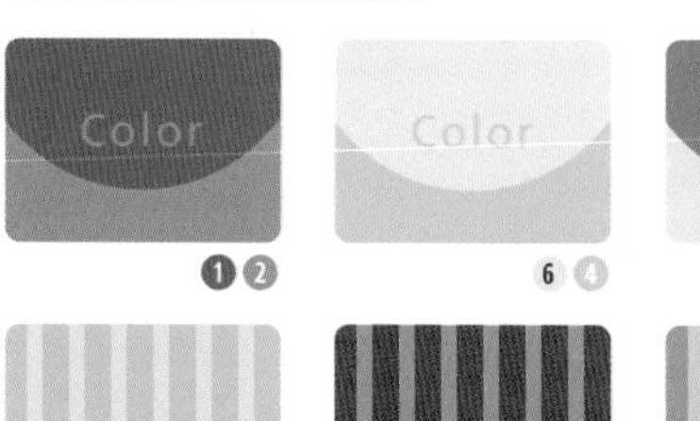
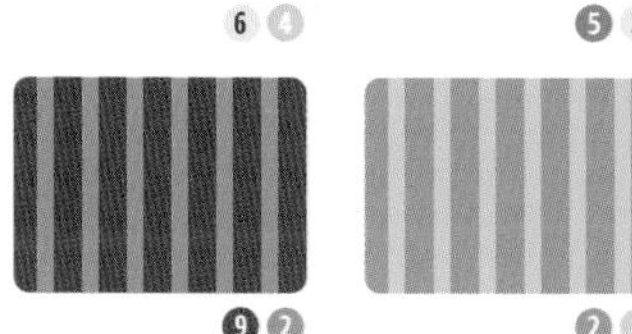
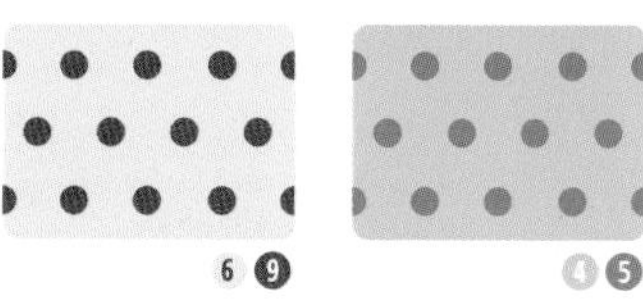
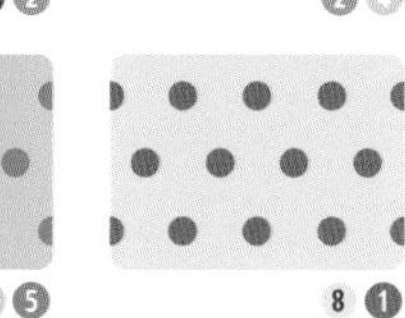

Three-color combinations

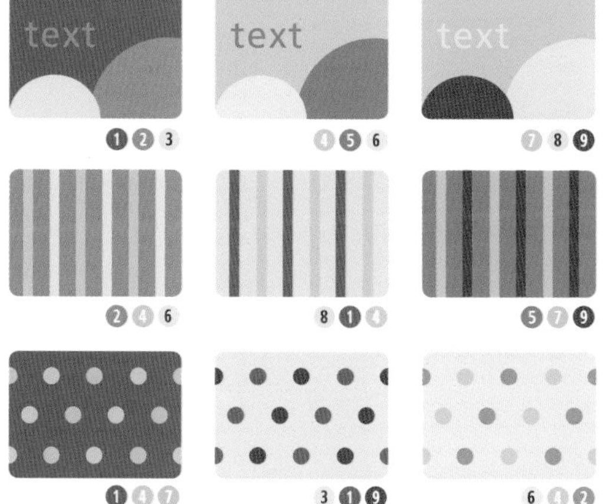

Designs

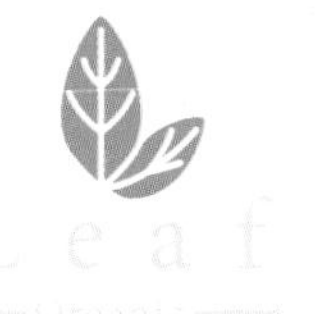

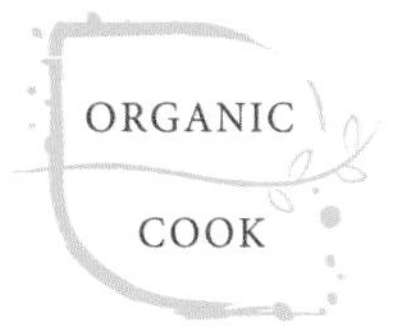

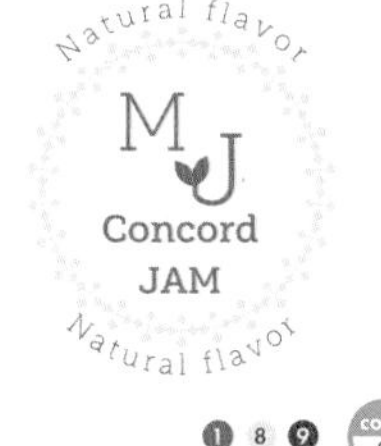

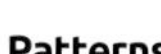

Patterns

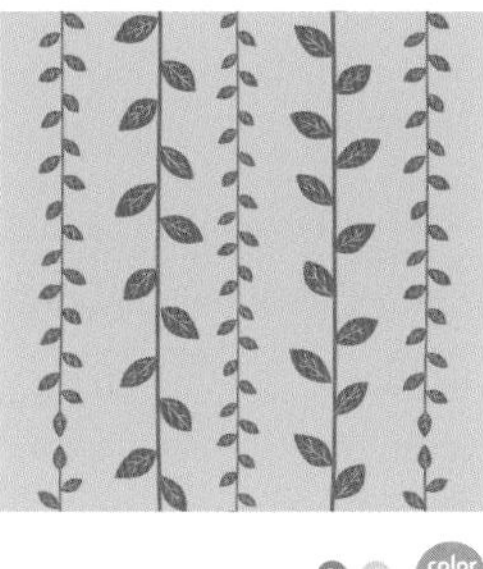
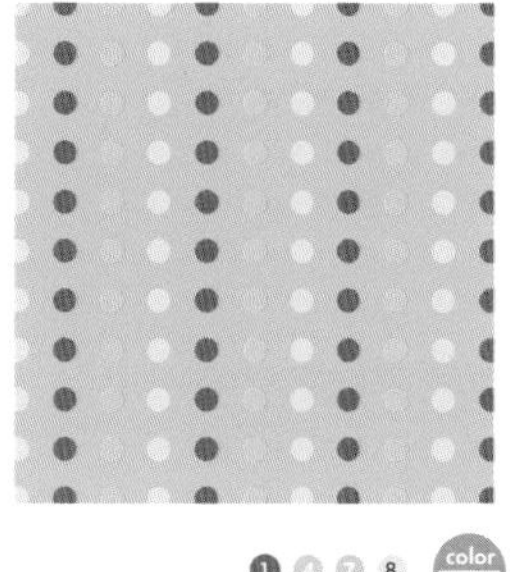

Illustration

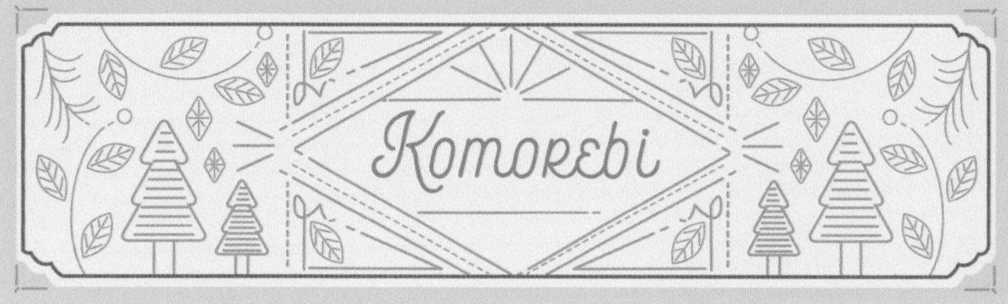

Recipe
034

Tropical Beach Resort

The Indian Ocean archipelago of the Maldives has limited its tourist industry to only one hotel on each island and is now known throughout the world as a first-rate resort area. Described as "the necklace of the Indian Ocean," "paradise on earth" and "the atolls of heaven," its beautiful colors have been used to form this palette.

- **FEELING** Clear, pellucid, expansive.
- **COMBINATIONS** Focus on light shades of blue with a sense of translucency.
- **TIPS** Use colors of different hues with high levels of brightness as accents.

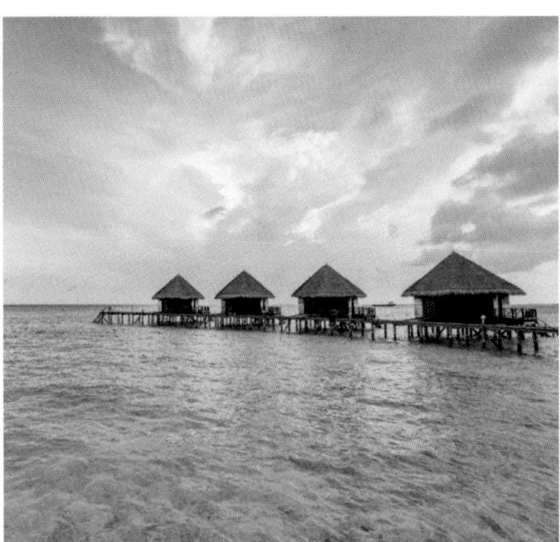

The ever-changing colors of the sea and sky can be enjoyed at leisure.

1 Indian Ocean
A blue that conjures the vast Indian Ocean.

2 Maldives Blue
The surprising blue of the sea; the blue of the heavenly Maldives.

3 Bright Turquoise
An intense blue that evokes the Tropics.

4 My Blue
My favorite is the blue found in the shallows.

5 Pieces of Blue
An extremely faint blue.

6 Blue Paradise
The blue of paradise can also symbolize the Virgin Mary.

7 Yogurt Smoothie
The color of the yogurt smoothie at breakfast.

8 Melon Juice
The green of fresh melon juice.

9 Orange Sherbet
The orange of cold, sweet sherbet.

1 — C70 M25 Y5 K0 / R66 G154 B208 / #419ACF

2 — C53 M3 Y0 K0 / R116 G199 B241 / #74C7F0

3 — C83 M0 Y0 K0 / R0 G173 B236 / #00ACEB

4 — C55 M0 Y25 K0 / R115 G198 B200 / #72C6C7

5 — C20 M0 Y9 K0 / R212 G236 B236 / #D4EBEC

6 — C90 M60 Y5 K0 / R0 G95 B168 / #005EA7

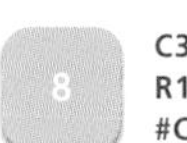

7 — C3 M10 Y15 K10 / R232 G220 B206 / #E8DBCD

8 — C30 M0 Y55 K0 / R193 G220 B141 / #C0DB8C

9 — C0 M40 Y50 K0 / R245 G175 B126 / #F5AF7D

Two-color combinations

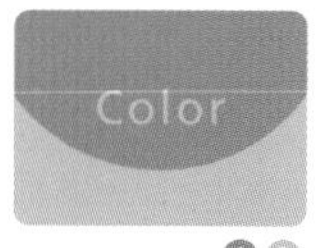

1 2

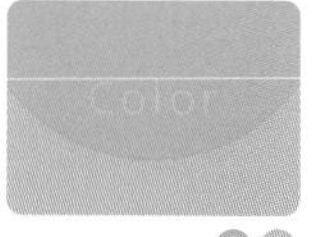

3 4

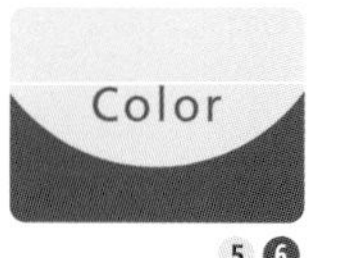

5 6

7 4

9 1

2 3

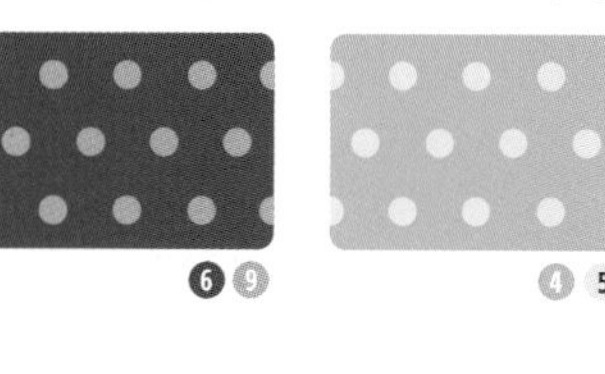
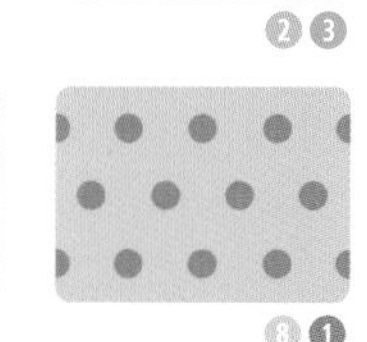

6 9

4 5

8 1

Three-color combinations

1 2 3

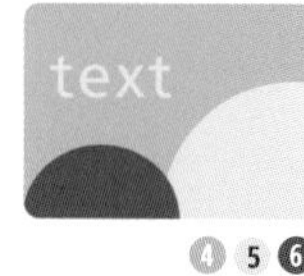

4 5 6

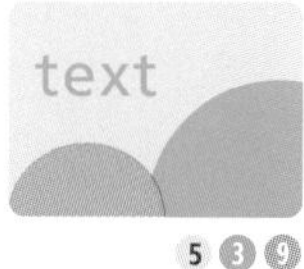
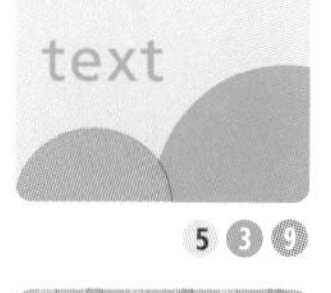

5 3 9

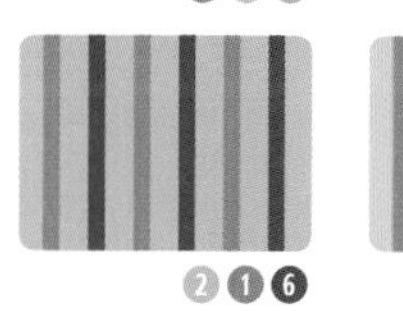

2 1 6

8 1 3

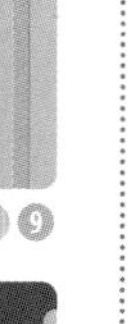

2 7 9

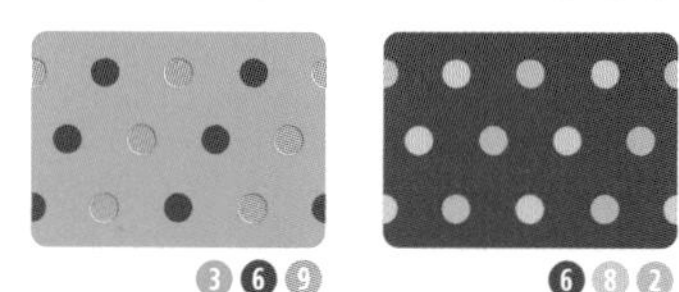

1 4 7

3 6 9

6 8 2

Designs

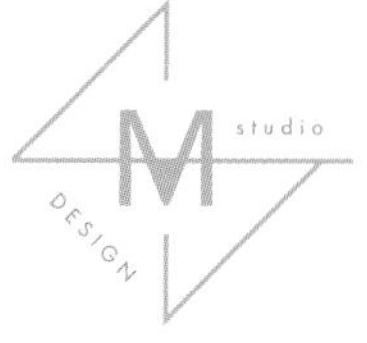

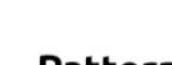
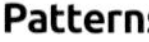

1 9 color 2

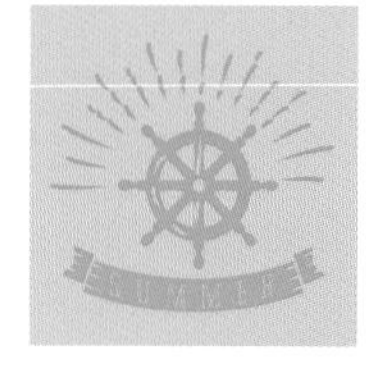

3 8 color 2

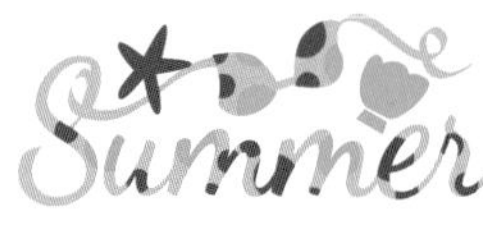

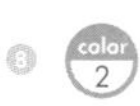
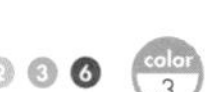

2 3 6 color 3

Patterns

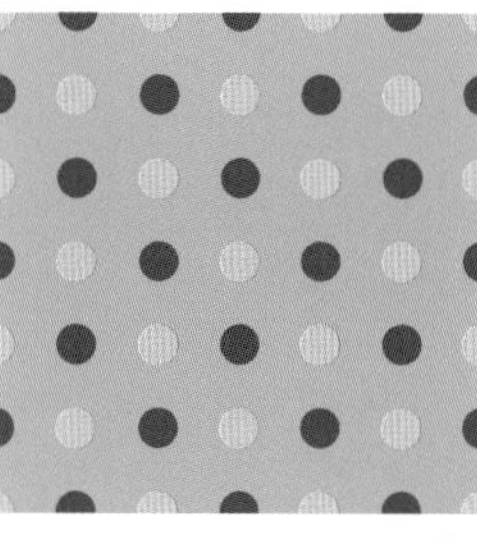

4 6 7 color 3

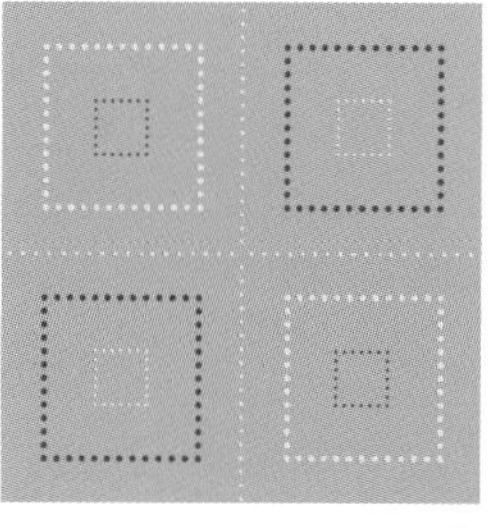

5 6 9 color 3

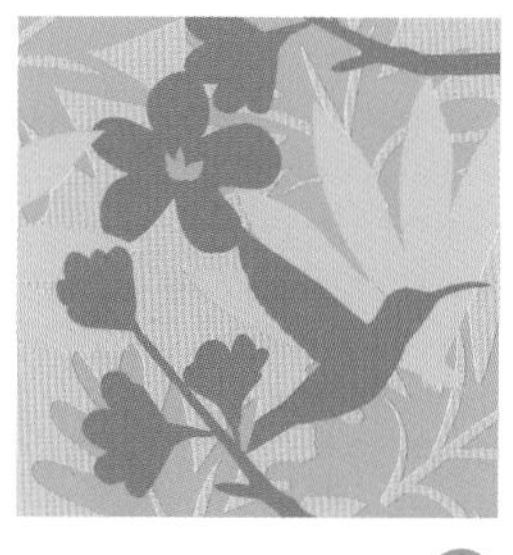

1 4 7 8 color 4

Illustration

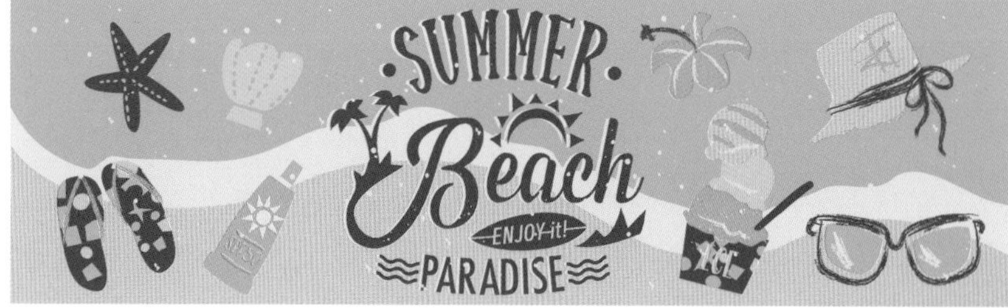

4 5 6 7 8 9 color 6

PART 04

FRESH + CLEAR

Recipe
035

Great Barrier Reef

It's not commonly known, but on Google Maps' "Street View," it's possible to walk through the water of the Great Barrier Reef. No flippers or oxygen tank are required to enjoy this fabulously uplifting view of the beautiful ocean. What should I do after playing with the adorable sea turtles and colorful tropical fish?

- **FEELING** Mother Nature, vast, magnificent.
- **COMBINATIONS** Colors of water are the focus.
- **TIPS** Work in accents to prevent the color scheme becoming dull.

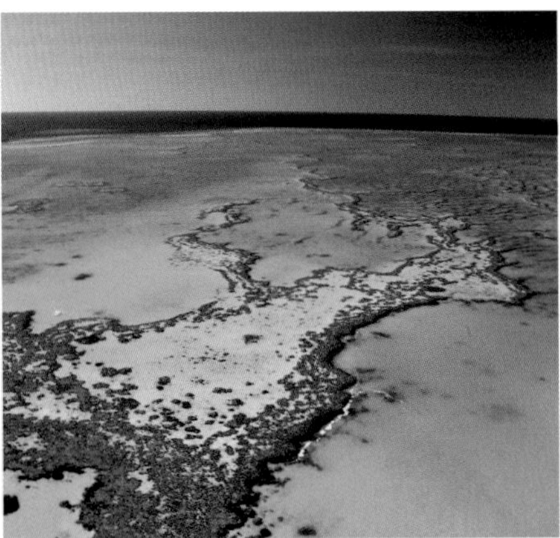

A combination of all kinds of blues suffuse this reef scene.

❶ **Lagoon**
The color of the sea surrounded by coral reefs; a beautiful emerald blue.

❷ **Spa Blue**
A blue that calls to mind the color of spas and pools in resort hotels.

❸ **Off the Coast**
A deep blue like that of the open sea on a fine day.

❹ **Horizon**
The blue of the horizon that appears particularly intense in color.

❺ **Dawn Blue**
The blue on the horizon at dawn.

❻ **Summer Shower**
A warm summer rain burned off by the heat of the sun.

❼ **Dawn Purple**
The faintly pink-purple tinge of the sky at dawn.

❽ **Chocolate Milk**
The color of sweet, chilled chocolate milk.

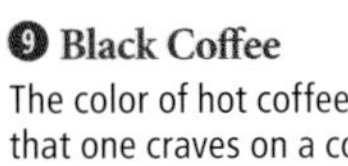

❾ **Black Coffee**
The color of hot coffee that one craves on a cold morning.

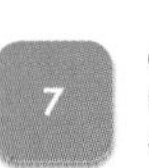
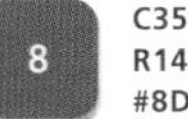

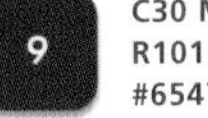

No.	CMYK	RGB	Hex
1	C75 M0 Y25 K0	R0 G179 B196	#00B2C4
2	C90 M0 Y8 K0	R0 G167 B222	#00A6DE
3	C90 M35 Y20 K0	R0 G128 B175	#0080AE
4	C83 M65 Y0 K0	R55 G89 B167	#3659A7
5	C60 M40 Y0 K2	R112 G139 B197	#708AC4
6	C45 M0 Y25 K0	R148 G209 B202	#94D0C9
7	C30 M40 Y5 K0	R187 G161 B197	#BBA0C5
8	C35 M40 Y45 K30	R141 G122 B107	#8D7A6A
9	C30 M50 Y50 K60	R101 G72 B60	#65473C

Two-color combinations

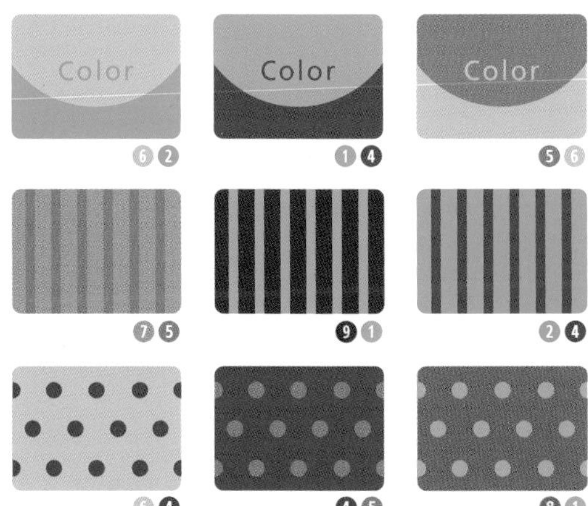

Three-color combinations

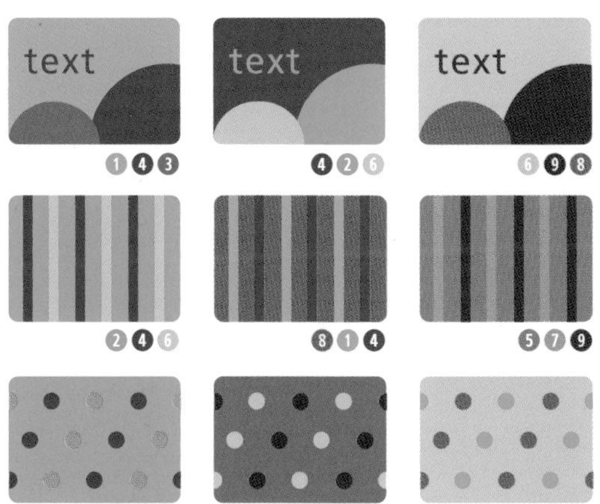

Designs

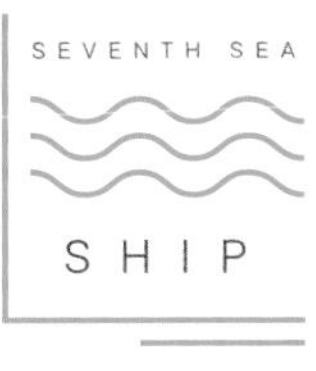

2 9 color 2

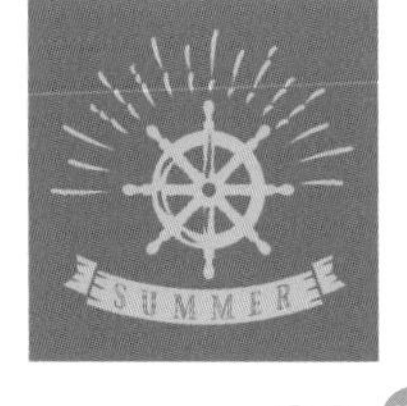

3 6 color 2

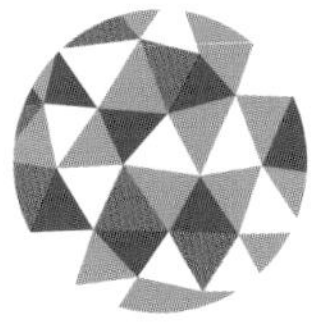
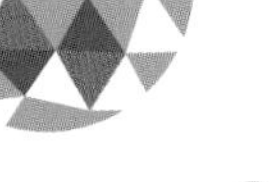
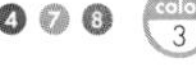

4 7 8 color 3

Patterns

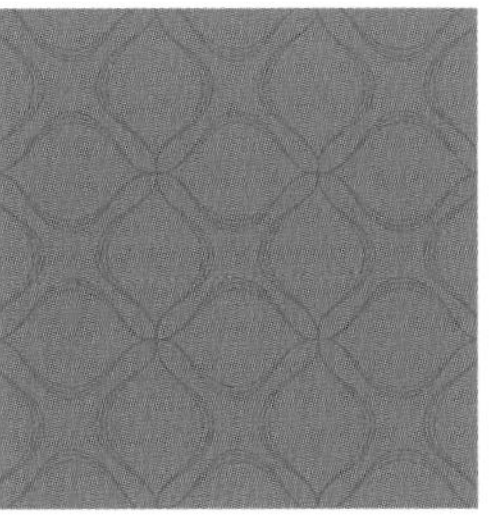

3 5 color 2

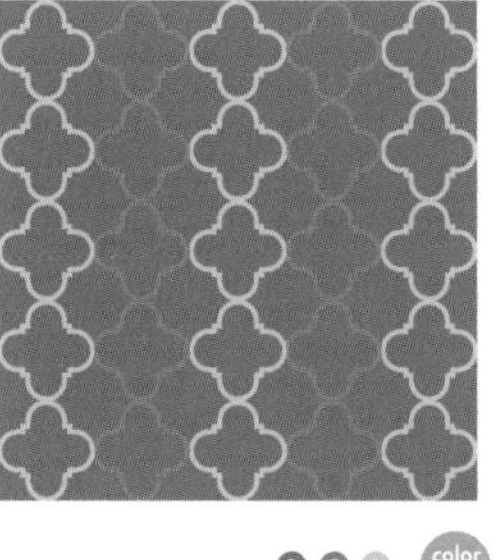

3 5 6 color 3

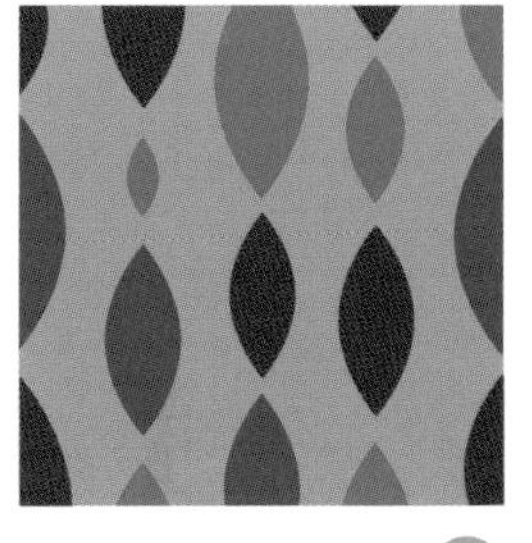

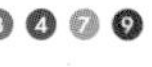

3 4 7 9 color 4

Illustration

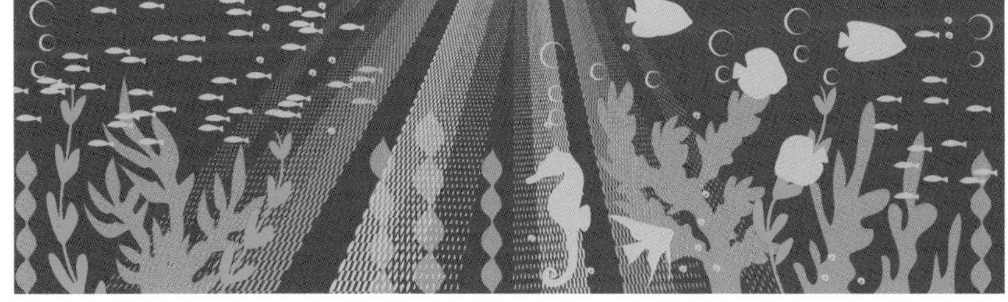

2 3 4 6 7 color 5

Recipe
036

Transparent Colors

The color of items is determined by which wavelength are reflected when light hits the object. However, transparent colors are slightly different as it depends on which components of a wavelength permeate them. Sometimes it's fun to try thinking of colors in a scientific way.

- **FEELING** Clear, refreshing, invigorating.
- **COMBINATIONS** Focus on cool shades with high levels of brightness and low to medium intensity.
- **TIPS** Use Colors 7 and 8 as accents.

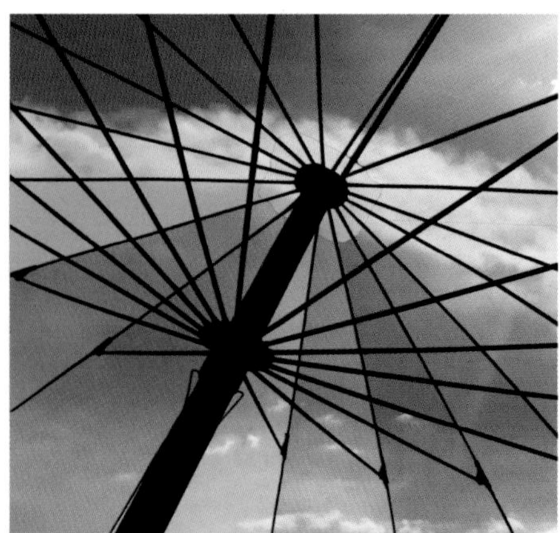

Focus on cool shades to express the sense of translucency.

❶ **Transparent Green**
Green with a sense of translucency.

❷ **Transparent Blue**
Blue with a sense of translucency.

❸ **Transparent Purple**
Purple with a sense of translucency.

❹ **Transparent Sky**
Sky blue with a sense of translucency.

❺ **Transparent Aqua**
Aqua blue with a sense of translucency.

❻ **Cloudy Green**
A slightly murky tone of green like that of a cloudy sky.

❼ **Cloudy Blue**
A slightly murky tone of gray blue like that of a cloudy sky.

❽ **Cloudy Beige**
A color made by mixing a lot of gray into orange.

⑨ **Transparent White**
A simple white that gives a sense of translucency.

No.	CMYK	RGB	Hex
1	C47 M0 Y60 K0	R148 G202 B130	#93CA82
2	C45 M23 Y0 K0	R150 G179 B221	#95B2DD
3	C30 M47 Y0 K0	R187 G147 B194	#BA93C2
4	C45 M37 Y0 K0	R153 G156 B205	#989BCC
5	C50 M0 Y0 K0	R126 G206 B244	#7DCDF3
6	C50 M0 Y25 K6	R127 G197 B194	#7FC4C1
7	C30 M0 Y0 K43	R127 G156 B172	#7E9CAB
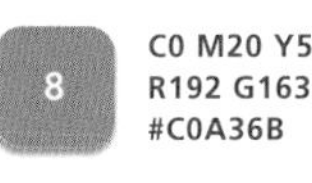 8	C0 M20 Y50 K33	R192 G163 B108	#C0A36B
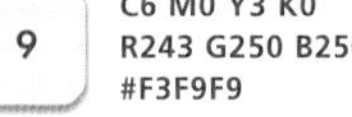 9	C6 M0 Y3 K0	R243 G250 B250	#F3F9F9

Two-color combinations

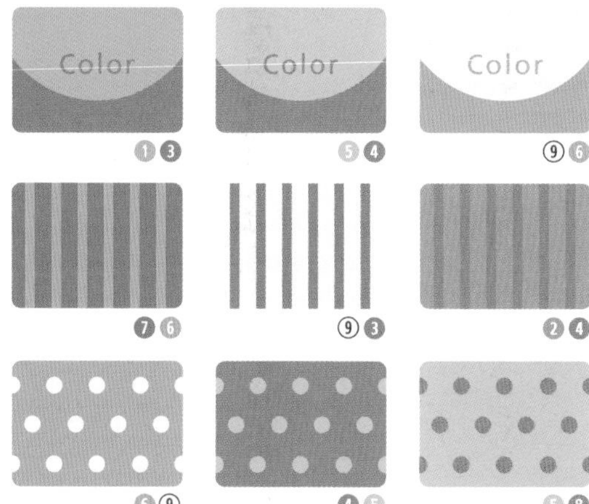

Three-color combinations

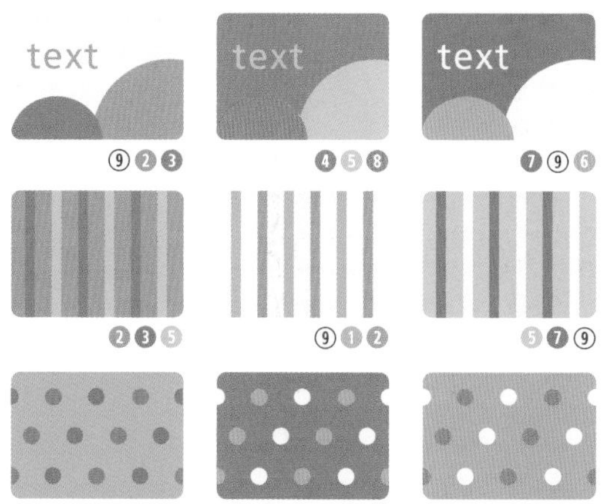

Designs

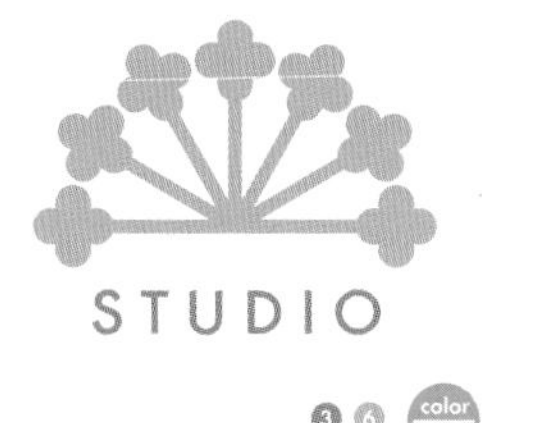

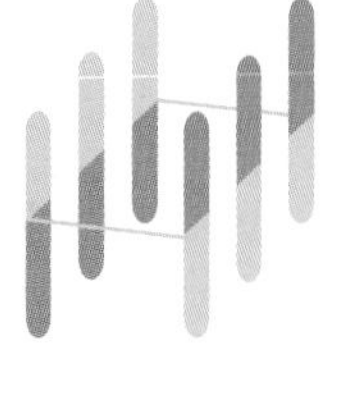

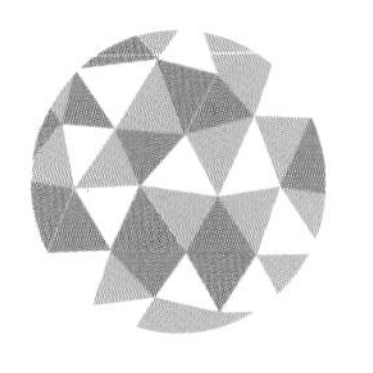

Patterns

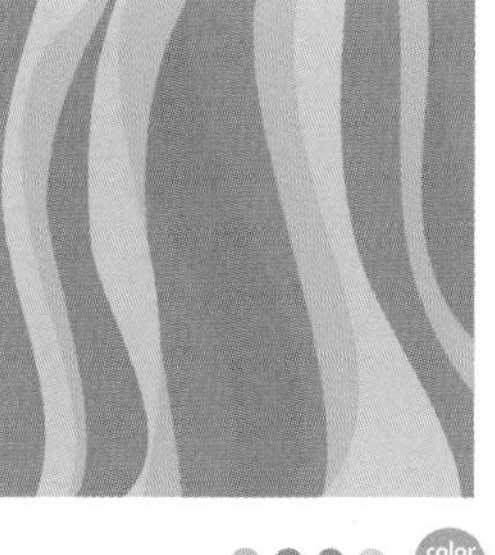

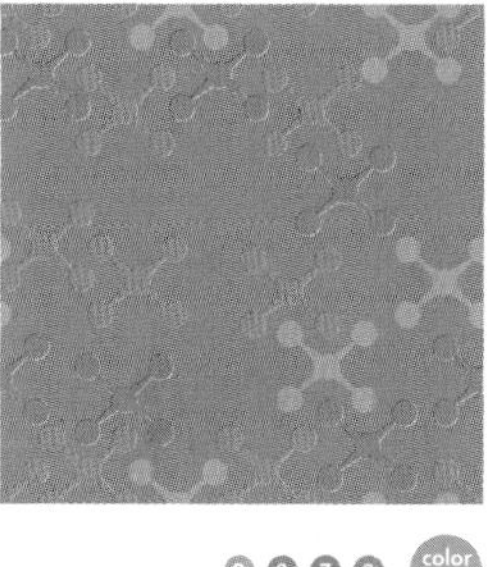

Illustration

Part

05

Elegant

These color palettes use shades of purple and grayish tones and can be used when a sophisticated, elegant look is desired. Delicate blossoms, makeup and nail polish are the motifs used here.

Color Schemes That are Sophisticated, Classy and Refined.

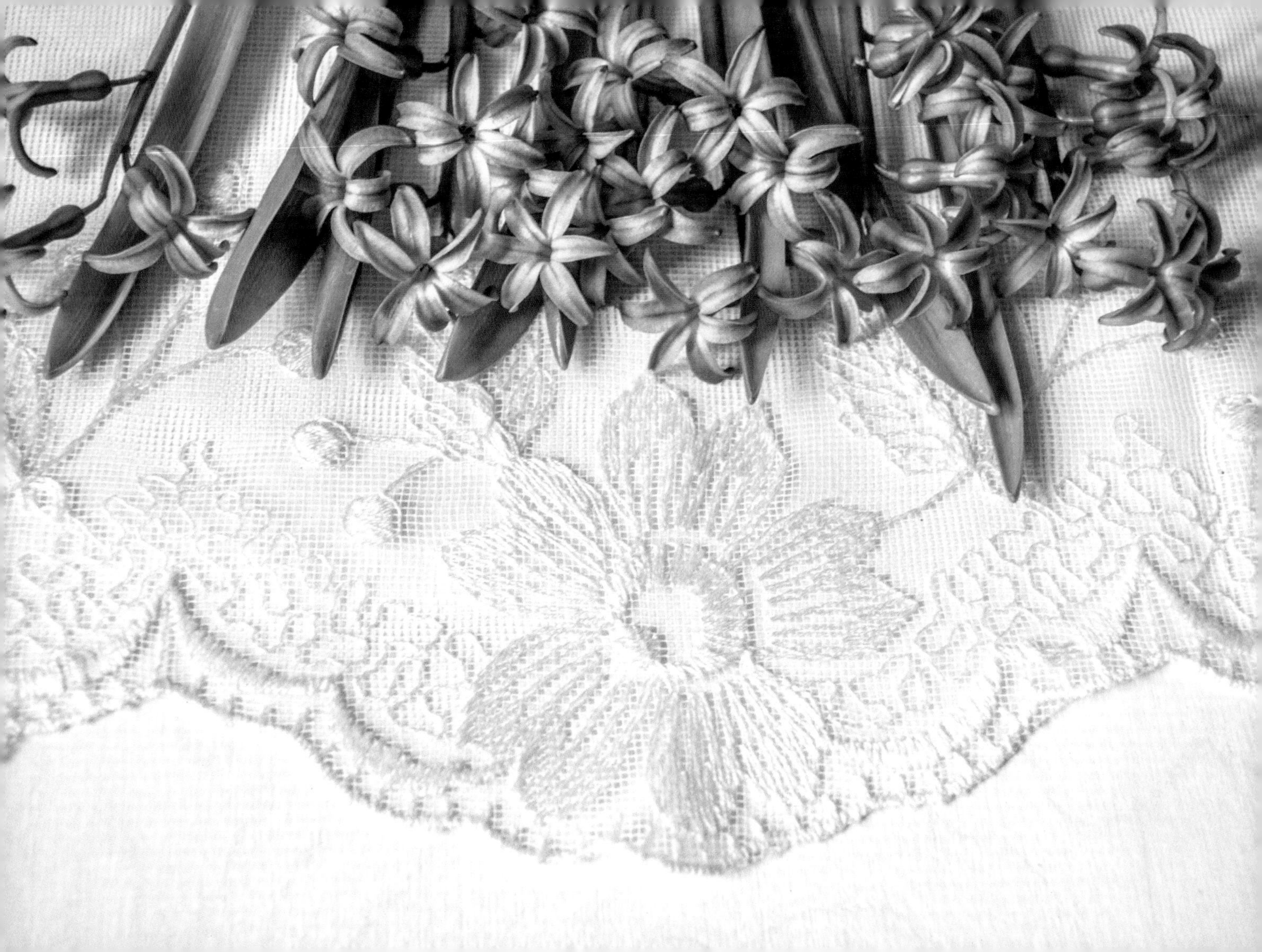

Recipe
037

Orchids

Held every February, the Japan Grand Prix International Orchid and Flower Show releases an original fragrance that has a different variety of orchid as its theme each year. It's hugely popular among passionate collectors. The colors on display are stunning. Here, the color scheme expresses the sophisticated aura of an orchid and captures its translucent splendor.

- **FEELING** Splendid, precious, gorgeous.
- **COMBINATIONS** Accent colors bring out splendor.
- **TIPS** Use light, bright shades as accent colors.

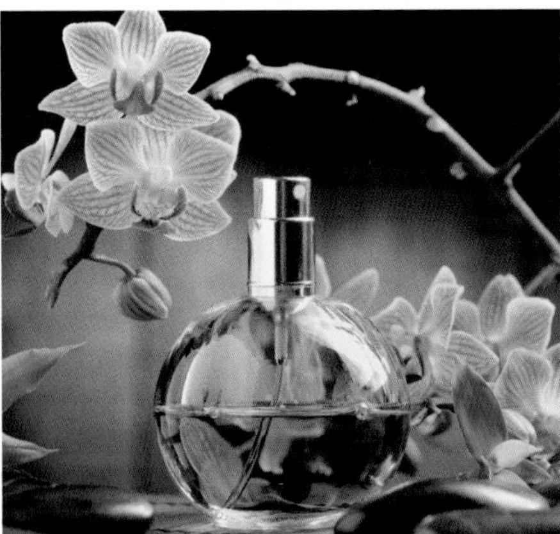

The various types of orchids number around 15,000.

❶ Orchid
This flower color is typical for an orchid.

❷ Bletilla Striata
A sturdy orchid that is easy to grow in pots and gardens.

❸ Cattleya
A deep purple like that of the cattleya flower from Central America.

❹ Cymbidium
Its petals are pale peach with dark stripes.

❺ Ao-Furan
Also known as Blue Moon, a Western orchid violet in color.

❻ Purple Elegance
A pale purple phalaenopsis called Purple Elegance.

❼ Ponerorchis Graminifolia
These orchids are native to mountain regions across Japan.

❽ Cymbidium
Available in various colors, this is one of the easily cultivated Western orchids.

❾ Grammatophyllum
Flowering in summer, this large orchid has light green blooms.

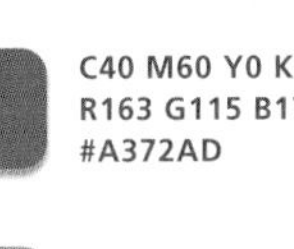
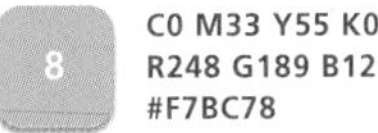
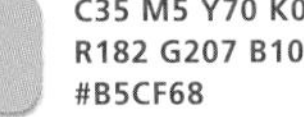

No.	CMYK	RGB	Hex
1	C15 M40 Y0 K0	R217 G170 B205	#D9AACD
2	C20 M65 Y0 K0	R203 G114 B171	#CB72AA
3	C20 M87 Y0 K0	R200 G57 B143	#C7398E
4	C10 M15 Y10 K0	R233 G221 B221	#E8DCDD
5	C40 M60 Y0 K3	R163 G115 B173	#A372AD
6	C35 M30 Y0 K3	R173 G173 B212	#ADACD3
7	C13 M73 Y0 K5	R208 G94 B156	#CF5E9B
8	C0 M33 Y55 K0	R248 G189 B121	#F7BC78
9	C35 M5 Y70 K0	R182 G207 B104	#B5CF68

Two-color combinations

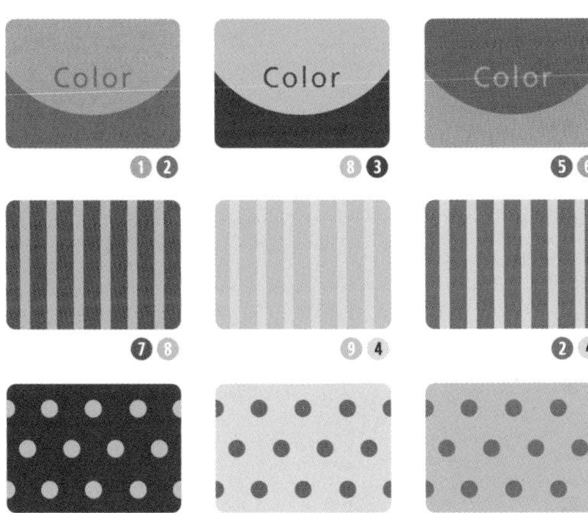

Three-color combinations

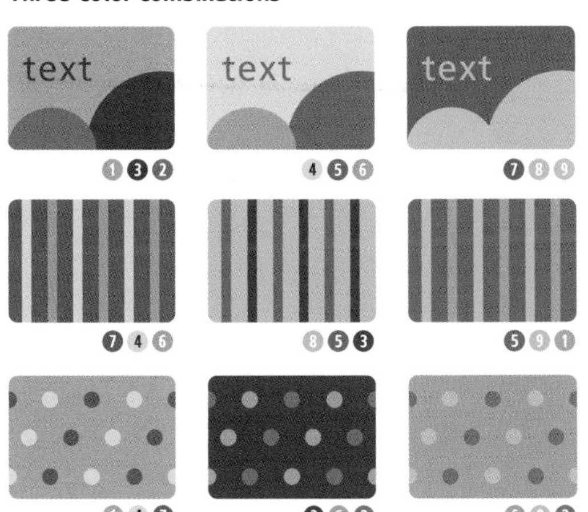

Designs

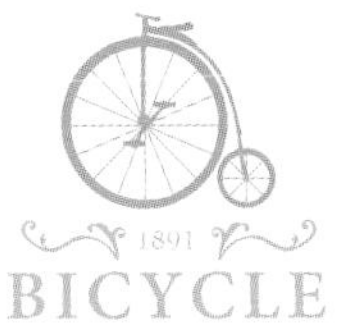

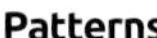

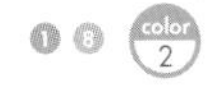

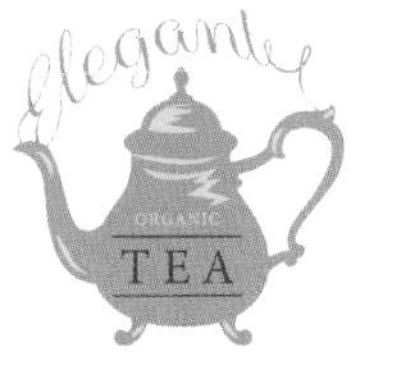

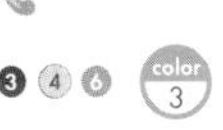

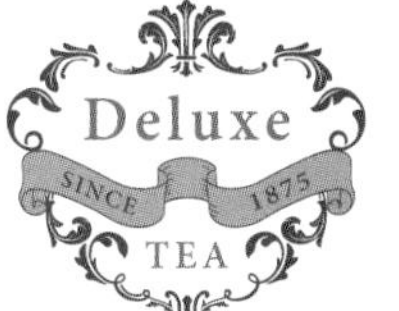

Patterns

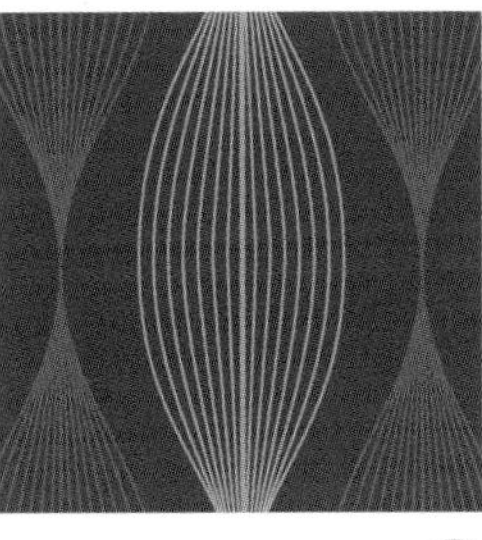

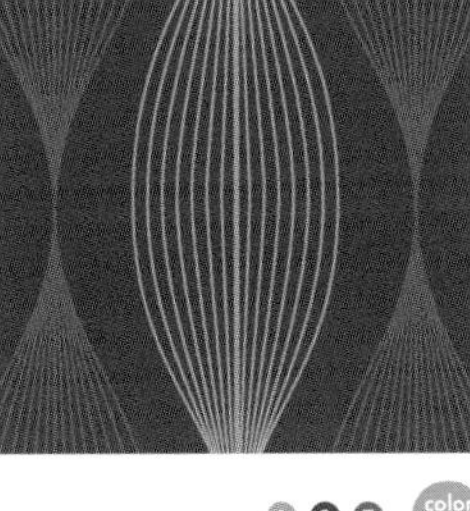

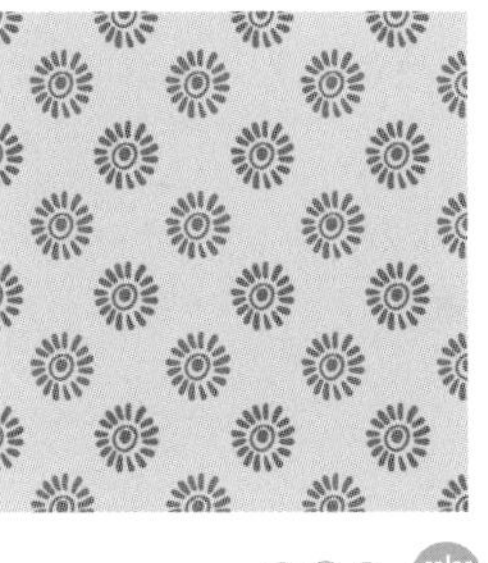

Illustration

Recipe
038

Lavender

My aromatherapist, who studied in England told me that essential oil from lavender is a cure-all that aids in everything from pain relief to relaxation. In Europe, it's commonly found in family medicine chests. Now, I always carry some with me as an amulet. When I open the little bottle, the lavender field is right there with me.

- **FEELING** Sense of security, calm, purity.
- **COMBINATIONS** Keep saturation levels in check to create a natural look.
- **TIPS** Match serene green with bluish purple.

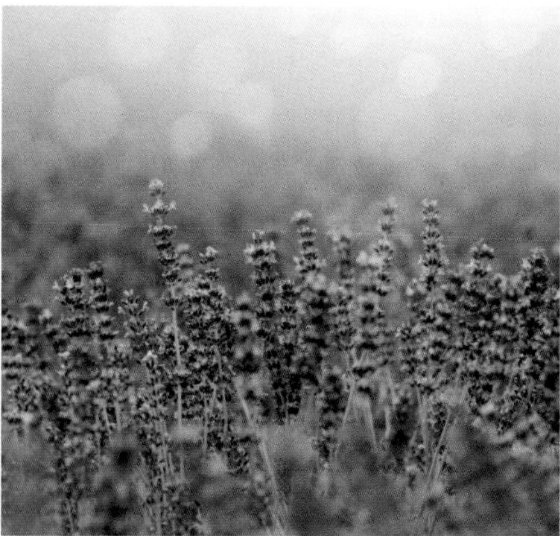

Aromatherapy is a natural method of treatment that has been used in Europe since ancient times.

❶ Uneasiness
A deep violet that expresses a sense of uneasiness.

❷ Worry
A color that expresses the state of emotion when burdened by worry.

❸ Stress
A color that expresses the difficult state of mind created by stress.

❹ Quiet Sleep
A purple to promote peaceful, deep sleep.

❺ Healing
A color that brings a sense of peace when troubled by uneasiness and worry.

❻ Pain Relief
A color that reflects the sensation of relieving pain or itchiness.

❼ Antibacterial
A purplish white with antiseptic undertones.

❽ Relax
A green that expresses a calm, quiet state of mind.

❾ Balance
The green of being oneself and not trying too hard.

	CMYK	RGB	Hex
1	C65 M65 Y0 K3	R108 G95 B166	#6C5EA5
2	C35 M55 Y0 K3	R173 G127 B180	#AD7EB4
3	C60 M75 Y0 K3	R122 G78 B155	#7A4E9A
4	C35 M40 Y0 K3	R174 G155 B199	#AD9AC7
5	C17 M30 Y0 K2	R213 G187 B216	#D4BAD8
6	C40 M35 Y0 K2	R163 G161 B206	#A3A1CE
7	C13 M15 Y0 K0	R226 G219 B237	#E1DBEC
8	C20 M5 Y30 K10	R200 G212 B181	#C8D4B4
9	C45 M0 Y55 K25	R126 G171 B117	#7DAA75

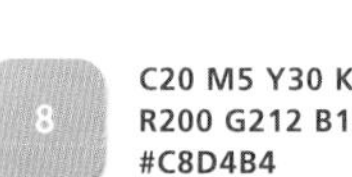
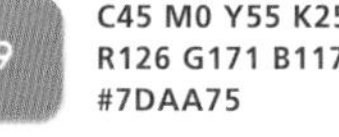

Two-color combinations

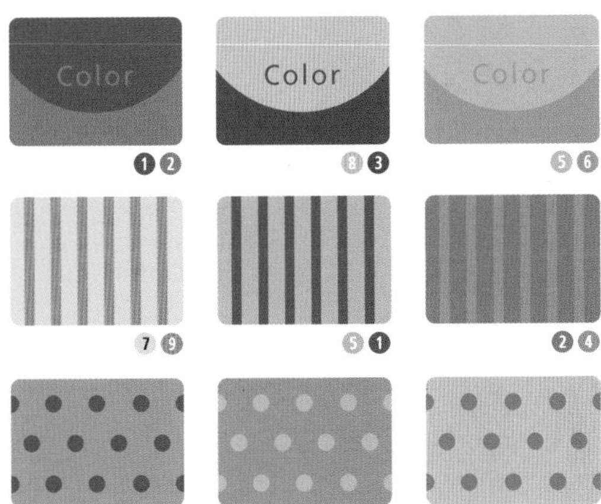

Three-color combinations

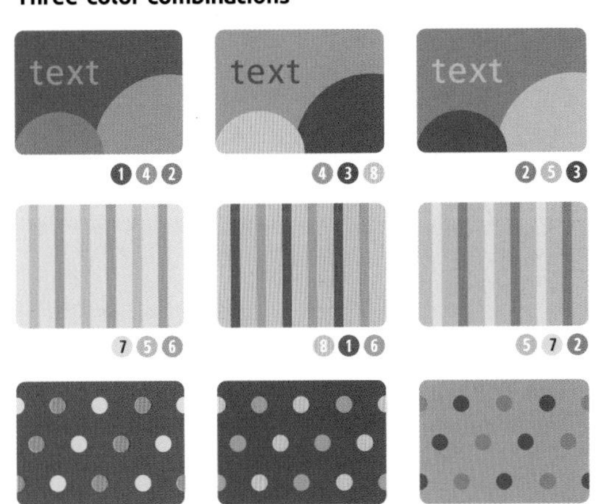

Designs

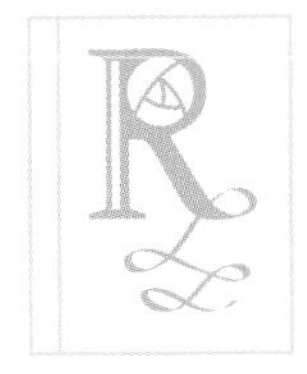
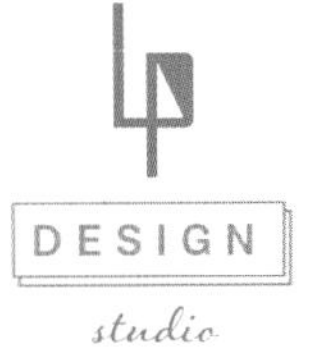

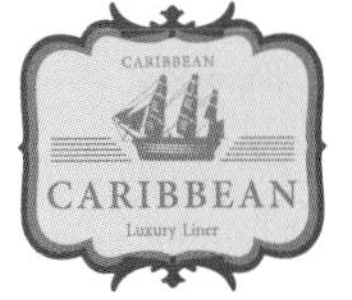

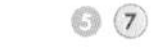
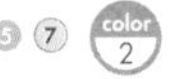
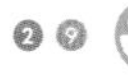
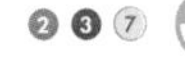

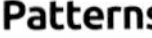

Patterns

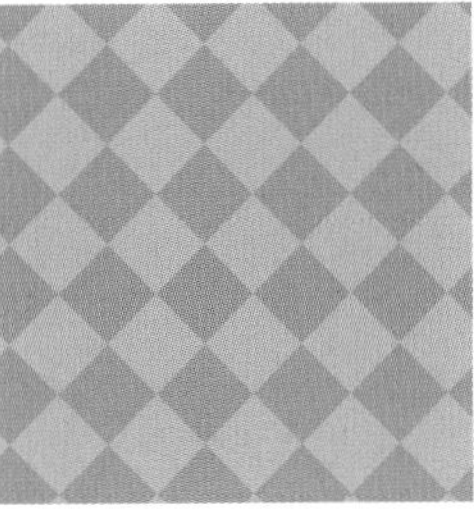
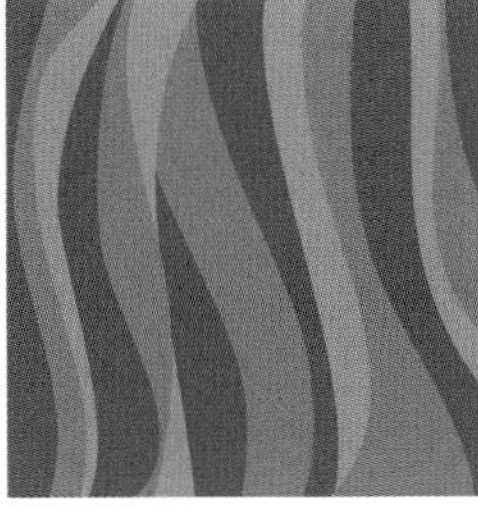
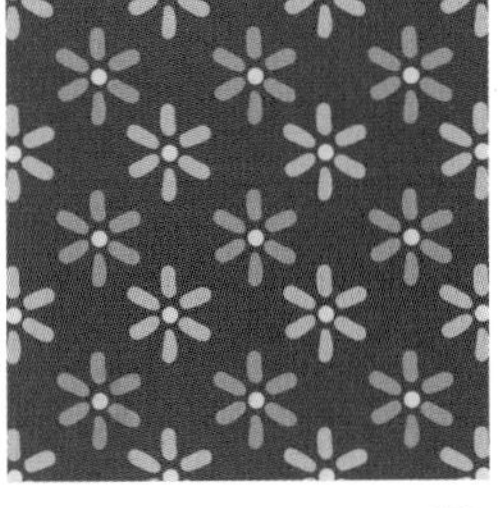
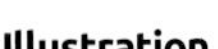

Illustration

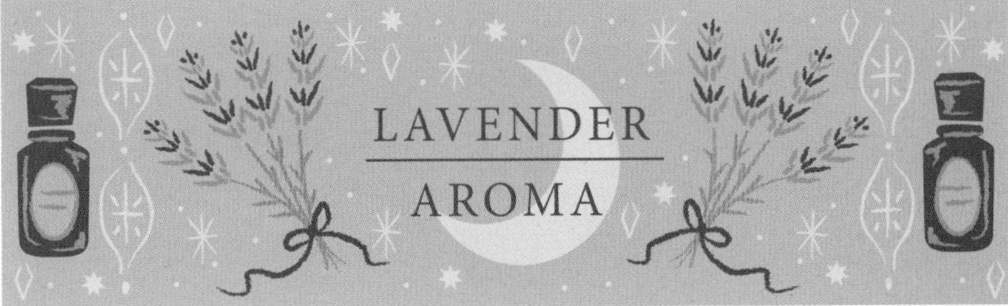

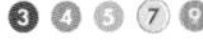
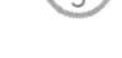

Recipe
039

Lilacs

Lilac is also known as lila. In Europe, it's often planted as a ornamental, blossoming into bursts of purple, pink and white blooms in spring. The flowers have four petals, but in rare cases they have five. This is a color palette that has been developed from hues that are similar.

- **FEELING** Elegant, soft, gentle.
- **COMBINATIONS** Combine colors with a focus on different shades of purple.
- **TIPS** Pull the look together by using similar hues and tones.

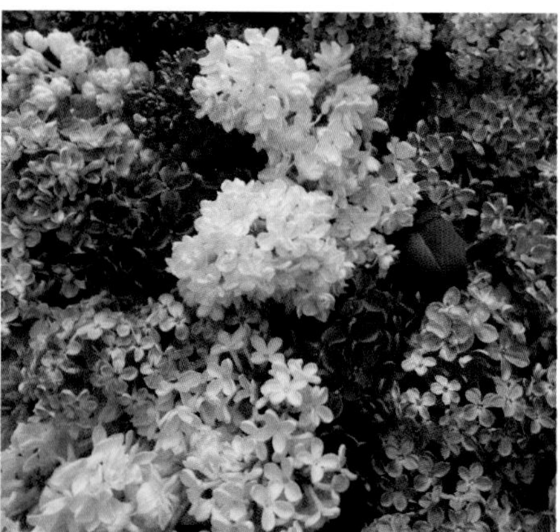

Lilac flowers are also used as an ingredient in perfume.

① **Whitish Pink**
A pink close to white. Makes for a stylish look when substituted in for white.

❷ **Deep Lilac**
A purple that is serene, elegant and refined.

❸ **Lilac Red**
A deep purple-tinged red like that of lilac flowers.

❹ **Lilac Purple**
A purple like that of lilac flowers.

❺ **Lilac Pink**
A purplish pink like that of lilac flowers.

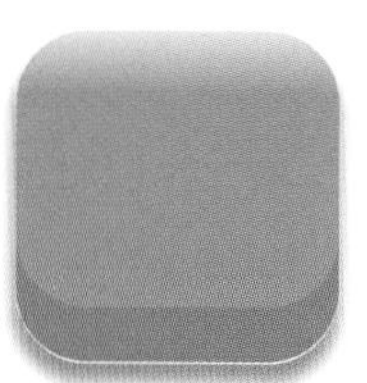

❻ **Cool Lilac**
A slightly blueish variation of indigo.

❼ **Perfume Pink**
A gentle pink like that of a faint perfume.

❽ **Fragrance Shadow**
A color that evokes the shadow of a lilac tree in full blossom.

❾ **Elegant lady**
This color evokes a mature woman with her own style.

1 C2 M13 Y4 K0 R249 G232 B235 #F8E7EB

2 C20 M60 Y10 K20 R178 G109 B145 #B16C90

3 C20 M85 Y0 K25 R167 G50 B121 #A63179

4 C30 M50 Y15 K0 R187 G142 B172 #BB8DAB

5 C20 M45 Y20 K3 R204 G154 B168 #CC9AA8

6 C35 M37 Y10 K0 R177 G163 B193 #B1A2C1

7 C10 M25 Y15 K0 R231 G202 B202 #E6C9CA

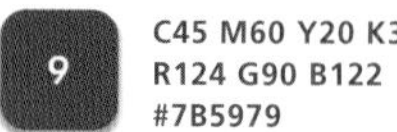

8 C30 M40 Y10 K60 R101 G84 B103 #645366

9 C45 M60 Y20 K30 R124 G90 B122 #7B5979

Two-color combinations

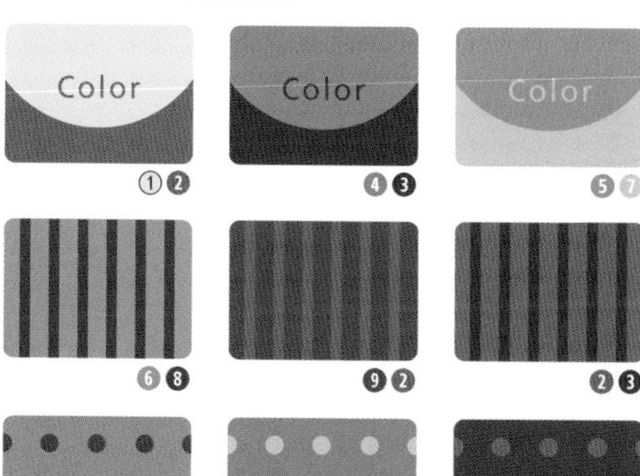

Three-color combinations

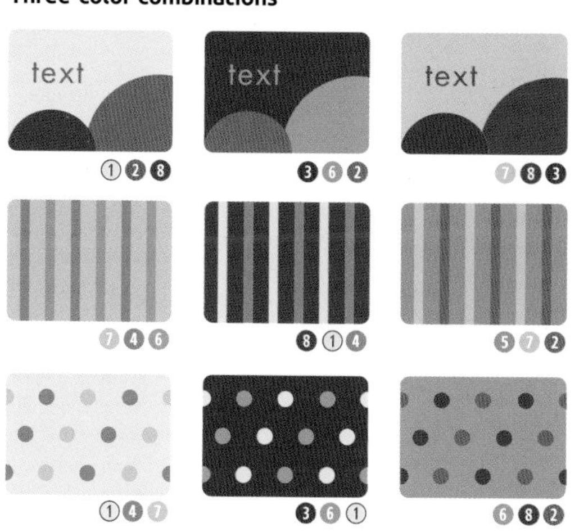

Designs

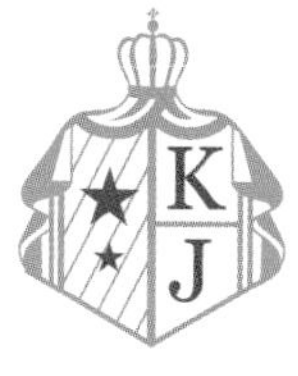

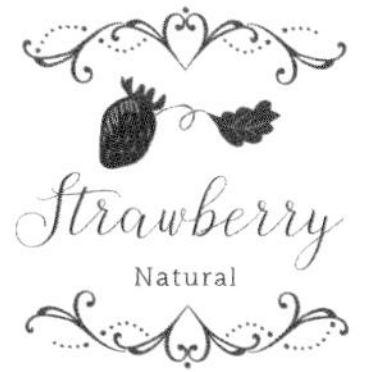

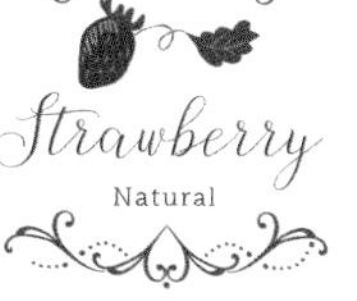

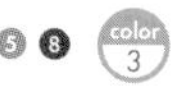

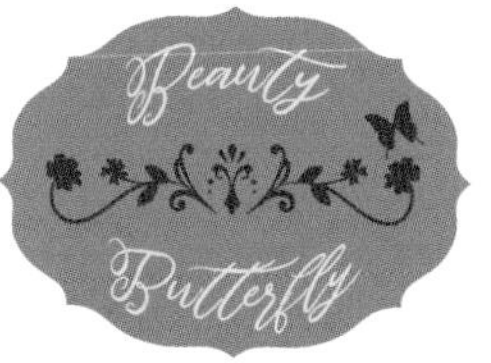

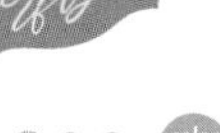

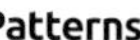

Patterns

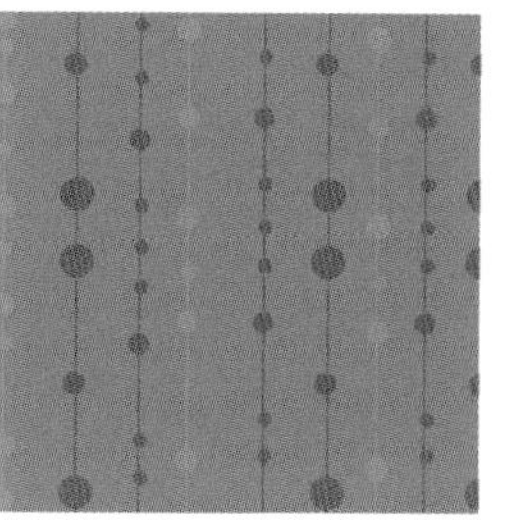

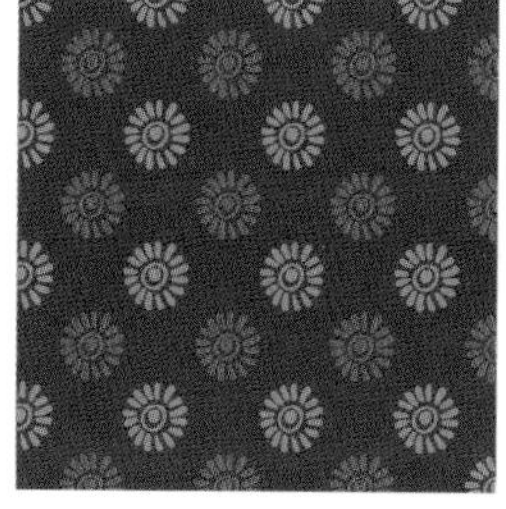

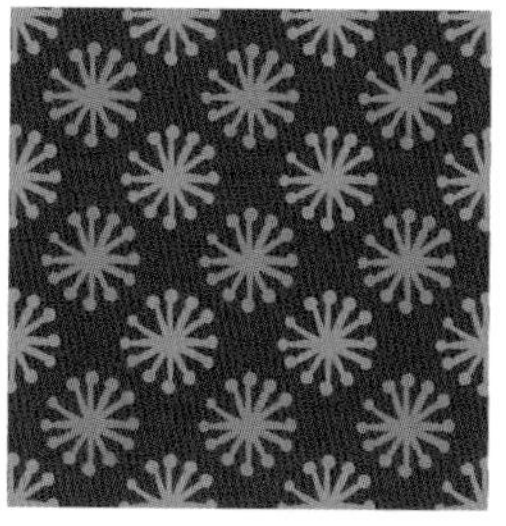

Illustration

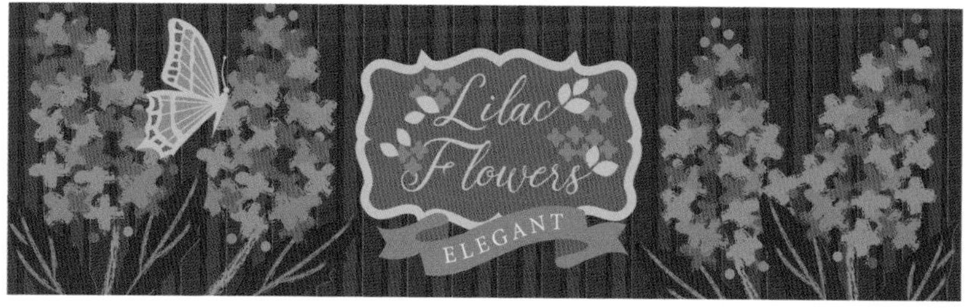

Recipe
040

Embroidered Cushions

My older sister has a beautiful cushion on her sofa that she made with her own clever hands. It's amazing what she can create. The use of elegant, gentle color is one of my sister's many talents. Someday I want to be the type of woman whom purples and blues suit.

- **FEELING** Elegant, refined, delicate.
- **COMBINATIONS** Focus on light grayish tones.
- **TIPS** Choose attractive shades as the accent colors.

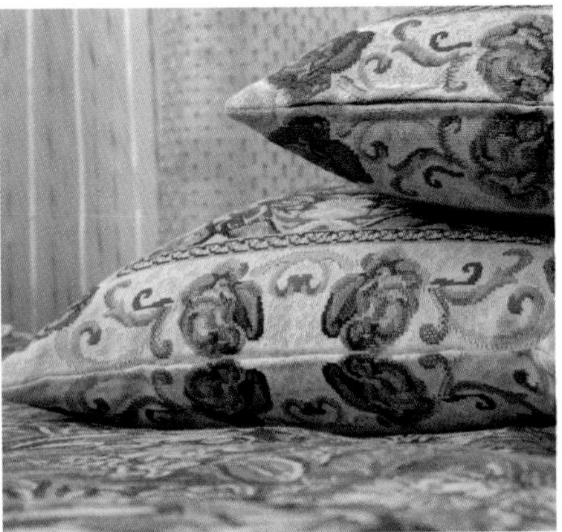

A color scheme that conjures the image of an elegance, delicacy and grace.

❶ Graceful Purple
A deep purple that evokes graceful refinement.

❷ Pink Beige
A red-tinged beige with a rich, refined feel.

❸ Bright Turquoise
A turquoise blue with an elegant sense of translucency.

❹ Feathery Violet
A violet shade that expresses delicacy and softness.

❺ Foggy Lavender
A grayish lavender color that appears to be enveloped in mist.

❻ Lady Blue
A hue between blue and violet with a deep sense of mystery.

❼ Mint Blue
Green-tinged blue with a fresh, clean feel like that of mint.

❽ Oyster White
White with a touch of gray like the flesh of an oyster.

❾ Luxury Gold
A yellow gold that brings luxury to the color scheme.

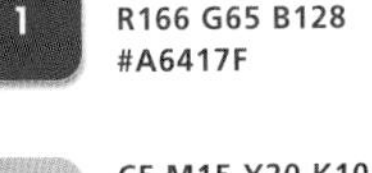

1 C40 M85 Y20 K0 R166 G65 B128 #A6417F

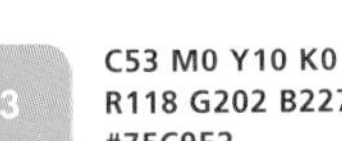

2 C5 M15 Y20 K10 R228 G209 B192 #E3D1C0

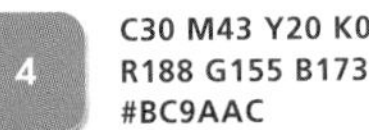

3 C53 M0 Y10 K0 R118 G202 B227 #75C9E2

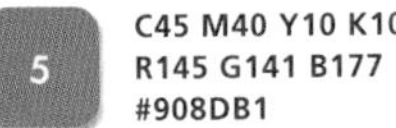

4 C30 M43 Y20 K0 R188 G155 B173 #BC9AAC

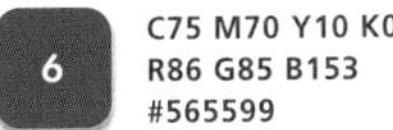

5 C45 M40 Y10 K10 R145 G141 B177 #908DB1

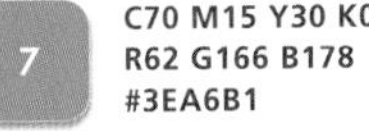

6 C75 M70 Y10 K0 R86 G85 B153 #565599

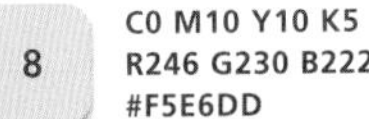

7 C70 M15 Y30 K0 R62 G166 B178 #3EA6B1

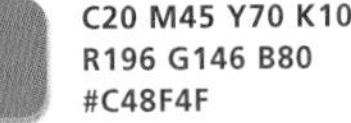

8 C0 M10 Y10 K5 R246 G230 B222 #F5E6DD

9 C20 M45 Y70 K10 R196 G146 B80 #C48F4F

Two-color combinations

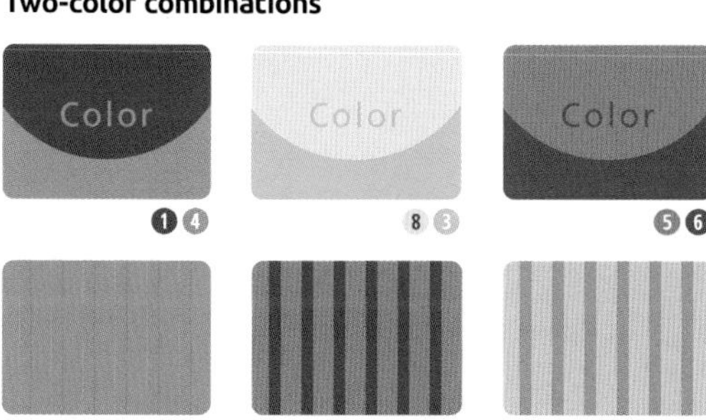

Three-color combinations

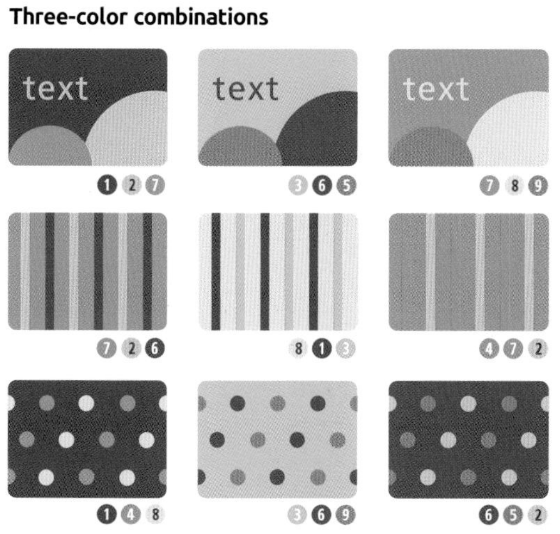

Designs

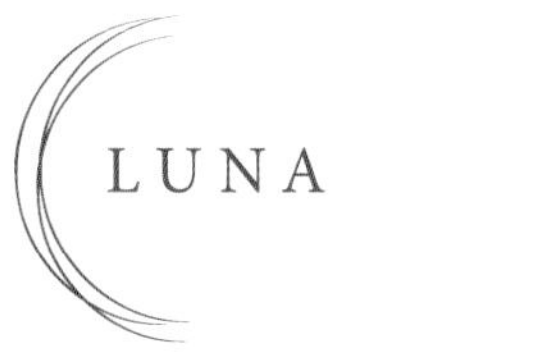

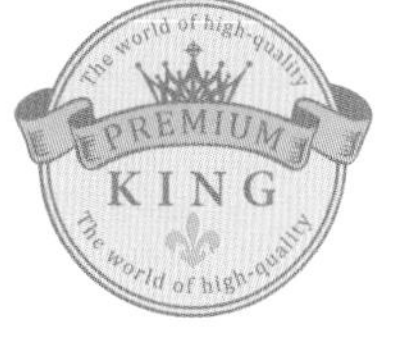

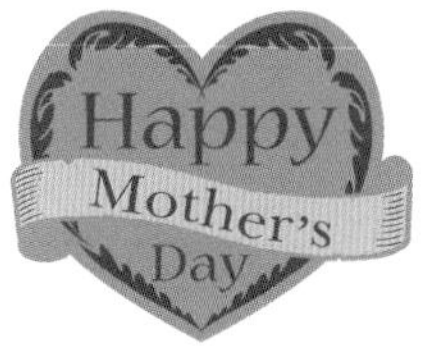

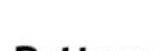

Patterns

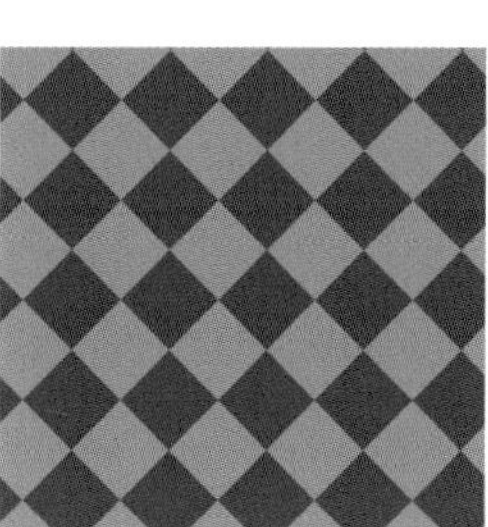

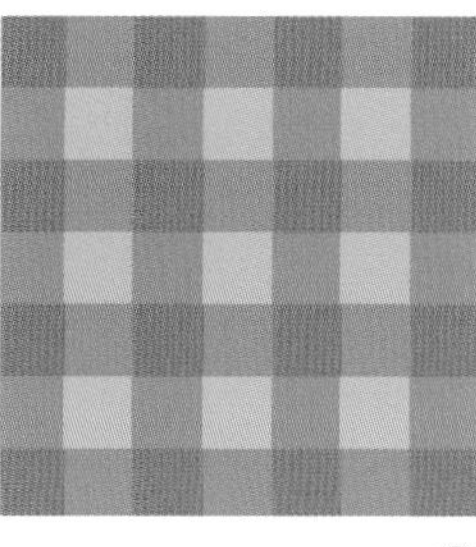

Illustration

PART 05

ELEGANT

Recipe
041

A Maiden's Prayer

On the Tokaido bullet train platforms at Tokyo and Shin Yokohama Stations, the safety barriers open and close to the tune of Polish composer Badarzewska's "A Maiden's Prayer." With its delicacy and grace, it's a classical piano standard. This color palette, too, is a mix of delicacy and gracefulness.

- **FEELING** Delicate, pretty, graceful.
- **COMBINATIONS** Use grayish colors over all.
- **TIPS** Using blue as the main color will create a mature look.

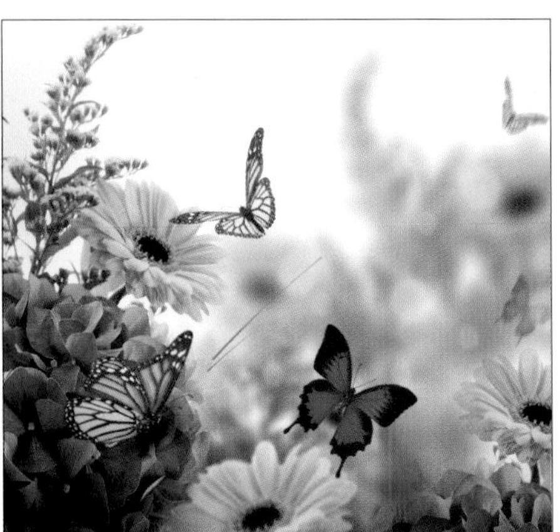

The combination of grayish pinks and blues strikes a soft and appealing contrast.

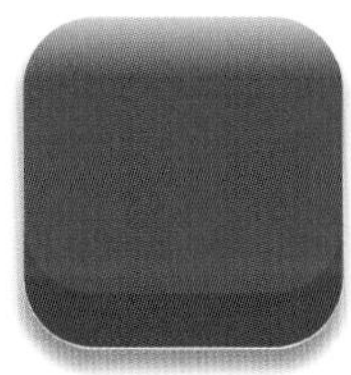

❶ **Hydrangea**
The blue of a hydrangea flower.

❷ **Of Uncertain Mind**
A delicate pink that expresses indecision and wavering.

❸ **Misty Green**
A green with a cast that is grayish, as if veiled in mist.

❹ **Silky Blue**
A pale blue with a silk-like gloss.

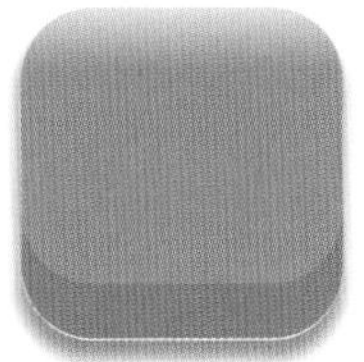

❺ **Misty Blue**
A grayish blue that creates a gentle, delicate impression.

❻ **Silky Pink**
A pale pink that is glossy and feminine.

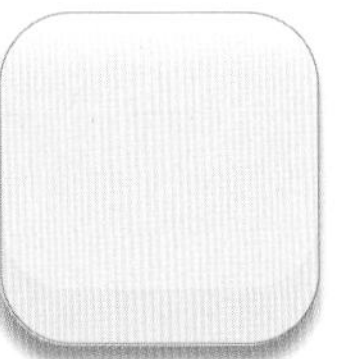

⑦ **Powder**
A white that creates a delicate, fine impression like that of powder.

❽ **Misty Purple**
A feminine, graceful purple of low intensity.

❾ **Makeup Pencil**
A grayish black like that of a cosmetic pencil.

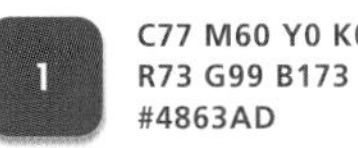

C77 M60 Y0 K0
R73 G99 B173
#4863AD

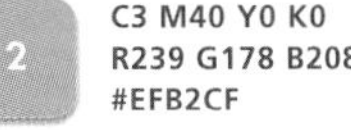

C3 M40 Y0 K0
R239 G178 B208
#EFB2CF

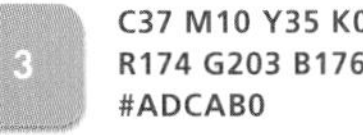

C37 M10 Y35 K0
R174 G203 B176
#ADCAB0

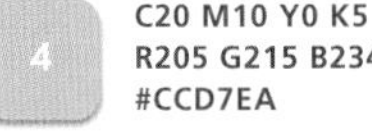

C20 M10 Y0 K5
R205 G215 B234
#CCD7EA

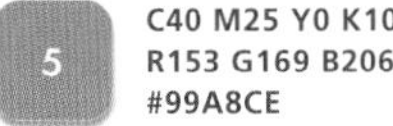

C40 M25 Y0 K10
R153 G169 B206
#99A8CE

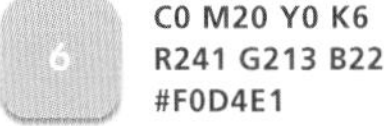

C0 M20 Y0 K6
R241 G213 B225
#F0D4E1

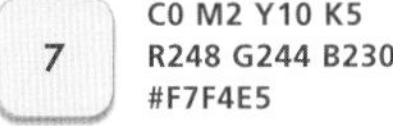

C0 M2 Y10 K5
R248 G244 B230
#F7F4E5

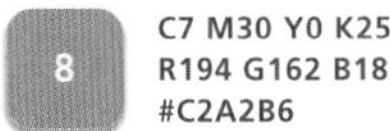

C7 M30 Y0 K25
R194 G162 B183
#C2A2B6

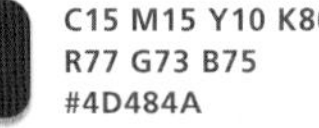

C15 M15 Y10 K80
R77 G73 B75
#4D484A

Two-color combinations

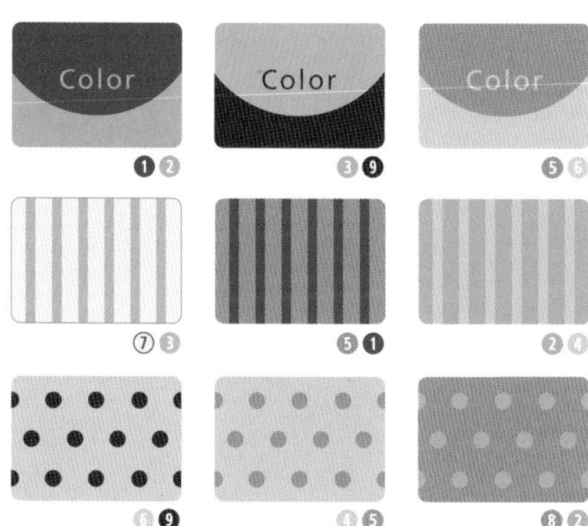

Three-color combinations

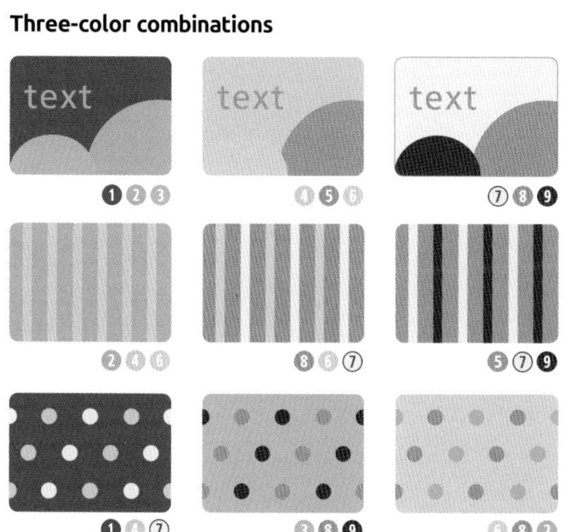

Designs

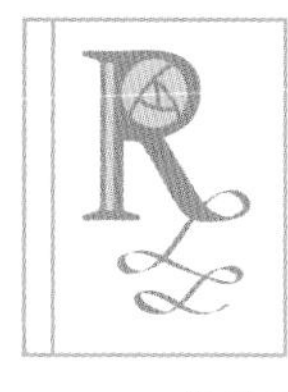

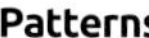

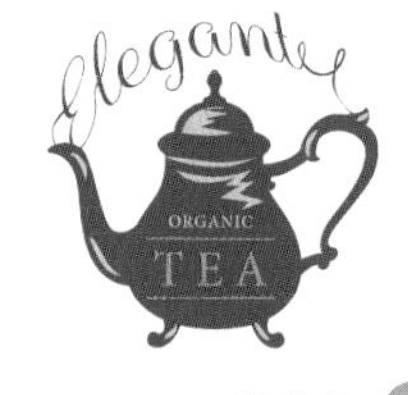

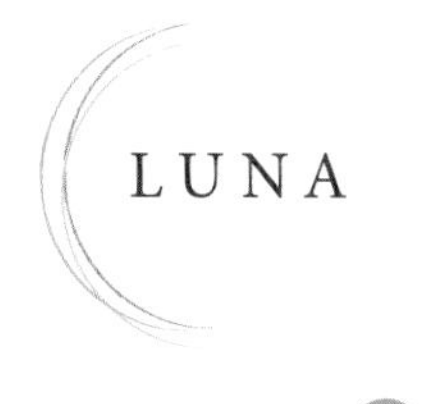

Patterns

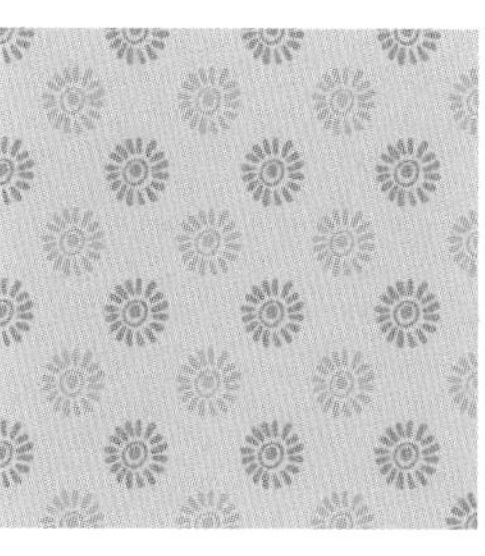

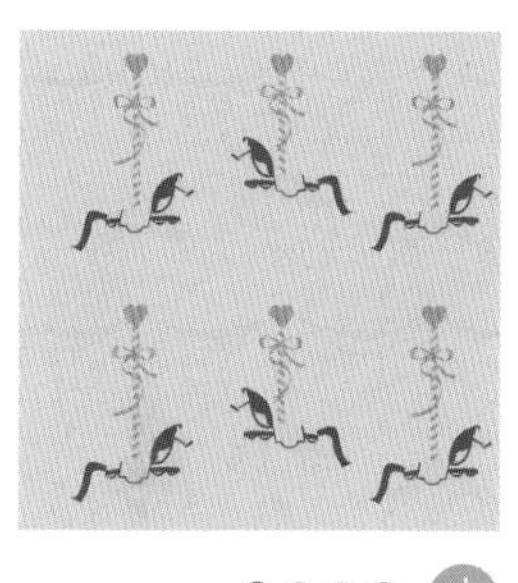

Illustration

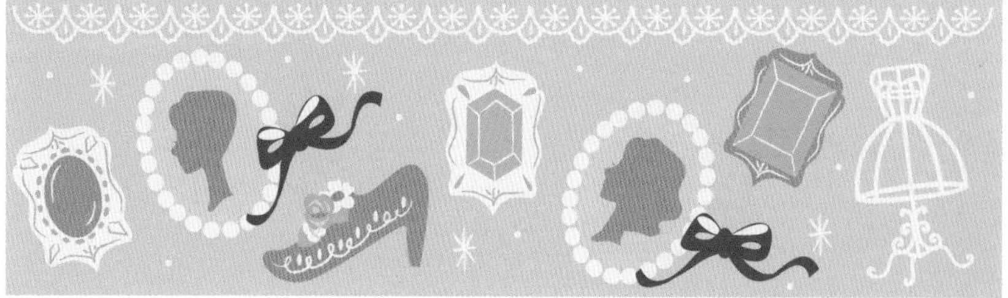

PART 05

ELEGANT

Recipe
042

The Magic of Makeup

Whenever I have a strong desire to transform the person I am now, I use new colors of eyeshadow and lipstick that I haven't tried before. I use the power of color to create a slightly different version of myself. It's good to have a range of options on hand. Who knows when the next time will be that I try to harness some magic power with new colors.

- **FEELING** Cool, mature, stylish.
- **COMBINATIONS** Focus on colors with a blue base.
- **TIPS** Somber colors with depth lend a sense of maturity.

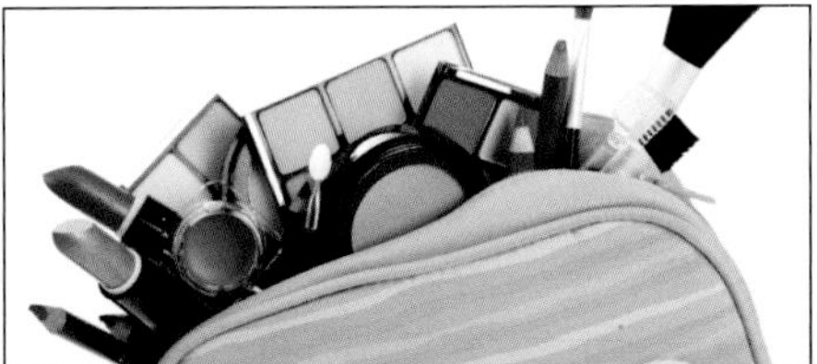

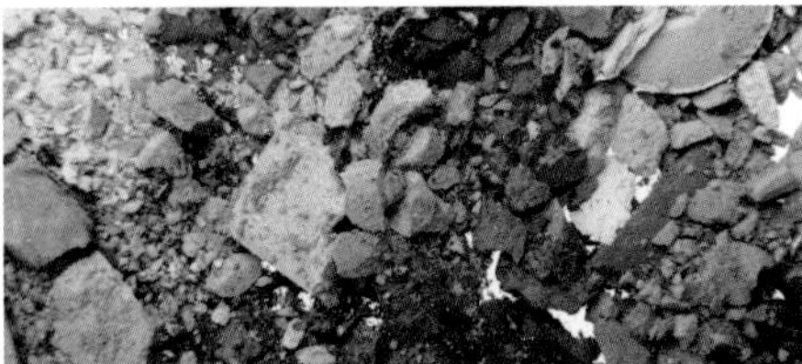

It's important to choose makeup colors that complement your skin tone.

❶ For Myself
A color that evokes the feeling of pampering oneself.

❷ Gloomy
A color that evokes gloomy emotions.

❸ Change
A color that evokes the strong desire to effect change.

❹ Next Stage
A color that evokes the desire to pursue the next new stage in life.

❺ Hot Pink
A vibrant, dazzling pink.

❻ New Feeling
New experiences and new feelings accom-panied by hesitation.

❼ Peacock Feather
The vivid blue green of a peacock feather.

❽ Rainy Day
A color that captures the melancholy air of a rainy morning.

❾ Space Gray
The vast, mysterious gray of the infinite universe.

1 C10 M50 Y15 K0 R225 G152 B173 #E097AD

2 C10 M50 Y15 K30 R178 G120 B138 #B17789

3 C25 M95 Y20 K0 R192 G32 B117 #BF1F75

4 C20 M43 Y0 K0 R207 G161 B201 #CEA1C8

5 C5 M85 Y20 K0 R225 G68 B126 #E0437D

6 C17 M17 Y0 K0 R217 G212 B234 #D8D4E9

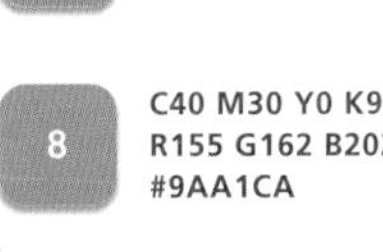

7 C75 M0 Y35 K10 R0 G167 B168 #00A7A8

8 C40 M30 Y0 K9 R155 G162 B202 #9AA1CA

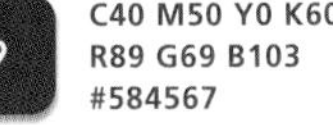

9 C40 M50 Y0 K60 R89 G69 B103 #584567

Two-color combinations

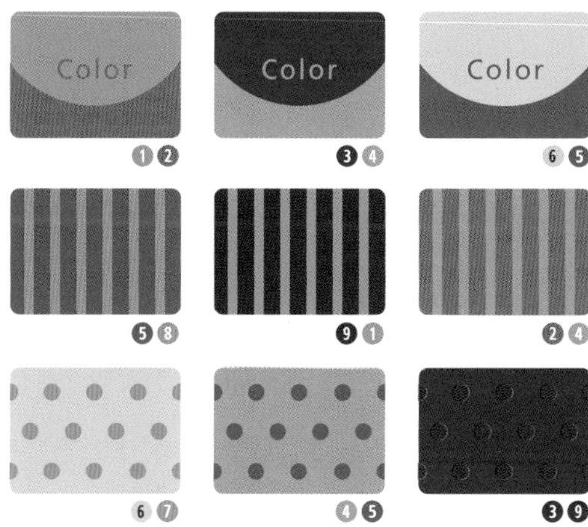

Three-color combinations

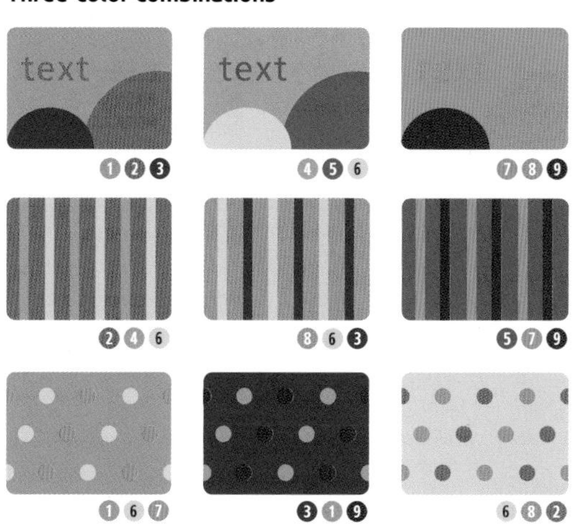

Designs

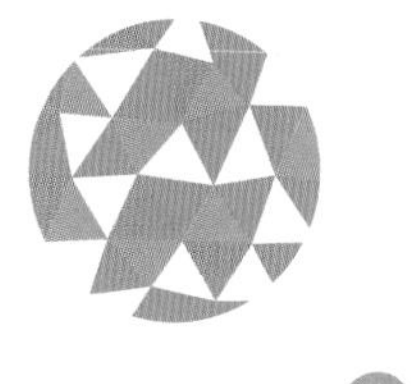

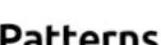

Patterns

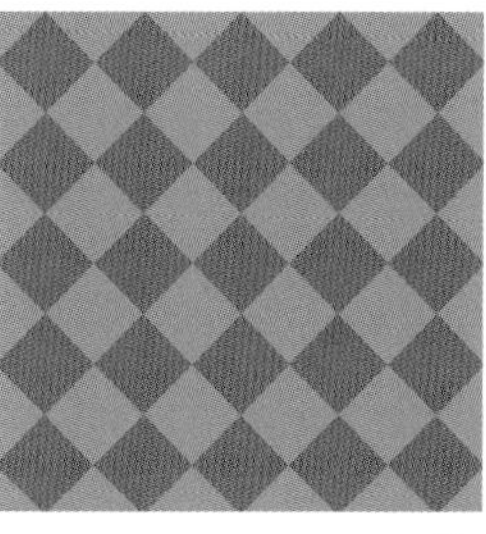

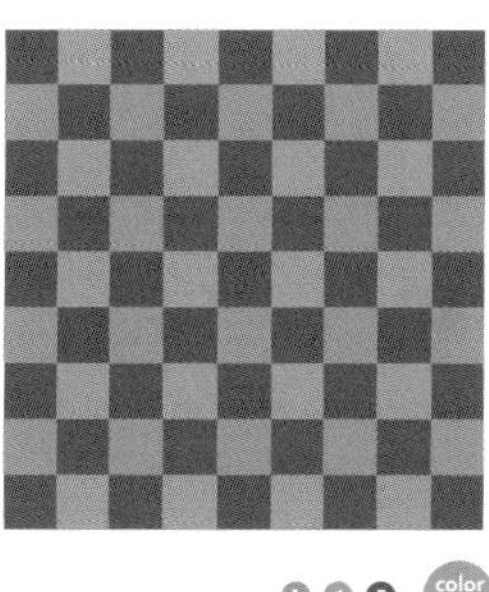

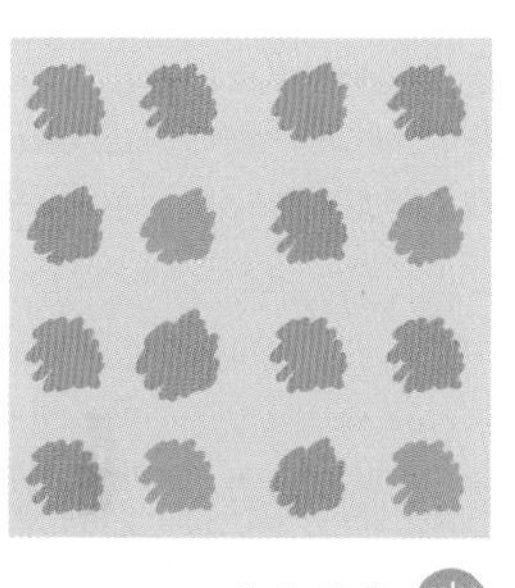

Illustration

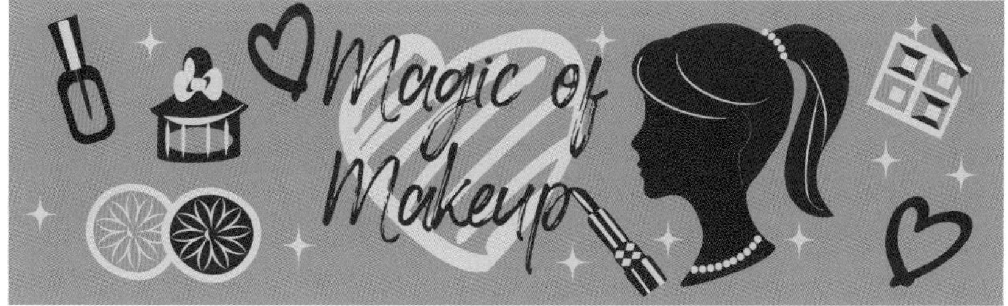

Recipe

043

Elegant Roses

In order to express elegance in a color scheme, add a little gray to each of the colors. In recent times, techniques for plant hybridization have advanced to create colors not found in the natural world. For example, violet-hued roses are called blue roses, and their associated meaning in the language of flowers is "to fulfill dreams."

- **FEELING** Serene, deep, silent.
- **COMBINATIONS** Focus on combining deep colors.
- **TIPS** Use Color 9 as an accent.

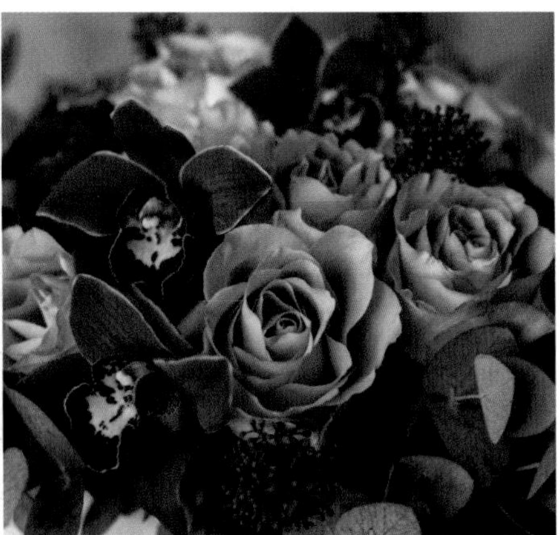

A mild, tranquil color scheme with a sense of gradation.

❶ Cattleya Red
The deep red seen on a cattleya flower.

❷ Blue Rose
The violet-hued rose that is a recent development.

❸ Grayish Green
The somber green of leaves with a whitish surface.

❹ Fulfilment
The fulfilment of a wish; a deep, quiet color.

❺ Cheers
Good wishes; a toast when drinking.

❻ Ripen
When fruits matures; or the expression "when the time is ripe."

❼ Calm Gray
A calm gray of medium brightness.

❽ Homage
Respect or regard, it's a medium-intensity purple.

❾ Grow White
A white which holds wishes for growth and development.

1	C40 M85 Y50 K40 R119 G43 B65 #772A41
2	C20 M30 Y5 K5 R203 G181 B205 #CAB4CC
3	C55 M20 Y30 K30 R97 G137 B140 #60898C
4	C55 M5 Y20 K65 R49 G95 B102 #315F66
5	C30 M90 Y30 K15 R167 G46 B101 #A62E65
6	C60 M70 Y30 K0 R125 G91 B131 #7C5B82
7	C20 M0 Y5 K40 R150 G168 B174 #95A8AD
8	C35 M75 Y25 K0 R176 G89 B132 #B05883
9	C9 M10 Y0 K0 R235 G231 B243 #EAE7F3

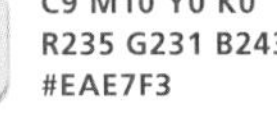

Two-color combinations

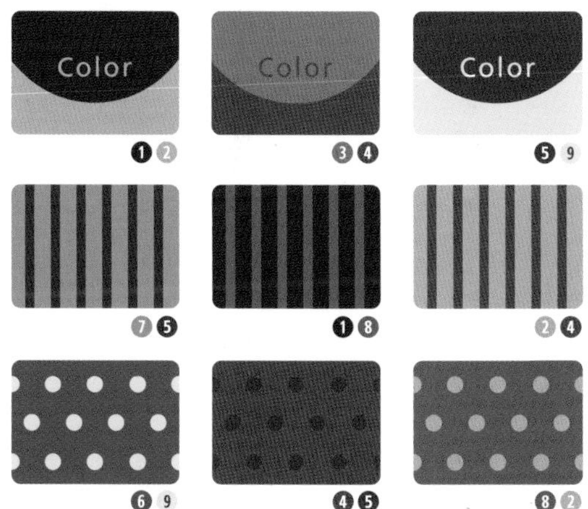

Three-color combinations

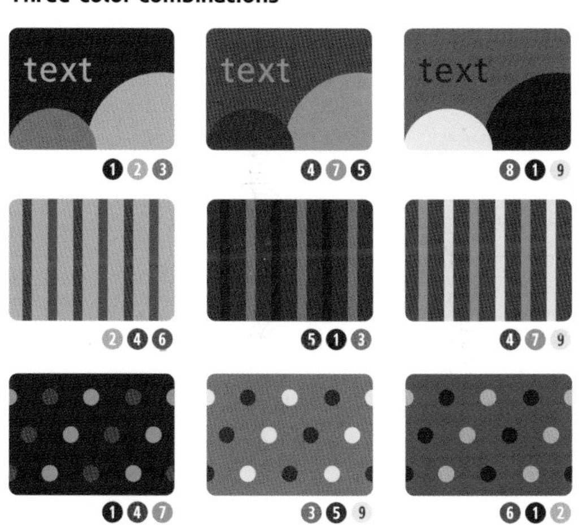

Designs

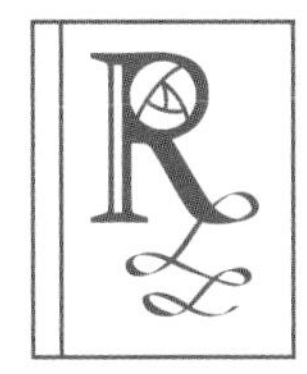
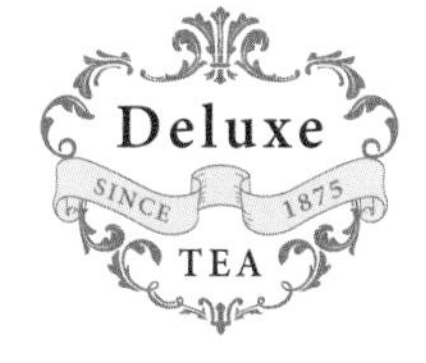

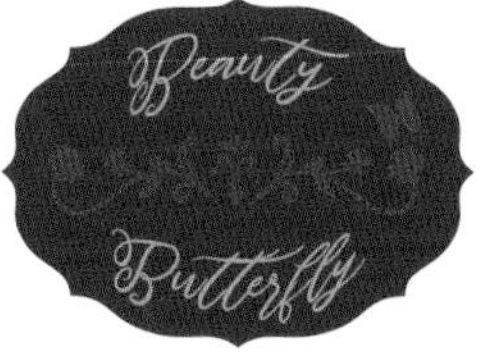

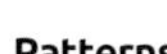
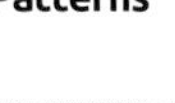

6 8 color 2 · 1 5 9 color 3 · 4 5 8 color 3

Patterns

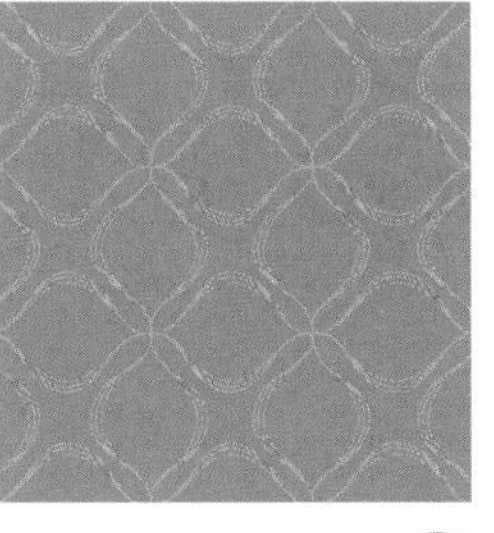
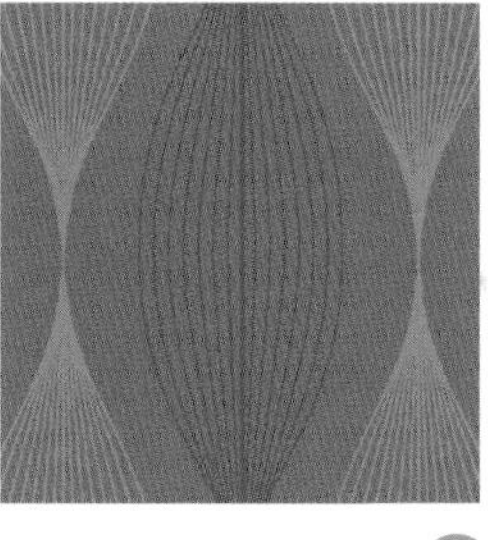
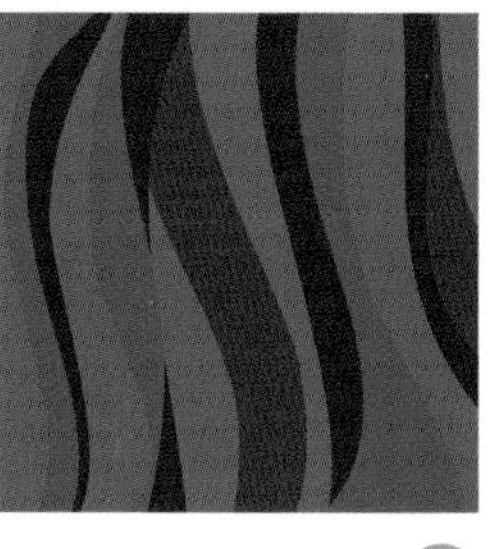
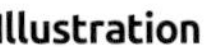

2 7 color 2 · 3 7 8 color 3 · 1 5 6 8 color 4

Illustration

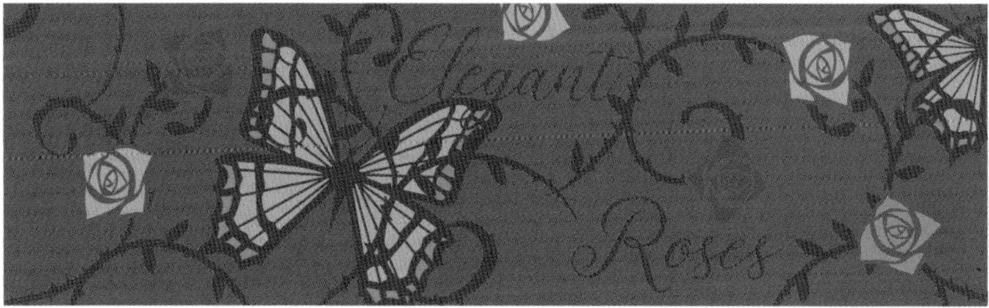

2 4 6 7 8 color 5

Recipe
044

A Dress Trimmed with Lace

When we think of wedding dresses, we think of white as the standard color. This has been the case ever since 1840, when Queen Victoria of England wore a wedding dress of pure white. White is seen as pure and unadulterated. A delicate color scheme with mere hints of color makes it possible to express the texture of lace and other fabrics.

- **FEELING** Neat, immaculate, pure.
- **COMBINATIONS** Use only light colors of hues that differ slightly from one another.
- **TIPS** Delicate when viewed up close, from a distance the details are obscured.

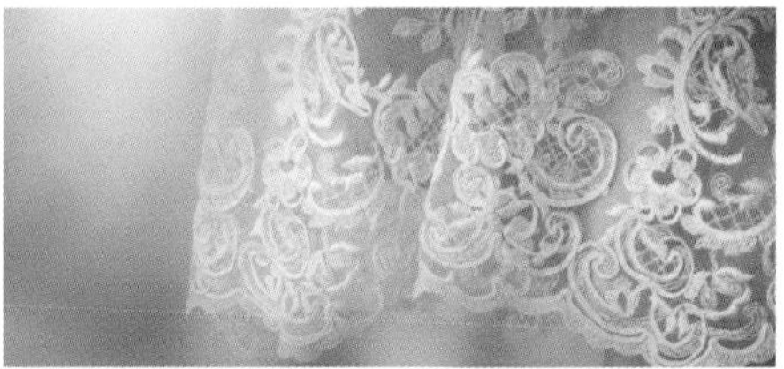

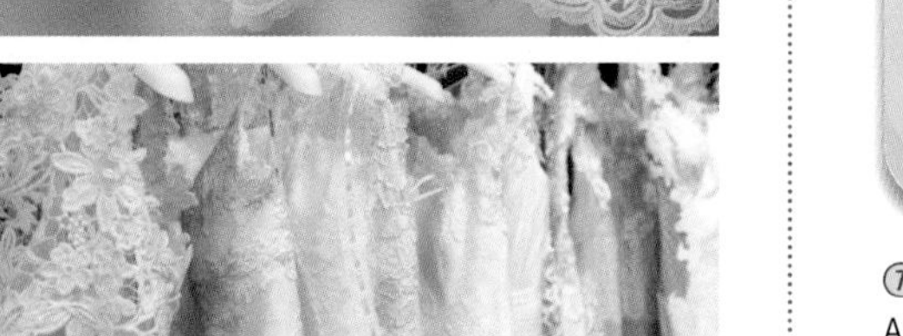

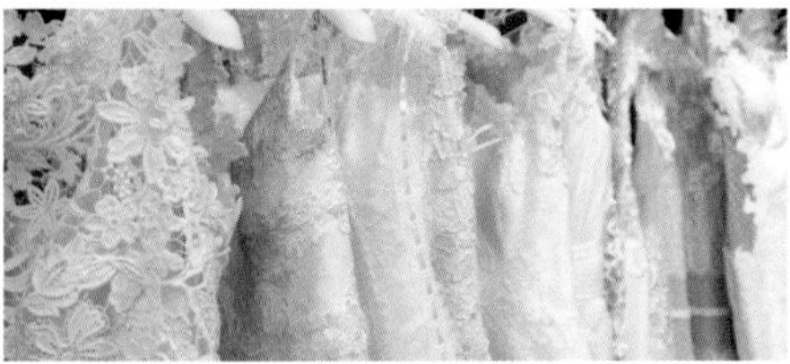

There are various nuances of whites, each with a different feel.

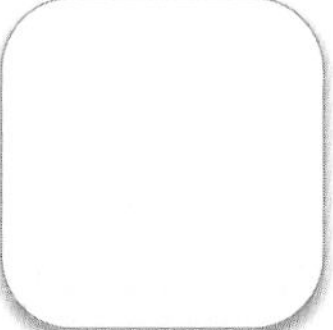

① Off White
Compared with pure white, this is a natural, calm shade.

② Soft White
A soft white with a faint tinge of color.

③ Ivory White
A warm white faintly tinged with yellow.

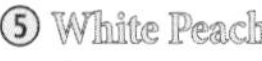

④ Champagne White
A white that is closer to beige than ivory white.

⑤ White Peach
A pale, pretty pink that is nearly white.

⑥ Pale Gray
A gray that is close to white, this color has a faint touch of blue to it.

⑦ Pale Blue
An extremely pale blue with an air of neatness and cleanness to it.

⑧ Pale Purple
An extremely pale purple that can be worn regardless of gender.

⑨ White Mocha
Mocha is a brand of coffee. This is a pale brown that is close to white.

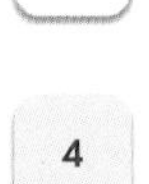

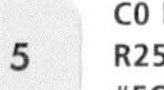

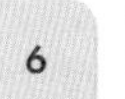

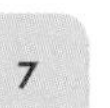

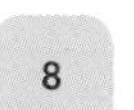

1	C3 M3 Y3 K0 R249 G248 B248 #F9F8F7
2	C0 M3 Y5 K0 R255 G250 B245 #FEFAF4
3	C0 M2 Y10 K0 R255 G251 B237 #FFFBEC
4	C0 M8 Y20 K0 R254 G239 B212 #FEEFD3
5	C0 M13 Y13 K0 R252 G232 B220 #FCE7DB
6	C10 M3 Y0 K8 R222 G230 B238 #DEE6EE
7	C23 M8 Y3 K0 R204 G222 B238 #CCDDEE
8	C5 M20 Y5 K0 R241 G216 B225 #F1D8E1
9	C0 M10 Y20 K10 R237 G221 B197 #EDDDC5

Two-color combinations

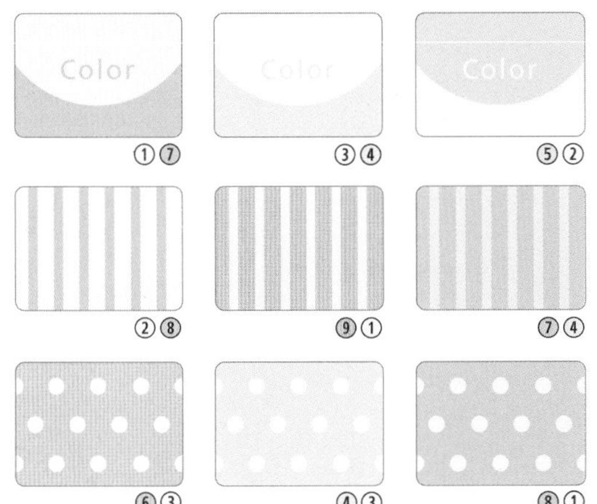

Three-color combinations

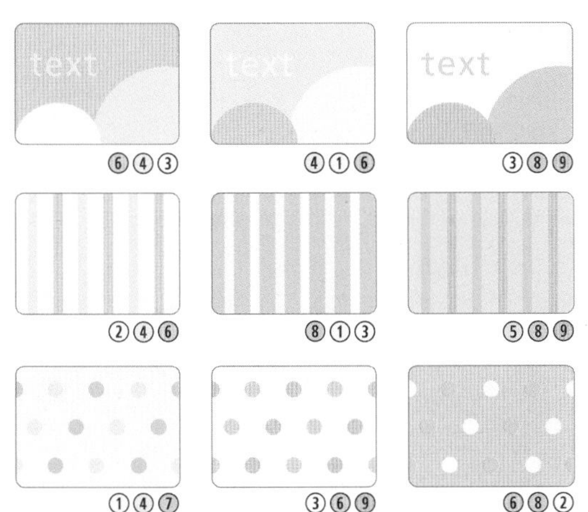

Designs

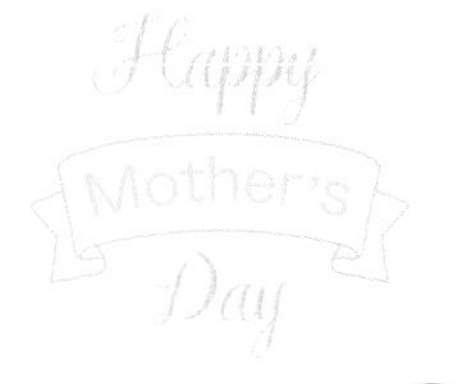

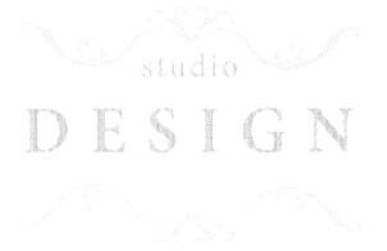

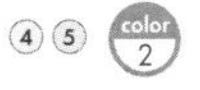

Patterns

①⑤⑥ color 3

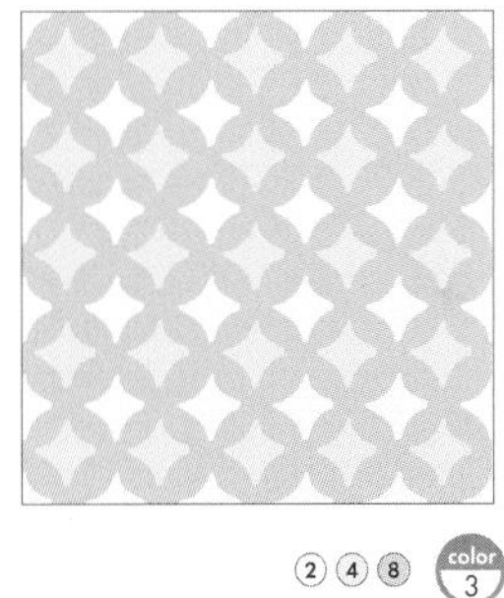

②④⑧ color 3

①③④⑧ color 4

Illustration

②④⑤⑥⑧ color 5

PART 05

ELEGANT

Recipe
045

Pretty Woman

As someone who spends a lot of time in front of a computer in an office, I visit a nail salon once a month. In blossom viewing season I have cherry-blossom-colored nails; at Christmas I go for a gorgeous look with lots of sparkling stones. But usually, I go for simple, "grown-up" colored nails.

- **FEELING** Simple, adult, serene.
- **COMBINATIONS** Team basic colors with grayish purples.
- **TIPS** Use beige and gray as the main colors.

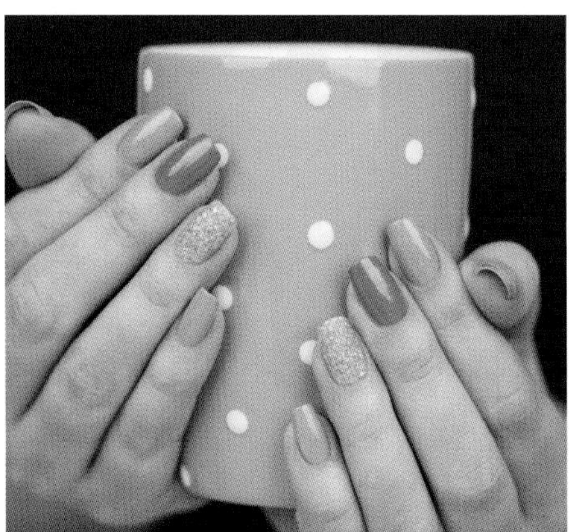

Add gold sparkles to beige and silver sparkles to gray.

❶ Girl's Beige
A sweet pink beige that pairs well with brighter colors.

❷ Magical Lavender
A violet that elegantly decorates the fingertips.

❸ Basic Gray
A standard fashion color, this is a gray that is easy to complement.

❹ Venus Purple
An elegant purple calls to mind the goddess of beauty.

❺ Calm Purple
A calm, serene grayish purple.

❻ Frost Purple
A purple that is low in saturation.

❼ Natural Gray
A color that helps one to remain relaxed.

❽ Drop of Purple
A color like that of white into which a drop of purple has been added.

❾ Royal Milk Tea
The color of black tea with plenty of milk.

1	C10 M20 Y17 K10 R217 G198 B192 #D9C5BF
2	C25 M30 Y5 K0 R199 G182 B210 #C6B6D2
3	C25 M8 Y5 K50 R124 G138 B148 #7C8993
4	C60 M90 Y45 K0 R128 G56 B99 #7F3762
5	C10 M25 Y10 K35 R173 G152 B159 #AC989F
6	C15 M30 Y10 K0 R220 G189 B204 #DBBDCC
7	C15 M10 Y10 K30 R176 G178 B179 #AFB1B3
8	C5 M10 Y0 K15 R219 G212 B220 #DBD3DC
9	C15 M25 Y30 K20 R192 G170 B153 #BFAA98

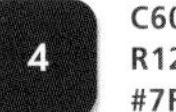
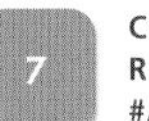

Two-color combinations

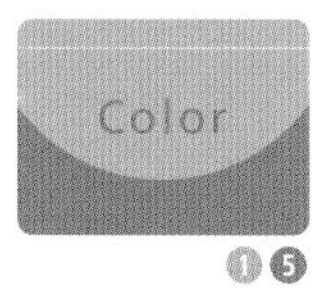

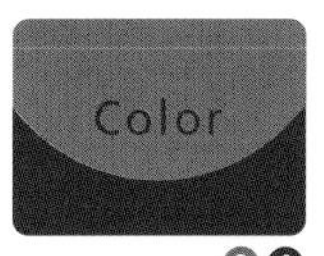

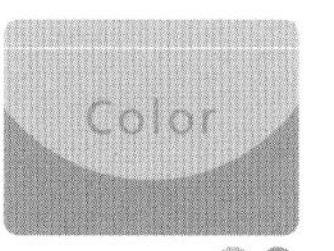

1 5 3 4 8 7

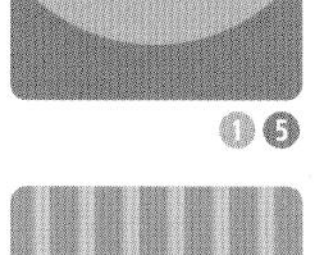

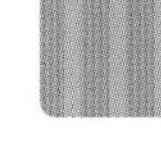
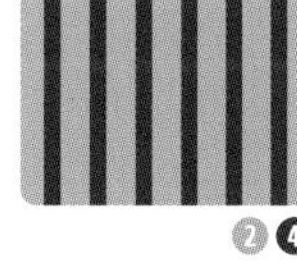

7 8 9 2 2 4

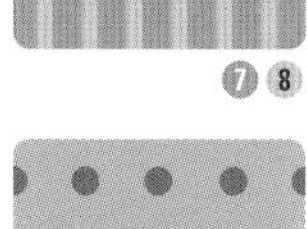
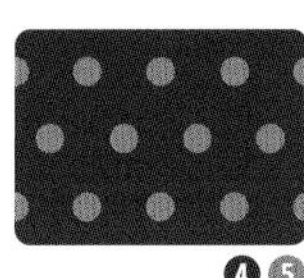
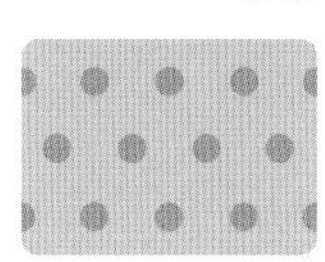

6 3 4 5 8 9

Three-color combinations

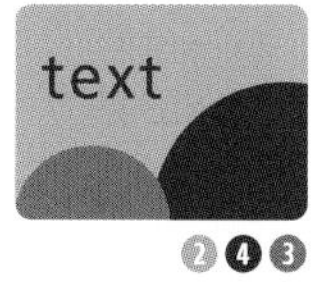

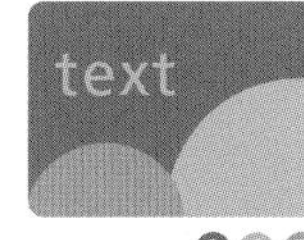

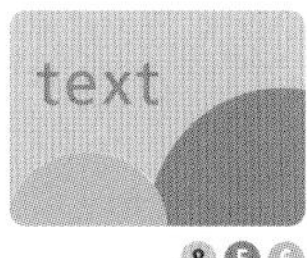

2 4 3 3 6 7 8 5 6

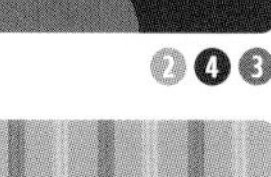

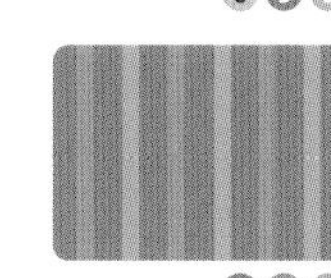

2 5 8 1 5 9 5 7 2

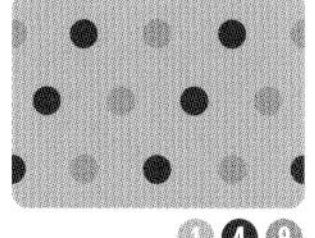
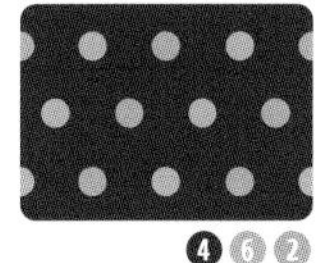
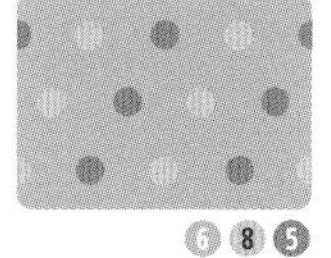

1 4 9 4 6 2 6 8 5

Designs

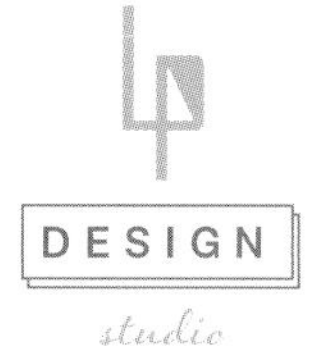

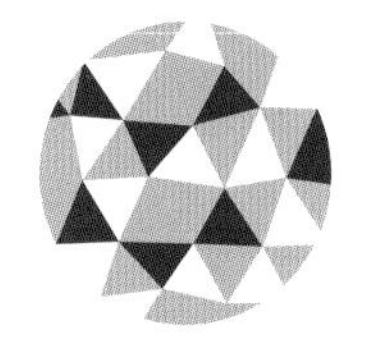

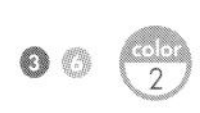
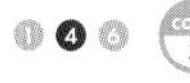

3 5 color 2 3 6 color 2 1 4 6 color 3

Patterns

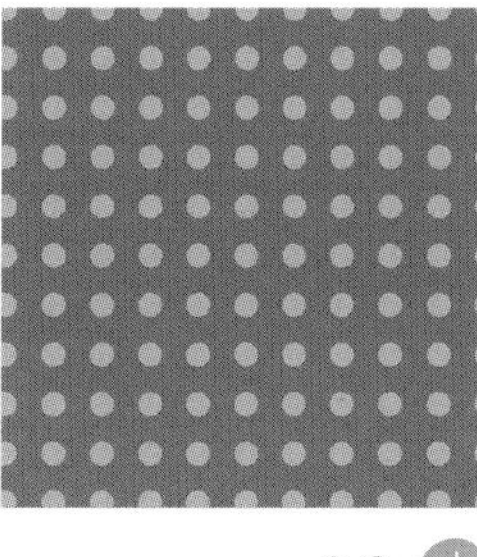
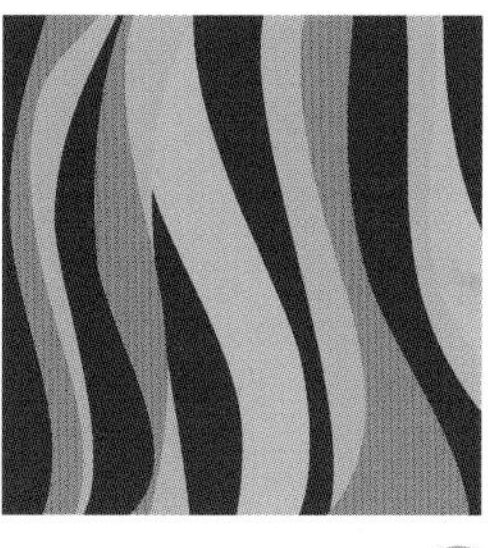
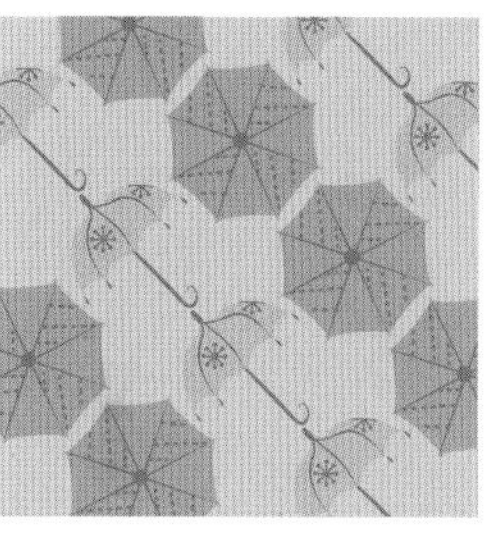
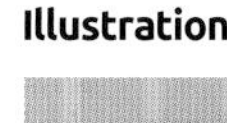

2 3 color 2 2 4 5 6 color 4 1 3 7 8 color 4

Illustration

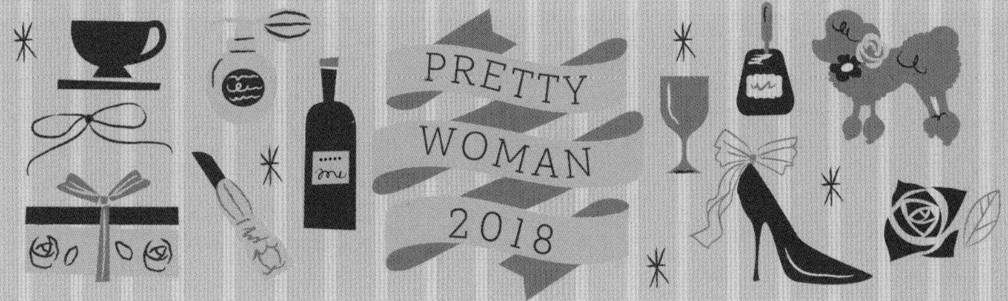

1 2 3 4 8 color 5

Recipe
046

Marbled Paper

The technique of floating paint on an aqueous solution of gum resin and capturing the created patterns by blotting them with paper is called marbling. Here, colors that appear in marbled patterns are picked out to form a color palette. There's a multitude of colors, but the similarity of tones allows for a relaxed, cohesive color scheme to be established.

- **FEELING** Calm, laidback, unobtrusive.
- **COMBINATIONS Use similar tones but different hues to create nuances.**
- **TIPS Keep the color scheme unfocused yet intricate.**

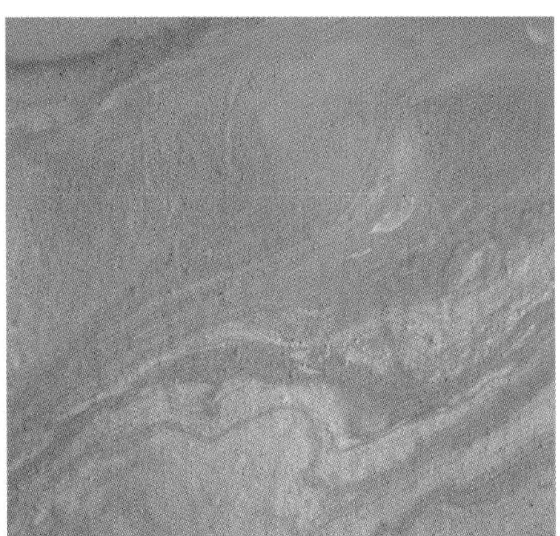

The naturally forming patterns are complex and unique.

❶ Grayish Purple
In Japanese, grayish indicates an ashy tinge.

❷ Grayish Rose
A grayish rose; a gentle, serene pink.

❸ Grayish Leaf
A yellow green tinged with gray that blends well in interiors.

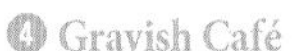
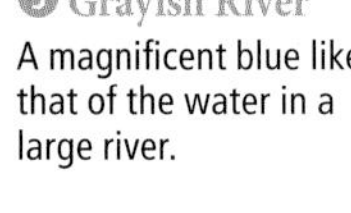

❹ Grayish Café
A warm gray beige with a hint of yellow.

❺ Grayish River
A magnificent blue like that of the water in a large river.

❻ Grayish Marron
A light brown with a touch of redness.

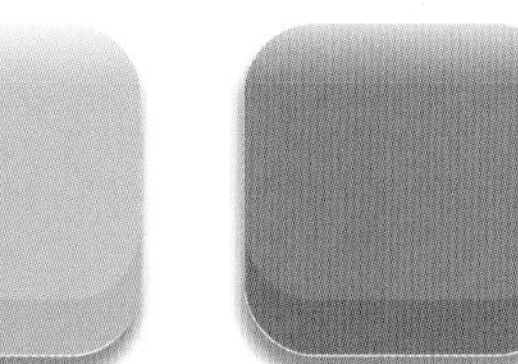

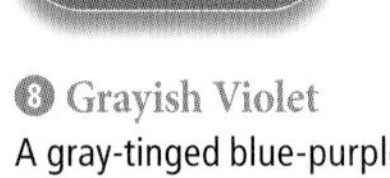
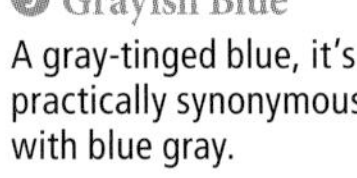

❼ Water Gray
A light gray with a gentle translucency to it.

❽ Grayish Violet
A gray-tinged blue-purple.

❾ Grayish Blue
A gray-tinged blue, it's practically synonymous with blue gray.

1 C20 M30 Y5 K10
R196 G175 B198
#C3AEC5

2 C5 M30 Y10 K10
R224 G184 B193
#DFB8C1

3 C35 M15 Y50 K2
R178 G193 B142
#B2C18E

4 C5 M10 Y35 K17
R217 G204 B160
#D8CCA0

5 C45 M10 Y20 K10
R140 G185 B191
#8CB8BE

6 C15 M25 Y20 K25
R183 G164 B161
#B6A4A0

7 C25 M15 Y5 K0
R199 G208 B227
#C7D0E3

8 C30 M35 Y0 K15
R169 G153 B190
#A999BD

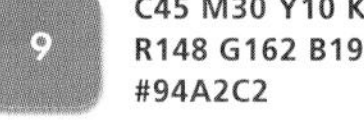

9 C45 M30 Y10 K5
R148 G162 B194
#94A2C2

Two-color combinations

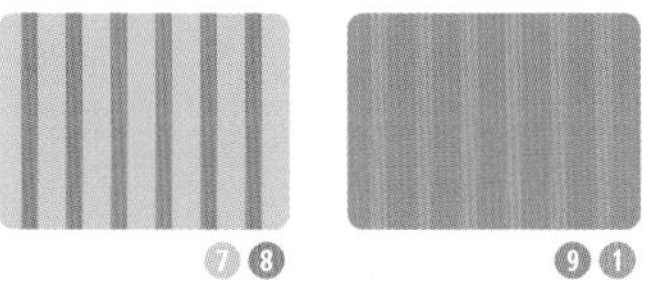

1 2 · 3 7 · 5 4

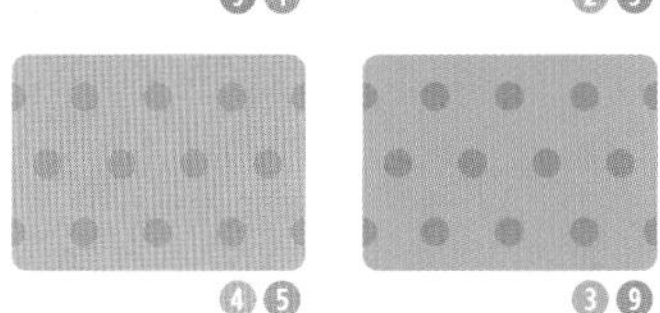

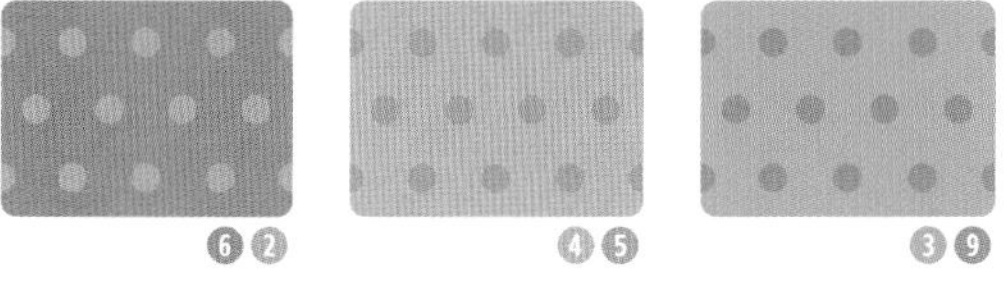

7 8 · 9 1 · 2 9

6 2 · 4 5 · 3 9

Three-color combinations

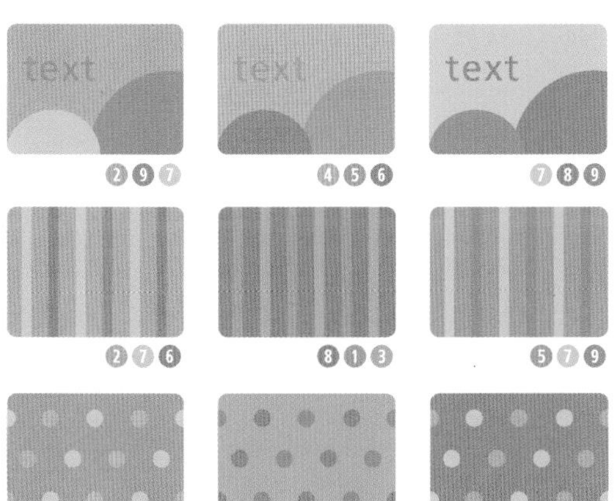

2 9 7 · 4 5 6 · 7 8 9

2 7 6 · 8 1 3 · 5 7 9

1 4 7 · 3 6 9 · 6 7 2

Designs

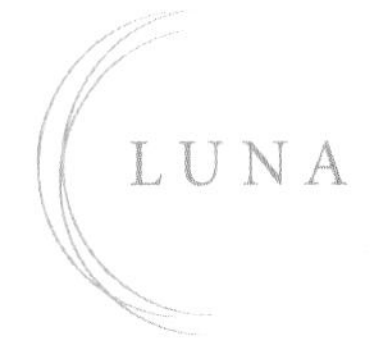

4 5 color 2

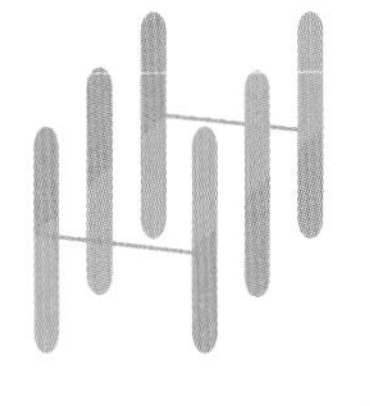

3 8 color 2

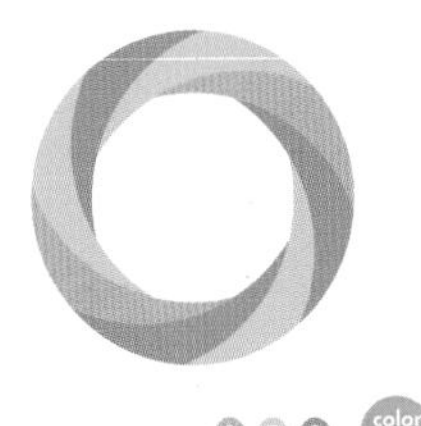

2 7 9 color 3

Patterns

3 8 color 2

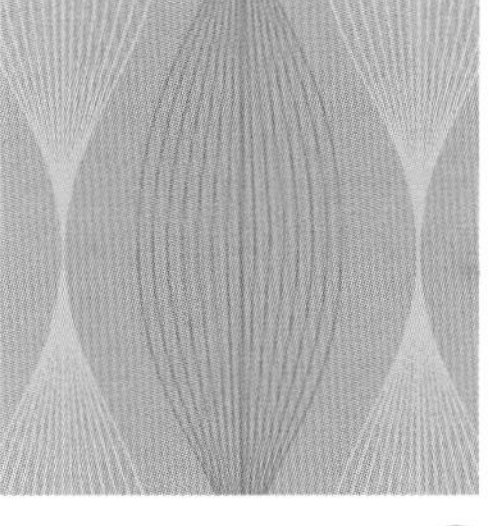

2 6 7 color 3

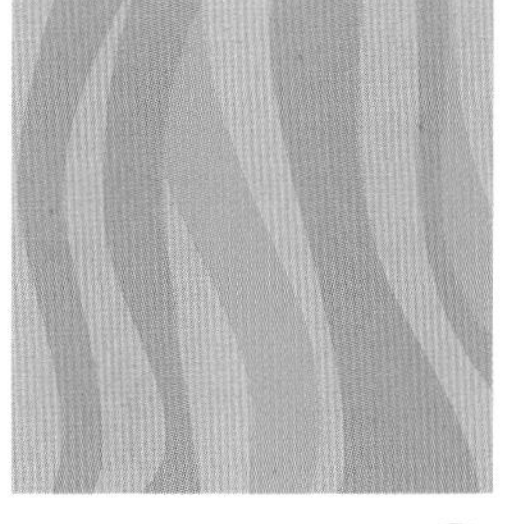

1 3 4 5 color 4

Illustration

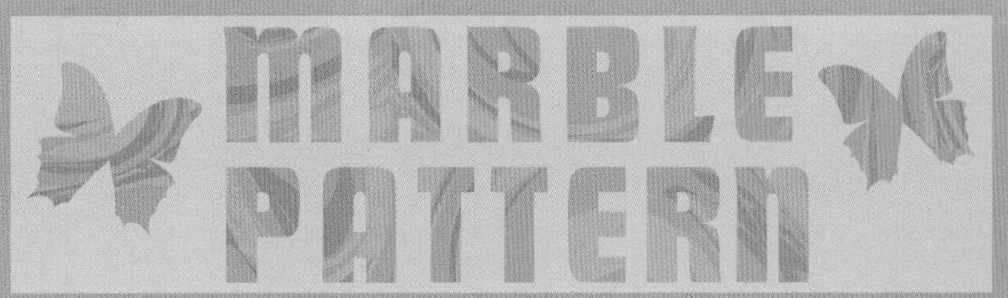

1 2 5 6 7 color 5

Color Scheme Techniques You Can Use Right Now

Extremely Popular Gradation: Color Scheme Terms Used in the World of Fashion

The gradation shown here is a color scheme technique in which the hues, brightness and levels of saturation change in a regular, gradated fashion from one color to the neighboring one in order to express flow and rhythm. Its easy-on-the-eye appearance makes it an extremely popular standard technique.

The color scheme terms covered on the next page have been used for years, mainly in the fashion industry, but they're all terms that can be widely applied to design work and hobbies as well.

If you're struggling with a concept for a color scheme, or feel that you're stuck in a rut, give these color schemes a try.

Gradation Where Colors Lighten and Darken Little by Little

This gradation is created by using one color and changing only the level of brightness in phases. Due to the effect of lighter sections appearing to be closer to the viewer and darker sections seeming to be farther away, this can be used when a sense of dimension is desired in a color scheme or design.

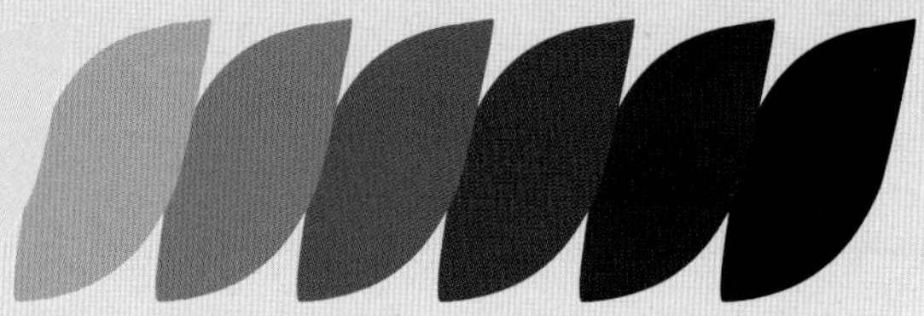

Boost the Mood with Rainbow Gradation

This standard gradation is created when hues change color in phases. The colors of the rainbow are symbols of good fortune and harmony. In Japan, there are seven colors in the rainbow (red, orange, yellow, green, blue, indigo and purple) but in the U.S., indigo is omitted to result in six colors being typical. This color scheme creates an image of fun and enjoyment.

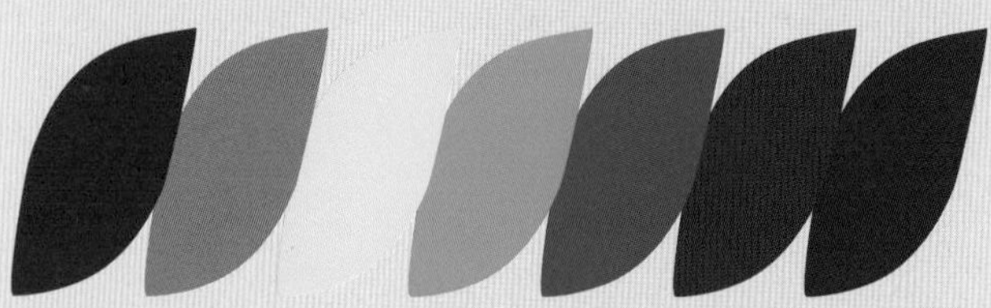

Gradation Where Colors Become Stronger and Weaker Little by Little

This gradation is created using one color and altering only the level of saturation in phases. The color on the right edge, vivid red (vv), is the most vibrant, while colors become closer to gray as they progress to the left. This can be used to give a polished finish to a color scheme.

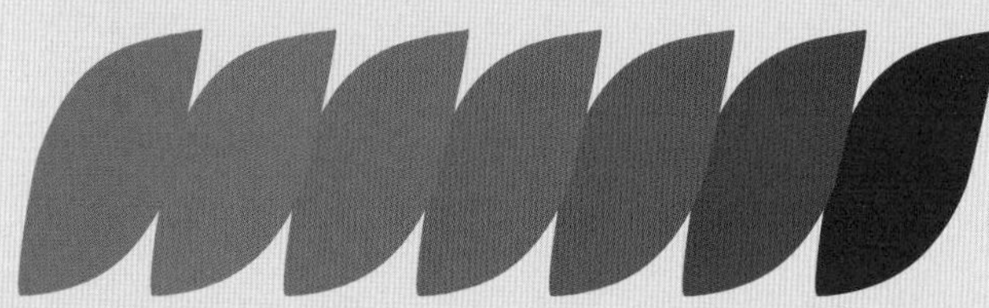

Tone on Tone

This refers to tones being layered one over the other in a color scheme that uses light and dark tones of the same color. Colors are cohesive, with tones creating a dynamic feel.

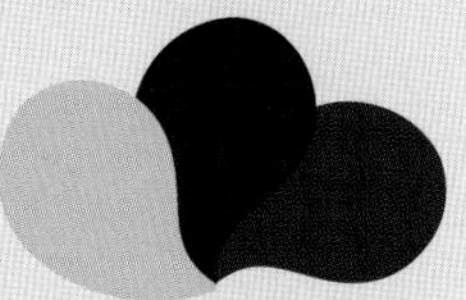
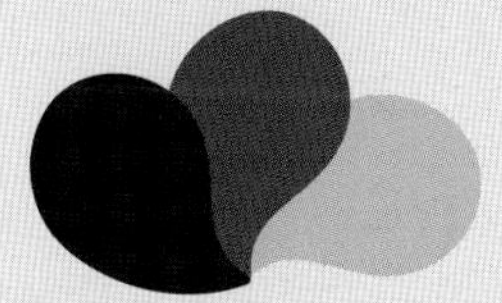

Tone on Tone

This refers to keeping within the one tone—using colors of the same tone but different hues. This is also handy when combining several colors.

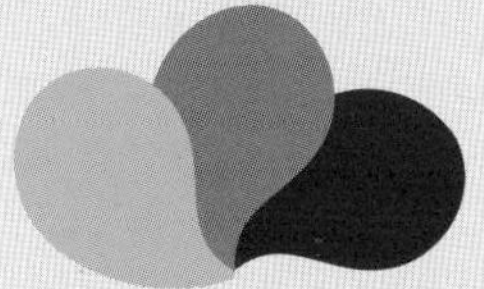

Tricolor

This refers to a three-color scheme with a sense of dynamism. Of the three colors, it's characteristic that one is white or black.

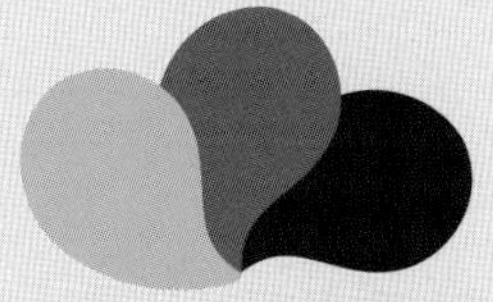

Camaieu

This is a combination of colors that are similar in hue, brightness and intensity. When viewed from a distance, this color scheme appears as a single color. It can be used to express subtle nuances.

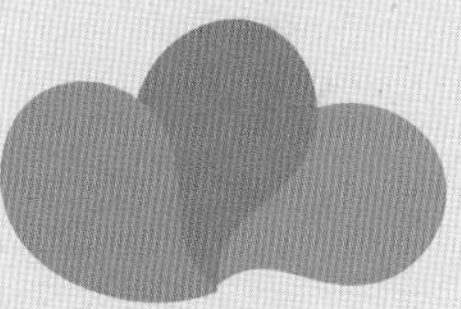

Faux Camaieu

Although there is more variation than in the Camaieu, this is a delicate color scheme. Faux means "false" in French.

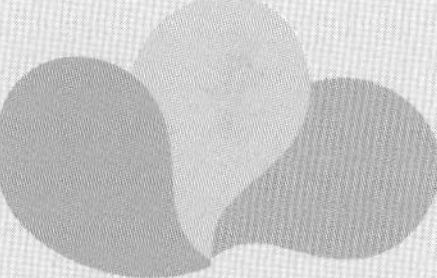

Tonal

This color scheme is composed of medium colors (sf, dl, lg, mg and dg on the tone chart on page 61) suggesting relaxed refinement.

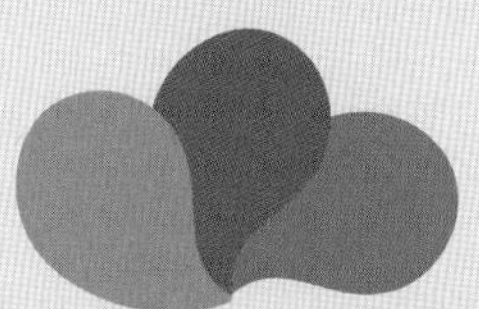
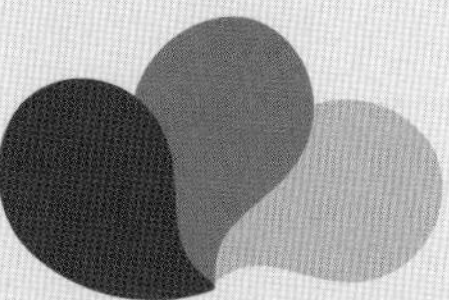

Part

06

Gorgeous + Luxury

This color palette evokes an image of gorgeousness. Compared with a casual color palette, it's characterized by its use of colors with depth and density. It's a color scheme that evokes a feeling of richness just by looking at it.

Color Schemes That Evoke Abundance and Flamboyance

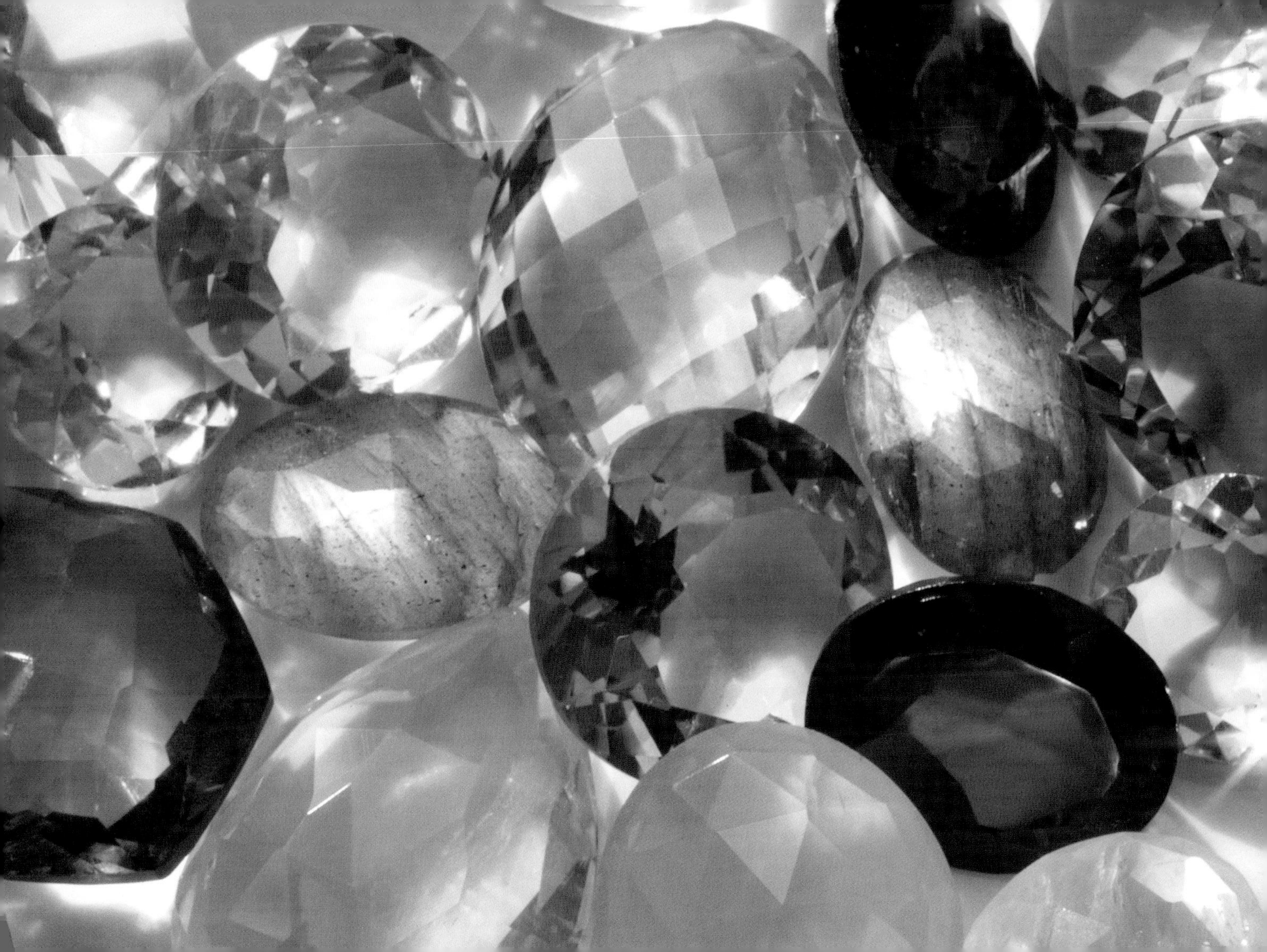

Recipe
047

A Future Star

In this world, some people have clear dreams or visions from the time they're young. They're extraordinary in that they have firm plans of what to achieve by when. Here, mainly colors with high levels of intensity have been selected. They're flamboyant and impactful to capture the strength of will needed to succeed.

- **FEELING** Splendid, pretty, dreamy.
- **COMBINATIONS** Focus on red to purple hues paired with warm beige.
- **TIPS** Simply using vibrant colors creates a flamboyant effect.

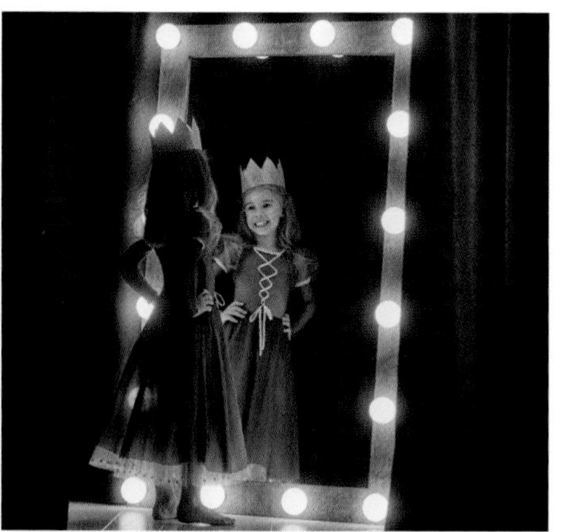

The key is to strike a pose and fully become the character.

❶ Raspberry Red
The red of ripe raspberries.

❷ Orchid Bloom
The color of a glossy orchid in full bloom.

❸ Biscuits
A light brown like that of crunchy biscuits.

❹ Lovely Violet
A color that evokes the courageous, pretty violet flower.

❺ Pink Lemonade
Lemonade in a cute, sweet pink color.

❻ Grape Juice
A deep, reddish purple like that of grape juice.

❼ Vanilla Ice Cream
The rich color of premium vanilla ice cream.

❽ Sweet Lilac
A color that conjures the pleasant fragrance of lilac.

❾ Rouge Red
The vibrant red of lipstick.

1 C7 M100 Y47 K35
R166 G0 B61
#A5003C

2 C35 M80 Y35 K0
R176 G79 B115
#B04E73

3 C15 M35 Y65 K0
R221 G175 B100
#DDAF63

4 C40 M70 Y20 K10
R157 G91 B134
#9C5B85

5 C10 M30 Y20 K0
R230 G192 B189
#E5C0BC

6 C20 M100 Y40 K40
R143 G0 B64
#8E0040

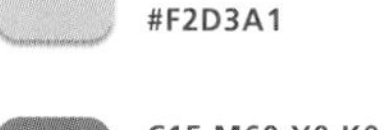

7 C5 M20 Y40 K0
R243 G212 B161
#F2D3A1

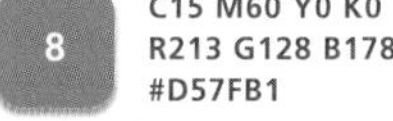

8 C15 M60 Y0 K0
R213 G128 B178
#D57FB1

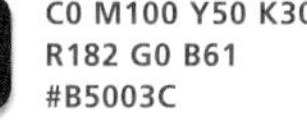

9 C0 M100 Y50 K30
R182 G0 B61
#B5003C

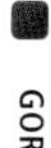

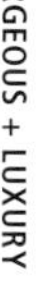

Two-color combinations

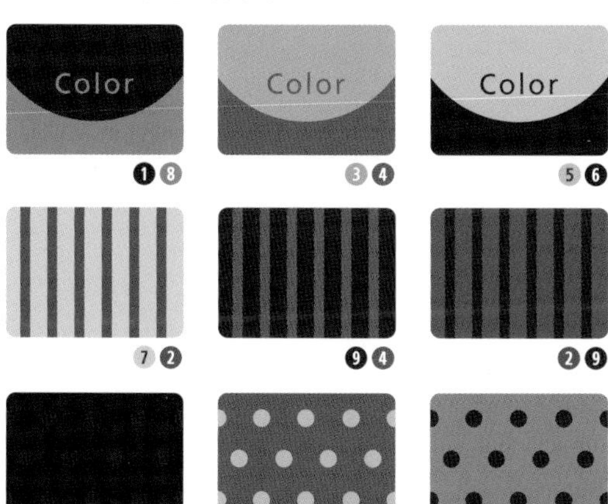

Three-color combinations

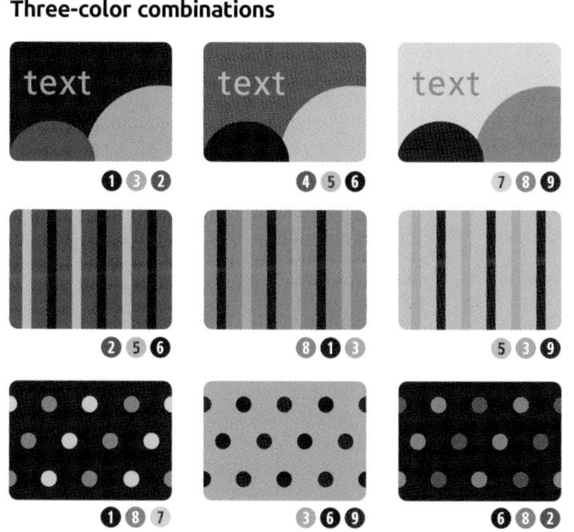

Designs

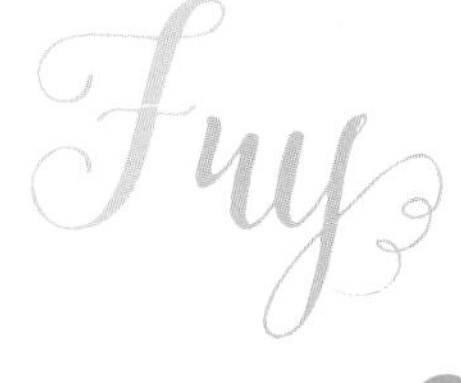

5 7 color 2

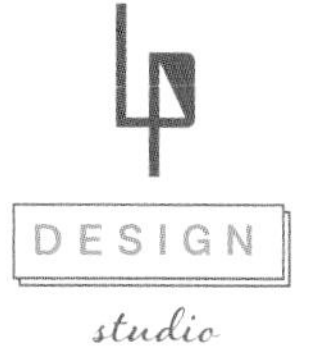

3 4 color 2

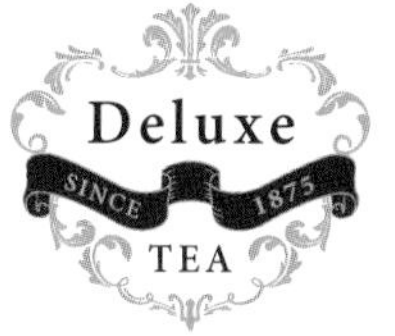

1 3 6 color 3

Patterns

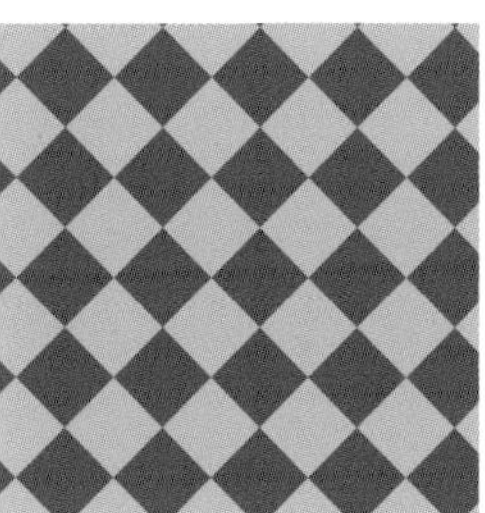

2 5 color 2

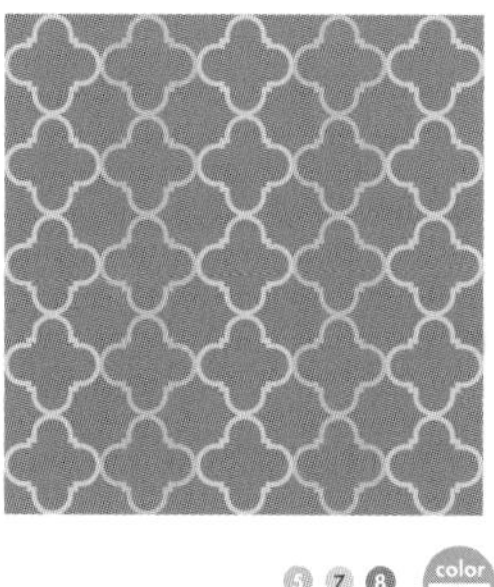

5 7 8 color 3

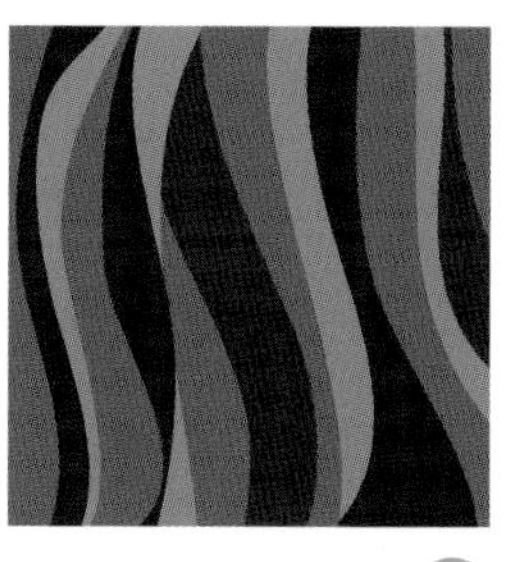

4 6 8 9 color 4

Illustration

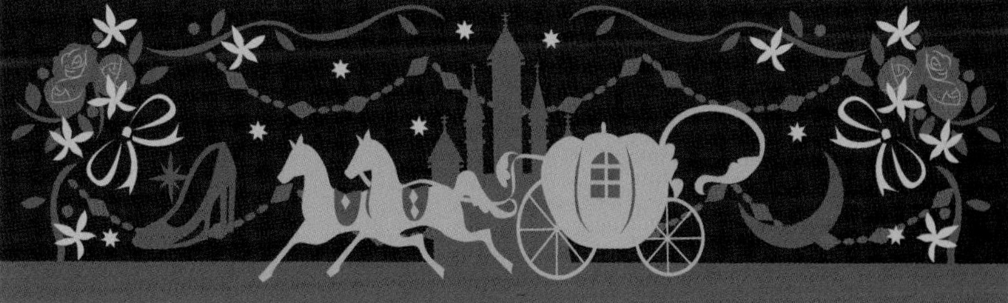

1 2 3 4 5 color 5

Recipe
048

Treasure Chest

In the movie "Spirited Away," the old woman who runs the bathhouse is a witch. She wears massive sparkling gemstones. As unlikely as it seems, their excessive gaudiness offers a glimpse of her sweet side. The owner of this treasure chest must be a a strong and sensitive woman. This gorgeous palette retains its sense of playfulness.

- **FEELING** Gorgeous, gaudy, impactful.
- **COMBINATIONS** Add gold shades to vivid colors.
- **TIPS** Use platinum and pearl white as accents.

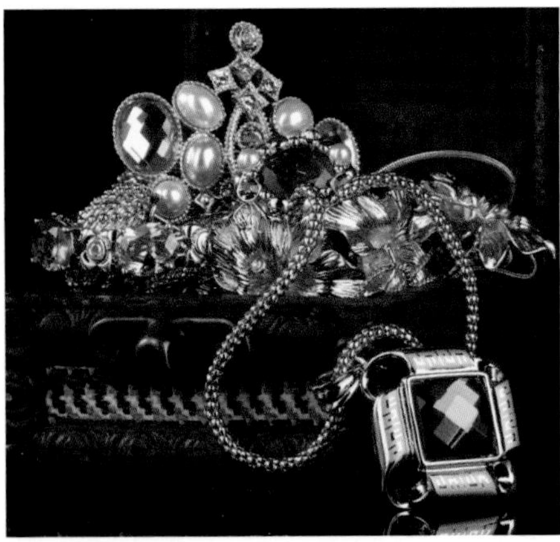

Add gorgeous accessories to adorn simple clothing.

❶ Love Romance
A red that suggests the moment that yearning turns into love.

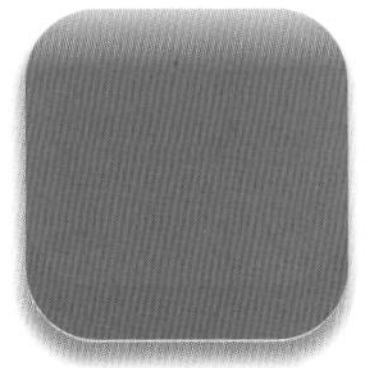

❷ Vital Green
A vivid green overflowing with energy.

❸ Beauty Pink
A color that evokes the enthusiastic pursuit of beauty.

❹ Golden Time
A color that evokes the prime time for beauty maintenance.

❺ Rich Gold
A yellow gold that suggests significant luxury.

❻ Premium Bronze
A color characterized by its calm red tinge.

❼ Platinum
A light gray that sparkles coolly like platinum.

⑧ Pearl White
A white like that of a pearl with an elegant lustre.

❾ Jewelry Box
The brown of a jewelry box that exudes an air of luxury.

1 C10 M100 Y60 K10 R202 G0 B65 #C90040

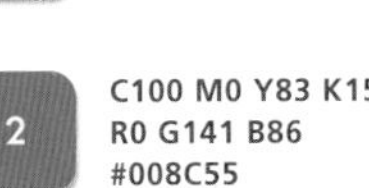

2 C100 M0 Y83 K15 R0 G141 B86 #008C55

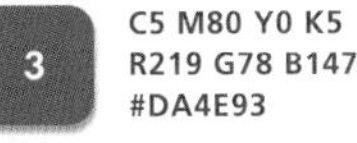

3 C5 M80 Y0 K5 R219 G78 B147 #DA4E93

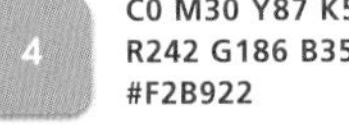

4 C0 M30 Y87 K5 R242 G186 B35 #F2B922

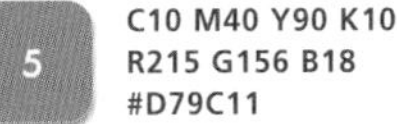

5 C10 M40 Y90 K10 R215 G156 B18 #D79C11

6 C0 M65 Y100 K30 R188 G93 B0 #BC5D00

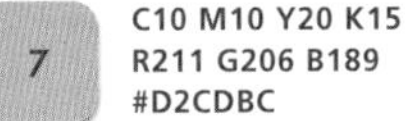

7 C10 M10 Y20 K15 R211 G206 B189 #D2CDBC

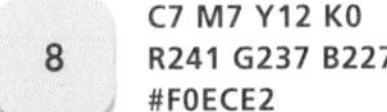

8 C7 M7 Y12 K0 R241 G237 B227 #F0ECE2

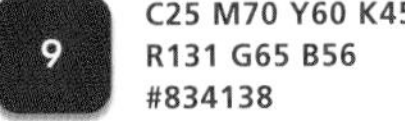

9 C25 M70 Y60 K45 R131 G65 B56 #834138

Two-color combinations

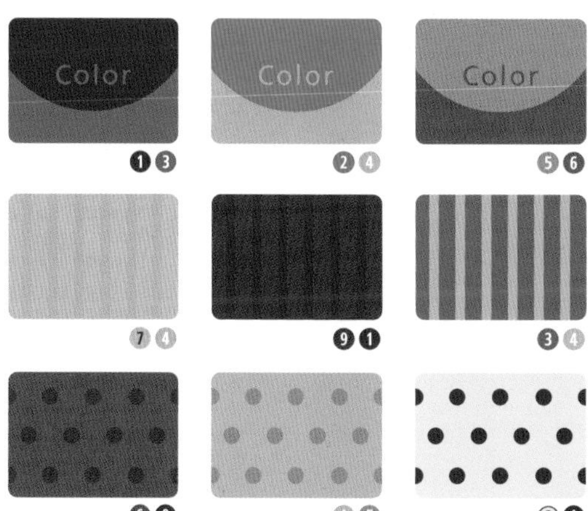

Three-color combinations

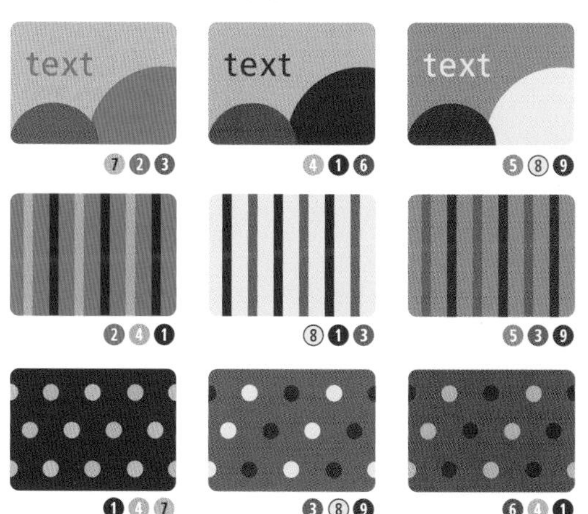

Designs

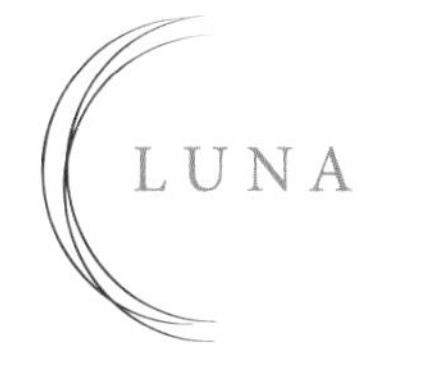

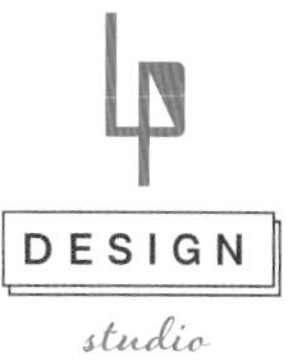

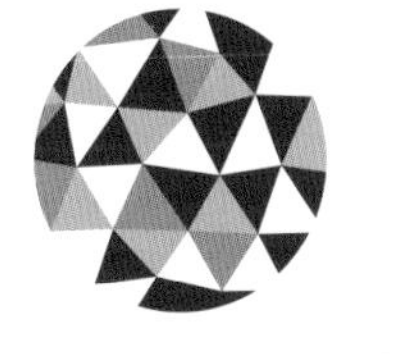

Patterns

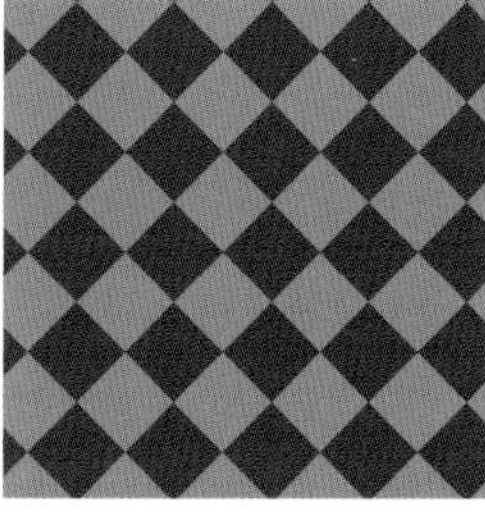

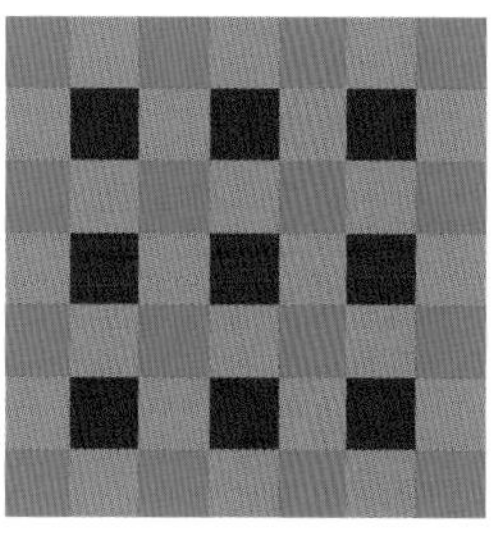

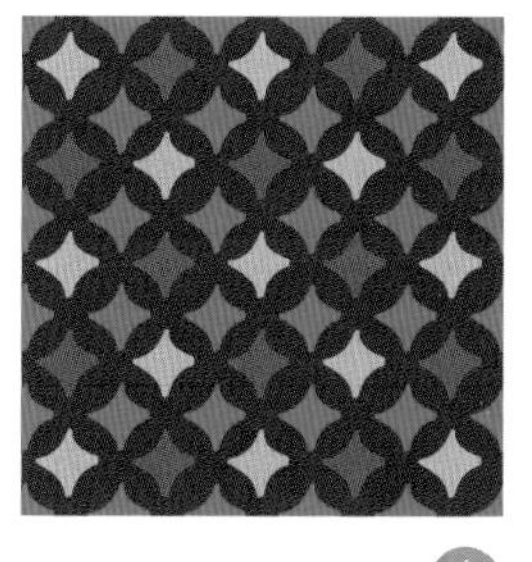

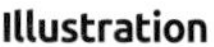

Illustration

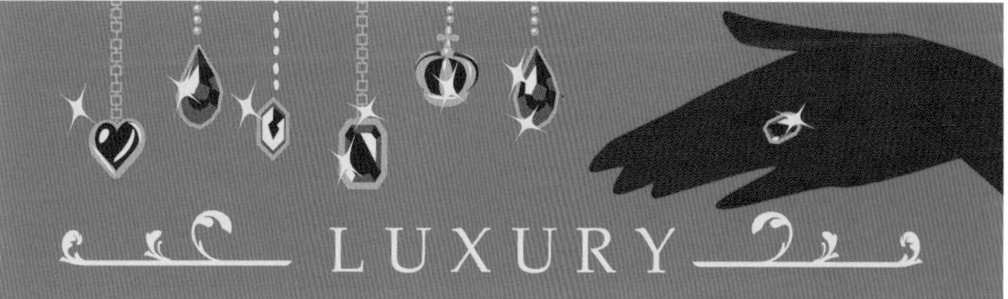

Recipe
049

Cocktails

The cocktails at tropical beach resorts are unapologetically colorful and gorgeous. I'd usually avoid blue cocktails, but I took the plunge and ordered one, charmed by its name, Blue Moon. My husband ordered the Gulf Stream, a cocktail that was created to suggest the blue ocean of the Caribbean. It seems that we were thinking the same thing.

- **FEELING** Vivid, gorgeous, colorful.
- **COMBINATIONS** Create color schemes combining vivid and deep hues.
- **TIPS** These are color schemes that are out of the ordinary.

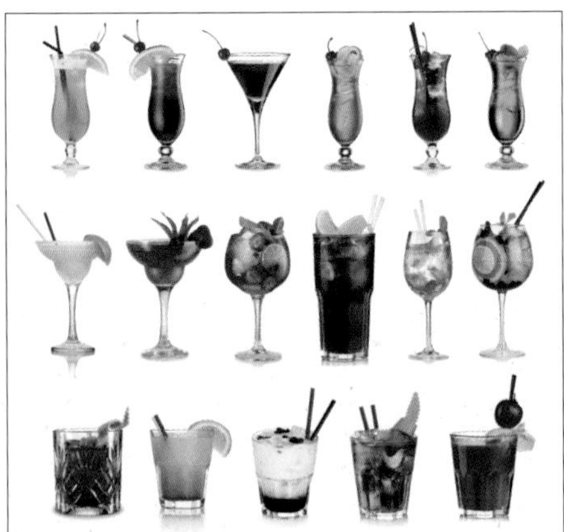

From standard cocktails to original creations, these are colorful adult beverages overflowing with fun.

❶ Sangria
A drink made from adding fruit and sweetener to red wine.

❷ Campari Orange
A standard cocktail made from orange juice and Campari.

❸ Blue Hawaii
This cocktail was trendy in the first half of the 1980s.

❹ Malibu Pineapple
Pineapple juice and coconut liqueur.

❺ Around the World
A green cocktail made from gin and mint liqueur.

❻ Blueberry Royale
A cocktail made from blueberry liqueur and Champagne.

❼ Lejay Cassis Tea
Cassis liqueur is added to ice tea to create this cocktail.

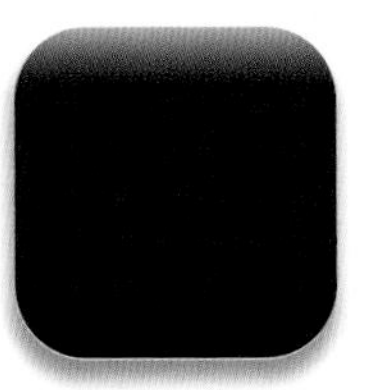

❽ Kahlua
This well-known drink is a type of coffee liqueur.

❾ Chichi
A cocktail made by adding coconut milk to a vodka base.

1 C25 M100 Y50 K0 R192 G14 B83 #BF0D52

2 C3 M55 Y90 K0 R237 G141 B31 #ED8C1F

3 C65 M15 Y10 K0 R80 G172 B211 #50ABD3

4 C10 M10 Y90 K0 R238 G219 B21 #EDDA15

5 C60 M8 Y50 K0 R106 G182 B147 #6AB592

6 C50 M100 Y50 K0 R148 G30 B87 #931E56

7 C0 M65 Y60 K40 R169 G83 B61 #A9533C

8 C0 M80 Y80 K80 R84 G9 B0 #540800

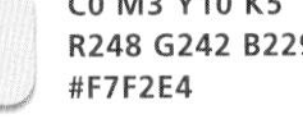

9 C0 M3 Y10 K5 R248 G242 B229 #F7F2E4

Two-color combinations

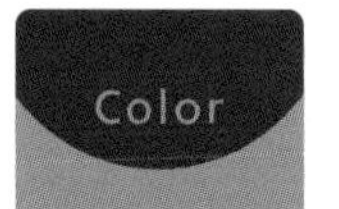

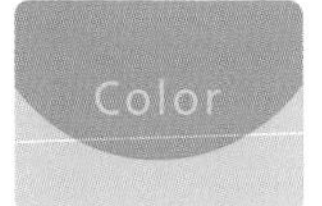

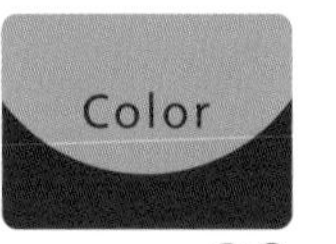

1 2 · 3 4 · 5 6

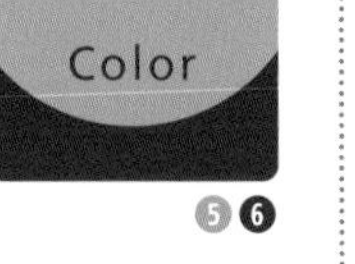
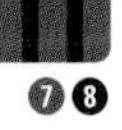
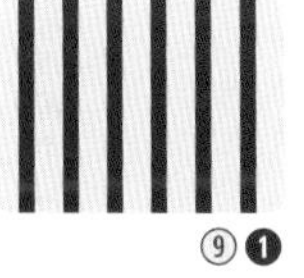
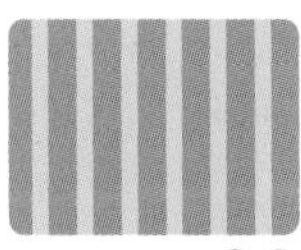

7 8 · 9 1 · 2 4

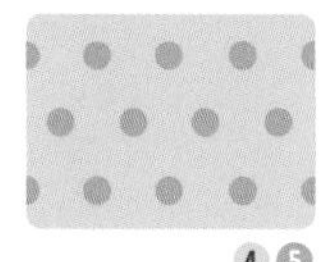
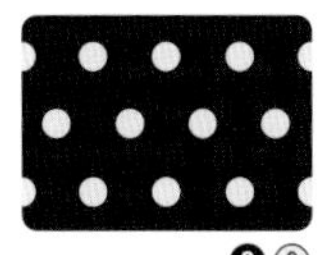

6 1 · 4 5 · 8 9

Three-color combinations

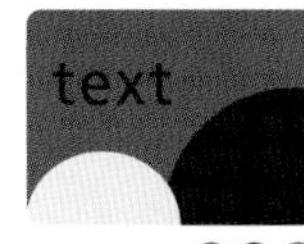

1 2 3 · 4 5 6 · 7 8 9

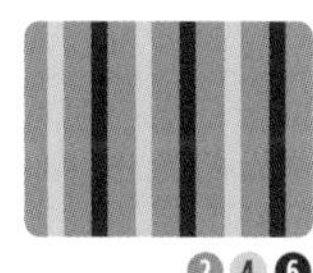
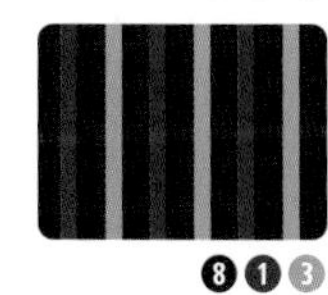
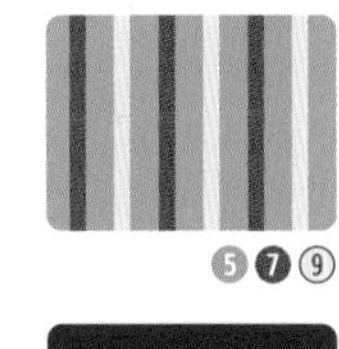

2 4 6 · 8 1 3 · 5 7 9

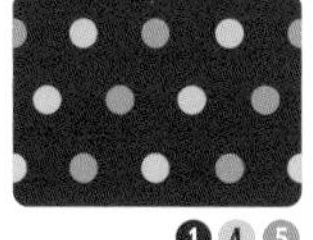
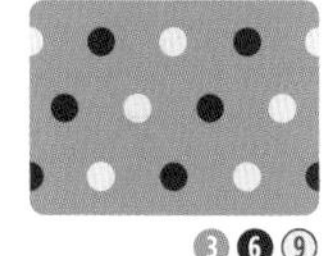
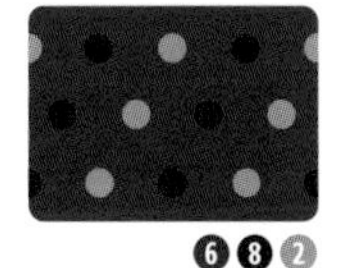

1 4 5 · 3 6 9 · 6 8 2

Designs

3 5 color 2

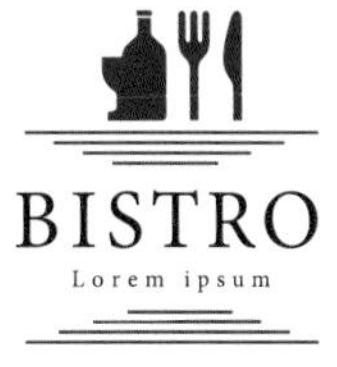

6 8 color 2

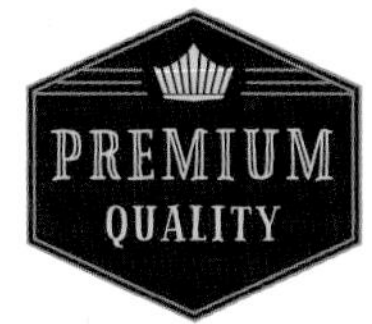

2 4 8 color 3

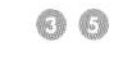

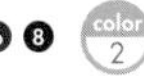
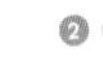

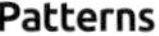

Patterns

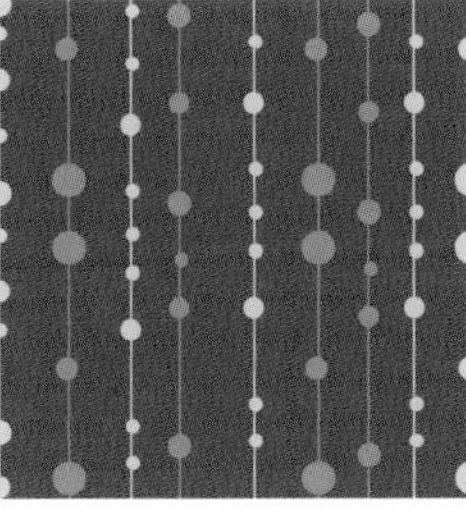
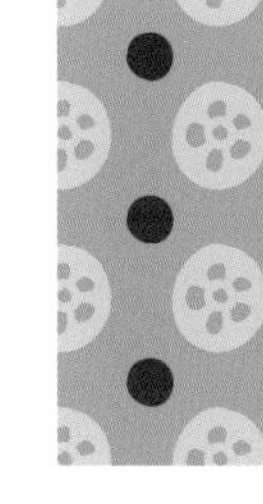
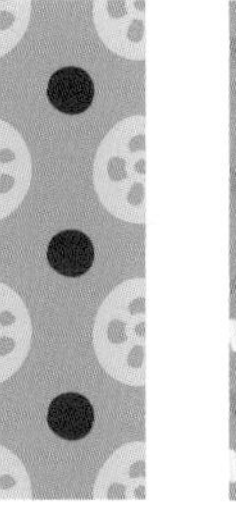
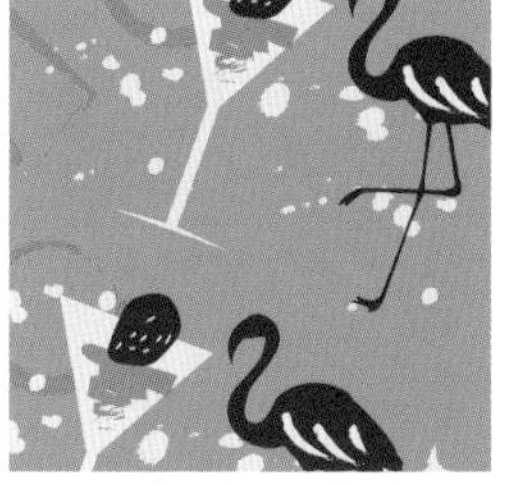
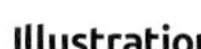

2 4 7 color 3 · 1 4 5 color 3 · 1 2 3 9 color 4

Illustration

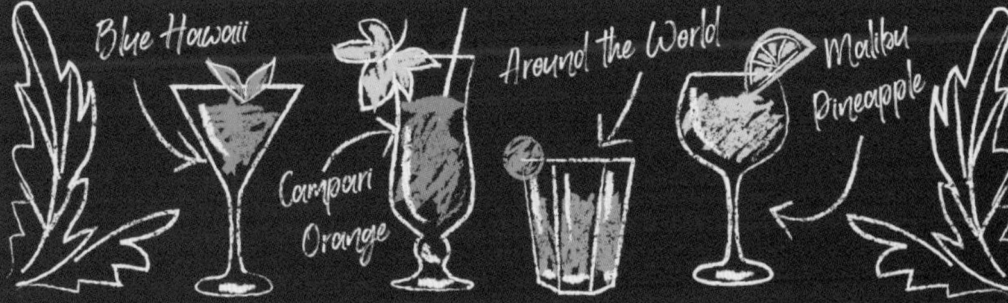

1 2 3 4 5 9 color 6

Recipe
050

Colorful Jewels

Certain precious stones have symbolic meanings. Garnet symbolizes blood and heightens vitality. Sapphire, with its blue that recalls the heavens, is considered to be the stone closest to the gods. Emerald has come to be used as an idiom for a natural paradise, a special place of wonder and enchantment.

- **FEELING** Gorgeous, luxurious, dazzling.
- **COMBINATIONS** Teaming similar colors makes for a cohesive look.
- **TIPS** The base color determines the overall air.

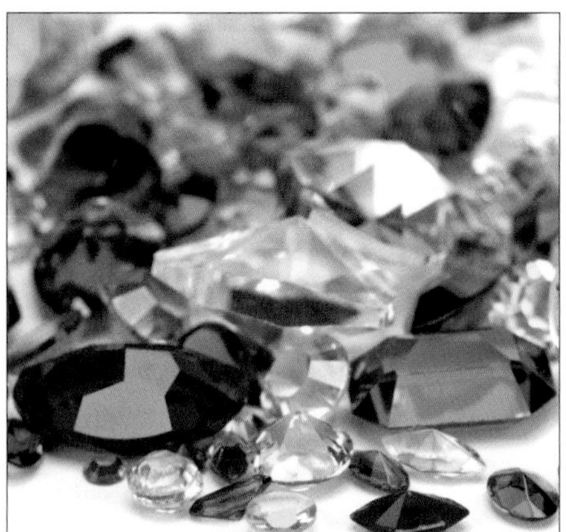

If the colors are too strong, add white to temper and tone down.

❶ Garnet
A deep red like that of a garnet, the birthstone for January.

❷ Sapphire
The name is derived from the Latin for the color blue.

❸ Topaz
In Japanese, this is known as "yellow gem."

❹ Blue Diamond
Blue diamonds are highly valued as they're exceedingly rare.

❺ Emerald
The emerald suggests fortune, happiness, hope and stability.

⑥ Diamond Light
The color of strong light emitted from a diamond.

❼ Amethyst
A stone that is believed to protect love.

❽ Aquamarine
The name of this stone is derived from the Latin for seawater.

❾ Ruby
The queen of precious stones, ruby is also said to elevate passion.

1. C10 M100 Y60 K35 / R162 G0 B49 / #A20031
2. C80 M70 Y0 K13 / R64 G75 B150 / #404A95
3. C0 M30 Y67 K0 / R249 G193 B95 / #F9C15F
4. C70 M47 Y0 K0 / R87 G123 B189 / #567ABD
5. C100 M0 Y75 K0 / R0 G155 B107 / #009B6B
6. C10 M3 Y0 K3 / R230 G238 B247 / #E6EEF6
7. C55 M85 Y0 K5 / R132 G58 B142 / #843A8E
8. C65 M5 Y10 K0 / R69 G184 B220 / #44B8DC
9. C5 M100 Y47 K0 / R222 G0 B83 / #DE0053

Two-color combinations

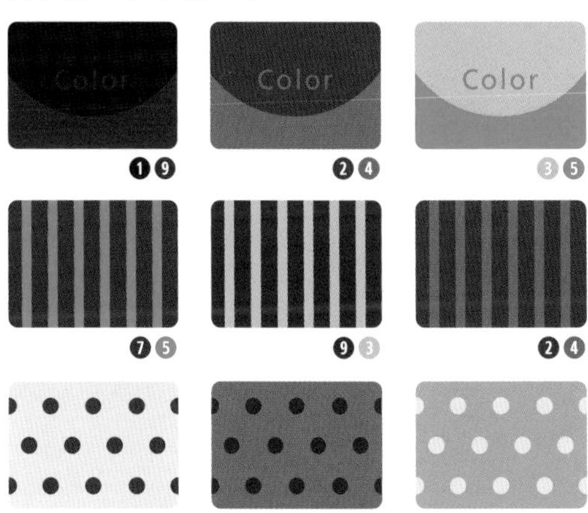

Three-color combinations

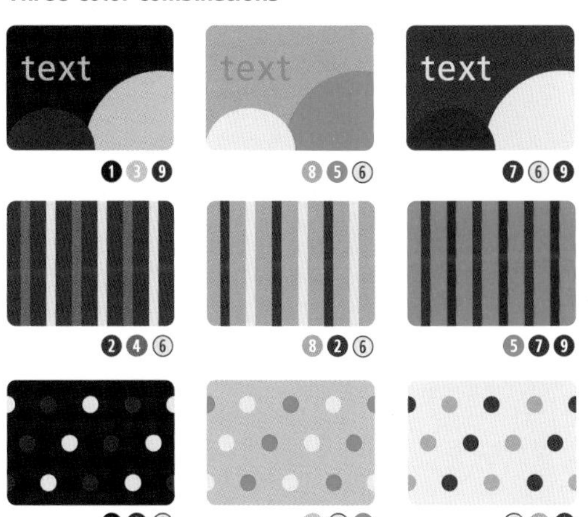

Designs

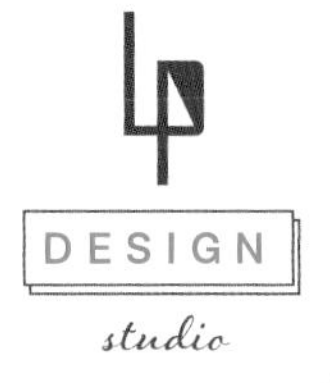

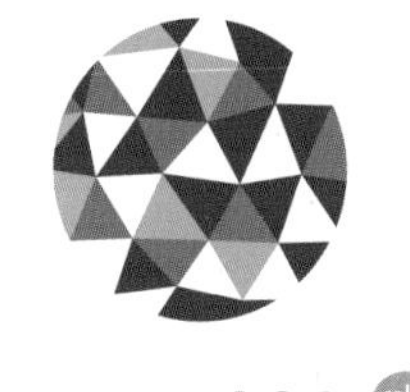

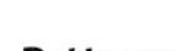

Patterns

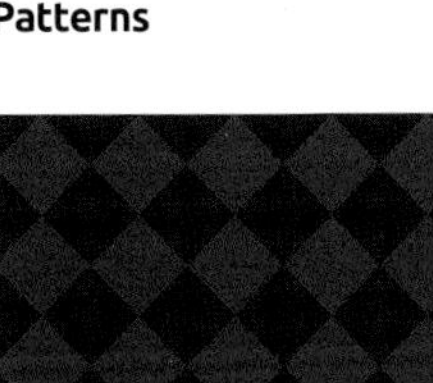

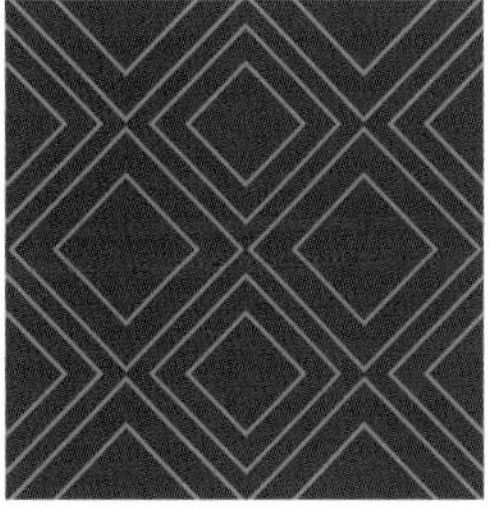

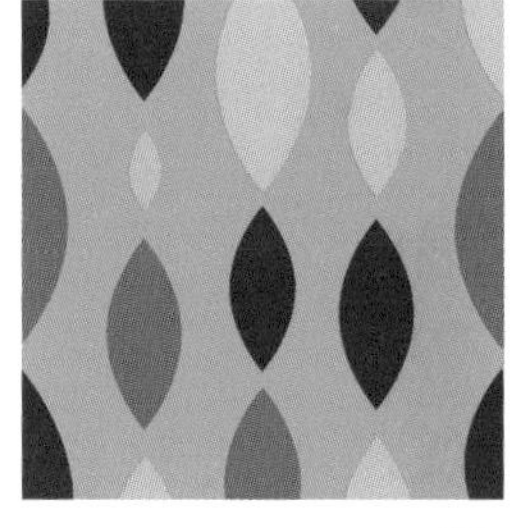

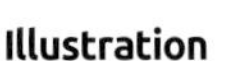

Illustration

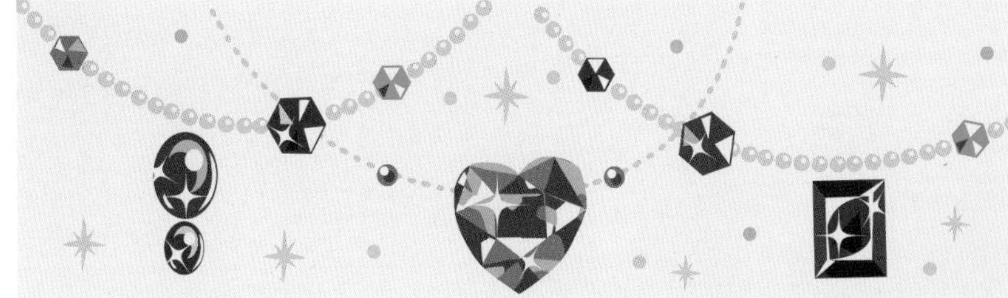

Recipe
051

Gold Brilliance

One of the methods for representing color is the Munsell System. It's incorporated into the Japan Industrial Standards (JIS), and its use allows colors to be accurately represented using codes and numerical values. However, the luster and shine of gold and silver are exceptions: they can't be substituted for codes and numerical values. That's what makes them such special colors.

- **FEELING** Special, glorious, powerful.
- **COMBINATIONS** Use more than three colors for an effective result.
- **TIPS** Pay attention to light and shade when combining colors.

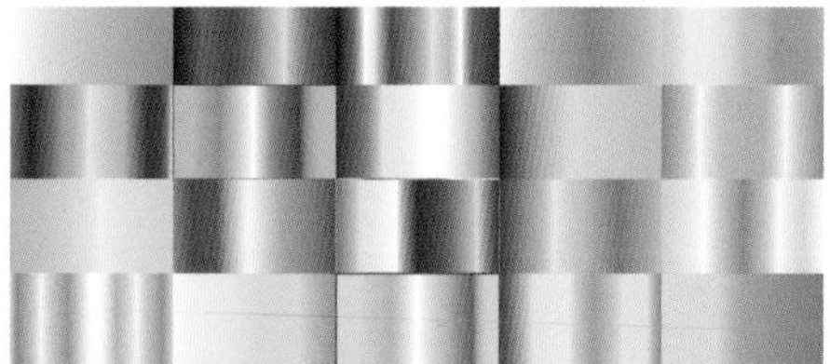

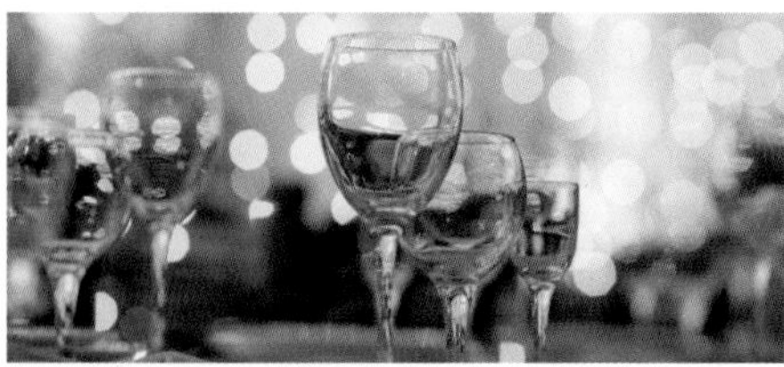

Gold has the power to enhance people's moods.

1 Yellow Gold
A gold with strong yellow tones. It creates an air of brilliance.

2 Inca Gold
A time-worn color like that of relics from the Inca empire.

3 Golden Glow
A color that gives the sense of glimpsing gold.

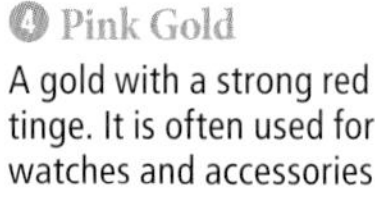

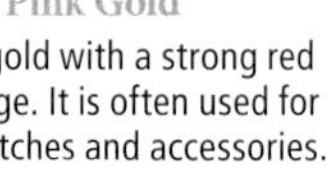

4 Pink Gold
A gold with a strong red tinge. It is often used for watches and accessories.

5 Antique Gold
This gold has a dullness and depth to it.

6 Shiny Gold
A brightly shining gold that dazzles the eyes.

7 Champagne Gold
Gold with pink tones like that of Champagne.

8 Coral Gold
A color that is like a mix of coral pink and gold.

9 Burnt Gold
A gold that is close to brown.

1 C5 M15 Y80 K5 R238 G209 B63 #EED13F

2 C10 M20 Y75 K10 R220 G191 B76 #DBBF4B

3 C20 M30 Y90 K25 R176 G148 B31 #B0941E

4 C0 M30 Y45 K15 R224 G176 B130 #DFB081

5 C0 M35 Y70 K23 R208 G154 B72 #D09A48

6 C0 M15 Y100 K4 R249 G212 B0 #F9D400

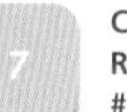

7 C0 M10 Y25 K10 R238 G220 B188 #EDDCBC

8 C0 M20 Y35 K15 R226 G195 B155 #E2C29B

9 C0 M35 Y90 K45 R165 G121 B0 #A57800

Two-color combinations

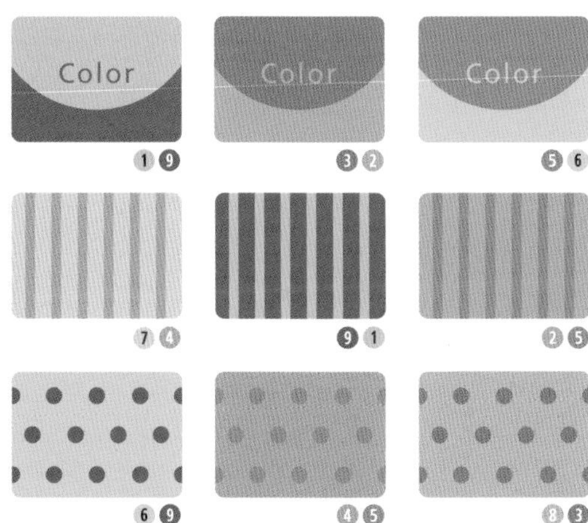

Three-color combinations

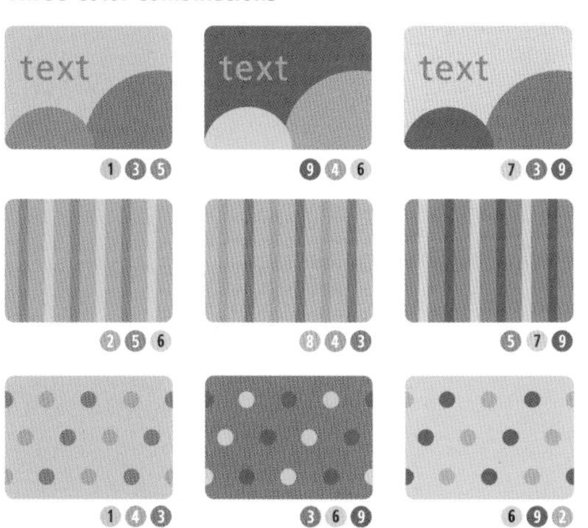

Designs

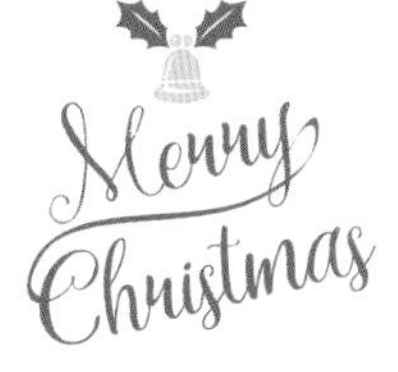

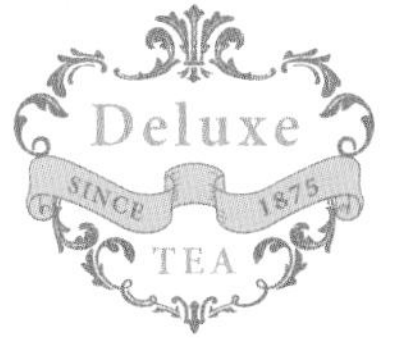

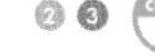

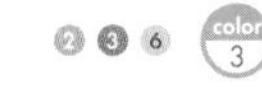

2 3 color 2 | 7 9 color 2 | 2 3 6 color 3

Patterns

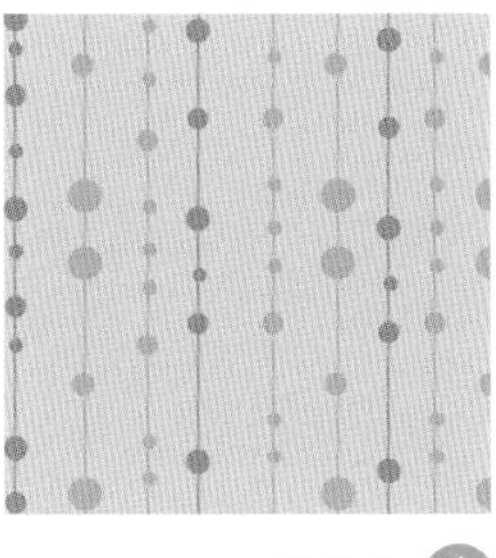

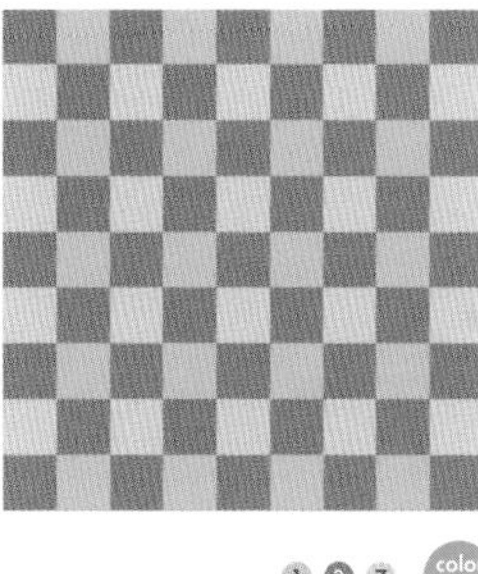

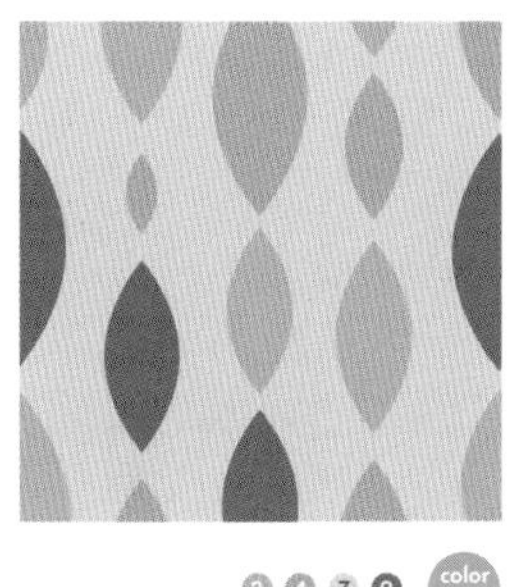

2 5 7 color 3 | 1 3 7 color 3 | 2 4 7 9 color 4

Illustration

1 2 5 7 9 color 5

Recipe
052

Rococo Interiors

Think of the age of Marie Antoinette, and you'll have a clear idea of Rococo style, which blossomed in Europe in the 18th century, with France at its heart. Its elegant, detailed interior design incorporated gorgeous, bright colors and soft pastel tones. The aristocrats of the day wore white wigs as part of their intricate outfits.

- **FEELING** Graceful, gorgeous, bright.
- **COMBINATIONS** Focus on using bright, brilliant colors.
- **TIPS** Grayish pastels also create an air of elegance.

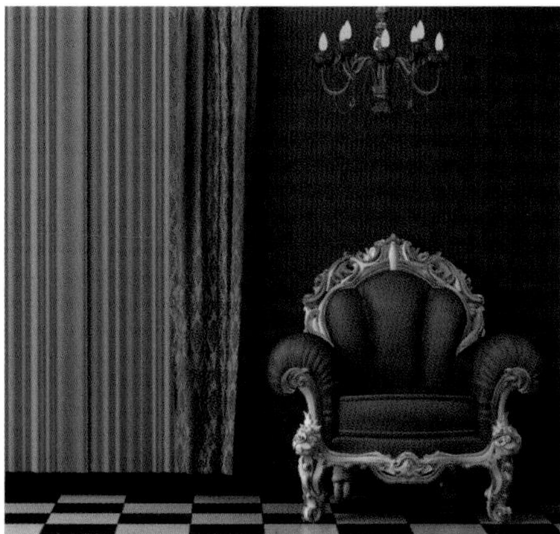

This style originated in the French court during the reign of King Louis the 15th.

❶ La Vie en Rose
A red the conjures rosy views of the world and future.

❷ Rococo White
White played the leading role in period interiors.

❸ Blonde Hair
A color that evokes light golden hair.

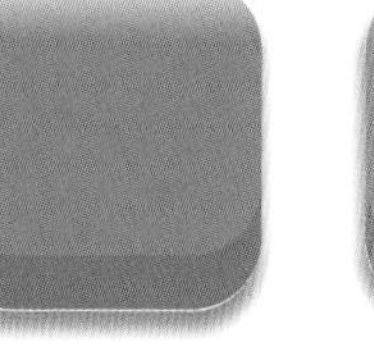

❹ Pompadour Pink
This color pink is associated with Madame Pompadour.

❺ Crème Brulee
In French, this means "scorched cream."

❻ Lilac Chiffon
A soft purple like that of silk chiffon.

❼ Macaron Pink
A macaron is a French confection.

❽ Opera
A type of chocolate cake created in France.

❾ Pale Green
A pale green color used in interiors and for clothing.

1 C25 M80 Y45 K0 R194 G81 B102 #C15066

2 C8 M10 Y10 K0 R238 G231 B227 #EDE7E3

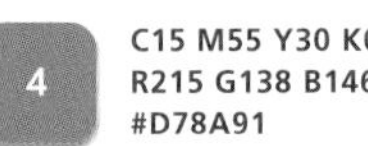

3 C0 M15 Y35 K10 R237 G211 B165 #ECD2A5

4 C15 M55 Y30 K0 R215 G138 B146 #D78A91

5 C10 M35 Y60 K10 R216 G167 B103 #D7A766

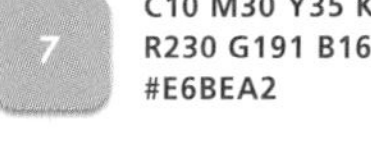

6 C5 M15 Y5 K5 R235 G219 B224 #EBDAE0

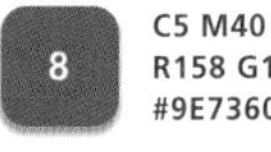

7 C10 M30 Y35 K0 R230 G191 B162 #E6BEA2

8 C5 M40 Y40 K45 R158 G115 B96 #9E7360

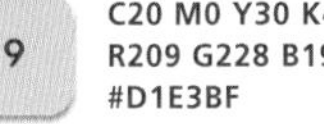

9 C20 M0 Y30 K4 R209 G228 B191 #D1E3BF

Two-color combinations

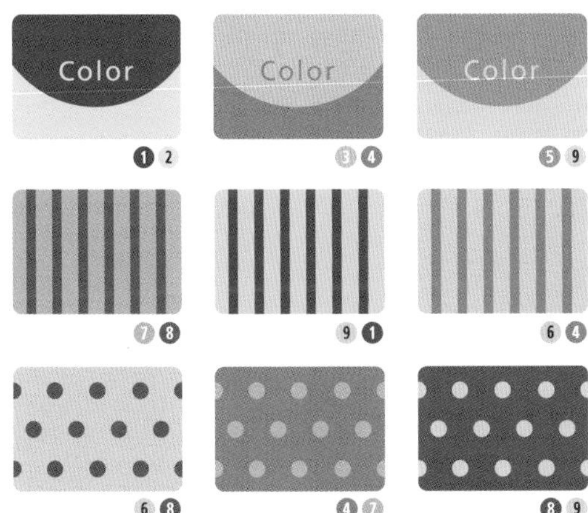

Three-color combinations

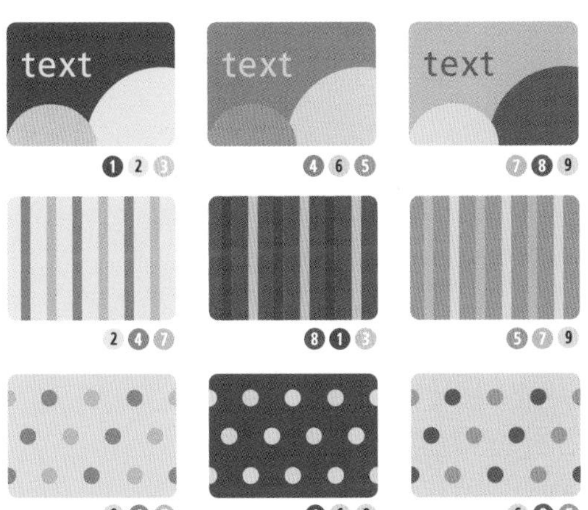

Designs

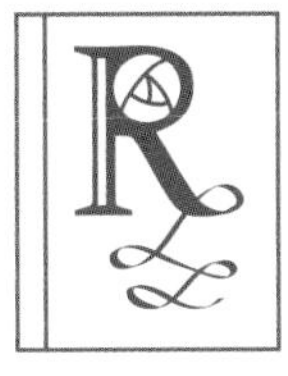
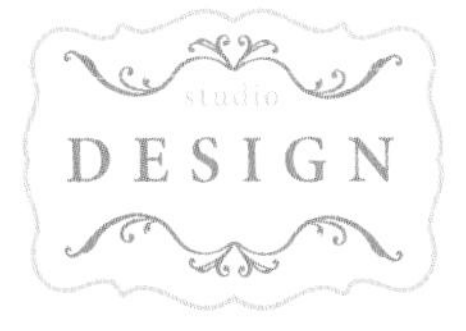

1 8 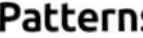  

5 9 

5 6 8 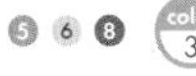

Patterns

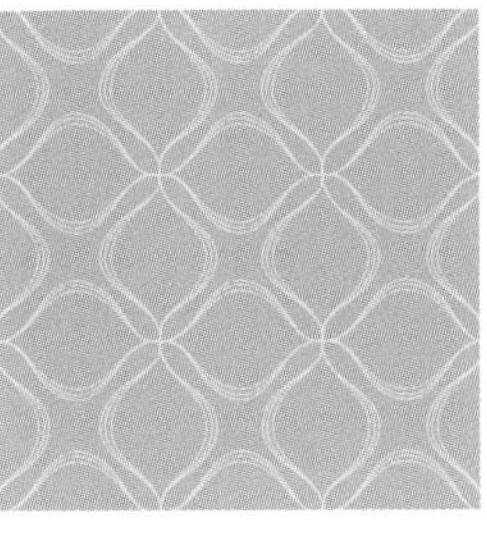

2 7 color 2

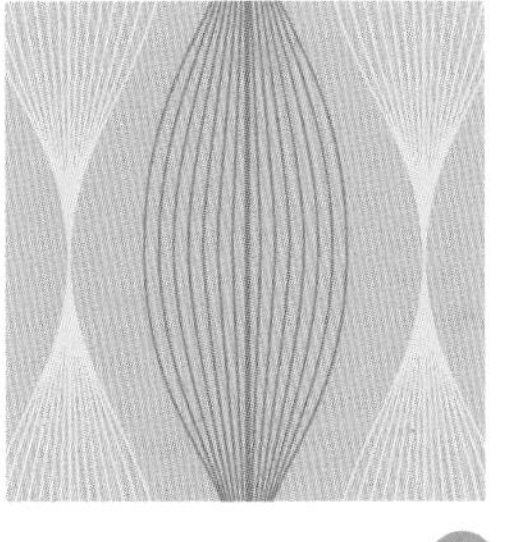

2 3 4 color 3

3 4 5 9 color 4

Illustration

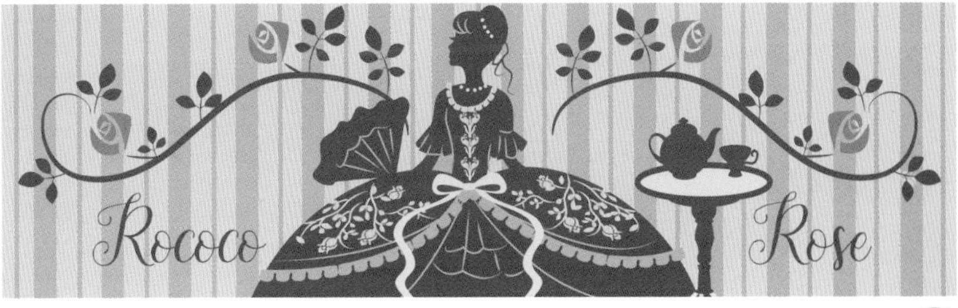

1 2 4 7 9 color 5

Recipe
053

Autumn Bouquets

Fall is harvest season, when plants that have soaked in the rays of the summer sun are heavy with fruit and grain. It's also a time for clear skies and clement weather. In order to express this sense of fulfilment and stability, warm, serene shades are the focus of this magnanimous color palette.

- **FEELING** Serene, assured, having depth.
- **COMBINATIONS** Create a composition using only warm, deep colors.
- **TIPS** Use white to accent the deep colors.

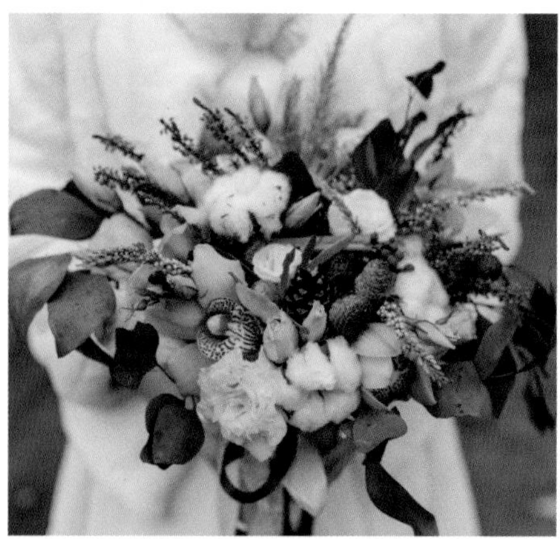

A serene color palette that brings together only fall colors.

❶ Evening Orange
The orange color that appears in the sky at dusk.

❷ Harvest Moon
In Japanese, this refers to the mid-fall harvest moon.

❸ Autumn Green
The green of leaves before they change color.

❹ Apple Cinnamon
The color of baked apples with plenty of cinnamon and sugar.

❺ Espresso
A deep color like that of espresso coffee.

❻ Persimmon
A reddish orange like that of ripe persimmon.

❼ Pumpkin
A deep orange like that of ripe pumpkin.

❽ Autumn Gray
A deep gray tinged with green that suggests late fall.

❾ Antique White
A smooth white with a mature air.

1 C10 M75 Y70 K0 R220 G95 B69 #DC5F45

2 C5 M30 Y75 K0 R241 G190 B77 #F1BD4C

3 C50 M27 Y70 K0 R145 G163 B99 #90A362

4 C10 M85 Y80 K35 R164 G50 B34 #A43121

5 C0 M60 Y80 K85 R74 G26 B0 #491A00

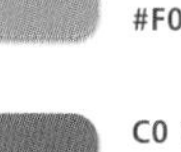

6 C0 M45 Y70 K3 R240 G161 B80 #F0A050

7 C0 M57 Y83 K15 R217 G124 B43 #D87C2B

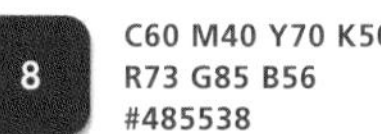

8 C60 M40 Y70 K50 R73 G85 B56 #485538

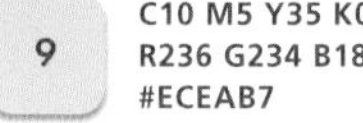

9 C10 M5 Y35 K0 R236 G234 B183 #ECEAB7

Two-color combinations

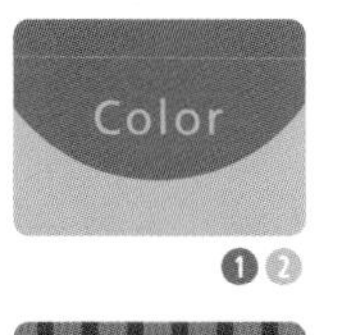

1 2

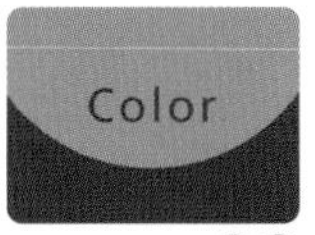

3 4

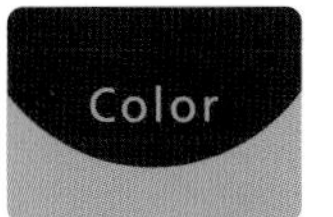

5 6

7 8

9 1

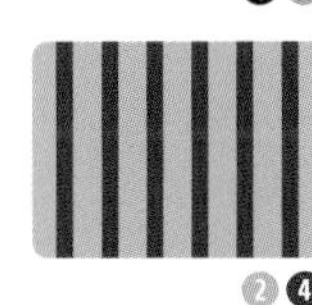

2 4

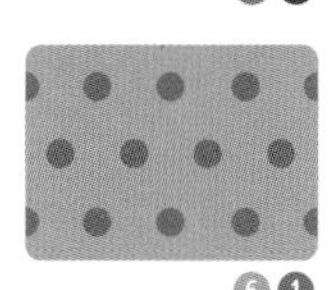

6 1

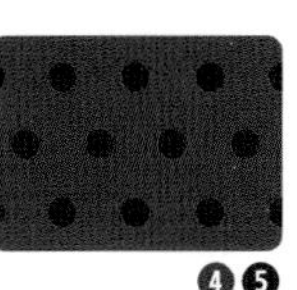

4 5

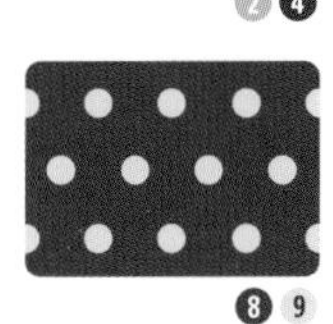

8 9

Three-color combinations

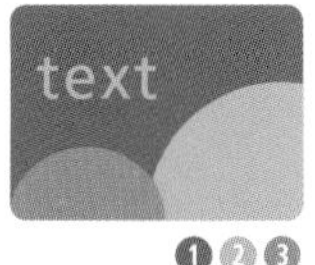

1 2 3

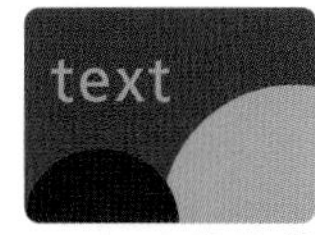

4 6 5

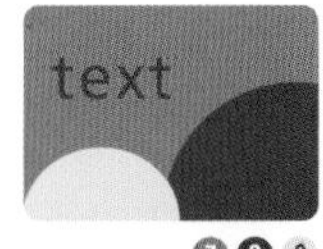

7 8 9

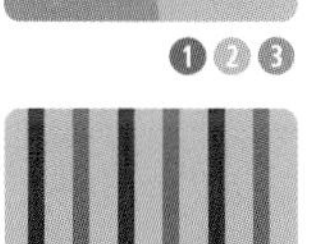

2 4 1

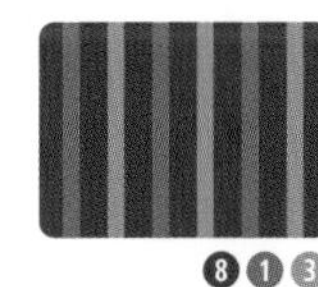

8 1 3

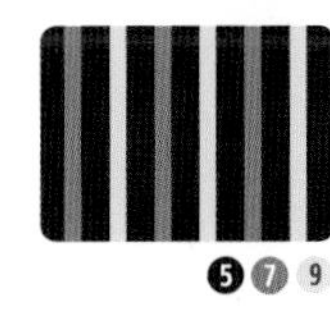

5 7 9

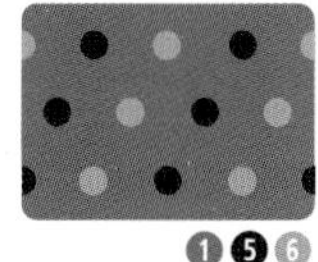

1 5 6

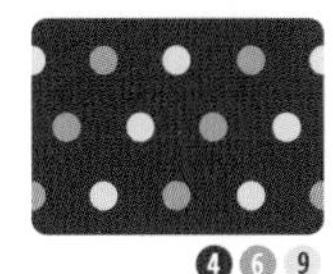

4 6 9

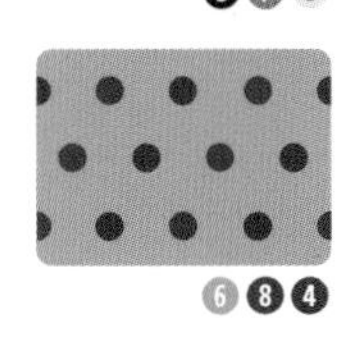

6 8 4

Designs

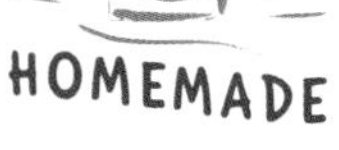

7 8 color 2

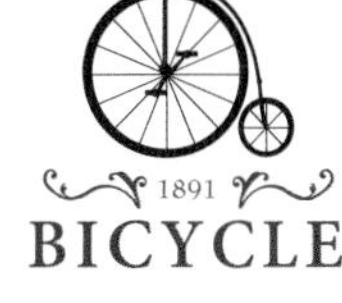

4 5 color 2

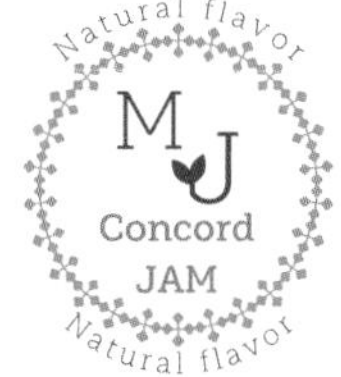
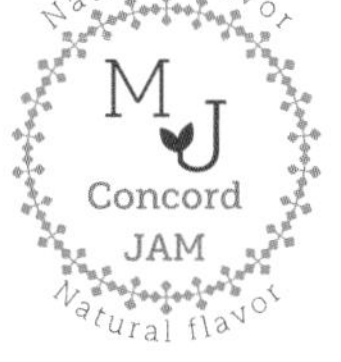

3 7 8 color 3

Patterns

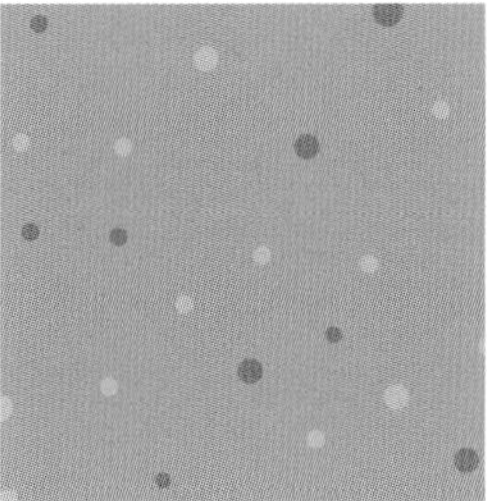

2 6 7 color 3

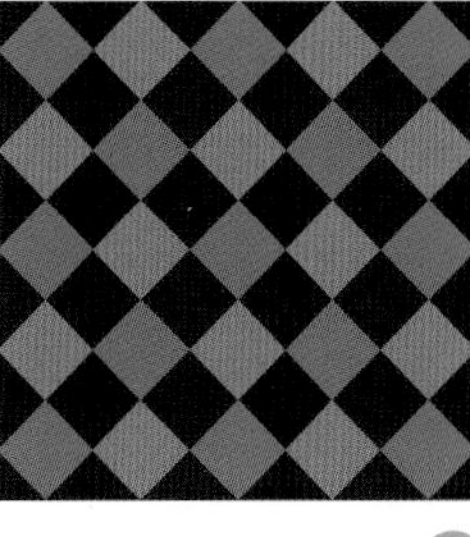

1 5 7 color 3

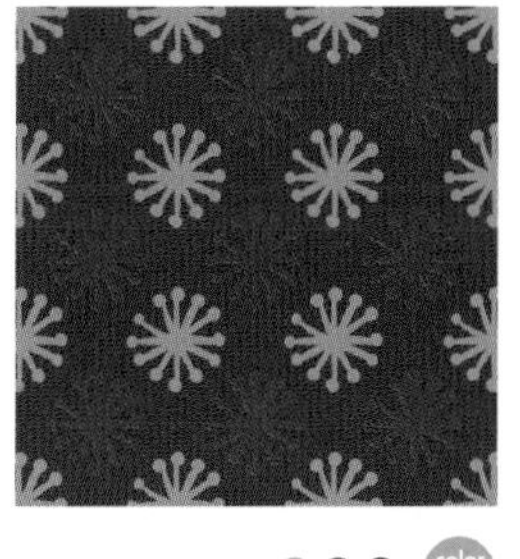

3 4 8 color 3

Illustration

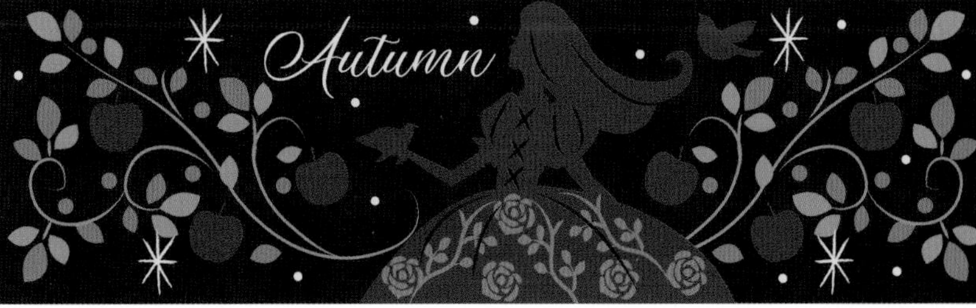

3 4 5 7 9 color 5

Part

07

Dynamic + Ethnic

This color palette has been created from a range of motifs and inspirations, including Indian spices, African fabric and Chinese talismans. The strength and power of the schemes and palettes can be felt in the bold use of color.

Color Schemes for a Bold, Ethnic Look.

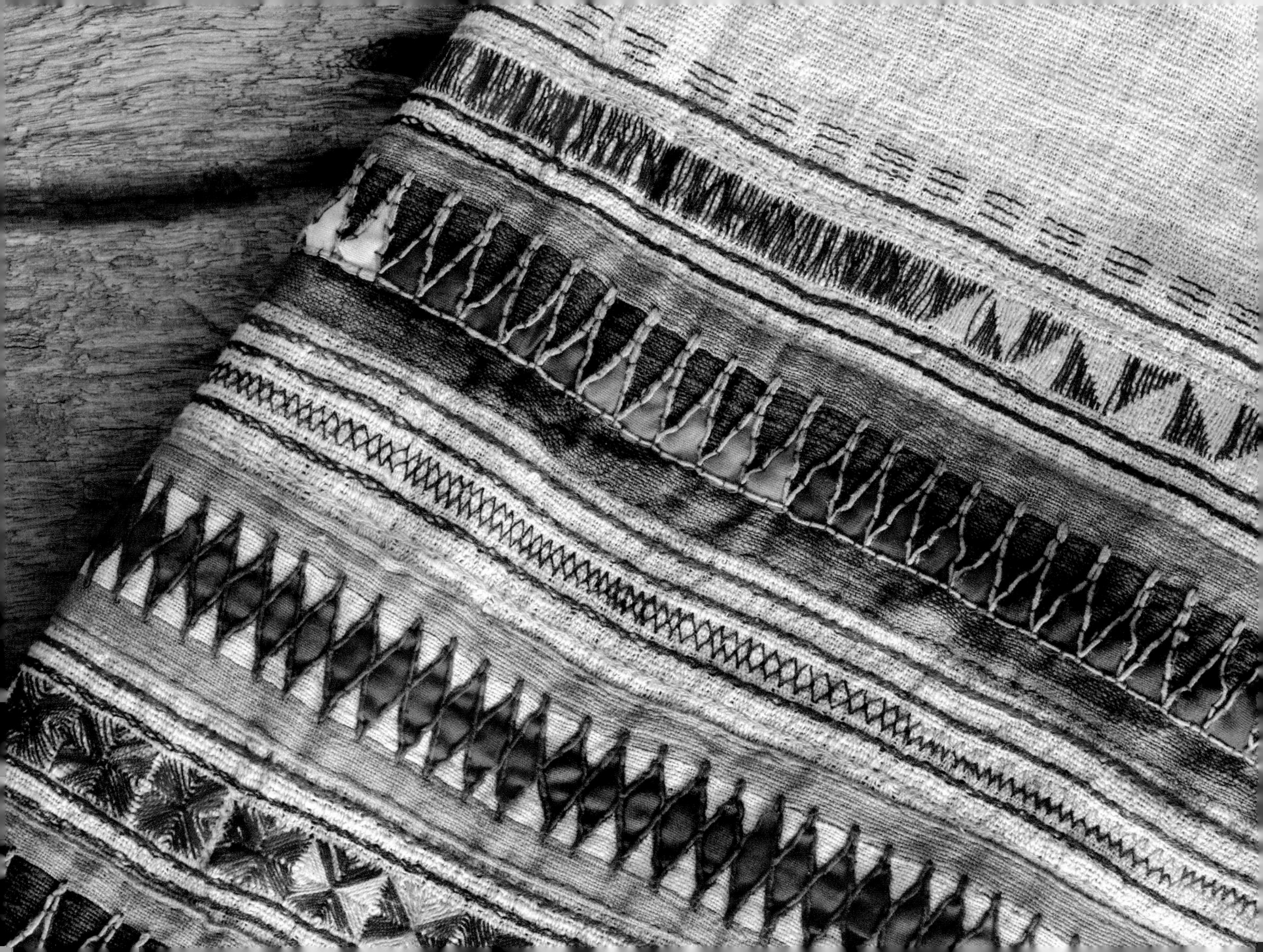

Recipe

054

Balinese Sunset

Tanah Lot Temple in Bali is a place where the sunset will stir the soul. Against a backdrop of a sky flushed red and a sparkling golden sea, the temple rises. As the sun sinks below the horizon line, the silhouette contrasts even more strongly against the background. This color palette evokes Bali and draws on those changing hues.

- **FEELING** Vast, earthy, ethnic.
- **COMBINATIONS** Create a color palette with shades contrasting from orange through to brown.
- **TIPS** Use blue shades as accent colors.

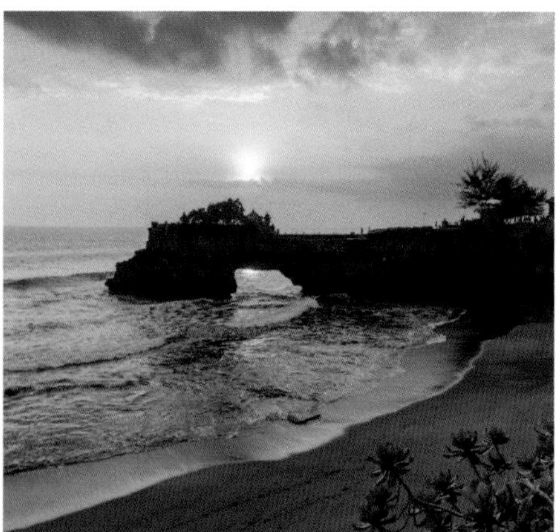

The entire landscape appears to have an orange filter applied to it.

❶ Cantaloupe Melon
The orange of melon flesh.

❷ Sunset Orange
The color of the glowing sky at the moment when the sun sets.

❸ Sunburn
Skin well browned while at a beach resort.

❹ Sand Brown
The color of a sandy beach; a light brown with a touch of gray.

❺ Terracotta
The kind of brown seen on terracotta plant pots.

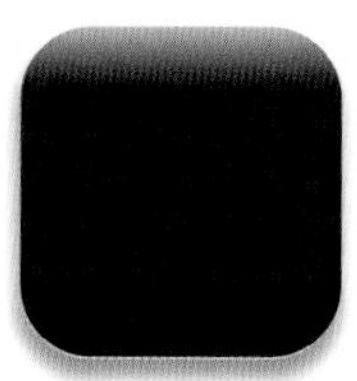

❻ Warm Brown
A strong brown with the faintest hint of yellow.

❼ Evening Cloud
Contrasting with orange, this is the color of a cloud that appears blue.

❽ Evening Sky
The color of the evening sky tinged with purple.

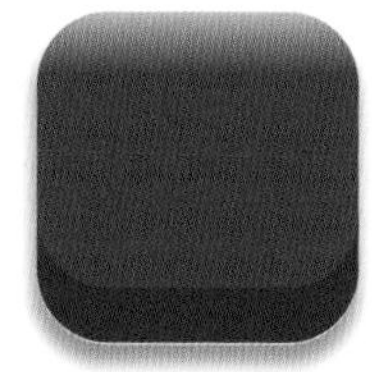

❾ Beach Green
The dull, faded green of foliage by the beach.

1 C0 M43 Y67 K0
R245 G168 B89
#F4A759

2 C0 M53 Y80 K15
R218 G132 B51
#D98332

3 C0 M37 Y80 K60
R133 G94 B19
#845D13

4 C0 M25 Y40 K40
R177 G146 B112
#B0916F

5 C0 M57 Y53 K30
R190 G109 B84
#BD6C53

6 C0 M40 Y100 K90
R62 G34 B0
#3D2100

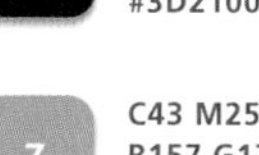

7 C43 M25 Y10 K0
R157 G177 B205
#9CB0CD

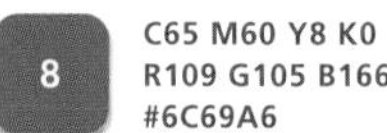

8 C65 M60 Y8 K0
R109 G105 B166
#6C69A6

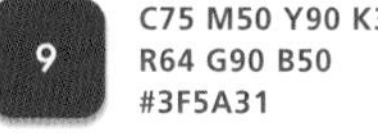

9 C75 M50 Y90 K30
R64 G90 B50
#3F5A31

Two-color combinations

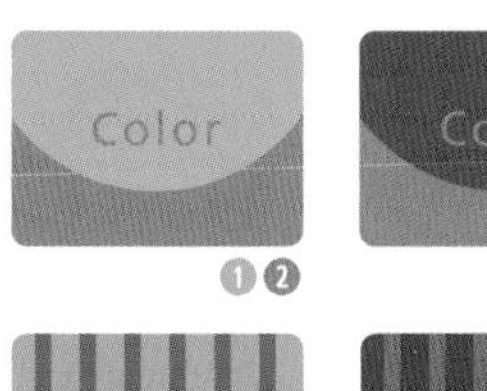
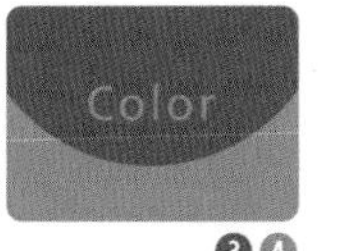
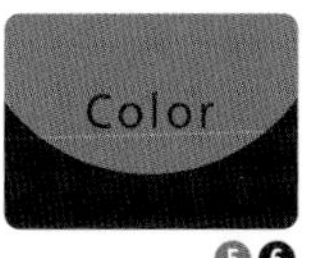
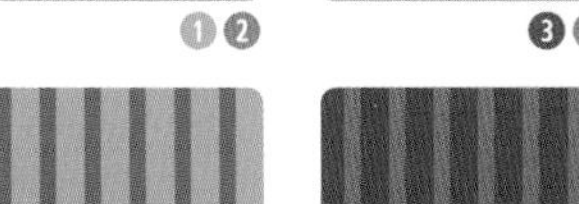
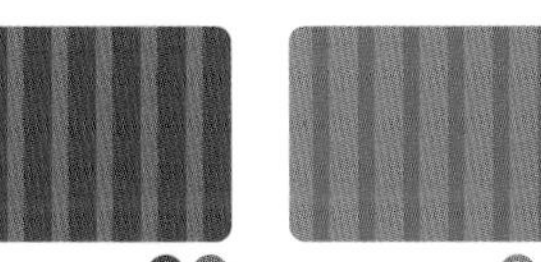
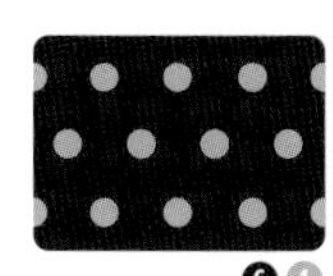
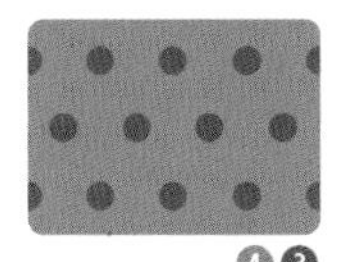
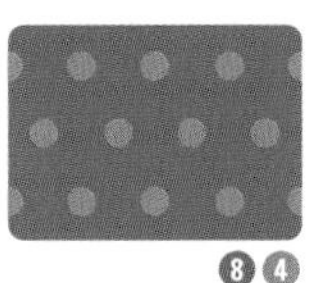

1 2 | 3 4 | 5 6

7 8 | 9 5 | 2 8

6 1 | 4 3 | 8 4

Three-color combinations

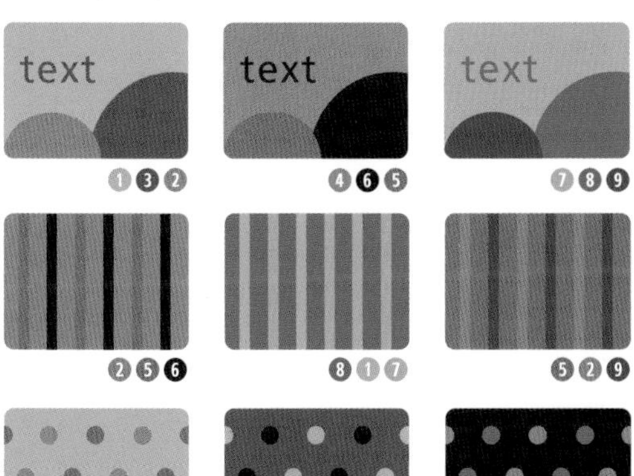

1 3 2 | 4 6 5 | 7 8 9

2 5 6 | 8 1 7 | 5 2 9

1 4 5 | 3 6 1 | 6 8 2

Designs

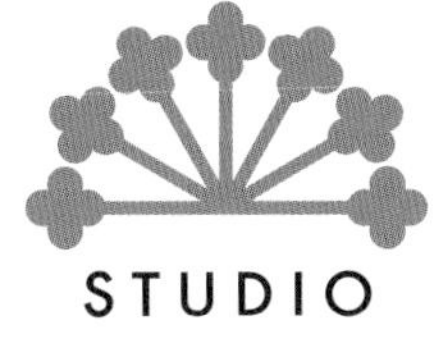

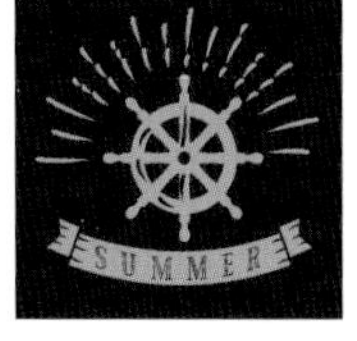
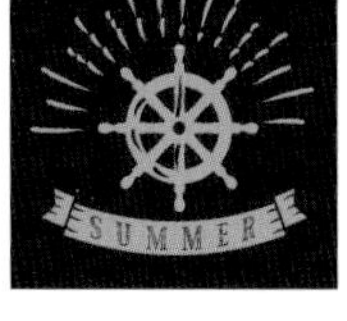

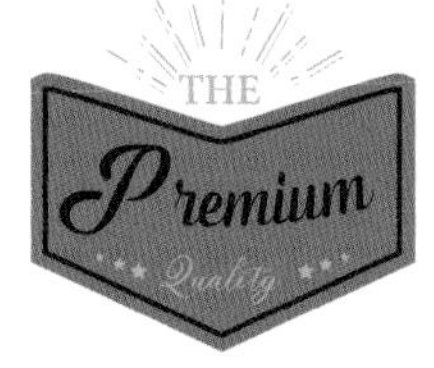

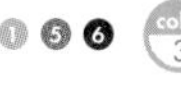

2 6 color 2 | 6 8 color 2 | 1 5 6 color 3

Patterns

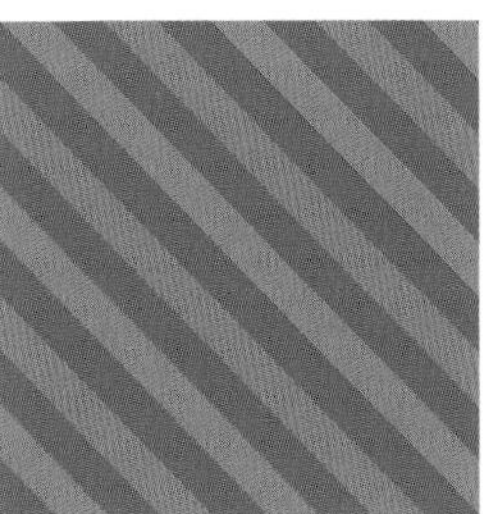
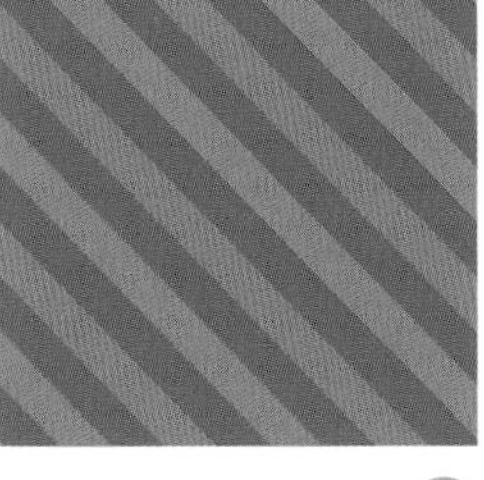
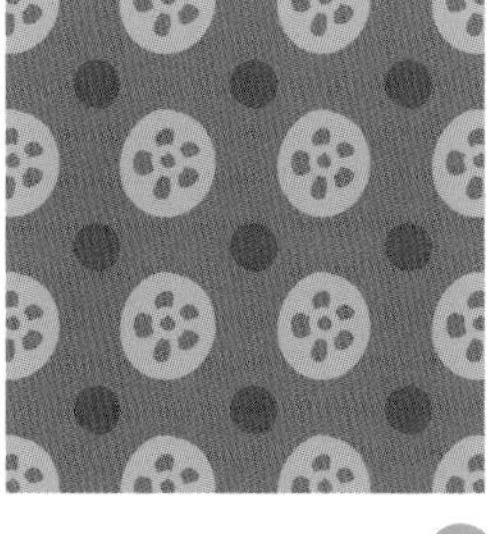
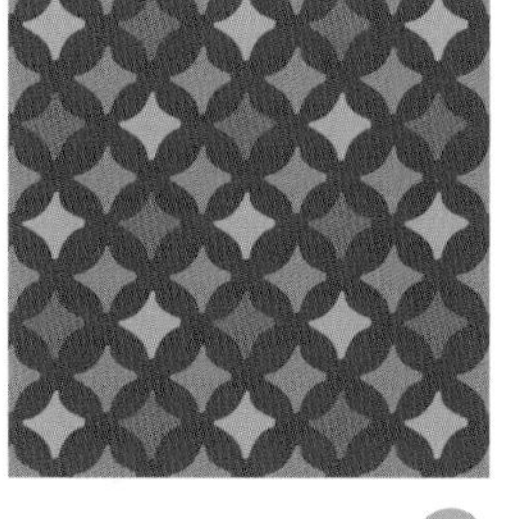

2 4 8 color 3 | 1 3 5 color 3 | 4 5 7 9 color 4

Illustration

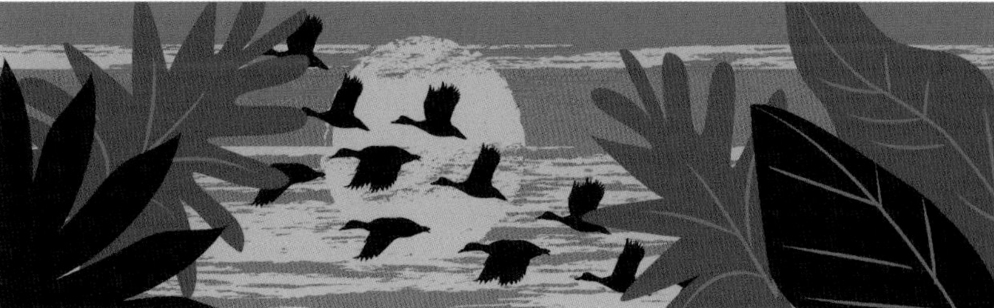

1 5 6 8 9 color 5

Recipe
055

Indian Spice Market

An everyday meal in India, curry is a dish made by simmering together plenty of vegetables and spices. Bubbling like water, the color changes depending on the combination of spices used. The type and amount of spices used depend on that day's weather and the available ingredients. A multitude of spices is sold by weight at markets.

- **FEELING** Ethnic, spicy, hot.
- **COMBINATIONS** Focus on deep, warm colors such as red, yellow and orange.
- **TIPS** Take special care to use dark colors and colors with depth.

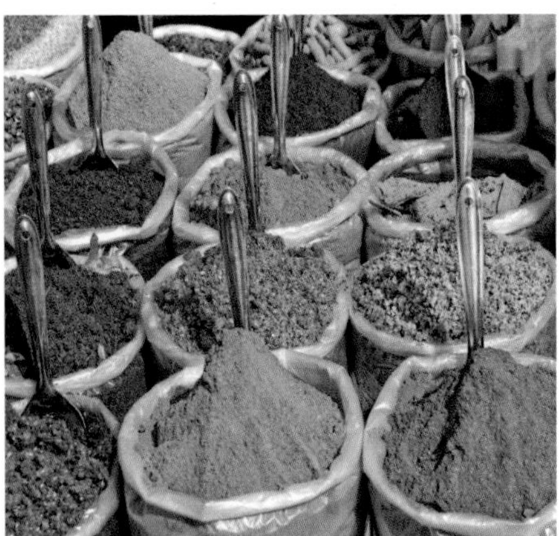

Indian cuisine derives its distinctive flavors from spices.

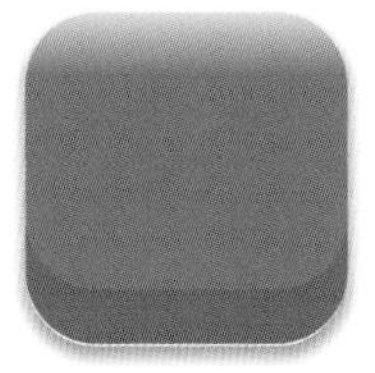

❶ **Turmeric**
A golden spice that gives curry its color.

❷ **Chili Pepper**
Red chili pepper that has been ground into a spicy powder.

❸ **Cayenne Pepper**
The powder of the cayenne variety of pepper.

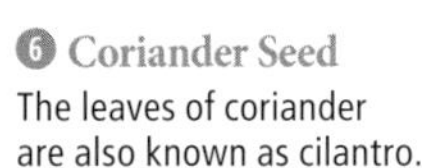

❹ **Cardamom**
The king of fragrances, this is also used in sweet, refreshing chai.

❺ **Bay Leaf**
A standard addition to soups and stewed dishes.

❻ **Coriander Seed**
The leaves of coriander are also known as cilantro.

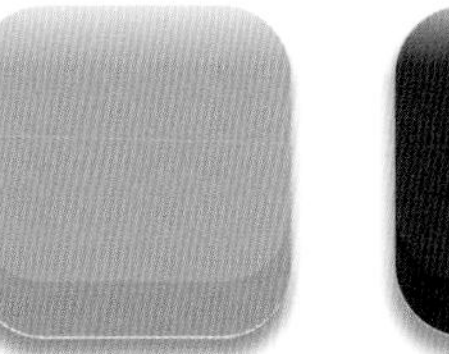

❼ **Cumin Seed**
The pleasing aroma of curry is helped by the addition of cumin seed.

❽ **Clove**
In 17th-century Europe, cloves were used to purify the air.

❾ **Garam Masala**
A mixed spice and an Indian staple.

1 C20 M30 Y100 K5 R207 G173 B0 #CFAC00

2 C25 M90 Y100 K0 R194 G58 B30 #C13A1E

3 C17 M60 Y100 K0 R211 G124 B11 #D27B0B

4 C65 M45 Y100 K0 R110 G126 B49 #6E7E31

5 C20 M3 Y70 K30 R170 G177 B80 #AAB050

6 C0 M15 Y80 K40 R179 G155 B42 #B39A29

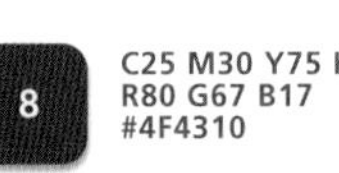

7 C20 M13 Y53 K13 R196 G193 B127 #C4C07E

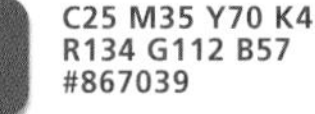

8 C25 M30 Y75 K75 R80 G67 B17 #4F4310

9 C25 M35 Y70 K45 R134 G112 B57 #867039

Two-color combinations

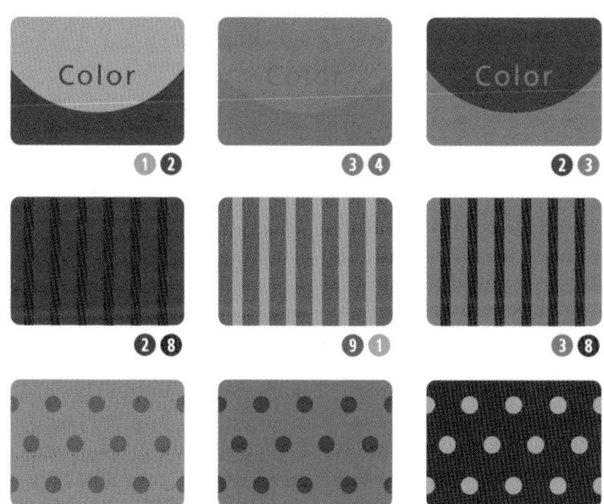

Three-color combinations

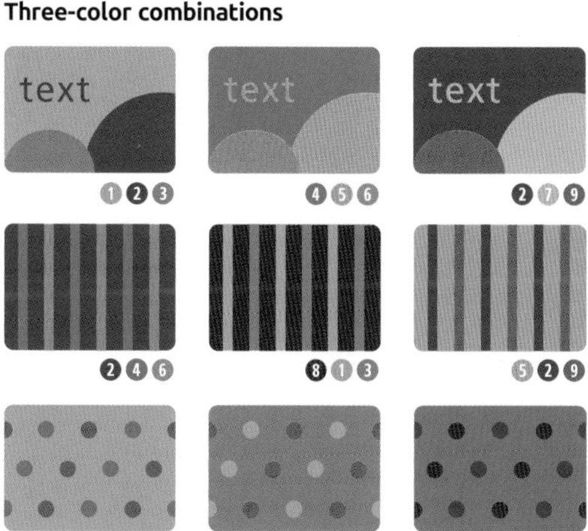

Designs

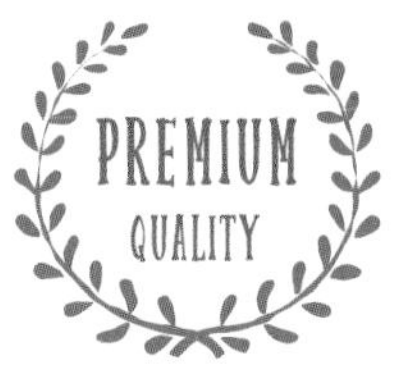

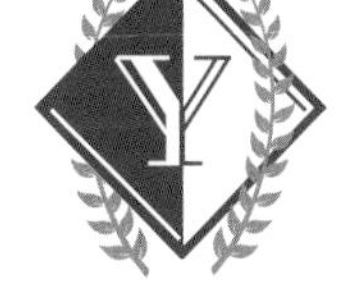

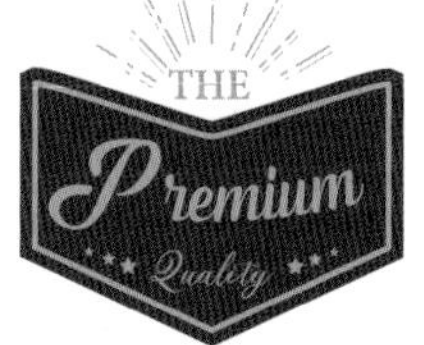

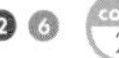

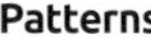

Patterns

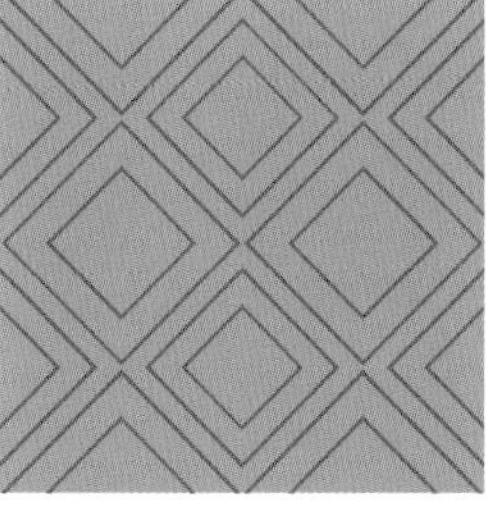

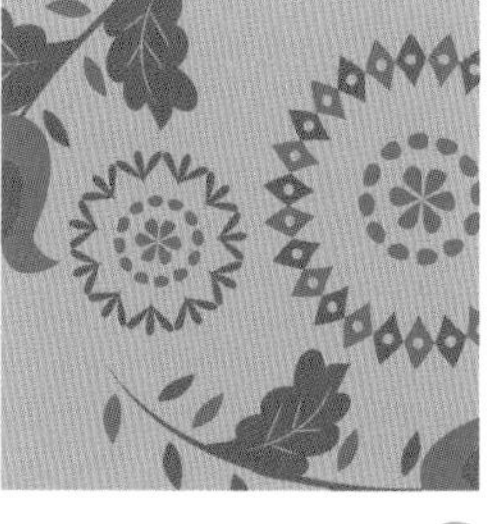

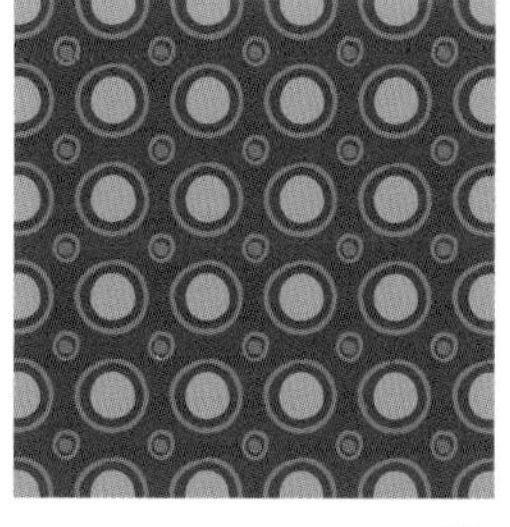

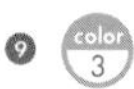

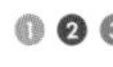

Illustration

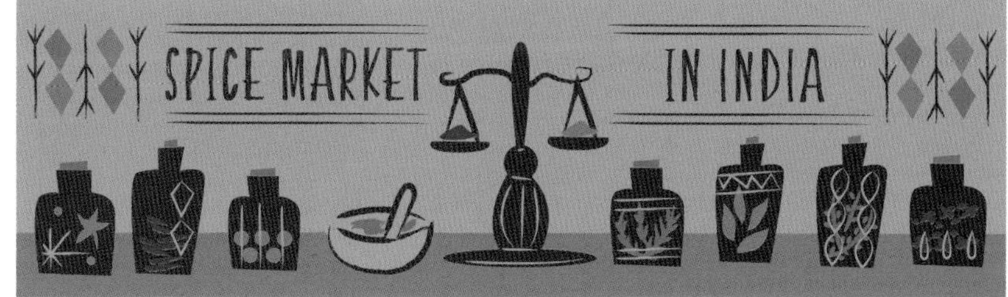

Recipe
056

Chinatown Good Luck Charm

In response to the question "What would be your country's national color?" 52.5 percent of Chinese answered "bright red." Barely a majority, but it shows how key to the culture the color is. Talismans are made in schemes of red with gold (or yellow), a pairing seen at Chinese New Year.

- **FEELING** Gaudy, good fortune, lively.
- **COMBINATIONS** Use red and gold over large surface areas for an authentic air.
- **TIPS** Yellow and ochre shades can substitute for gold.

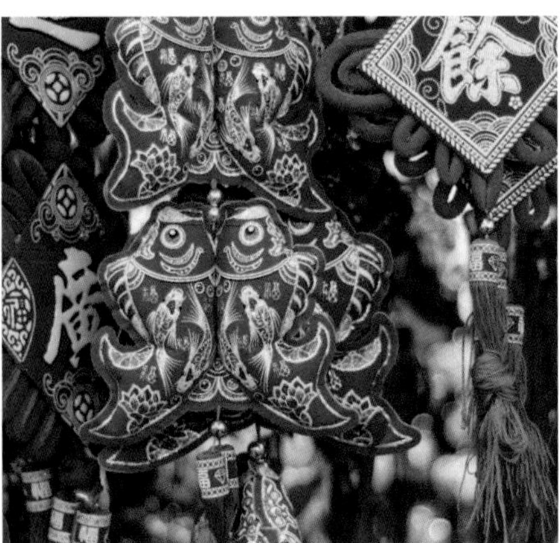

Red and gold are the main colors for Chinese lucky charms.

❶ Chinese Red
A vermilion made using a pigment made from a mineral called cinnabar.

❷ Good Luck Yellow
A bright yellow that would seem to usher in happiness.

❸ Chinese Blue
A greenish blue that is more vibrant than turquoise blue.

❹ Better Fortune
A deep, dense yellow that indicates good times ahead.

❺ Orient Purple
A vivid purple with reddish tones that makes a showy impression.

❻ Warm Red
A red tinged with yellow that has a warm feel.

❼ Signal Red
The red of a traffic light, a color that really stands out.

❽ Pure Green
A green like that squeezed out of a paint tube.

❾ Vivid Blue
A vivid blue that adds accent to warm colors.

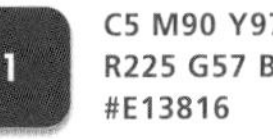

1 C5 M90 Y97 K0
R225 G57 B22
#E13816

2 C15 M10 Y97 K0
R228 G214 B0
#E3D600

3 C97 M20 Y0 K0
R0 G141 B215
#008DD6

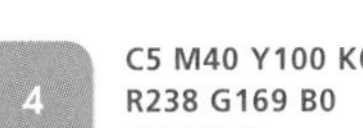

4 C5 M40 Y100 K0
R238 G169 B0
#EEA800

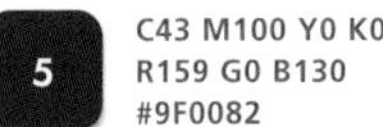

5 C43 M100 Y0 K0
R159 G0 B130
#9F0082

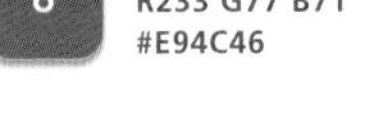

6 C0 M83 Y65 K0
R233 G77 B71
#E94C46

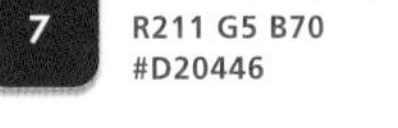

7 C13 M100 Y60 K0
R211 G5 B70
#D20446

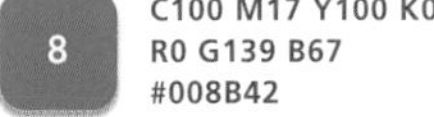

8 C100 M17 Y100 K0
R0 G139 B67
#008B42

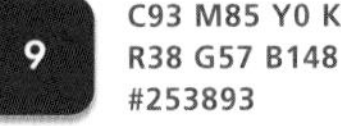

9 C93 M85 Y0 K0
R38 G57 B148
#253893

Two-color combinations

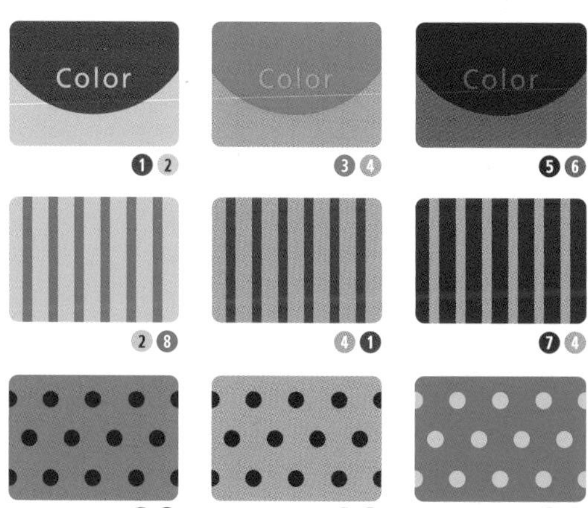

Three-color combinations

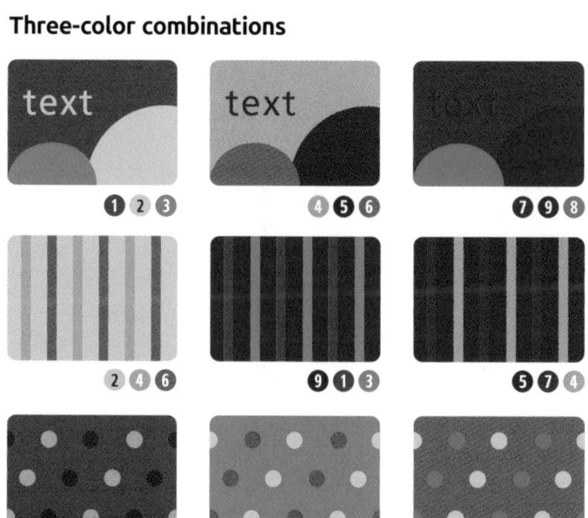

Designs

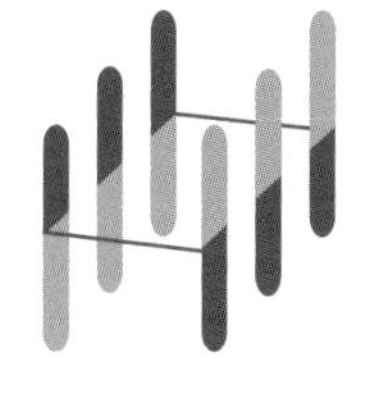

1 4 color 2

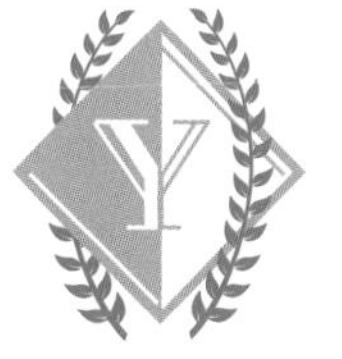

4 8 color 2

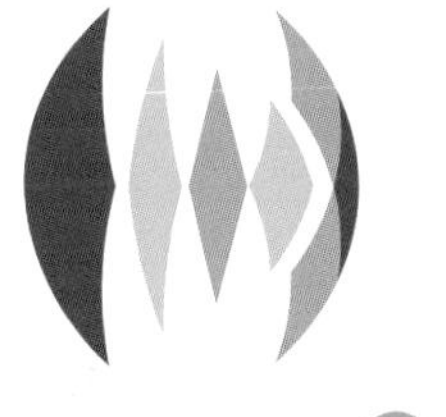

1 2 4 color 3

Patterns

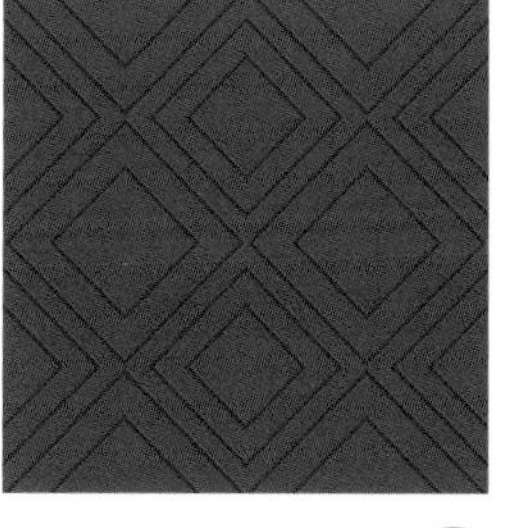

1 9 color 2

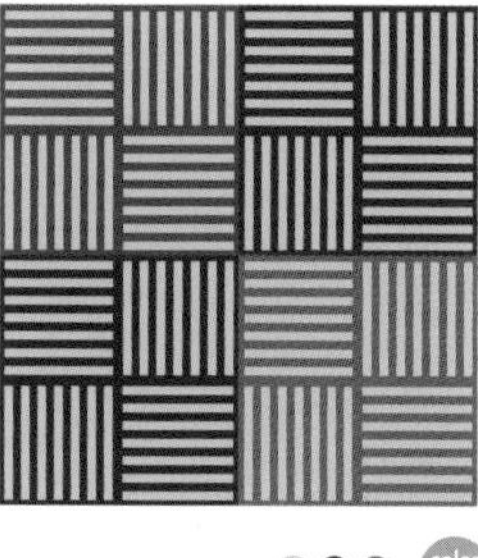

2 5 6 color 3

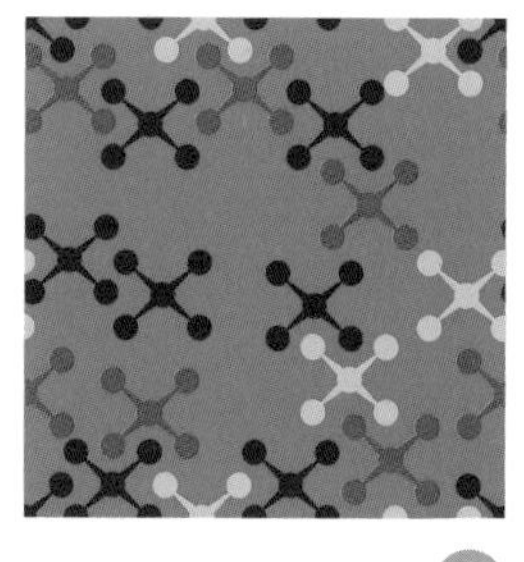

2 3 5 6 color 4

Illustration

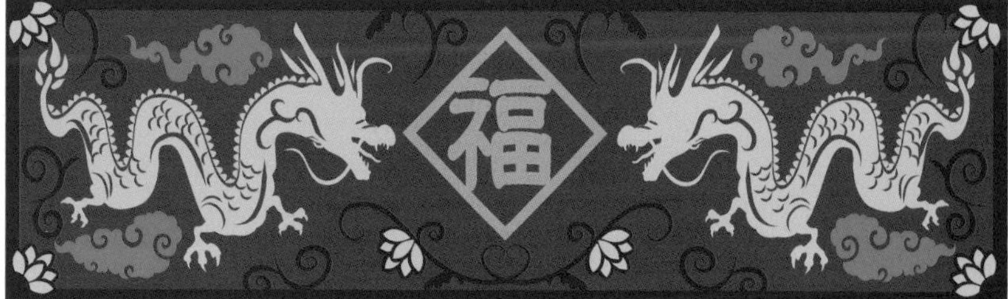

1 2 3 4 9 

Recipe
057

African Dresses

African fabrics have distinctive patterns and coloration. Earth tones are offset and highlighted with warm or rich tones. In Japan, colors that complement one's particular skin tone are called personal colors. According to that philosophy, the palette on this page is made up of colors with a yellow base that are categorized as fall colors.

- **FEELING** Having depth, powerful, a sense of stability.
- **COMBINATIONS** Use deep warm colors, focusing on shades of brown.
- **TIPS** White also works well as an accent color.

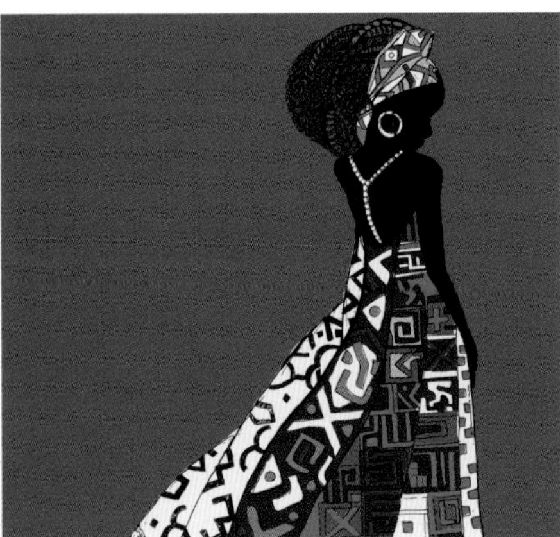

A cohesive look can be created when multiple colors are used because of their commonality.

❶ Mahogany
A brown with strong, red timber-like tones.

❷ Carbon Black
Carbon is used as a coloring agent.

❸ Nile River
A deep greenish blue that recalls the upper Nile River.

❹ Rooibos Tea
A tea from southern Africa that has excellent antioxidant effects.

❺ Dark Brown
A brown that is close to a black with low levels of luminosity.

❻ Shrimp Pink
A pink tinged with orange like that of a shrimp.

❼ Mustard Gold
A gold with yellow tones like mustard.

❽ Cacao
In Greek, cacao is theobroma, which means "food of the gods."

❾ Safari Pink
The kind of pink seen on birds such as flamingos.

1 C55 M97 Y95 K0 R139 G45 B47 #8A2D2F

2 C0 M2 Y0 K95 R47 G38 B36 #2E2624

3 C70 M0 Y40 K23 R35 G155 B145 #239A90

4 C30 M80 Y77 K0 R186 G81 B62 #BA503D

5 C35 M60 Y45 K75 R70 G38 B40 #462628

6 C10 M35 Y50 K0 R230 G180 B130 #E5B381

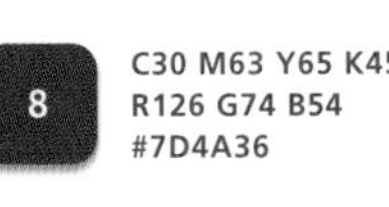

7 C30 M50 Y87 K30 R151 G109 B39 #966C26

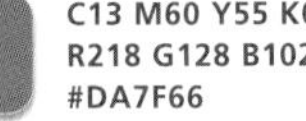

8 C30 M63 Y65 K45 R126 G74 B54 #7D4A36

9 C13 M60 Y55 K0 R218 G128 B102 #DA7F66

Two-color combinations

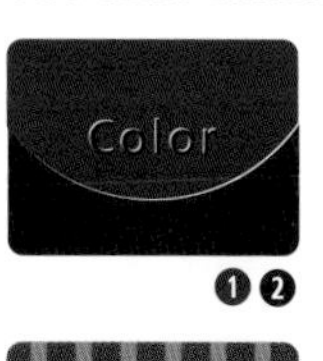

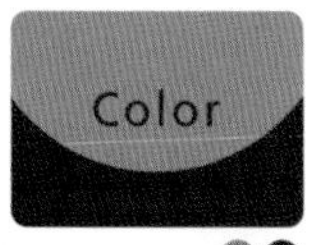

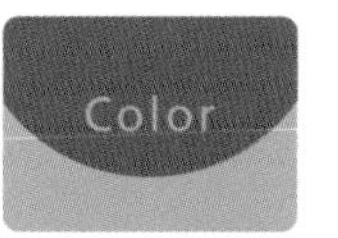

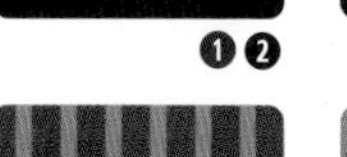
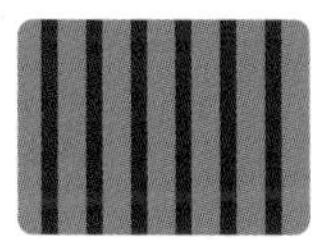
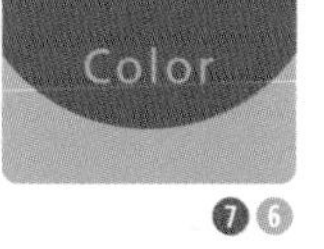
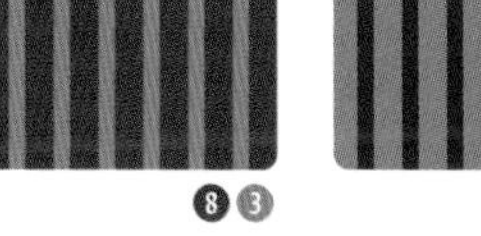
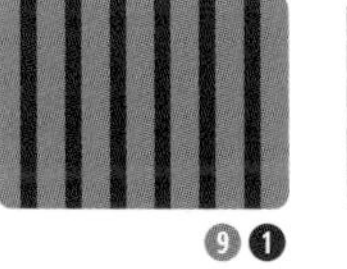
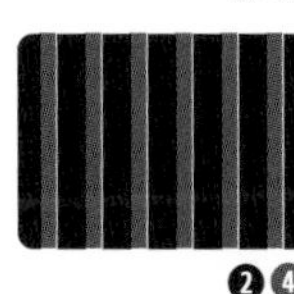
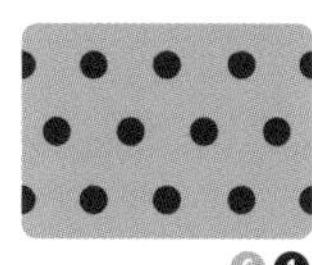
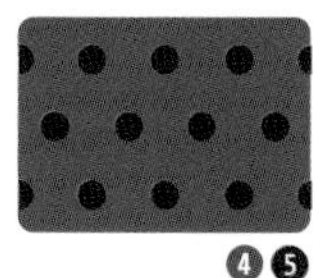
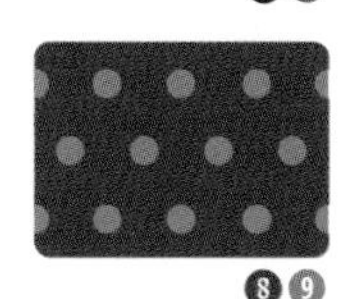

1 2 · 3 5 · 7 6

8 3 · 9 1 · 2 4

6 1 · 4 5 · 8 9

Three-color combinations

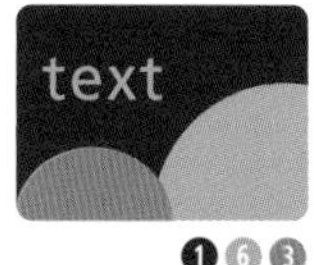

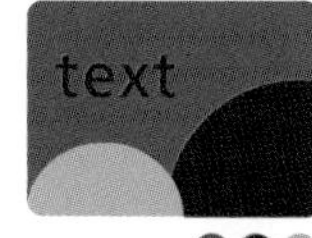

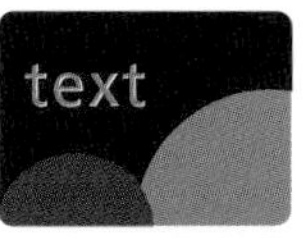

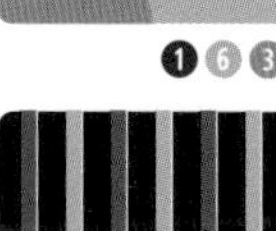

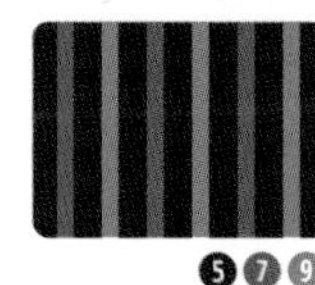
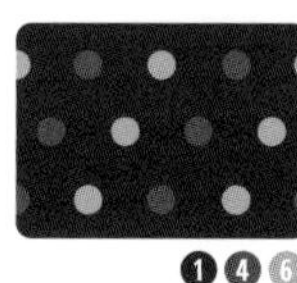
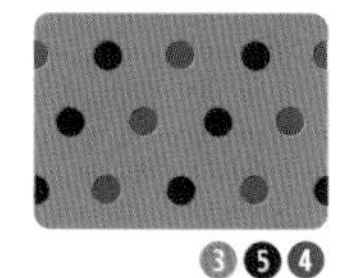
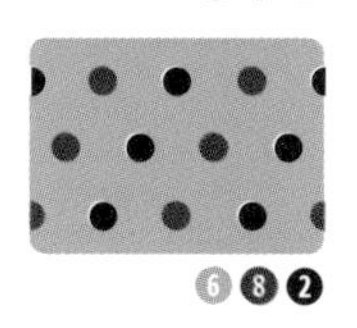

1 6 3 · 4 5 6 · 2 9 8

2 4 6 · 6 1 3 · 5 7 9

1 4 6 · 3 5 4 · 6 8 2

Designs

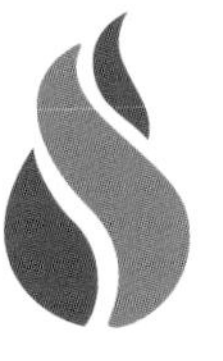

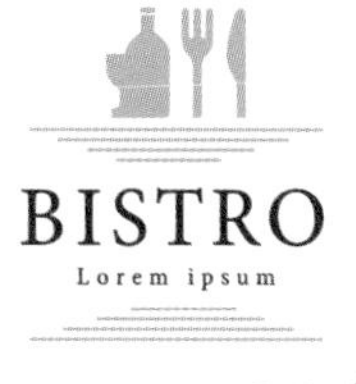

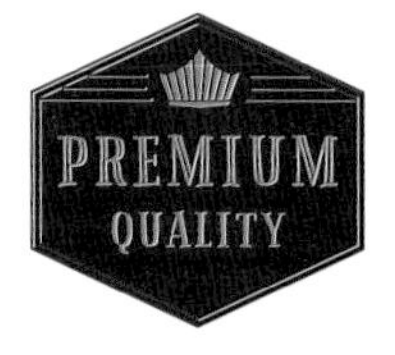

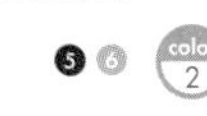
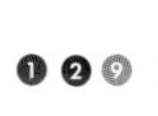

4 9 color 2 · 5 6 color 2 · 1 2 9 color 3

Patterns

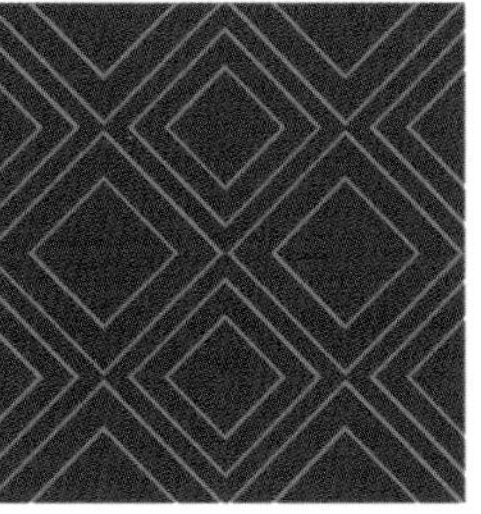
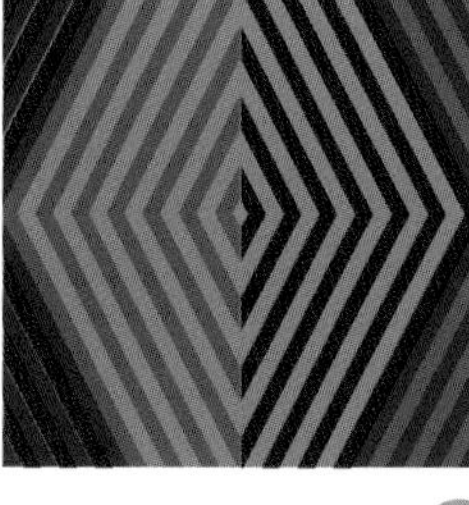
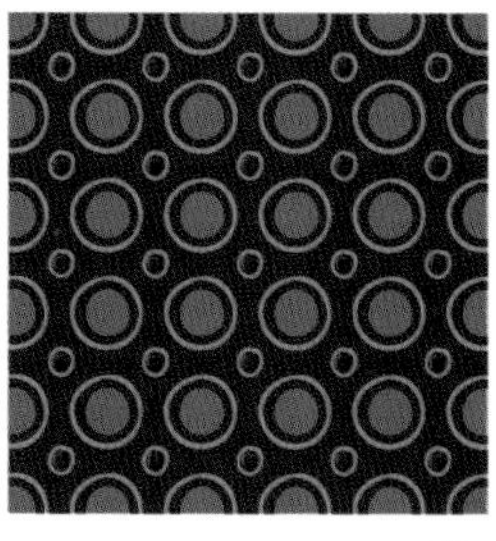
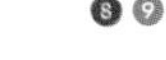

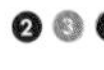

8 9 color 2 · 1 4 5 9 color 4 · 2 3 5 7 color 4

Illustration

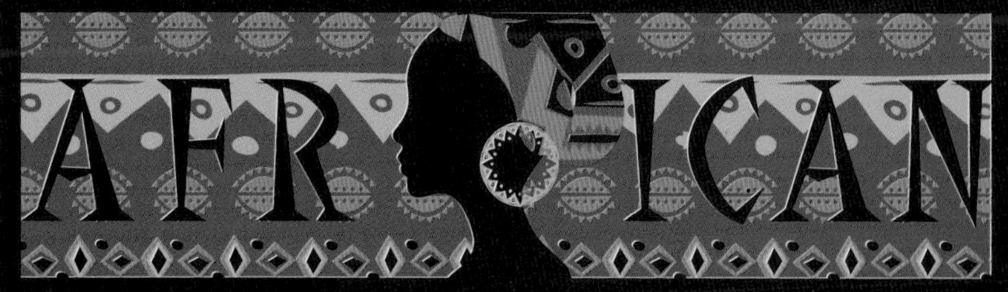

2 3 4 6 7 color 5

Recipe
058

Friendship Bracelets

Friendship bracelets originated in Brazil. Once they're tied on, they're customarily worn until the threads break. In Japan, they became widely known due to Brazilian-born soccer players wearing them, and many people wear them as accessories. For wishes related to love, bracelets containing red or pink are tied around the wrist of the dominant hand.

- **FEELING** Connected, powerful, understated.
- **COMBINATIONS** Use a multiple of medium colors for a muted look.
- **TIPS** All the colors are medium to low intensity, so select hues freely.

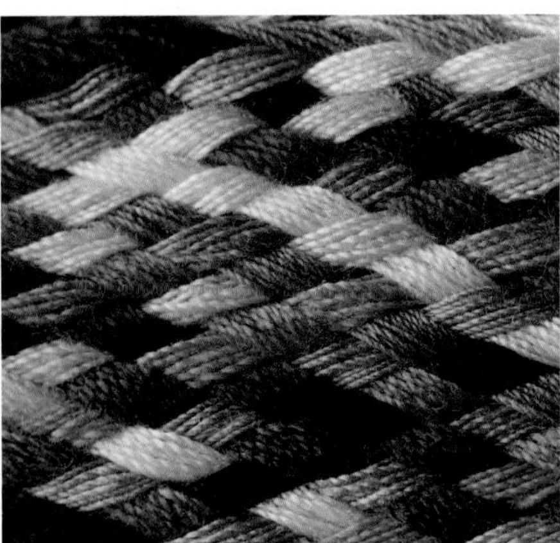

Medium colors refer to those to which gray has been added to form a dull shade for a peaceful, chic impression.

❶ Chestnut
The brown of a chestnut casing.

❷ Toy Poodle
The color of the fluffy coat of a toy poodle.

❸ Deep Forest
The color of a deep forest thick with trees.

❹ Red Ochre
The first color used in the history of humankind; red earth.

❺ Red Fox
A brown with strong red tones like that of a red fox's fur.

❻ Dusty Pink
A dusty, dull pink.

❼ Egyptian Blue
One of the oldest synthetic pigments in human history.

❽ Navy Blue
The color of the uniforms worn by the British Navy.

❾ Dried Herb
The faded green of dried herbs.

1 C40 M85 Y60 K55 R98 G31 B43 #611E2A

2 C20 M35 Y45 K20 R182 G150 B121 #B69678

3 C77 M45 Y75 K40 R46 G86 B61 #2E553C

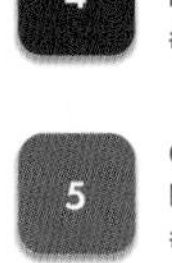

4 C15 M90 Y80 K30 R166 G41 B37 #A62925

5 C0 M60 Y75 K27 R195 G106 B51 #C26A32

6 C23 M70 Y37 K0 R199 G103 B121 #C66778

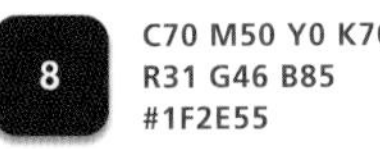

7 C70 M20 Y25 K30 R50 G128 B146 #317F91

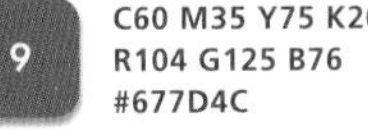

8 C70 M50 Y0 K70 R31 G46 B85 #1F2E55

9 C60 M35 Y75 K20 R104 G125 B76 #677D4C

Two-color combinations

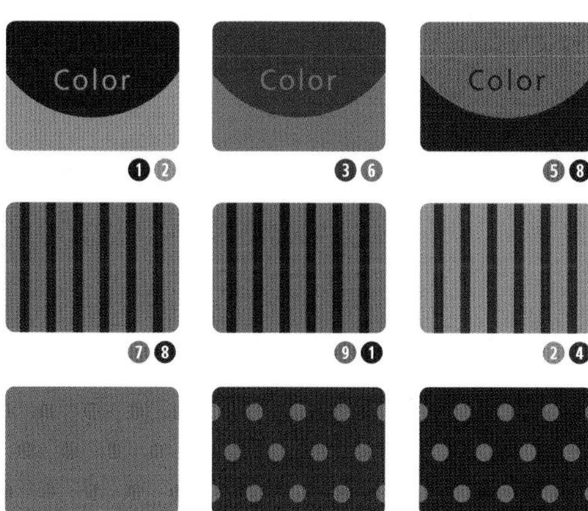

Three-color combinations

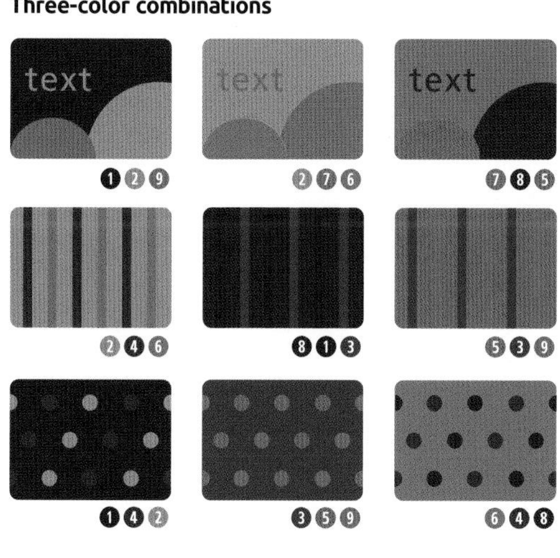

Designs

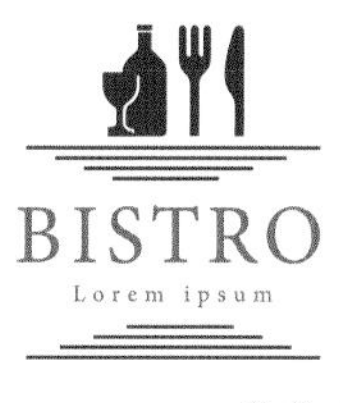

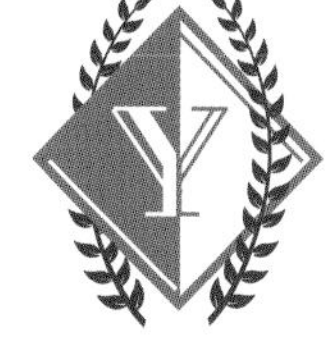

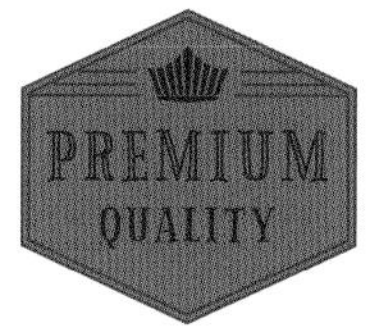

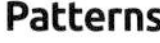

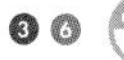

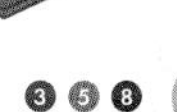

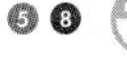

Patterns

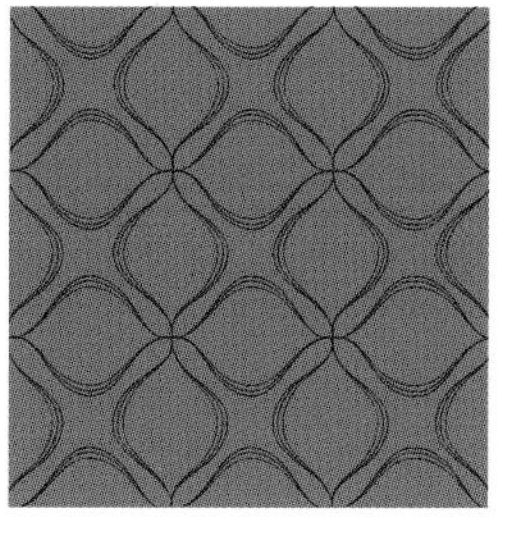

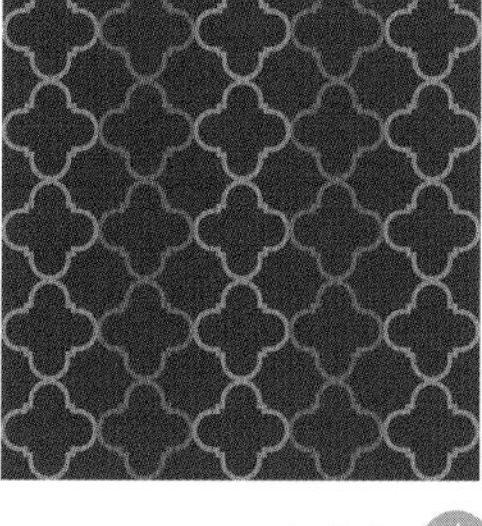

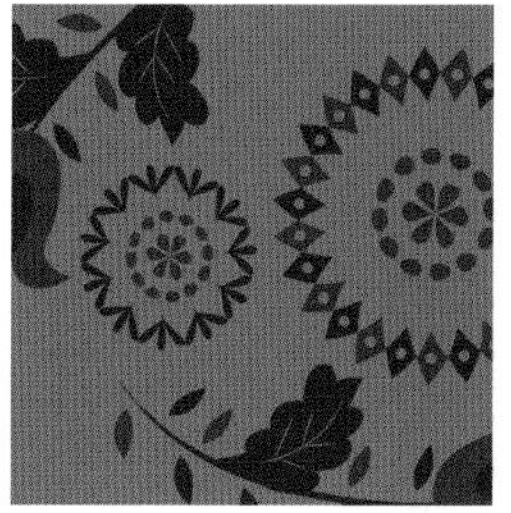

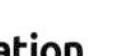

2 3 9 color 3

1 4 7 color 3

Illustration

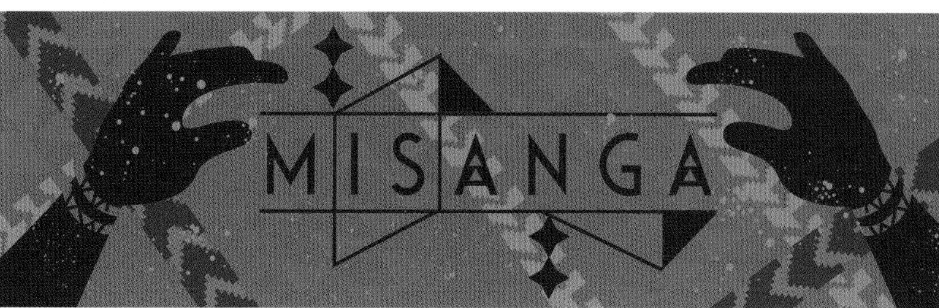

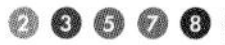

PART 07

DYNAMIC + ETHNIC

Recipe
059

Beadwork Pendants

The pendants the locals make are full of energy and color. I can't resist touching them! I know that once I go back to Japan, I'll never wear them as they're so gaudy, but I can't stop myself from buying them. Rising above the rules for color schemes, these fun pendants seem to exist simply to take in the power of color.

- **FEELING** Colorful, bold, energetic.
- **COMBINATIONS** Freely combine vivid colors.
- **TIPS** Ideal for when an eye-catching color scheme is needed.

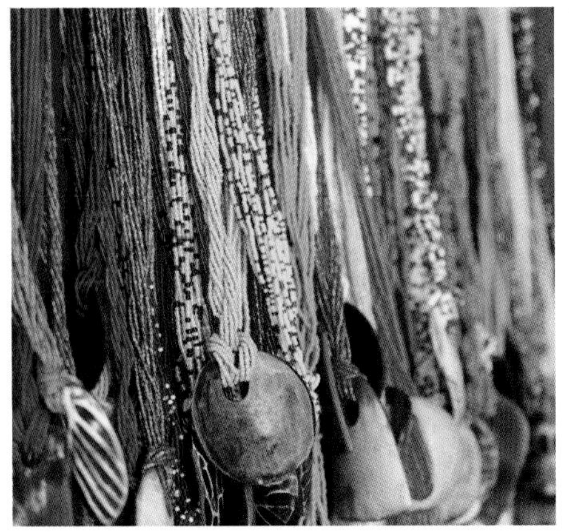

The chaotic jumble of colors makes a powerful impression.

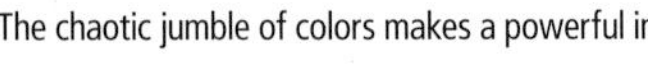

❶ Caribbean Sea
A deep, dense blue like that of the Caribbean Sea.

❷ Mango Yellow
A rich, dense yellow like that of a ripe mango.

❸ Vivid Red
A vivid red like that of a hibiscus flower.

❹ Jungle Green
A powerful green like that of a lush, dense jungle.

❺ Citrus Orange
The color of a fresh, juicy orange.

❻ Equator Blue
A color evoking the sky shimmering in the heat in equatorial countries.

❼ Dusty Lavender
A lavender color that appears faded from the strong sunlight.

❽ Coconut White
The white of the edible flesh inside a coconut.

❾ Coconut Brown
The deep reddish brown of the outer section of a coconut shell.

1	C65 M35 Y0 K10 R89 G135 B191 #5887BF
2	C3 M23 Y90 K0 R248 G202 B18 #F7CA11
3	C5 M70 Y75 K0 R229 G108 B62 #E56C3E
4	C75 M25 Y80 K3 R62 G144 B86 #3D9055
5	C2 M55 Y90 K0 R239 G141 B30 #EE8D1E
6	C50 M10 Y20 K0 R135 G192 B202 #86BFC9
7	C53 M70 Y35 K0 R140 G94 B125 #8C5D7C
8	C0 M3 Y5 K5 R247 G243 B237 #F7F3ED
9	C20 M65 Y70 K45 R138 G74 B46 #89492E

Two-color combinations

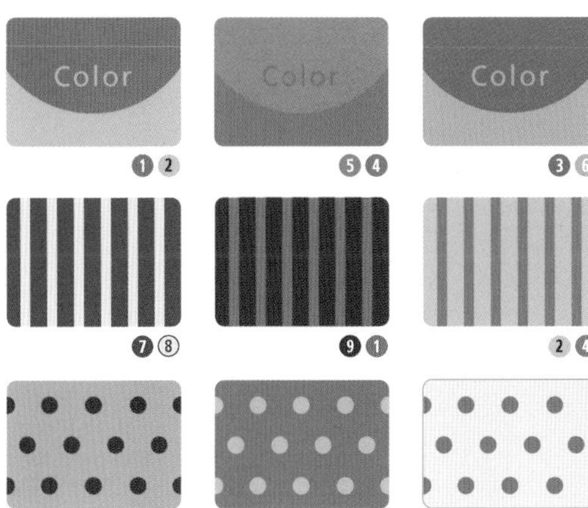

Three-color combinations

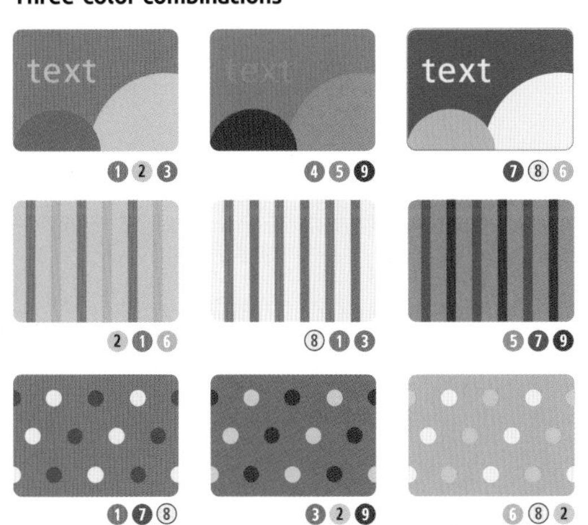

Designs

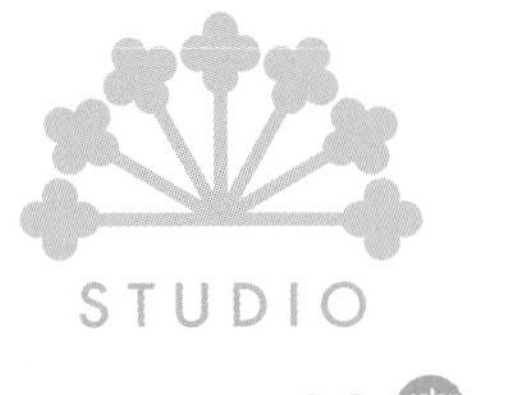

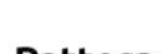

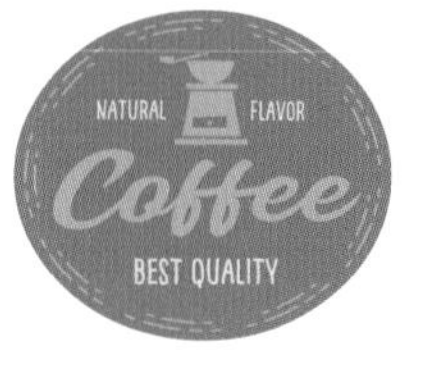

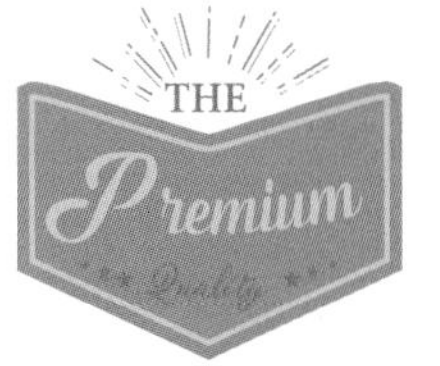

Patterns

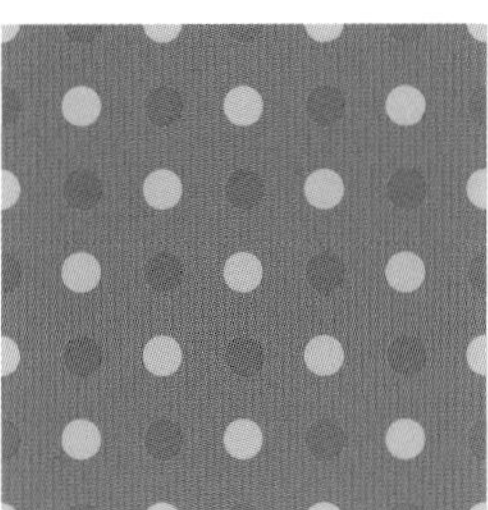

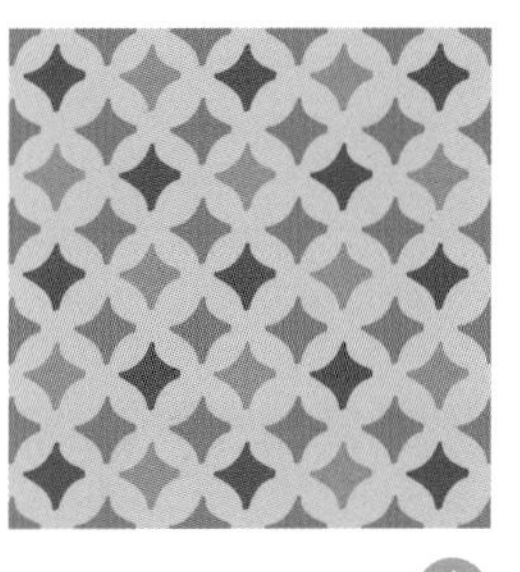

Illustration

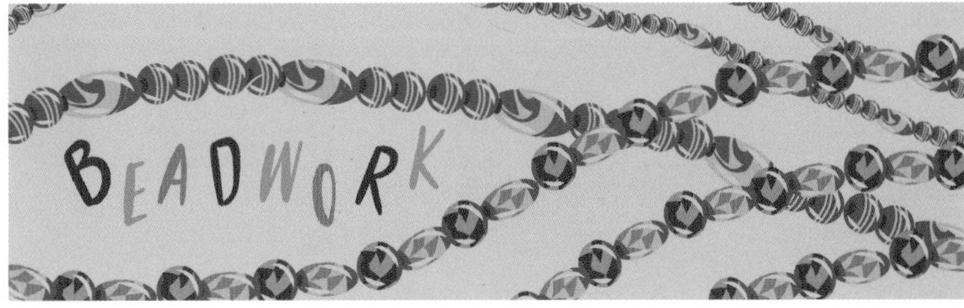

Recipe
060

Ethnic Fabrics

Simply looking at the fabrics in Asian countries perks me up. I'll make a cosmetics pouch from the vivid pink and deep green cloth, and maybe coasters from the eye-popping yellow fabric with purple accents. On fall nights, at the sewing machine, my thoughts drift to my Asian travels.

- **FEELING** Lively, fun, festive.
- **COMBINATIONS** Use vivid colors, focusing on warm shades.
- **TIPS** Yellow based colors are also effective.

Dark colors serve as accents to pull together the overall color scheme.

❶ Orange Red
An orange close to red that exudes warmth and heat.

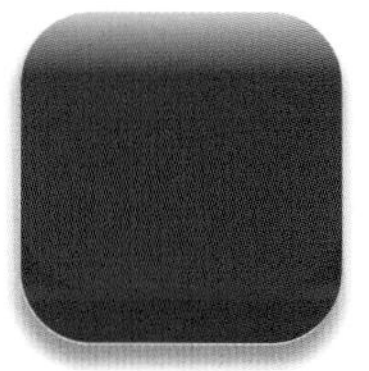

❷ Awakening Purple
A vibrant, eye-catching purple.

❸ Saffron Yellow
The yellow of pigment harvested from saffron flowers.

❹ Yellow Green
A bright, brilliant yellow green that appears to sparkle.

❺ Psychedelic Pink
Psychedelic colors are colors that were popular in the 1960s.

❻ Bright Coral
A color that is more intense than coral pink.

❼ Chai
Indian-style milk tea that is sweet and spicy.

❽ Caramel
The brown of sweet caramel.

❾ Ivy Green
The deep, dark green of ivy leaves.

No.	CMYK	RGB	Hex
1	C0 M85 Y100 K5	R226 G69 B8	#E24507
2	C40 M90 Y0 K3	R163 G47 B138	#A22E8A
3	C5 M23 Y100 K0	R244 G200 B0	#F3C800
4	C47 M5 Y100 K0	R152 G193 B27	#98C01A
5	C5 M100 Y0 K6	R214 G0 B123	#D5007A
6	C3 M67 Y63 K5	R226 G112 B81	#E26F50
7	C5 M30 Y47 K25	R198 G159 B116	#C69F73
8	C0 M63 Y90 K40	R170 G86 B10	#A9560A
9	C80 M40 Y90 K40	R34 G89 B47	#21592E

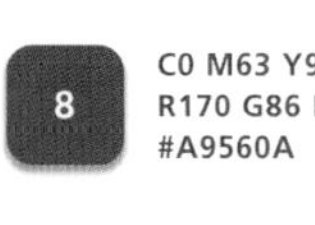

Two-color combinations

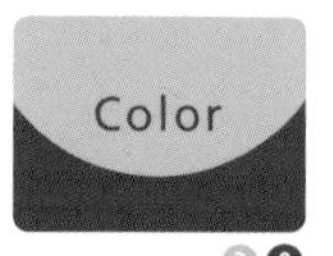

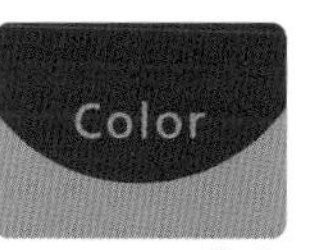

1 2 | 3 9 | 5 7

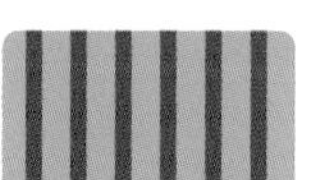

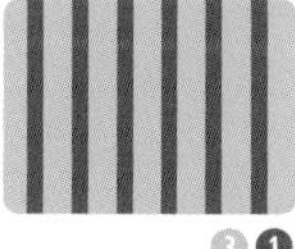

4 8 | 3 1 | 2 5

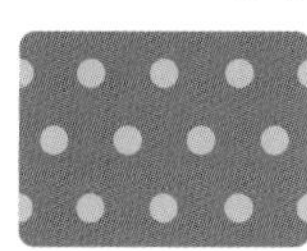

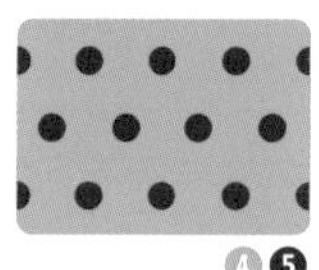

6 3 | 4 5 | 8 9

Three-color combinations

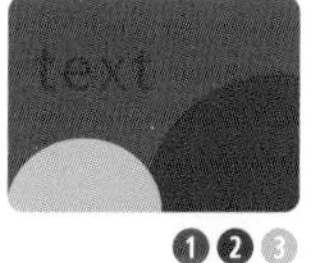

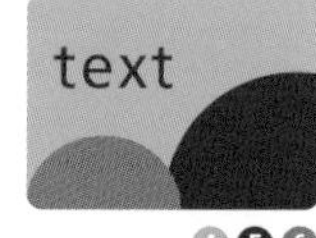

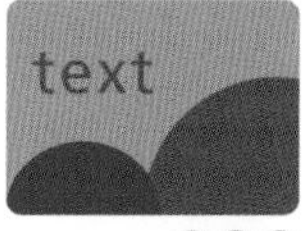

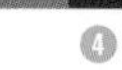

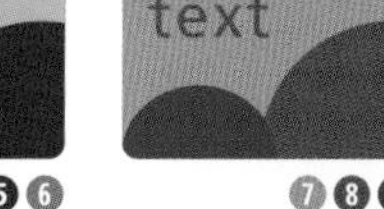

1 2 3 | 4 5 6 | 7 8 9

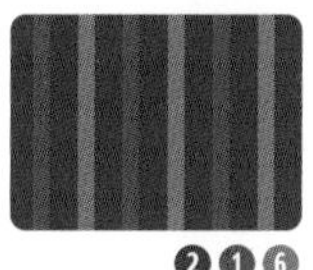

2 1 6 | 8 6 2 | 5 1 9

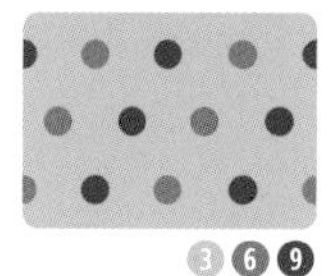

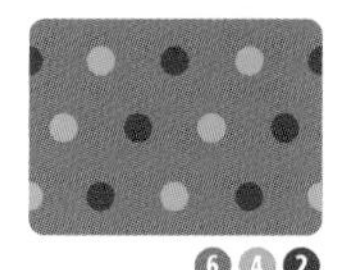

1 4 3 | 3 6 9 | 6 4 2

Designs

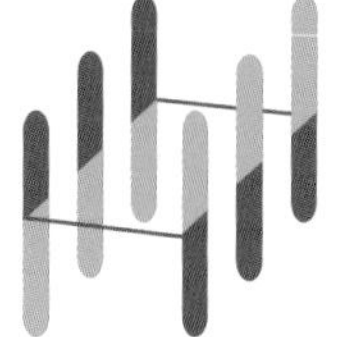

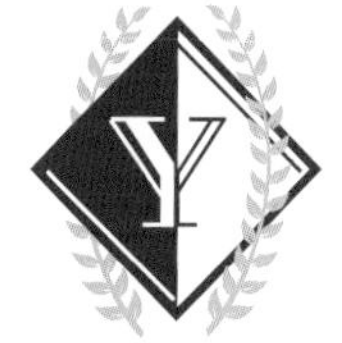

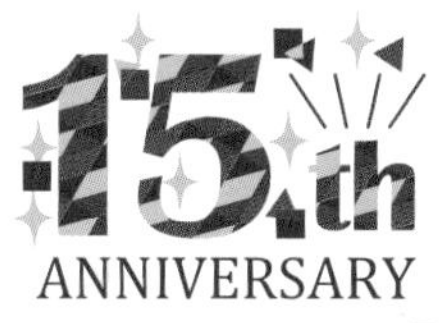

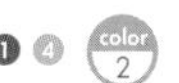

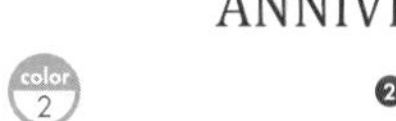

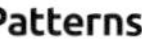

1 4 color 2 | 3 5 color 2 | 2 3 5 8 color 4

Patterns

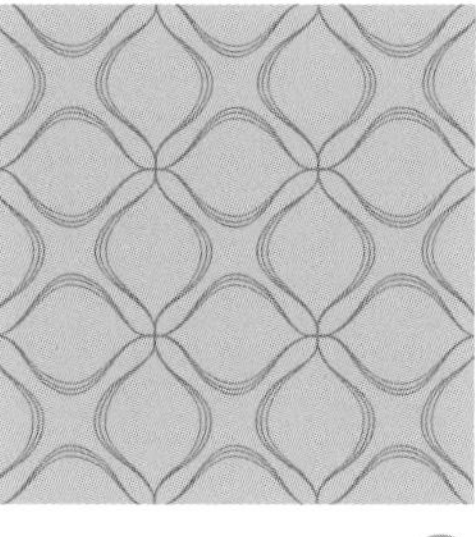

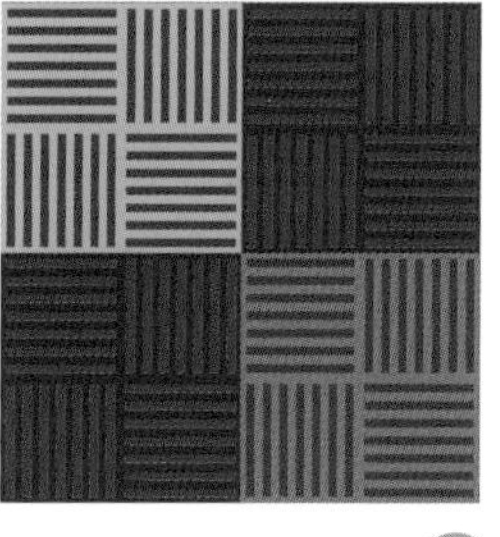

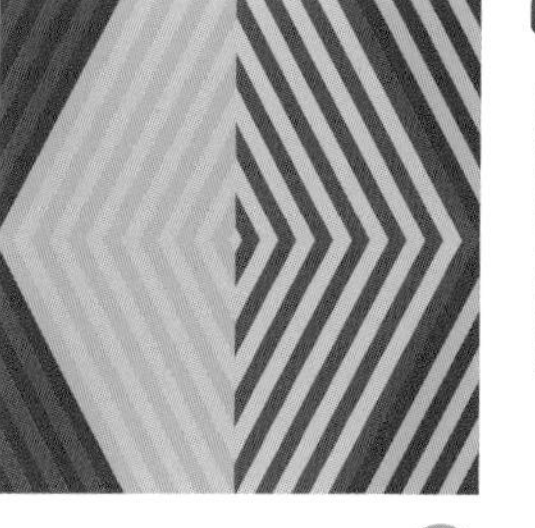

3 6 color 2 | 4 5 6 9 color 4 | 1 3 4 9 color 4

Illustration

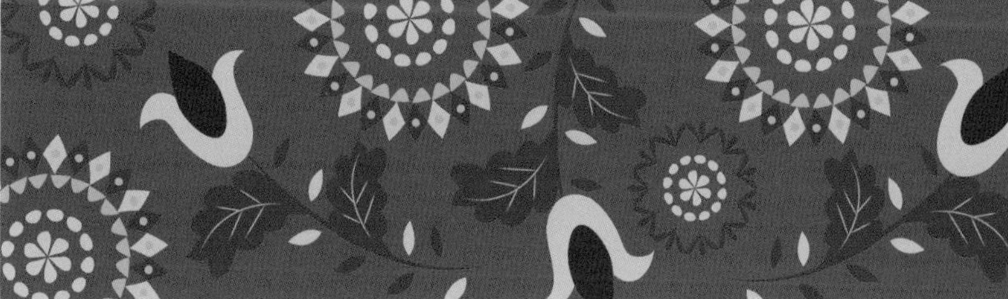

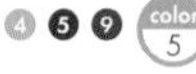

1 3 4 5 9 color 5

Part
08

Classic + Chic

This color palette conjures old and traditional items and treasured keepsakes. The understated, deep tones convey a classic impression. Old maps, fountain pens, men's suits open the door to nostalgia's many hues.

Color Schemes With a Traditional, Authentic, Refined Feel.

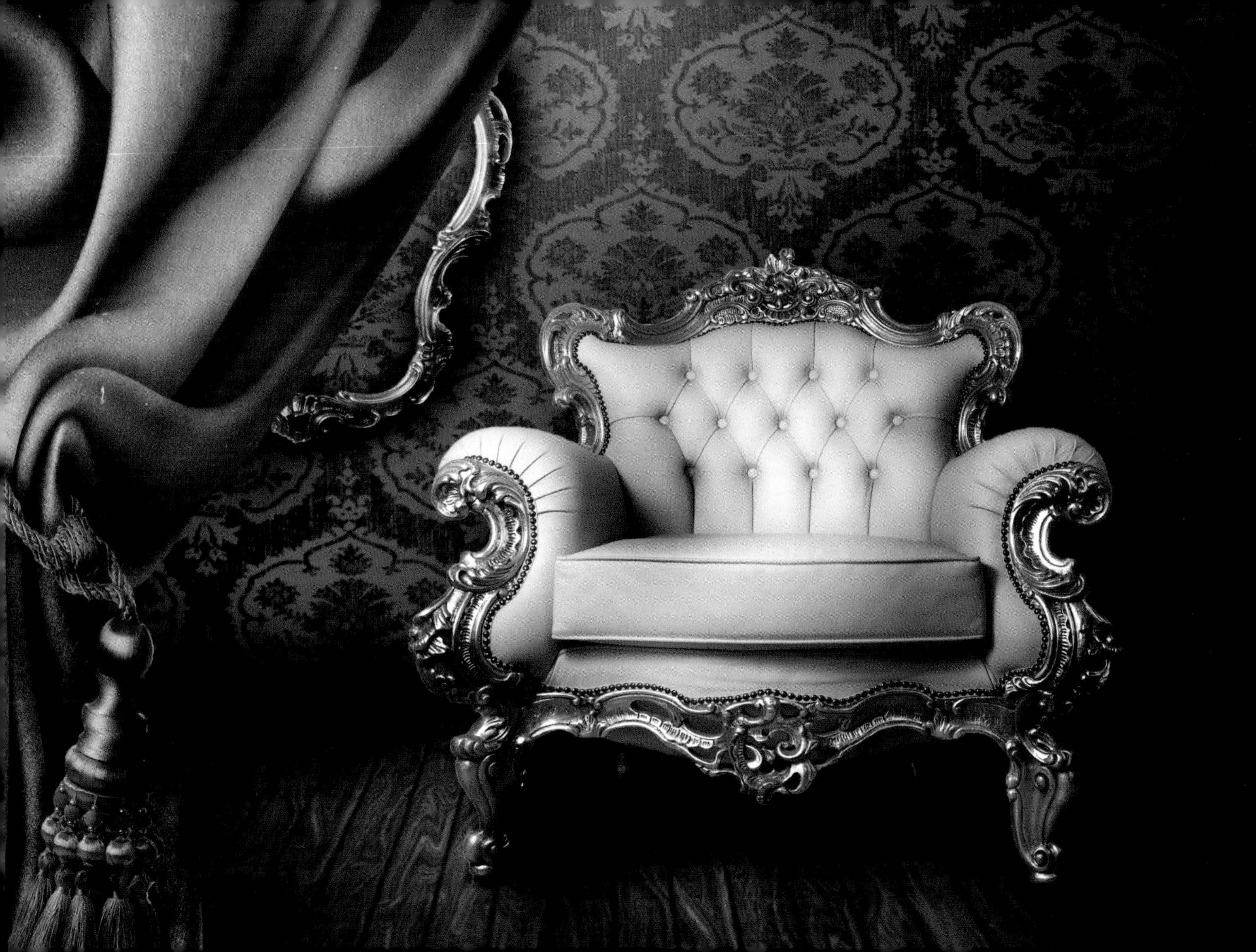

Recipe
061

Antiques

The antiques I find myself attracted to are not those from Japan, but rather from overseas. In a 1934 American trade agreement, an antique is defined as a handicraft, artifact or work of art older than 100 years. Items that have been passed down over generations have a calm warmth to them. Their slightly yellowed, weathered look soothes.

- **FEELING** Tranquil, stable, dignified.
- **COMBINATIONS** Combine dark, dignified colors.
- **TIPS** These colors create a sense of stability but take care that they don't appear too drab.

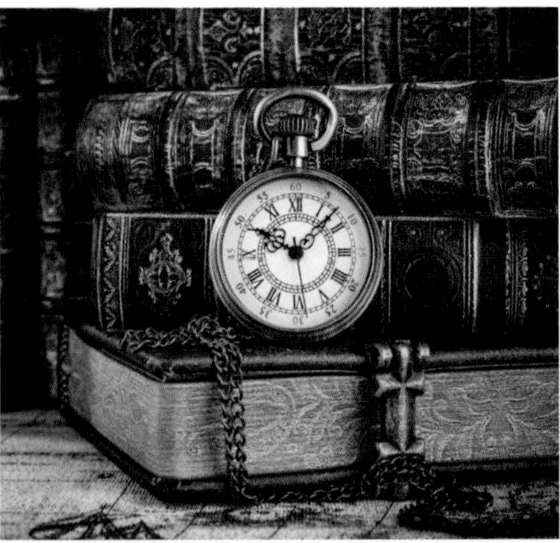

Faded gold exudes a burnished, refined, antique air.

❶ Cigarette Brown
A deep brown like that of dried tobacco leaves.

❷ Historical Brown
A dignified brown that creates the sense of the weight of history.

❸ Old Books
The color of the pages of old books that have aged over many years.

❹ Bordeaux
A dark red like that of wine from Bordeaux.

❺ Calfskin
A lustrous deep color like that of calfskin leather.

❻ Forest Black
A color that suggests a dark night deep in a forest.

❼ Black Olives
The color of ripe, black olives.

❽ Greige
A color in between gray and beige.

❾ Coffee Beans
The dark brown, almost black color of coffee beans.

1 C30 M45 Y75 K30 R151 G116 B60 #96743B

2 C15 M40 Y90 K80 R78 G52 B0 #4D3400

3 C0 M5 Y27 K15 R230 G220 B182 #E5DBB5

4 C0 M70 Y50 K75 R97 G31 B28 #601F1C

5 C0 M35 Y45 K65 R122 G89 B64 #795840

6 C70 M33 Y53 K55 R42 G82 B73 #2A5249

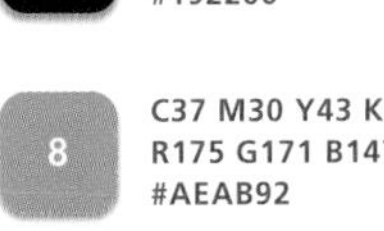

7 C50 M25 Y100 K90 R25 G34 B0 #192200

8 C37 M30 Y43 K0 R175 G171 B147 #AEAB92

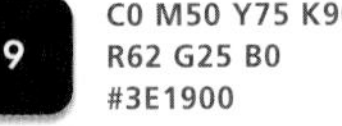

9 C0 M50 Y75 K90 R62 G25 B0 #3E1900

Two-color combinations

Three-color combinations

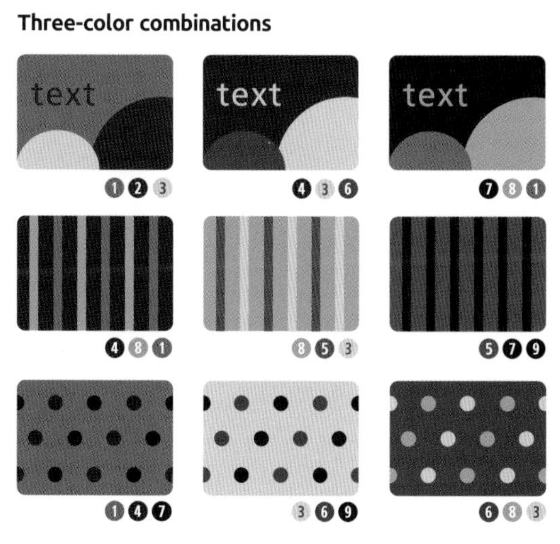

Designs

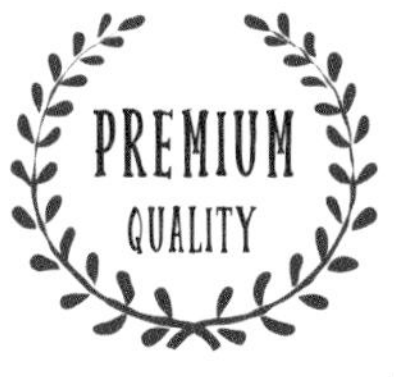

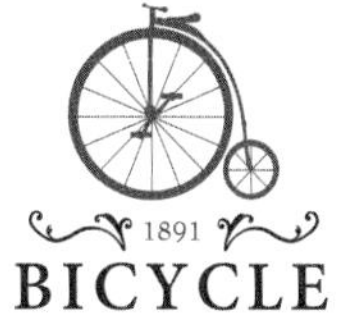

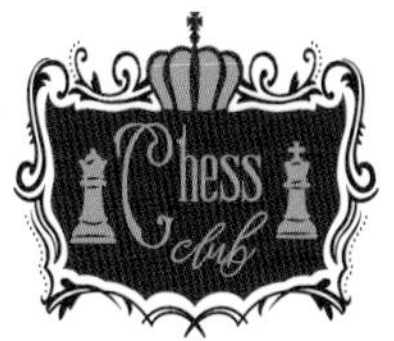

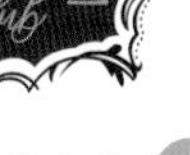

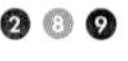

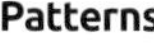

Patterns

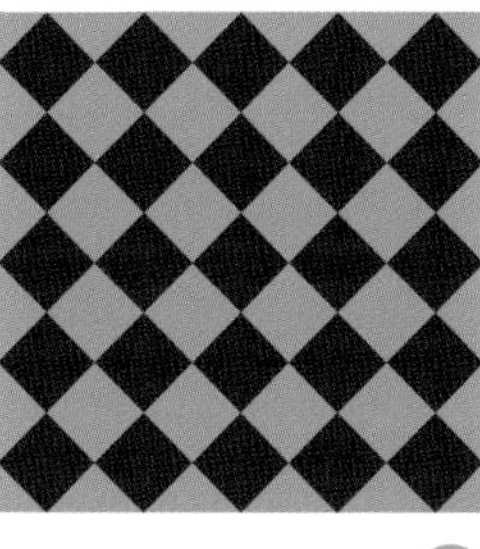

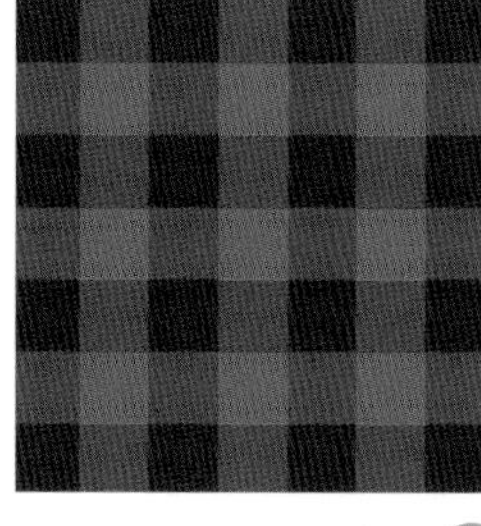

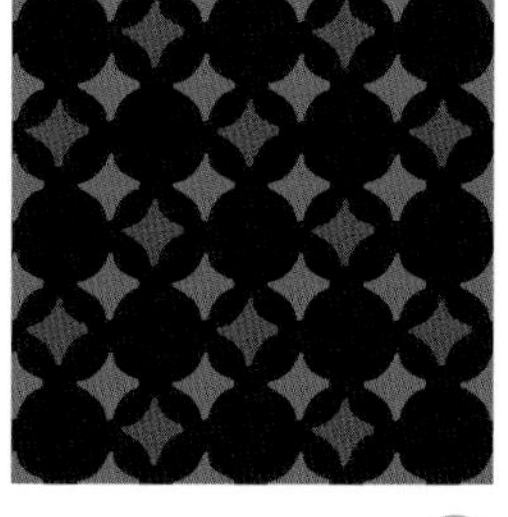

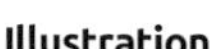

Illustration

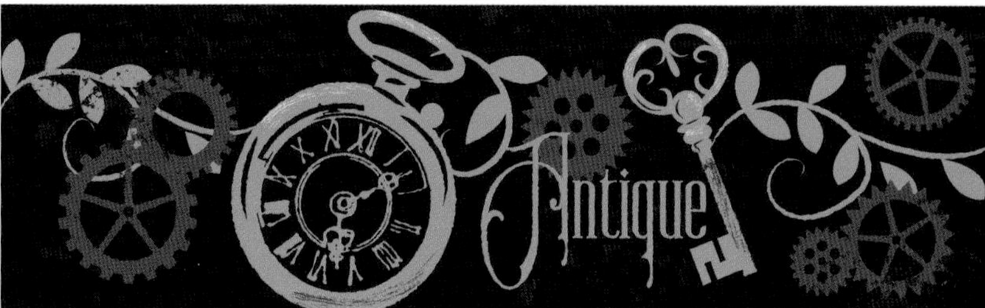

Recipe

062

Fountain Pens

Writer Shotaro Ikenami is quoted as saying, "The fountain pen is man's greatest weapon." A letter written with a fountain pen conveys the amount of pressure used and the quirks of penmanship, making the writer seem more present. Here, chic tones are used as base colors combined with sophisticated accents to develop the scheme.

- **FEELING** Dignified, chic, having depth.
- **COMBINATIONS** Create contrasts in hue and tone.
- **TIPS** Use Colors 7, 8 and 9 as effective accents.

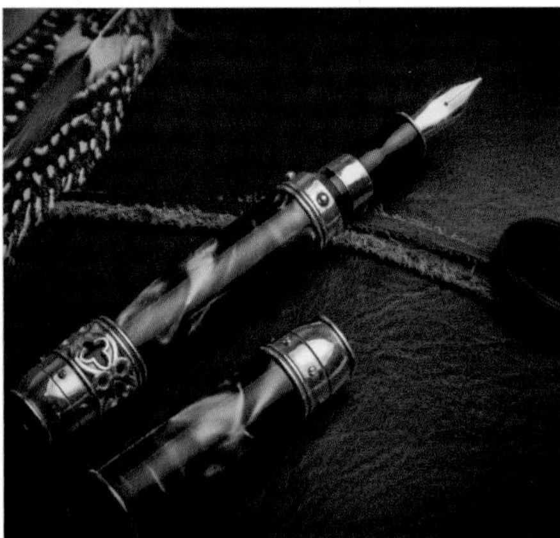

A much-used fountain pen reflects its owners quirks.

❶ Dandy Brown
A burnt brown that approaches black.

❷ Yellow Brown
A warm brown with strong yellow tones.

③ Platinum White
A white that evokes the brilliance of platinum.

❹ Lamb's Wool
A pale yellow beige like that of unbleached lamb's wool.

❺ Red Brown
A reddish brown with an air of cool.

❻ London Fog
A gray that calls to mind the misty London air.

❼ Antique Red
A deep red that evokes a dignified serenity.

❽ Ink Blue
A deep, tranquil blue like that of fountain pen ink.

❾ Blue Green
A cool color halfway between blue and green.

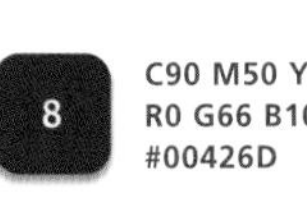

No.	CMYK	RGB	Hex
1	C27 M45 Y70 K75	R78 G55 B20	#4D3614
2	C10 M25 Y55 K30	R183 G156 B100	#B69B63
3	C8 M8 Y6 K0	R238 G235 B236	#EDEAEC
4	C0 M10 Y30 K13	R232 G215 B175	#E8D6AE
5	C30 M55 Y45 K55	R109 G73 B69	#6D4845
6	C10 M15 Y15 K35	R174 G165 B161	#AEA5A0
7	C10 M90 Y85 K30	R172 G41 B30	#AC291D
8	C90 M50 Y13 K50	R0 G66 B109	#00426D
9	C90 M20 Y60 K33	R0 G111 B95	#006F5F

Two-color combinations

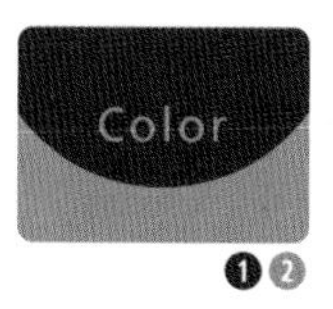
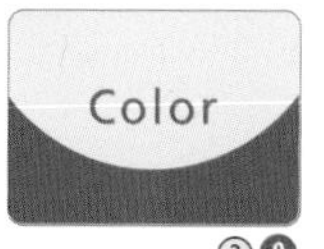
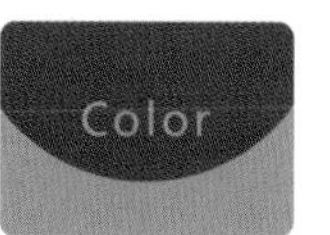
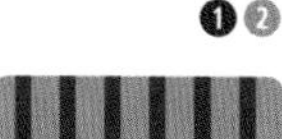
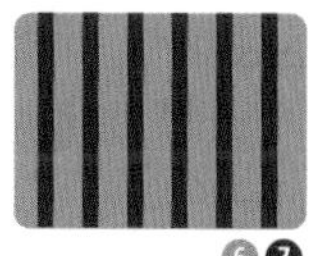
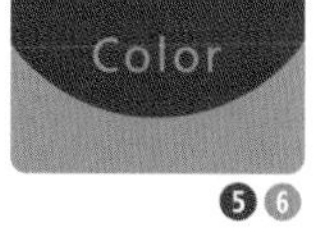
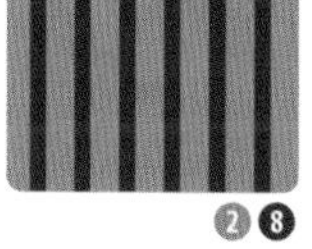
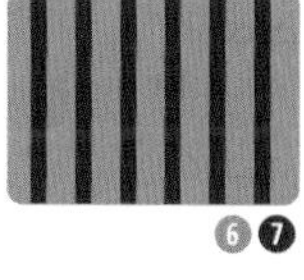
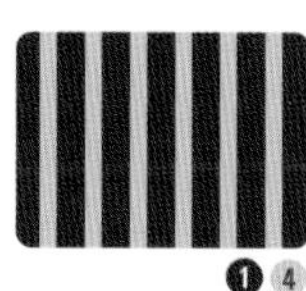
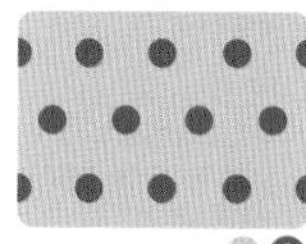

Three-color combinations

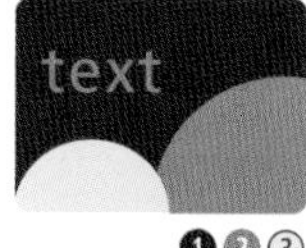
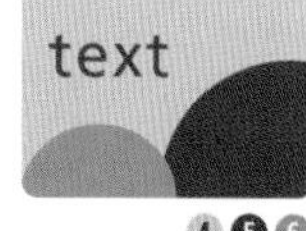
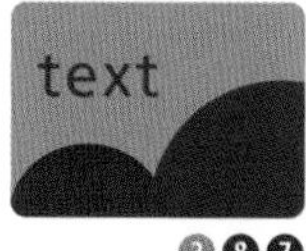
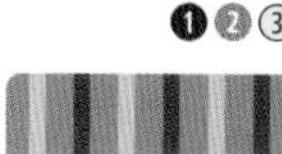

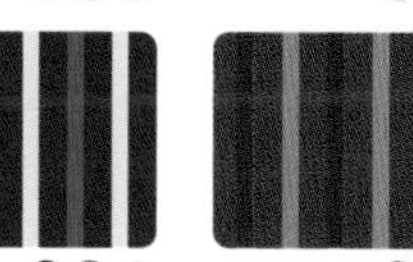
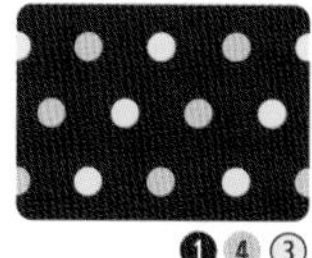
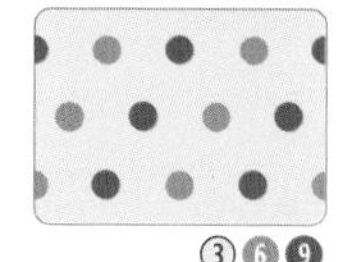
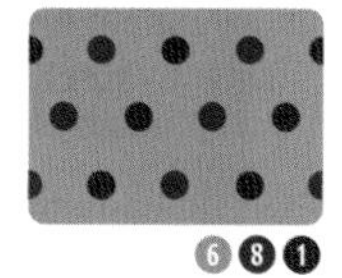

Designs

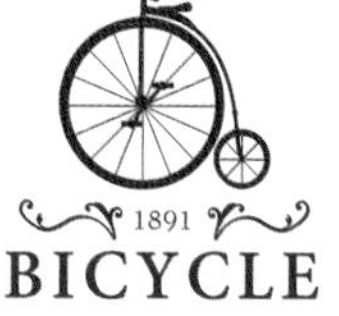

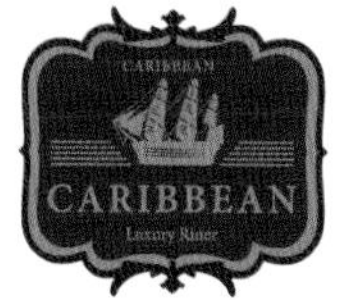

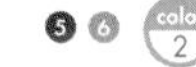
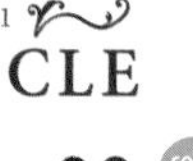

Patterns

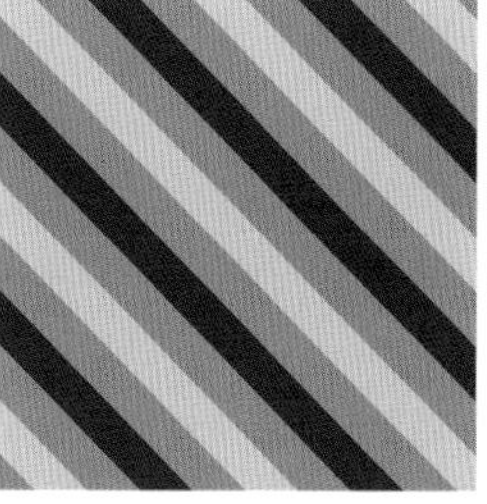
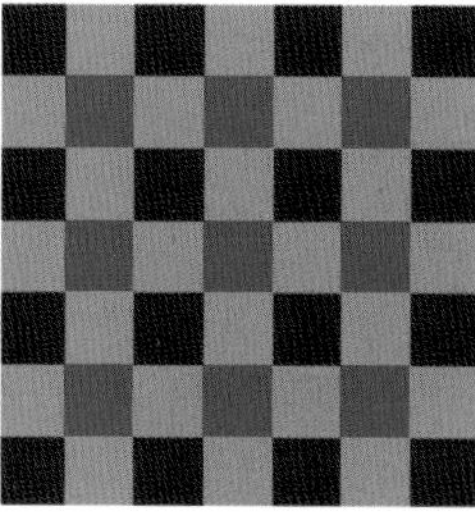
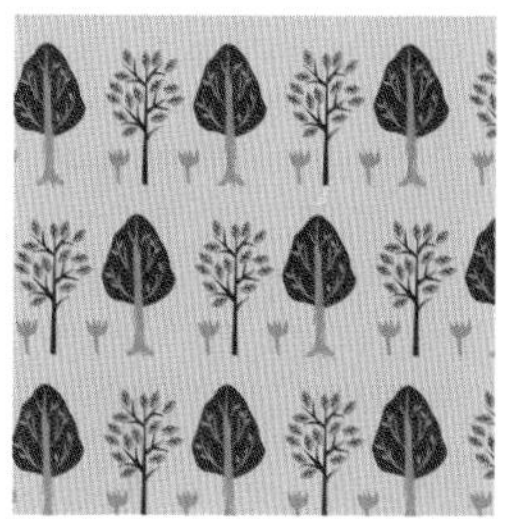
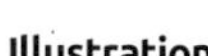

Illustration

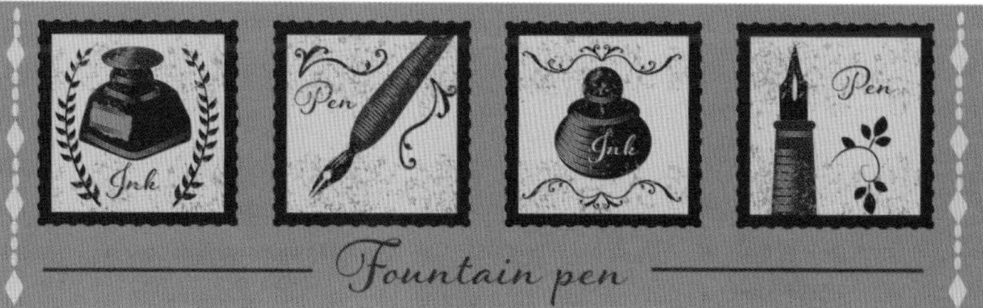

Recipe
063

Men's Suits

Charcoal gray and navy are standard colors for business suits, and the shirts worn with them are overwhelmingly white or a very pale blue, though that palette has expanded in recent years to include patterns and hints of pastel. This basic color scheme creates a fresh and neat impression.

- **FEELING** Orthodox, precise, neat.
- **COMBINATIONS** Use gray and navy over large surface areas.
- **TIPS** The necktie creates the accent color(s).

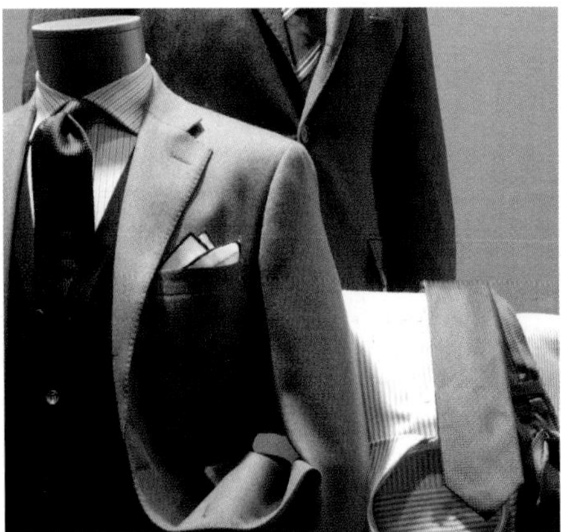

Brown is another suit basic, allowing for richer tones in the colder months and lighter tan and khaki tones for summer.

❶ Summer Suits
In the summer, suits in pale colors make for a cooler look.

❷ Basic Navy
Representing sincerity and intellect, navy gets the job done in style.

❸ Basic Charcoal
Regardless of the color of the tie worn with it, a fail-safe suit hue.

❹ Silver
Make silver the main color when using metallics.

❺ Lavender Gray
An extremely pale gray with a hint of lavender.

❻ Basic Tie
A quiet blue is another standard color for a necktie.

❼ Creator's Brown
This chic reddish brown works well with navy.

❽ Accent Navy
Highly saturated navy is an attractive color for a necktie.

❾ Shirt Blue
A light blue with a neat, refreshing feel.

	CMYK	RGB	Hex
1	C7 M15 Y0 K65	R117 G109 B117	#756D74
2	C35 M25 Y0 K80	R59 G60 B77	#3A3C4C
3	C0 M15 Y0 K83	R81 G69 B73	#504548
4	C20 M20 Y5 K15	R190 G184 B201	#BDB8C9
5	C7 M7 Y0 K15	R216 G215 B223	#D8D6DE
6	C40 M40 Y0 K40	R117 G109 B145	#756C91
7	C47 M57 Y60 K0	R154 G119 B100	#997663
8	C70 M55 Y0 K75	R28 G34 B73	#1B2249
9	C20 M10 Y0 K0	R211 G222 B241	#D2DDF1

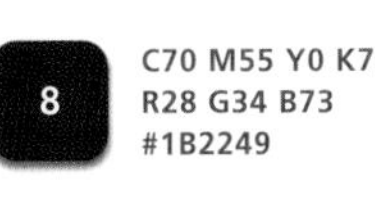
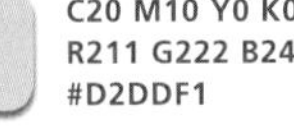

Two-color combinations

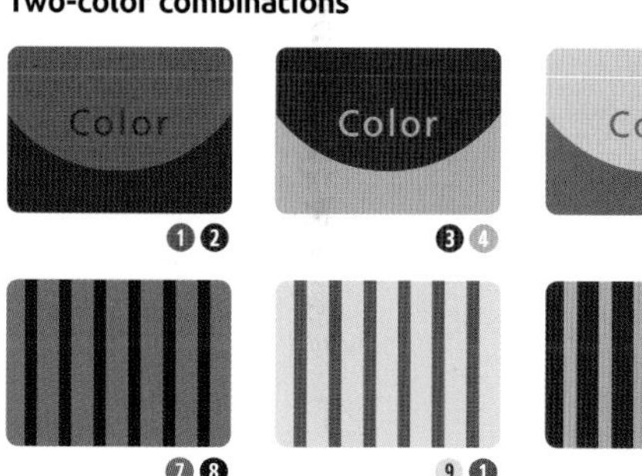

Three-color combinations

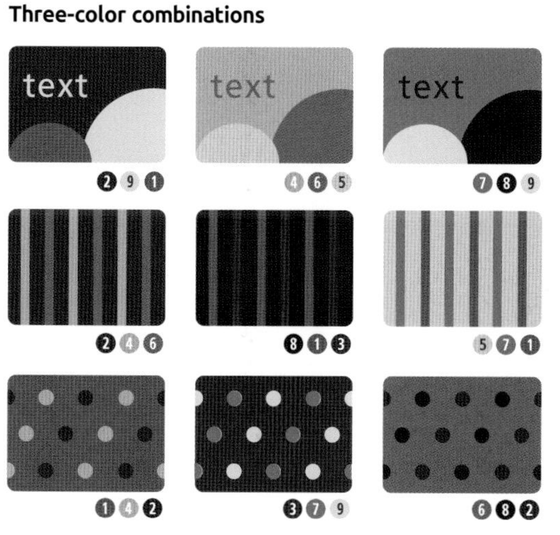

Designs

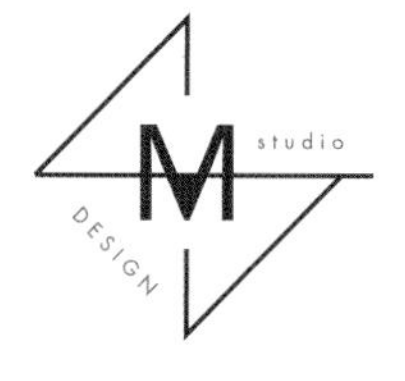

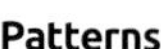

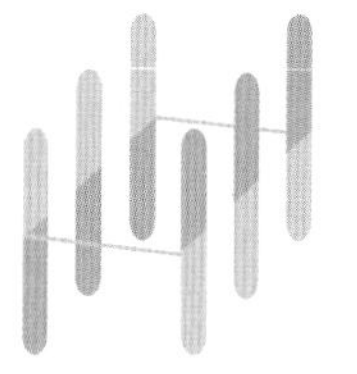

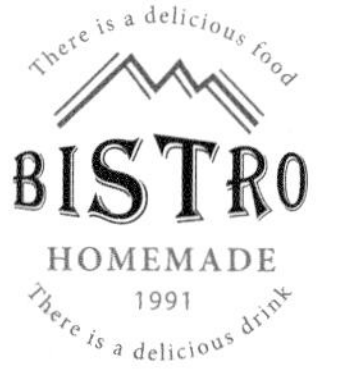

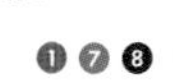

Patterns

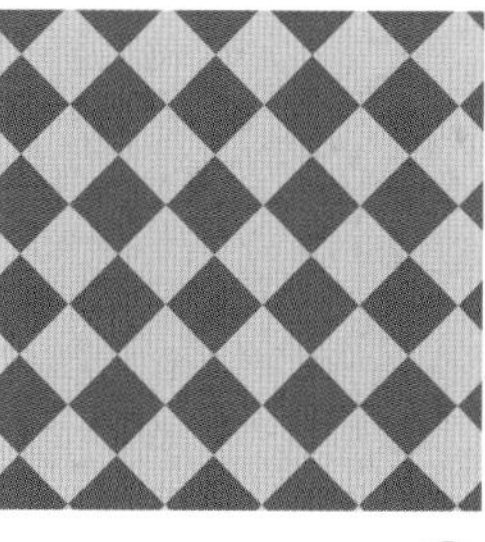

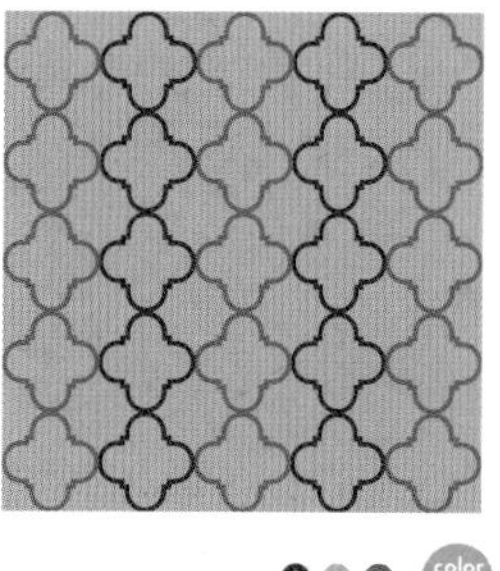

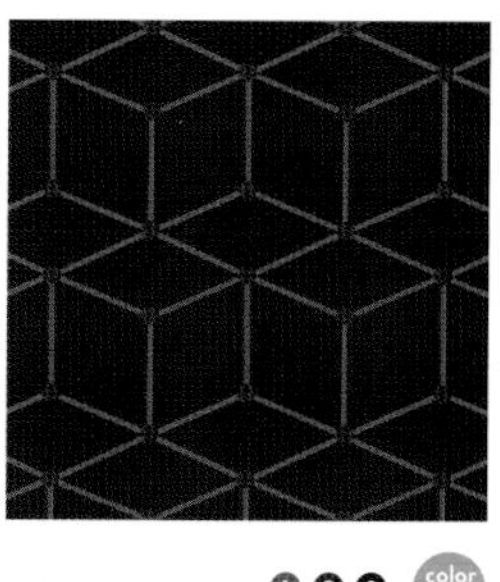

Illustration

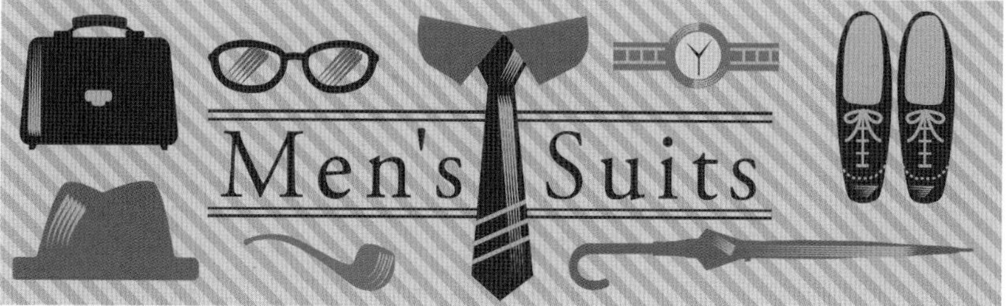

PART 08

CLASSIC + CHIC

Recipe
064

Autumn Leaves

There are many words in Japanese that express nature's changing colors. There are "yellow leaves," "brown leaves" and for leaves like maples that turn red, "red leaves," which is the general term used to describe the almost psychedelic transformations. Fall leaves offer up an indelible palette all their own.

- **FEELING** Autumnal, deep, rich.
- **COMBINATIONS** Make deep red and yellow the main colors.
- **TIPS** Use a moderate amount of brown shades as the sub-colors.

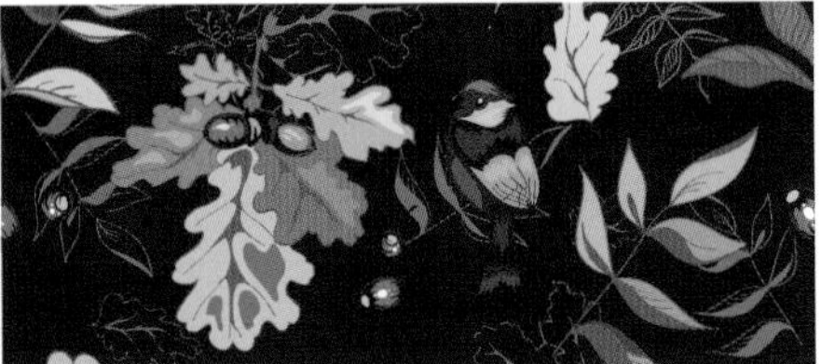

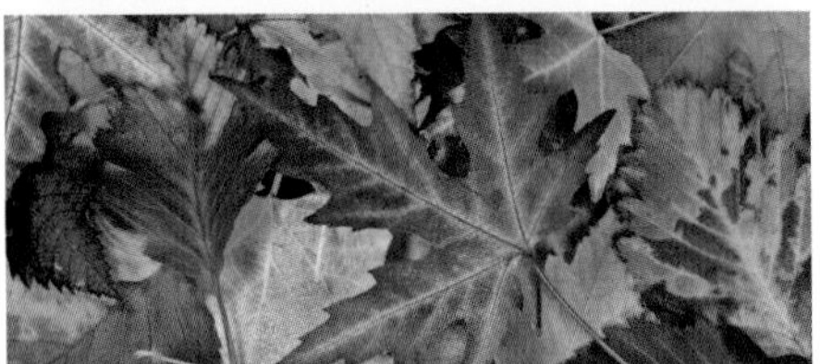

It's hard to replicate the intricate veins and details of the color gradations that appear each fall.

❶ Red Leaves
Maple trees turn red due to the compound anthocyanin.

❷ Yellow Leaves
Ginkgo leaves turn yellow due to a predominance of carotenoid.

❸ Brown Leaves
Among the fall tones, brown leaves offer a stark counterpoint.

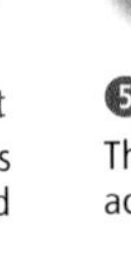

❹ Fallen Chestnut
The color of chestnuts that have ripened and fallen to the ground.

❺ Acorn
The light brown of acorns.

❻ Wild Boar
A brown like that of wild boar's hair.

❼ Russet
In Japanese, this color refers to fallen leaves, it's a traditional color.

❽ Green Russet
Russet colors with a strong touch of green.

❾ Red Russet
Russet colors with a strong touch of red.

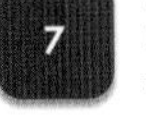

No.	CMYK	RGB	Hex
1	C0 M77 Y70 K40	R167 G62 B43	#A73D2A
2	C0 M30 Y90 K8	R237 G182 B18	#EDB512
3	C10 M20 Y50 K55	R135 G119 B79	#86774F
4	C15 M45 Y60 K60	R117 G81 B50	#755132
5	C0 M45 Y65 K50	R153 G101 B53	#986435
6	C15 M40 Y55 K55	R127 G95 B64	#7F5F40
7	C25 M20 Y50 K70	R89 G86 B58	#58553A
8	C50 M25 Y90 K50	R89 G103 B30	#59671E
9	C25 M50 Y40 K55	R115 G80 B77	#73504C

Two-color combinations

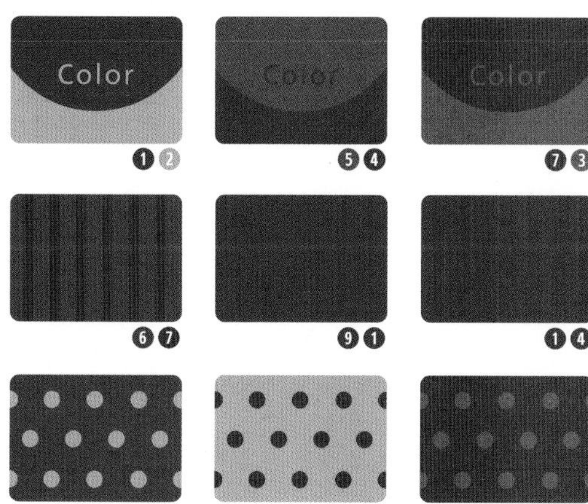

Three-color combinations

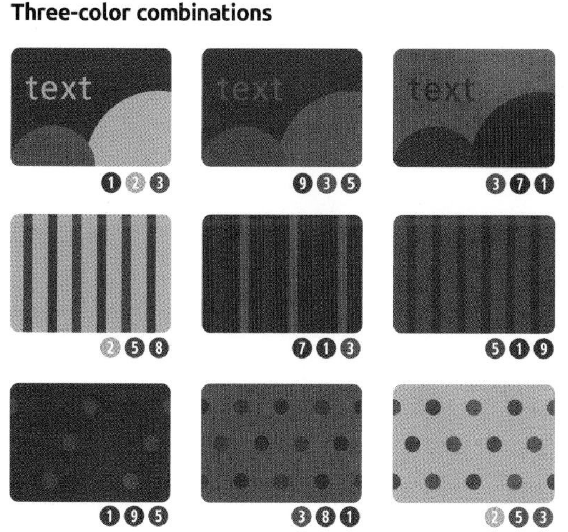

Designs

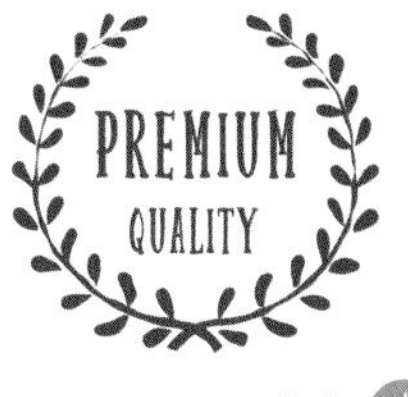

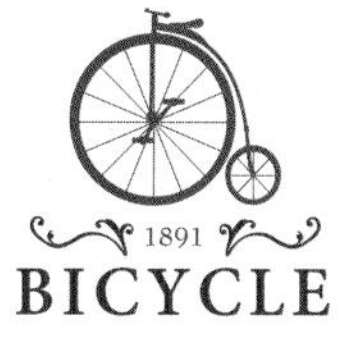

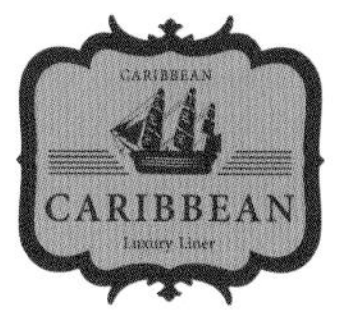

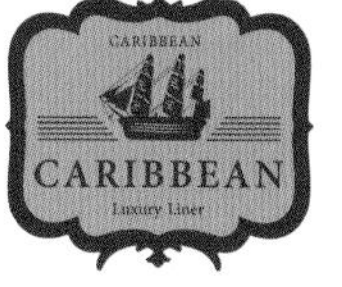

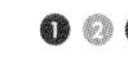

Patterns

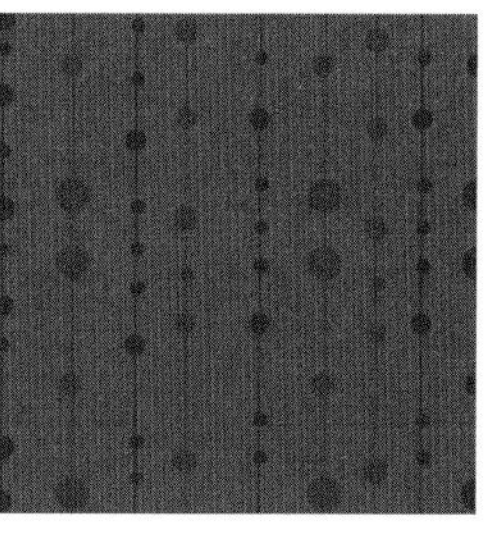

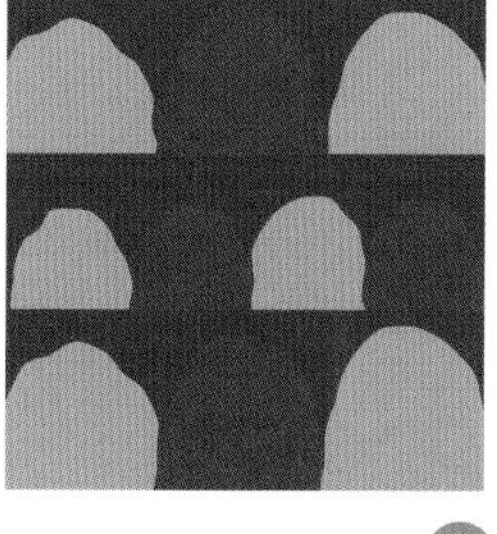

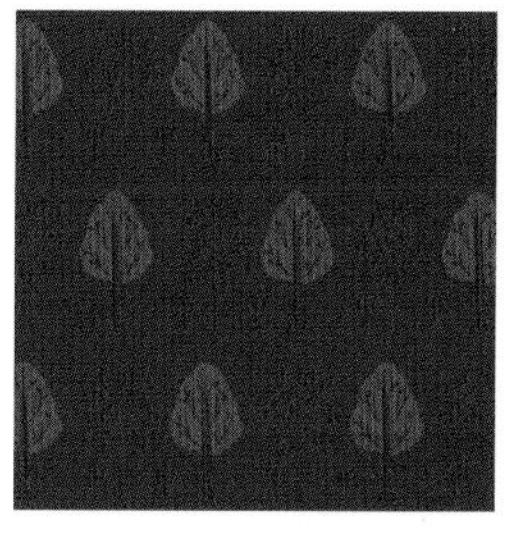

Illustration

Recipe
065

Old Maps of Paris

I like looking at maps. Last year on a trip to Paris, I got my hands on an old map. Carefully unfolding it and in deep concentration, I followed the names of the alleys with my eyes: Where is the art supplies store? And where was that antiques shop? I find my heart wandering back there on long fall nights.

- **FEELING** Nostalgic, aged, retro.
- **COMBINATIONS** Combine indistinct colors in a dreamy fashion.
- **TIPS** Dark colors add definition and pull the overall scheme together.

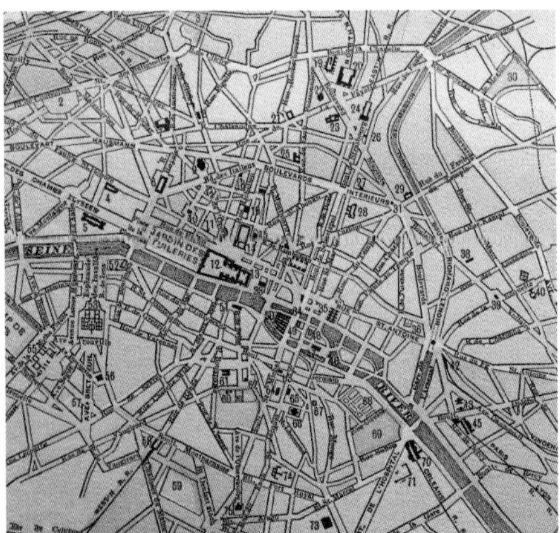

An aged, hazy color scheme lends a retro air.

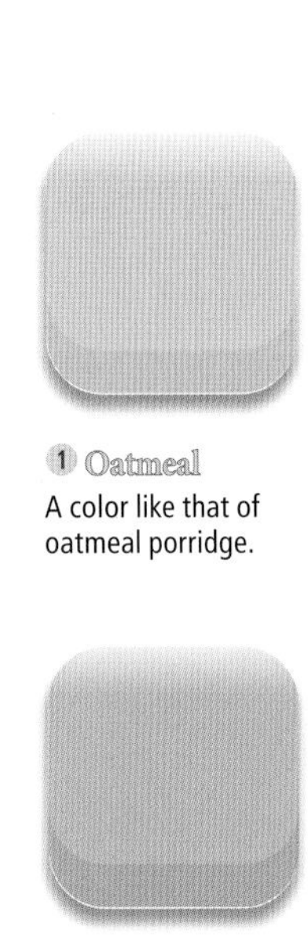

1 Oatmeal
A color like that of oatmeal porridge.

2 Nostalgic Orange
An indistinct, soft orange.

3 Nostalgic Beige
An indistinct, soft beige.

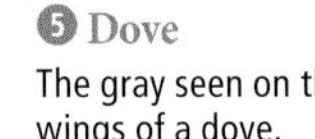

4 Nostalgic Pink
An indistinct, soft pink.

5 Dove
The gray seen on the wings of a dove.

6 Ginger Candy
A candy made with plenty of ginger and honey.

7 Almond
The color of fragrant roast almonds.

8 Macadamia Nuts
The color of macadamia nuts once the shell is removed.

9 Aging Black
The black of ink that has faded over many years.

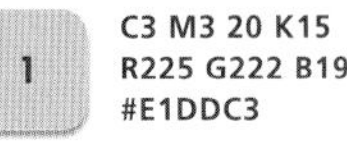

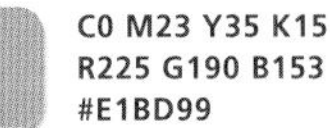

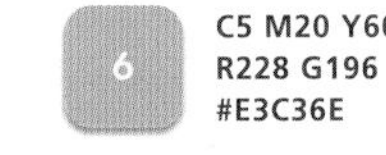

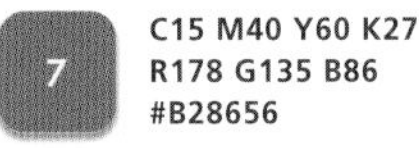

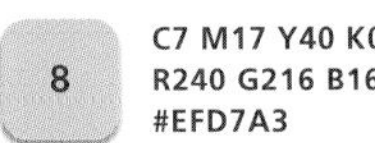

1 C3 M3 20 K15
R225 G222 B196
#E1DDC3

2 C0 M23 Y35 K15
R225 G190 B153
#E1BD99

3 C0 M10 Y40 K15
R229 G210 B153
#E4D299

4 C0 M25 Y20 K10
R233 G195 B183
#E9C3B7

5 C10 M15 Y20 K40
R165 G156 B146
#A49B91

6 C5 M20 Y60 K10
R228 G196 B110
#E3C36E

7 C15 M40 Y60 K27
R178 G135 B86
#B28656

8 C7 M17 Y40 K0
R240 G216 B163
#EFD7A3

9 C17 M15 Y25 K70
R97 G93 B85
#605D54

Two-color combinations

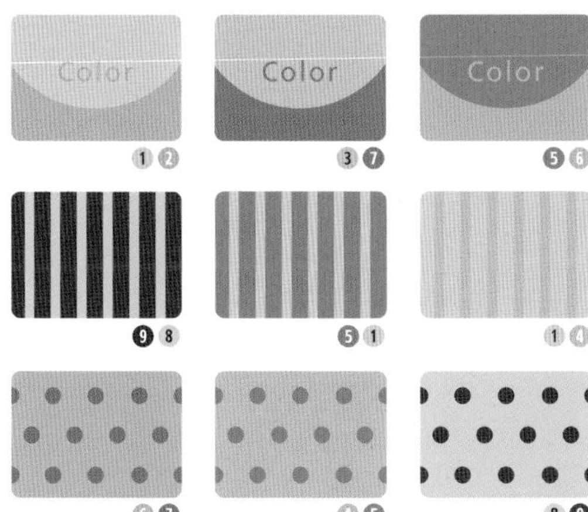

Three-color combinations

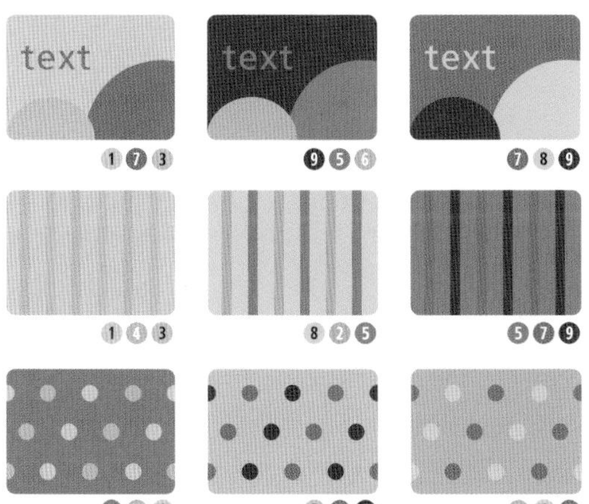

Designs

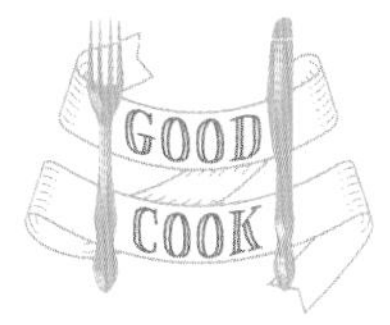

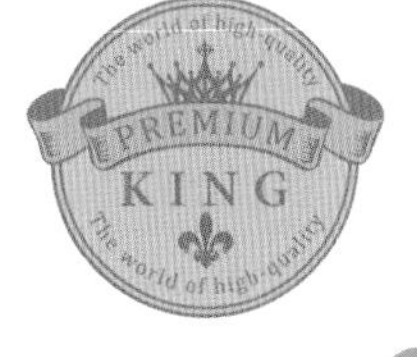

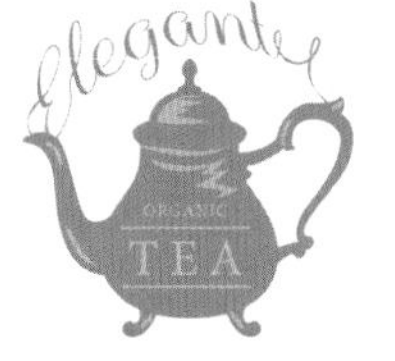

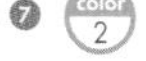
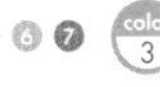
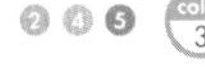

Patterns

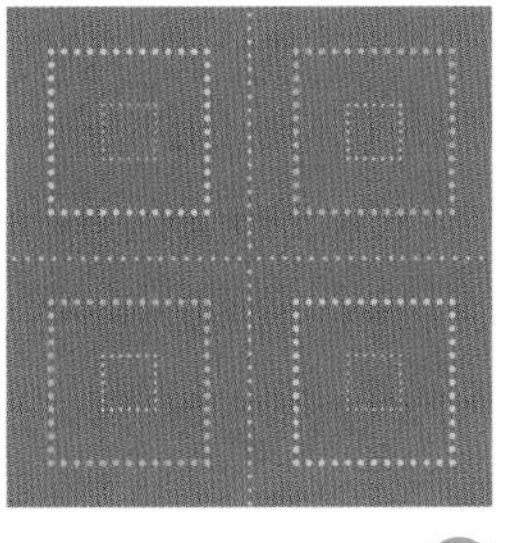
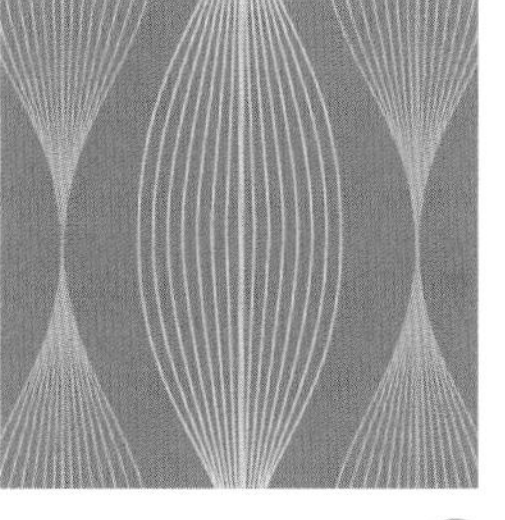
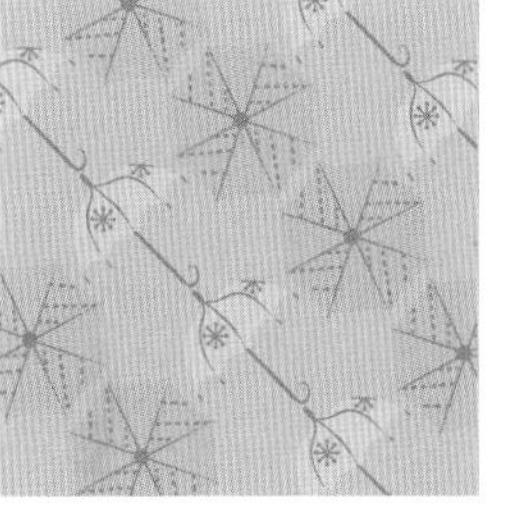
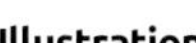

Illustration

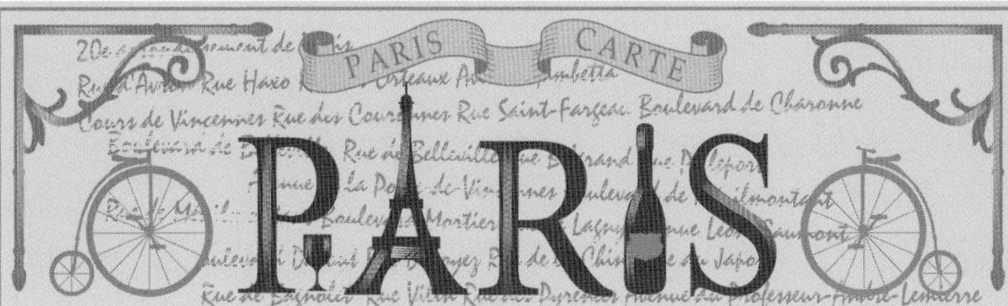

Colors that Work on the Soul and Colors that Resonate

Visual Experiences with Color and the Activation of the Subconscious Through the Rich Colors of a Mandala

At the German Bauhaus (a school established in 1919 with the aim of general education in the fine arts and architecture), Johannes Itten, who taught color science, said the following in his book "The Art of Color" about the stained glass in medieval European churches:

"Stained glass windows could be understood by everyone, they were twinkling pictographs. Their mysterious beauty afforded Christians a sublime spiritual experience. This visual experience was a direct invitation to a highly spiritual life. . . ."

For the mostly illiterate population of the time, the Bible stories expressed via stained glass pictures were guides to their faith. One can imagine that the colorful rays of light streaming through the windows into the dim space would've been deeply moving.

The psychologist Carl Jung believed that rich colors could activate the workings of the unconscious mind and researched mandalas, including them in experimental treatments at his clinic.

In Tibetan Buddhism, monks use richly colored sands to create mandalas, but their creations aren't ornamental; rather they're made for ascetic purposes.

The colors in stained glass are "permeating rays" while those in the sand of a mandala are "reflecting rays," so we can interpret the true nature of color that resonates as being light itself.

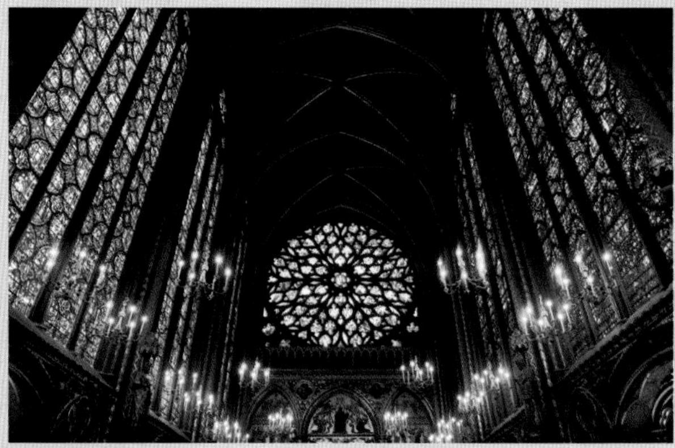

The rays of colored light streaming through stained glass are mysterious, spiritual and, for many, soul-stirring.

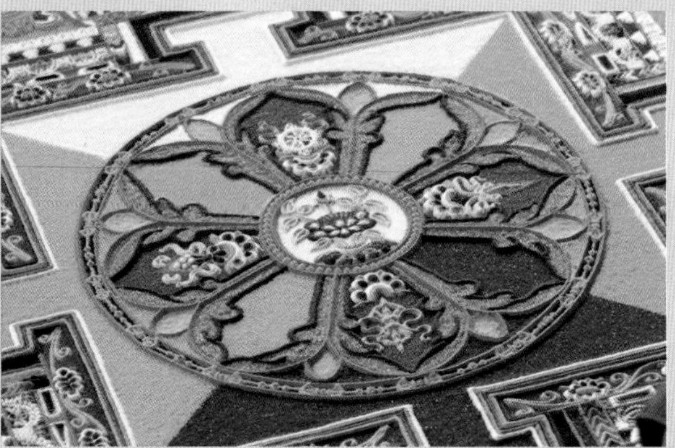

Jung believed that schemes composed of rich colors stimulated the unconscious.

The Pink Breathing Method

The pink breathing method was devised by an American woman whose continued practice resulted in improved skin color and radiance and a more youthful appearance. The method is extremely simple:

① Think of your favorite shade of pink.
② Breathe the color into your whole body.
③ Once areas of concern are filled with that color . . .
④ . . . comfortably release the breath.
Why not try gazing at the image below to try it for yourself?

Cherish the Colors You Love or That Interest You

There are colors all around us. In the sense that we usually don't take particular notice of them, colors might seem to exist just like air, but if you happen to be noticing that out of all these colors, you're suddenly drawn to a bright yellow green or feel attracted to turquoise blue, maybe there's a reason you're drawn to them or seek them out.

Part of art therapy involves the concept of using color to better understand oneself and restore one's mental state. Recently, the term "color therapy" has become more widespread and healing through the use of color is gaining attention and proponents.

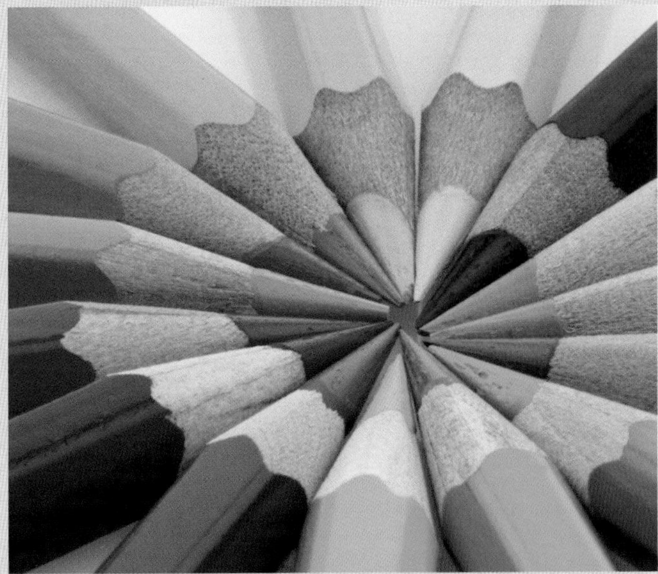

Part

09

Mysterious

These mysterious schemes bring together motifs such as Halloween, witches and the Arabian Nights. Deep, dark colors are the focus, but there are novel approaches to the spooky hues and dark tones too.

Mysterious, Imaginative Color Schemes

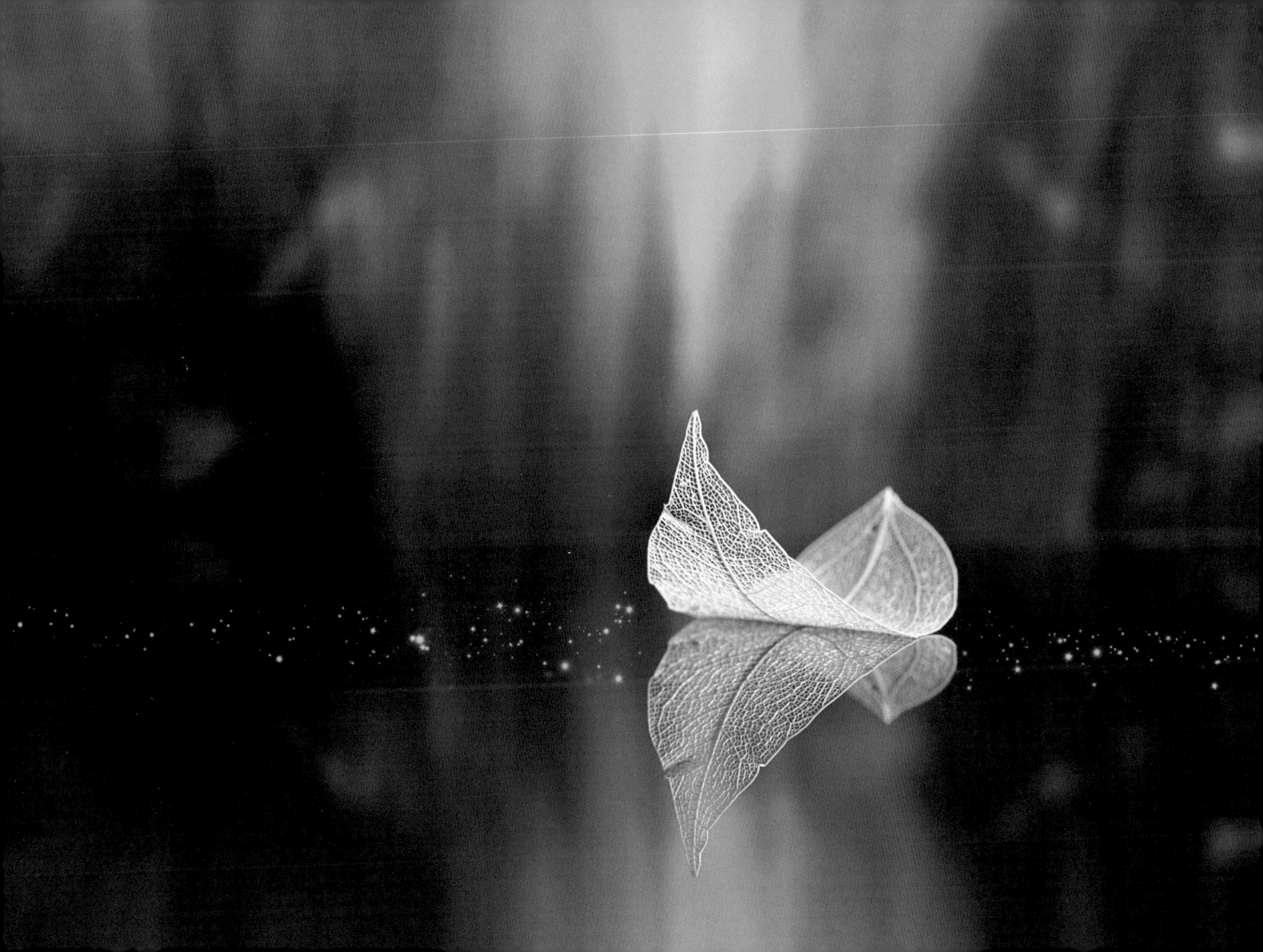

Recipe
066

Halloween

Halloween is celebrated the day before All Hallows' Day, but it originates from the Celtic harvest festival. For the Celts, October 31 marked the end of the year, and it was believed that on that night, the spirits of the dead would return and witches and goblins would emerge. So these spooky and supernatural spirits have earned a place among the seasonal sights.

- **FEELING** Mysterious, impactful.
- **COMBINATIONS** Focus on orange, purple and black.
- **TIPS** Orange and purple are contrasting colors.

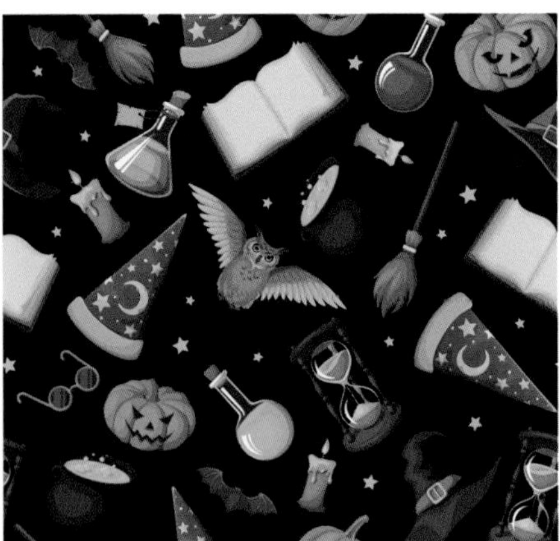

Alchemy, magic and the supernatural provide a treasure trove of imagery.

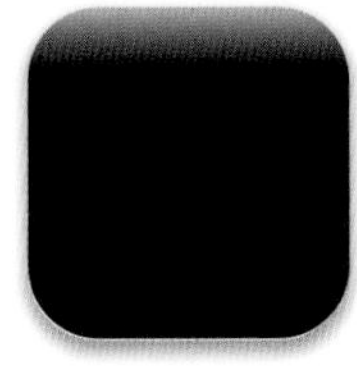

❶ Halloween Purple
A standard Halloween color used in proportion with black.

❷ Halloween Orange
Symbolic of the Protestant Movement in Northern Ireland. The color of the harvest.

❸ Dark Night
Black symbolizes darkness, night, death, magic and evil spirits.

❹ Harvest Purple
The purple of fruits that ripen in fall.

❺ Harvest Gold
Gold symbolizes an abundant crop.

❻ Jack-O'-Lantern
A silly or scary lantern made by hollowing out a pumpkin.

❼ Aphrodisiac
This word has its origins in the Greek goddess Aphrodite.

❽ Owl
Owls appear as the servants of witches. This is the color of an owl's wing.

❾ Bat
The gray of a bat's fur.

1 C55 M90 Y0 K13 R126 G42 B130 #7D2A82

2 C0 M55 Y90 K10 R226 G133 B27 #E2841A

3 C30 M30 Y0 K95 R29 G19 B32 #1D121F

4 C30 M63 Y0 K10 R174 G107 B162 #AD6BA2

5 C0 M17 Y100 K10 R238 G200 B0 #EEC800

6 C0 M37 Y90 K15 R223 G161 B20 #DEA014

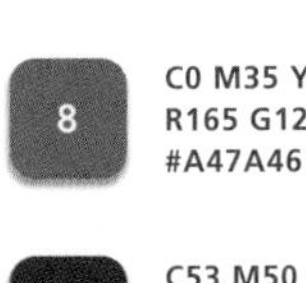

7 C45 M0 Y95 K20 R136 G175 B34 #87AE22

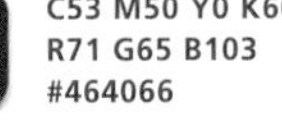

8 C0 M35 Y60 K45 R165 G122 B71 #A47A46

9 C53 M50 Y0 K60 R71 G65 B103 #464066

Two-color combinations

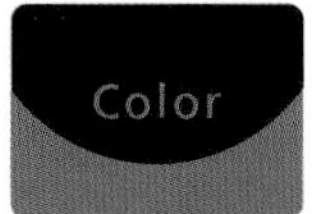
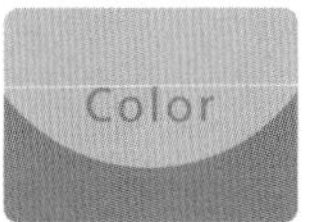
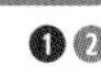

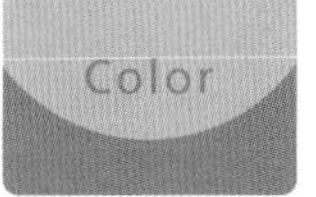

1 2 · 3 4 · 5 2

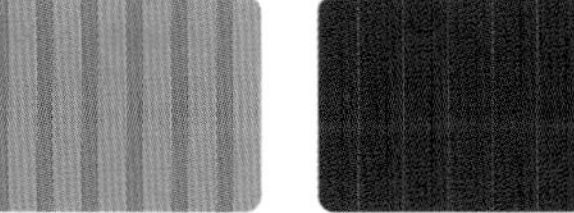

7 8 · 9 1 · 2 4

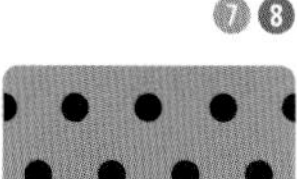
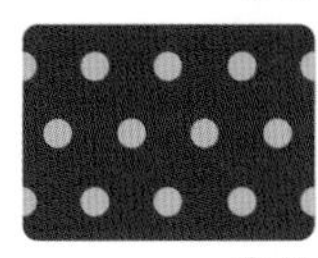
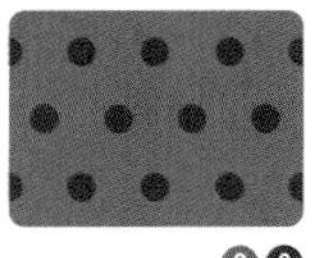

6 3 · 1 5 · 8 9

Three-color combinations

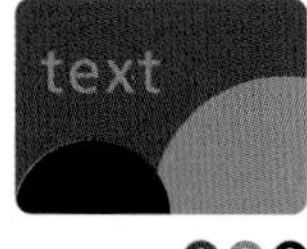
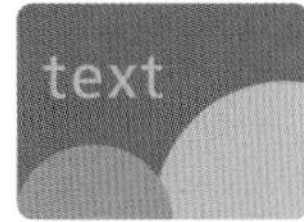
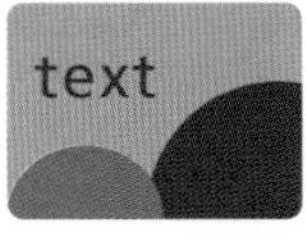

1 2 3 · 4 5 6 · 7 9 8

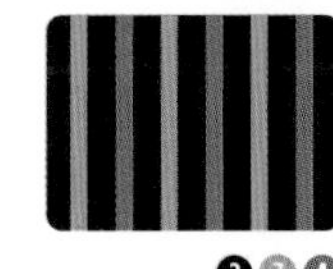

2 4 3 · 8 1 9 · 3 7 4

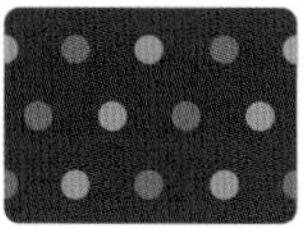
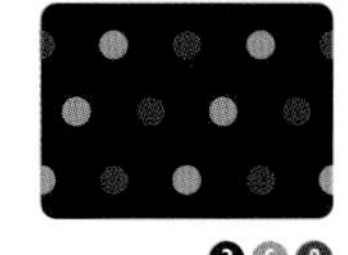
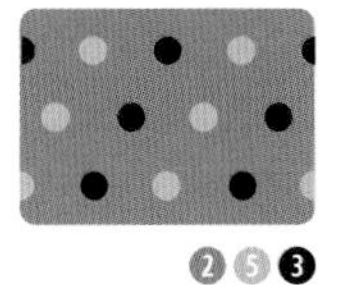

1 4 7 · 3 6 9 · 2 5 3

Designs

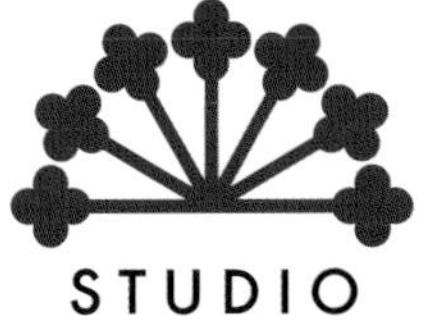

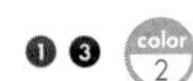

1 3 color 2

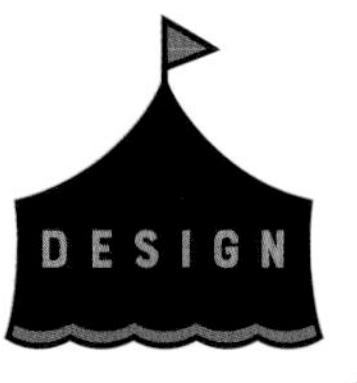

3 4 7 color 3

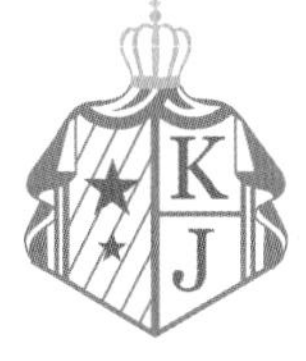

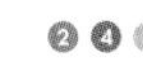
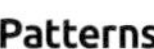

2 4 5 color 3

Patterns

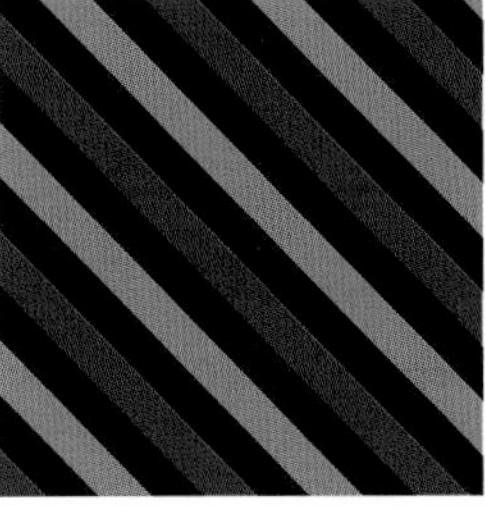

2 3 4 color 3

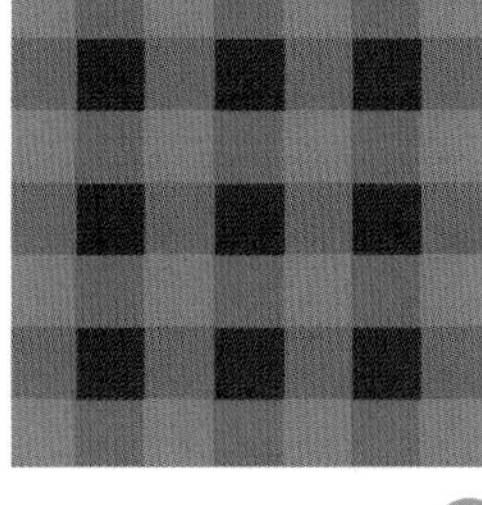

2 4 9 color 3

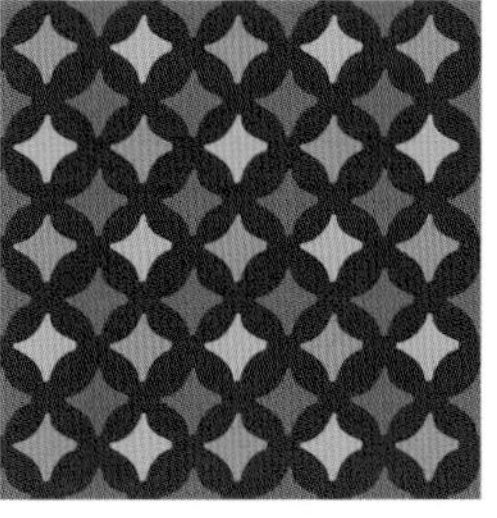

1 4 5 7 color 4

Illustration

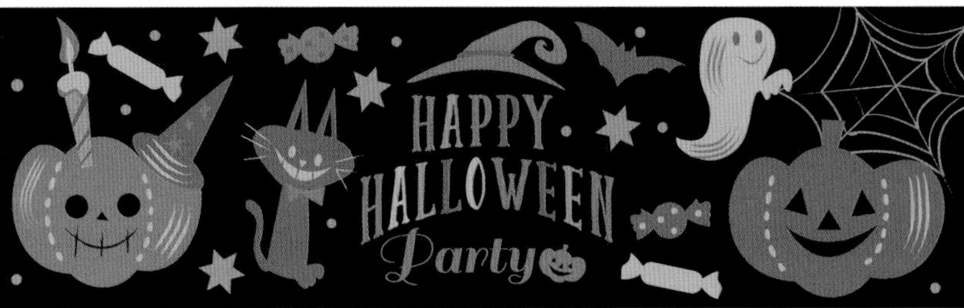

1 2 3 5 7 color 5

Recipe
067

Trick or Treat

"Trick or treat" is what children say when they visit houses on Halloween night, meaning "if you don't give us candy, we'll play a trick on you." Like the Obon festival in Japan, Halloween is thought to be a time when spirits can travel between this world and the next, originating as a ceremony to ward off evil spirits.

- **FEELING** Fruitful, abundant, having warmth.
- **COMBINATIONS** Use fall-like colors in similar hues and tones.
- **TIPS** Create a color scheme that fully embraces the rich colors.

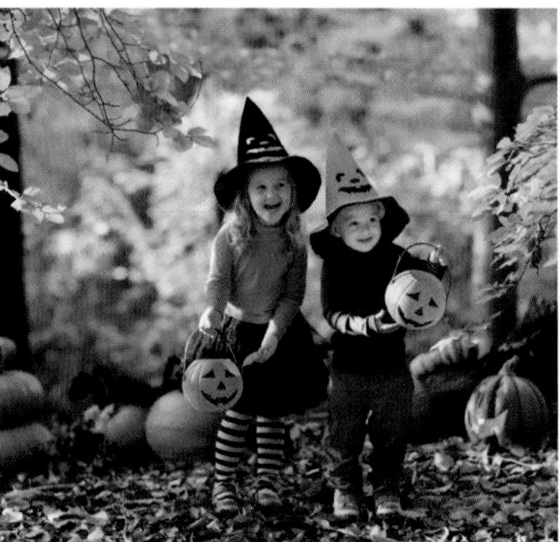

A jack-o'-lantern was once thought to drive away evil spirits.

❶ Pumpkin Red
The color of a pumpkin; a dense reddish orange.

❷ Terracotta
In Italian, this means "baked earth." It's a brownish orange.

❸ Dark Chocolate
A dark brown approaching black.

❹ Chocolate Donut
The color of a donut slathered in chocolate glaze.

❺ Cocoa Cookies
A cookie made using a generous amount of cocoa powder.

❻ Milk Cocoa
The color of cocoa diluted in milk, a seasonal treat.

❼ Olive
A dark, dull yellowish green like that of an olive.

❽ Owl
Ranging from a strong green to a color close to brown, similar to khaki.

❾ Wool Beige
The color of wool fabric made from undyed wool.

1 — C0 M80 Y100 K10, R220 G79 B3, #DB4E02

2 — C0 M95 Y90 K30, R183 G24 B20, #B61713

3 — C20 M45 Y97 K83, R67 G41 B0, #422900

4 — C20 M80 Y70 K80, R73 G6 B0, #480600

5 — C10 M60 Y80 K60, R121 G64 B17, #784011

6 — C27 M50 Y57 K35, R146 G105 B79, #92694F

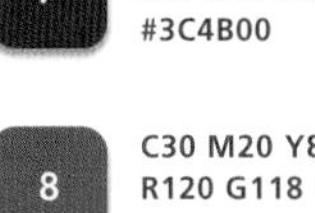

7 — C50 M20 Y95 K70, R61 G75 B0, #3C4B00

8 — C30 M20 Y85 K50, R120 G118 B31, #78751F

9 — C23 M20 Y50 K15, R186 G178 B127, #BAB17E

Two-color combinations

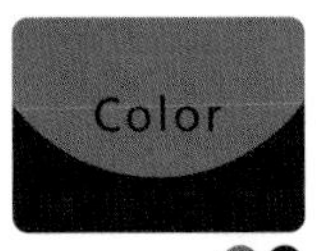

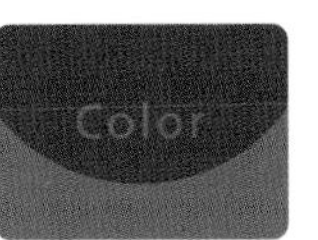

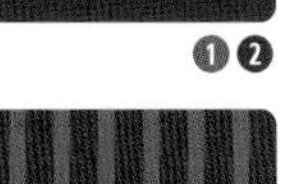

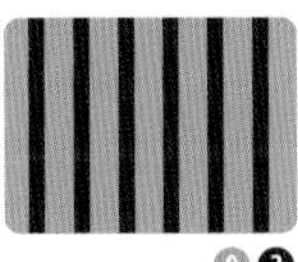

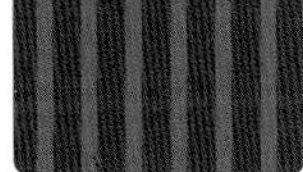

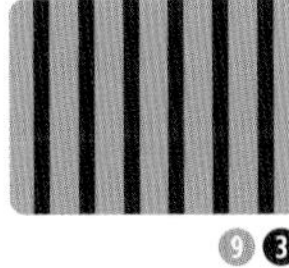

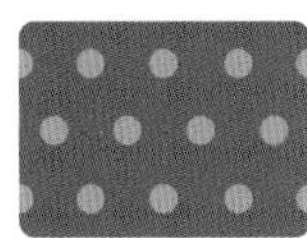

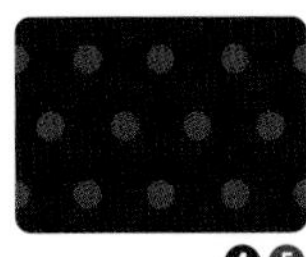

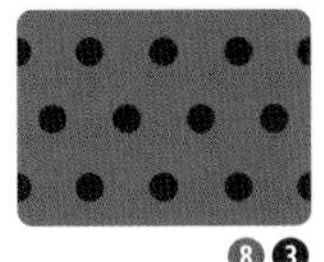

Three-color combinations

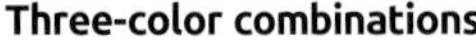

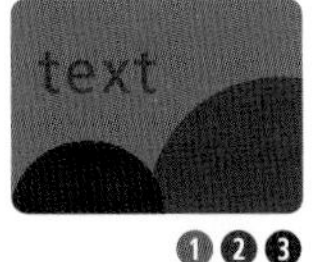

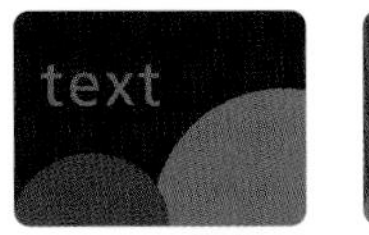

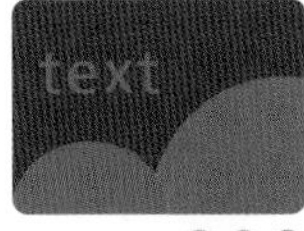

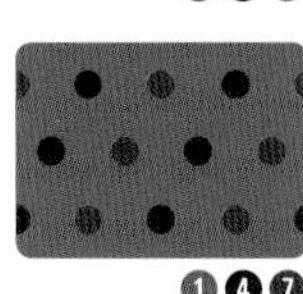

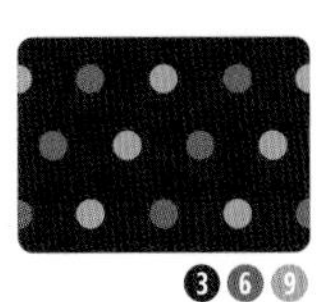

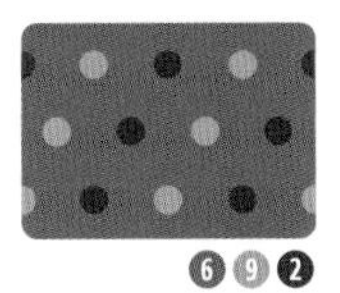

Designs

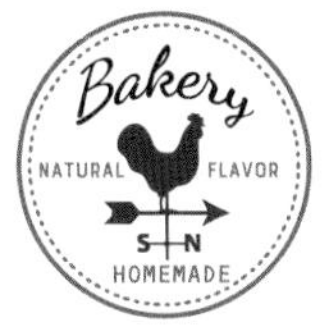

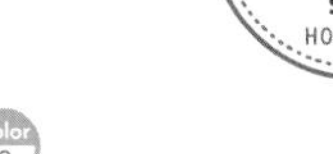

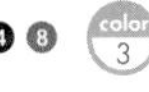

Patterns

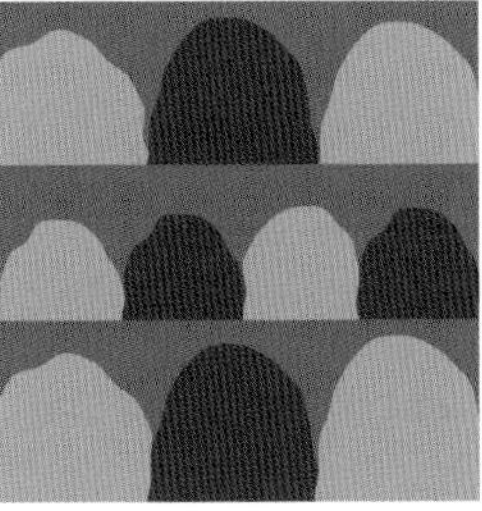

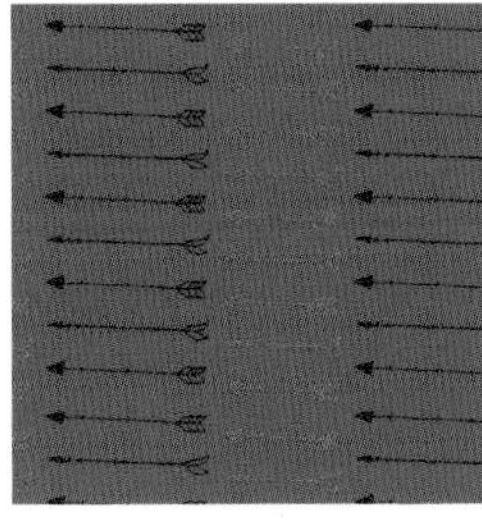

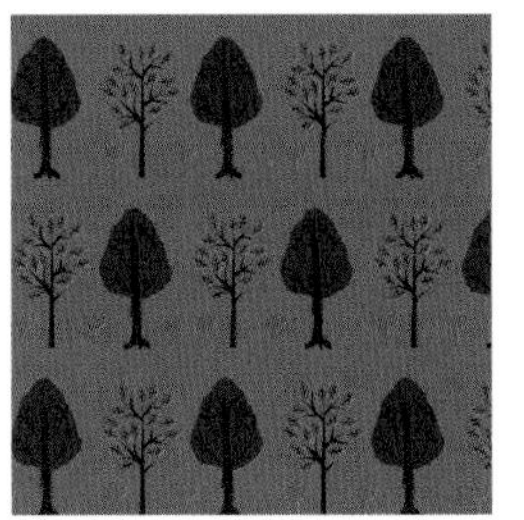

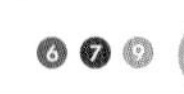

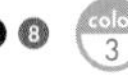

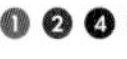

Illustration

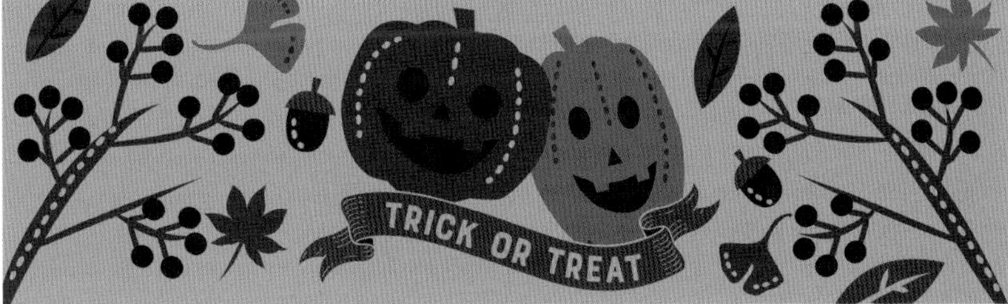

Recipe

068

Full Moon

There's a theory that the waxing and waning of the moon influences people's feelings and behaviors. Emotions run high at the time of the full moon, and our ability to absorb nutrients improves. Whatever your view of the moon's influence on our lives, this color palette brings together only shades of blue associated with the night sky and the lunar orb seen glowing in its midst.

- **FEELING Mysterious, secret, dark.**
- **COMBINATIONS Combine colors with a focus on different shades of blue-gray.**
- **TIPS Aim for the look of a black-and-white photograph.**

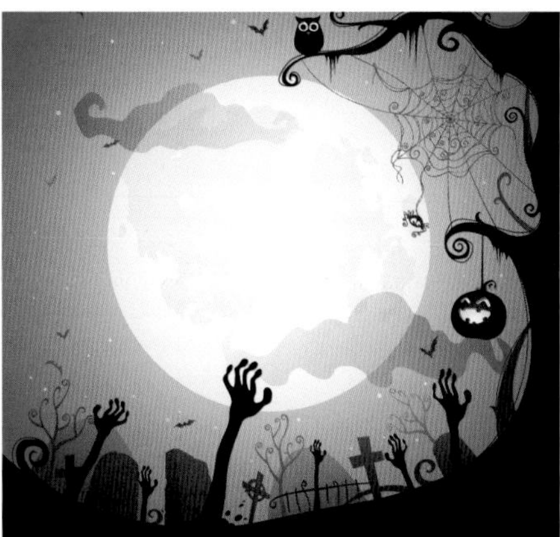

Halloween motifs take on a different look depending on the color scheme used.

❶ Dark Shadow
The color of a dark shadow with a touch of blue.

❷ Twilight
The blue of the sky when nocturnal animals start to emerge.

③ Fog
A white like that of fog completely concealing the moon.

❹ Breaking Dawn
The color of the sky at daybreak when the moon is still shining white.

❺ Midnight
The color of the sky in the middle of the night, a deep blue-black.

❻ Grave Marker
The color of stone used to mark graves, tombs and monuments.

⑦ Moonlight
On the night of a full moon, the color that lights up the night streets.

❽ Moon Mist
A light gray like that of mist covering the moon.

❾ Moon Shadow
The color of shadows where moonlight does not reach.

No.	CMYK	RGB	Hex
1	C70 M10 Y0 K87	R0 G43 B65	#002B40
2	C60 M10 Y0 K40	R64 G132 B167	#3F83A6
3	C15 M0 Y10 K5	R217 G233 B229	#D9E9E5
4	C50 M0 Y0 K20	R109 G179 B212	#6CB2D3
5	C65 M23 Y0 K67	R30 G75 B105	#1D4B69
6	C20 M0 Y0 K23	R178 G200 B212	#B1C7D4
7	C0 M0 Y15 K7	R245 G242 B219	#F4F2DB
8	C15 M0 Y0 K45	R149 G162 B169	#94A1A9
9	C25 M0 Y0 K80	R67 G80 B87	#424F56

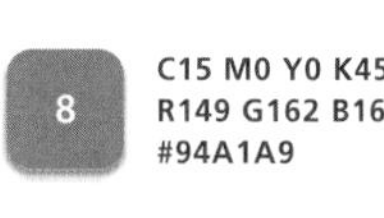
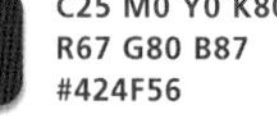

Two-color combinations

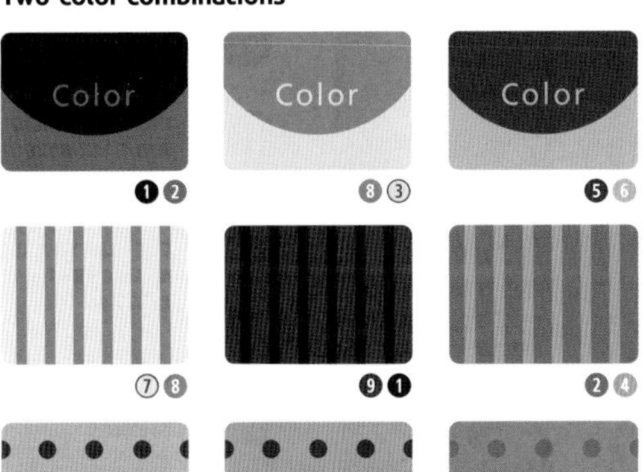

Three-color combinations

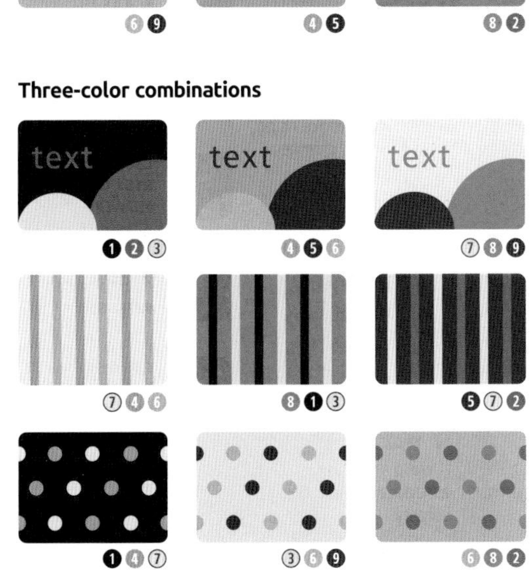

Designs

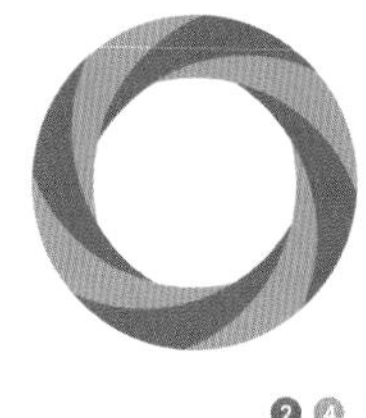

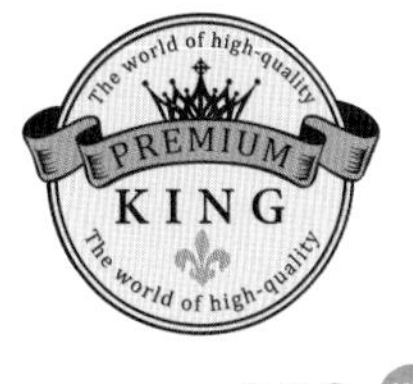

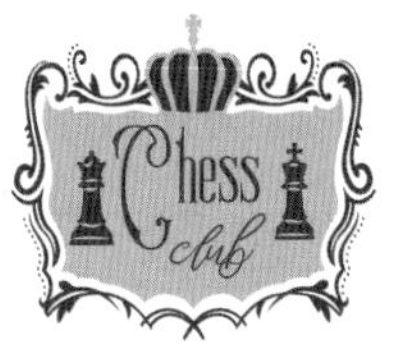

1 2 7 color 3

5 6 9 color 3

Patterns

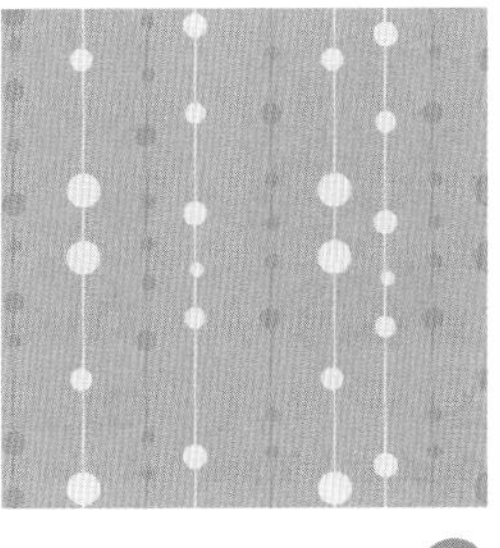

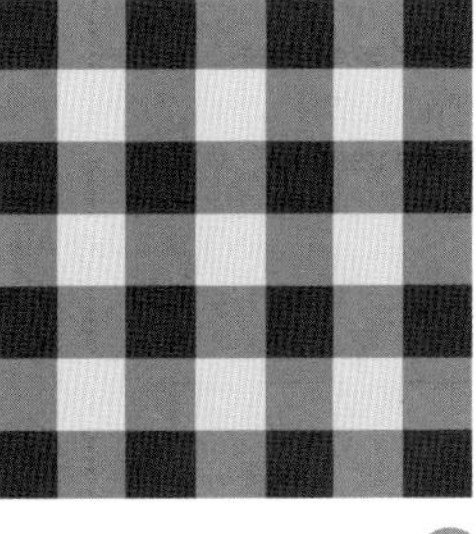

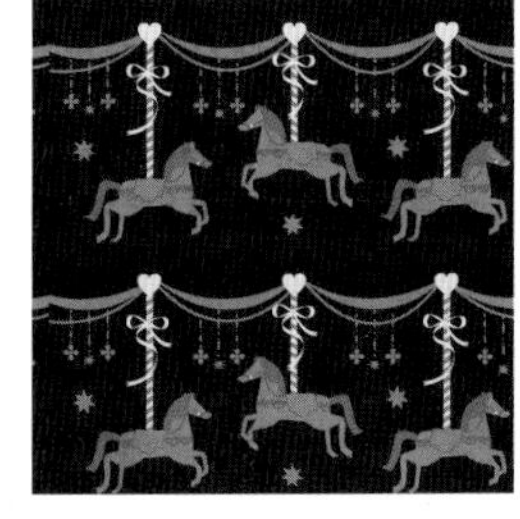

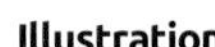

4 6 7 color 3

3 5 8 color 3

1 2 7 8 color 4

Illustration

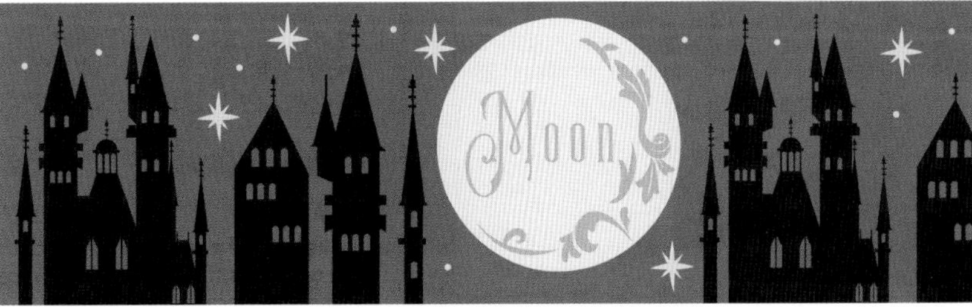

1 2 3 6 7 

PART 09 MYSTERIOUS

Recipe
069

Witch's Brew

With her cape, pointed hat and supernatural powers, the witch inhabits the world of fantasy and fairy tale. In Romania, where the culture of the witch is rooted in ancient tradition and folklore, 70 percent of the population believe in witches. Clearly, the image of the witch as a conjurer of magic retains its powerful allure.

- **FEELING** Suspicious, secretive, dark.
- **COMBINATIONS** Utilize dull, dark shades of blue and blue green to effect.
- **TIPS** This is a color scheme that can be used to express a sense of the unexpected.

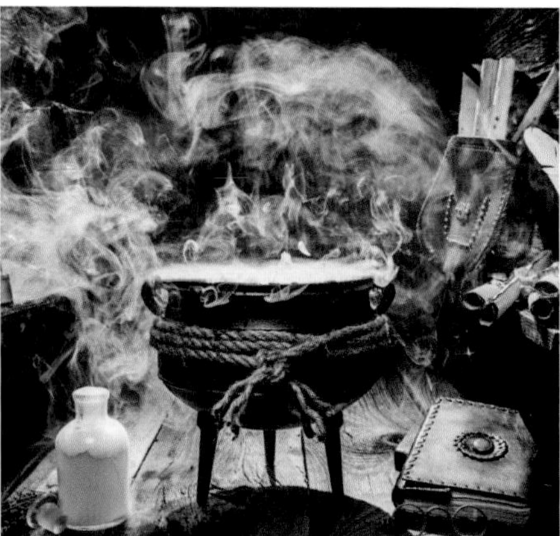

Blue and green smoke rise from a witch's caldron. What potion or elixir is being concocted this time?

❶ Orient Blue

The color of the walls at a witch's lair, similar to Oriental indigo.

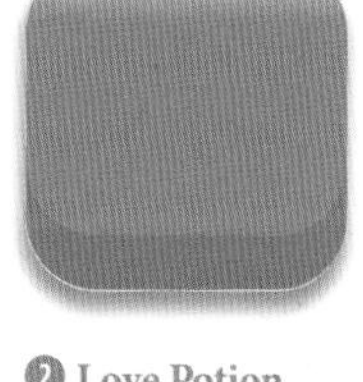

❷ Love Potion

Love potions are some witches' areas of expertise, elixirs promising passion.

❸ Black Cat

Well known as the witch's partner. This is the black of a cat's fure.

❹ Ash

The gray of ash left after a fire.

❺ Failed Work

A color that evokes something that didn't go according to plan.

❻ Silver Smoke

The silver of smoke rising from a witch's chimney.

❼ Tips

The cover of a notebook a witch uses to record spells and incantations.

❽ Elixir of Life

The color of a potion being prepared by a witch.

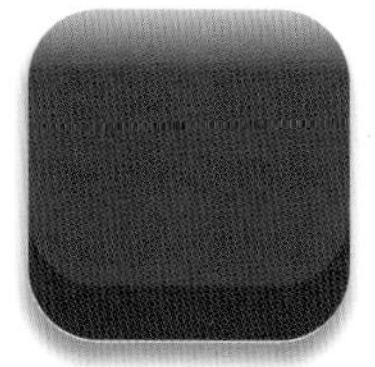

❾ Witchcraft

A word and color associated with magic or sorcery.

No.	CMYK	RGB	Hex
1	C63 M30 Y0 K50	R57 G96 B134	#395F85
2	C65 M0 Y53 K20	R70 G162 B126	#45A17E
3	C45 M25 Y0 K85	R38 G46 B64	#262D40
4	C30 M15 Y0 K37	R137 G151 B172	#8996AC
5	C35 M0 Y20 K30	R138 G174 B169	#8AAEA9
6	C10 M4 Y0 K15	R211 G217 B225	#D2D9E1
7	C30 M0 Y53 K30	R151 G174 B115	#97AE73
8	C60 M0 Y23 K40	R63 G139 B146	#3F8B92
9	C40 M30 Y0 K63	R82 G86 B110	#52556E

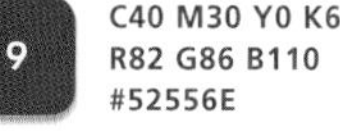

Two-color combinations

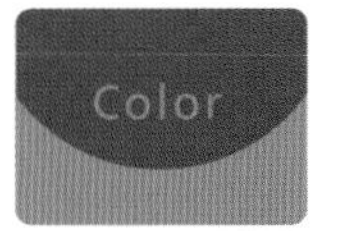

1 2

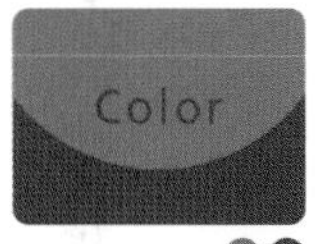

8 9

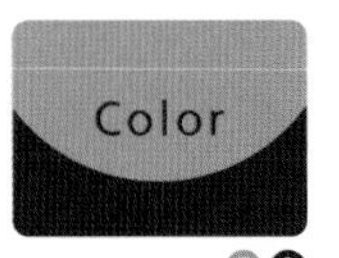

5 3

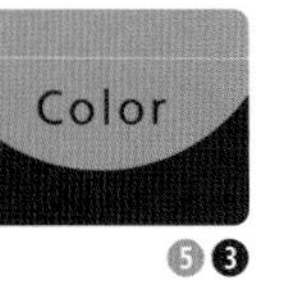

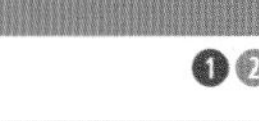
7 8

3 1

2 5

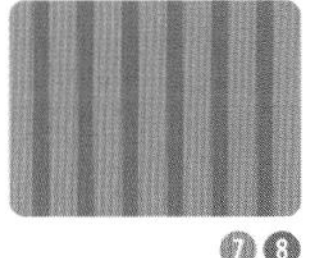
6 9

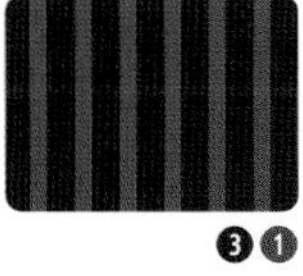
4 5

8 9

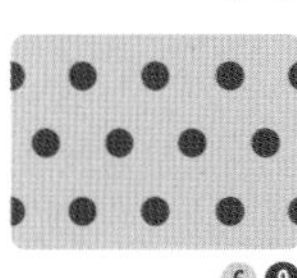

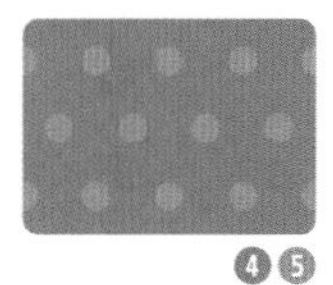

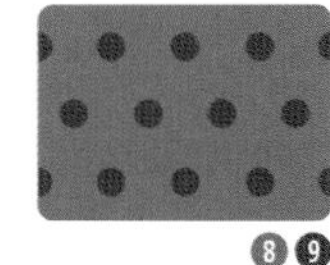

Three-color combinations

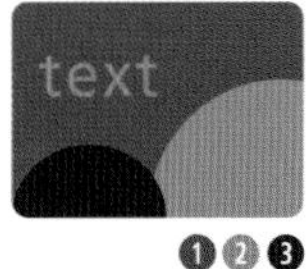

1 2 3

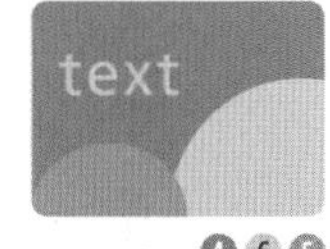

4 6 5

7 8 9

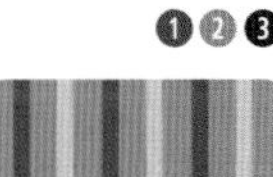
2 1 6

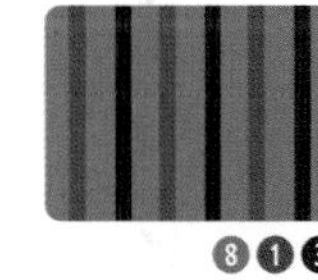
8 1 3

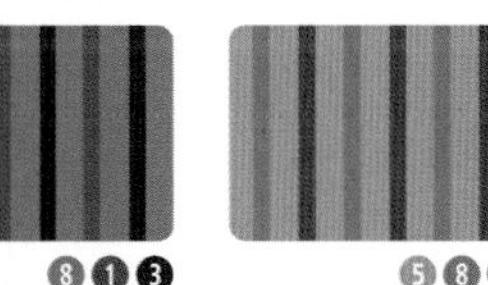
5 8 9

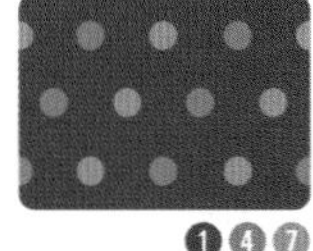
1 4 7

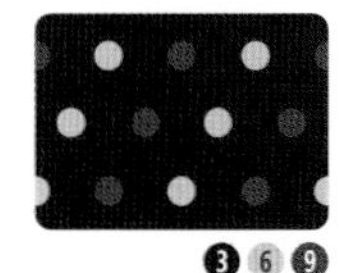
3 6 9

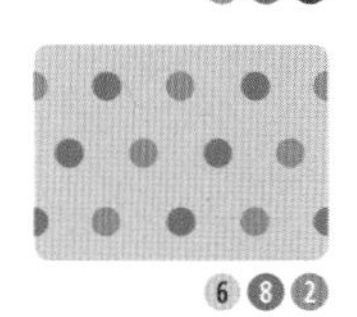
6 8 2

Designs

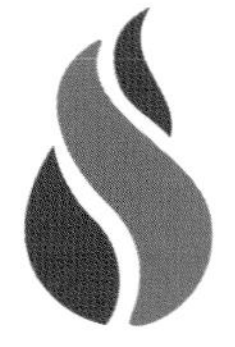
8 9 color 2

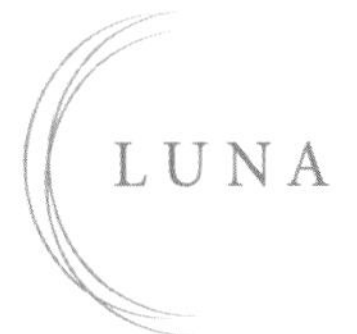

4 5 color 2

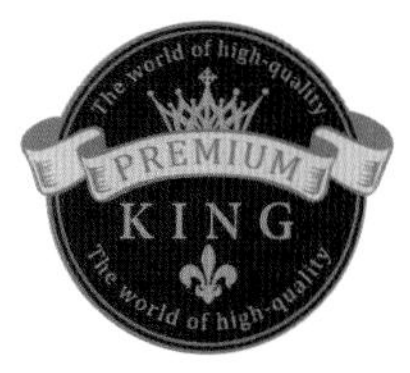

3 7 8 color 3

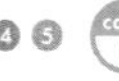

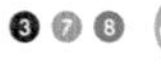

Patterns

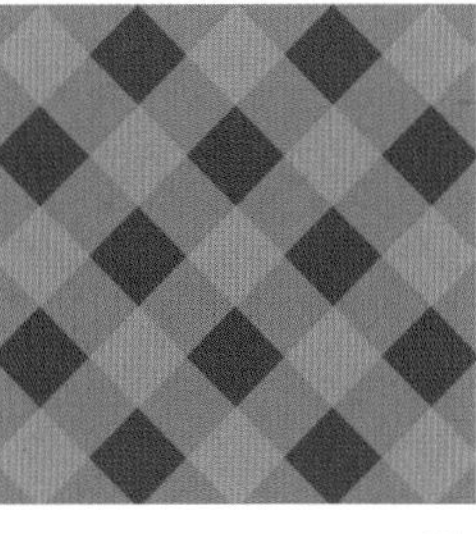
1 4 7 color 3

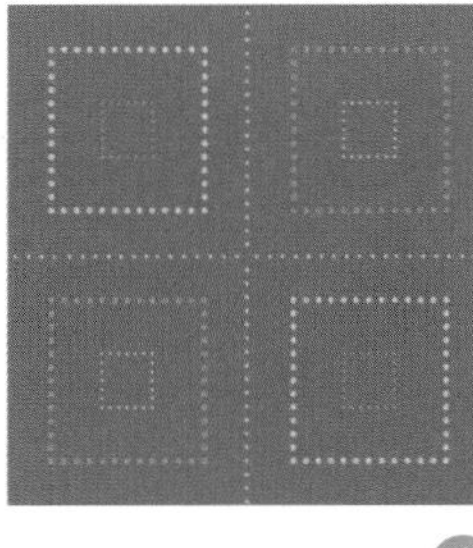
6 7 8 color 3

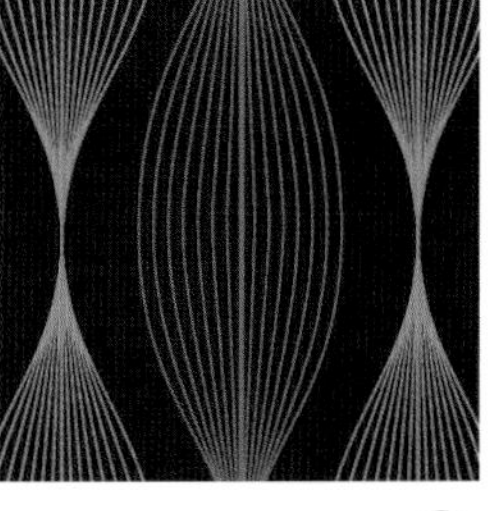
3 7 8 color 3

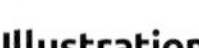

Illustration

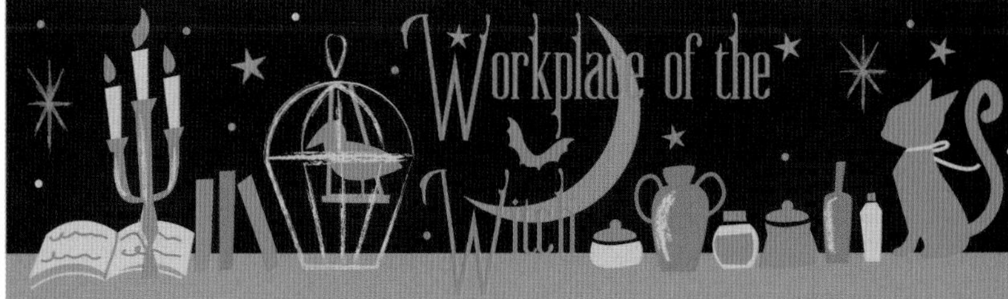

2 3 4 5 6 7 color 6

PART 09

MYSTERIOUS

Recipe
070

Arabian Nights

The Arabian Nights is also known by the title "1,001 Nights." In this beloved work, a storyteller entertains a king with fascinating tales every night, purposely stopping at the climax then resuming the exciting story again the next evening. Finally, after 1,001 stories, the pair live happily ever after.

- **FEELING** Mysterious, exotic, magical.
- **COMBINATIONS** Add black to shades from blue to purple.
- **TIPS** Use camel as an accent color.

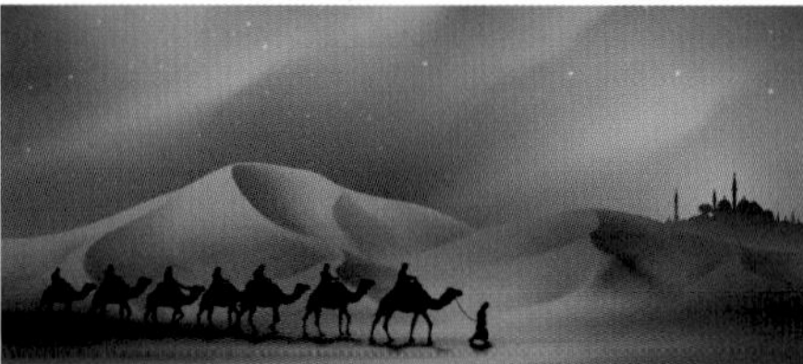

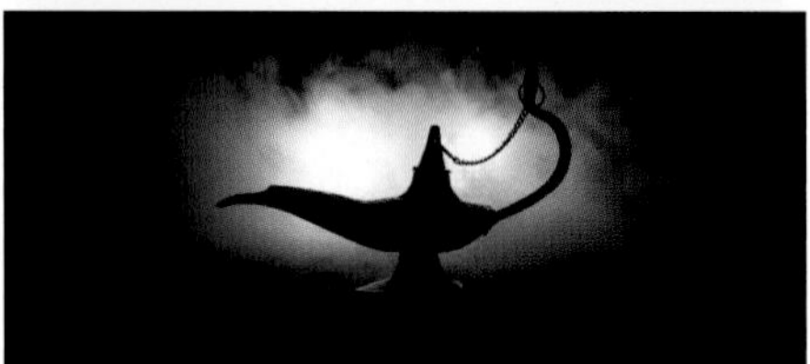

This color scheme can conjure the look of other realms.

1 Magic Hour
The pale brightness of the sky that appears briefly after sunset.

2 Islam Blue
The deep blue used in tiles with geometric motifs.

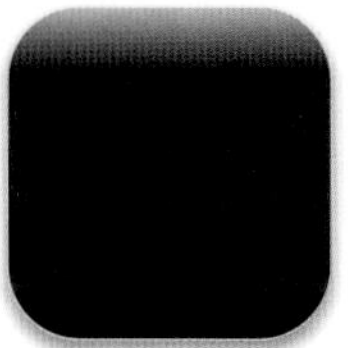

3 Moonless Night
Dark black that evokes the total darkness that accompanies a new moon.

4 Jasmine
The name of the princess who appears in *Aladdin and the Wonderful Lamp.*

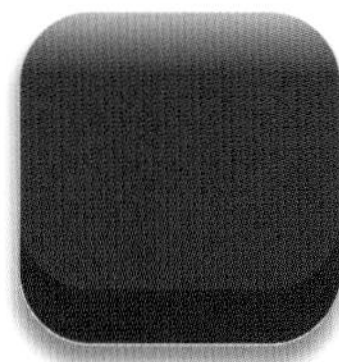

5 Aladdin
The youth whose life changes completely due to the magic of the lamp.

6 Camel
The color of a camel, this is one of fashion's standard colors.

7 Night Dune
The color of sand dunes at night, this is a gray visible by starlight.

8 Arabian Nights
The mysterious color of the night sky, evoking a distant land.

9 Cave Brown
The color of the giant cave in which the magic lamp slumbers.

1 C50 M30 Y0 K25 R114 G136 B177 #7187B0

2 C80 M65 Y0 K10 R62 G84 B158 #3D549D

3 C15 M15 Y0 K93 R45 G36 B42 #2C242A

4 C50 M0 Y5 K25 R105 G171 B197 #68ABC4

5 C50 M70 Y15 K30 R116 G72 B118 #734876

6 C0 M20 Y55 K25 R208 G176 B107 #CFB06A

7 C40 M20 Y8 K50 R101 G117 B135 #657587

8 C40 M0 Y5 K75 R59 G86 B96 #3A555F

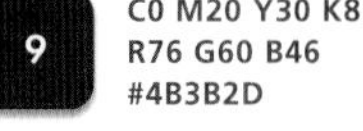

9 C0 M20 Y30 K85 R76 G60 B46 #4B3B2D

Two-color combinations

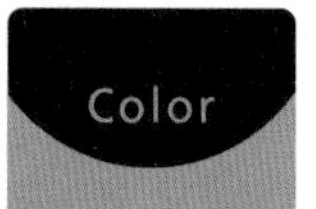

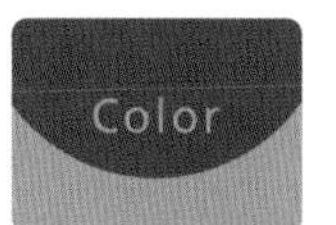

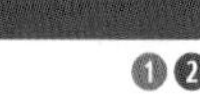
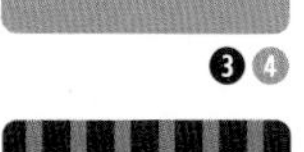

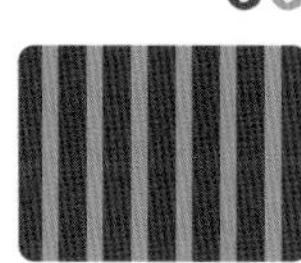
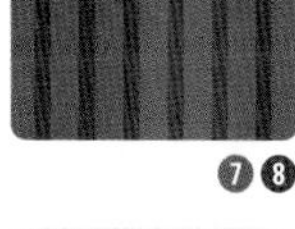
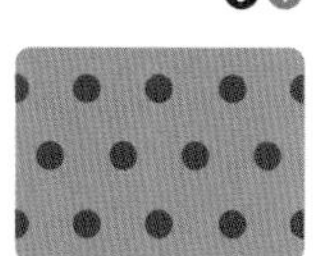
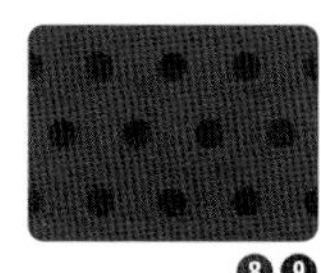

1 2 · 3 4 · 5 6
7 8 · 9 1 · 8 4
6 9 · 4 5 · 8 9

Three-color combinations

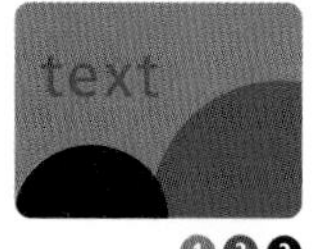

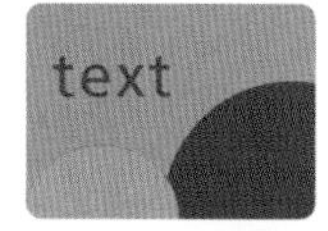

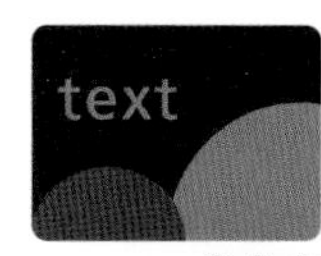

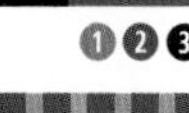
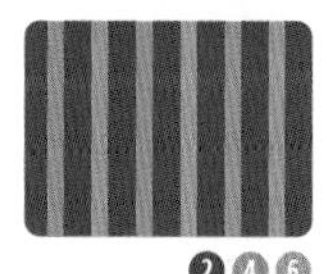
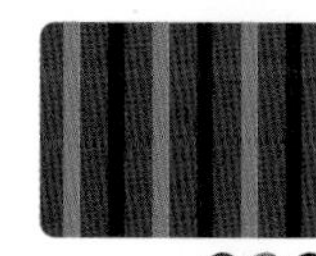

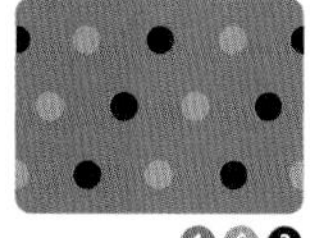
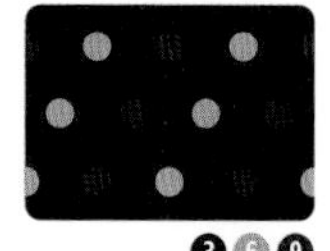
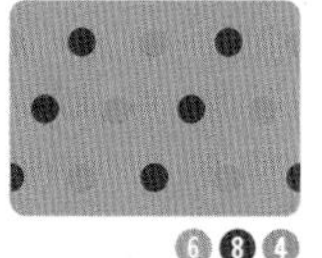

1 2 3 · 4 5 6 · 3 1 8
2 4 6 · 8 1 3 · 5 7 9
1 6 3 · 3 6 9 · 6 8 4

Designs

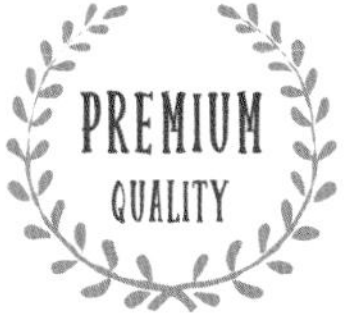

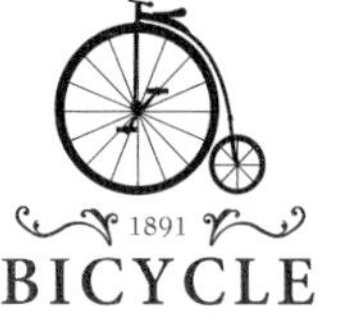

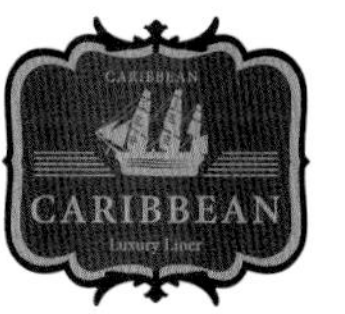

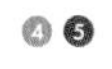

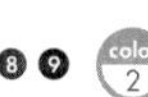
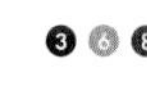

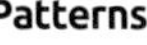

4 5 color 2 · 8 9 color 2 · 3 6 8 color 3

Patterns

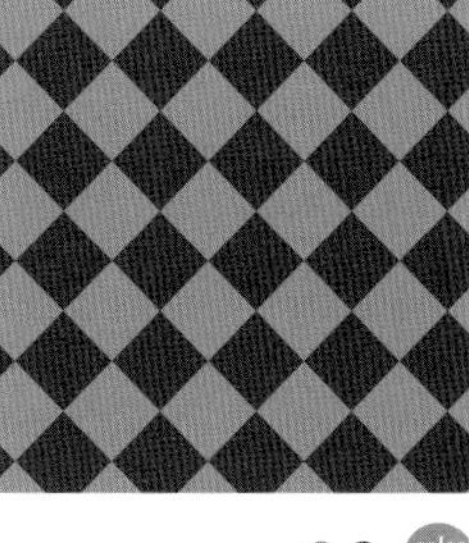
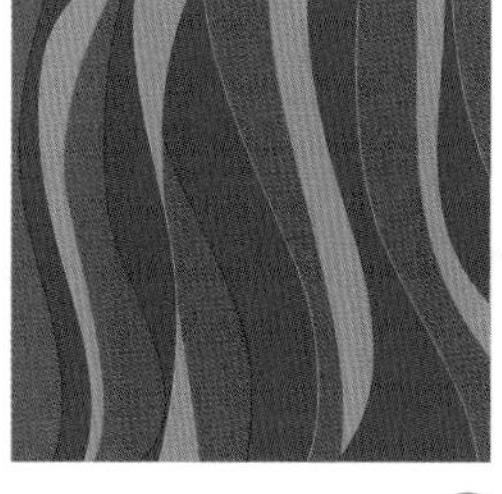
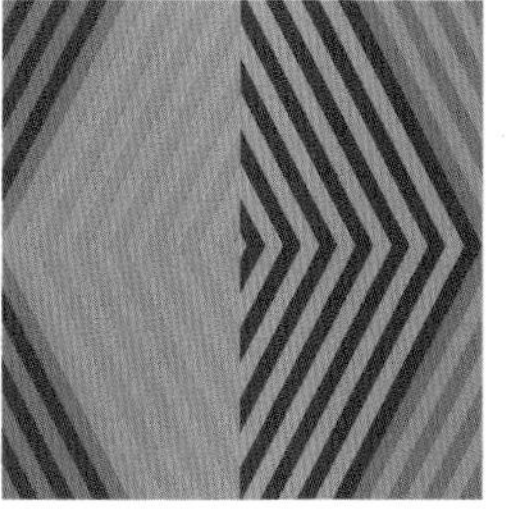
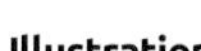

4 8 color 2 · 2 4 7 color 3 · 1 4 5 8 color 4

Illustration

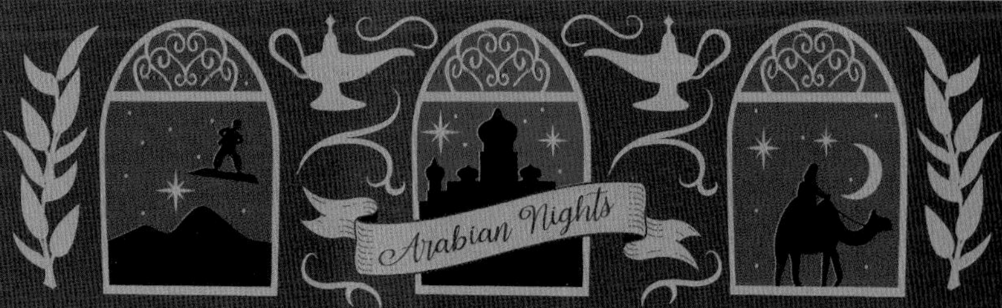

2 3 5 6 8 color 5

Part

10

Sharp + Modern

Taking its motifs from New York skyscrapers and from modern interiors, these are stylish, sophisticated color palettes. As a bonus, there are also plenty of hints here on the effective use of grays and monotones.

Cool, Neo-futuristic Color Schemes.

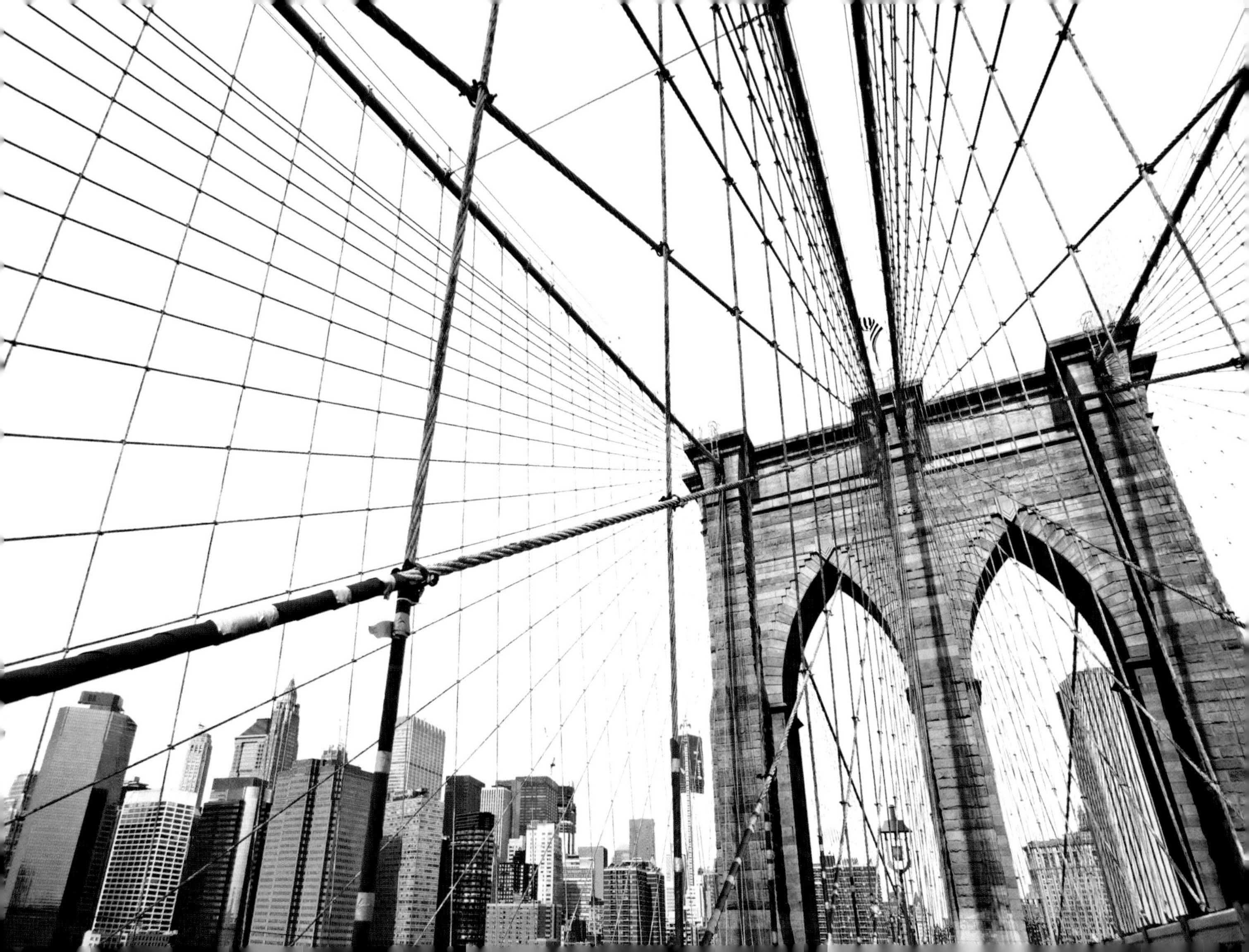

Recipe
072

Planet Earth

The Earth is a planet of water, once referred to as the Big Blue Marble. Blue is the color of the orb as seen from space, but that's a view afforded only to astronauts. The walls of the space station where astronauts temporarily live are a color chosen for minimum stress. To contrast with the blue and green, it's an off-white with the faintest hint of yellow.

- **FEELING** Mysterious, splendid, divine.
- **COMBINATIONS** Focus on intermediate colors such as blue and green.
- **TIPS** Avoid overly vibrant, vivid colors.

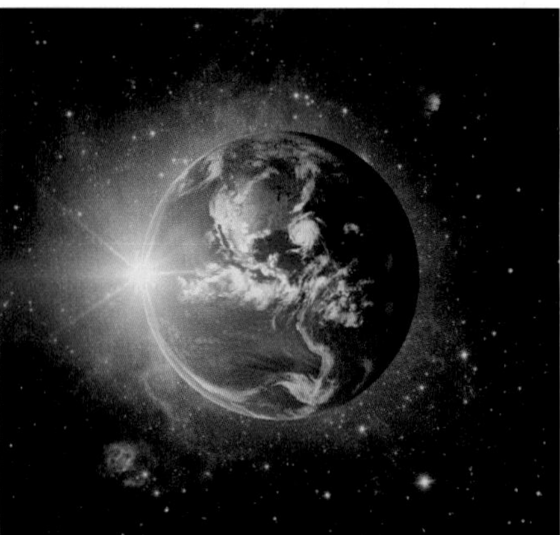

The sun peeks out from behind the planet, lighting up a palette of earthy and otherworldly tones.

❶ Cosmic Blue
A deep, dark blue that suggests outer space.

❷ Blue Planet
A mysterious, powerful blue that evokes the ocean-covered planet.

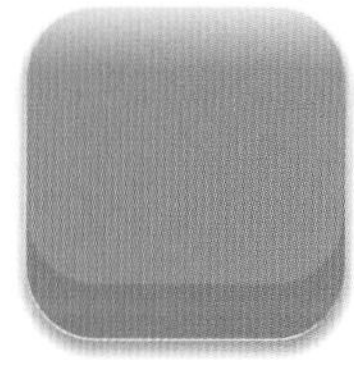

❸ Blue Star
The color of a star sparkling bluish white in space.

4 Cloud White
The color of clouds covering Earth; a white with a blue tinge.

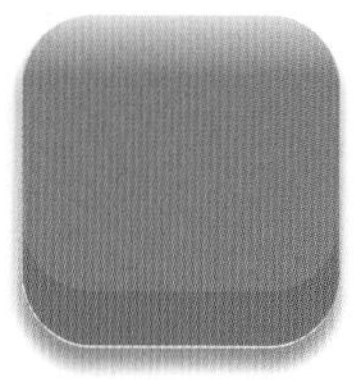

❺ Deep Sea
A blue that suggests an ocean trench or the deep.

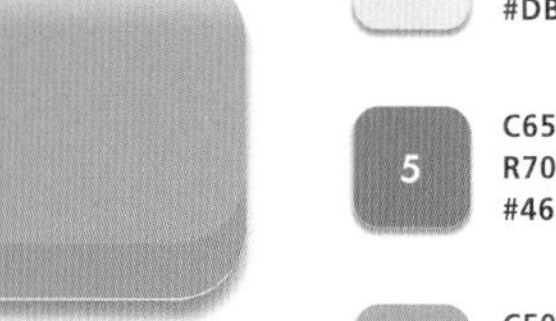

❻ Shallow Sea
A blue that calls to mind a bright, shallow sea.

❼ Oasis
A place of rest, a color associated with sustenance.

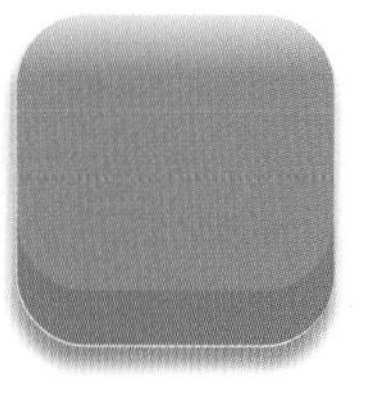

❽ City
The grayish green of an urban center.

❾ Soil
A color that evokes land seen from outer space.

1 C90 M60 Y3 K60 / R0 G45 B95 / #002D5E

2 C83 M50 Y0 K20 / R23 G96 B161 / #1760A0

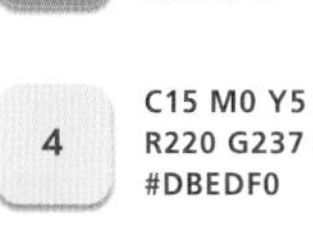

3 C45 M20 Y10 K10 / R141 G171 B197 / #8DABC5

4 C15 M0 Y5 K3 / R220 G237 B240 / #DBEDF0

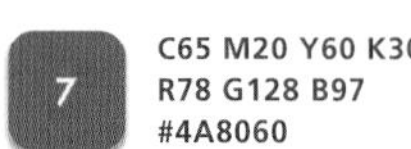

5 C65 M17 Y0 K15 / R70 G153 B202 / #4699CA

6 C50 M5 Y15 K5 / R128 G193 B209 / #7FC1D0

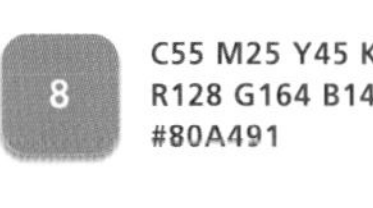

7 C65 M20 Y60 K30 / R78 G128 B97 / #4A8060

8 C55 M25 Y45 K0 / R128 G164 B146 / #80A491

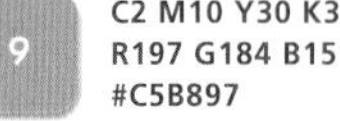

9 C2 M10 Y30 K30 / R197 G184 B151 / #C5B897

Two-color combinations

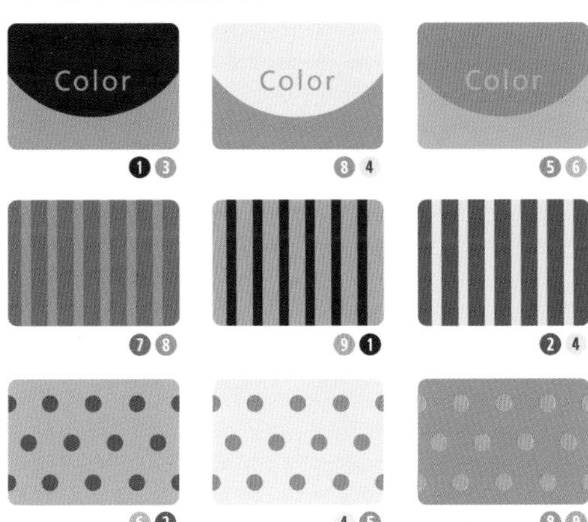

Three-color combinations

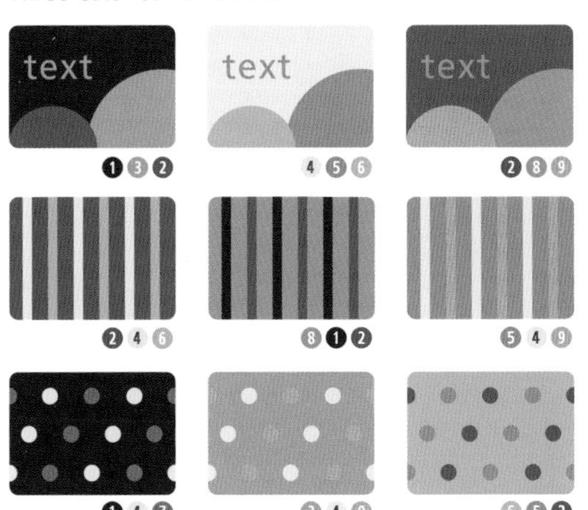

Designs

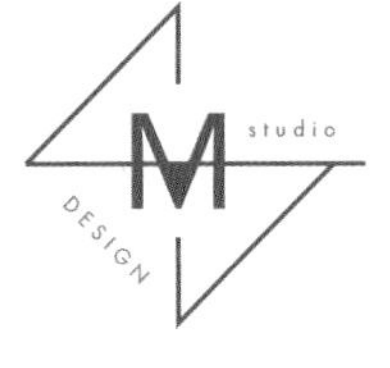

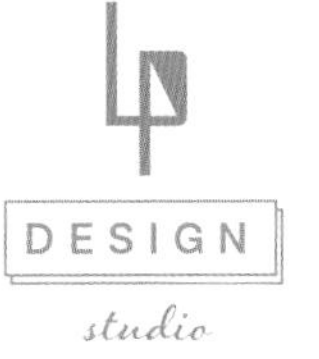

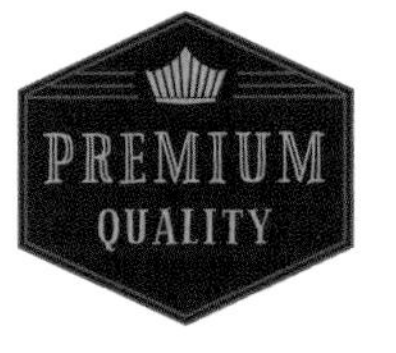

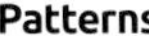

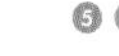

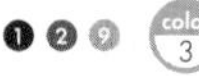

Patterns

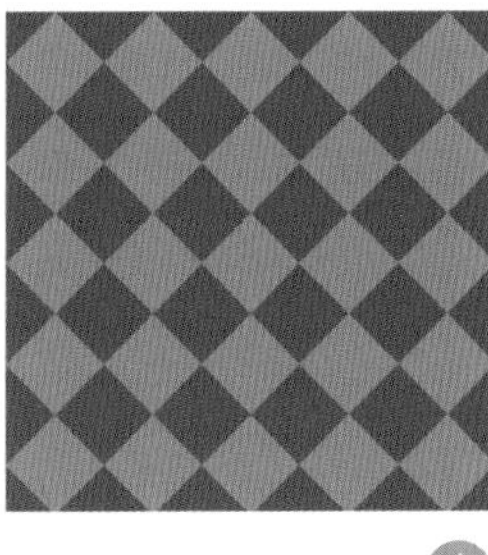

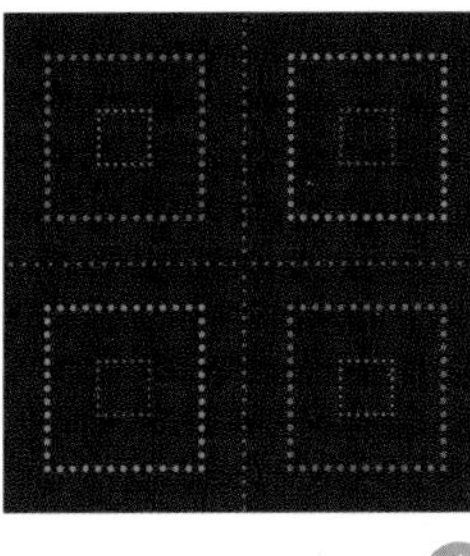

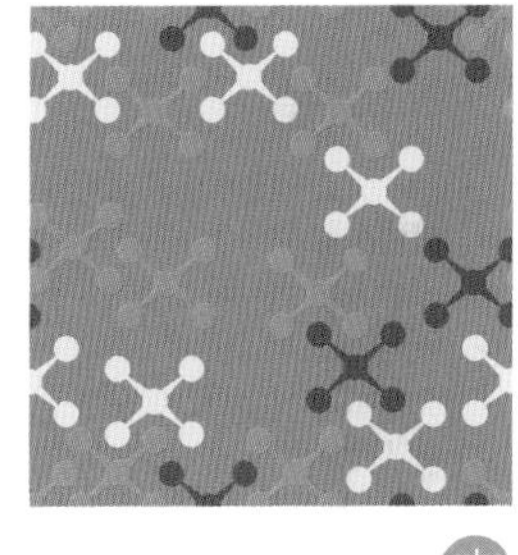

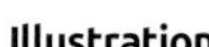

color 3

color 4

Illustration

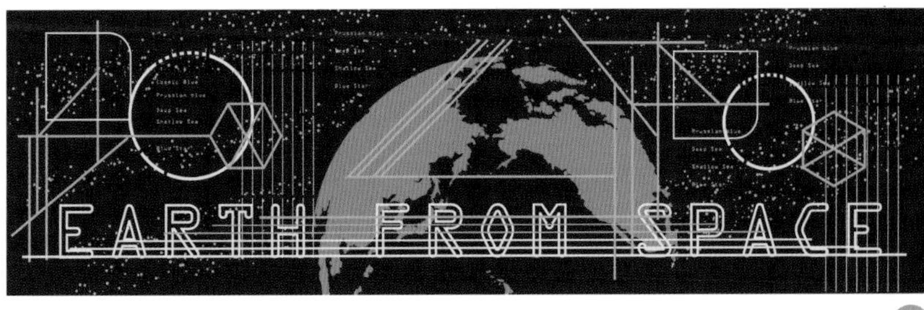

color 5

PART 10

SHARP + MODERN

Recipe
073

Modern Interiors

Colors can be divided into two main groupings: chromatic and achromatic. Achromatic colors are white, black and gray—colors lacking in hue. In color schemes for modern interiors, associated tones are added, also known as off-neutral colors. These are chromatic colors that have a very faint hue.

- **FEELING** Simple, cool, modern.
- **COMBINATIONS** Create a color scheme using only off-neutral colors.
- **TIPS** Create contrasts in brightness to pull the colors together.

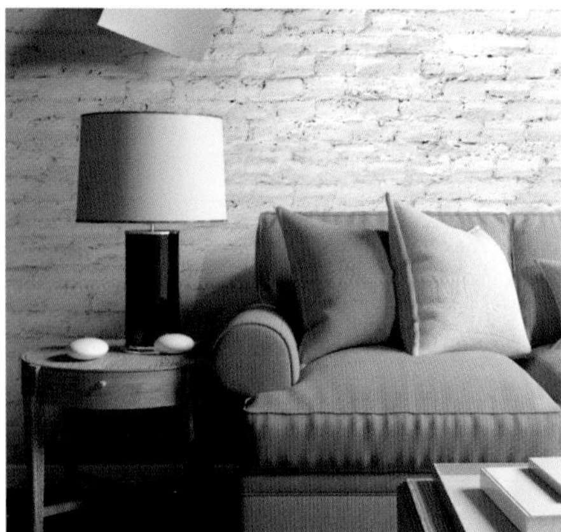

In a living space where colors overlap and possibly compete, it's a good idea to consciously keep tones low-key.

1 Simple Gray
An intermediate, neutral gray.

2 Grayish Wall
Often used in interiors, this is an extremely pale gray.

3 Light Blue Gray
Among the blue grays, this is a gray that has a high level of brightness.

4 Basic Black
In interiors that keep color to a minimum, this becomes an accent.

5 Dark Blue Gray
Among the blue grays, this is a gray that has a low level of brightness.

6 Rose Brown
Rose but without the pink tones, a brown with a reddish tinge.

7 Light Cool Gray
A light, bluish gray that makes a cool impression.

8 Light Warm Gray
A light, yellowish gray that makes a warm impression.

9 Grayish Brown
A brown that is easy to use and highly versatile in interiors.

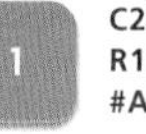
1 C20 M15 Y15 K25 R175 G176 B176 #AEAFAF

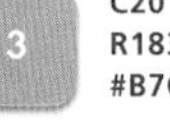
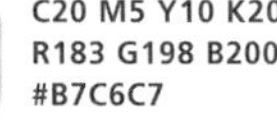
2 C10 M5 Y10 K5 R228 G231 B225 #E3E6E1

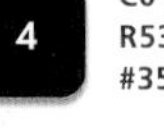
3 C20 M5 Y10 K20 R183 G198 B200 #B7C6C7

4 C0 M0 Y5 K93 R53 G47 B43 #352E2B

5 C35 M5 Y10 K70 R75 G95 B102 #4B5F65

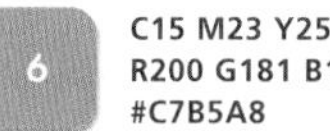
6 C15 M23 Y25 K15 R200 G181 B169 #C7B5A8

7 C13 M9 Y0 K25 R187 G190 B202 #BBBECA

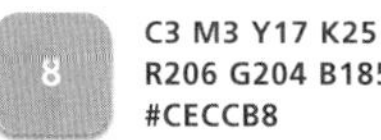
8 C3 M3 Y17 K25 R206 G204 B185 #CECCB8

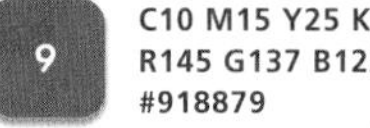
9 C10 M15 Y25 K50 R145 G137 B122 #918879

Two-color combinations

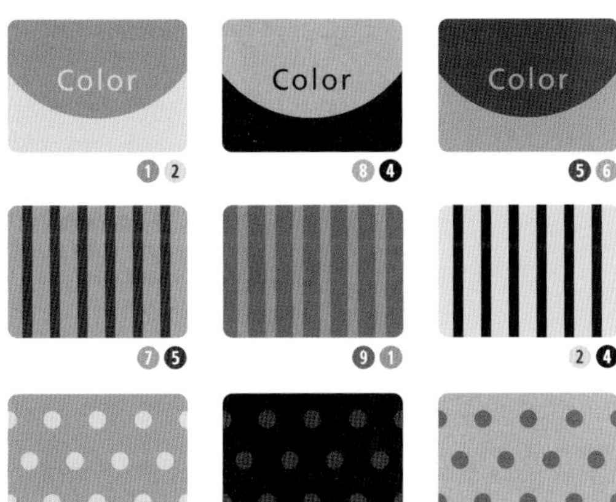

Three-color combinations

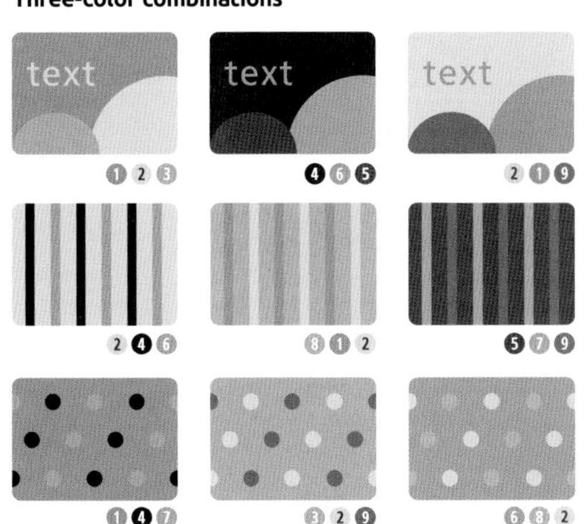

Designs

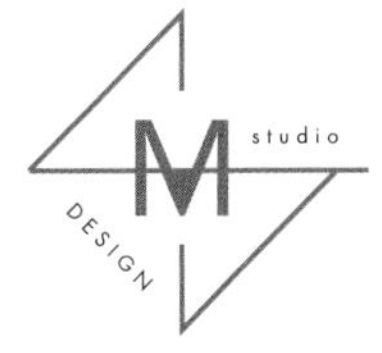

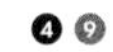

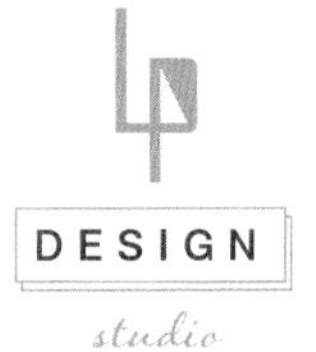

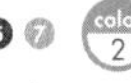

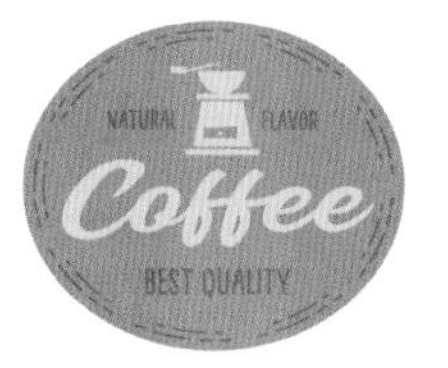

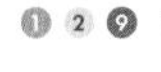

Patterns

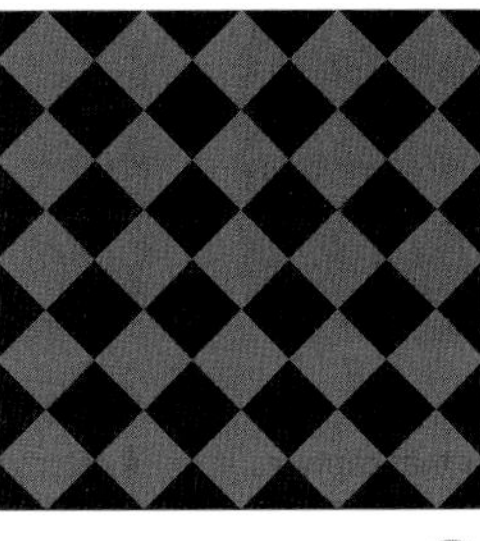
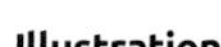

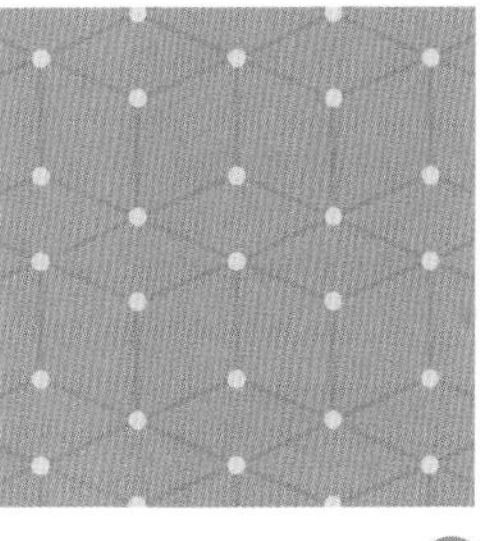

1 2 6 color 3

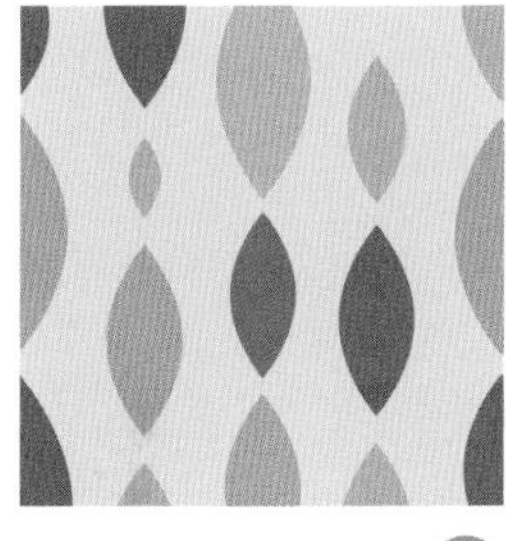

2 3 6 9 color 4

Illustration

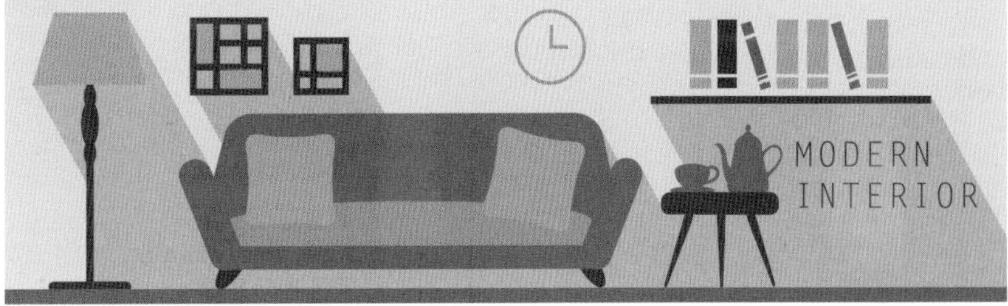

1 2 5 6 8 color 5

PART 10

SHARP + MODERN

Recipe
074

New York Skyscrapers

In the 1960s, a specific red was thrown into the spotlight, the red of the necktie or "power tie" worn by politicians. Even today it's widely used as a color that creates a sense of passion, strength and a driving force. With the colors of the sunset-drenched Manhattan buildings as a base, this palette adds red—a symbol of success and victory—as an accent color.

- **FEELING** Hopes for tomorrow, fulfilling, metropolitan.
- **COMBINATIONS** Add red as an accent to off-neutral colors.
- **TIPS** Put gray with a touch of color in the leading role.

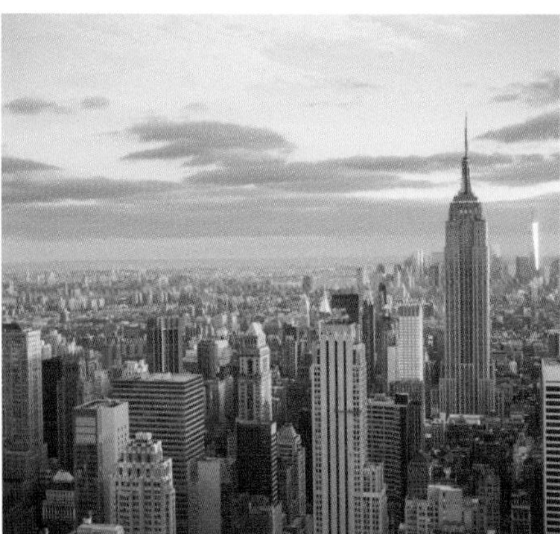

The clusters of buildings in Manhattan take on a different appearance depending on the colors of the light and time of day.

❶ Urbane Brown
A brown with a stylish air.

❷ Rose Beige
Tinged with red, this beige makes a sophisticated impression.

❸ Greenish Gray
A gray tinged with green that sets off shades of red.

❹ Neutral
A color that captures and expresses a sense of impartiality, neither light nor dark.

❺ Old Building
A color with depth, like that of an old building.

❻ Ink Black
A black resembling fountain pen ink.

❼ Reddish Gray
A gray tinged with red, seen in the spaces between buildings at sundown.

❽ Power Tie
This color often makes an appearance at a president's inaugural address.

❾ Make it Happen
A color to make dreams into reality.

No.	CMYK	RGB	Hex
1	C35 M45 Y30 K35	R134 G110 B117	#856E75
2	C13 M20 Y30 K20	R196 G179 B157	#C3B39C
3	C30 M0 Y20 K15	R170 G203 B193	#AACBC1
4	C10 M5 Y10 K23	R197 G201 B196	#C5C8C4
5	C40 M5 Y30 K40	R115 G148 B136	#739488
6	C35 M40 Y15 K70	R78 G66 B81	#4D4150
7	C15 M30 Y25 K55	R128 G108 B104	#7F6C68
8	C3 M100 Y100 K25	R188 G0 B10	#BB0009
9	C0 M90 Y87 K0	R232 G56 B37	#E73825

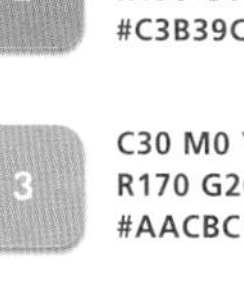

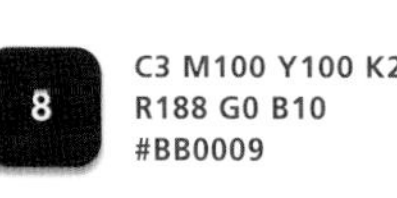

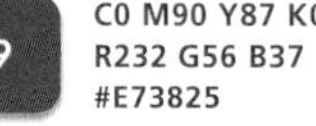

Two-color combinations

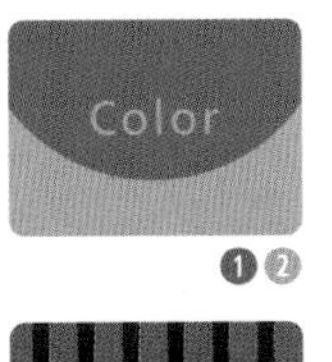

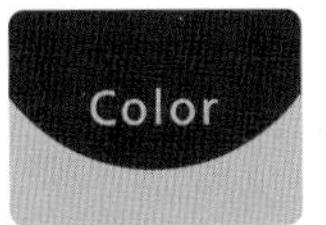

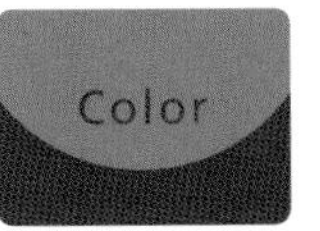

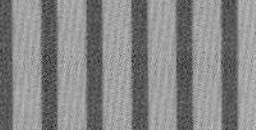

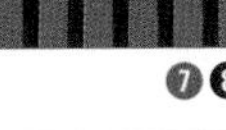

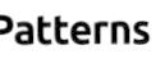

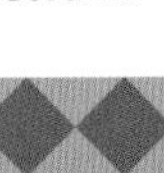

Three-color combinations

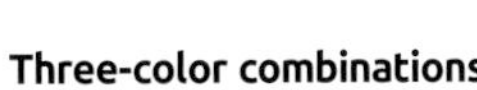

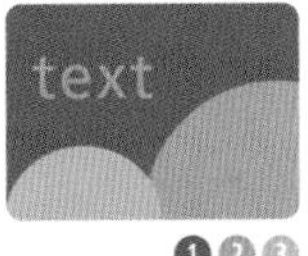

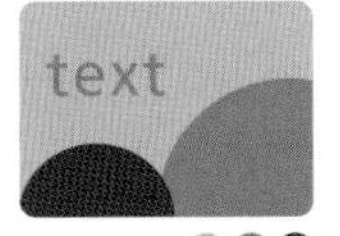

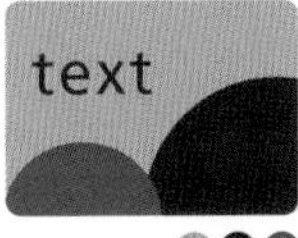

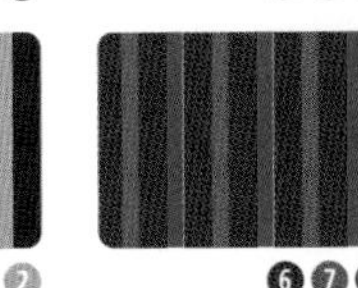

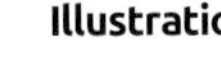

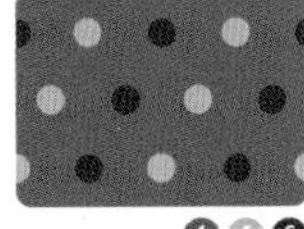

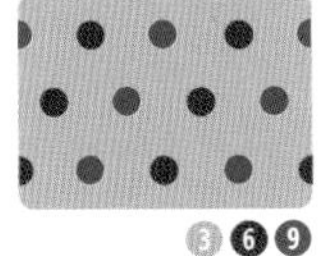

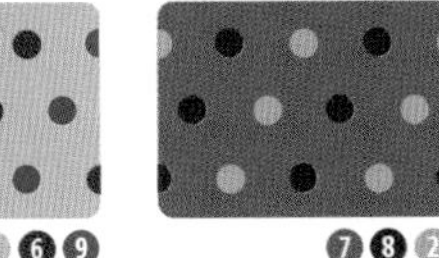

Designs

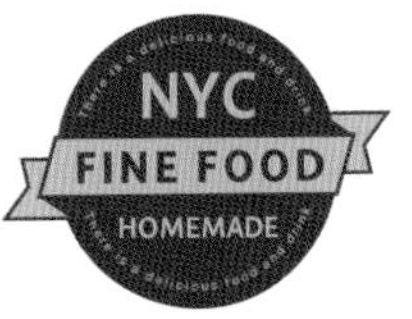

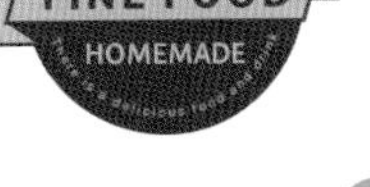

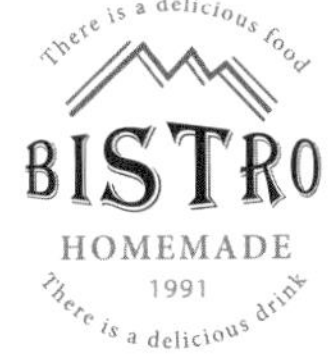

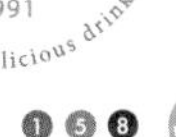

Patterns

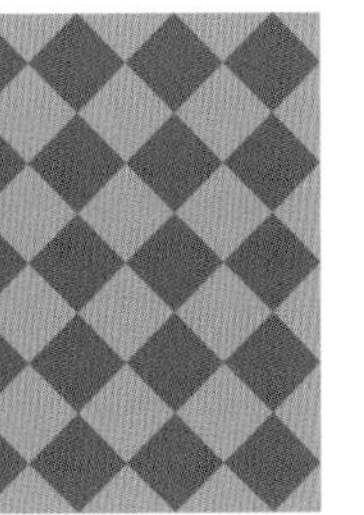

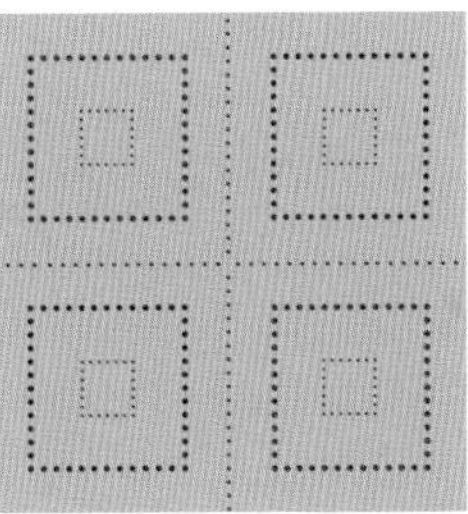

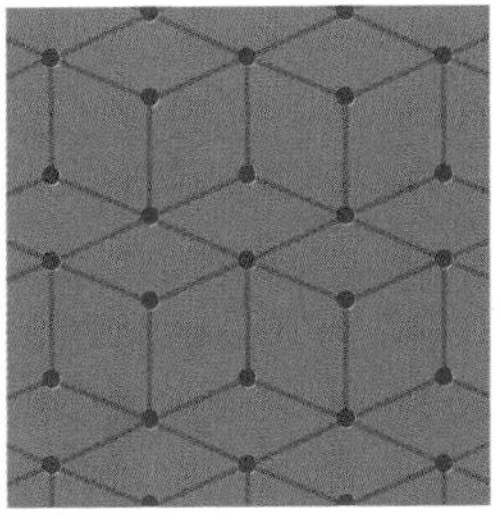

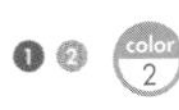

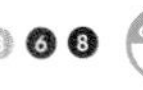

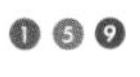

Illustration

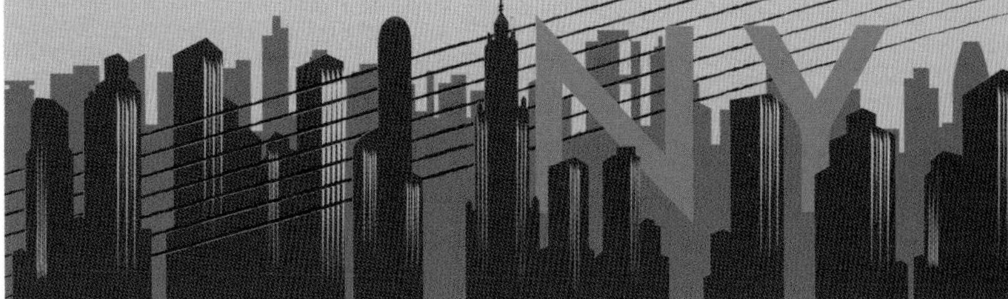

Recipe
075

Nordic Modern

The winters are long and dark in Scandinavia. Areas near the Arctic Circle experience "white nights" in summer when the sun doesn't set all night, but in winter, the sun never rises above the horizon. The vivid, warm colors favored in Scandinavian design are one way of making the living environment brighter.

- **FEELING** Natural, exuding warmth, magnanimous.
- **COMBINATIONS** Focus on warm, yellow-based colors.
- **TIPS** Turquoise shades work well with browns.

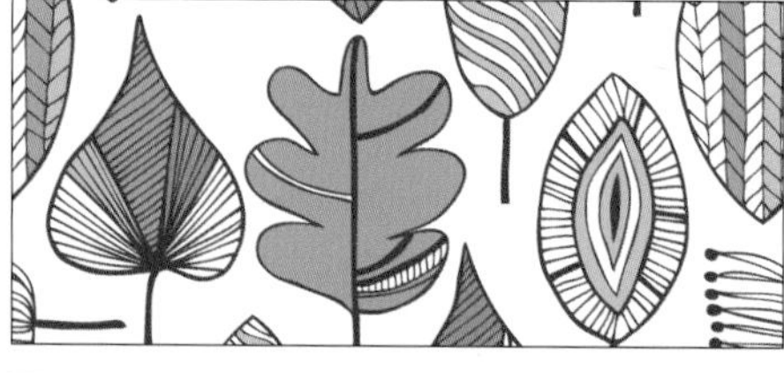

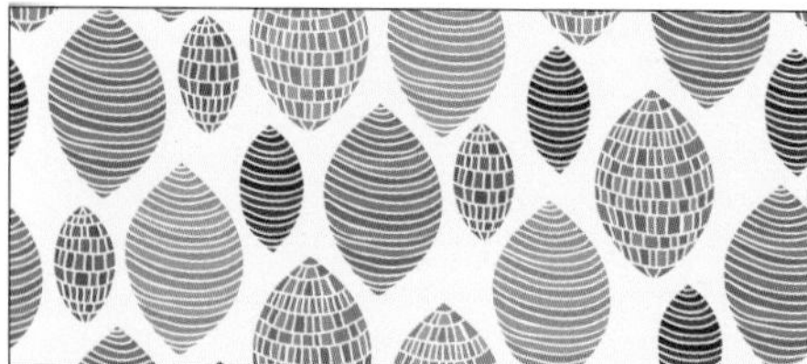

Abstracted natural motifs feature heavily in Scandinavian designs.

1 Nordic Blue
A greenish blue tinged with gray, this color has a sense of warmth to it.

2 Grass Green
In Japanese this green is called grass green.

3 Straw Yellow
The faded yellow of straw.

4 Autumn Brown
The base color in forests from fall through to the start of winter.

5 Autumn Leaf
The color of trees just before they lose their leaves.

6 Teal Green
The green seen on duck wings.

7 Teal Blue
The greenish blue seen on duck wings.

8 Nordic Night
A color evoking the night sky in the northern latitudes.

9 Pine Cone
The color of pine cones; a deep brown with a reddish tint.

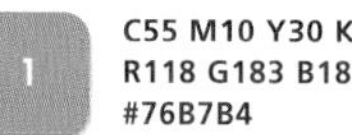

No.	CMYK	RGB	Hex
1	C55 M10 Y30 K3	R118 G183 B181	#76B7B4
2	C50 M20 Y70 K2	R143 G171 B101	#8EAB64
3	C20 M15 Y75 K0	R215 G204 B85	#D7CC55
4	C17 M30 Y70 K30	R172 G144 B71	#AC8F47
5	C40 M15 Y70 K40	R119 G135 B71	#778646
6	C75 M25 Y50 K0	R55 G148 B137	#369488
7	C65 M15 Y15 K27	R65 G141 B167	#408CA6
8	C60 M20 Y40 K63	R49 G85 B80	#305450
9	C13 M25 Y35 K80	R79 G65 B52	#4E4134

Two-color combinations

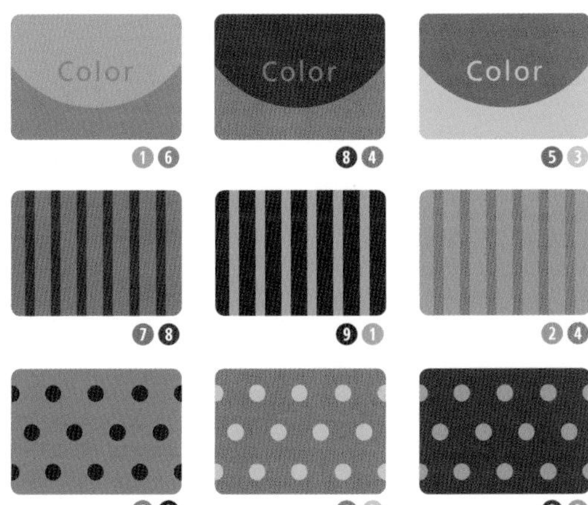

1 6 · 8 4 · 5 3
7 8 · 9 1 · 2 4
6 9 · 4 3 · 8 2

Three-color combinations

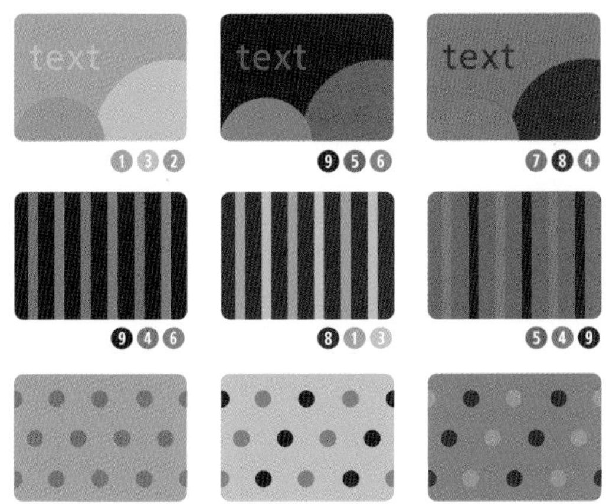

1 3 2 · 9 5 6 · 7 8 4
9 4 6 · 8 1 3 · 5 4 9
1 4 7 · 3 6 9 · 6 8 2

Designs

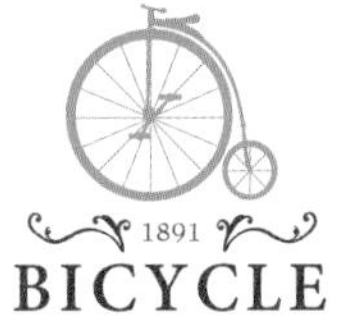
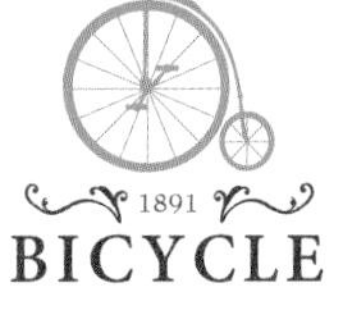

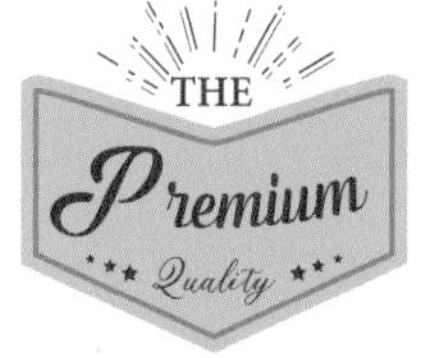

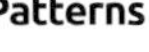

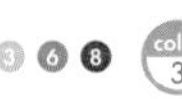

6 7 color 2 · 2 8 color 2 · 3 6 8 color 3

Patterns

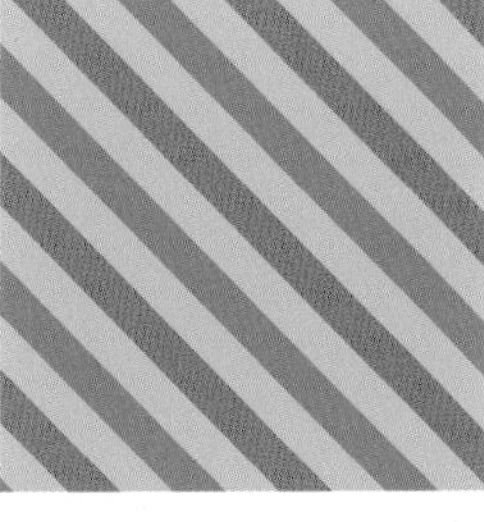
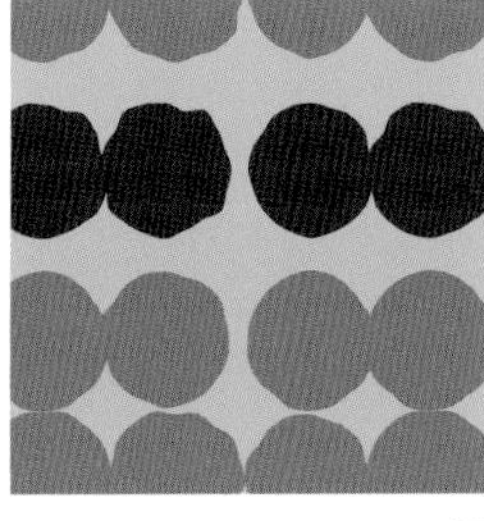
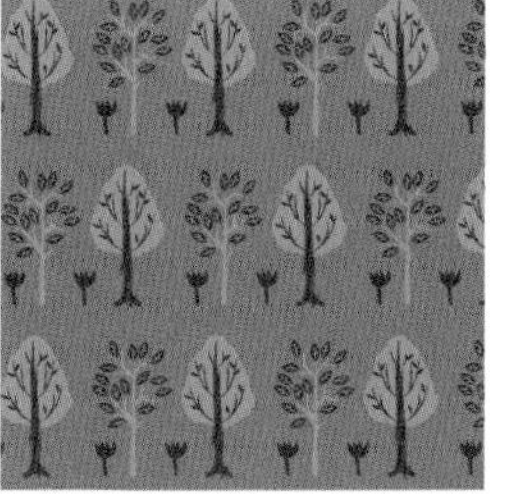

3 5 6 color 3 · 3 7 9 color 3 · 2 4 8 color 3

Illustration

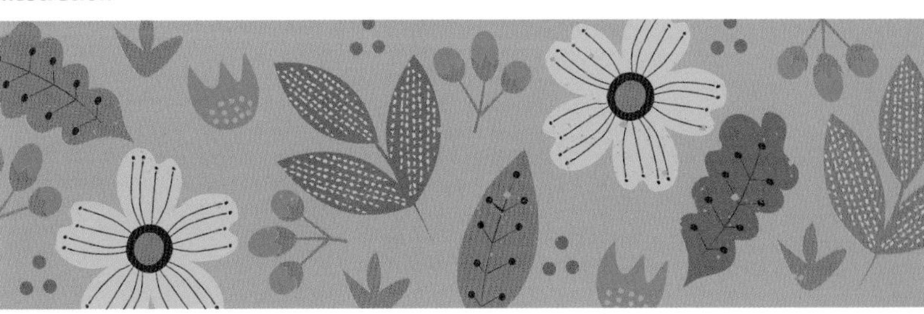
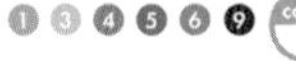

1 3 4 5 6 9 color 6

Part

11

The World Around Us

These color palettes evoke the landscapes and events of Japan's four seasons and use color to take us on a journey around the world. Notice how national and cultural differences can alter how the same color groupings appear.

Colors of Japan and the World

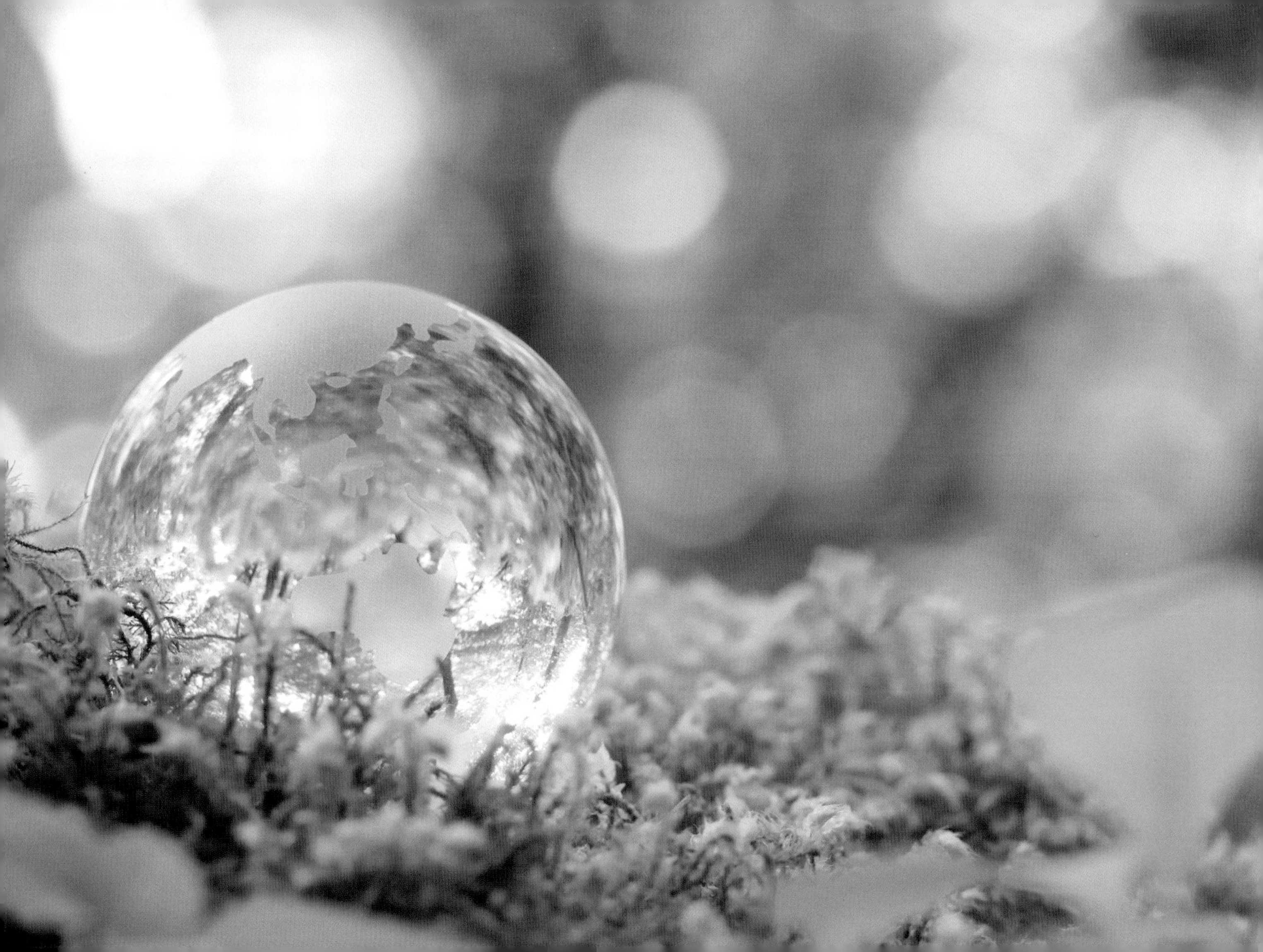

Recipe
076

Springtime in Japan

Spring scenery in Japan typically calls to mind the collaboration of cherry blossoms in full bloom with rapeseed flowers. Somei Yoshino cherries blossom only for a single week and then shed their blooms in a moment. It was Japanese people who came to see the cherry blossoms as a metaphor for life, perseverance in preparing to fulfill one's brief role.

- **FEELING** Bright, soft, twinkling.
- **COMBINATIONS** Use light pinks and yellow greens as base colors.
- **TIPS** Use vibrant yellows and violets as accent colors.

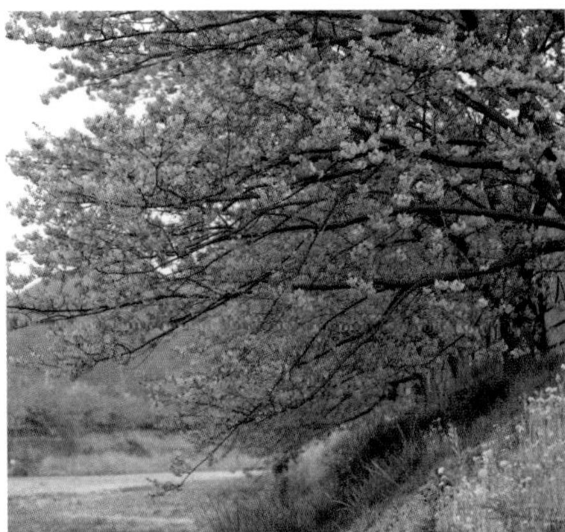

The wave of spring cherry blossoms, spreading to the north as the season progresses, is called the Sakura Front.

1 Rapeseed Flower
Also called the seed oil plant, this is the raw material for rapeseed oil.

2 Young Leaf
Deciduous trees start sprouting leaves along with the arrival of spring.

3 Petal
A color suggesting cherry blossom petals, it's more highly saturated than the actual petals.

4 Full Bloom
A color expressing the joy of people viewing cherry trees in full bloom.

5 Spring Haze
The hazy sky of spring, a color phrase used since the Heian era.

6 Budding
The time when wild vegetables send out pale yellow-green buds.

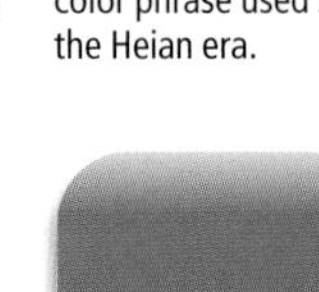

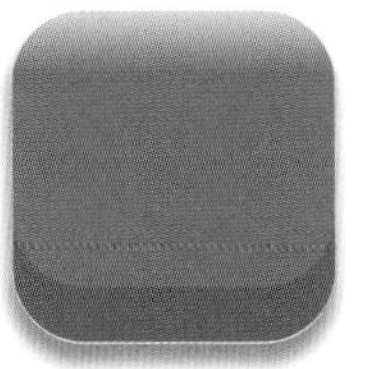

7 Bamboo Shoot
The edible shoots of bamboo emerge from the ground at the start of spring.

8 Princess Violet
The color of little violets that grow on the sides of paths.

9 Cuckoo
A gray like that of a cuckoo's wing.

1
C0 M4 Y90 K0
R255 G236 B0
#FFEC00

2
C45 M5 Y77 K0
R156 G197 B90
#9CC45A

3
C0 M20 Y3 K0
R250 G220 B229
#FADCE5

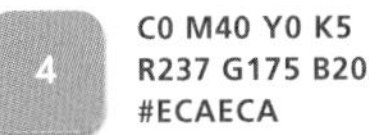

4
C0 M40 Y0 K5
R237 G175 B202
#ECAECA

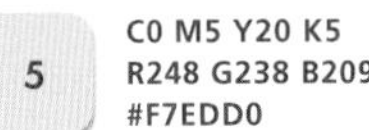

5
C0 M5 Y20 K5
R248 G238 B209
#F7EDD0

6
C20 M2 Y60 K0
R216 G226 B128
#D8E27F

7
C0 M25 Y50 K30
R197 G161 B108
#C4A16C

8
C45 M55 Y2 K0
R155 G124 B180
#9B7BB4

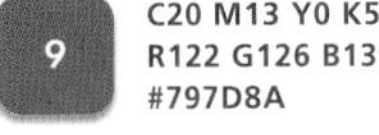

9
C20 M13 Y0 K55
R122 G126 B139
#797D8A

Two-color combinations

Color — 1 4

Color — 8 3

Color — 5 2

7 6

3 4

6 1

3 9

1 2

8 5

Three-color combinations

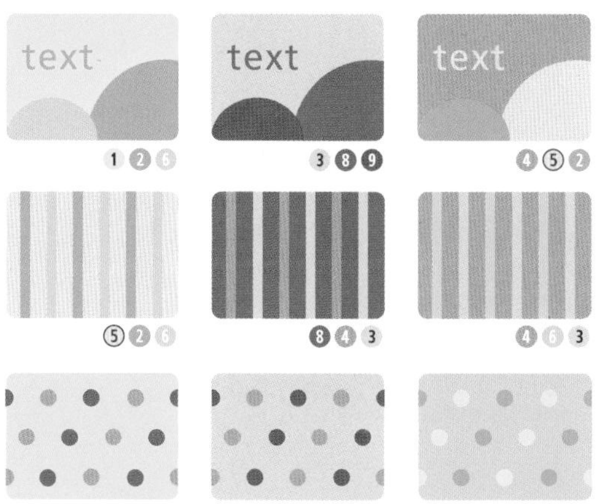

1 2 6 · 3 8 9 · 4 5 2

5 2 6 · 8 4 3 · 4 6 3

1 4 8 · 3 4 9 · 6 1 2

Designs

3 4 color 2

6 9 color 2

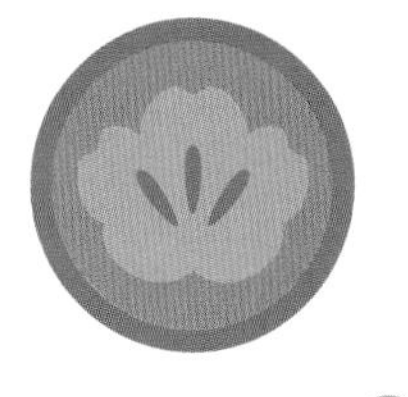

4 7 8 color 3

Patterns

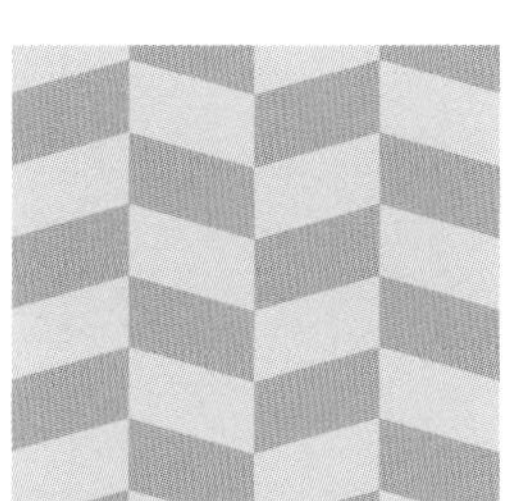

3 4 color 2

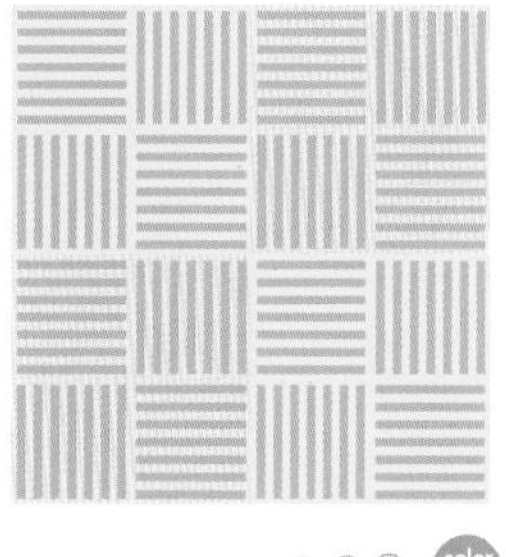

1 2 5 color 3

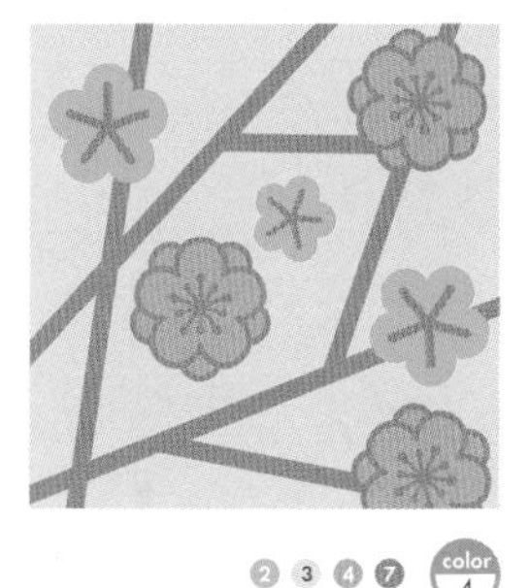

2 3 4 7 color 4

Illustration

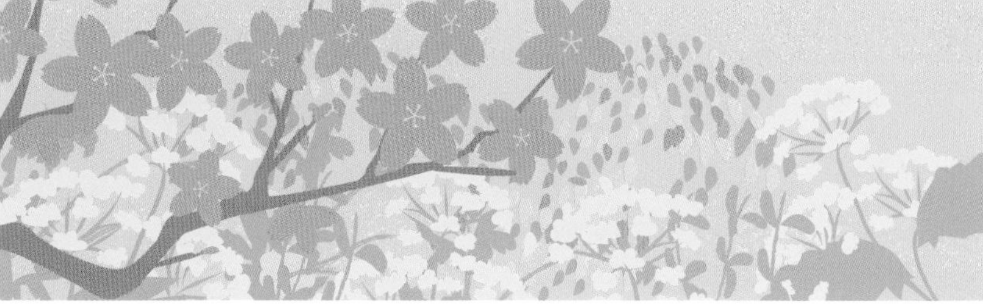

1 2 3 4 5 7 color 6

Recipe
077

Spring Festivals and Events

In Japan, spring marks the end, and restart of, the school and business year. I can easily become harried at this time of the year, because I need to focus on staff reshuffling and the start of new projects. Without even thinking, I put on a crisp white shirt to motivate myself or a strong blue color to gather my thoughts.

- **FEELING** Wishes fulfilled, fresh, clear.
- **COMBINATIONS** Create a color scheme that contrasts light and strong colors.
- **TIPS** Create variations through the tones used.

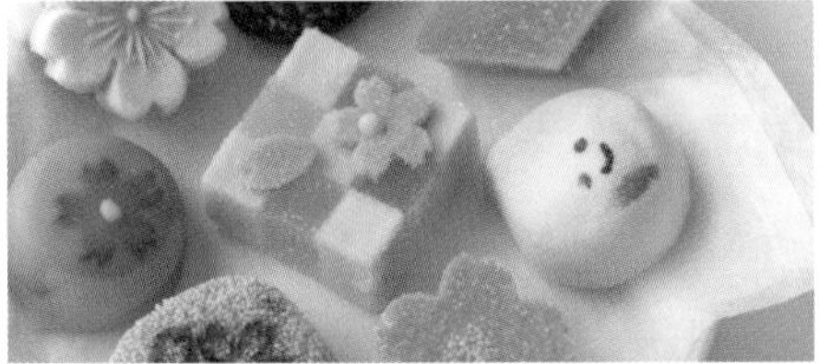

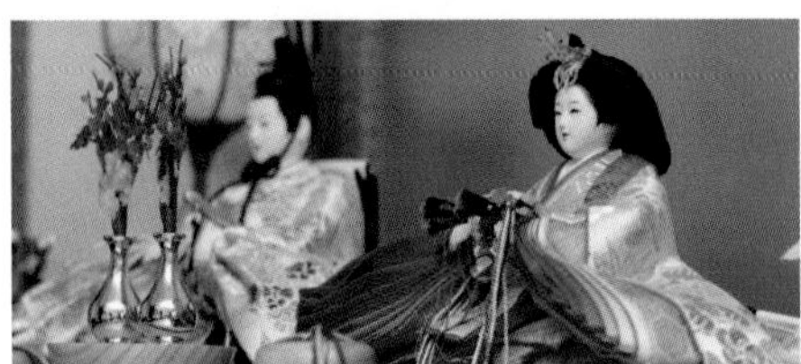

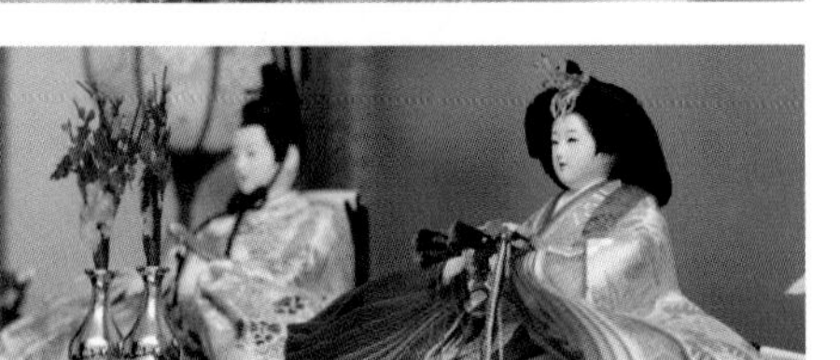

Tears and laughter: Spring is a season of farewells and new encounters.

① Doll Festival
A festival to pray for the health and well-being of girls.

② Lingering Snow
The snow that falls in spring, or the snow that remains.

③ Beneath the Snow
The color of plants preparing to bud beneath the snow.

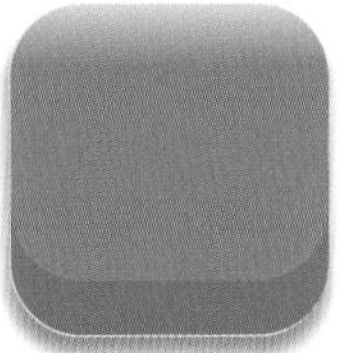

④ Rice Cake Wrapped in Oak Leaf
The oak is seen as a symbol of fertility or the prosperity of inheritance.

⑤ Carp Streamers
The color of carp streamers used to pray for the health of boys.

⑥ Uniform
A basic uniform color, deep navy.

⑦ Mother's Day
Gifts for mothers who are living are red, while mothers who have died are honored with white.

⑧ New School Semester
A color conjuring the mix of nervousness and excitement on the morning of a new school semester.

⑨ School Satchel
Elementary school students' satchels were all once this color.

1 C0 M45 Y13 K0 R243 G168 B183 #F2A7B7

2 C0 M0 Y7 K0 R255 G254 B243 #FFFEF3

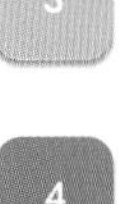

3 C30 M0 Y55 K8 R183 G209 B134 #B7D185

4 C57 M30 Y75 K0 R127 G153 B90 #7E995A

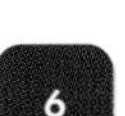

5 C60 M55 Y0 K2 R118 G115 B179 #7673B3

6 C70 M43 Y0 K60 R38 G67 B107 #25426B

7 C0 M87 Y55 K0 R232 G64 B82 #E84051

8 C15 M0 Y3 K0 R223 G241 B248 #DFF1F7

9 C4 M75 Y40 K0 R229 G96 B111 #E4606F

Two-color combinations

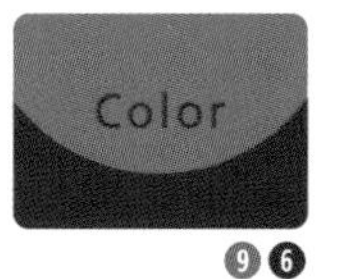
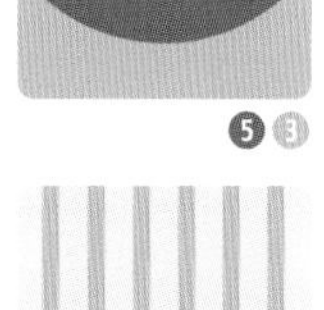
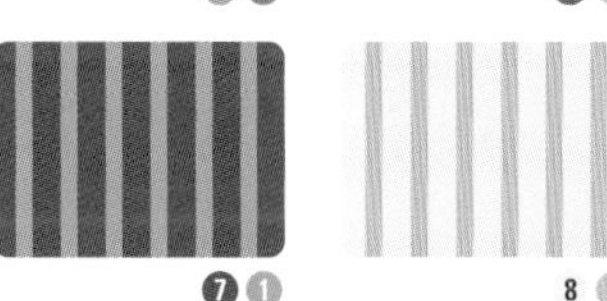
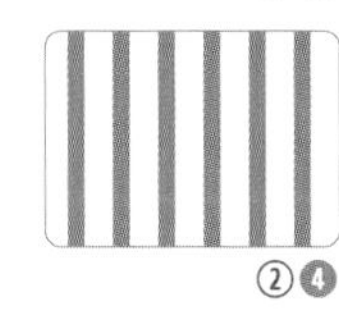
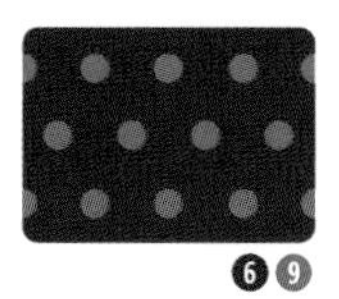
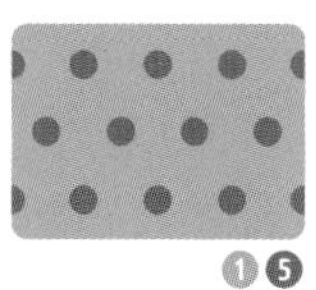
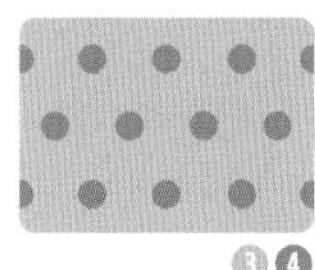

Three-color combinations

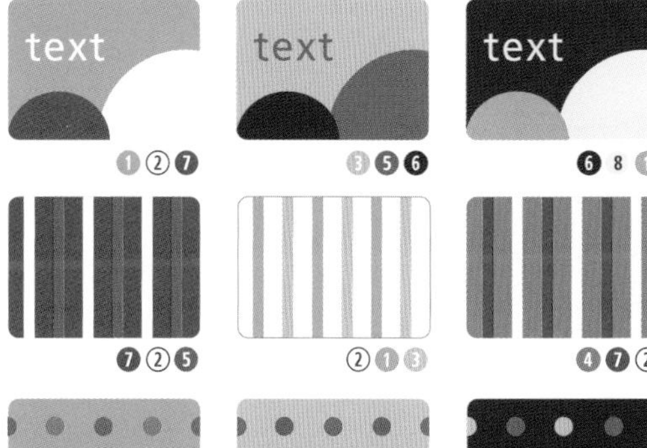

Designs

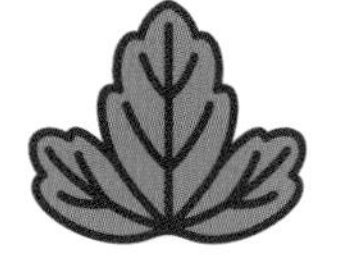

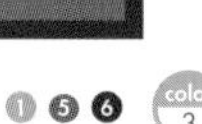

Patterns

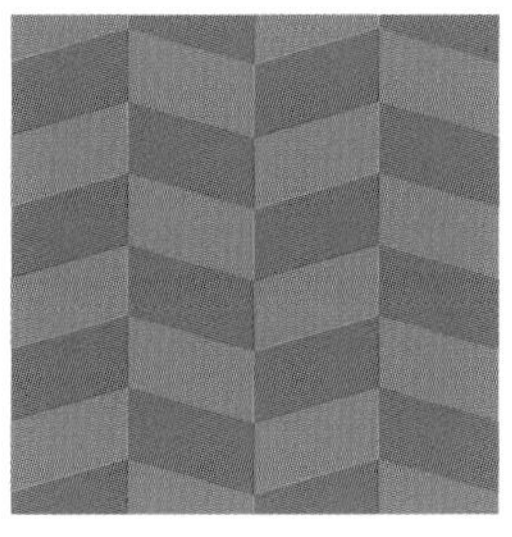
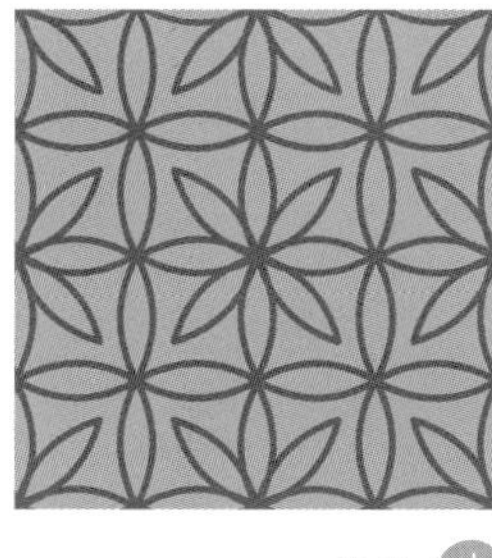
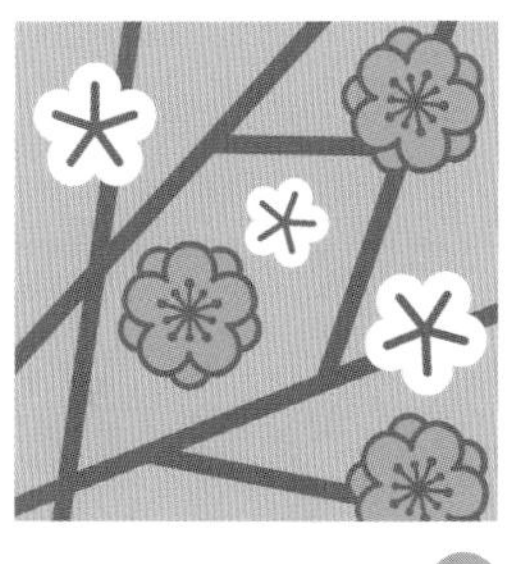

Illustration

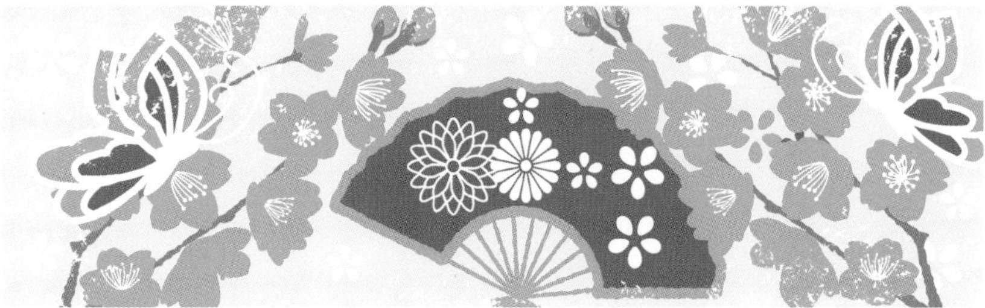

Recipe
078

Summer in Japan

Japanese people are adept at using color to create a sense of coolness even in summer. In *kaiseki-ryori* (multi-course cuisine), green bamboo is laid on the plate or green maple leaves are used as an accent to an arrangement of food. Red to yellow are warmer colors, while shades of blue are considered cooler hues. Depending on how it's used, green can be a cool, refreshing summer color.

- **FEELING** Refreshing, cooling, calm.
- **COMBINATIONS** Light colors that contain gray.
- **TIPS** If using green or purple, use shades that tend toward blue or other cool colors.

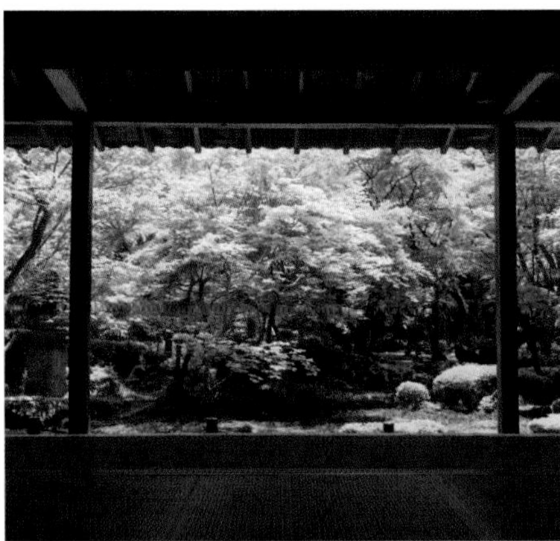

The strong rays of summer sunlight create attractive contrasting patterns and tones of light and dark.

❶ Mosquito Coil
The deep blue-green of the familiar mosquito coil sending up smoke.

❷ Green Maple
The fresh green of the maple at this time can be a cooling hue.

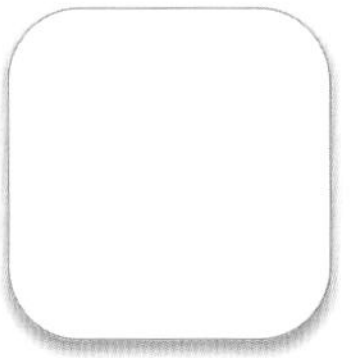

③ Somen Noodles
A color like that of somen noodles.

❹ Yukata
The deep blue that is not quite indigo or the purple used for a yukata.

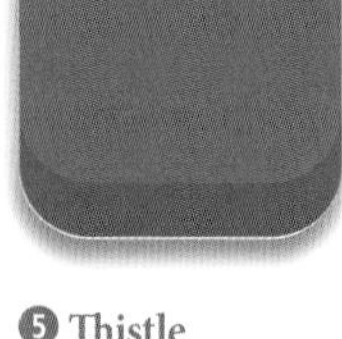

❺ Thistle
The intense purple of a thistle flower.

❻ Fan
A color evoking a sandal-wood fan.

❼ Colored Carp
Colored carp originated in Ojiya City in Niigata prefecture.

❽ The Color of a Wind Bell's Ring
A pale blue that suggests the sound of a wind chime.

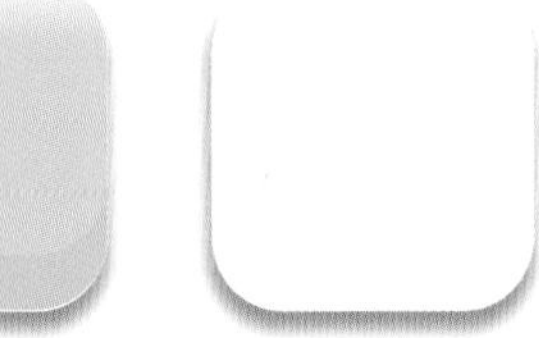

⑨ Firefly's Light
A color evoking the mysterious light emitted by fireflies on summer nights.

1 C65 M0 Y45 K20
R67 G162 B140
#43A28C

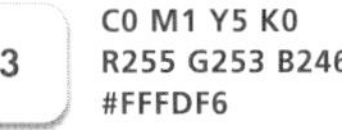

2 C60 M0 Y70 K0
R107 G188 B110
#6ABC6E

3 C0 M1 Y5 K0
R255 G253 B246
#FFFDF6

4 C40 M40 Y0 K50
R103 G95 B128
#675F80

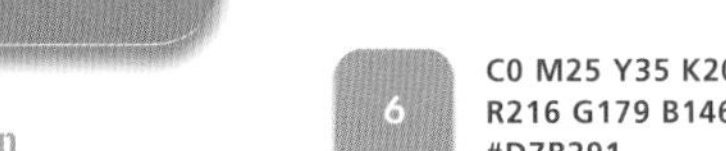

5 C20 M70 Y0 K0
R202 G103 B164
#CA66A3

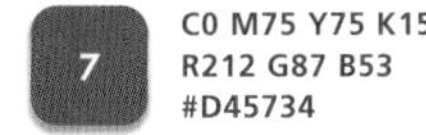

6 C0 M25 Y35 K20
R216 G179 B146
#D7B291

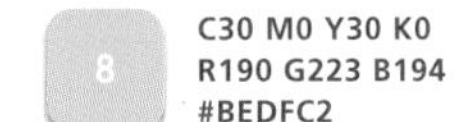

7 C0 M75 Y75 K15
R212 G87 B53
#D45734

8 C30 M0 Y30 K0
R190 G223 B194
#BEDFC2

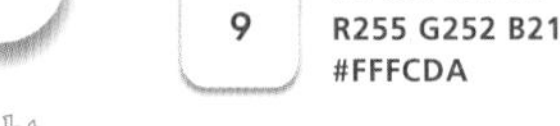

9 C0 M0 Y20 K0
R255 G252 B219
#FFFCDA

Two-color combinations

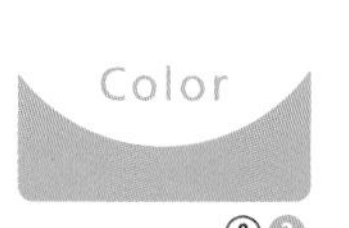

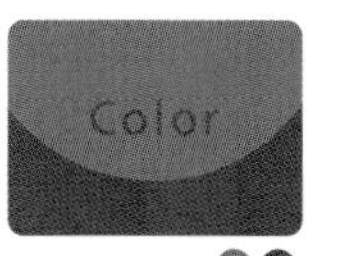

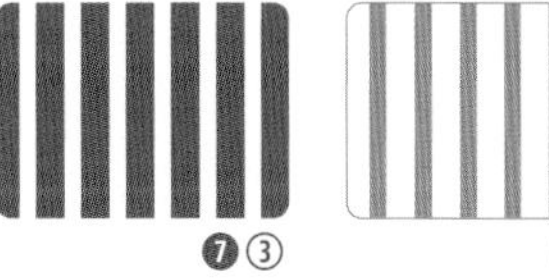
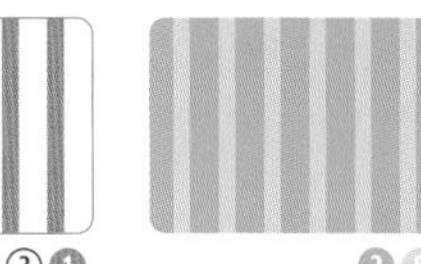
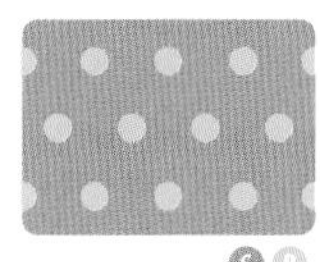
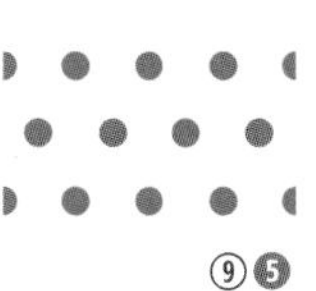
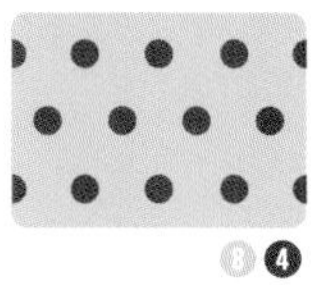
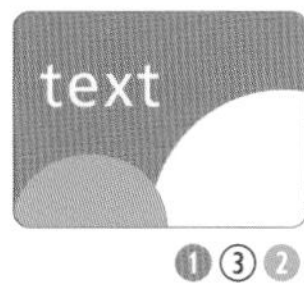
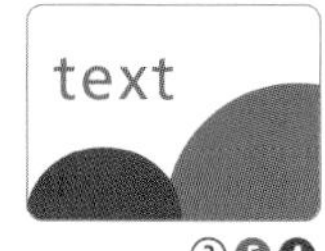
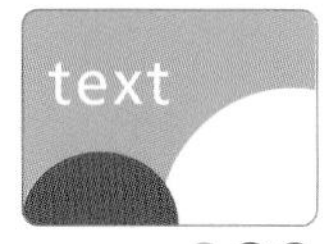

Three-color combinations

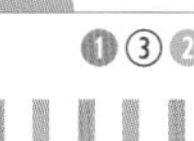
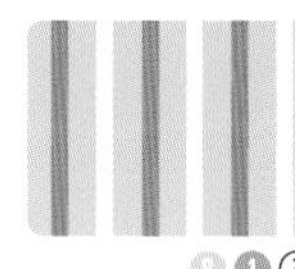

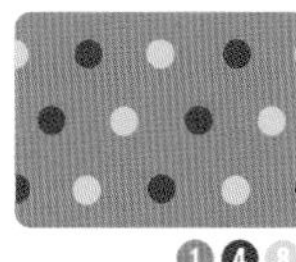
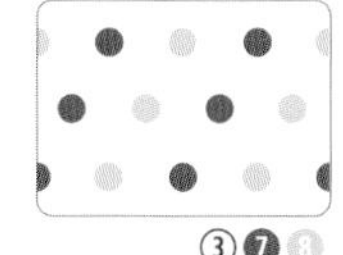
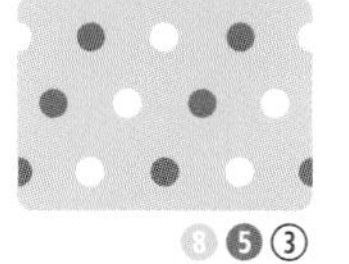

Designs

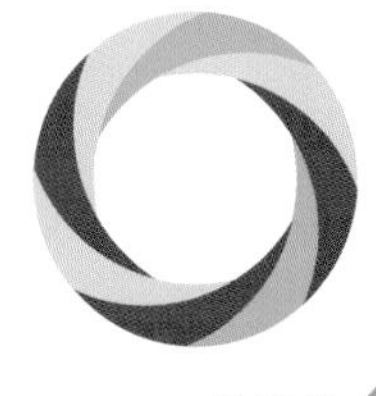

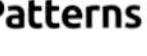

Patterns

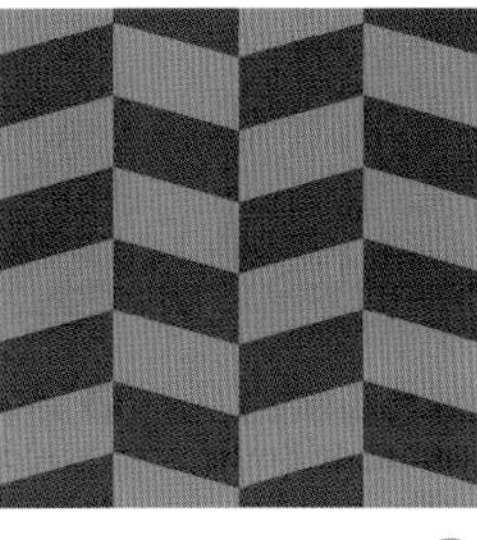

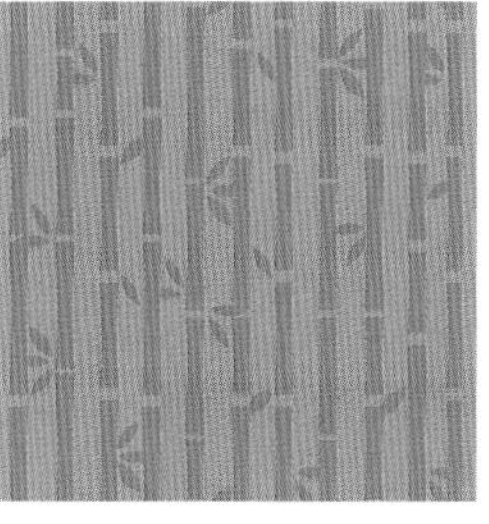
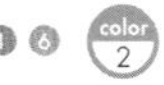

Illustration

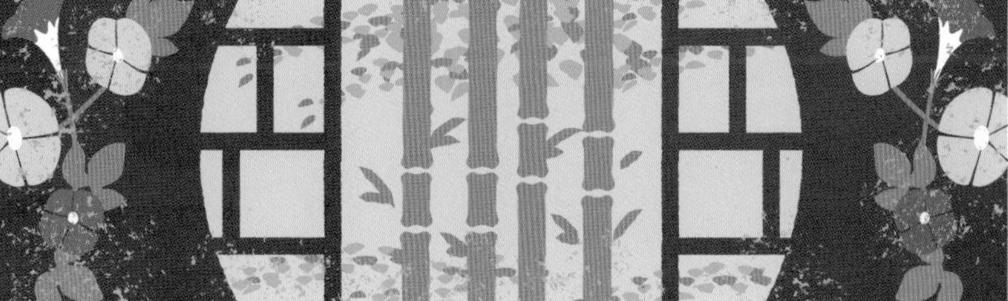
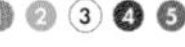

Recipe
079

Summer Festivals and Events

I love the beach. Some people love mountains, but I've decided I belong at the seaside. Recently I took the plunge and ordered a surfboard. The base color is a simple white, but I was very thorough in choosing a design to accent it, so I can't wait to see the end result. These are some of the colors that inspired my choice.

- **FEELING** Spirited, eye-catching, fun.
- **COMBINATIONS** Go all out combining vivid colors.
- **TIPS** Decide on one color as the main, base tone.

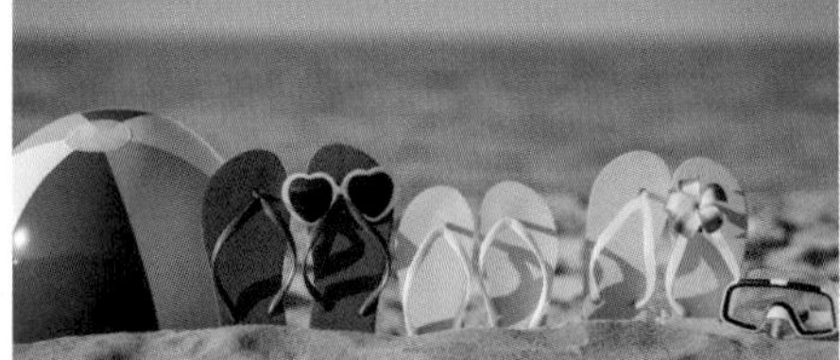

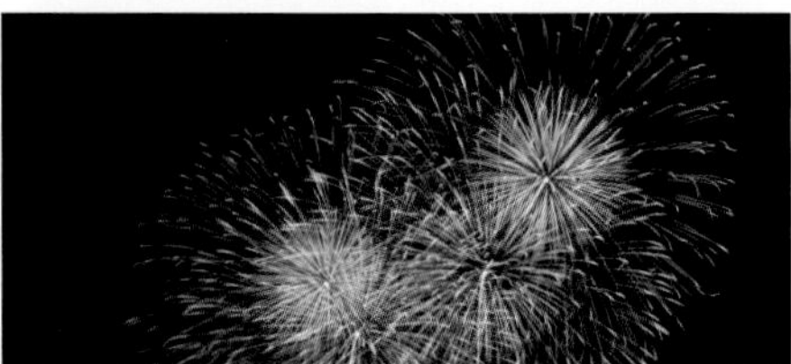

Vivid colors help set the tone and the stage for relaxation, frivolity and amusement.

1 Ocean Swimming
A blue that evokes the deep sea in summer.

2 Thundercloud
A color that evokes a giant, rising thundercloud.

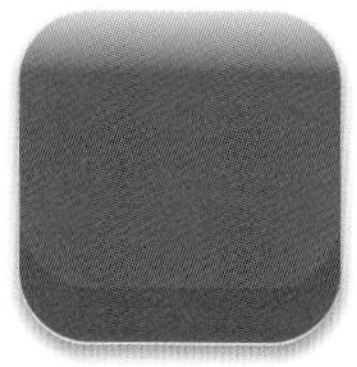

3 Watermelon
The sweet flesh of a perfectly ripe melon.

4 Old-Fashioned Lemonade Bottle
A color like that of a nostalgic, retro lemonade bottle.

5 Morning Glory (red)
One looks forward to seeing how many flowers will open each morning.

6 Morning Glory (blue)
The violet of a morning glory, known as heavenly blue.

7 Strawberry Syrup
Strawberry syrup for shaved ice desserts, it turns the tongue red.

8 Blue Hawaii
Also the name for a cocktail, it's associated with the blues of Hawaii.

9 Lemon Syrup
Does this really taste like lemon? The color at least suggests its sourness.

	CMYK	RGB	Hex
1	C75 M35 Y0 K0	R51 G137 B202	#3389CA
2	C8 M0 Y0 K3	R235 G244 B250	#EAF4F9
3	C0 M85 Y70 K0	R233 G71 B63	#E8473E
4	C40 M0 Y25 K19	R142 G188 B178	#8EBBB1
5	C10 M90 Y0 K1	R215 G46 B138	#D62E8A
6	C80 M83 Y0 K0	R78 G62 B149	#4E3D95
7	C0 M90 Y40 K0	R231 G52 B98	#E73462
8	C70 M0 Y0 K0	R0 G185 B239	#00B8EE
9	C3 M0 Y70 K0	R254 G242 B99	#FDF262

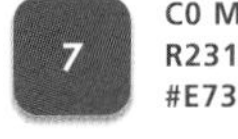
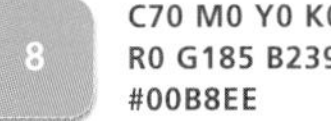
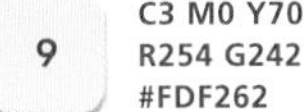

Two-color combinations

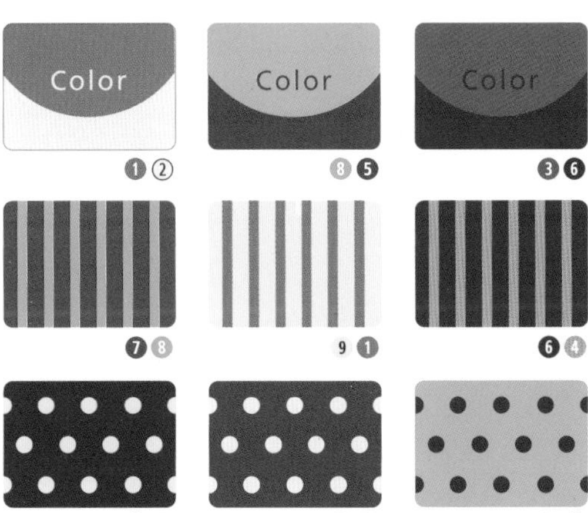

Three-color combinations

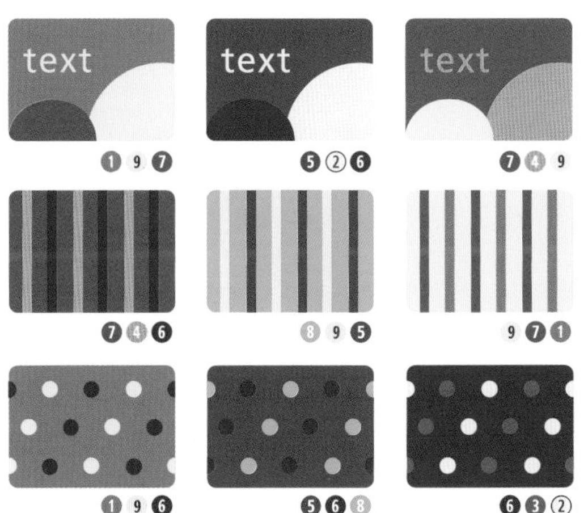

Designs

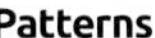

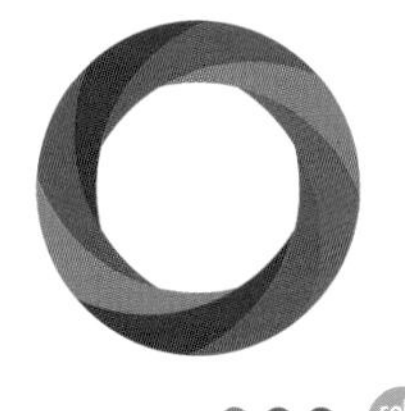

Patterns

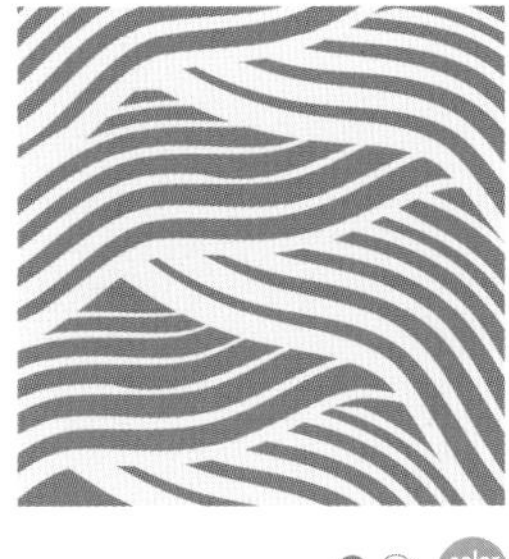
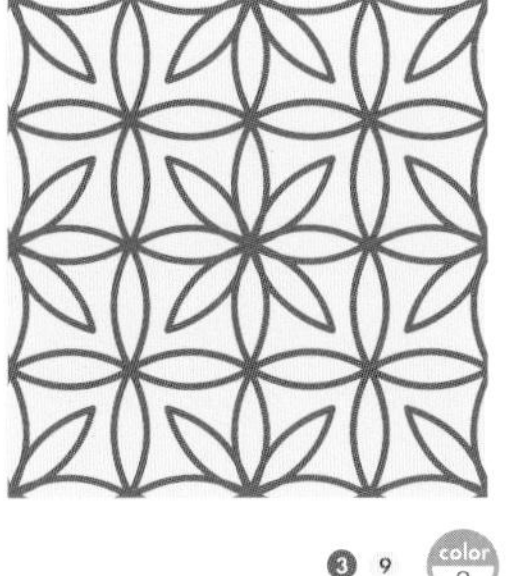
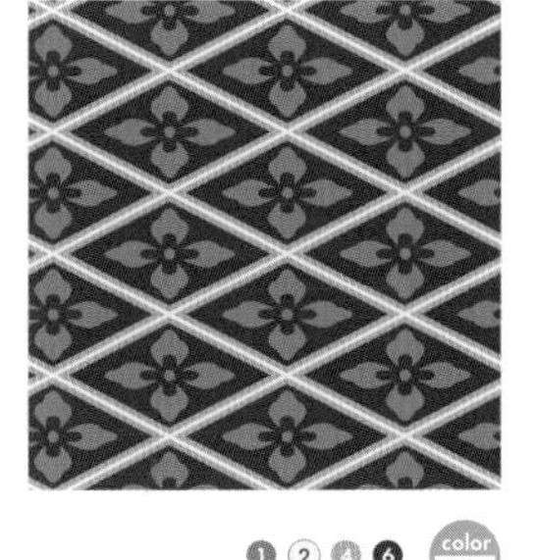

Illustration

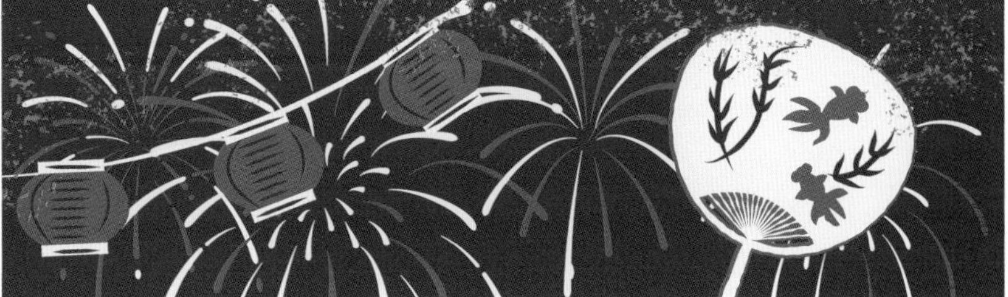

PART 11

THE WORLD AROUND US

Recipe
080

Autumn in Japan

When creating a fall-like color scheme, the rule is to make all the colors deep and dense. In order to evoke the seasons, for spring and fall, create color palettes that conjure the changing natural landscape (such as cherry trees in full bloom or trees with leaves changing color). Conversely, colors that suggest seasonal events are invaluable for winter and summer palettes (such as fireworks displays and festive Christmas colors).

- **FEELING** Bountiful, fulfilled, having depth.
- **COMBINATIONS** Gather lively harvest festival hues.
- **TIPS** If similarly deep tones are used, the colors can be chosen freely.

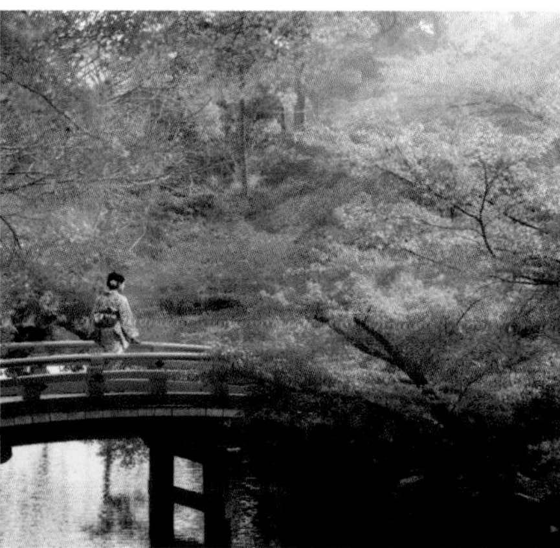

When the leaves change color, the prime places for viewing the transforming foliage broadcast fall-color reports.

❶ Red Dragonfly
A color like that of the red dragonfly flitting among lily pads.

❷ Sawtooth Acorns
These acorns are large and round, another sign of the season.

❸ Persimmon
The color of ripe persimmon fruit, an orange that is very close to red.

❹ Ginkgo Nut
A whitish brown like that of a ginkgo nut.

❺ Fragrant Olive
As the fall season deepens, olive flowers release a pleasant fragrance.

❻ Grape (black)
Grapes that are a purple like Concord grapes.

❼ Grape (green)
Green grapes like muscats.

❽ Grape (red)
Small red grapes like the Delaware variety.

❾ Fig
The color of figs that are on the market from June to October.

No.	CMYK	RGB	Hex
1	C0 M85 Y75 K20	R202 G60 B47	#C93C2E
2	C0 M55 Y60 K50	R151 G87 B56	#965738
3	C0 M75 Y100 K5	R229 G94 B0	#E45D00
4	C2 M10 Y25 K10	R235 G219 B188	#EADBBB
5	C0 M35 Y75 K0	R248 G183 B74	#F7B749
6	C75 M80 Y55 K0	R92 G72 B95	#5C485F
7	C47 M0 Y85 K0	R150 G200 B73	#96C748
8	C30 M85 Y35 K35	R139 G46 B83	#8B2E52
9	C30 M80 Y55 K0	R186 G80 B90	#B9505A

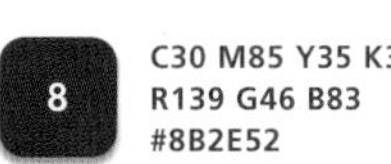

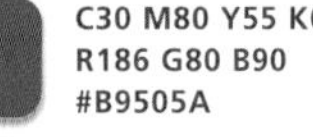

Two-color combinations

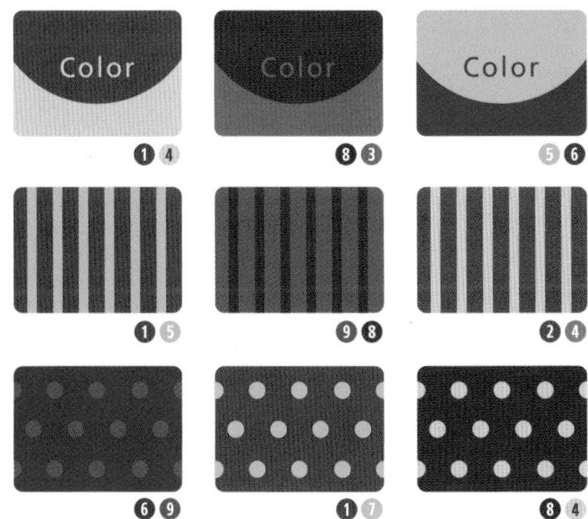

Three-color combinations

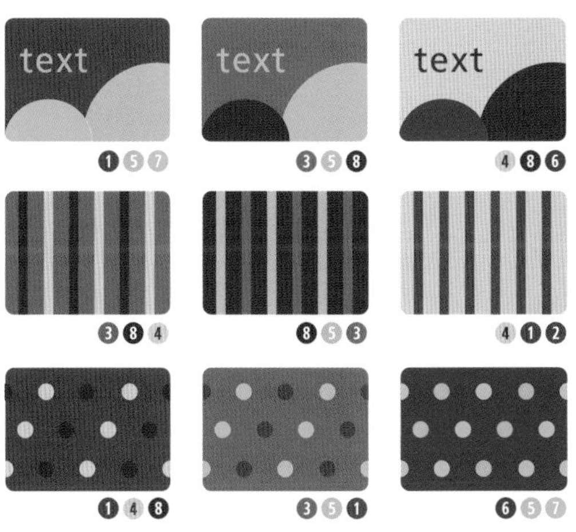

Designs

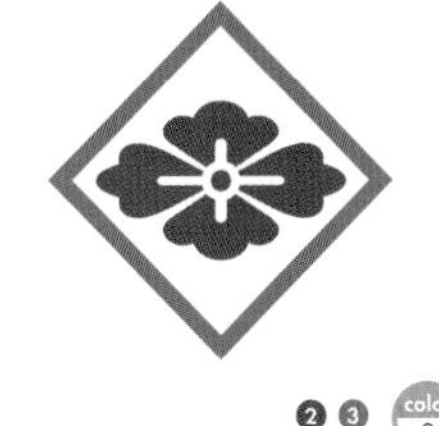

2 3 color 2

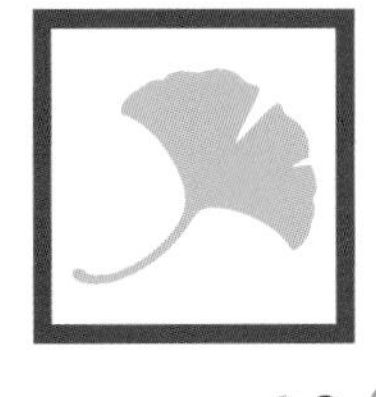

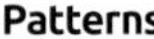

5 6 color 2

1 8 9 color 3

Patterns

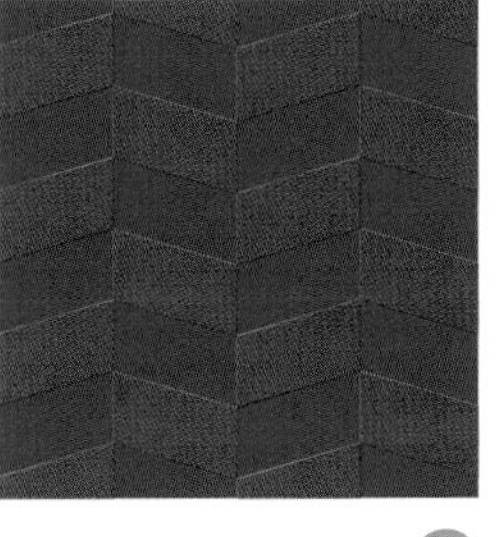

2 6 color 2

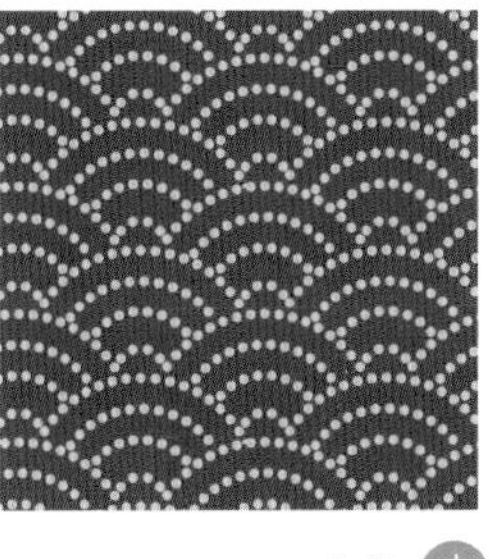

1 4 color 2

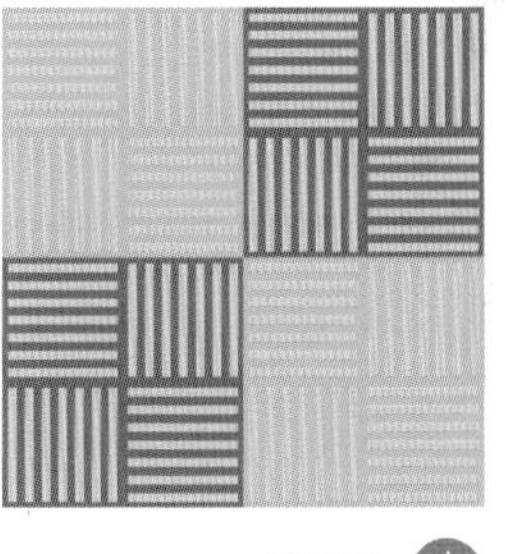

3 4 5 color 3

Illustration

1 3 5 8 9  color 5

PART 11

THE WORLD AROUND US

Recipe
081

Autumn Festivals and Events

The contrasting tones of fall seep into our work and lives. I notice the influence in my project presentations and try using different colors that conjure as much boldness as they do softness and simplicity. One formula for creating a vividly distinctive color scheme is to find a suitable amount of variation within a sense of uniformity. Simple, right?

- **FEELING** Gentle, dignified, having warmth.
- **COMBINATIONS** Use beige or light yellow shades for the base.
- **TIPS** Use warm, powerful colors as accents.

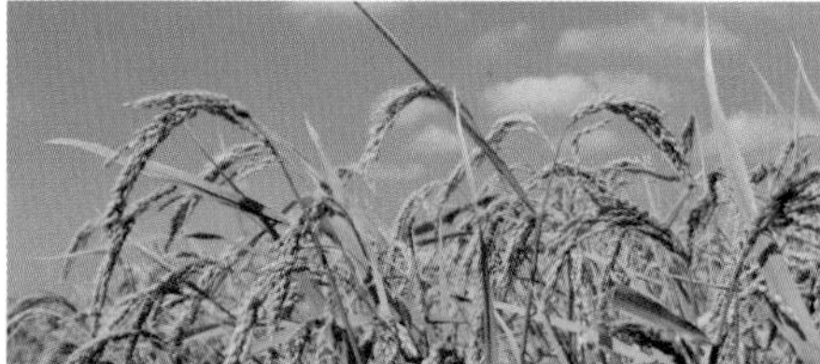

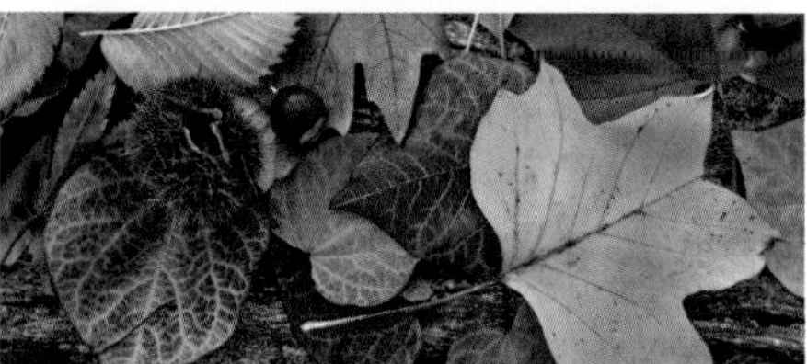

Harvesttime beckons as the wheat grows heavy with grain. The quickening wind sends colored leaves like confetti skittering by.

① **Harvest Moon**
The color of the harvest moon that lit up the mid-autumn night sky.

② **Moon-Viewing Dumplings**
The custom of making offerings to the moon began during the Heian period.

③ **Pampas Grass**
The color of pampas grass, which was offered along with dumplings.

④ **Maple Leaves**
The color of maple leaves that have taken on fall colors.

⑤ **Ginkgo Trees**
A color that evokes the vibrant yellow of ginkgo leaves.

⑥ **Digging Potatoes**
The deep, intense purple of sweet potato skins.

⑦ **Chestnut**
A dark brown tinged with red like the shells of chestnuts.

⑧ **Ears of Rice**
The golden yellow of ripened rice ears awaiting harvest.

⑨ **Fine Fall Day**
The brisk blue sky at around the time of fall sporting events.

1	C0 M5 Y35 K2 R253 G240 B182 #FDF0B6
2	C0 M4 Y10 K2 R252 G246 B232 #FCF5E8
3	C0 M15 Y30 K10 R237 G209 B135 #EDD086
4	C0 M80 Y80 K15 R211 G76 B44 #D34B2B
5	C0 M25 Y80 K0 R251 G201 B62 #FBC93D
6	C35 M85 Y40 K0 R176 G67 B105 #B04369
7	C0 M85 Y85 K65 R116 G22 B0 #741600
8	C0 M10 Y70 K23 R215 G192 B80 #D6C050
9	C60 M25 Y15 K0 R108 G162 B195 #6CA2C2

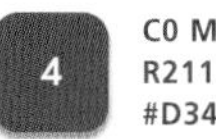
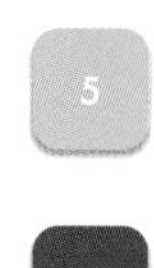
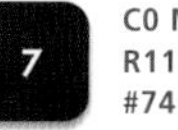
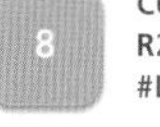

Two-color combinations

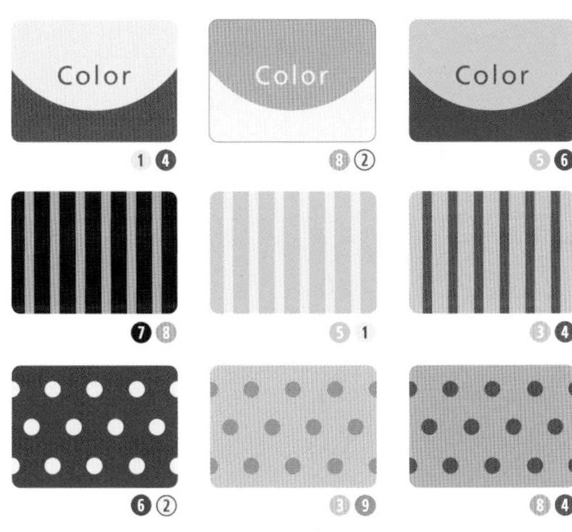

Three-color combinations

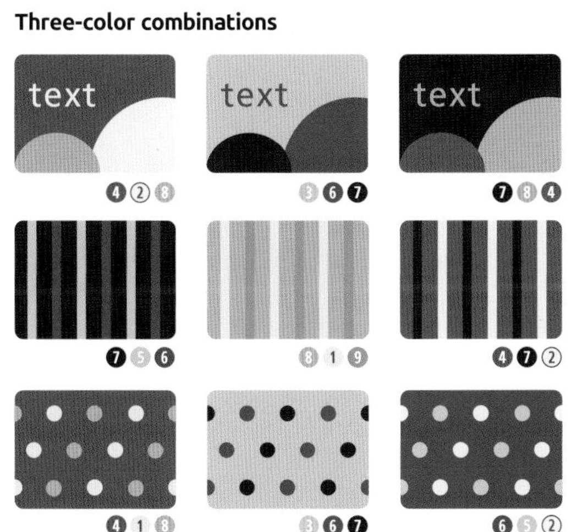

Designs

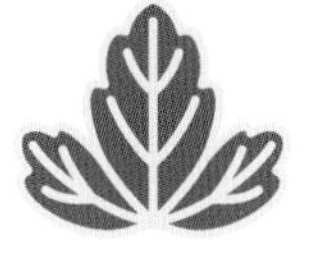

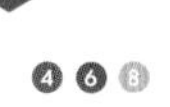

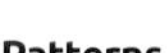

Patterns

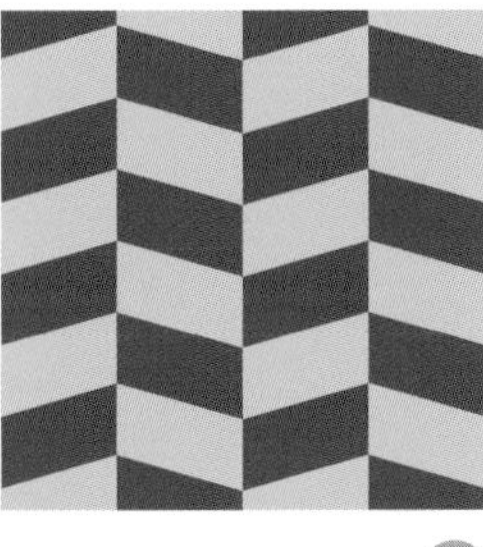

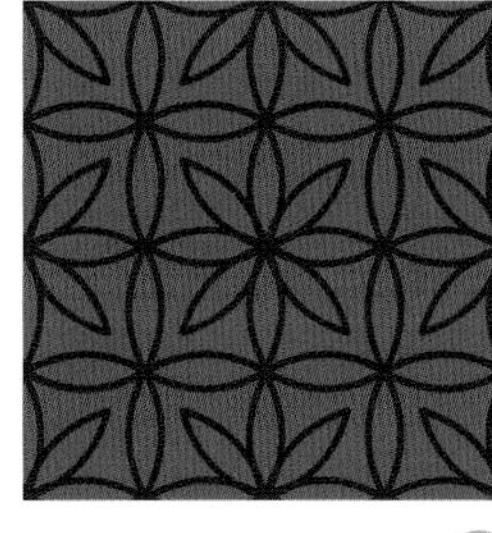

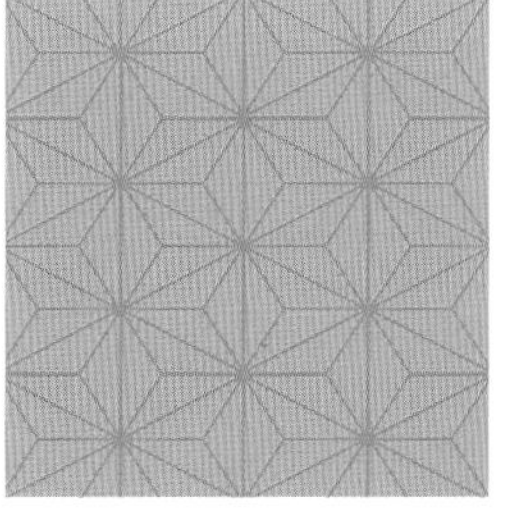

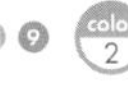

Illustration

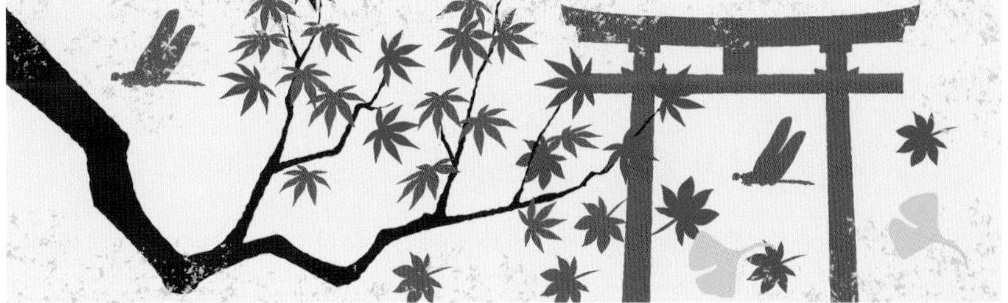

Recipe

082

Winter in Japan

In Japanese, there are many ways of describing snow. In terms of the time and place where snow falls, it's categorized into first snow, first snow to settle on a mountain, early snow, late snow and lingering snow. The way it falls is divided into powder snow, light snowfall, large snowflakes, snowballs, heavy snowfall and blizzard. There are also words to describe the snow's condition such as corn snow and perpetual snow. This sense for detail is something to be treasured.

- **FEELING** Orderly, pulled together, quiet.
- **COMBINATIONS** Use off-neutrals as key colors.
- **TIPS** Use deep red or dark blue as accents.

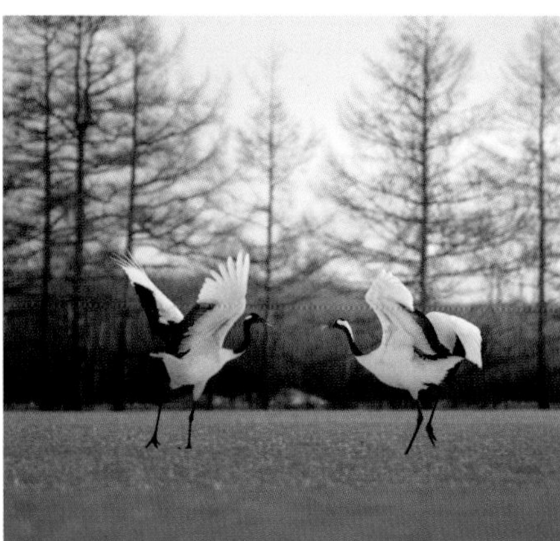

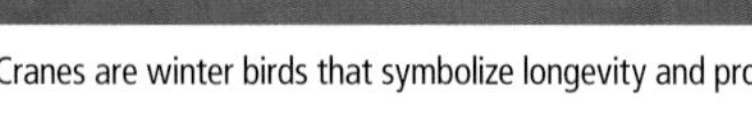

Cranes are winter birds that symbolize longevity and prosperity.

① **New Snow**
The clear white of snow that has just fallen.

② **Icicle**
Icicles that form beneath the eaves are proof of cold air.

③ **North Wind**
A color that evokes the cold wind blowing from the north.

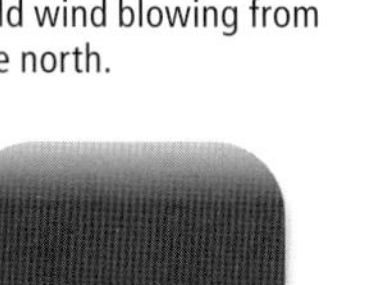

④ **Firewood**
The crackle and pop of wood giving in to the fire's flame.

⑤ **Blizzard**
Not just a snowstorm, but a visibility-reducing whiteout.

⑥ **Winter Solstice**
The shortest day of the year. In Sapporo, it's roughly nine hours.

⑦ **Fireplace**
A color evoking the warm, comfortable space a fireplace creates.

⑧ **Open-Air Market**
The feel of the open-air market alive with vendors.

⑨ **First Sunrise**
Calling to mind the auspicious sunrise of the first day of the year.

No.	CMYK	RGB	Hex
1	C3 M0 Y0 K2	R247 G250 B252	F7FAFC
2	C20 M4 Y0 K0	R211 G231 B248	#D3E7F7
3	C30 M15 Y0 K20	R162 G177 B202	#A1B1CA
4	C0 M20 Y40 K45	R167 G143 B108	#A78F6B
5	C5 M0 Y0 K10	R230 G235 B238	#E5EBEE
6	C9 M0 Y0 K80	R82 G85 B87	#525457
7	C3 M15 Y35 K0	R248 G223 B176	#F7DEAF
8	C15 M90 Y75 K25	R174 G44 B45	#AE2B2D
9	C0 M60 Y63 K0	R239 G132 B87	#EF8457

Two-color combinations

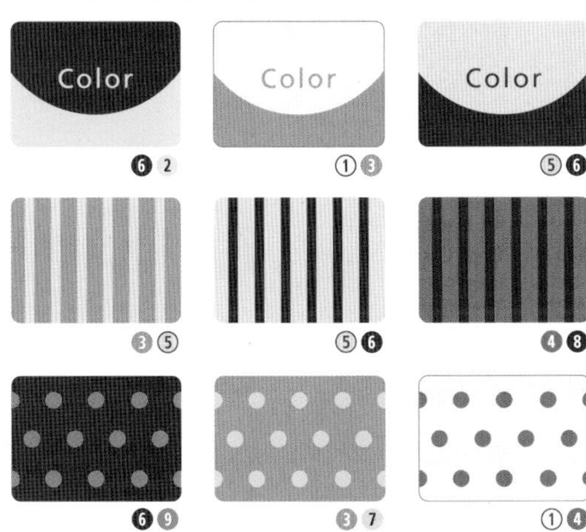

Three-color combinations

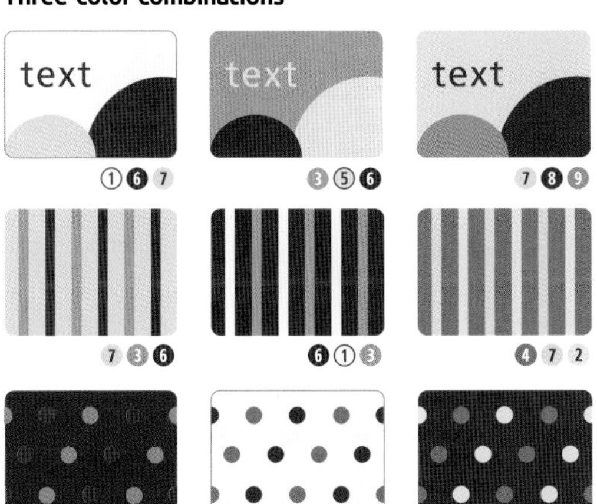

Designs

Patterns

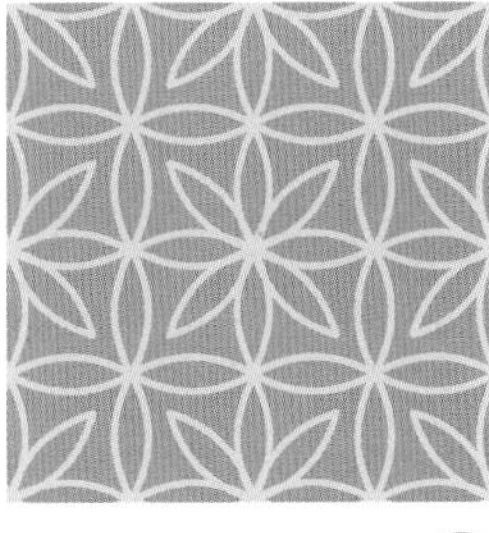

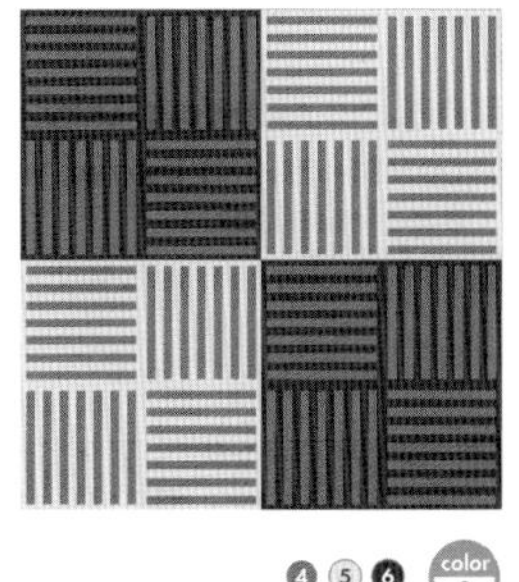

Illustration

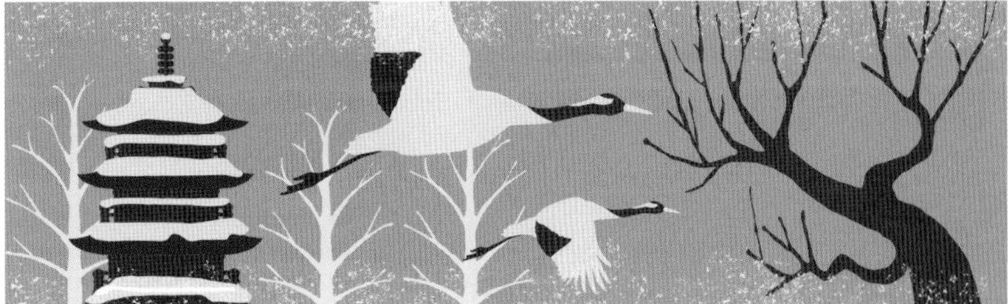

Recipe
083

Winter Festivals and Events

End-of-the-year gatherings and Christmas parties start as soon as December approaches. Then once the holidays are over, there are the celebrations to start the year. Just as I was thinking it was all starting yet again, a gym opened at my nearest train station. I'm going to try to go regularly to make things different this year. To combine the new with the traditional is a good way to approach the tones of the season too.

- **FEELING** Auspicious, lucky, dignified.
- **COMBINATIONS** Use red, white, gold and black for a Japanese look.
- **TIPS** Strong contrasts lend visual appeal.

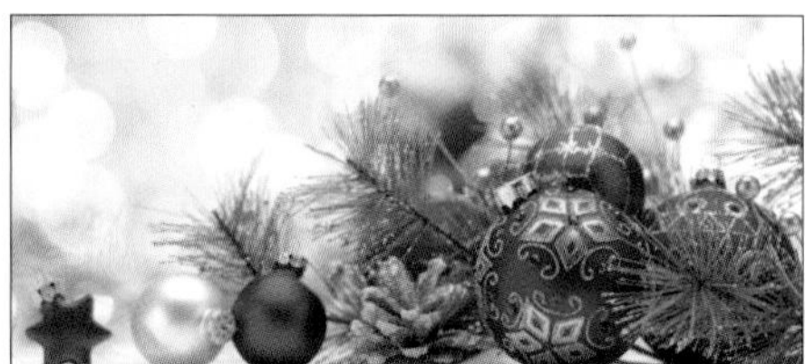

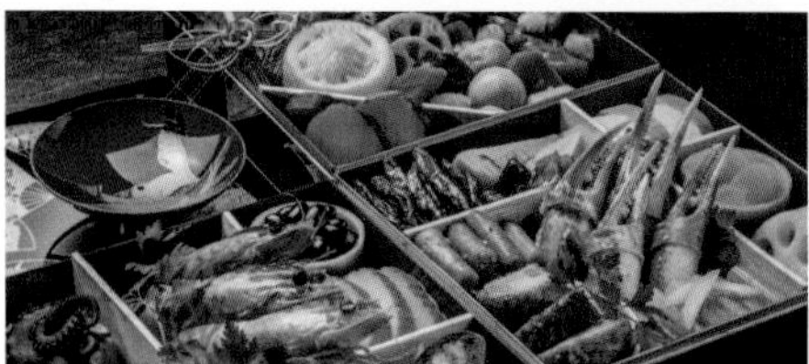

This is the season when "lucky" colors are prominently on hand.

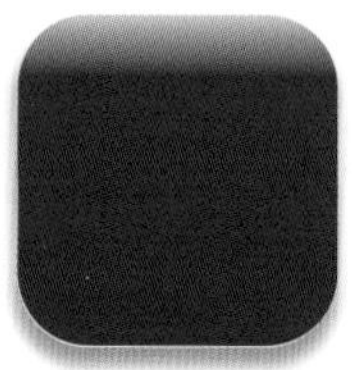

❶ Crabapple
The color of the small apples used in Christmas wreaths.

❷ Holly
The color of holly used in Christmas wreaths and for Bean-Throwing Night.

❸ Lucky Charm
Once Christmas is over, everyone slips into New Year mode.

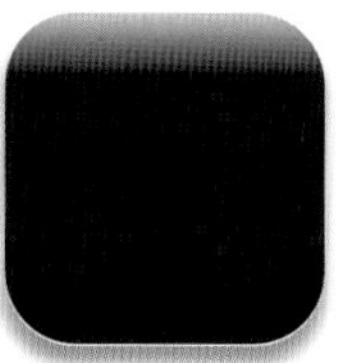

❹ Calligraphy
A black like that of India ink, which is created from charcoal.

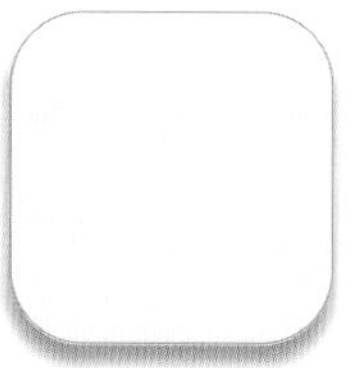

⑤ Rice Cakes
The white of rice cakes offered to the god Toshi-gami at New Year.

❻ Japan
In English, lacquering is known as japanning, a traditional handicraft.

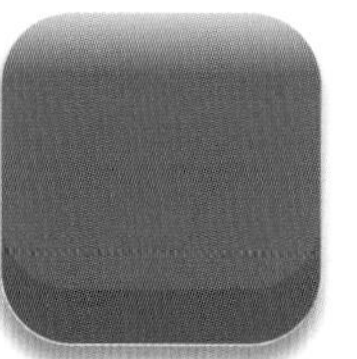

❼ Illumination
The color of lights sparkling brightly at light shows in winter.

❽ Cold Wind
The cold, drying wind of winter.

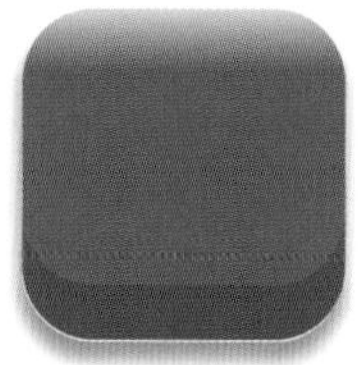

❾ Furoshiki
A color recalling the *furoshiki* cloth used to wrap and deliver year-end gifts.

1 C30 M100 Y75 K0 R184 G26 B58 #B71939

2 C100 M45 Y90 K0 R0 G111 B73 #006E49

3 C0 M25 Y65 K25 R207 G168 B85 #CEA754

4 C0 M3 Y0 K95 R47 G38 B36 #2F2524

5 C0 M0 Y10 K2 R253 G251 B236 #FDFBEB

6 C0 M95 Y100 K20 R200 G29 B9 #C81D09

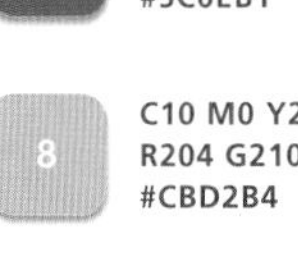

7 C70 M55 Y0 K3 R92 G111 B177 #5C6EB1

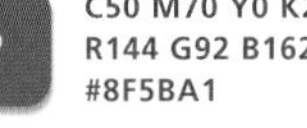

8 C10 M0 Y25 K20 R204 G210 B180 #CBD2B4

9 C50 M70 Y0 K2 R144 G92 B162 #8F5BA1

Two-color combinations

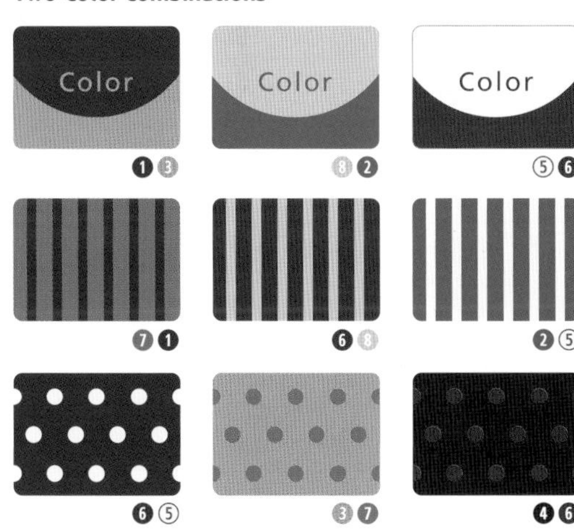

Three-color combinations

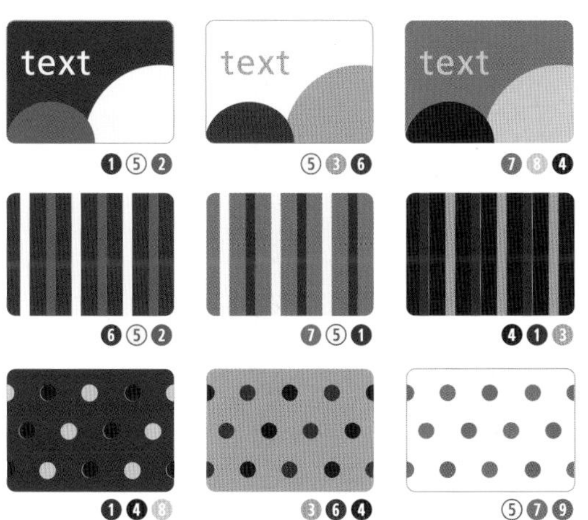

Designs

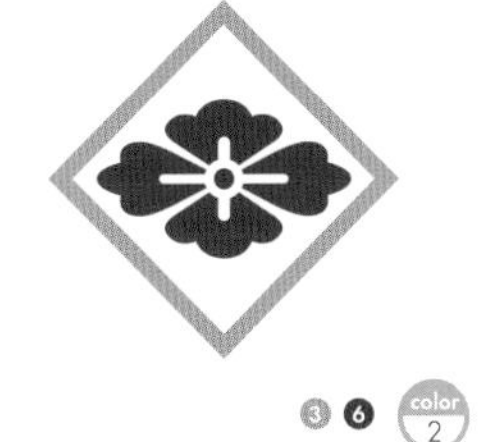

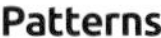

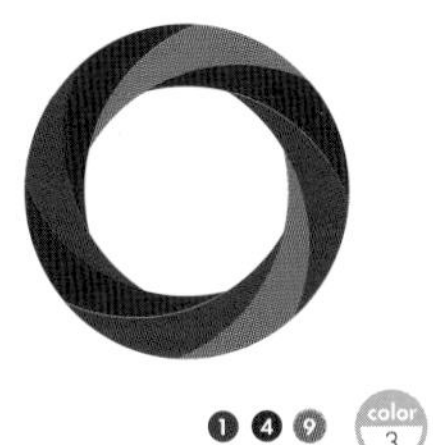

Patterns

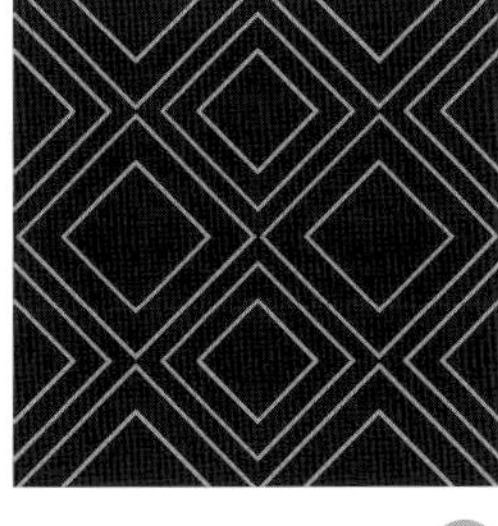

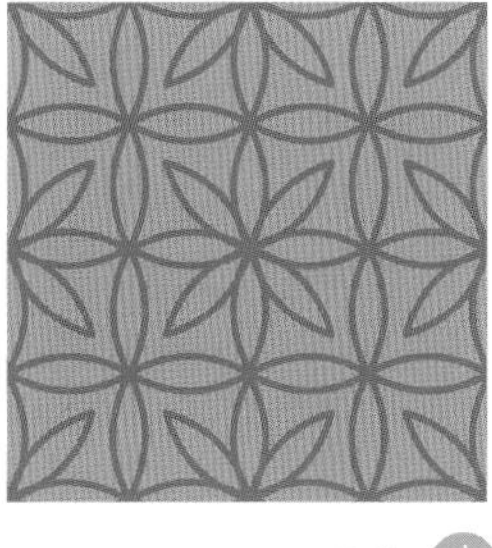

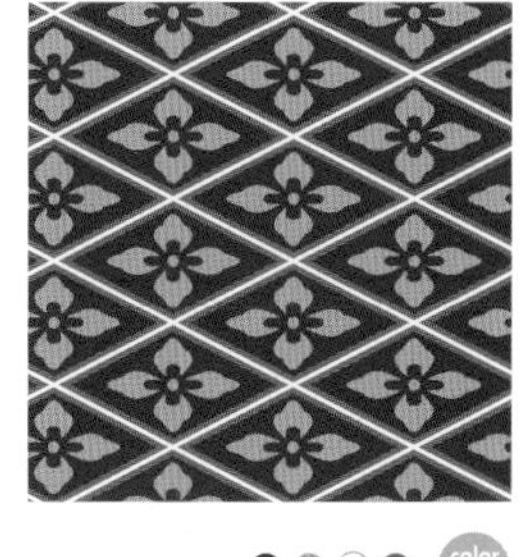

Illustration

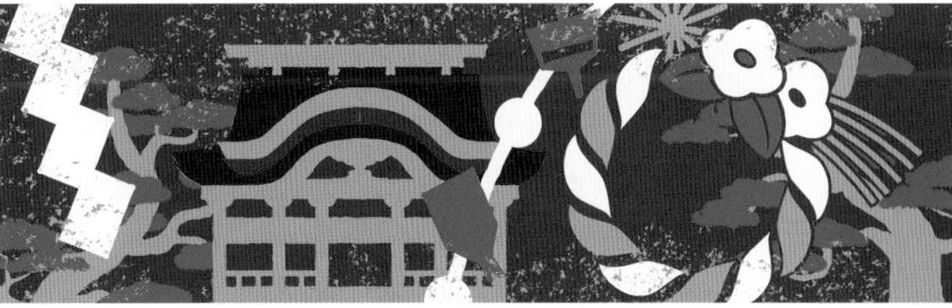

Recipe
084

Heian Era Elegance

In the Heian period, it was standard practice for the costumes of aristocratic women serving in the inner palace to be made up of multiple layers. The combination of colors was determined in minute detail depending on the season and each color scheme was given a tasteful name such as "pine combination" and "the fragrance of red plums." Attire that didn't adhere to these rules was seen as a breach of etiquette.

- **FEELING** Flamboyant, lustrous, bright.
- **COMBINATIONS** Combine colors that are bright and have high levels of saturation.
- **TIPS** Take care to create a sense of the seasons.

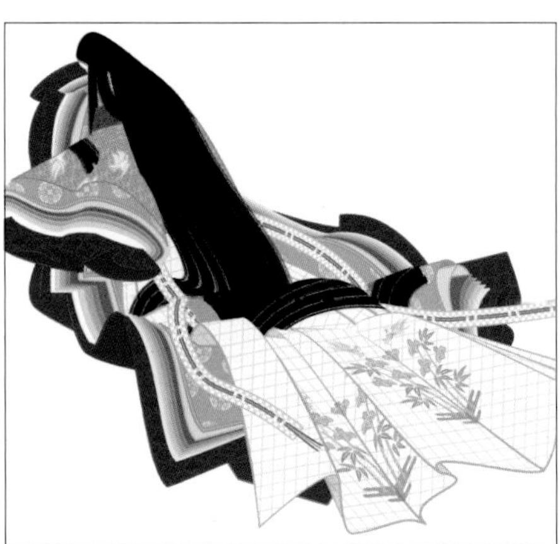

Women's court robes weighed as much as 45 pounds (20 kg).

❶ Crimson
A color created from the red pigment of the safflower.

❷ Ouni
Dyed using safflower and gardenia seeds, this is the color of robes worn by the Crown Prince.

❸ Sprout Yellow
In the Heian era, this was a color worn by a young person.

❹ Imayo-iro
Imayo means "to be popular or to be in vogue" so this means "a popular color."

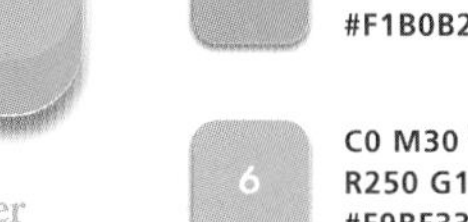

❺ Ikkonzome
Refers to the pale red resulting from one pound of safflower being used to dye one pound of silk.

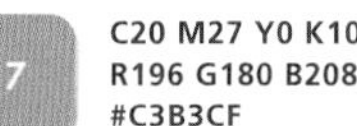
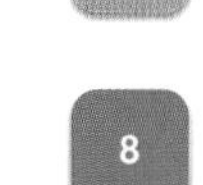

❻ Globeflower
The color of globeflowers, also used to describe the gold color of small coins.

❼ Pale
During the Heian period, "pale" or "light" indicated a purple hue.

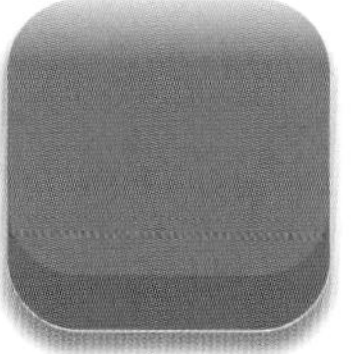

❽ Wisteria
The violet seen in wisteria flowers.

❾ Reddish Indigo
The purple color resulting from a dye that combines indigo and crimson.

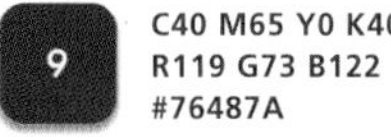

1 C2 M100 Y90 K0 / R227 G0 B33 / #E30021

2 C0 M65 Y70 K0 / R238 G121 B72 / #EE7948

3 C38 M0 Y84 K0 / R175 G209 B71 / #AFD147

4 C0 M75 Y35 K20 / R203 G83 B102 / #CB5266

5 C2 M40 Y20 K0 / R242 G177 B178 / #F1B0B2

6 C0 M30 Y83 K0 / R250 G192 B52 / #F9BF33

7 C20 M27 Y0 K10 / R196 G180 B208 / #C3B3CF

8 C43 M50 Y0 K0 / R159 G134 B189 / #9F86BC

9 C40 M65 Y0 K40 / R119 G73 B122 / #76487A

Two-color combinations

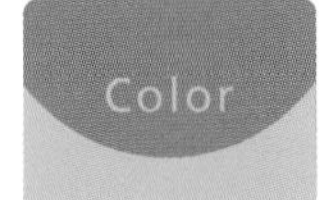
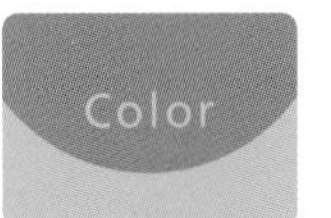
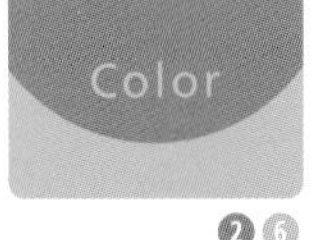
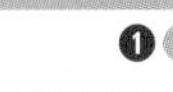
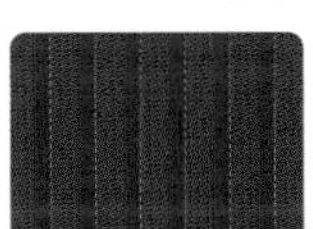

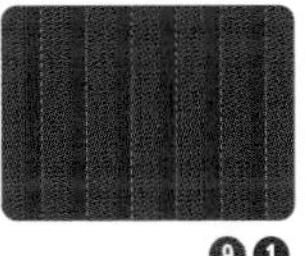
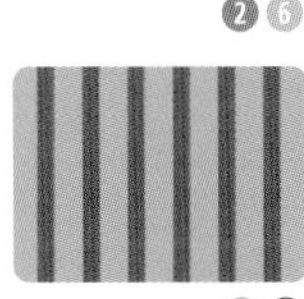
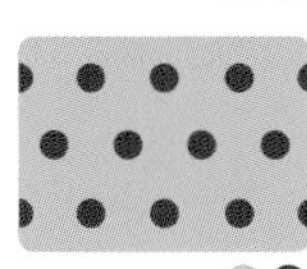
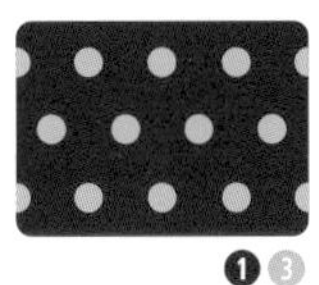
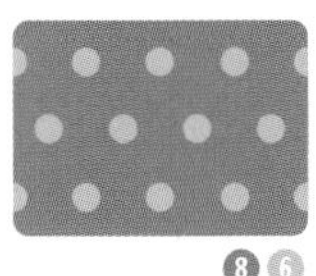

Three-color combinations

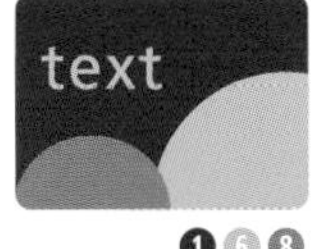
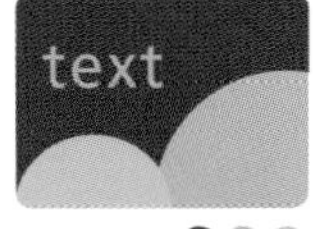
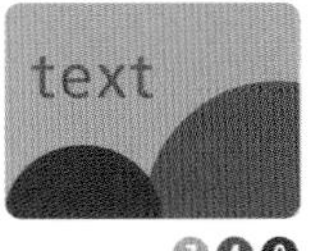
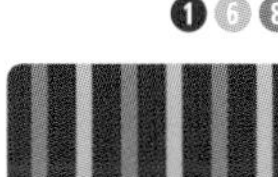
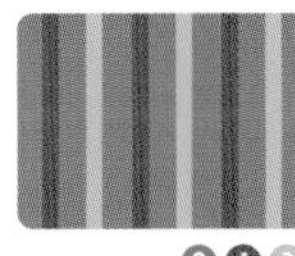

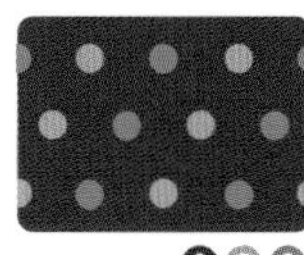
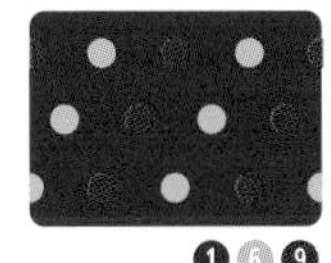
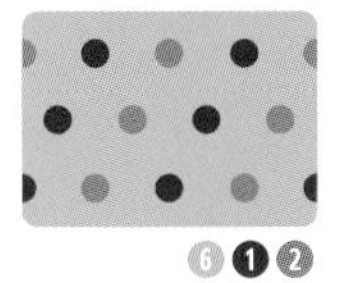

Designs

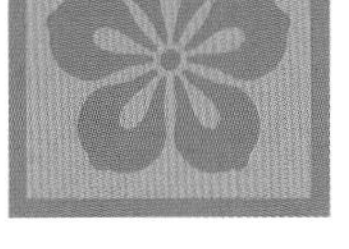

Patterns

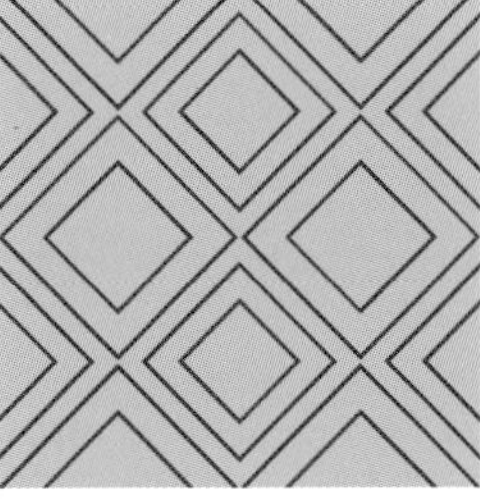
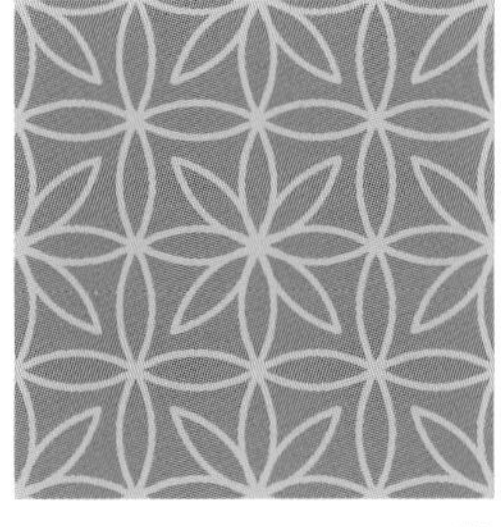

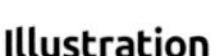

Illustration

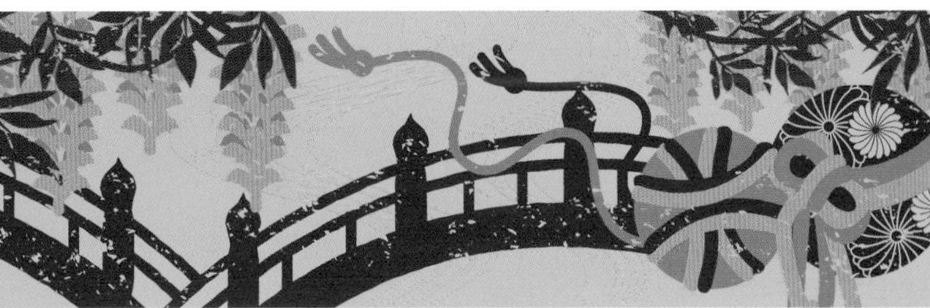

Recipe
085

Cool Colors of the Edo Period

Under the sumptuary regulations imposed by the shogunate government of the Edo period, commoners' kimonos could only be made of cotton or linen in colors limited to brown, gray or indigo. In response, the people created a multitude of variations of those colors, giving rise to a saying of the day that translates as "48 teas and 100 mice" (tea=brown, mouse=gray).

- **FEELING** Subdued, plain, serene.
- **COMBINATIONS** Combine various browns and grays.
- **TIPS** Keep accent colors low-key.

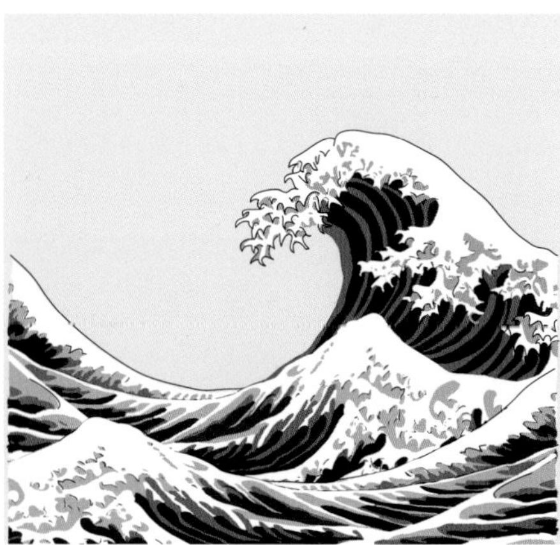

The famous woodcuts and artwork of the era also reflect the influence of the prevailing period palette.

❶ Plum Gray
A red-tinged gray like that of red plum flowers, this color was popular in the Edo period.

❷ Fukagawa Gray
A greenish gray that was popular with young people and geisha.

❸ Indigo Gray
A gray tinged with an indigo-like blue.

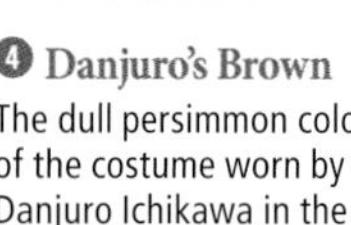

❹ Danjuro's Brown
The dull persimmon color of the costume worn by Danjuro Ichikawa in the play *Shibaraku.*

❺ Rokou's Brown
Kikunojo Segawa wore this color to play Rokou in *Greengrocer Oshichi.*

❻ Shikan's Brown
A brown beloved by Utaemon Nakamura IV, his stage name was Shikan.

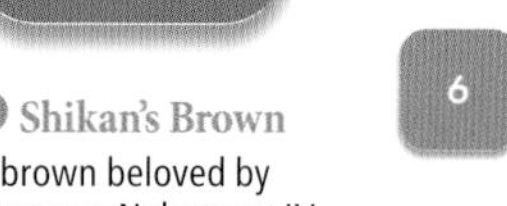

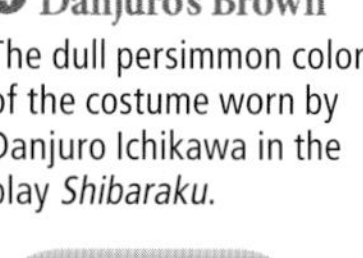

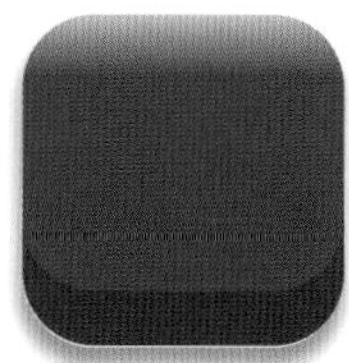

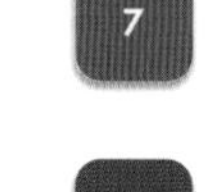

❼ Rikan's Brown
A brown beloved by Kichisaburo Arashi, whose stage name was Rikan.

❽ Indigo
An indigo that is also known as Japan blue.

❾ Storeroom
Formerly known as *nando* and giving this color its name, the word for storeroom in modern Japanese is *oshi-ire.*

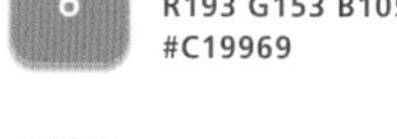

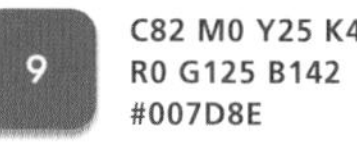

	CMYK	RGB	Hex
1	C0 M30 Y4 K30	R195 G158 B171	#C39EAB
2	C23 M0 Y15 K45	R136 G156 B151	#889B97
3	C35 M0 Y5 K55	R99 G130 B141	#63818C
4	C2 M50 Y60 K45	R160 G101 B64	#A0643F
5	C0 M20 Y70 K55	R146 G122 B48	#927930
6	C2 M30 Y50 K30	R193 G153 B105	#C19969
7	C0 M3 Y60 K70	R114 G107 B49	#726A31
8	C70 M20 Y0 K60	R15 G87 B121	#0F5779
9	C82 M0 Y25 K40	R0 G125 B142	#007D8E

Two-color combinations

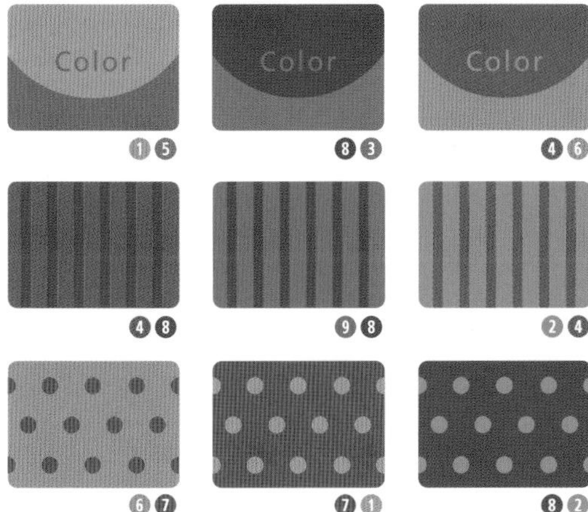

Three-color combinations

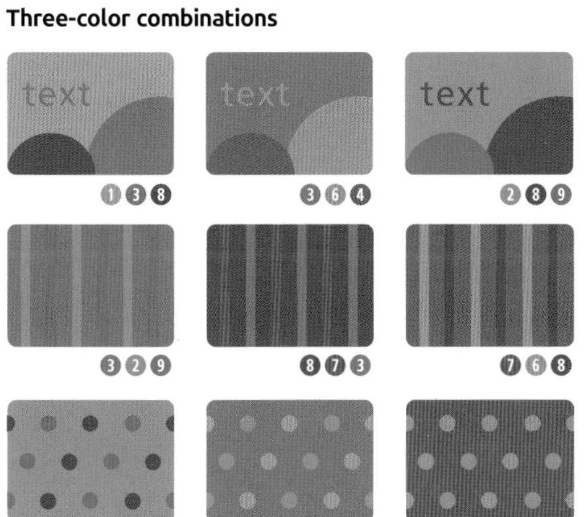

Designs

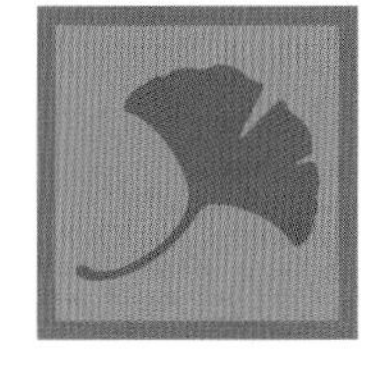

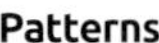

3 8 color 2

4 5 6 color 3

1 3 8 color 3

Patterns

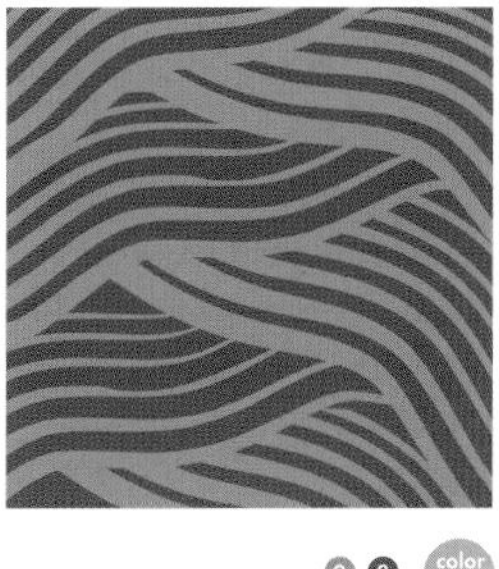

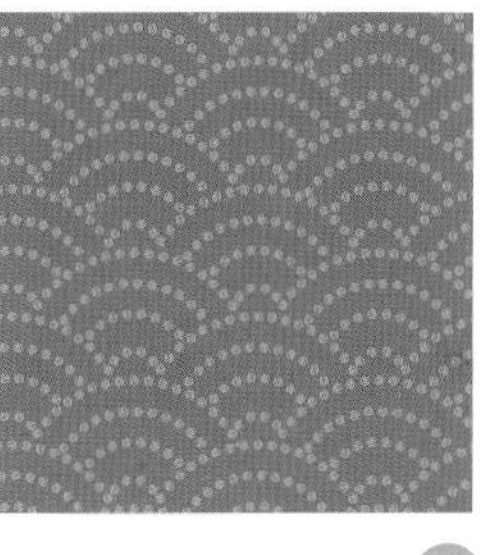

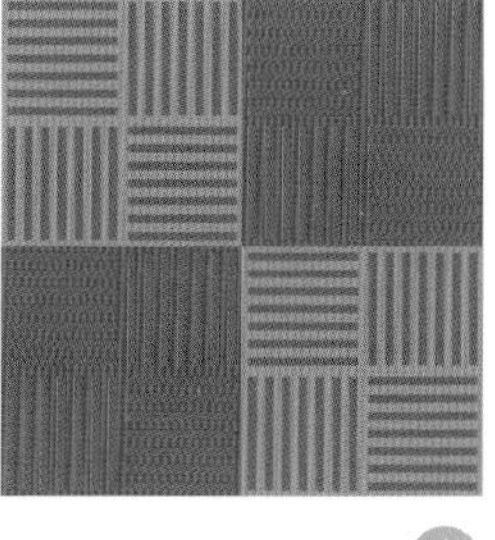

2 8 color 2

1 3 color 2

4 6 7 color 3

Illustration

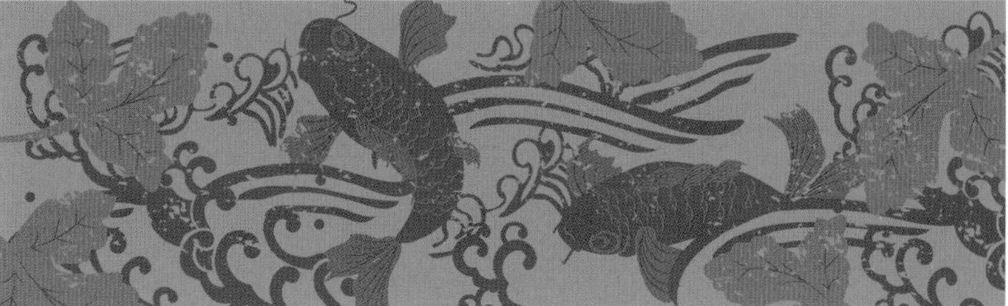

2 4 5 8 color 4

Recipe
086

Modern Colors of the Meiji Era

In the Age of Enlightenment, there were many innovations made in the field of color. 1873 marked the arrival of the first color sciences course using a color chart. Synthetic dyes also began to be imported, altering fashion forever with their vibrant shades. In cities, Western-style architecture favored bricks and gas lights and lamps became a common sight.

- **FEELING** Retro, nostalgic, having warmth.
- **COMBINATIONS** Add vibrant colors to shades of dull brown.
- **TIPS** Use strong colors like those of synthetic pigments as accents.

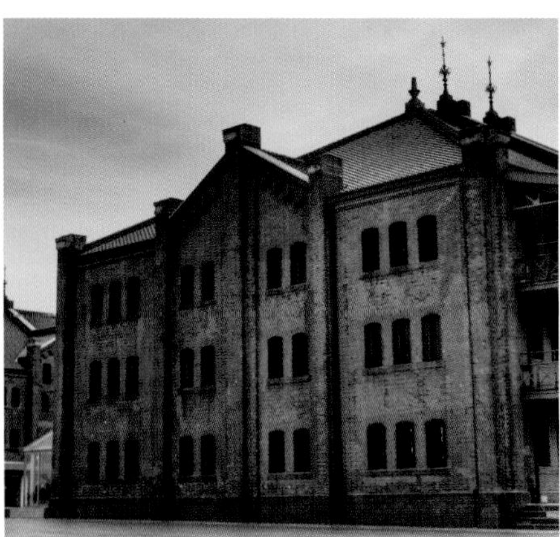

For the people of the day, the red of brickwork was novel, while today it conjures a retro impression.

❶ Maroon
Hakama were popular among students who became known as "girls in maroon skirts."

❷ Arrow Cloth
Attire patterned with arrows and worn with maroon *hakama*.

❸ Leather Brown
The brown of leather lace-up boots.

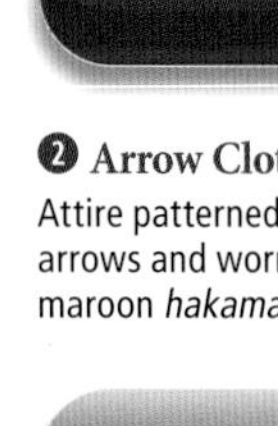

❹ Camellia
Art Deco-style abstracted camellia motifs were popular.

❺ This Spring
Another name for a popular color also called shinbashi.

❻ Evening Primrose
A well-known poem by Takehisa Yumeji that was set to music.

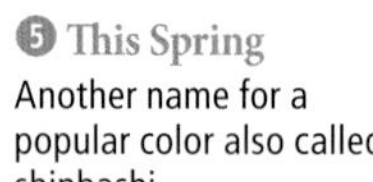

❼ Rickshaw Black
The color of rickshaw carriages, which were a means of transport at the time.

❽ Cafe
Western-style cafes serving coffee and Western confections became popular.

❾ Tin
Toys made of tin appeared at the start of the Meiji era.

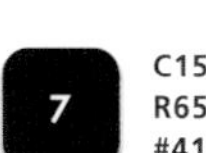

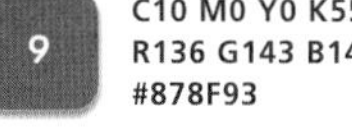

No.	CMYK	RGB	Hex
1	C0 M60 Y50 K60	R129 G67 B54	#814336
2	C60 M80 Y25 K20	R110 G62 B112	#6D3D6F
3	C0 M30 Y65 K55	R144 G111 B53	#906F35
4	C0 M80 Y50 K5	R227 G81 B91	#E2515A
5	C55 M0 Y15 K25	R92 G166 B182	#5BA6B5
6	C0 M15 Y70 K10	R238 G206 B88	#EDCE57
7	C15 M20 Y10 K85	R65 G57 B60	#41383B
8	C0 M25 Y50 K40	R177 G145 B97	#B09060
9	C10 M0 Y0 K55	R136 G143 B148	#878F93

Two-color combinations

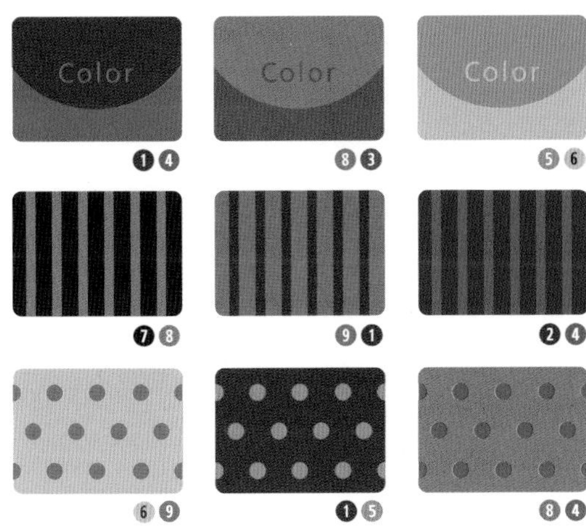

Three-color combinations

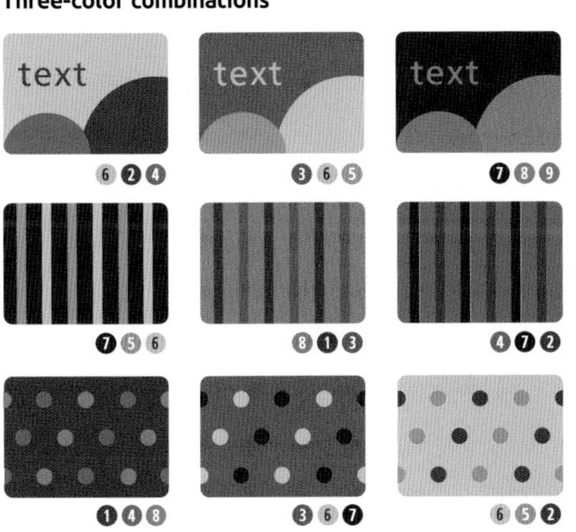

Designs

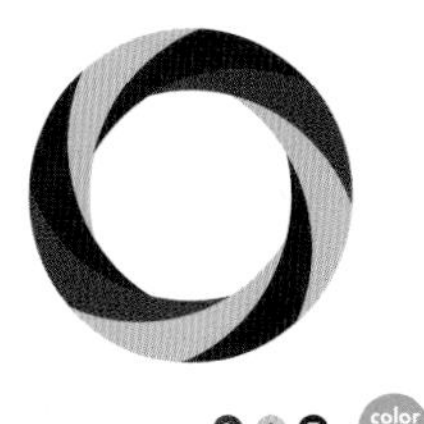

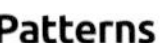

Patterns

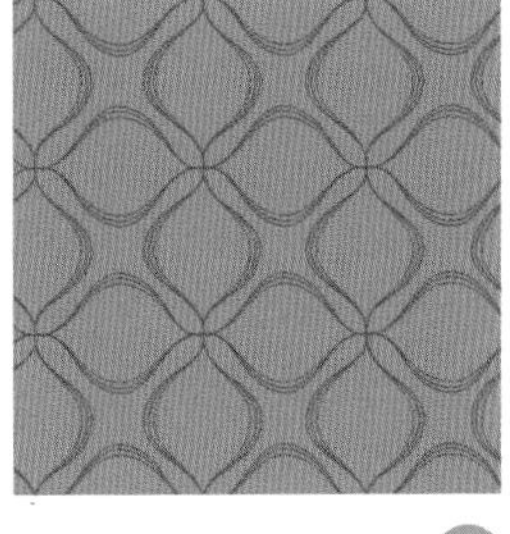

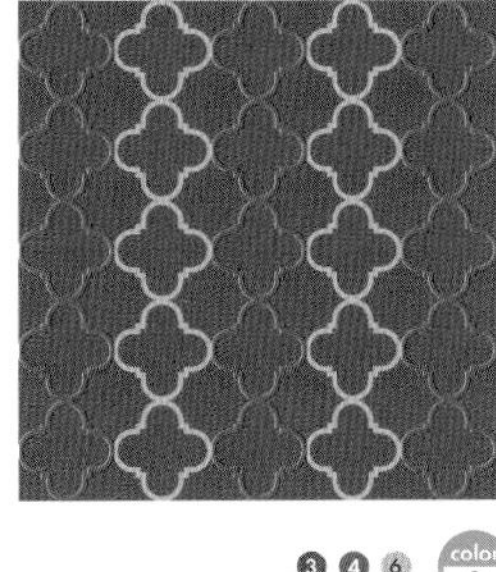

Illustration

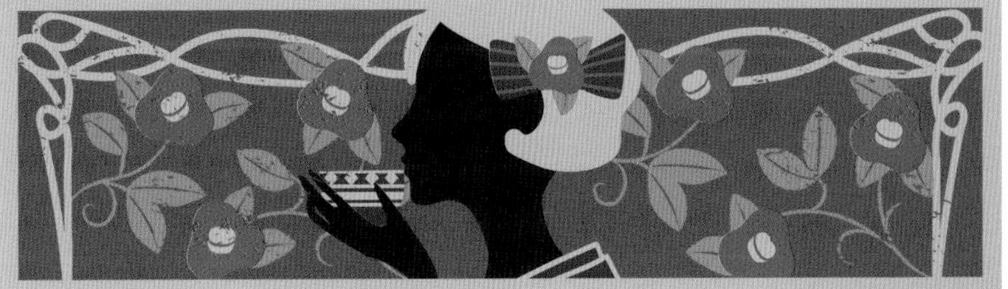

Recipe
087

A Theme Park Palette

The setting for *Moomins on the Riviera*, a film made in 2014 to commemorate the 100th anniversary of Moomins' creator Tove Jansson, is the southern French resort area, the Riviera. The illustrations in the original book are in black and white, but in the film the sand on the beach and the water of the sea all have a yellow sparkle. Red, orange and yellow all fall within the range of warm colors.

- **FEELING** Cheerful, affectionate, casual.
- **COMBINATIONS** Colors 2, 3 and 6 bring out a relaxed casual feel.
- **TIPS** In Northern Europe, deep colors predominate.

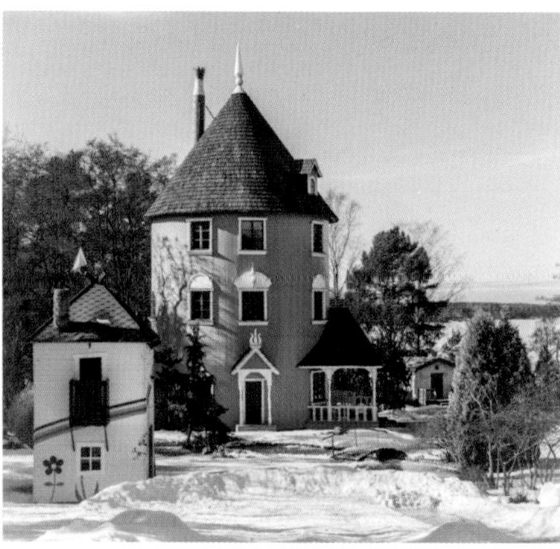

The quaint charms of a fairy tale village.

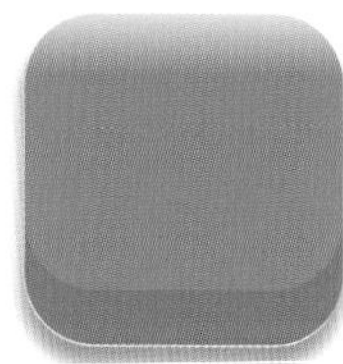

❶ **Blue Wall**
The house's outer wall is a color like the bright blue of the sky.

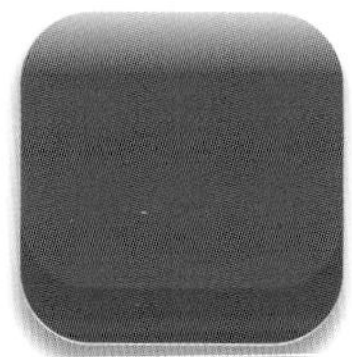

❷ **Peaked Roof**
Standing out even from a distance, the roof is a deep red.

❸ **Hair in a Topknot**
The color of red hair tied in an up-do.

④ **Boy's Pale Blue**
A white faintly tinged with blue that calls to mind a boy's pallor.

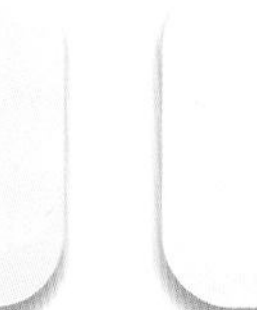

⑤ **Girl's Pale Yellow**
A faint, gentle cream that calls to mind a girl's pallor

❻ **Traveler's Hat**
A color between gray and green with a sense of calm.

❼ **Striped Apron**
The red of mom's much loved apron.

❽ **Reindeer**
A warm brown like that of a reindeer.

❾ **Finland Blue**
The blue of the Finnish national flag.

1. C65 M35 Y3 K0 / R95 G144 B201 / #5F90C8
2. C27 M80 Y100 K0 / R192 G81 B29 / #BF501D
3. C15 M55 Y95 K6 / R209 G130 B22 / #D18215
4. C13 M0 Y5 K0 / R228 G243 B245 / #E4F2F4
5. C4 M0 Y20 K0 / R249 G249 B218 / #F8F9DA
6. C35 M0 Y55 K37 / R131 G159 B104 / #839E67

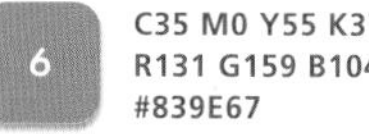

7. C0 M85 Y80 K15 / R210 G63 B43 / #D23F2A

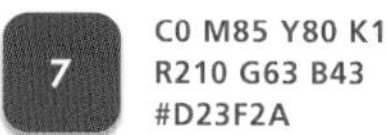

8. C2 M30 Y45 K25 / R203 G161 B119 / #CAA177
9. C85 M73 Y0 K0 / R56 G77 B159 / #384D9F

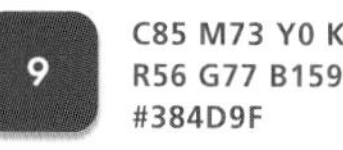

Two-color combinations

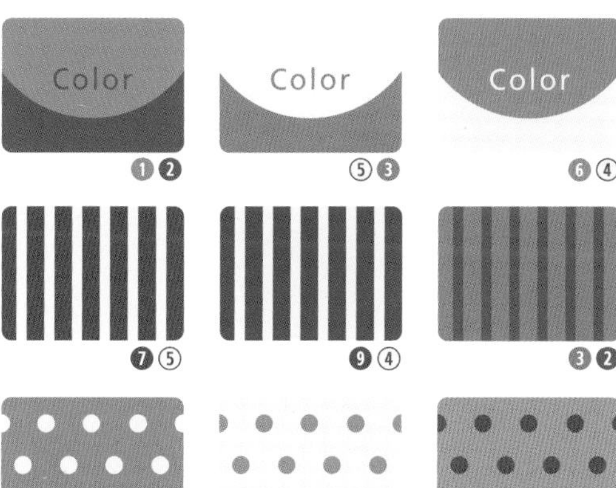

Three-color combinations

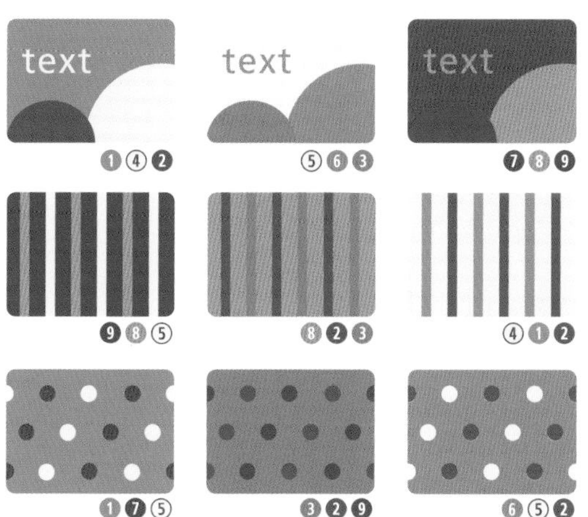

Designs

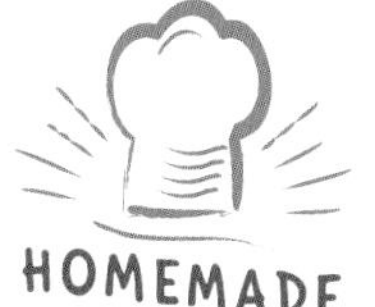

3 7 color 2

2 6 color 2

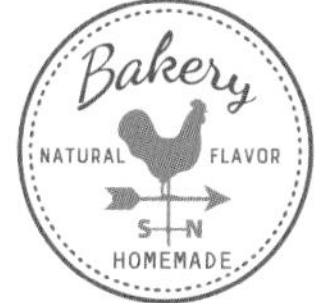
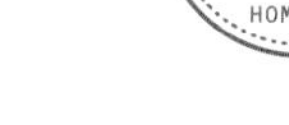
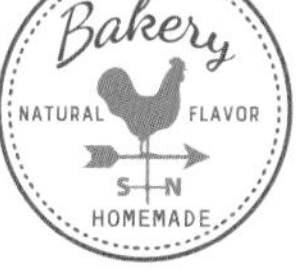

3 7 9 color 3

Patterns

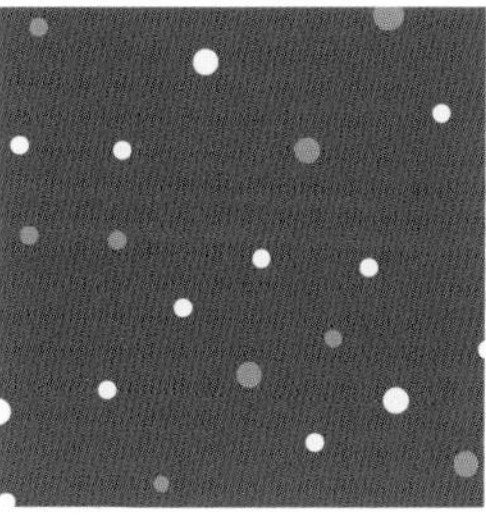

1 5 8 color 3

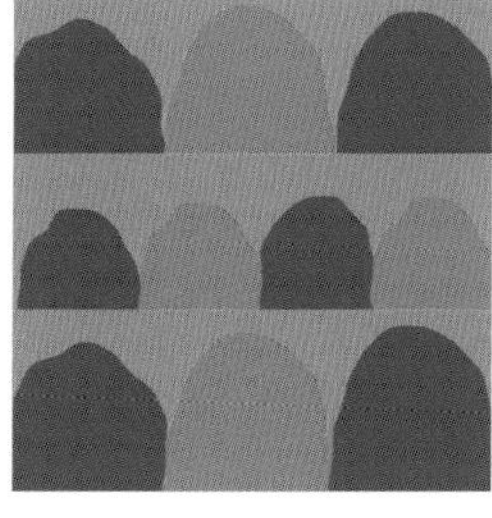

3 6 9 color 3

1 3 5 9 color 4

Illustration

1 5 7 8 color 4

Recipe

088

Northern Lights

The beautiful light of the aurora filling the sky "will change how you view life" says a researcher who has observed the effect over many years. I watched it on video but it wasn't the same as witnessing it firsthand. Maybe it's because humans are creatures who need all five senses to be fully working in order to experience things. Time to book a trip to the Northern Lights then!

- **FEELING** Mysterious, fantastical, magical.
- **COMBINATIONS** Use clear, cool colors with a focus on blue green.
- **TIPS** Use deep blue as a base color.

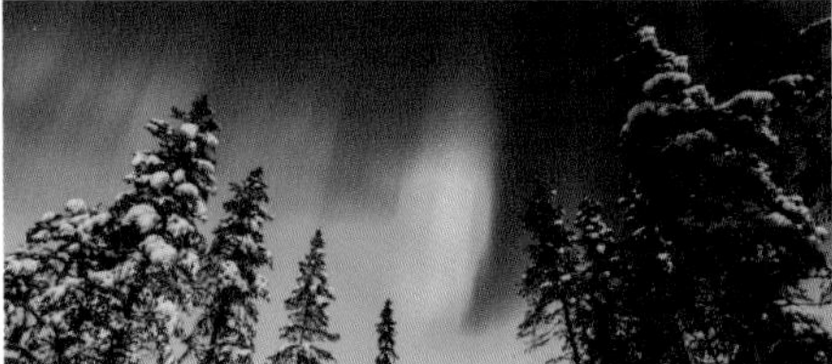

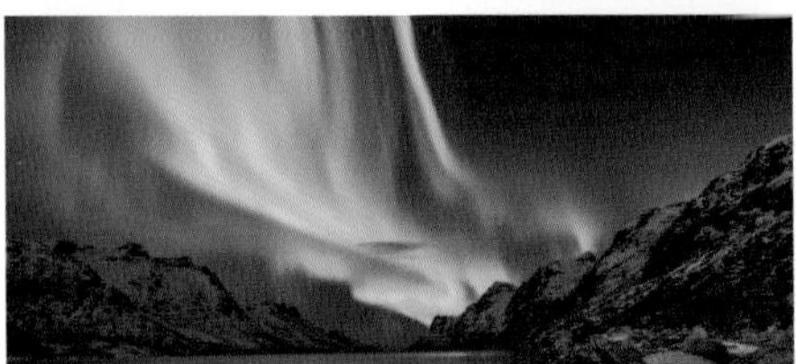

The ghostly, otherworldly colors and effects of the Northern Lights have captivated observers for ages.

❶ Starry Sky
A deep blue suggesting a starry sky.

❷ Northern Lights
The Northern Lights is another name for the mystical aurora.

❸ Aurora Green
The bright, gentle green light pulsing in the aurora.

❹ White Night
This refers to the sun shining all night long, also called Midnight Sun.

❺ Aurora Blue
A translucent light described as both blue and green.

❻ Shiny Purple
A mystical purple light that appears occasionally.

❼ Polar Night
This refers to the sun never rising above the horizon line in winter.

❽ Fjord
A strong blue that suggests the surface of the water in a fjord.

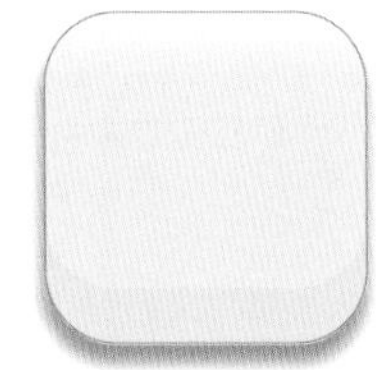

⑨ Snow Crystal
No two snow crystals are exactly alike.

1. C95 M50 Y20 K30 / R0 G85 B129 / #005481
2. C75 M10 Y50 K0 / R26 G166 B146 / #19A591
3. C35 M3 Y35 K0 / R178 G215 B182 / #B2D6B5
4. C35 M20 Y0 K0 / R175 G192 B227 / #AFC0E2
5. C40 M10 Y25 K0 / R165 G201 B195 / #A4C8C2
6. C45 M63 Y0 K0 / R155 G108 B172 / #9B6CAB
7. C50 M30 Y0 K45 / R91 G109 B144 / #5A6D8F
8. C63 M0 Y0 K25 / R55 G161 B200 / #37A0C8

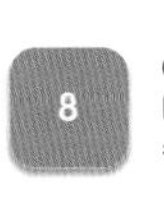

9. C6 M3 Y0 K3 / R239 G242 B247 / #EEF1F7

Two-color combinations

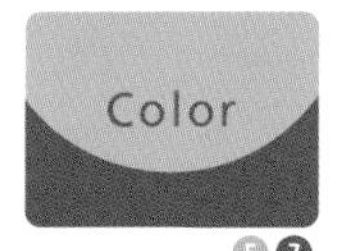

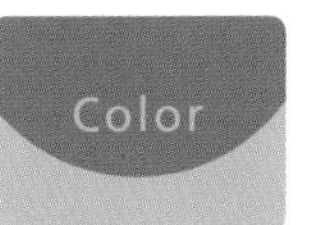

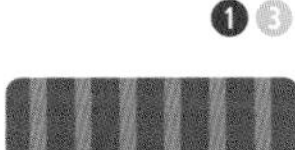

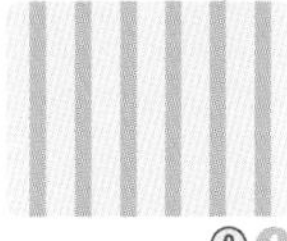

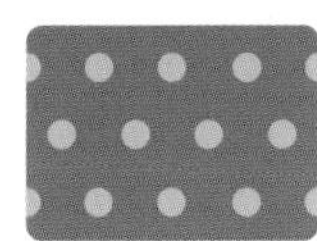

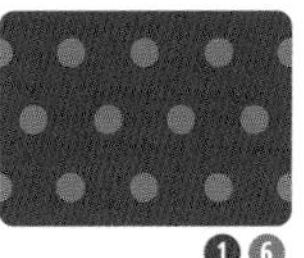

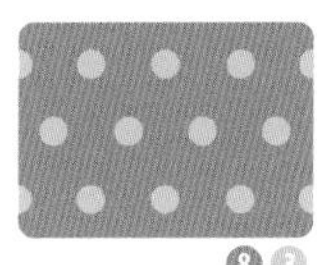

1 3 · 5 7 · 6 4

7 8 · 9 4 · 4 2

6 4 · 1 6 · 8 3

Three-color combinations

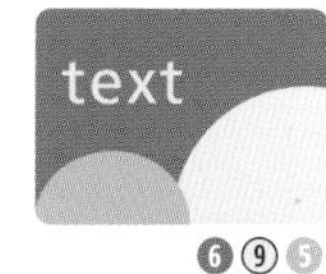

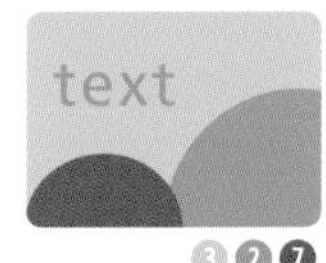

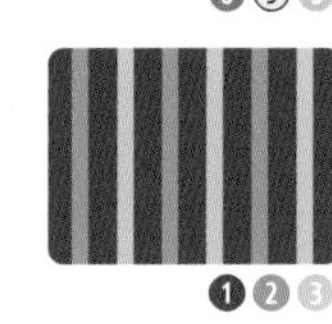

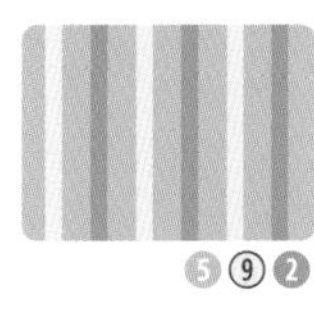

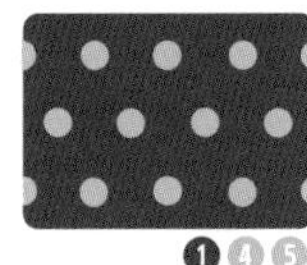

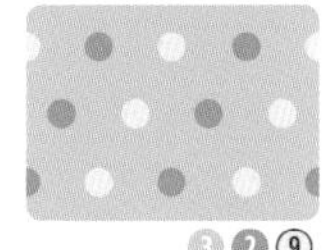

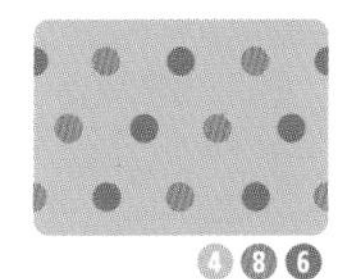

1 4 3 · 6 9 5 · 3 2 7

9 8 5 · 1 2 3 · 5 9 2

1 4 5 · 3 2 9 · 4 8 6

Designs

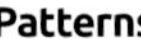

1 2 color 2

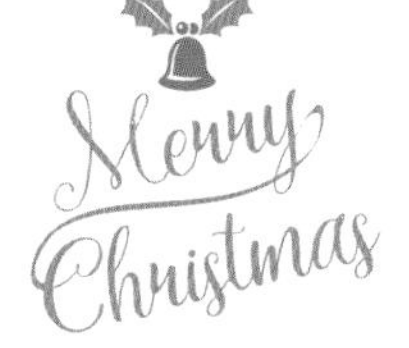

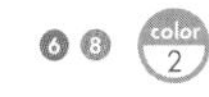

6 8 color 2

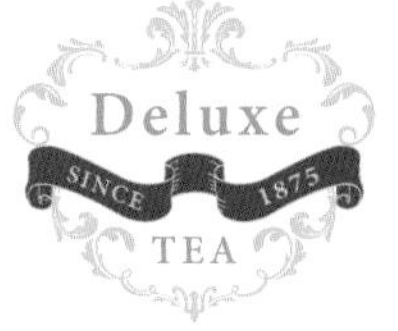

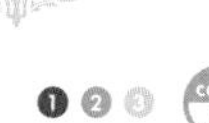

1 2 3 color 3

Patterns

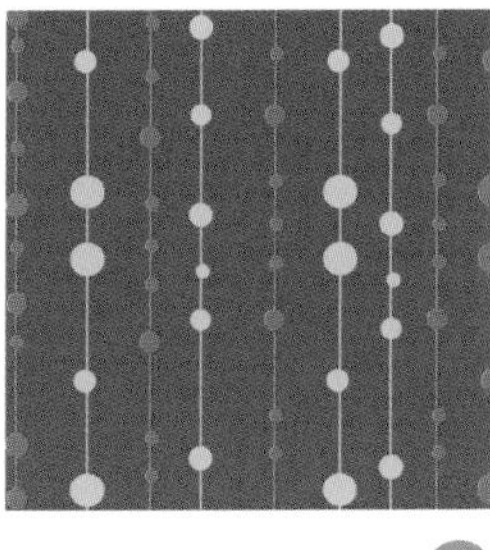

3 6 7 color 3

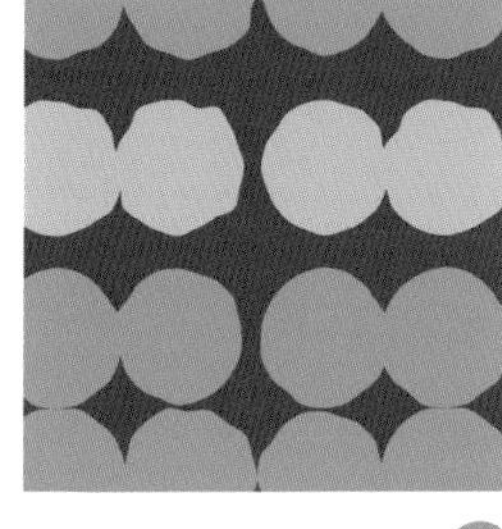

1 2 4 color 3

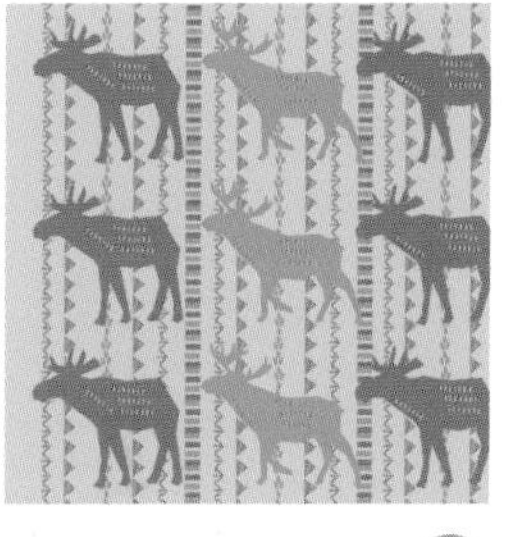

2 3 6 8 color 4

Illustration

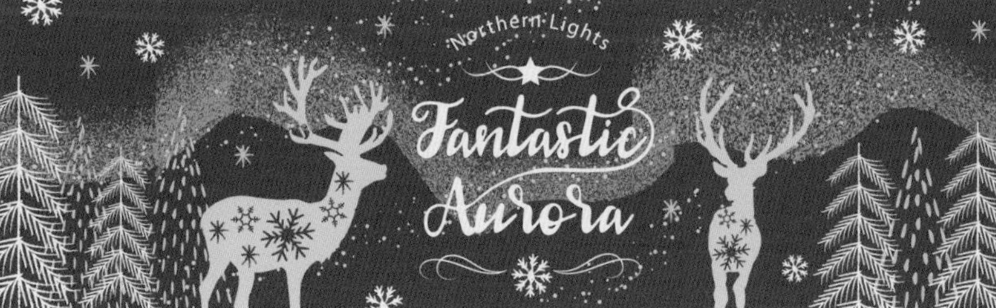

1 2 3 4 9 color 5

Recipe

089

Rosenborg Castle

Apparently, lots of Danish people like going for walks. When I asked at the tourist information center which bus to take to get to the castle, I was told, "You can walk there. It's not far. It's more of a hassle to get the bus." They were right. After walking a little way, a field of purple flowers burst into view and before I knew it, I'd arrived at the castle.

- **FEELING** Gentle, elegant, tranquil.
- **COMBINATIONS** Use intermediate colors such as green and purple.
- **TIPS** If things appear too indistinct, use navy to pull colors together.

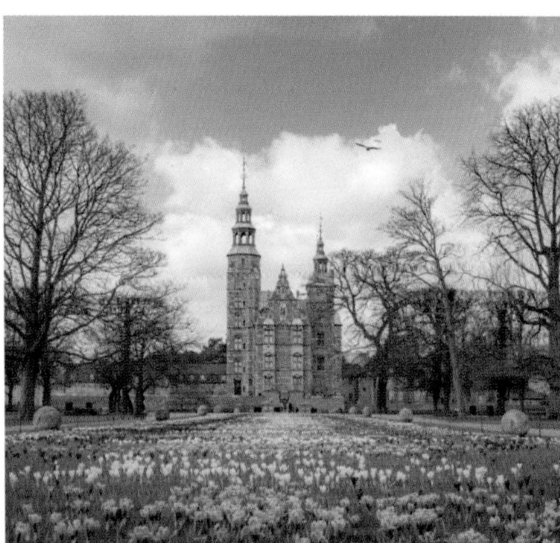

Rosenborg Castle is in the heart of Copenhagen.

❶ **Rosenborg Castle**
A building in the Dutch Renaissance style.

❷ **Pansy**
The deep purple seen on pansies.

❸ **Copenhagen Blue**
A blue like that of Royal Copenhagen porcelain.

❹ **Steeple**
A blue green like that of Rosenborg Castle's steeple.

❺ **Lawn**
The yellow green of a well-maintained lawn.

❻ **Iris**
The light violet of an iris flower.

❼ **Northern Sky**
The color of the sky at the higher latitudes of northern Europe.

❽ **Danish**
A color like that of the danish, the sweet treat that originated here.

❾ **Peacock**
Peacocks roam freely in the vast Tivoli Gardens.

1	C20 M33 Y50 K0 R211 G177 B131 #D3B083
2	C40 M55 Y0 K20 R144 G109 B159 #906C9E
3	C85 M60 Y0 K30 R27 G75 B139 #1B4A8B
4	C50 M0 Y40 K13 R124 G185 B158 #7BB99D
5	C40 M0 Y65 K0 R168 G209 B118 #A8D076
6	C27 M40 Y0 K1 R193 G162 B203 #C0A1CA
7	C40 M25 Y0 K3 R161 G177 B217 #A0B0D8
8	C20 M40 Y67 K8 R200 G155 B89 #C89A59
9	C67 M15 Y50 K0 R84 G167 B143 #53A68E

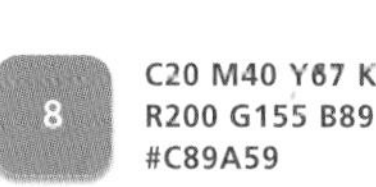
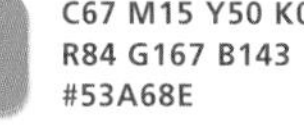

Two-color combinations

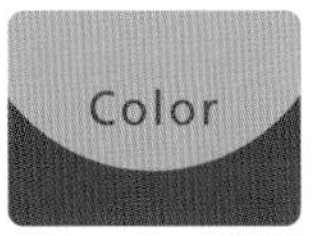
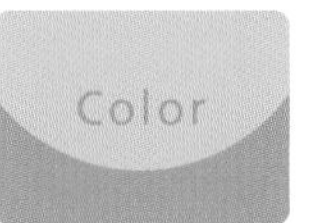
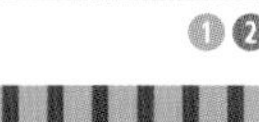

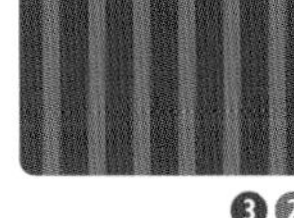
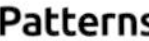
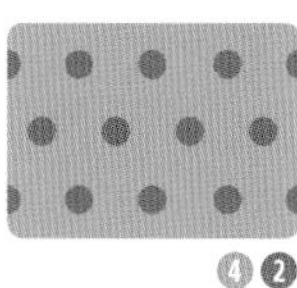
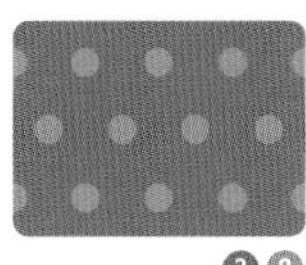
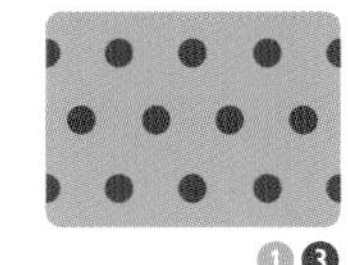

Three-color combinations

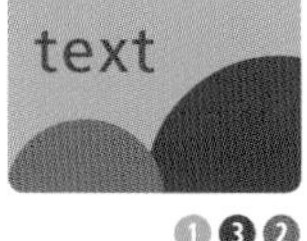
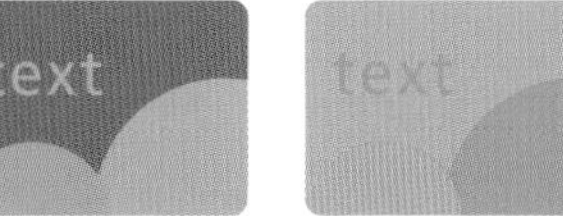

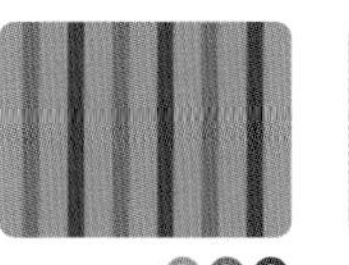
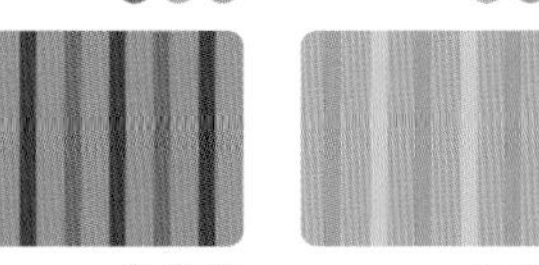
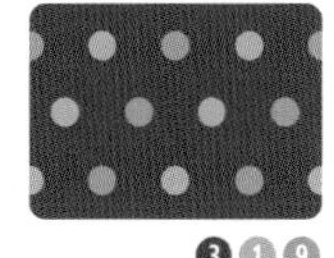
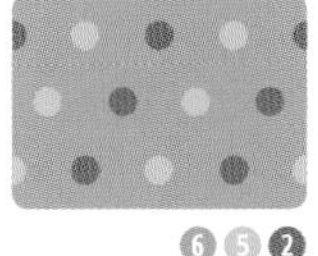

Designs

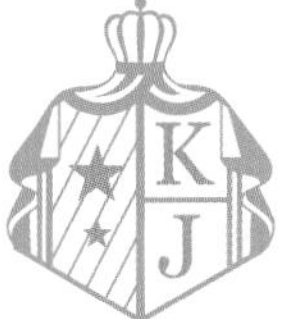

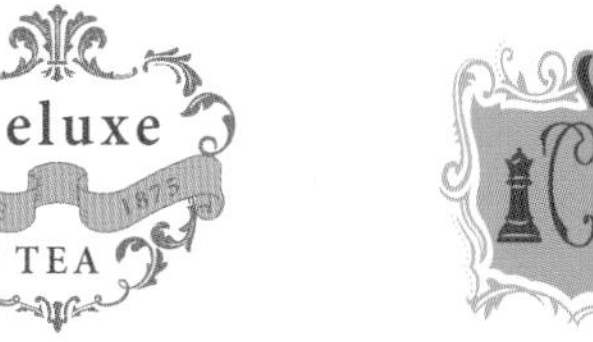

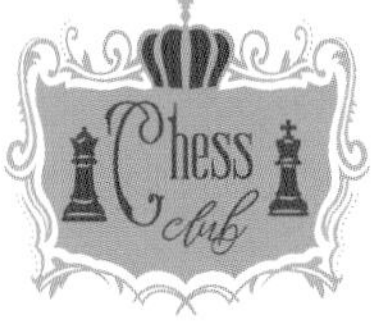

Patterns

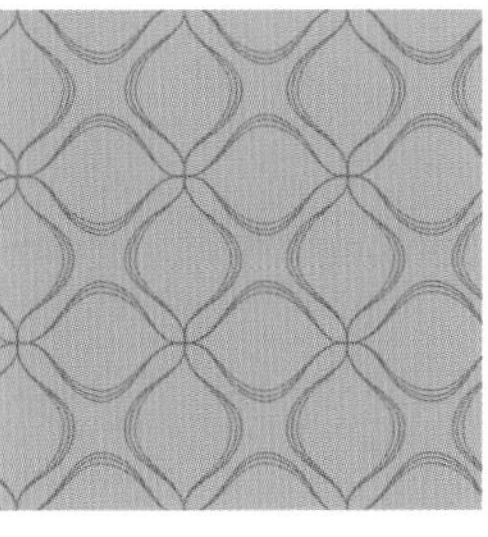

Illustration

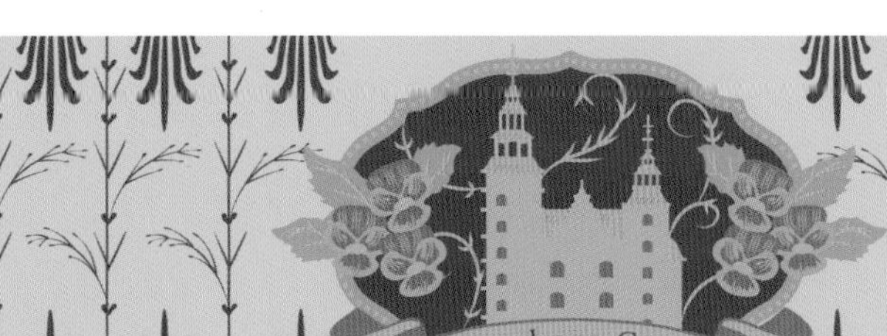

PART 11 THE WORLD AROUND US

Recipe
090

Old Stockholm

In Stockholm, Sweden, the Gamla Stan district has buildings that still remain from the 17th and 18th centuries and the streets are paved with cobblestones. In the central square is the museum of Alfred Nobel, known for the Nobel Prize. The adorable use of color creates a sense of traveling back to the Middle Ages, and the whole city abounds in color schemes that are serene and warm.

- **FEELING** Traditional, tranquil, medieval.
- **COMBINATIONS** Combine warm browns in light and dark shades.
- **TIPS** Use glorious reds, yellows and blues as accents.

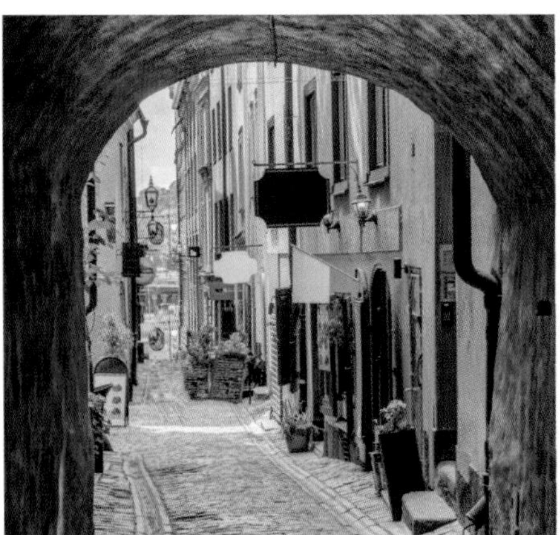

The walls in shades of brown and the texture of the narrow, cobblestone paved alleys conjure an Old World charm.

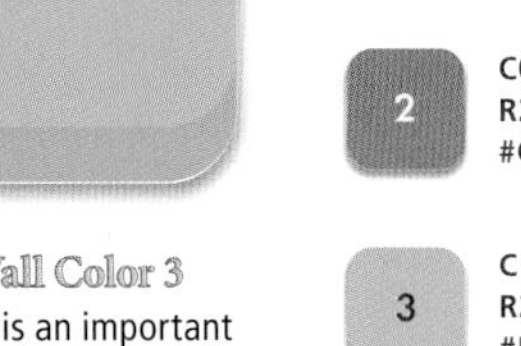

1 Wall Color 1
A warm wall color with a slightly high level of saturation.

2 Wall Color 2
In winter, it's dark and daylight hours are short; a brown complements.

3 Wall Color 3
Color is an important element for living comfortably.

4 Stone Paving
A color evoking the cobblestones of Gamla Stan's alleys.

5 Traditional House
The color of walls in a traditional Swedish timber house.

6 Roof
This is a color scheme for the roofs of vacation houses.

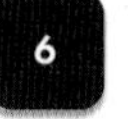

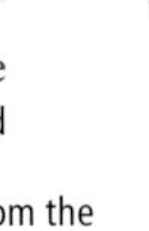

7 Mailbox (domestic)
Two mailboxes—blue and yellow—are installed next to each other.

8 Mailbox (international)
Blue and yellow is also the color scheme for Sweden's national flag.

9 Dalana Horse
The color of carved wooden horses, a traditional craft from the Dalana region.

No.	CMYK	RGB	Hex
1	C5 M10 Y45 K0	R246 G229 B158	#F5E49E
2	C0 M40 Y45 K25	R203 G145 B112	#CA9170
3	C15 M25 Y40 K0	R222 G196 B157	#DEC39C
4	C0 M0 Y15 K25	R211 G209 B190	#D3D1BD
5	C15 M70 Y65 K0	R213 G105 B80	#D56950
6	C0 M0 Y3 K85	R76 G73 B71	#4B4846
7	C50 M30 Y1 K0	R138 G163 B212	#89A3D3
8	C17 M0 Y70 K0	R224 G230 B102	#E0E565
9	C10 M95 Y80 K0	R217 G39 B49	#D82630

Two-color combinations

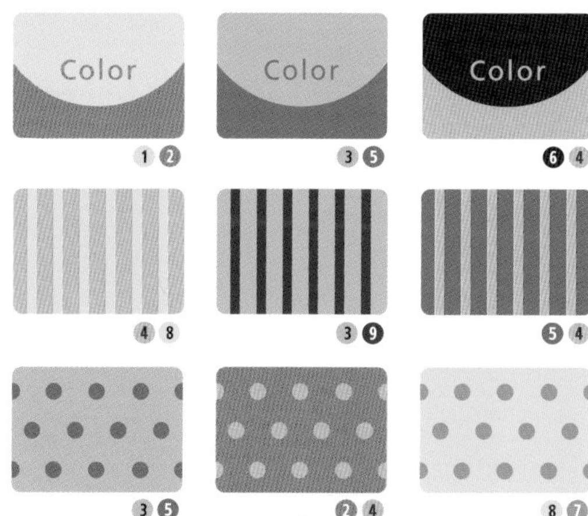

Three-color combinations

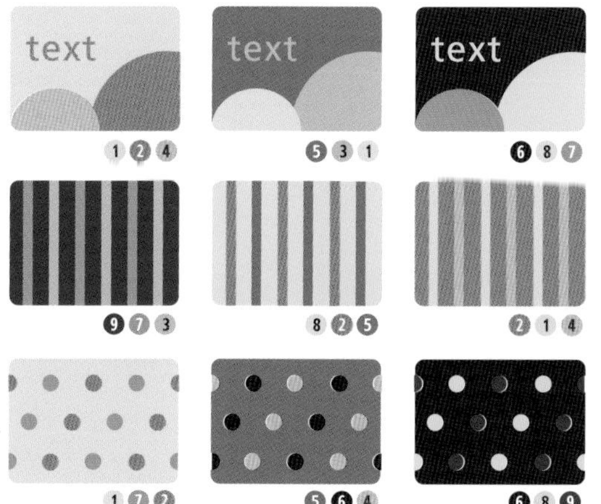

Designs

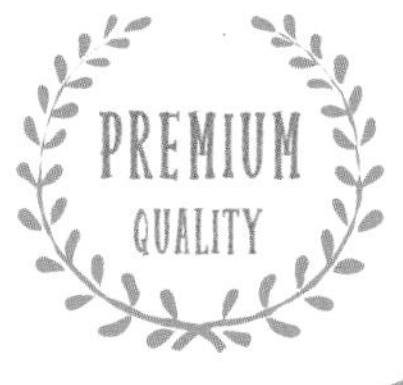

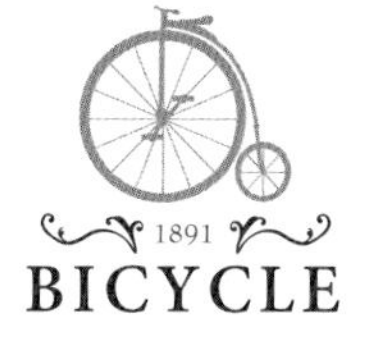

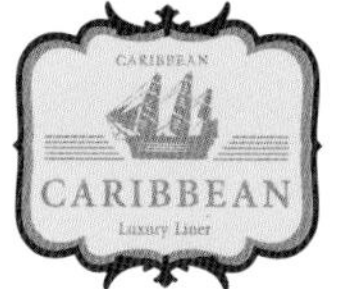

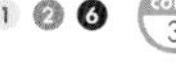

Patterns

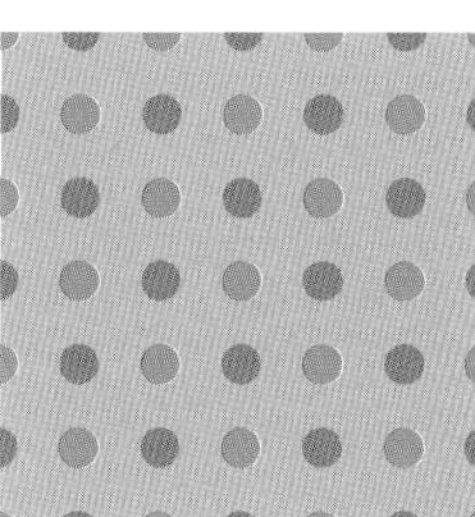

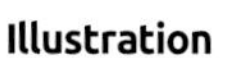

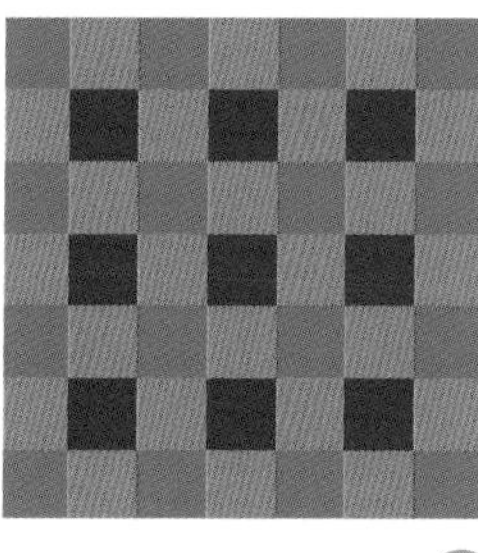

Illustration

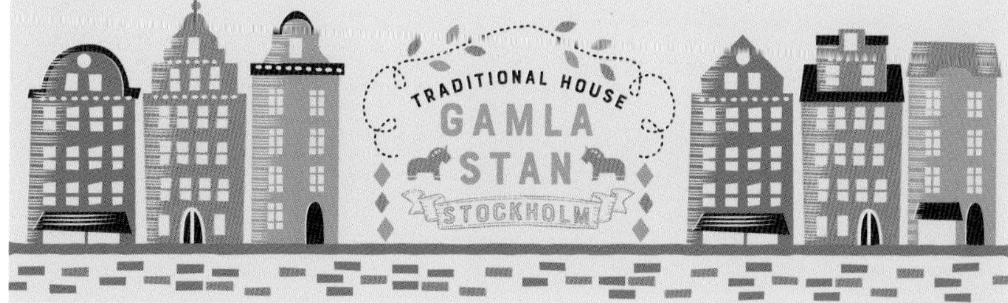

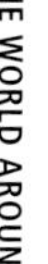

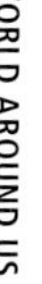

Recipe
091

Venice

Venice is a leading tourist destination. Every year, from the end of February to the start of March, people gather for Carnival in colorful costumes and masks. A ferry ride away from the main island, Burano Island is a remote enclave whose houses are all different colors. According to the wisdom of the fishermen, even if the fog is thick, you'll be able to find your own house.

- **FEELING** Calm, amiable, nostalgic.
- **COMBINATIONS** Add brown and beige to shades of blue.
- **TIPS** Use green blue to indicate the water of Venice.

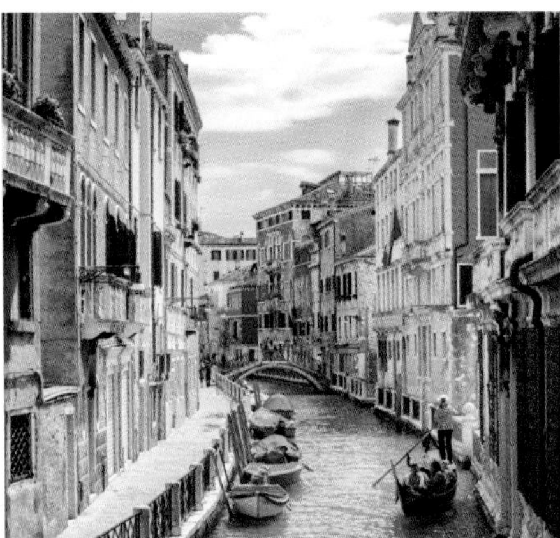

Gondolas are a means of moving freely through the intricate network of canals.

① Venetian Blue
The canals crisscross the waterways in the city in northeast Italy.

② Grand Canal
The largest canal in Venice, it equates to a major arterial road.

③ Vacation Blue
Italians enjoy two to three weeks of vacation in summer.

④ Beige
The color of buildings' outer walls is in harmony with the green blue of the water.

⑤ Italian Red
A deep red that creates a sense of history and style.

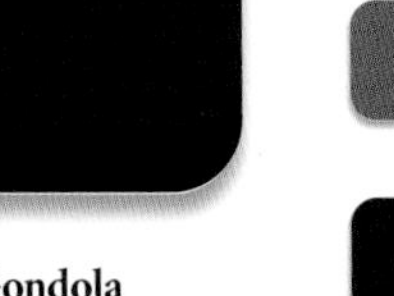

⑥ Gondola
The color of the hull of gondolas, which allow free movement through the narrow waterways.

⑦ Pasta
Typical Italian fare. There are over 650 types.

⑧ Tomato Sauce
A typical Italian tomato is the San Marzano variety.

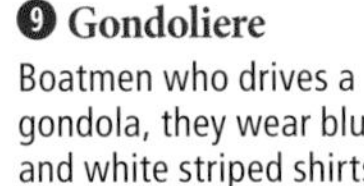

⑨ Gondoliere
Boatmen who drives a gondola, they wear blue and white striped shirts.

No.	CMYK	RGB	Hex
1	C50 M0 Y40 K0	R135 G202 B172	#87C9AB
2	C45 M0 Y20 K25	R121 G174 B176	#79AEAF
3	C70 M40 Y0 K5	R78 G130 B192	#4E81BF
4	C0 M15 Y35 K10	R237 G211 B165	#ECD2A5
5	C0 M70 Y70 K30	R187 G85 B53	#BA5434
6	C0 M60 Y70 K90	R62 G15 B0	#3D0E00
7	C0 M15 Y60 K10	R237 G207 B112	#EDCF70
8	C0 M90 Y90 K20	R201 G47 B25	#C82F19
9	C100 M70 Y0 K40	R0 G52 B119	#003376

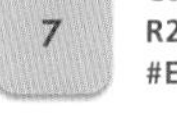
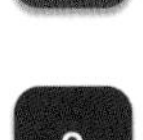

Two-color combinations

Color

1 4

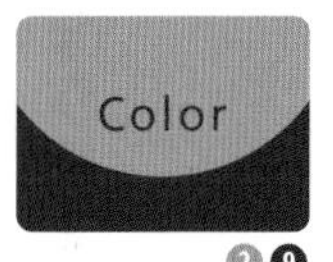

2 9

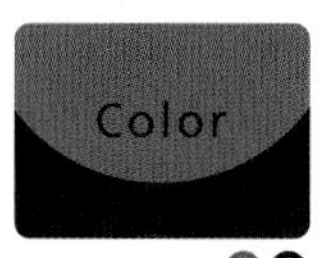

5 6

7 8

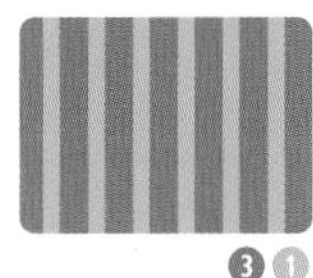

3 1

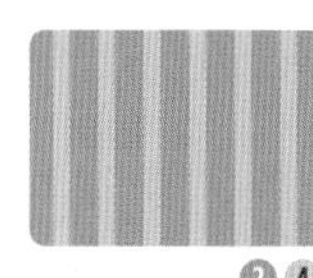

2 4

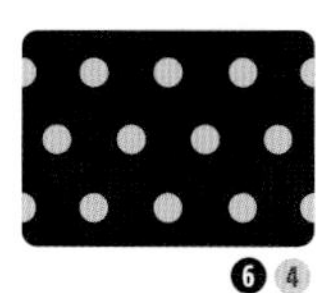

6 4

1 7

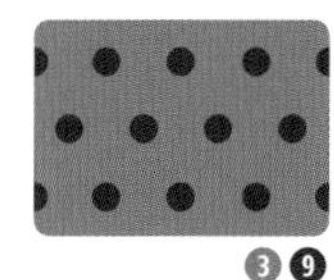

3 9

Three-color combinations

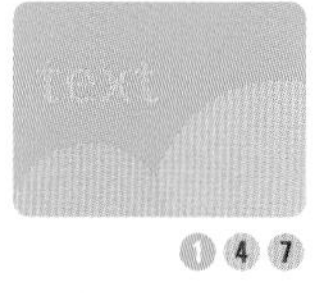

1 4 7

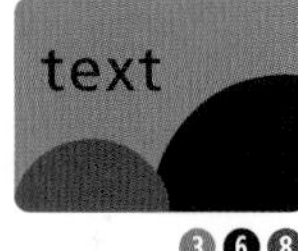

3 6 8

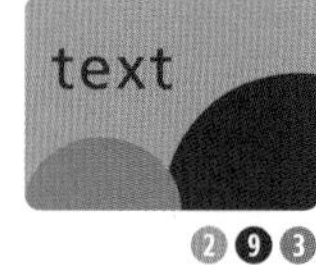

2 9 3

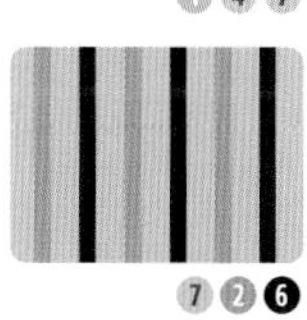

7 2 6

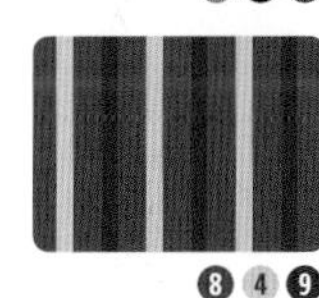

8 4 9

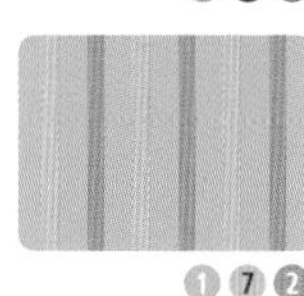

1 7 2

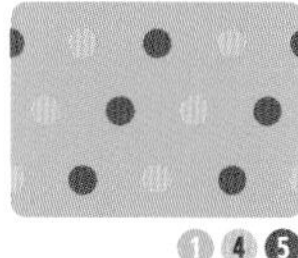

1 4 5

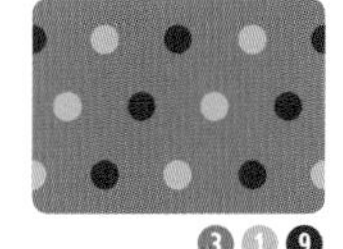

3 1 9

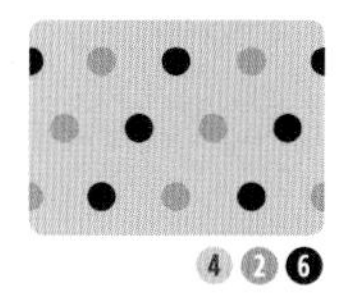

4 2 6

Designs

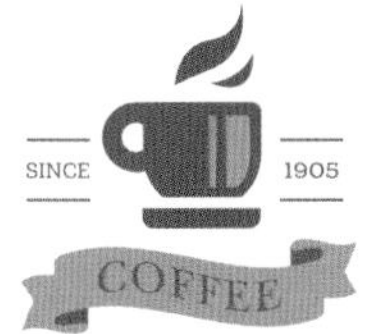

2 5 color 2

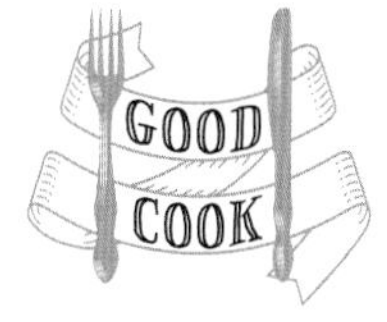

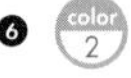

2 6 color 2

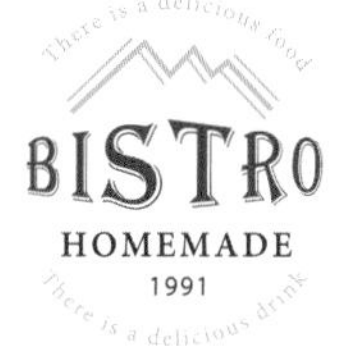

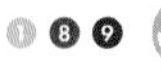

1 8 9 color 3

Patterns

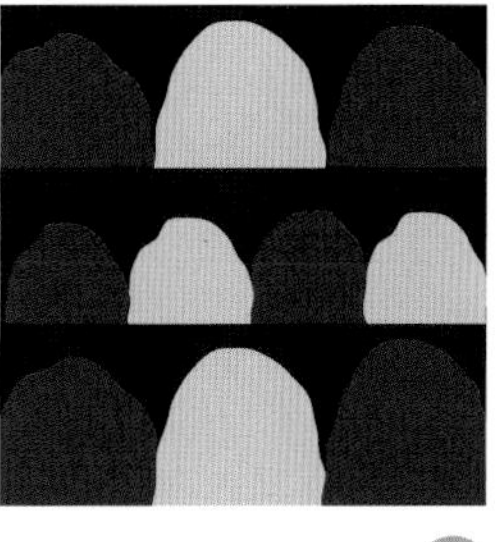

6 7 9 color 3

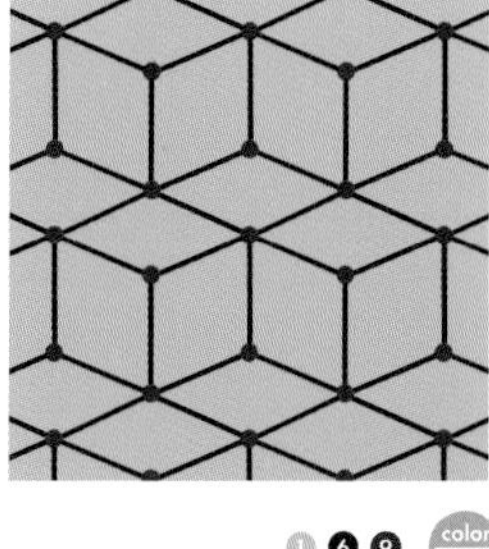

1 6 9 color 3

2 4 5 color 3

Illustration

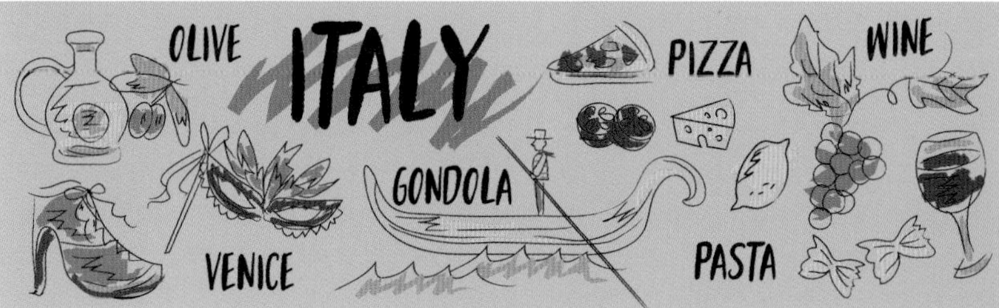

1 2 3 6 7 8 color 6

Recipe

092

The Swiss Alps

In *Heidi, Girl of the Alps*, there's a scene in which the grandfather is toasting cheese in the fireplace. This type of cheese is raclette, and in Swiss cuisine the melted cheese is scraped off with a knife and eaten with potatoes. The long winter in the Alps comes to an end between the end of June and the middle of July, when the snow melts and the alpine plants all blossom at once. I've drawn on the spring scenery to develop this color palette.

- **FEELING** Expansive, cheerful, natural.
- **COMBINATIONS** Use the blue sky, white clouds and green meadows as base colors.
- **TIPS** Create a color palette that replicates the tran quility of the scenery.

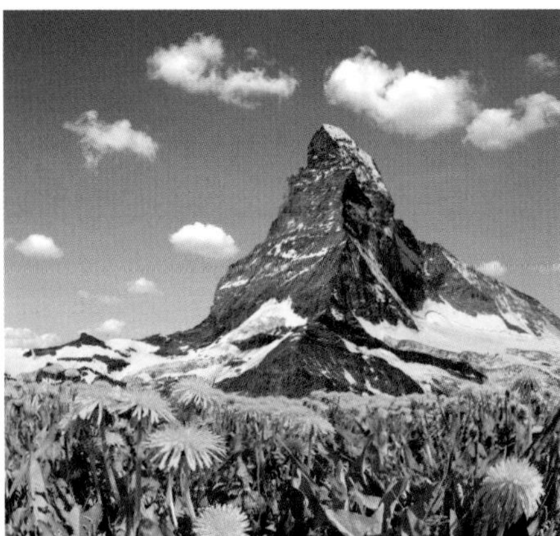

Below a clear sky, all the colors seem to come to life.

1 Mountain Breeze
A fresh breeze that blows through mountainous areas.

2 Edelweiss
The national flower of Switzerland. In German, it means "noble white."

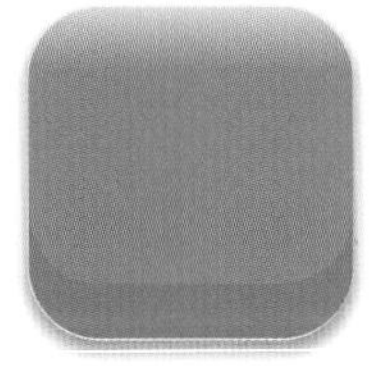

3 Alps Green
All kinds of flowers bloom in the alpine grasslands once the snow melts.

4 Raclette Cheese
The color of raclette cheese, which is eaten by warming a cut section until it melts.

5 Matterhorn Gray
The color of the sheer rock face of the Matter-horn.

6 Marmot
A member of the squirrel family that eats grass, fruit, tree roots and flowers.

7 Alpenhorn
A long wind instrument originally used by cow-herds.

8 Sun Kiss
The color of bright flowers blooming in the sun.

9 Traditional Black
Blue, red and black are commonly used in traditional garments.

1 C65 M30 Y0 K8
R86 G144 B200
#5690C7

2 C7 M0 Y4 K0
R241 G249 B248
#F1F8F7

3 C65 M20 Y90 K0
R101 G159 B68
#649F44

4 C0 M15 Y55 K0
R254 G222 B132
#FDDE83

5 C10 M5 Y7 K0
R125 G127 B127
#7D7F7F

6 C15 M20 Y25 K40
R157 G146 B135
#9D9287

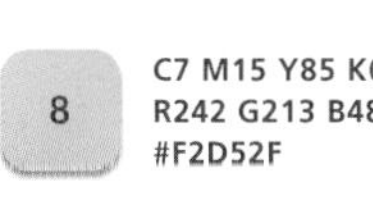

7 C0 M25 Y60 K25
R207 G168 B95
#CEA85E

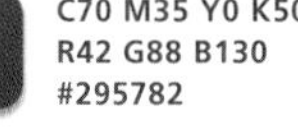

8 C7 M15 Y85 K0
R242 G213 B48
#F2D52F

9 C70 M35 Y0 K50
R42 G88 B130
#295782

Two-color combinations

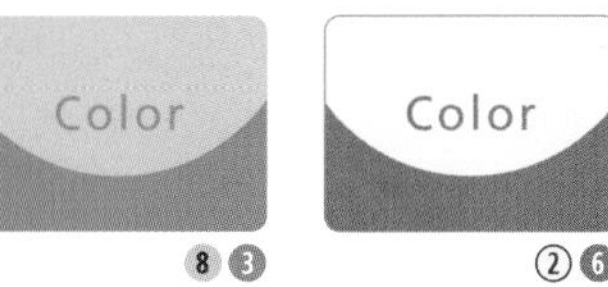
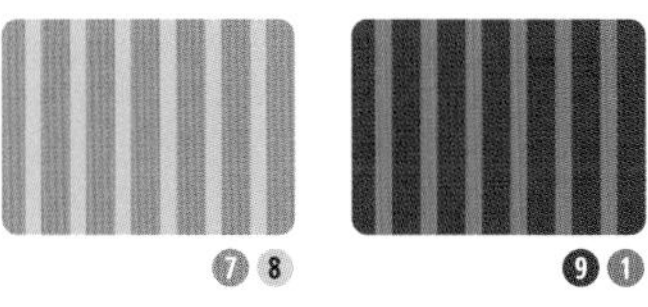
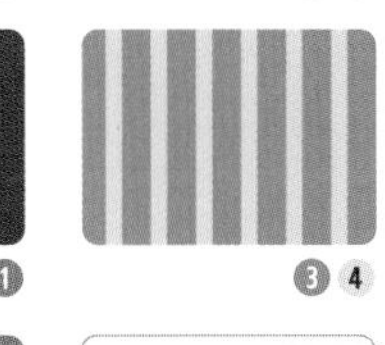

Three-color combinations

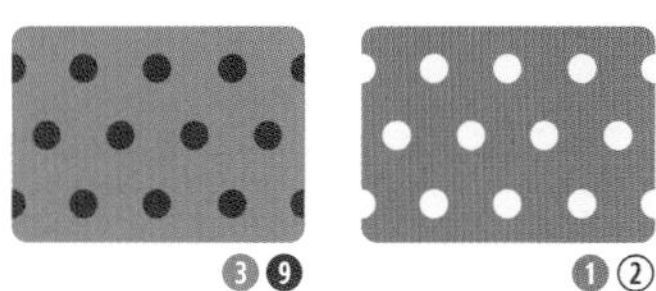
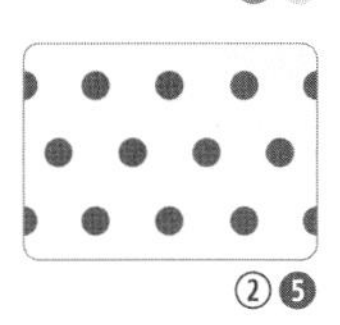
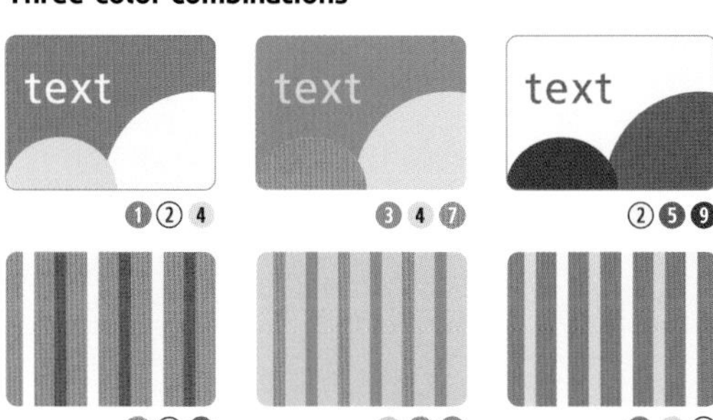

Designs

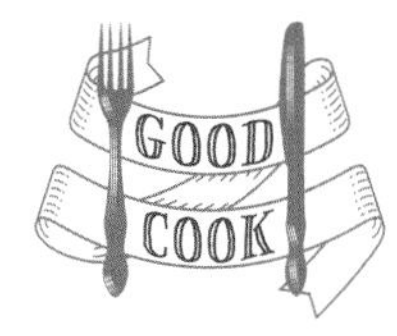

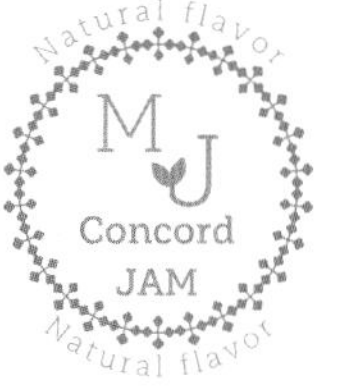

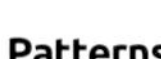

Patterns

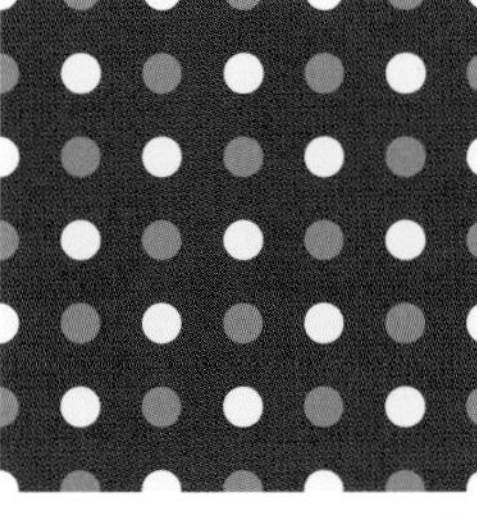
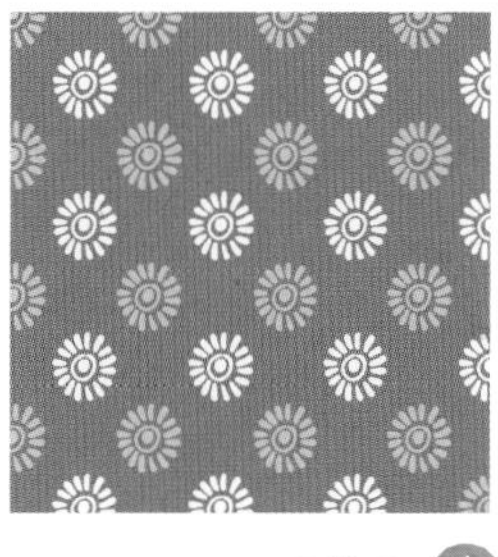

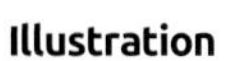

Illustration

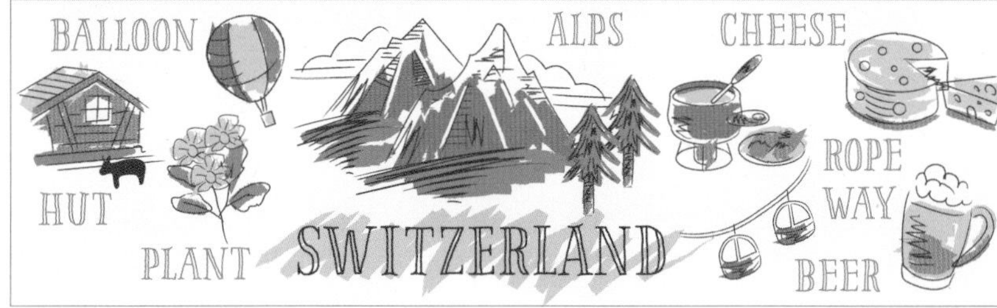

Recipe
093

Provence

The lavender fields of Provence in southern France were described to me as one of the landscapes I should see at least once. It's not only the beauty of the color, but being enveloped by the fragrance that guarantees a heavenly holiday. The word "lavender" derives from the Latin for "to wash," as lavender was used as an aromatic in washing and for bathing. The people of ancient Rome also made this color part of their lives.

- **FEELING** Soft, romantic, fable-like.
- **COMBINATIONS** Use pastel colors with a focus on purple.
- **TIPS** Keep tones similar for a cohesive look.

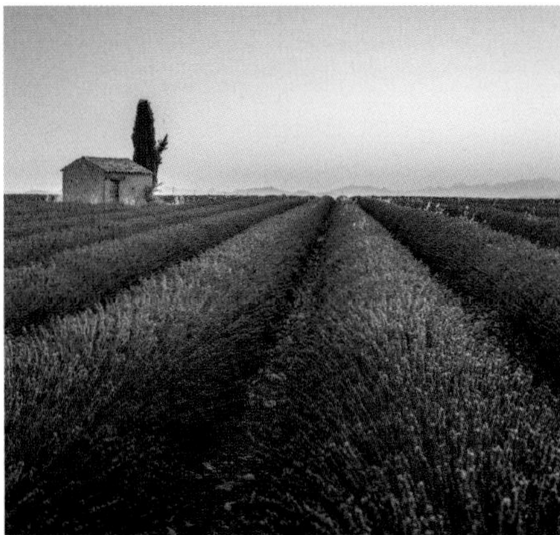

Purple stretches as far as the eye can see in a beautiful field of lavender.

1 French Lavender
This variety has two petals that spring out like rabbit ears.

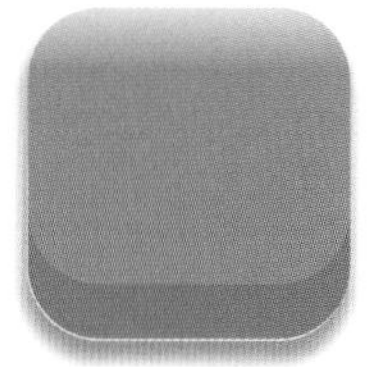

2 Spike Lavender
Grayish flowers that have a refreshing scent.

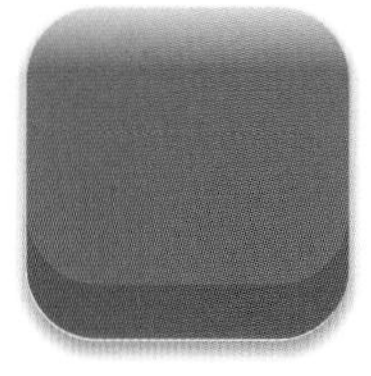

3 Lavender Extra
Characterized by a fresh, gentle fragrance.

4 Sachet
A small bag filled with dried lavender flowers.

5 Flamingo
The pink of flamingos who migrate to Provence.

6 Rosé
The color of rosé wine, frequently drunk in summer in France.

7 Ochre
Colored clay particular to southern France. The color differs depending on the region.

8 Sleeping Beauty
Sleeping Beauty is set in the Loire region of France.

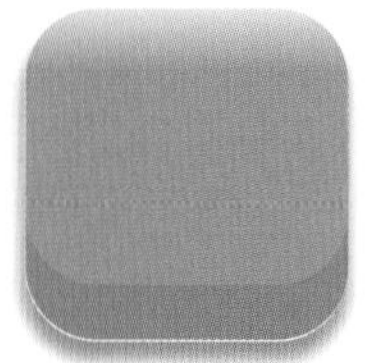

9 Cote d'Azur
Literally translated, this means "azure coast."

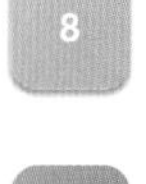

No.	CMYK	RGB	Hex
1	C35 M50 Y3 K0	R177 G139 B187	#B08ABA
2	C40 M40 Y5 K0	R166 G154 B196	#A59AC3
3	C55 M55 Y0 K0	R132 G118 B181	#8376B5
4	C10 M15 Y0 K5	R225 G215 B231	#E1D7E6
5	C0 M15 Y20 K0	R252 G227 B205	#FCE2CC
6	C0 M33 Y30 K10	R231 G179 B159	#E7B39E
7	C0 M35 Y55 K20	R213 G160 B104	#D59F67
8	C35 M10 Y0 K8	R166 G198 B226	#A5C5E2
9	C50 M25 Y8 K4	R134 G167 B202	#86A7CA

Two-color combinations

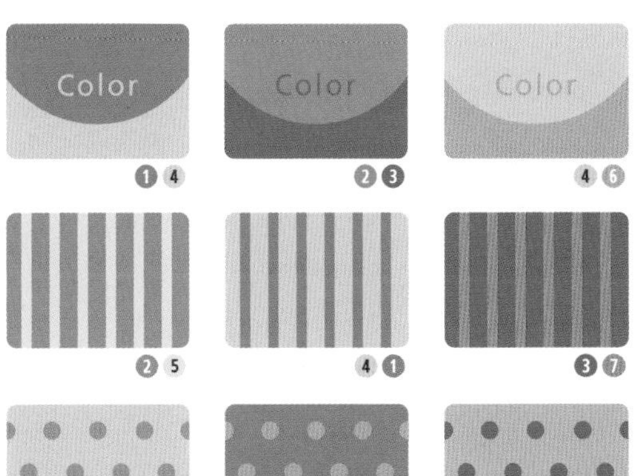

Three-color combinations

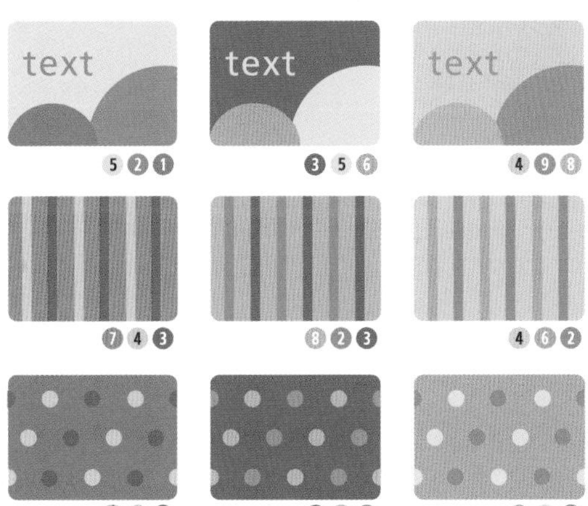

Designs

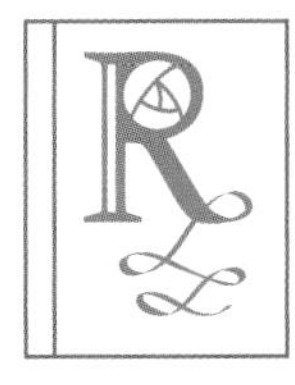

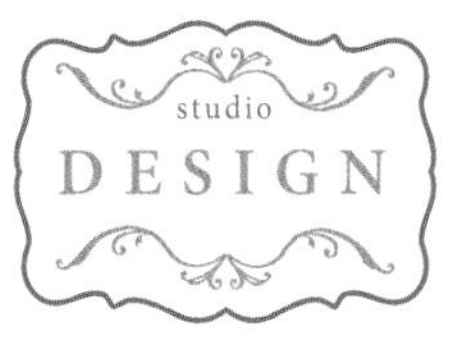

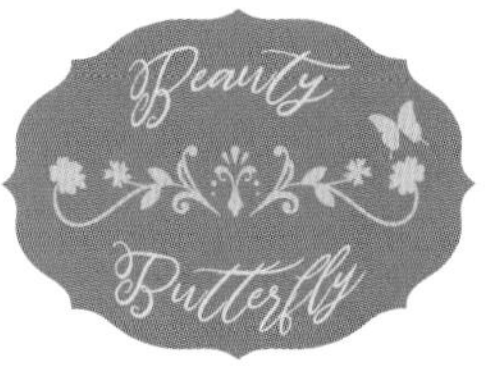

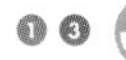

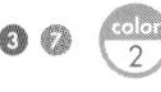

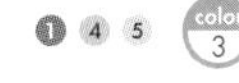

Patterns

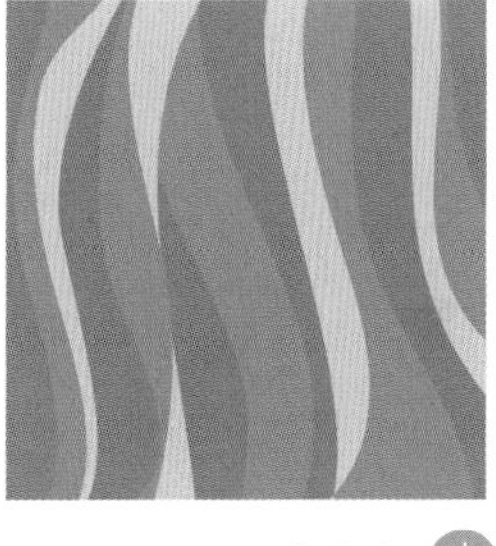

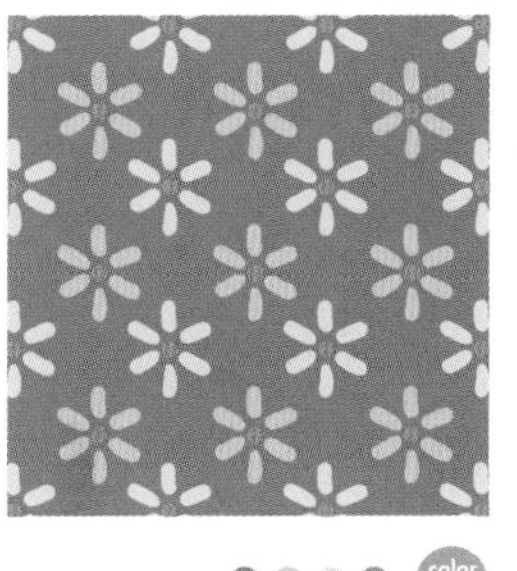

Illustration

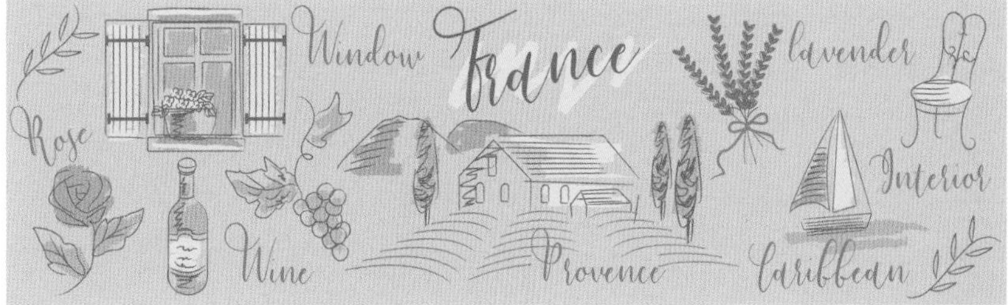

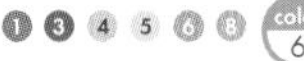

Recipe
094

Santorini

The first major purchase I made when I started work was a picture. As its motif, it features the Greek island of Mykonos, otherwise known as the pearl of the Aegean Sea, with scenery of a white cafe terrace overlooking the blue ocean. Whenever I'm feeling tired, I always conjure up the image of that place. The tension melts from my shoulders, and I breathe easy.

- **FEELING** **Clear, lucid, decided.**
- **COMBINATIONS** **Take cues from the scenery to combine colors with a focus on blue and white.**
- **TIPS** **Use pale brown and shades of pink as accents.**

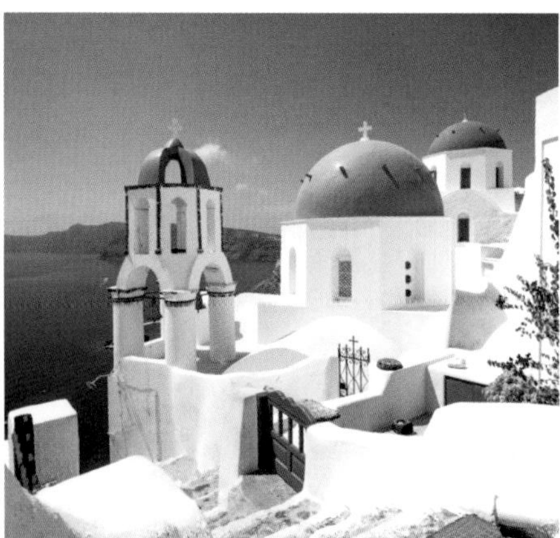

The beautiful scenery provides the ideal setting for the starkly contrasting blue-and-white style of the coastal villages.

❶ Greek Blue
The blue of the sea synonymous with the Greek coast.

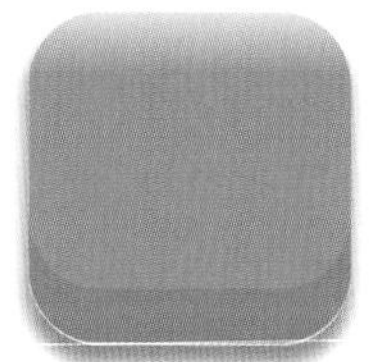

❷ Blue Eyes
The color of Zeus' eyes, the king of the gods in Greek mythology.

③ Sacred White
In Greek mythology, white symbolized the gods.

④ Limestone
Lime is used to create the white coating on the walls of buildings.

❺ Parthenon
This ancient ruin was vividly decorated back in the day.

❻ Acropolis
A brown that recalls the fortress of an ancient city.

❼ Stone Pavement
A blue-tinged gray that suggests the cobblestones of a pavement.

⑧ Morning Well
A color evoking the white walls of houses tinted by the sunrise.

❾ Bougainvillea
The color of bougainvillea flowers that bloom in profusion in the alleys.

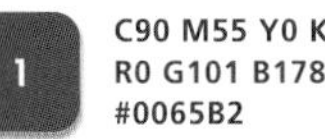

C90 M55 Y0 K0
R0 G101 B178
#0065B2

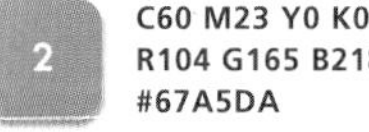

C60 M23 Y0 K0
R104 G165 B218
#67A5DA

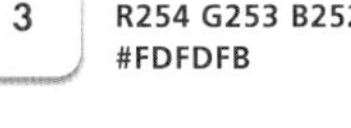

C1 M1 Y2 K0
R254 G253 B252
#FDFDFB

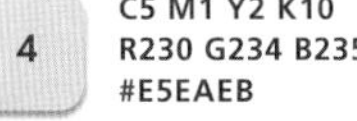

C5 M1 Y2 K10
R230 G234 B235
#E5EAEB

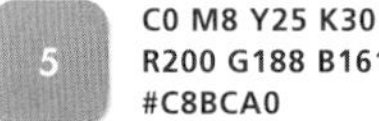

C0 M8 Y25 K30
R200 G188 B161
#C8BCA0

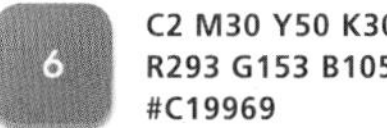

C2 M30 Y50 K30
R293 G153 B105
#C19969

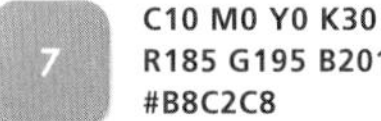

C10 M0 Y0 K30
R185 G195 B201
#B8C2C8

C0 M15 Y8 K0
R252 G229 B226
#FBE4E2

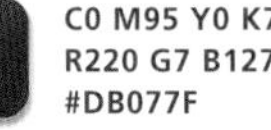

C0 M95 Y0 K7
R220 G7 B127
#DB077F

Two-color combinations

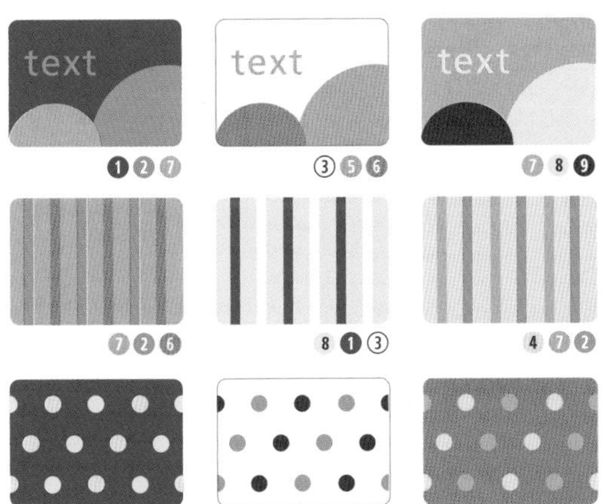

Three-color combinations

Designs

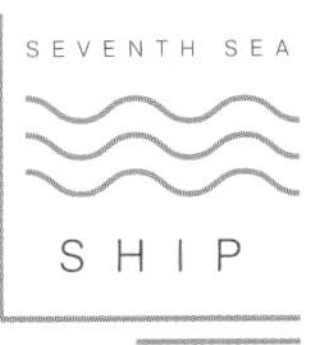

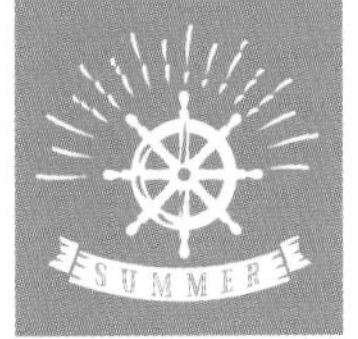

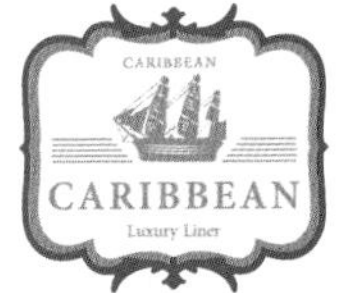

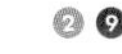

Patterns

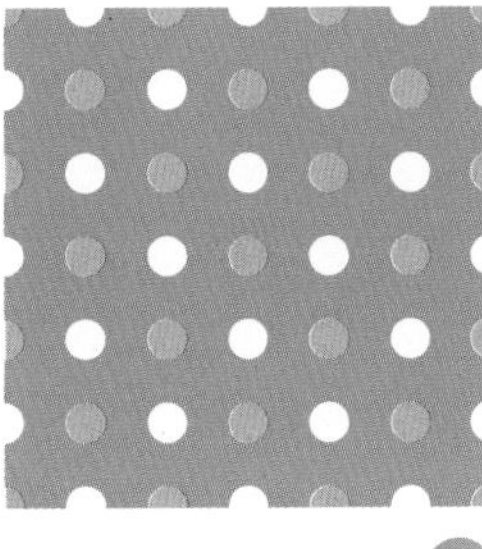

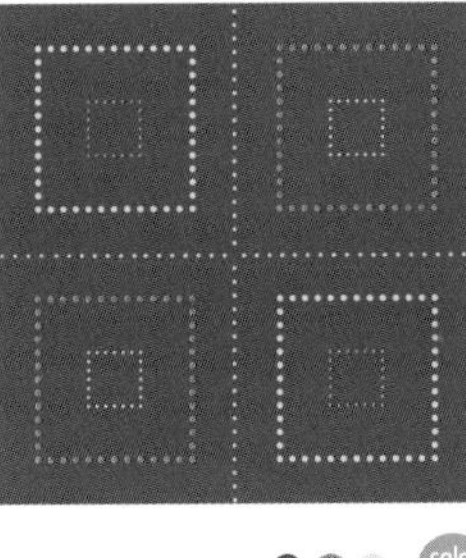

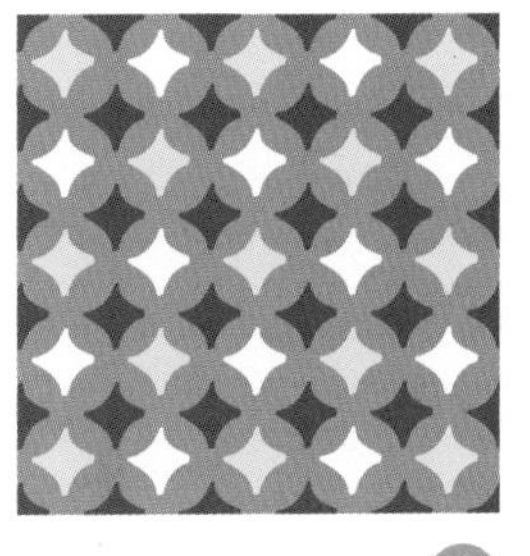

Illustration

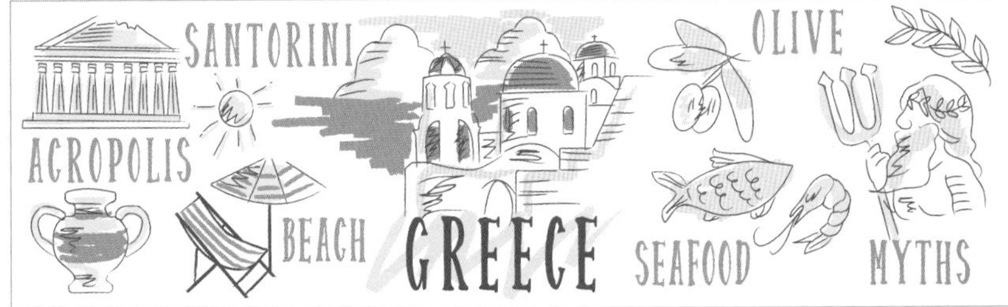

Recipe
095

Carnival in Rio

The Japanese phrase "Gin bura" is derived not from the meaning of wandering aimlessly (*bura bura*) around Ginza (which is its contemporary meaning), but from drinking Brazilian coffee in Ginza. Many local government municipalities have established sister-city agreements with Brazilian counterparts. Here, the colors that symbolize Brazil are used in the scheme.

- **FEELING** Cheerful, powerful, flamboyant.
- **COMBINATIONS** Use brilliant, deep colors.
- **TIPS** Deep colors express a unity with the earth.

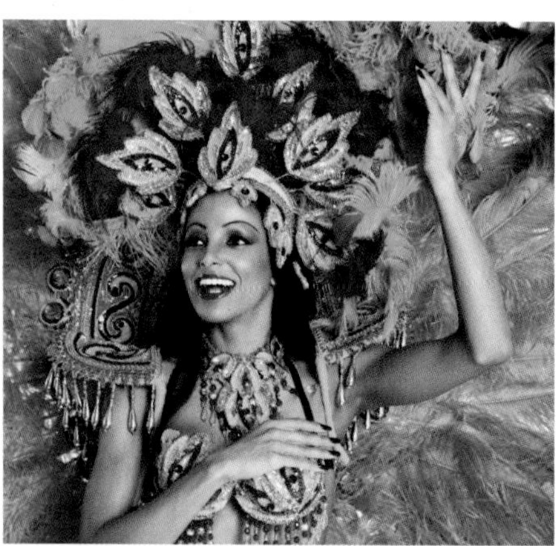

Carnival also involves contests where the dancing is judged.

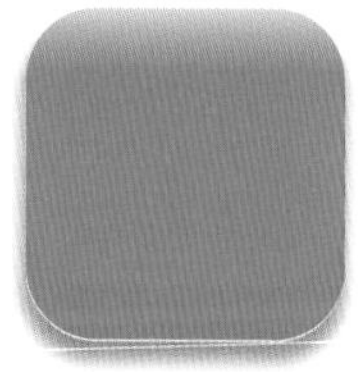

1 Rainforest
A green evoking Brazil's tropical rainforests.

2 Brazilian Yellow
A yellow evoking rich mineral resources.

3 Passion
A red suggesting dancers passionately engaged in the samba.

4 Rio Blue
The blue circle in the center of the national flag symbolizes the sky of Rio de Janeiro.

5 Soccer Field
In a rain forest or on an urban field, soccer matches pop up anywhere.

6 Coffee Plantation
One-third of the world's coffee is produced in Brazil.

7 Jacaranda
The tropical version of cherry blossoms, this is the color of jacaranda flowers.

8 Carnival Pink
The color of feather decorations swaying flamboyantly.

9 Samba Orange
An orange that calls to mind the bright rhythms of the samba.

1	C100 M0 Y75 K5 R0 G151 B104 #009768
2	C3 M0 Y100 K37 R185 G175 B0 #B9AE00
3	C8 M95 Y90 K15 R198 G33 B31 #C6211E
4	C95 M90 Y0 K6 R34 G46 B139 #222E8A
5	C60 M0 Y90 K6 R106 G180 B65 #69B341
6	C0 M35 Y70 K73 R104 G73 B21 #684915
7	C40 M60 Y0 K2 R164 G115 B174 #A473AE
8	C0 M80 Y40 K2 R231 G83 B106 #E75269
9	C0 M57 Y90 K0 R241 G138 B30 #F0891D

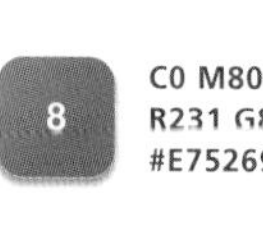
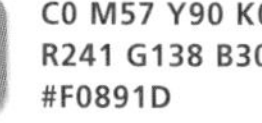

Two-color combinations

1 2

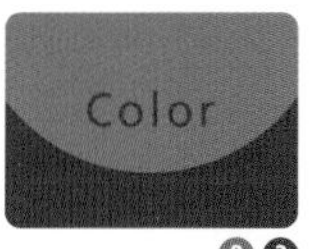

8 3

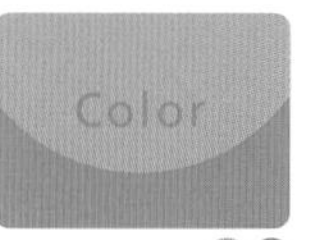

5 1

7 8

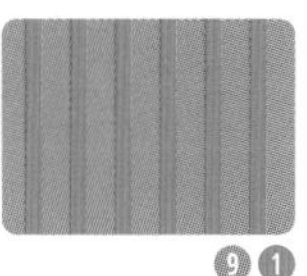
9 1

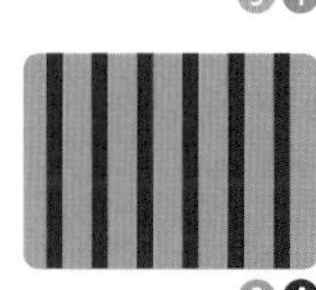
2 4

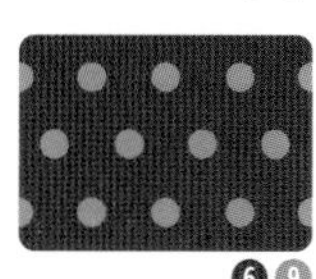
6 9

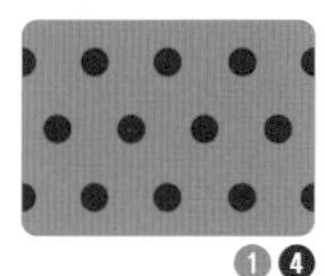
1 4

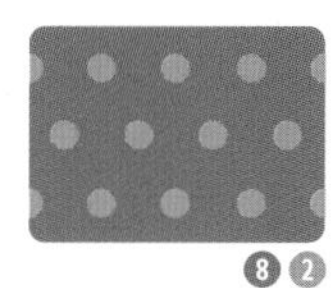
8 2

Three-color combinations

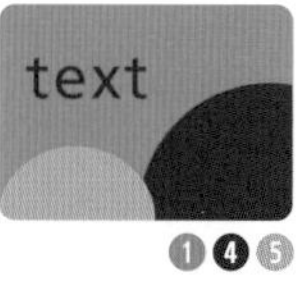

1 4 5

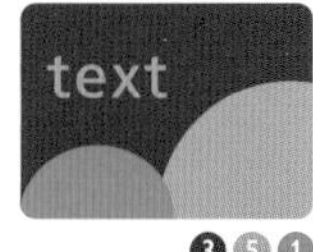

3 5 1

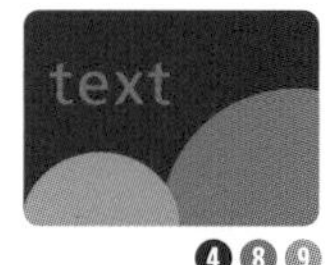

4 8 9

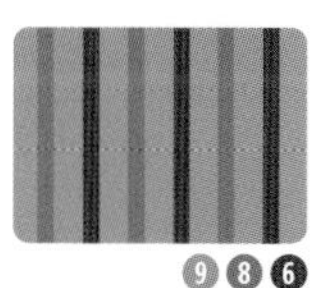
9 8 6

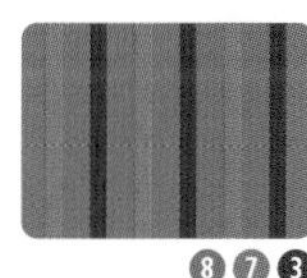
8 7 3

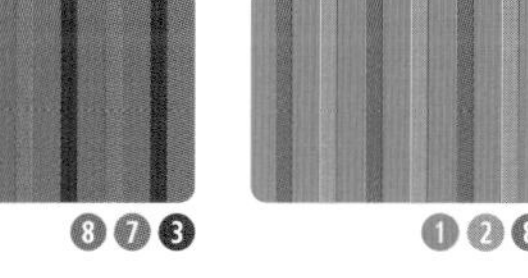
1 2 8

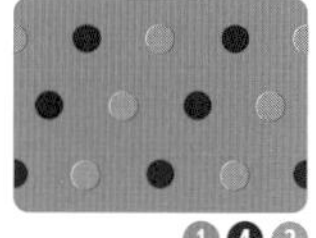
1 4 2

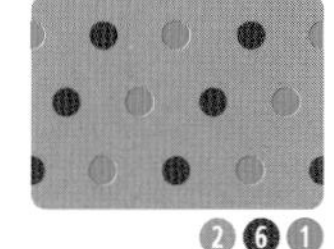
2 6 1

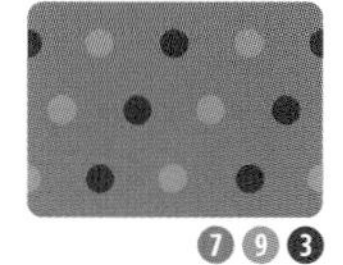
7 9 3

Designs

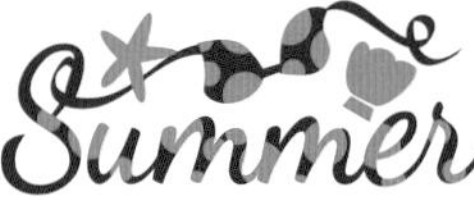

1 4 color 2

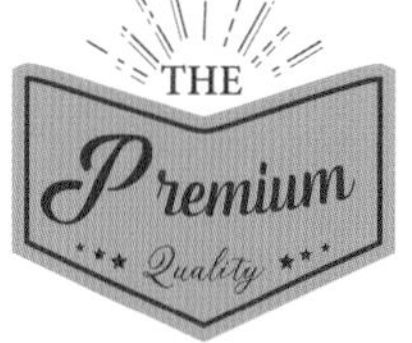
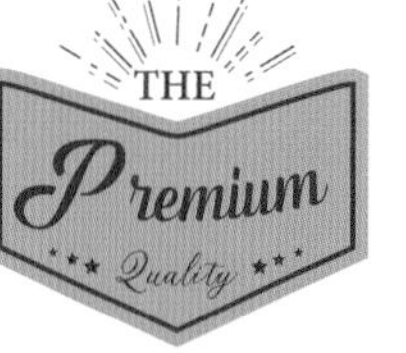

3 5 6 color 3

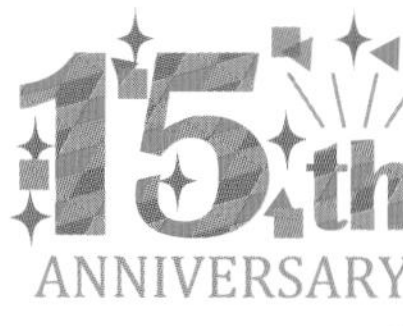

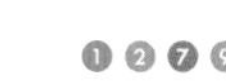
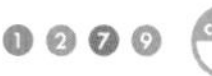
1 2 7 9 color 4

Patterns

1 2 color 2

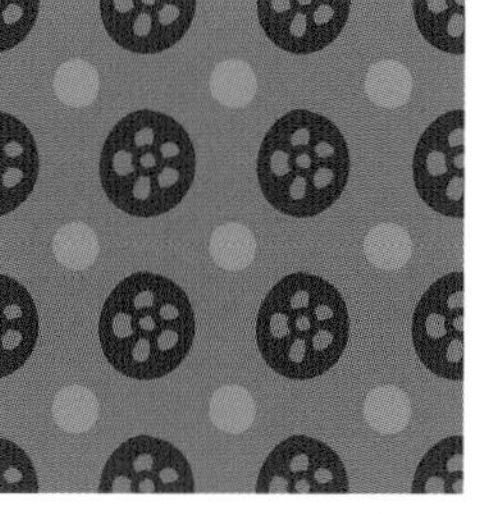
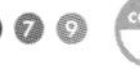
3 7 9 color 3

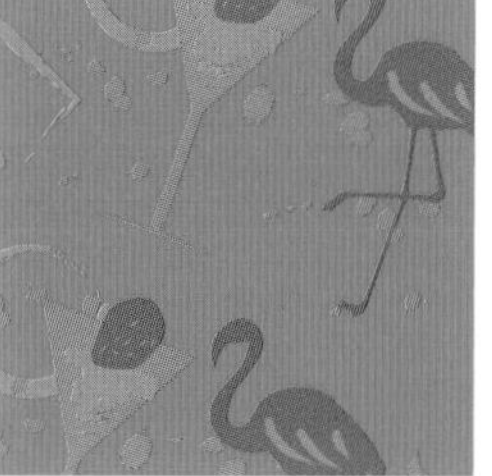

1 2 8 9 color 4

Illustration

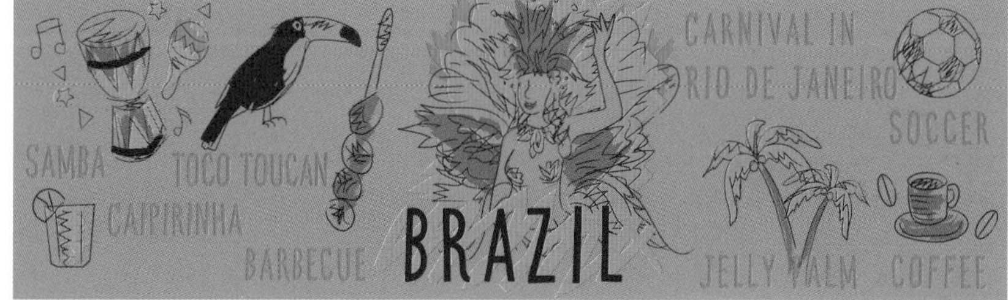

1 2 4 8 9 color 5

Recipe
096

Machu Picchu

The ruins of an Incan outpost, Machu Picchu is located high in the Andes. Irrigation brought the terraced fields of corn and potatoes to life, and there was a shrine to the sun where the winter and summer solstices could be observed. As there was no written language associated with this highly developed civilization, many mysteries remain to this day.

- **FEELING** Ancient, unembellished, alpine.
- **COMBINATIONS** Create an unadorned air using deep colors with warmth.
- **TIPS** Use similar tones, adding variation through different hues.

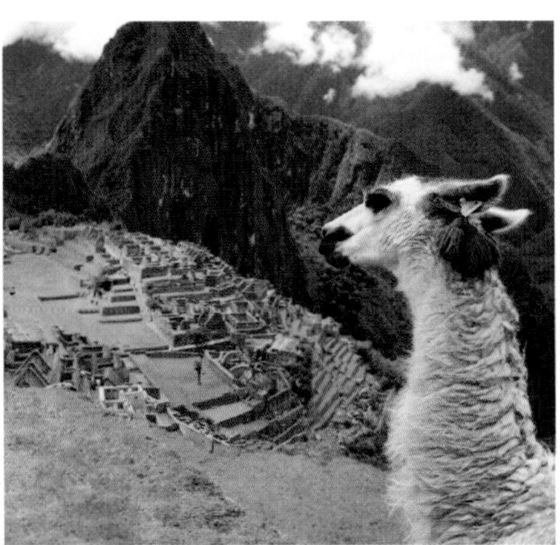

The stone ruins are surrounded by the deep greens and browns of the mountains.

1 Machu Picchu Gold
The emperor was thought to be the descendant of the sun god, Inti.

2 Nazca Brown
A brown like that of the soil at Nazca, famous for its geoglyphs.

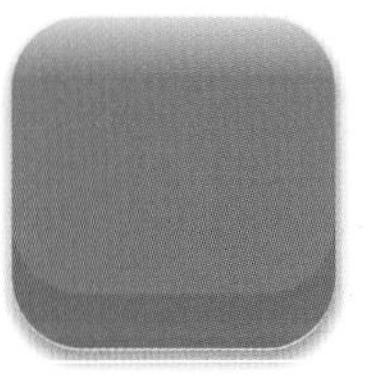

3 Highland Green
The slightly faded green seen at high-altitude locations.

4 Treasure
A gold evoking the treasure of the Incan Empire.

5 Hummingbird
The wings of the hummingbird feature in the geoglyphs at Nazca also.

6 Spirit
A blue evoking the spirit that dwells in nature.

7 Alpaca
A domestic animal similar to a llama, they graze in the highlands of the Andes.

8 Cock-of-the-Rock
The color of the wings of the Andean cock-of-the-rock, the national bird of Peru.

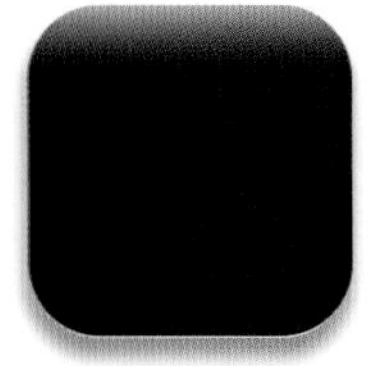

9 Chicha Morada
A national drink made from malted purple corn.

1
C53 M45 Y90 K0
R140 G133 B59
#8C853B

2
C0 M20 Y47 K40
R178 G152 B104
#B19767

3
C65 M30 Y95 K0
R105 G147 B58
#699239

4
C0 M15 Y80 K20
R219 G189 B54
#DBBD36

5
C70 M0 Y50 K30
R37 G145 B121
#249078

6
C70 M0 Y10 K45
R0 G126 B152
#007D98

7
C0 M10 Y30 K8
R241 G223 B181
#F1DEB5

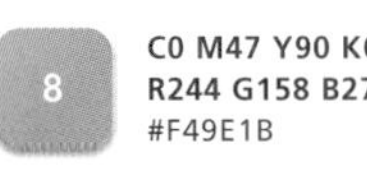

C0 M47 Y90 K0
R244 G158 B27
#F49E1B

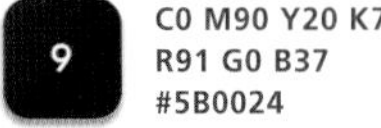

C0 M90 Y20 K77
R91 G0 B37
#5B0024

Two-color combinations

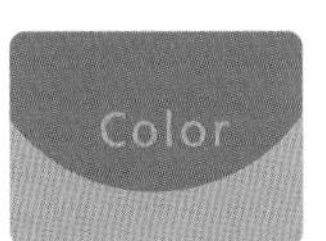

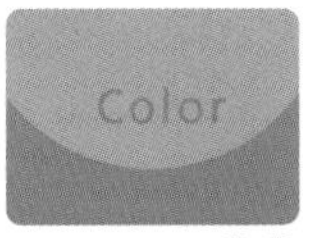

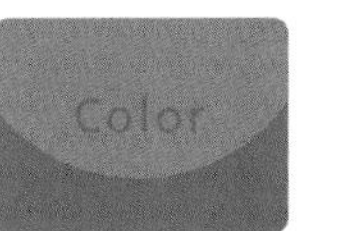

1 4　8 3　2 6

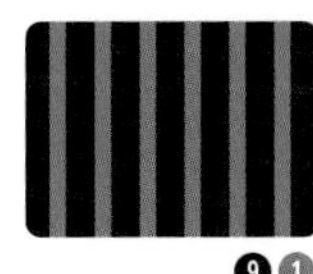

7 8　9 1　2 4

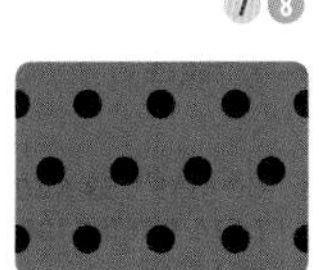
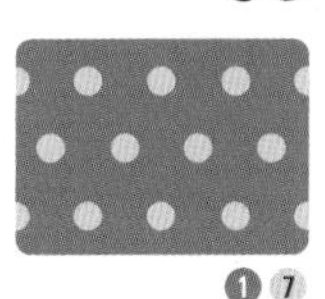
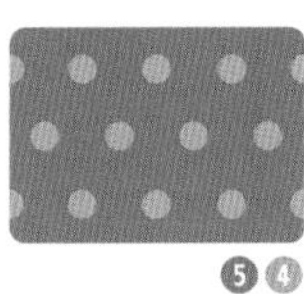

6 9　1 7　5 4

Three-color combinations

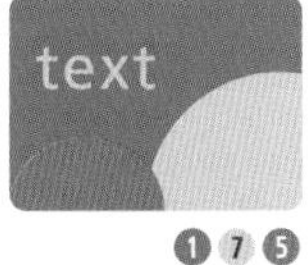

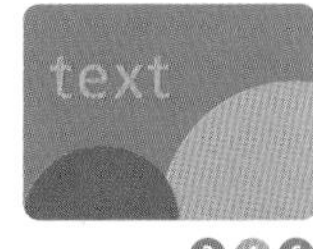

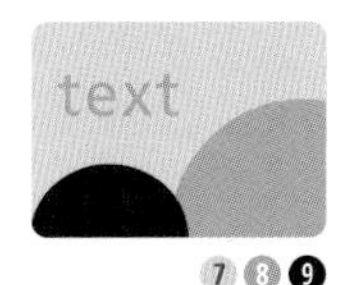

1 7 5　3 4 6　7 8 9

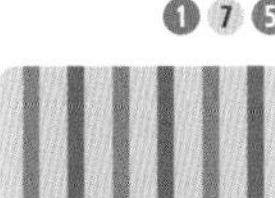
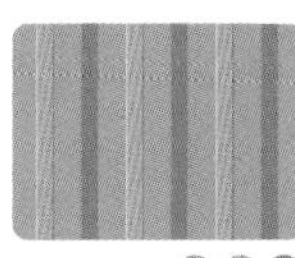
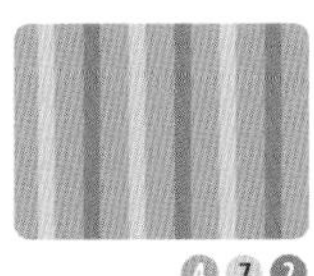

7 2 6　8 4 3　4 7 2

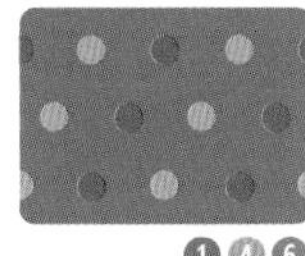
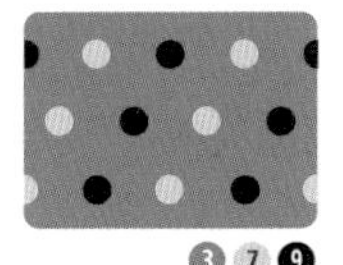
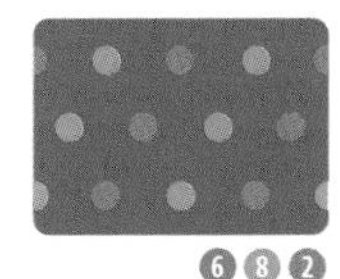

1 4 6　3 7 9　6 8 2

Designs

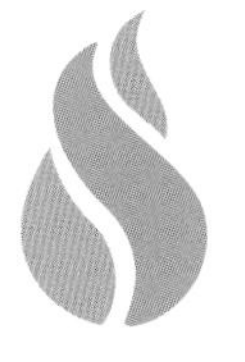

4 8 color 2

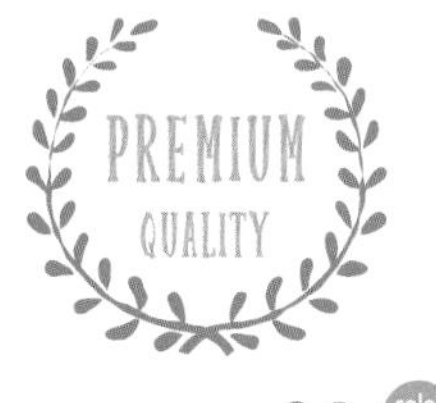

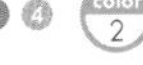

3 4 color 2

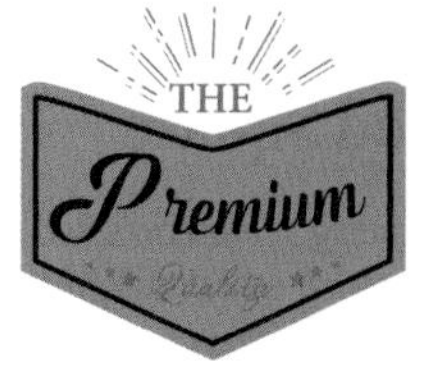

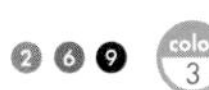

2 6 9 color 3

Patterns

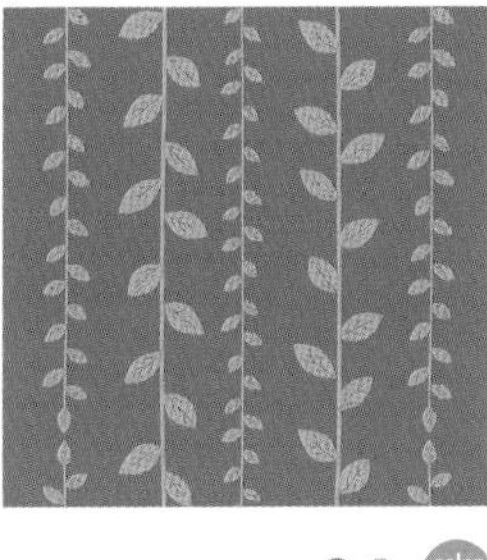
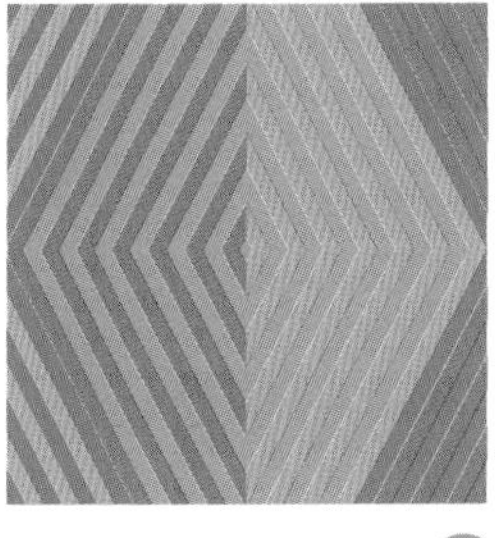
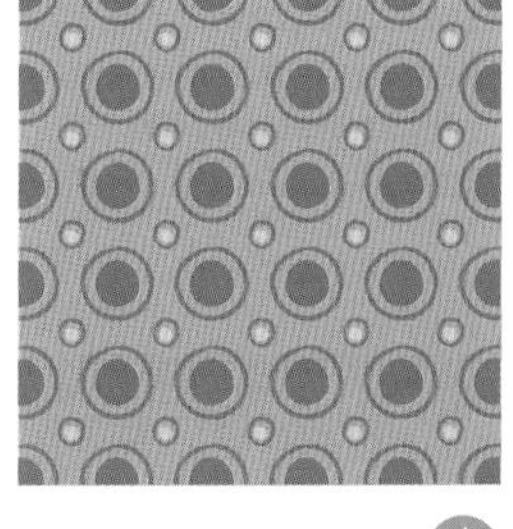
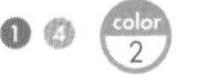

1 4 color 2

2 3 4 8 color 4

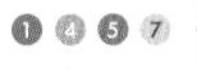

1 4 5 7 color 4

Illustration

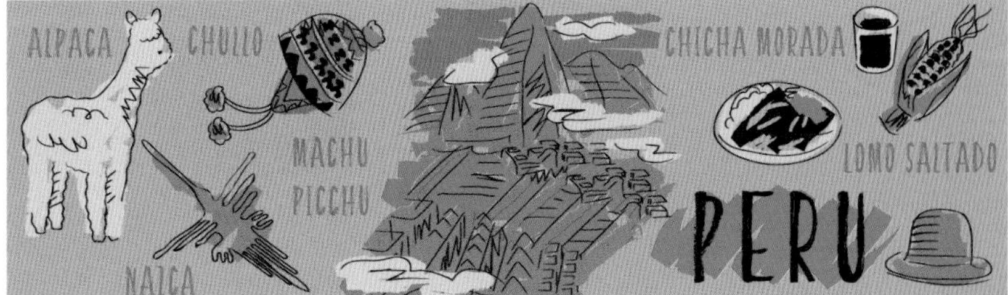

2 3 4 5 7 9 color 6

Recipe
097

Red Square

Standing in Moscow's Red Square, Saint Basil's Cathedral contains eight smaller churches arranged around a larger central one. All the churches differ in height and decoration to form an elaborate design. In Russian, "red" also means "beautiful," so Red Square originally meant "beautiful square." The brick-red color is set off by the blue of the sky.

- **FEELING** Colorful, fun, having an exotic atmosphere.
- **COMBINATIONS** Make the reddish brown of the bricks the base color.
- **TIPS** White makes an effective accent color.

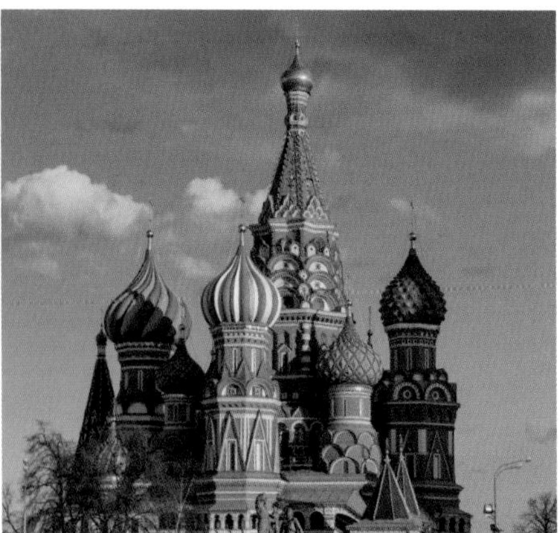

St. Basil's Cathedral not only typifies the Russian palette, it's a symbol of the nation's imperial past as well.

① Brick Red
The color of bricks. The church roofs are all made of brick.

② Onion
The silhouette of the tower resembles an onion.

③ Kremlin Green
The green of pointed roofs stand out among the red of the fortress.

④ White Goose
With its harsh winters, Siberia is famous for producing down.

⑤ Piroshki
The color of this daily dish of wheat dumplings with various fillings.

⑥ Borscht
A red soup and a Russian staple made from beets.

⑦ Light Blue
In Russian, there is a different word for blue depending on whether it is dark or light.

⑧ Caviar
The salted eggs of the sturgeon are a Russian delicacy.

⑨ Sacred Black
Russian icons of the Virgin Mary are dressed in black.

1	C0 M60 Y70 K13	R219 G121 B68	#DB7843
2	C0 M20 Y55 K6	R243 G205 B124	#F2CD7C
3	C63 M0 Y50 K15	R81 G170 B137	#50AA88
4	C0 M0 Y3 K8	R242 G242 B238	#F2F2EE
5	C0 M35 Y57 K20	R214 G160 B100	#D59F63
6	C2 M65 Y50 K30	R186 G94 B83	#B95D52
7	C65 M23 Y0 K0	R85 G161 B217	#54A1D9
8	C50 M40 Y55 K55	R82 G83 B67	#525242
9	C0 M7 Y0 K97	R41 G28 B27	#291B1B

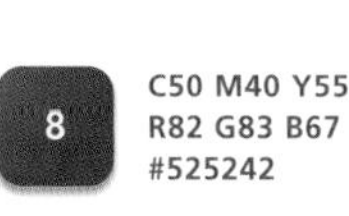

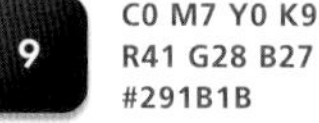

Two-color combinations

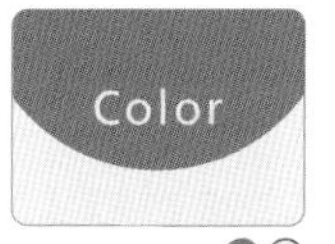

1 4

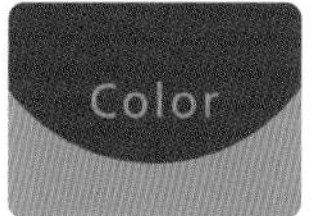

8 3

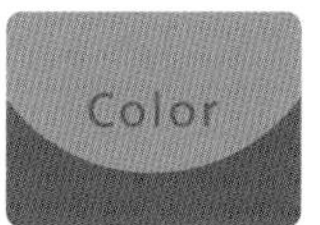

5 6

7 8

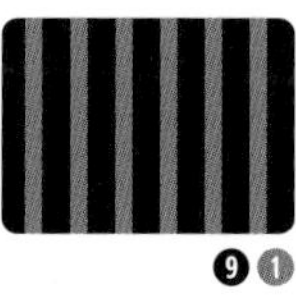
9 1

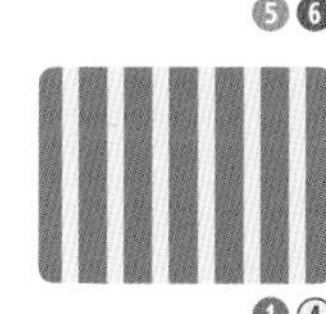
1 4

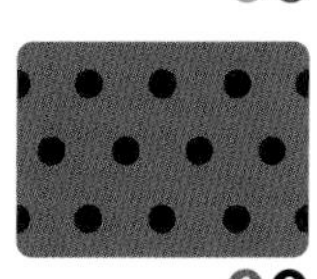
6 9

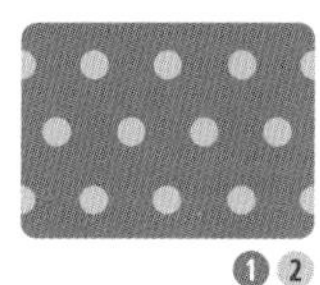
1 2

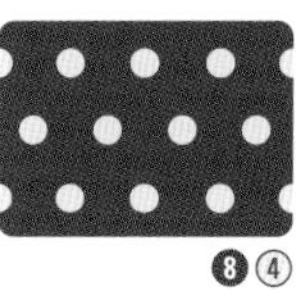
8 4

Three-color combinations

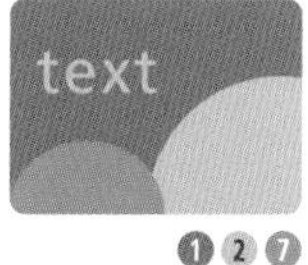

1 2 7

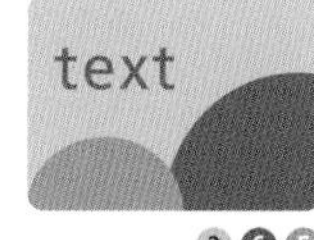

2 6 5

7 8 1

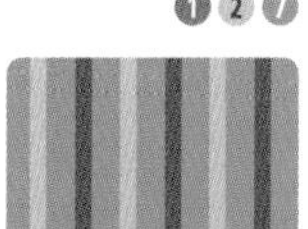
7 2 6

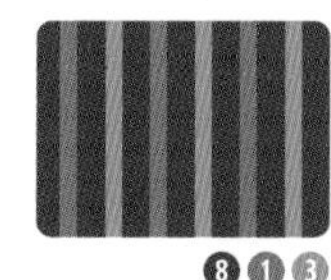
8 1 3

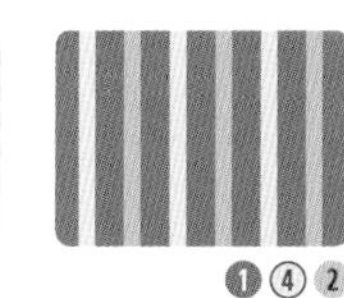
1 4 2

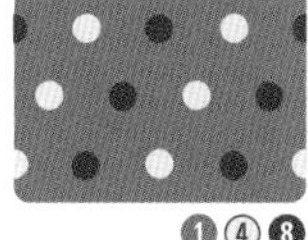
1 4 8

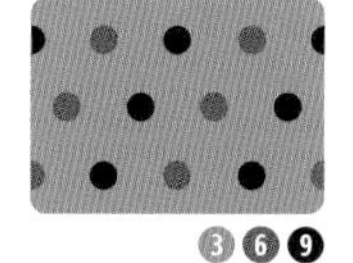
3 6 9

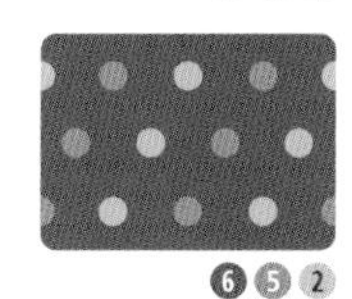
6 5 2

Designs

6 7 color 2

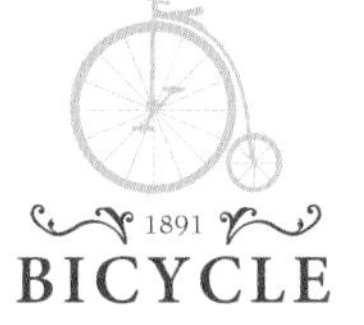

5 8 color 2

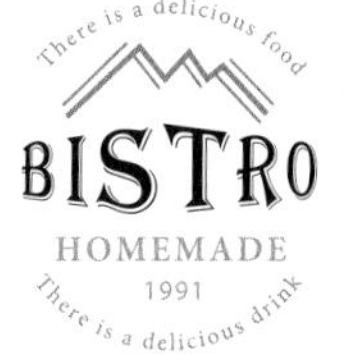

1 3 9 color 3

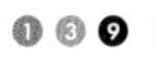
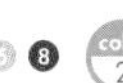

Patterns

1 2 3 color 3

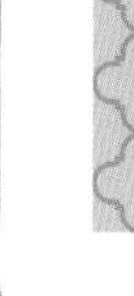
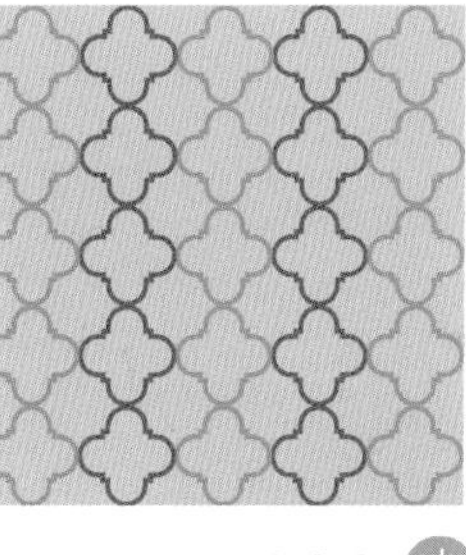
2 6 7 color 3

1 4 5 6 color 4

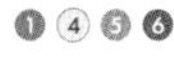

Illustration

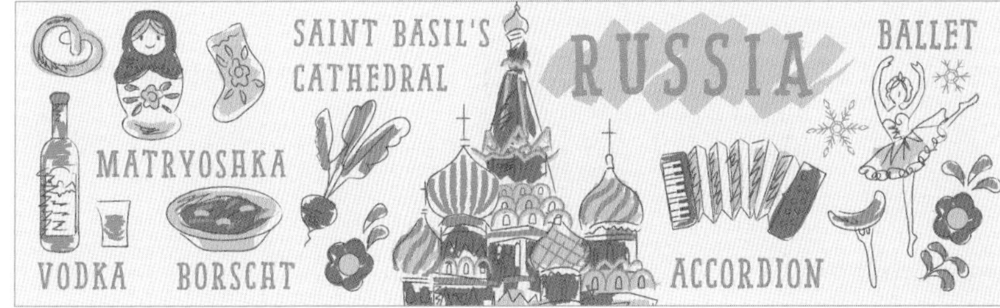

1 2 3 4 6 7 color 6

PART 11

THE WORLD AROUND US

Recipe
098

Little India, Singapore

In Singapore is an Indian quarter called Little India where the buildings are brilliantly colored and the temples overflowing with floral offerings. It's a place to experience the colors of India, with restaurants serving up southern Indian style lunches on huge banana leaves and shops selling knickknacks and traditional saris in vibrant hues.

- **FEELING** Invigorating, lively, energetic.
- **COMBINATIONS** Use mainly highly saturated colors with a touch of depth.
- **TIPS** Adding pastel shades tones things down.

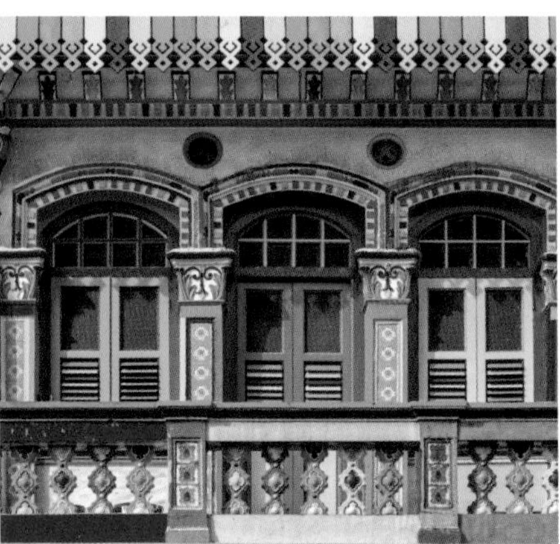

Singapore's charm lies in the mix of different cultures as reflected in the bursts of its color schemes.

❶ Singapore Red
Symbolizing equality and unity, the red of the national flag.

❷ Golden Lion
The name Singapore is derived from *singa*, which means "lion."

❸ Sentosa Beach
A large beach resort in Singapore.

❹ Zoo Forest
Singapore Zoo is famous for its lack of fences and cages.

❺ Laksa
A spicy noodle dish flavored with coconut milk.

❻ Raffles Hotel
The roof of the famous colonial-style Raffles Hotel.

⑦ Plumeria
A typically tropical white flower with five petals. It has a pleasant fragrance.

❽ Ganesha Pink
Ganesha is a god with the head of an elephant. Pink governs wealth, prosperity and wisdom.

❾ Peranakan Green
Delicately patterned porcelain draws on the traditions of the Peranakan culture.

No.	CMYK	RGB	Hex
1	C0 M100 Y70 K4	R224 G0 B55	#E00037
2	C0 M15 Y90 K23	R214 G184 B4	#D5B703
3	C83 M20 Y0 K20	R0 G131 B189	#0083BC
4	C65 M0 Y60 K25	R68 G154 B109	#439A6D
5	C0 M55 Y70 K10	R226 G134 B72	#E18547
6	C0 M57 Y65 K35	R180 G103 B62	#B4663E
7	C0 M0 Y17 K2	R254 G250 B223	#FDFADE
8	C3 M30 Y15 K10	R227 G185 B186	#E3B9B9
9	C55 M0 Y53 K0	R121 G195 B145	#78C391

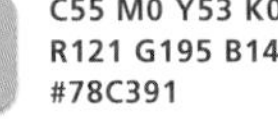

Two-color combinations

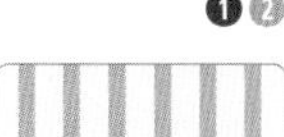
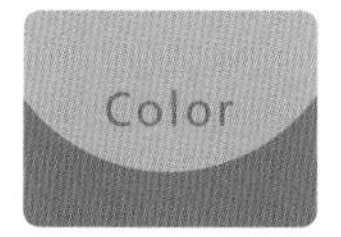

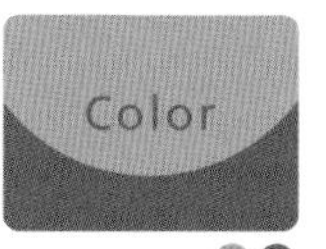

1 2 · 8 3 · 2 6

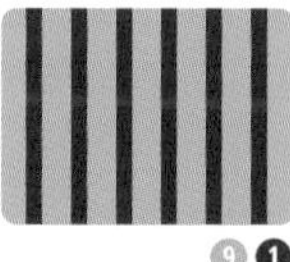

7 8 · 9 1 · 2 4

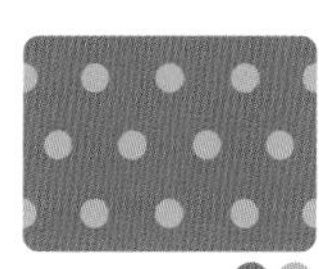
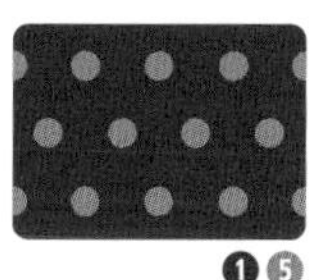
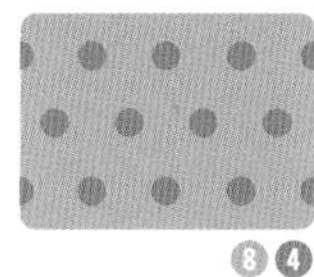

3 9 · 1 5 · 8 4

Three-color combinations

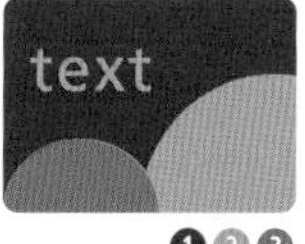

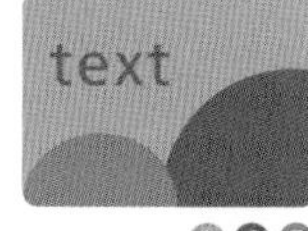

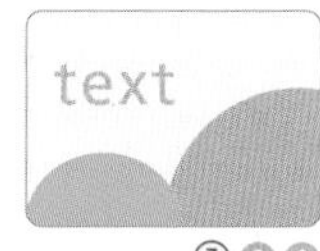

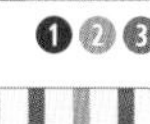

1 2 3 · 2 6 5 · 7 8 9

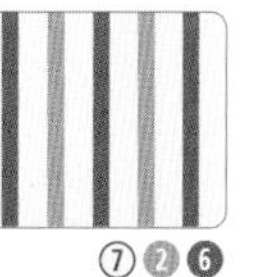
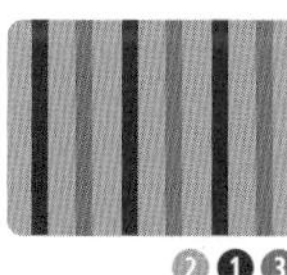
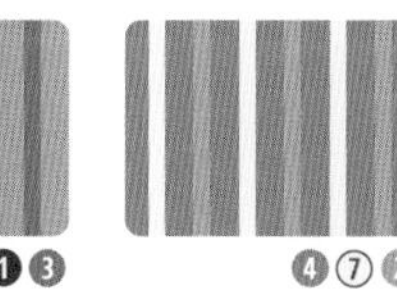

7 2 6 · 2 1 3 · 4 7 2

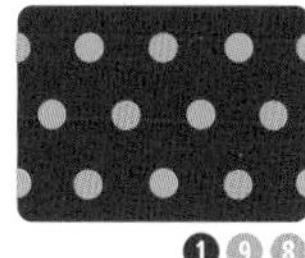
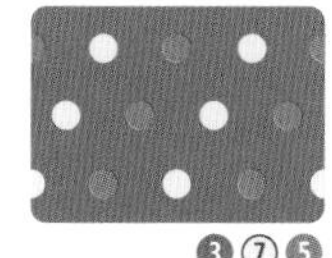
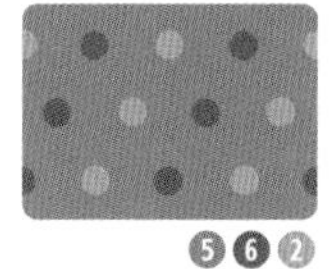

1 9 8 · 3 7 5 · 5 6 2

Designs

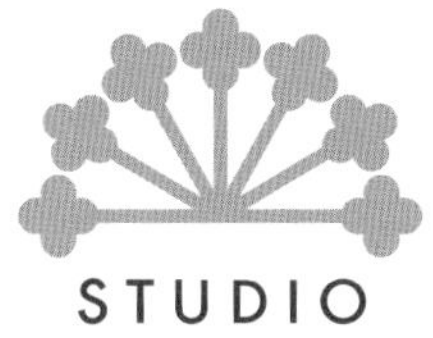
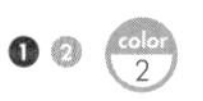

1 2 color 2

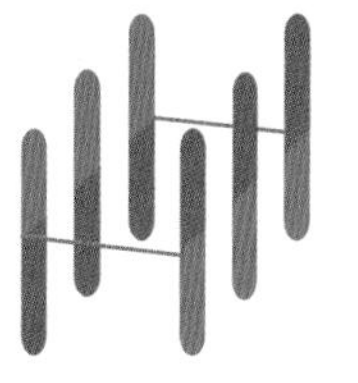
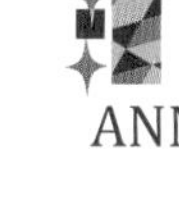

3 6 color 2

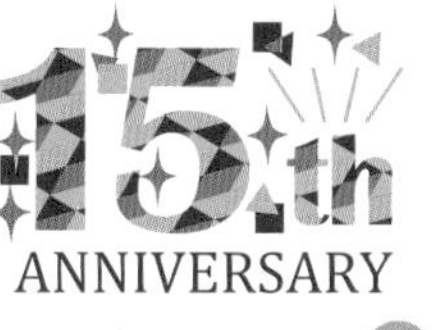

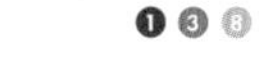

1 3 8 9 color 4

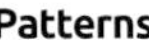

Patterns

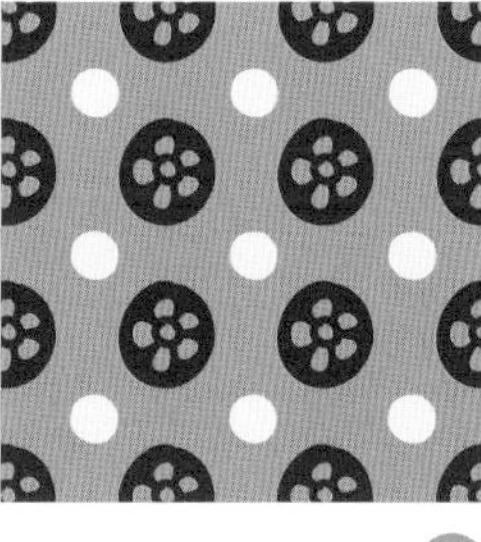

1 2 7 color 3

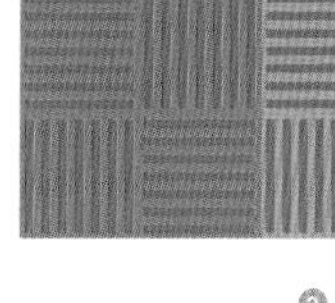

2 3 5 color 3

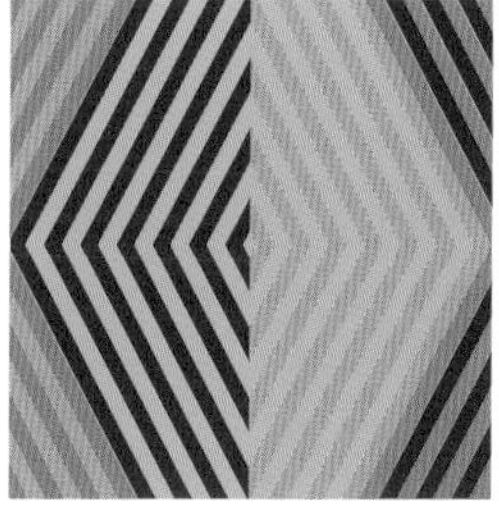
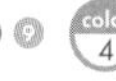

1 2 4 9 color 4

Illustration

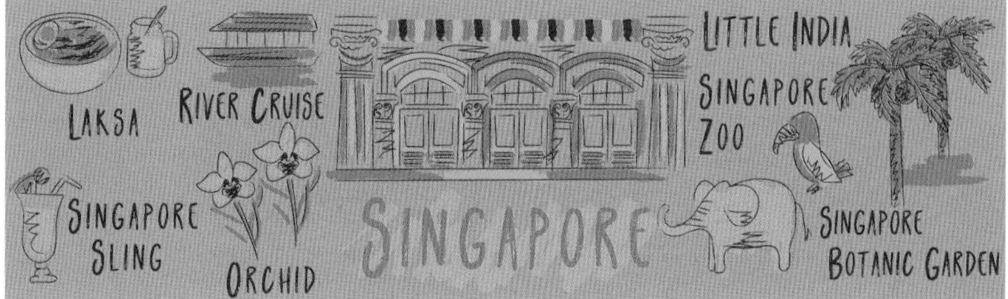

1 2 4 5 8 9 color 6

PART 11 THE WORLD AROUND US

A Closer Look at Japanese Sensibility and Color

A Love of the Seasons and a Place to Enjoy the Changing Scenery

In Japanese, *kacho fugetsu* is a term that refers to the beauty of scenery. It can be loosely translated as: "Experience the beauties of nature and in doing so, discover yourself."

The winter moon, the autumn landscape, spring buds, cherry blossoms, these reflect the aesthetic sensibilities of the Japanese people.

The Takarazuka Revue was established in 1914. The group made the performance into a two-part system in 1921. The first part was named Flower Troupe and the second part was referred to as Moon Troupe. The names of many colors can be traced back to the Heian period, most derived from flowers and plants.

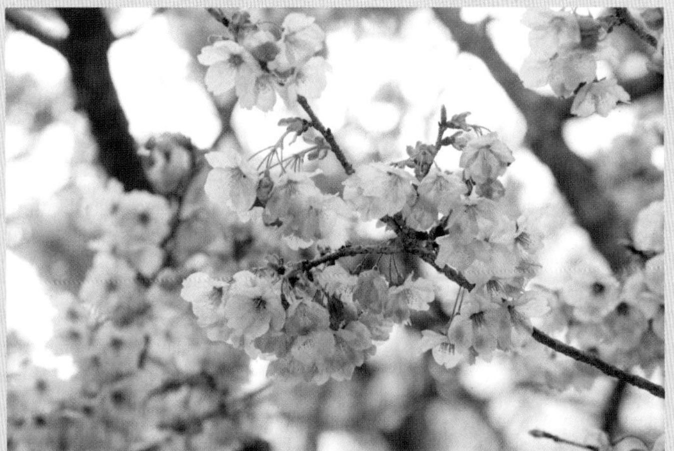

Since the Heian period, the word "flower" has come to mean and be synonymous with the symbolic cherry blossom.

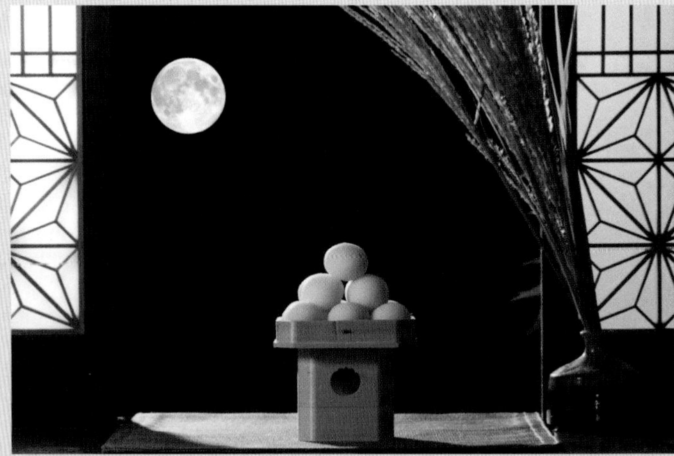

Since fall in the lunar calendar occurs from June to September, the mid-autumn moon shows itself around August 15.

Red Fuji

Mt. Fuji, long a symbol of Japan, is also referred to by an ancient name. From late summer to early autumn, the mountain's entire surface is illuminated by the morning sun, casting off a ruddy glow known as Red Fuji. The version depicted in "Make this: "South Wind, Clear Sky" (see page 260) is deservedly famous. In winter the effect changes. When covered in snow, the mountain takes on a pinkish hue during sunrise and sunset.

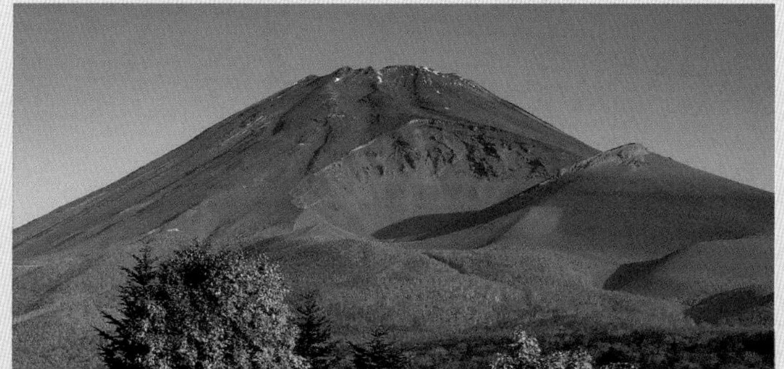

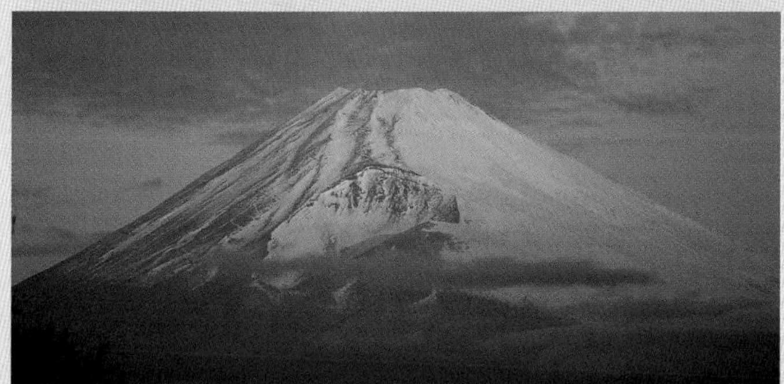

Two opposite-season visions of "Red Fuji."
Photo courtesy of Susono City Tourism Association.

Japanese Bento is Now World Bento

Bento has been embraced by people around the world. Anime helped to spread the craze. Fans saw favorite characters eating lunch that way and wanted to follow suit.

I'm thrilled that Japanese food culture is being so enthusiastically adopted and introduced to new places.

In terms of the color scheme, there's a trick to making your bento lunch look delicious. The basic palette of a bento box is 1) the white rice and 2) the various sides, which are often of an less-than-appealing shade of brown. Lean liberally on the "three primary colors of food"—red, yellow and green—and arrange to create a well-balanced meal, visually!

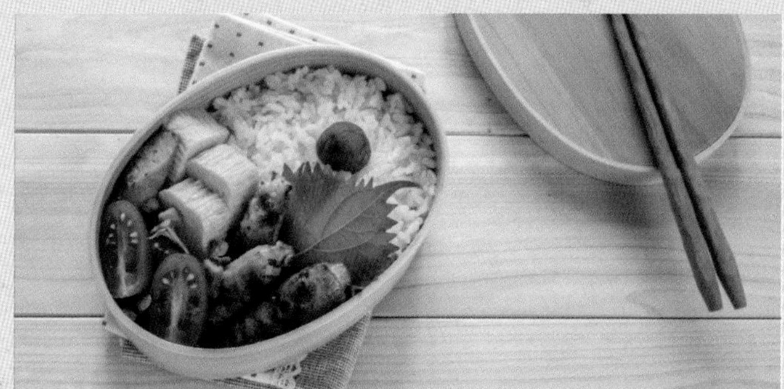

Red, yellow and green morsels pop out of a bland white-rice background.

Part
12

Colors from History

These color schemes have been created from art and design movements that were popular at a certain period in time, such as Art Nouveau and Midcentury Modern. Let's see what we can learn from the colors of art history.

Colors Associated with Movements and Artwork

1995 2000 2005 2010 2015 2020 2025 2030

Recipe
099

Art Nouveau

Meaning "new art," Art Nouveau was a decorative movement at the end of the 19th century characterized by designs with organic curves and floral and botanical motifs along with elaborate decoration. Standout colors included dull yellows, beiges and purples. The posters of Alphonse Mucha and the glassware of Emile Galle are some of the items that typify the period.

- **FEELING** Graceful, noble, nostalgic.
- **COMBINATIONS** Use dull yellows and beiges as base colors.
- **TIPS** Add accents of purple, black and shades of blue.

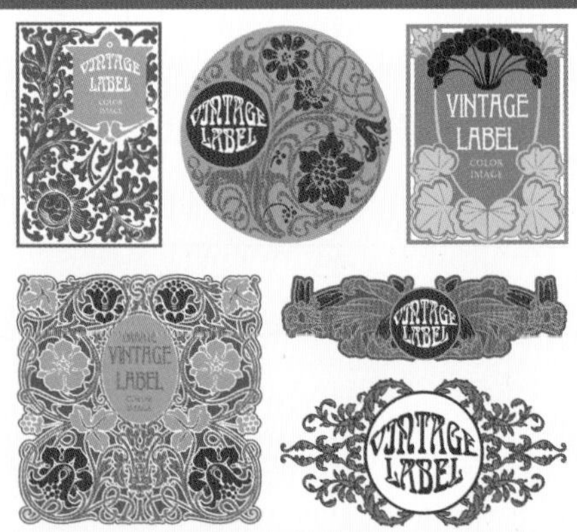

The high level of decoration was a reaction to the mass production sparked by the Industrial Revolution.

❶ French Marigold
A deep yellow like that of a marigold flower.

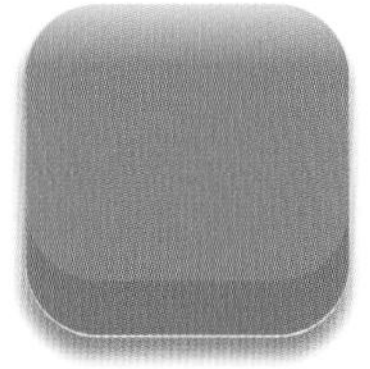

❷ Stem Green
A dull yellow green like that of plant stems.

❸ Berry Syrup
A color conjuring the tart taste of raspberries.

❹ Foggy Moon
The soft off-white of a moon veiled in fog.

❺ Spring Dust
A color expressing the dusty feel of the air in early spring.

❻ Black Olive
A black tinged with green like that of a black olive.

❼ Blue Angel
A pale blue calling to mind the wings of an angel.

❽ Mocha
A port city in Yemen where coffee was packed and exported.

❾ Hot Wine
A deep red like that of hot spiced or mulled wine.

1 C0 M35 Y70 K5
R240 G178 B84
#F0B253

2 C50 M25 Y70 K3
R142 G163 B98
#8EA362

3 C2 M75 Y30 K35
R175 G70 B94
#AE465D

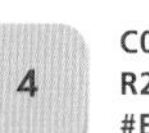

4 C0 M7 Y30 K10
R239 G225 B181
#EEE0B5

5 C0 M27 Y75 K33
R191 G151 B57
#BE9738

6 C25 M0 Y45 K75
R79 G89 B61
#4E593C

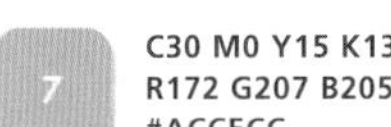

7 C30 M0 Y15 K13
R172 G207 B205
#ACCECC

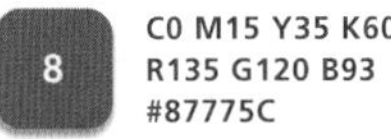

8 C0 M15 Y35 K60
R135 G120 B93
#87775C

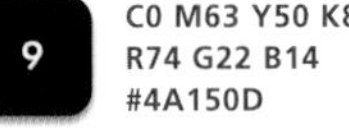

9 C0 M63 Y50 K85
R74 G22 B14
#4A150D

Two-color combinations

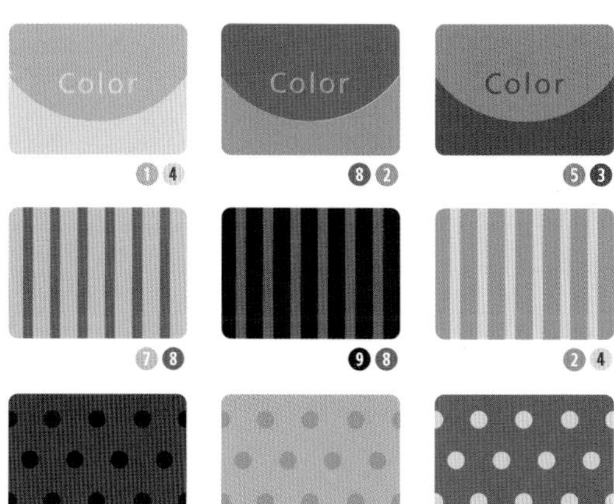

Three-color combinations

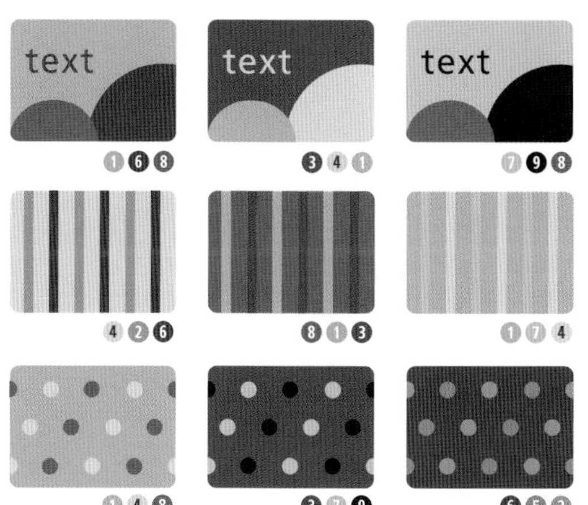

Designs

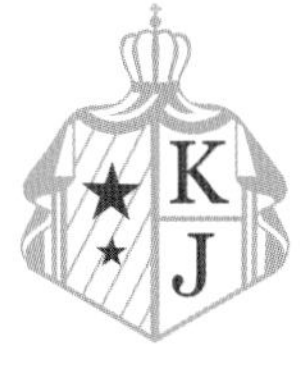

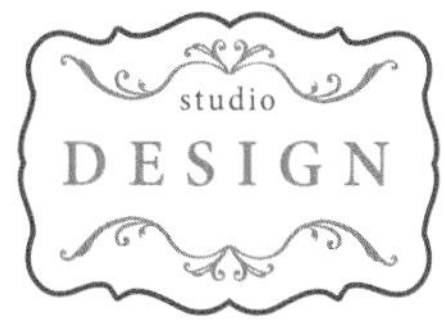

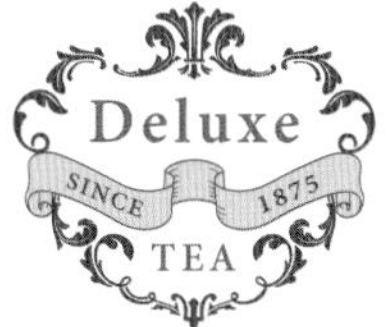

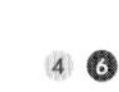

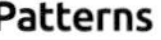

Patterns

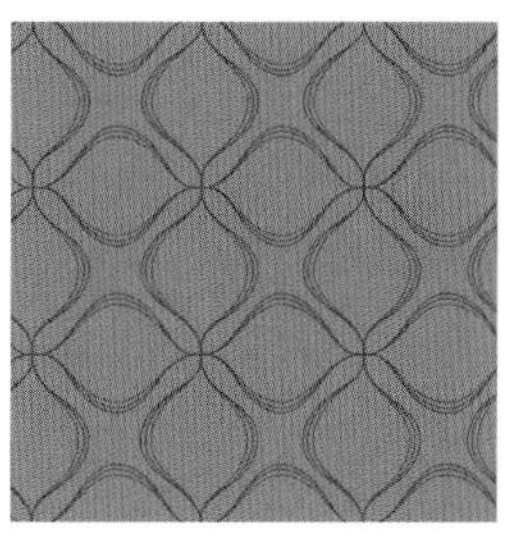
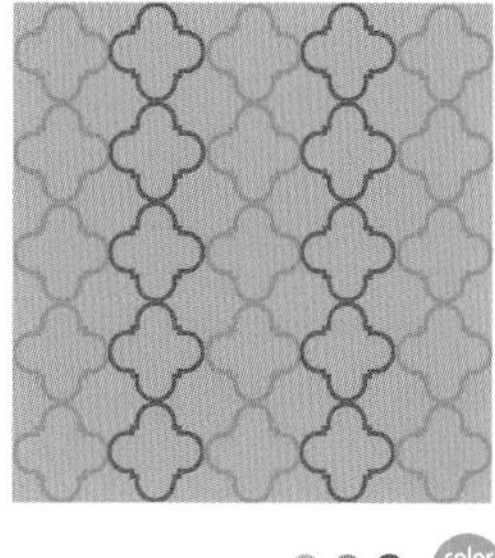

Illustration

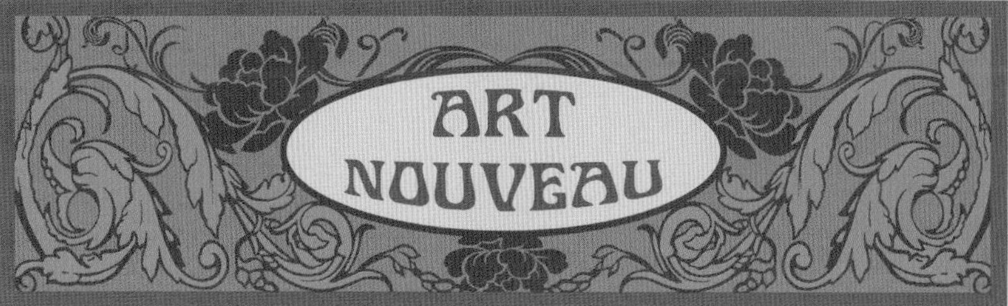

Recipe
100

Art Deco

Unsuited to mass production due to its high level of decoration, Art Nouveau declined with the outbreak of World War I and gave rise to Art Deco. This movement was characterized by linear, rational designs, geometric patterns, monotones, metallic shades and contrasting colors. As it gained popularity at the World's Fair in Paris in 1925, it is also called 1925 Style.

- **FEELING** Sophisticated, stylish, modern.
- **COMBINATIONS** Make conscious use of monotones and metallic shades.
- **TIPS** Use near-futuristic blue as an accent color.

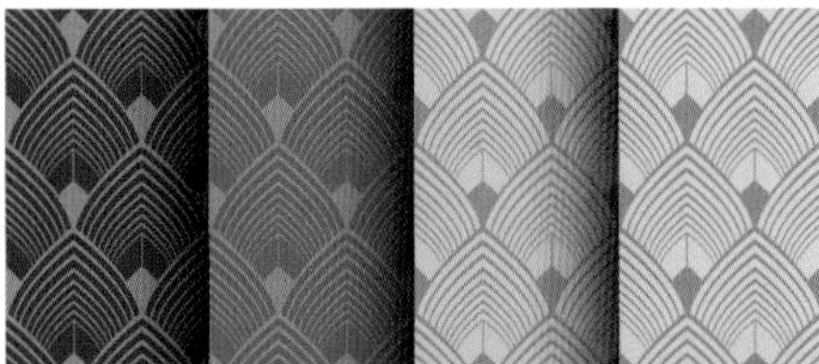

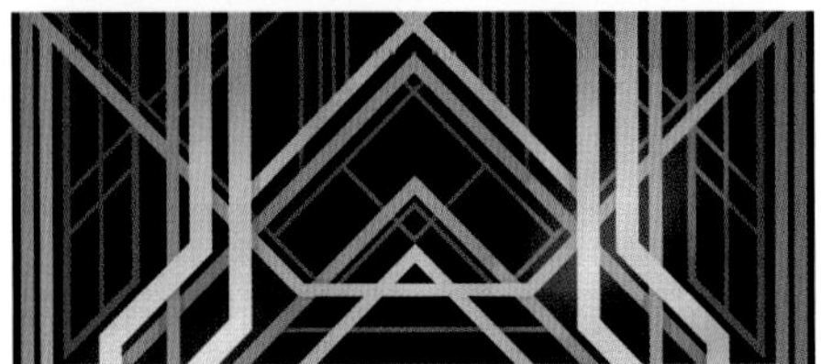

The geometric shapes meant designs could retain a sophisticated feel while allowing for mass production.

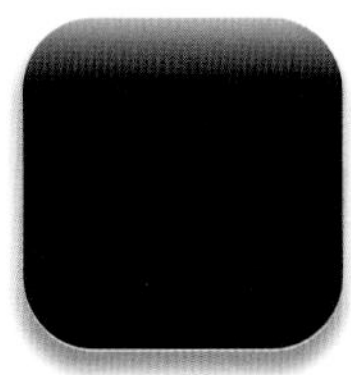

❶ Black Panther
A color like that of a sleek, nimble black panther.

❷ Calm
A color suggesting a gentle, quiet, restful state.

❸ Apple Crisp
A dessert made in American households typically in fall.

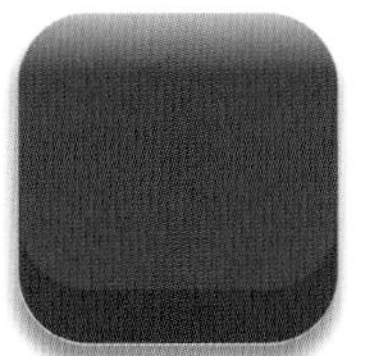

❹ Royal Blue
Traditionally used by the British royal family, this is a deep blue.

❺ Yosemite Blue
A U.S. national park that is a standout location for rock climbing.

❻ Innocence
A blue suggesting an unembellished, plain state.

❼ Shell Pink
The faint pink like that seen inside a shell.

❽ Manhattan Gray
A gray evoking New York's skyscrapers.

❾ Ebony
A hardwood that was used as timber but also as a material for making jewelry.

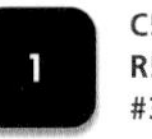

1 C5 M15 Y5 K93
R51 G38 B39
#332627

2 C0 M3 Y15 K10
R239 G233 B212
#EEE9D4

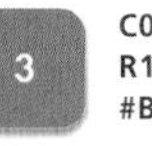

3 C0 M25 Y53 K35
R187 G153 B98
#BB9861

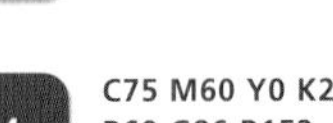

4 C75 M60 Y0 K20
R69 G86 B152
#445597

5 C70 M0 Y17 K35
R2 G140 B161
#028CA1

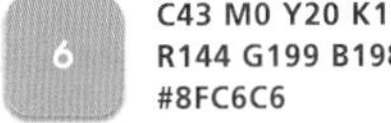

6 C43 M0 Y20 K10
R144 G199 B198
#8FC6C6

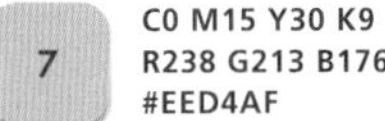

7 C0 M15 Y30 K9
R238 G213 B176
#EED4AF

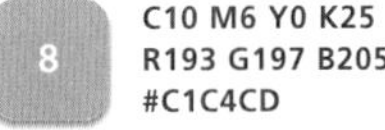

8 C10 M6 Y0 K25
R193 G197 B205
#C1C4CD

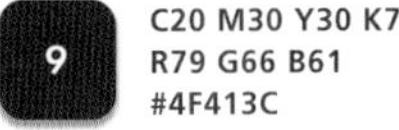

9 C20 M30 Y30 K77
R79 G66 B61
#4F413C

Two-color combinations

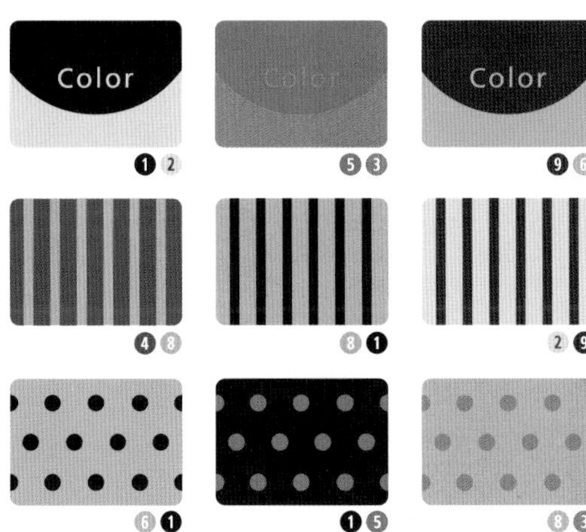

Three-color combinations

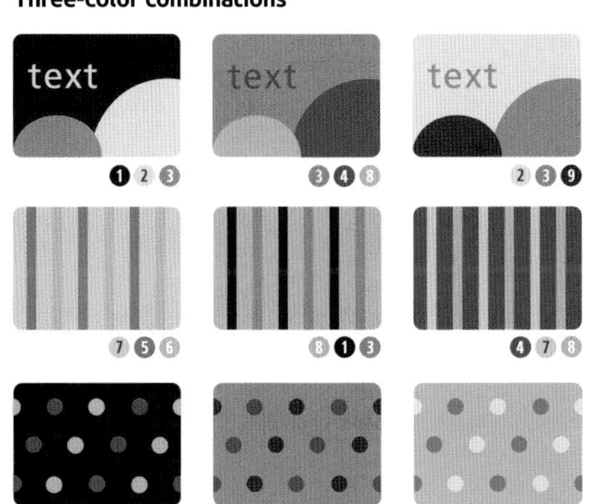

Designs

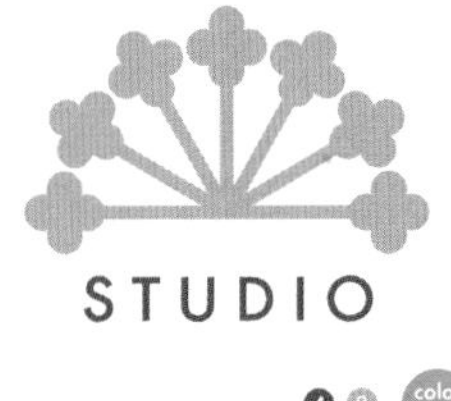

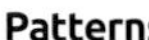

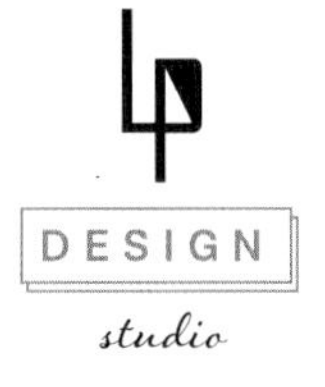

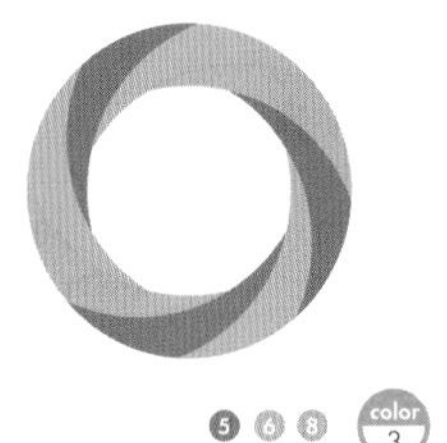

Patterns

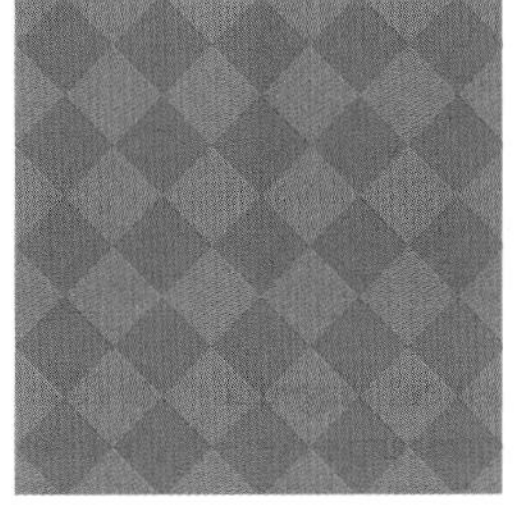

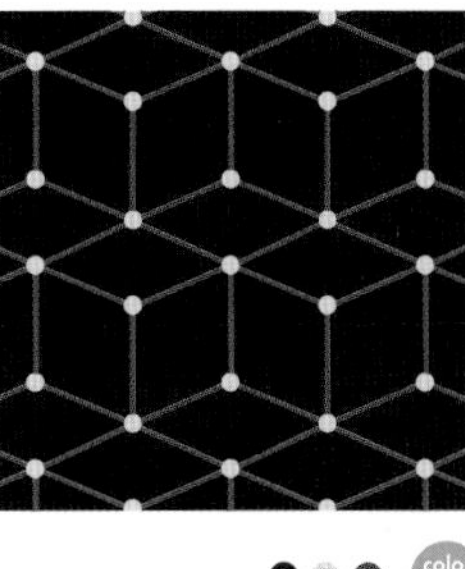

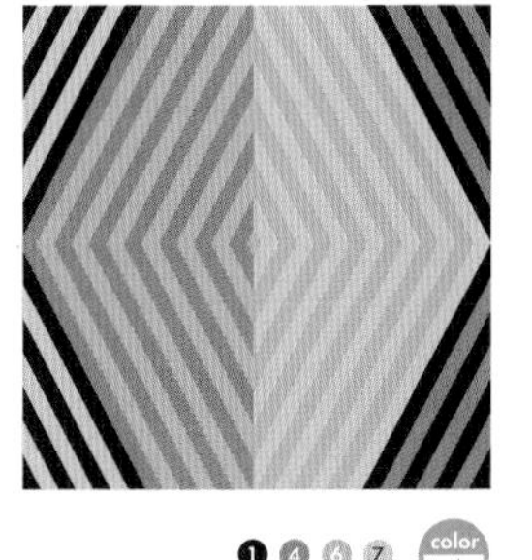

Illustration

Recipe
101

Pop Art

The Pop Art movement developed in the first half of the 1960s, centering on New York. It was characterized by the use of primary colors in a way that made them seem to pop. Andy Warhol produced work drawing on familiar, mass-produced and consumerist items such as Campbell's soup cans, while Roy Lichtenstein presented mass entertainment in comic-strip form.

- **FEELING** Pop, fun, energetic.
- **COMBINATIONS** Draw heavily on the three primary colors used in printing.
- **TIPS** Make use of achromatic colors—use black to pull things together and white to space things out.

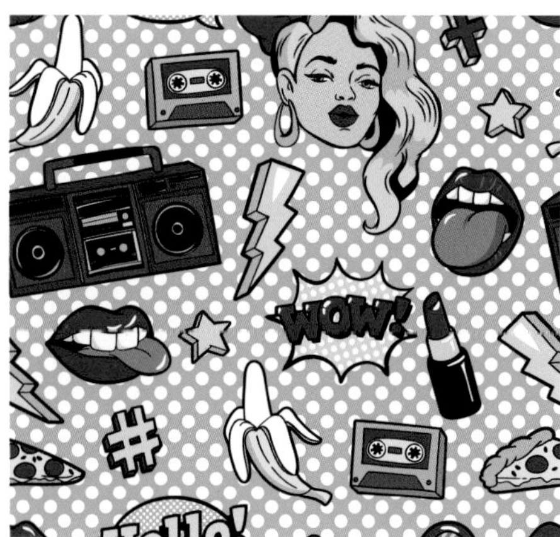

Pop Art is characterized by its use of primary colors and familiar motifs.

1 Pigment Yellow
A nearly blinding yellow like that of painter's pigment.

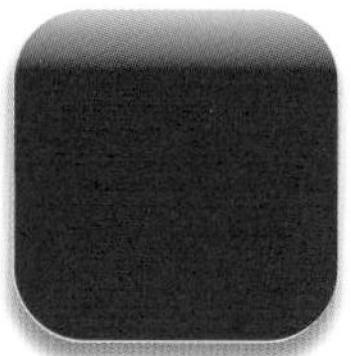

2 Lipstick Red
Bright red lipstick became popular at the same time as rock 'n' roll.

3 Pigment Cyan
A vivid greenish blue like that of cyan toner.

4 Pigment Magenta
A splendid purple like that of magenta toner.

5 Blue in the Blue
The bluest of blues, pure and deep.

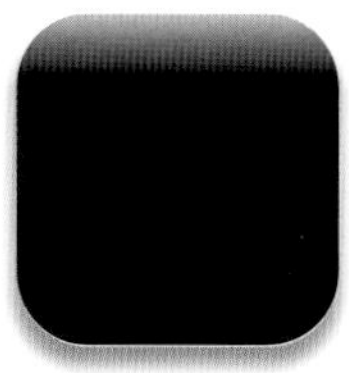

6 Black Ink
In printing ink, in addition to the three primary colors, black is vital.

7 Pure Purple
A fresh, bright purple.

8 Brilliant Orange
A vibrant reddish orange that seems to pop.

9 White Base
The white of paper or of a base.

No.	CMYK	RGB	Hex
1	C0 M0 Y97 K0	R255 G241 B0	#FFF000
2	C0 M100 Y83 K0	R230 G0 B41	#E50029
3	C97 M0 Y0 K0	R0 G162 B233	#00A2E9
4	C0 M97 Y0 K0	R229 G0 B130	#E40081
5	C100 M97 Y0 K0	R26 G37 B138	#192489
6	C0 M0 Y0 K97	R41 G31 B29	#281F1C
7	C63 M100 Y0 K0	R121 G18 B133	#791284
8	C0 M63 Y100 K0	R239 G124 B0	#EE7B00
9	C0 M0 Y2 K0	R255 G255 B252	#FFFEFC

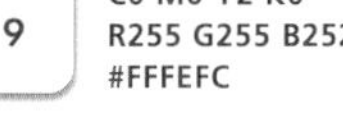

Two-color combinations

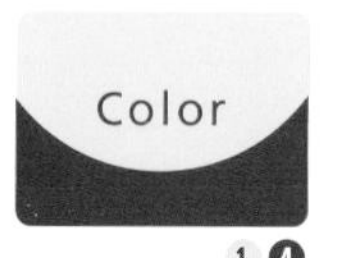

1 4

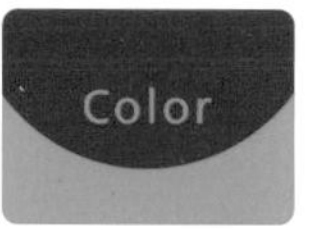

2 3

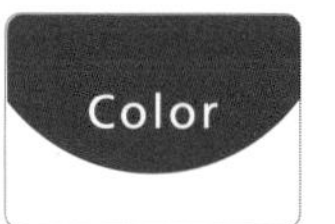
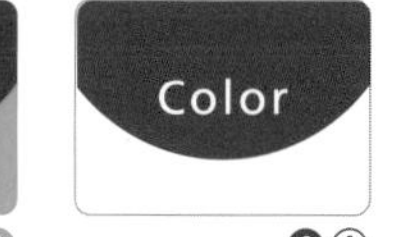

4 9

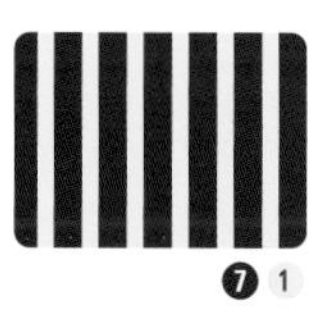
7 1

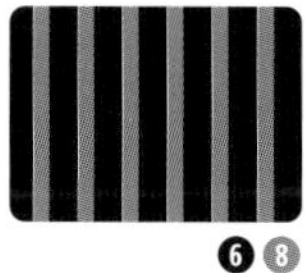
6 8

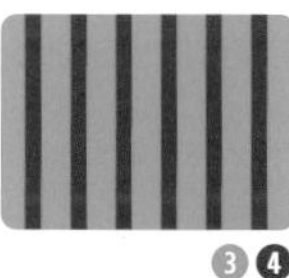
3 4

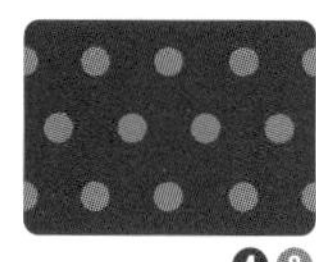
4 8

1 3

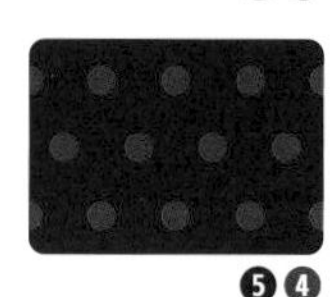
5 4

Three-color combinations

1 4 7

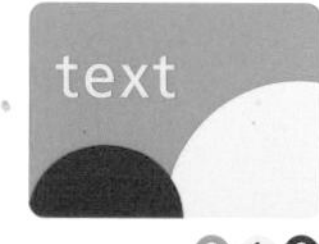

3 1 2

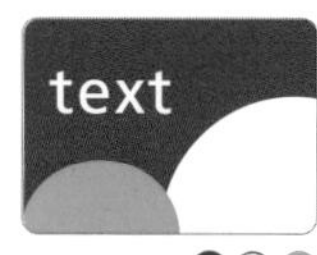

4 9 3

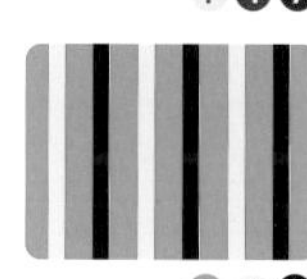
3 1 6

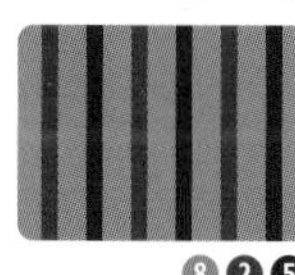
8 2 5

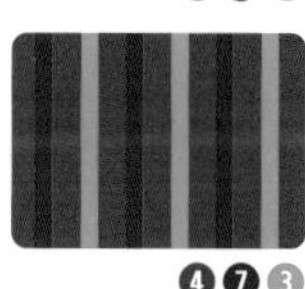
4 7 3

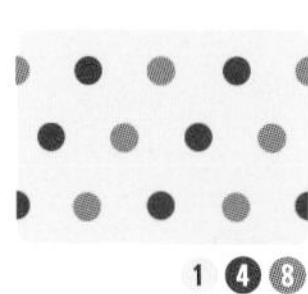
1 4 8

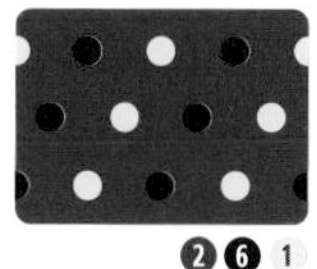
2 6 1

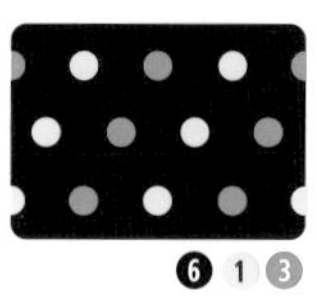
6 1 3

Designs

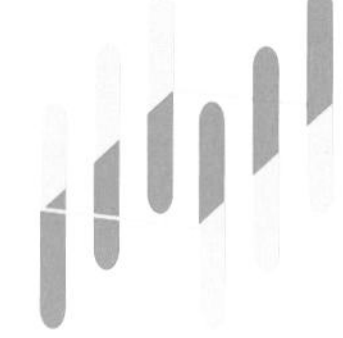
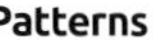
1 3
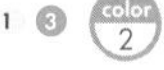

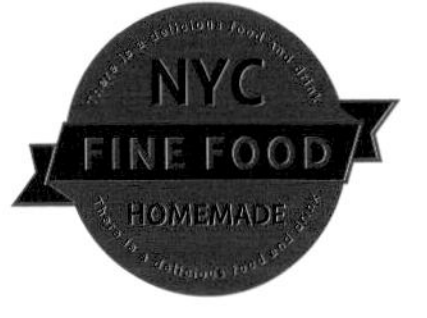

2 6
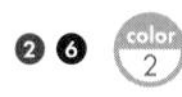

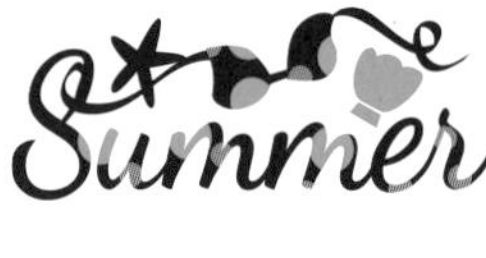

3 5 8
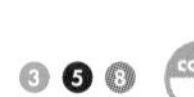

Patterns

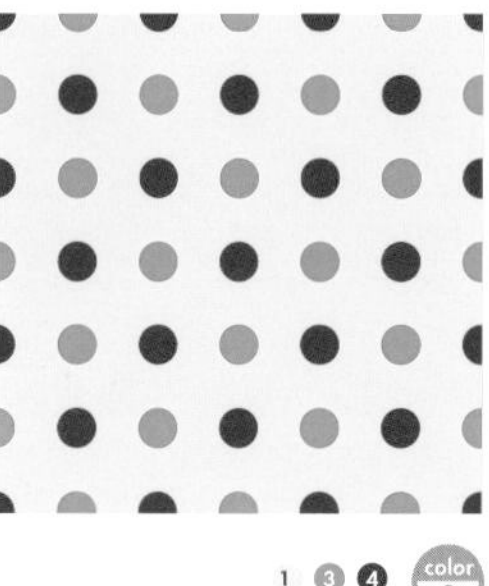
1 3 4 color 3

2 3 9 color 3

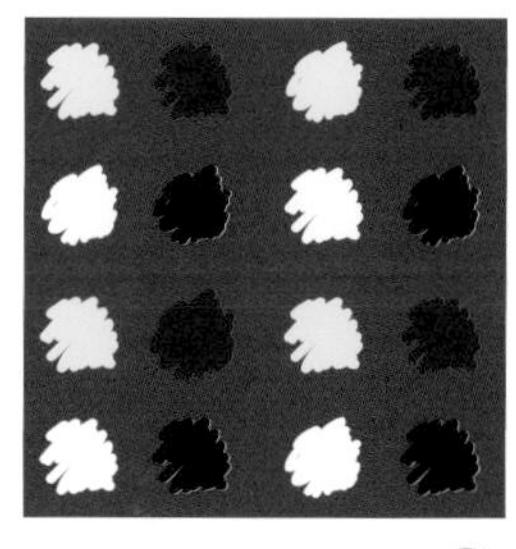
1 4 5 9 color 4

Illustration

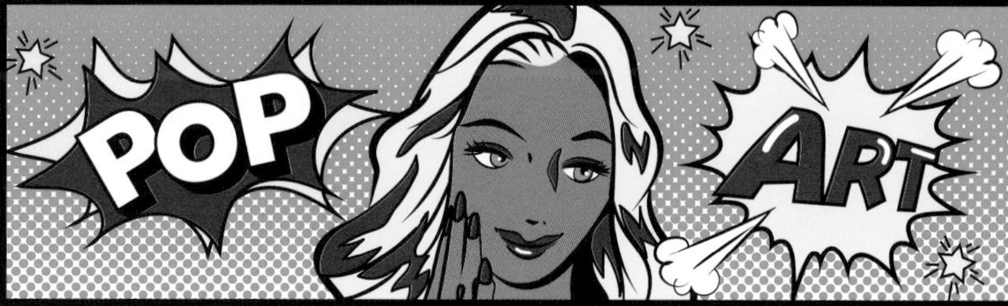

1 3 4 6 9 color 5

Recipe
102

Midcentury Modern

As its name suggests, this simple, functional style emerged in the middle of the century in 1950s America. The colorful furniture and other decorative items along with curved forms gained iconic status. Designers Charles and Ray Eames were well-known proponents of the style, but Scandinavian designers really made their mark during this period.

- **FEELING Retro, warm, nostalgic.**
- **COMBINATIONS Team natural colors like those of timber with strong, artificial shades.**
- **TIPS Use black if you want to create impact.**

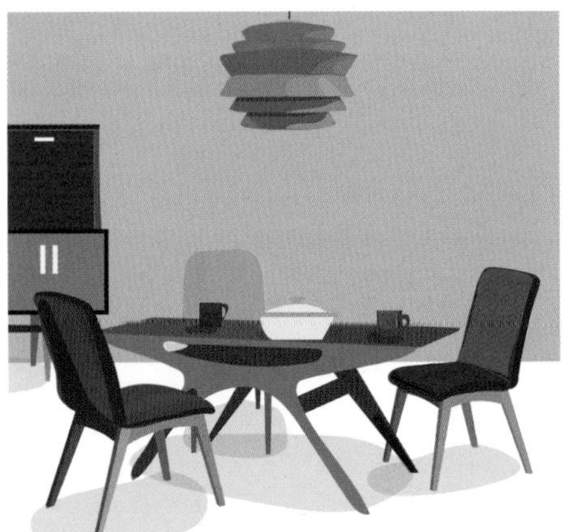

Midcentury furniture teams well with contemporary Scandinavian style.

1 Grape Green
A bright yellow green like that of grapes.

2 Plain Wood
A light beige like that of plain timber.

3 Gray Mist
A gray that appears soft like mist.

4 Forest Moss
A green like that of moss growing deep in a forest; a serene yellow green.

5 Warm Comfort
The special seat in front of a warm, comfortable fireplace.

6 Tear Drop
Pale, diaphanous, the color of tears.

7 Classic Burgundy
A color evoking a mature, deep red wine.

8 Blue Lake
A blue that calls to mind the calm surface of a big lake.

9 Peanut Butter
A common spread for sandwiches or toast.

1 C15 M0 Y70 K17
R202 G206 B90
#CACD5A

2 C0 M15 Y37 K27
R205 G182 B140
#CCB68C

3 C3 M0 Y10 K15
R225 G227 B215
#E1E2D6

4 C20 M0 Y80 K45
R144 G151 B46
#90972E

5 C0 M83 Y90 K10
R219 G72 B29
#DA471D

6 C20 M0 Y7 K20
R183 G205 B208
#B7CCCF

7 C0 M60 Y70 K70
R108 G52 B18
#6C3411

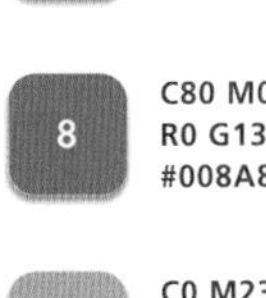

8 C80 M0 Y43 K30
R0 G138 B131
#008A82

9 C0 M23 Y63 K15
R226 G186 B98
#E2BA61

Two-color combinations

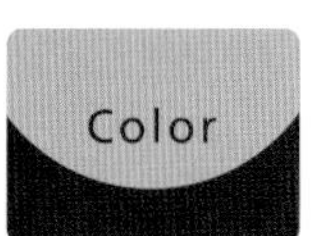

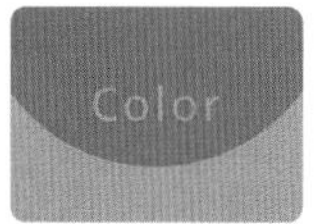

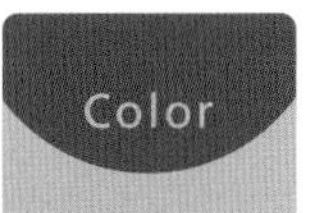
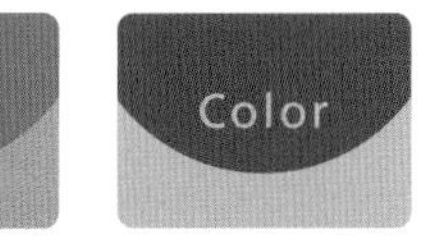

1 7 8 2 5 6

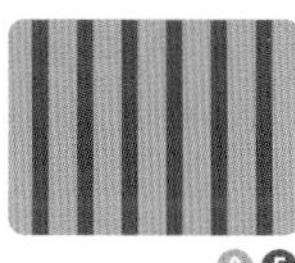
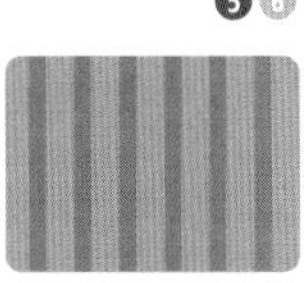

3 1 9 5 2 4

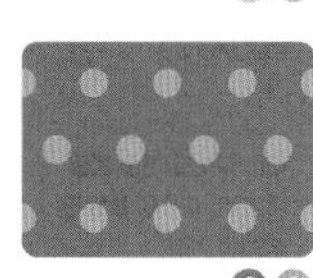
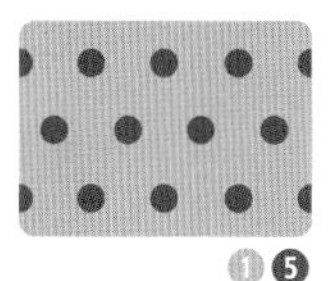
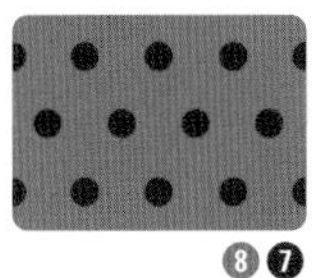

4 9 1 5 8 7

Three-color combinations

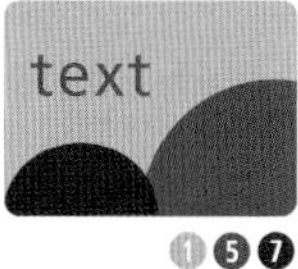

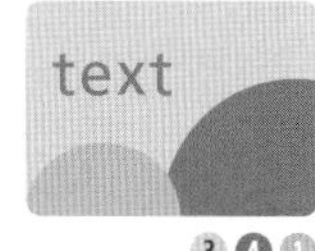

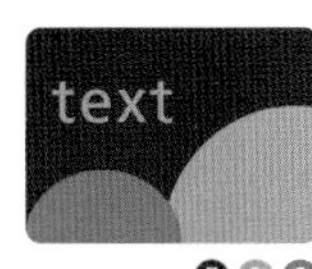

1 5 7 3 4 1 7 2 8

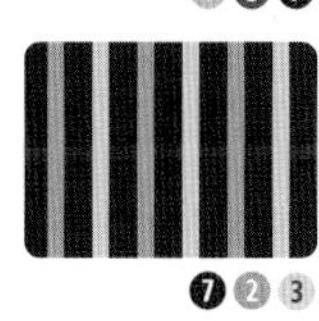
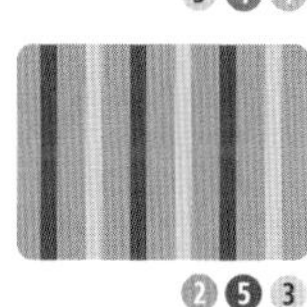
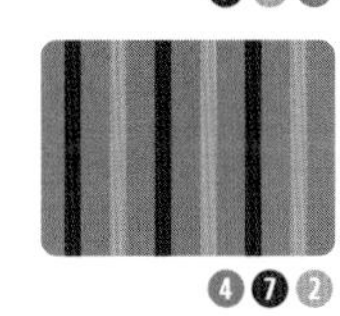

7 2 3 2 5 3 4 7 2

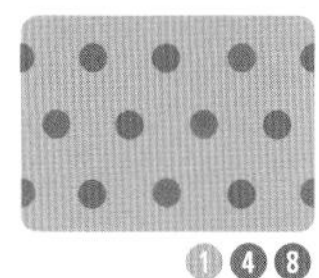
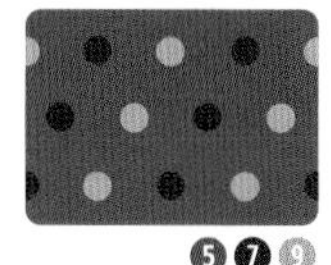
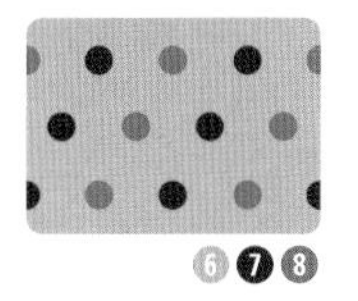

1 4 8 5 7 9 6 7 8

Designs

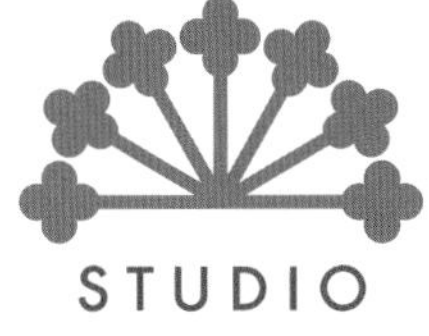

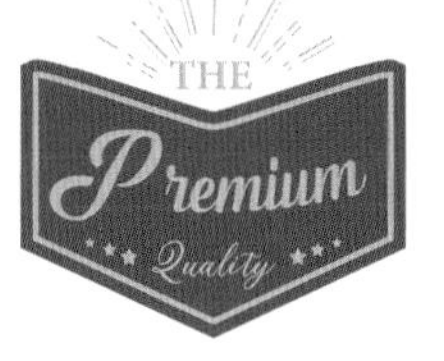

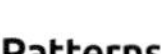
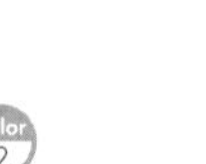
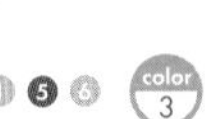

5 8 color 2 4 7 color 2 1 5 6 color 3

Patterns

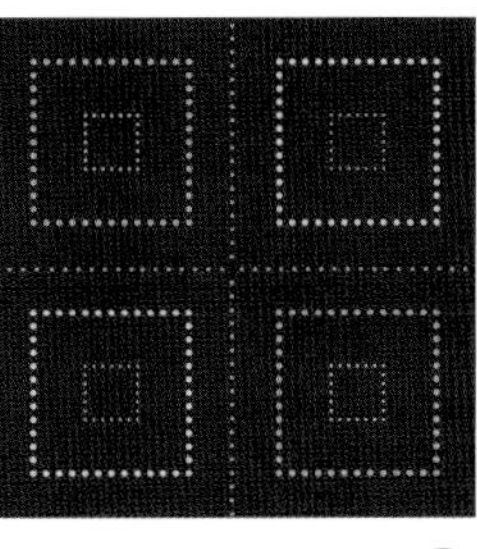
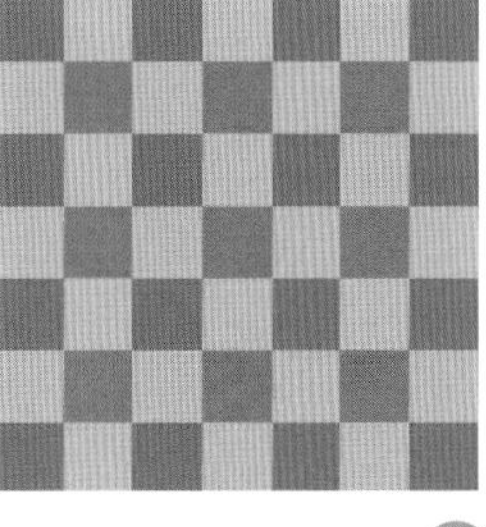
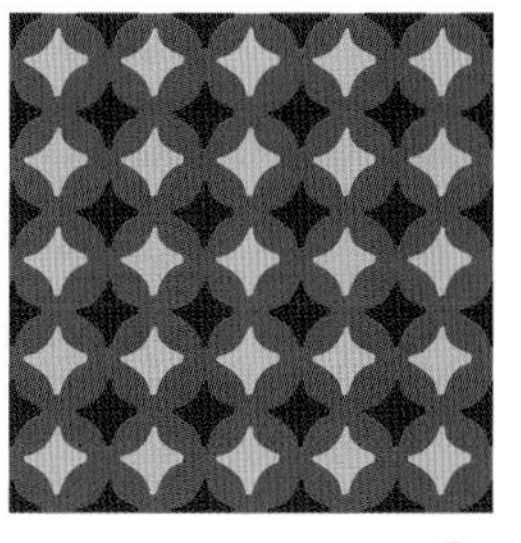

3 7 9 color 3 1 4 8 color 3 1 5 6 7 color 4

Illustration

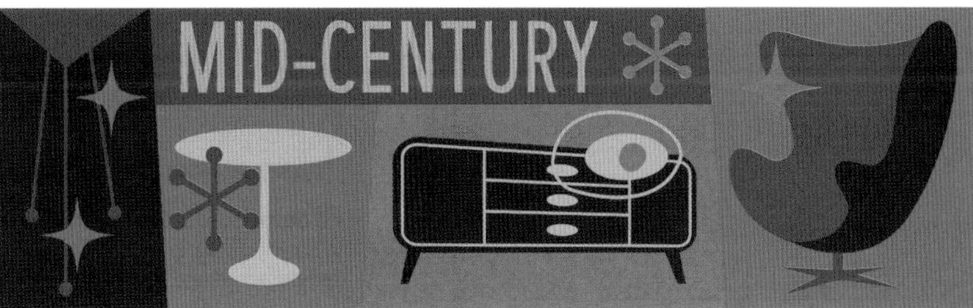

4 5 6 7 8 9 color 6

Recipe
103

Psychedelic 60s

Psychedelic is a term for art or music that suggests or references a hallucinogenic state. Beginning with the hippies on America's West Coast, the term and movement spread in the latter half of the 1960s, with artists such as Yokoo Tadanori and Peter Max creating works using unusual clashes of primary and fluorescent colors.

- **FEELING** Hallucinatory, bewitching, chaotic.
- **COMBINATIONS** Use many colors in highly saturated and fluorescent hues.
- **TIPS** Place complementary colors such as red and green, yellow and purple next to one another.

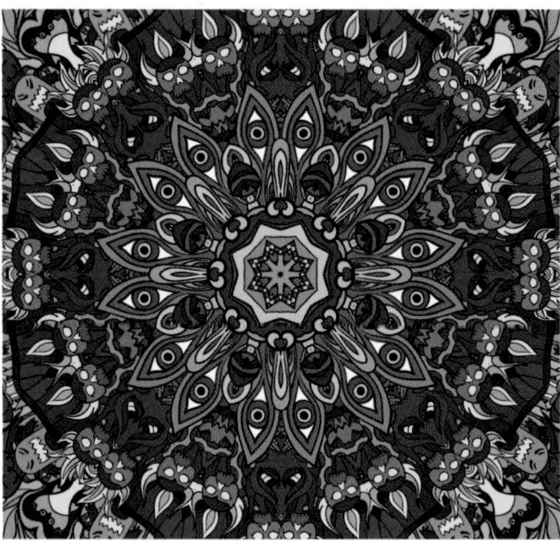

Extremely saturated colors swirl around and around in this psychedelic image.

❶ Neon Purple
A color recalling the purple of neon lights in the city at night.

② Yellow Submarine
The yellow that appears in the animated film starring the Beatles.

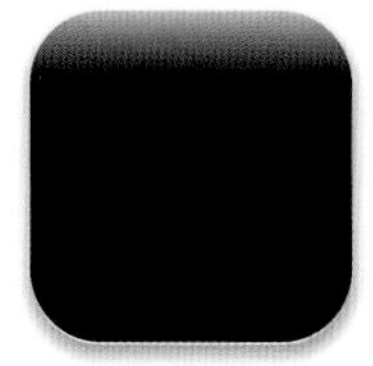

❸ Darkness
A deep black that seems to swallow everything up.

❹ Illuminant Green
A blue green that suggests foresight and illumination.

❺ Fluorescent Pink
Fluorescent pink, a rosy, dreamlike glow.

❻ Universe
A blue signifiying outer space, the universe and all its people.

❼ Surprise Orange
A bright, strong, glowing red-tinged orange.

❽ Electric Green
An electric yellow green.

❾ Magical Turquoise
A turquoise that exudes an air of wonder.

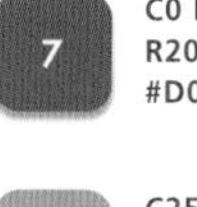
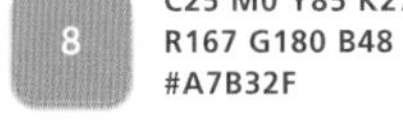
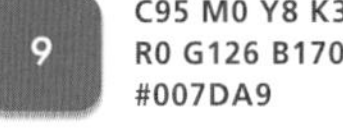

	CMYK	RGB	Hex
1	C35 M93 Y0 K0	R174 G37 B137	#AE2488
2	C17 M0 Y100 K0	R225 G227 B0	#E1E200
3	C0 M40 Y0 K95	R47 G14 B25	#2F0E19
4	C75 M0 Y60 K0	R0 G175 B132	#00AF83
5	C0 M85 Y3 K0	R231 G66 B143	#E7428E
6	C75 M83 Y0 K0	R91 G62 B149	#5B3E95
7	C0 M75 Y85 K17	R209 G86 B36	#D05523
8	C25 M0 Y85 K27	R167 G180 B48	#A7B32F
9	C95 M0 Y8 K35	R0 G126 B170	#007DA9

Two-color combinations

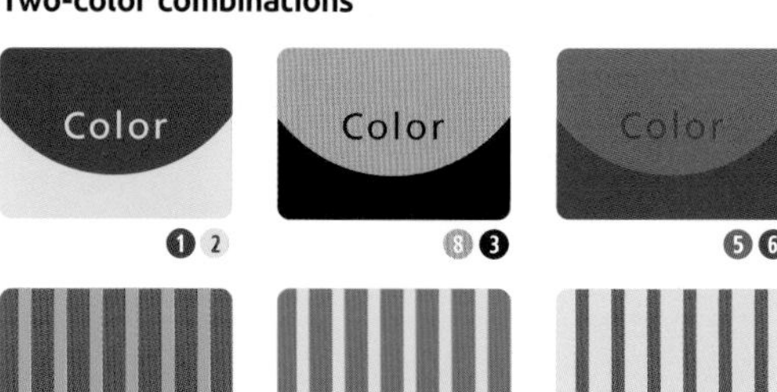

1 2 · 8 3 · 5 6

7 4 · 9 2 · 2 7

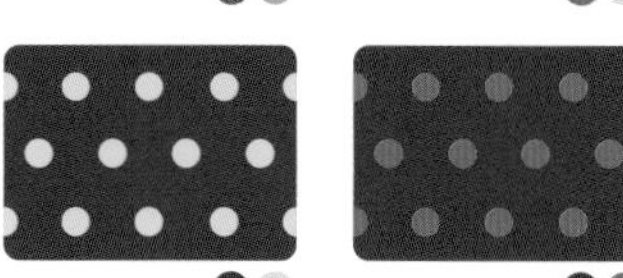

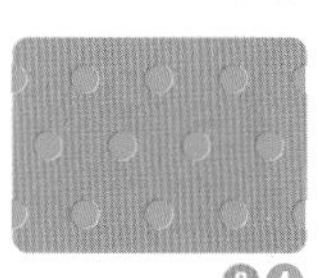

6 2 · 1 9 · 8 4

Three-color combinations

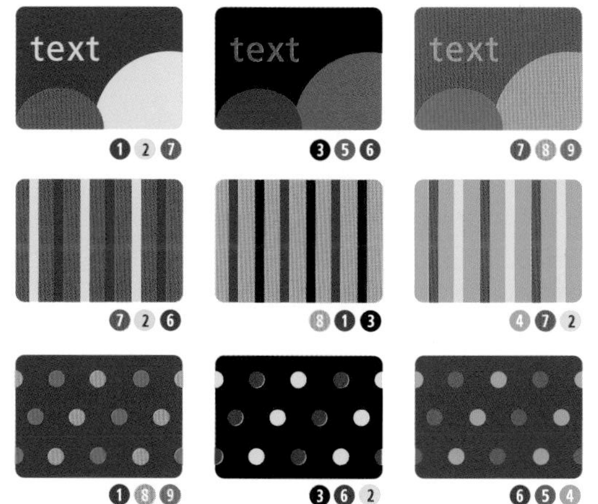

1 2 7 · 3 5 6 · 7 8 9

7 2 6 · 8 1 3 · 4 7 2

1 8 9 · 3 6 2 · 6 5 4

Designs

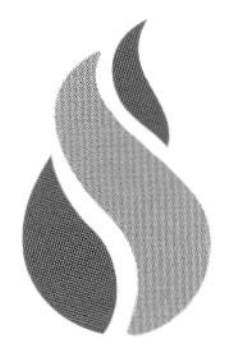

5 8 color 2

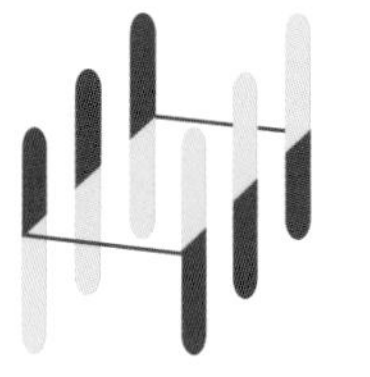

2 6 color 2

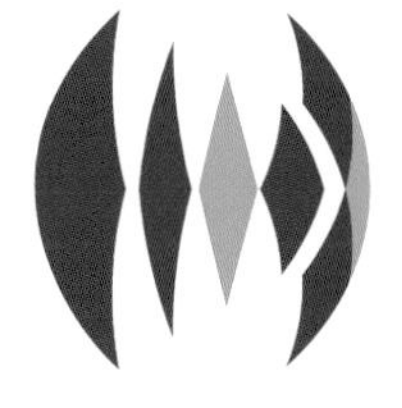

1 4 6 color 3

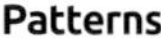

Patterns

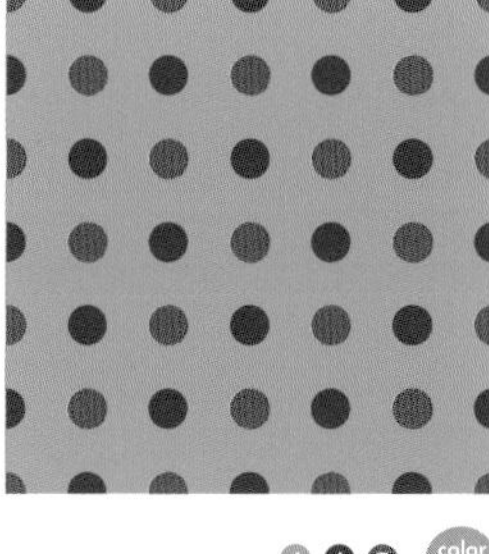

4 6 7 color 3

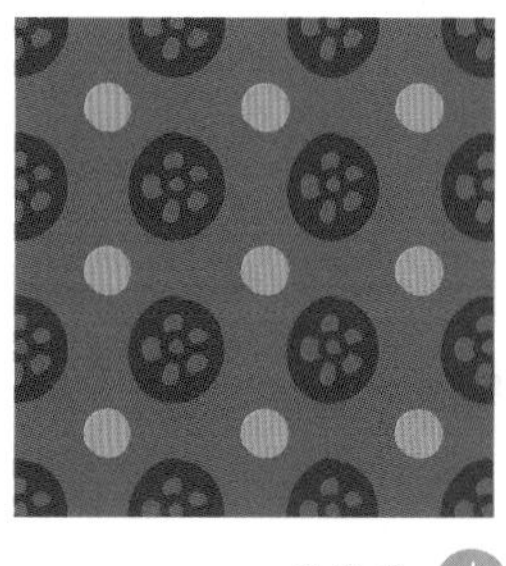

5 6 8 color 3

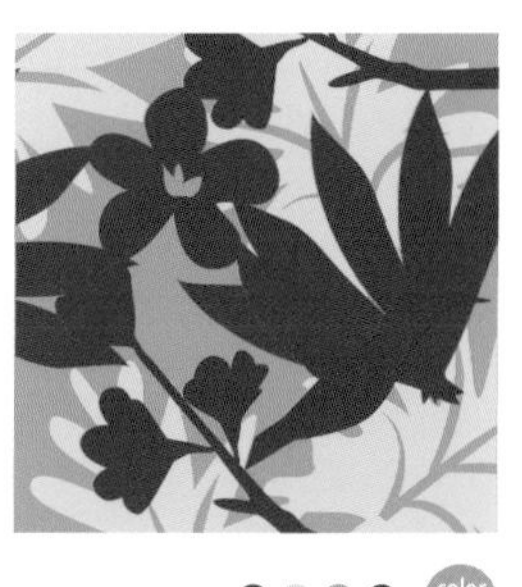

1 2 4 6 color 4

Illustration

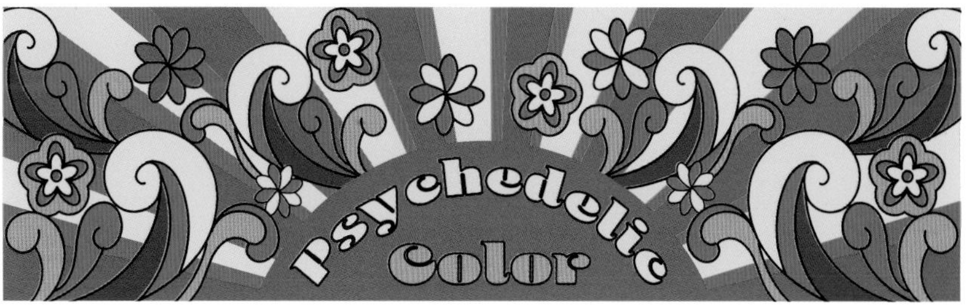

2 3 5 6 8 9 color 6

Recipe
104

Earth Tones

Toward the end of the 1960s, environmental pollution started to become a problem in Japan. Then, under the influence of the second major oil shock in 1973, consumerism slumped and attention turned to the environment and its preservation. At this time, earth colors became popular, centering on shades of brown. This was true not only for fashion but also for interiors.

- **FEELING** Natural, tranquil, secure.
- **COMBINATIONS** Focus on shades of brown and add khaki and olive.
- **TIPS** Create a cohesive look by using similar hues in dull tones.

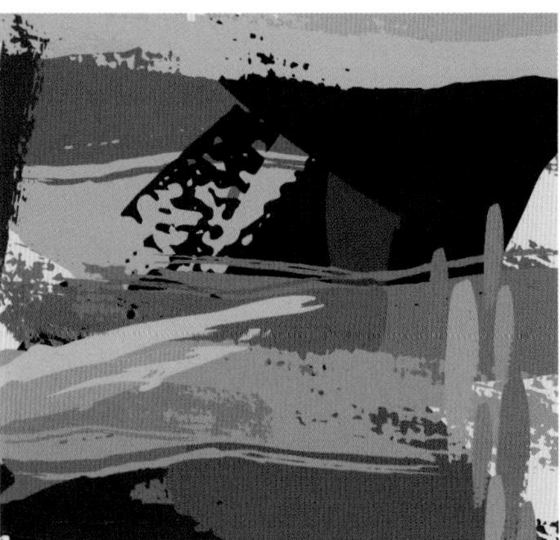

Natural colors such as that of unbleached cloth also became popular at this time.

❶ Okutama
The color of soil gathered in the Okutama region of Tokyo.

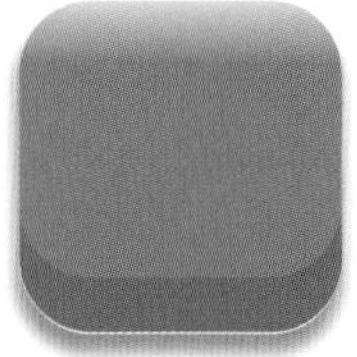

❷ Tosa
The color of soil gathered in the Tosa region of Kochi prefecture.

❸ Ishigaki
The color of soil gathered on Ishigaki Island in Okinawa prefecture.

❹ Tokoname
The color of soil gathered in the Tokoname region of Aichi prefecture.

❺ Asahi
The color of soil gathered in the Asahi region of Shimane prefecture.

❻ Tateyama
The color of soil gathered in the Tateyama region of Toyama prefecture.

❼ Awaji
The color of soil gathered in the Awaji region of Hyogo prefecture.

❽ Obihiro
The color of soil gathered in the Obihiro region of Hokkaido.

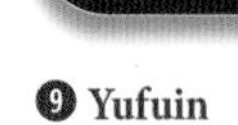

❾ Yufuin
The color of soil gathered in the Yufuin area of Oita prefecture.

1 — C0 M40 Y65 K70, R110 G74 B32, #6E4A1F

2 — C40 M40 Y70 K2, R168 G149 B91, #A8945A

3 — C13 M60 Y65 K40, R156 G89 B58, #9B5839

4 — C0 M50 Y83 K20, R210 G132 B42, #D28329

5 — C0 M40 Y47 K20, R212 G152 B114, #D39772

6 — C0 M9 Y25 K15, R229 G214 B182, #E4D5B6

7 — C3 M25 Y55 K35, R184 G151 B94, #B7975E

8 — C20 M43 Y50 K70, R93 G67 B49, #5D4231

9 — C33 M15 Y50 K70, R80 G87 B60, #4F563C

Two-color combinations

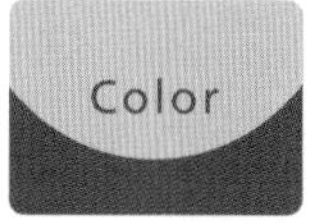
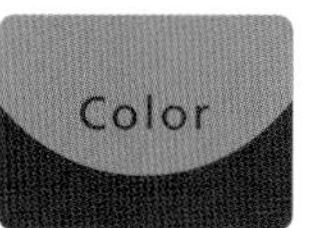

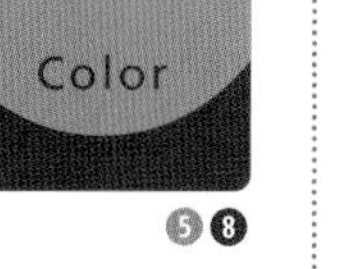

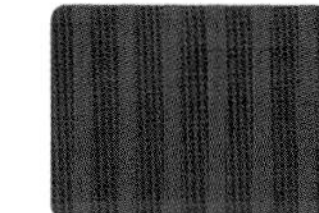

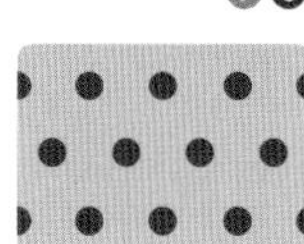
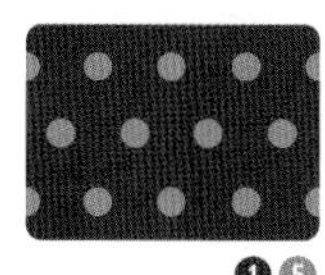
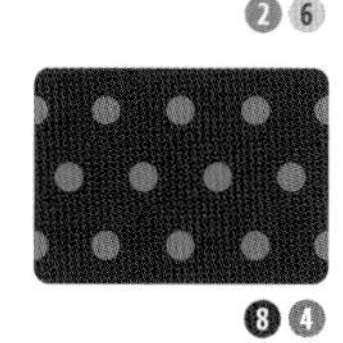

Three-color combinations

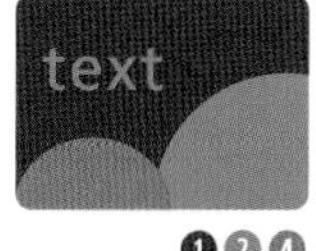
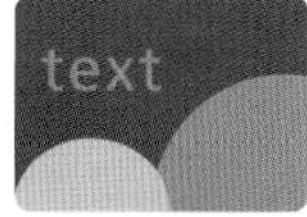
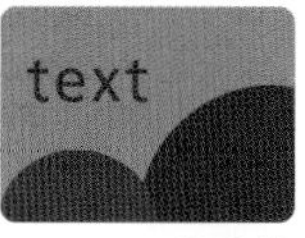
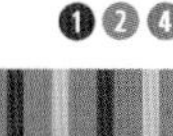

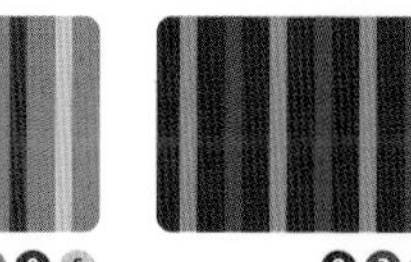
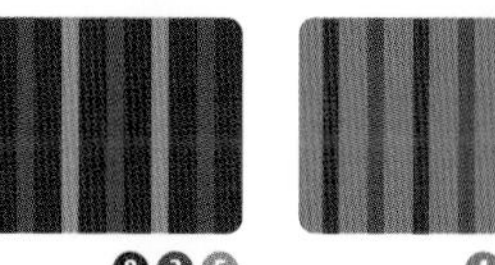

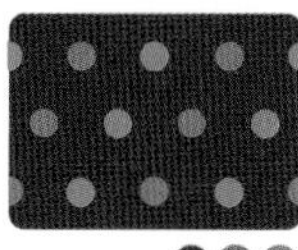
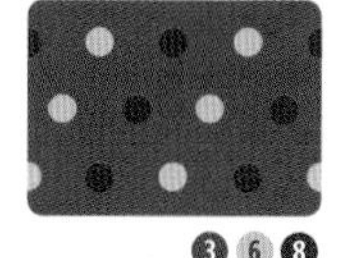
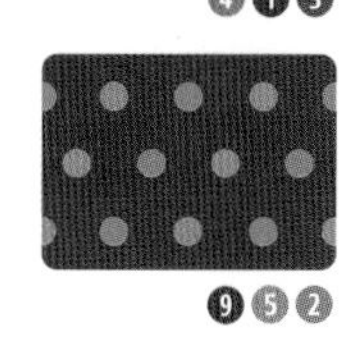

Designs

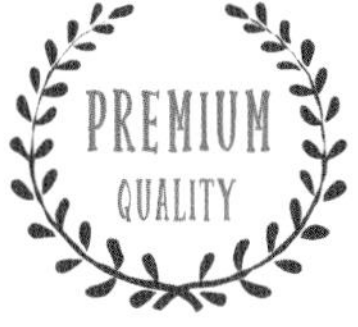

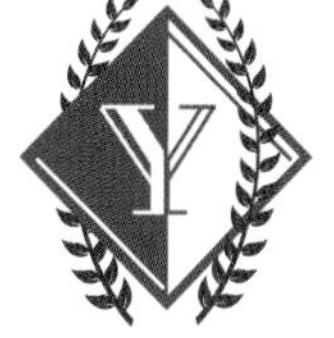

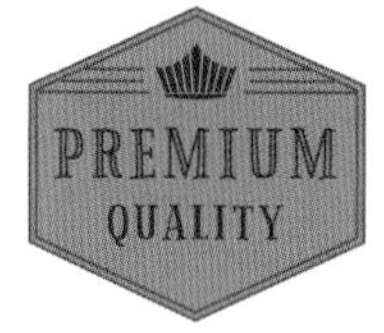

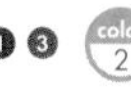
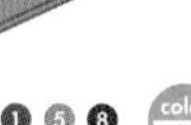

Patterns

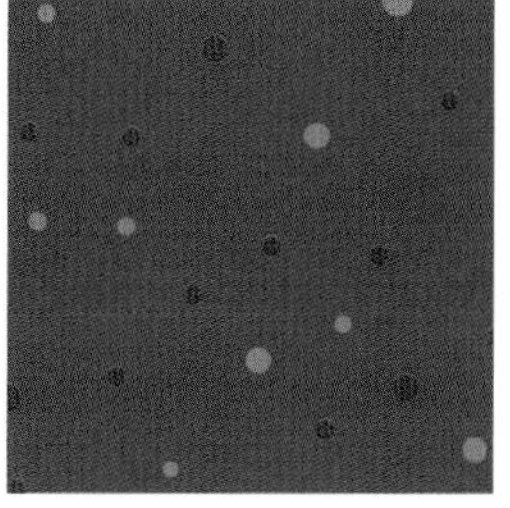

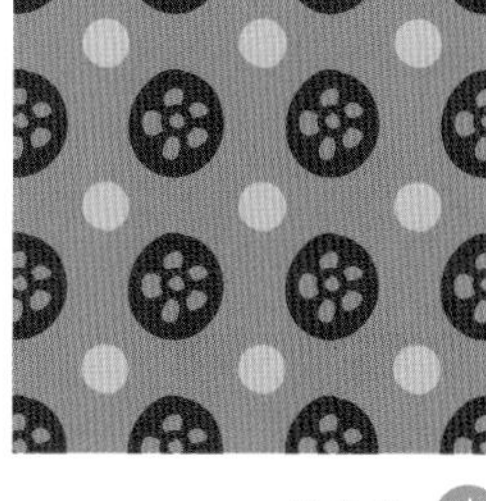

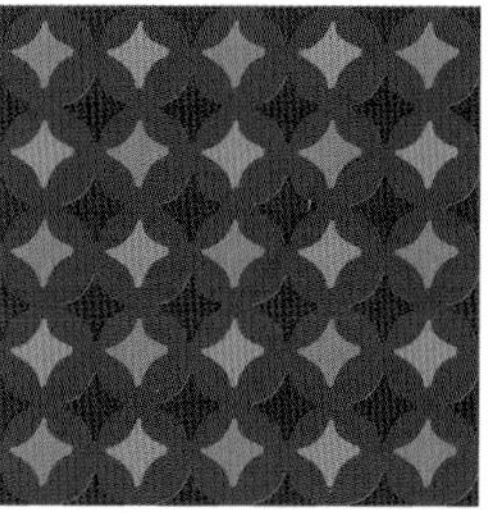

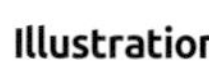

Illustration

Recipe
105

Black and Bright

The pieces presented by Yohji Yamamoto and Rei Kawakubo at the 1982 spring fashion collections in Paris were dubbed "black shock" and helped establish a worldwide trend. Soon after, Japan experienced a period of unprecedented economic growth known as the bubble economy. The legendary disco, Juliana Tokyo, is an enduring symbol of the bubble period.

- **FEELING** Flamboyant, fantastic, feminine.
- **COMBINATIONS** Add black to bright, glorious colors.
- **TIPS** Create high contrasts in brightness and levels of saturation.

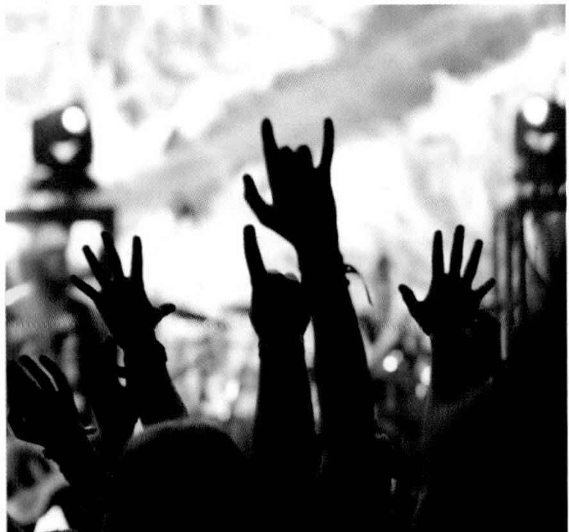

At a live concert, vivid colors play over the top of contrasting light and shade.

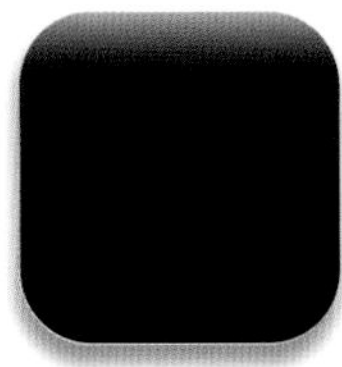

❶ Oriental Black
At this time, dyed hair wasn't the trend, and black hair prevailed.

❷ American Pink
American-made cosmetics and nail colors were trendy at the time.

❸ Lavender Dream
A color evoking bittersweet memories.

❹ Marina Bay
The color of the calm sea and the rows of gently bobbing boats.

5 Crescent Moon
A three-day-old moon. The start of a magical night.

❻ Mirror Ball
Sparkling lights in the middle of a dance club, a disco era holdover.

❼ Feather Fan Pink
The feather fans women held as they danced on podiums.

❽ Body Conscious
A one-piece dress in a primary color that fits tightly to the body.

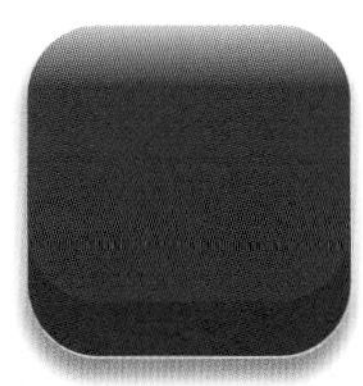

❾ Twinkle Purple
Earrings that twinkle in the spotlight.

1 C25 M75 Y0 K93 R40 G0 B23 #280017

2 C10 M53 Y0 K0 R223 G146 B188 #DF91BC

3 C30 M33 Y0 K0 R187 G174 B212 #BBADD4

4 C37 M0 Y25 K0 R171 G217 B203 #ABD9CB

5 C5 M0 Y40 K0 R248 G245 B176 #F7F5B0

6 C0 M0 Y0 K33 R195 G196 B196 #C3C3C4

7 C2 M85 Y0 K0 R229 G66 B145 #E44191

8 C0 M93 Y50 K0 R231 G42 B84 #E62954

9 C60 M87 Y0 K0 R126 G56 B145 #7D3790

Two-color combinations

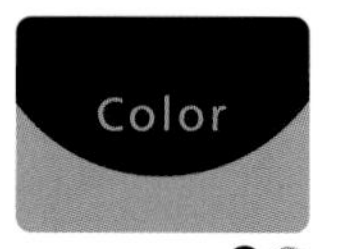

1 2

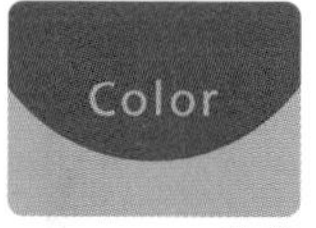

8 3

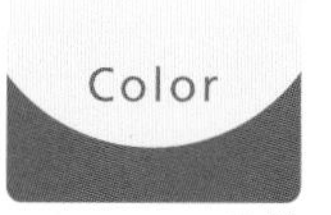
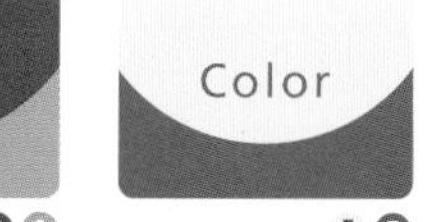

5 7

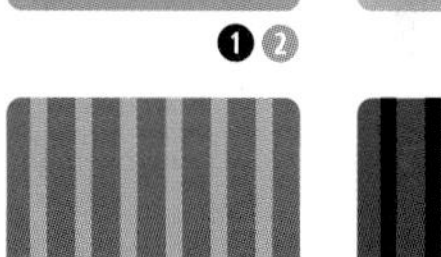

7 3

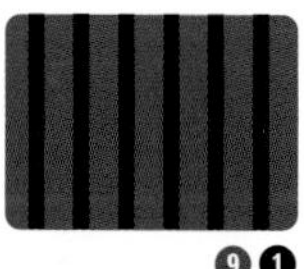

9 1

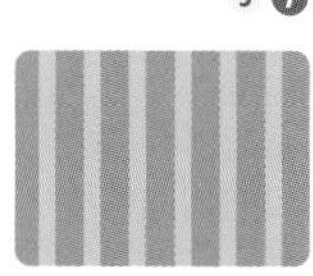

2 4

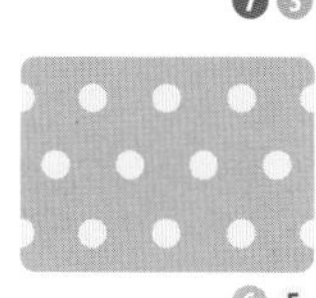

6 5

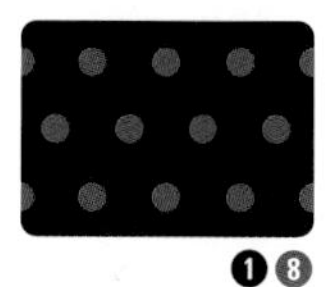

1 8

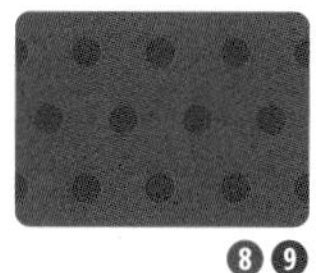

8 9

Three-color combinations

1 2 7

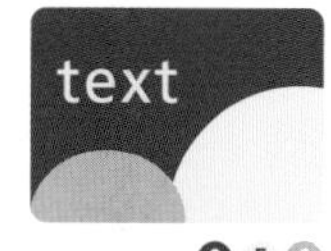

9 5 6

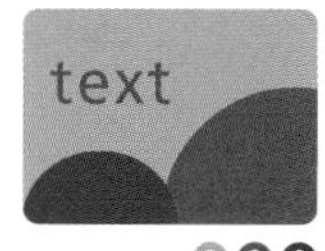

3 8 9

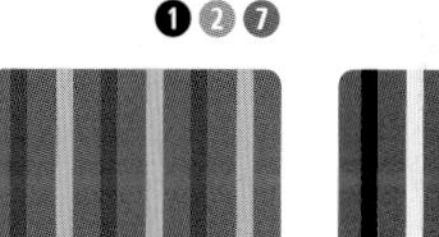

7 9 6

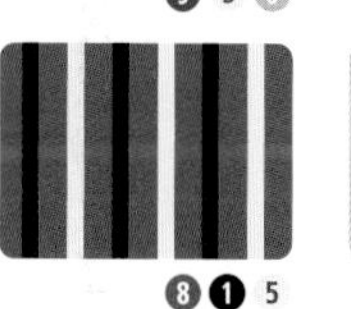

8 1 5

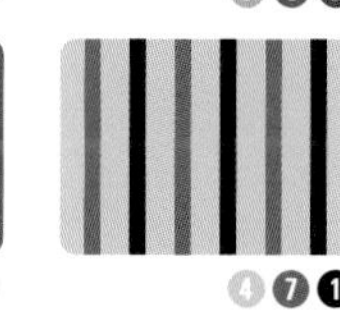

4 7 1

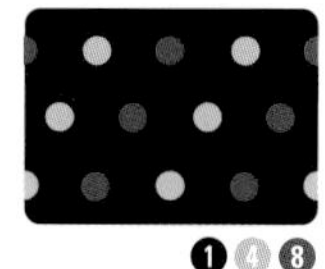

1 4 8

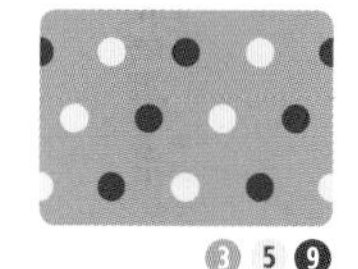

3 5 9

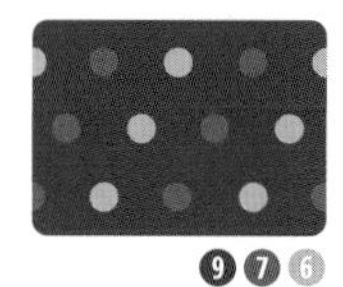

9 7 6

Designs

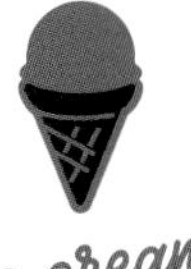
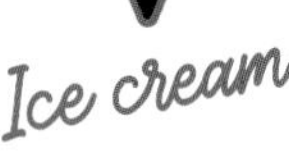

1 7 color 2

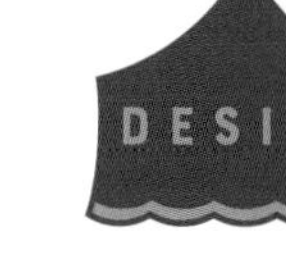
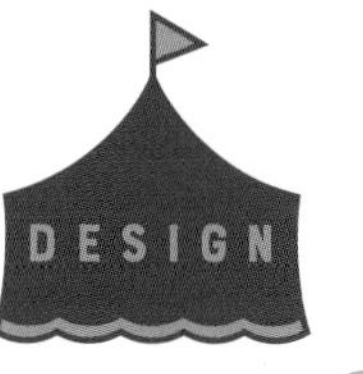

2 9 color 2

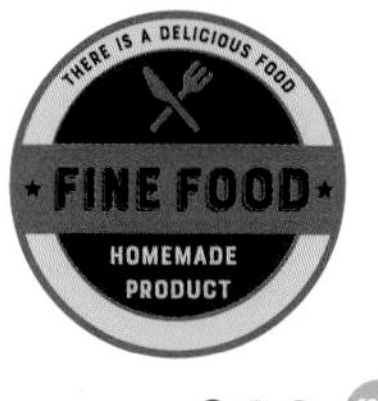

1 4 8 color 3

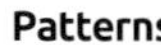

Patterns

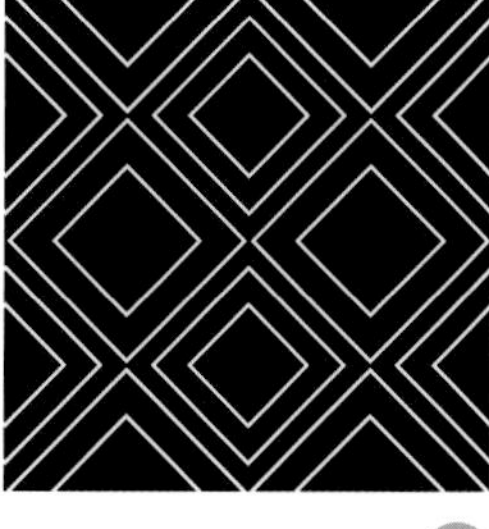

1 5 color 2

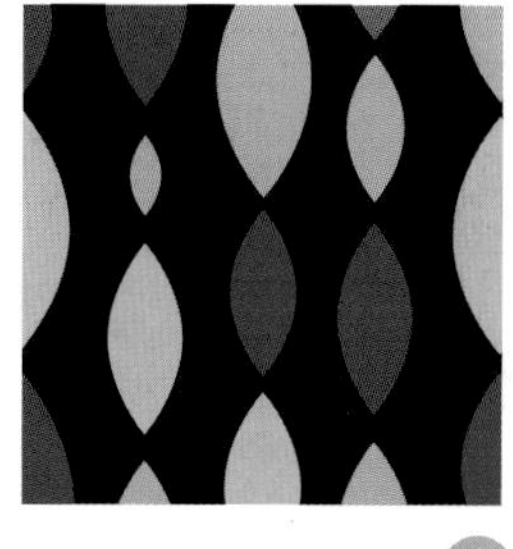

1 3 9 color 3

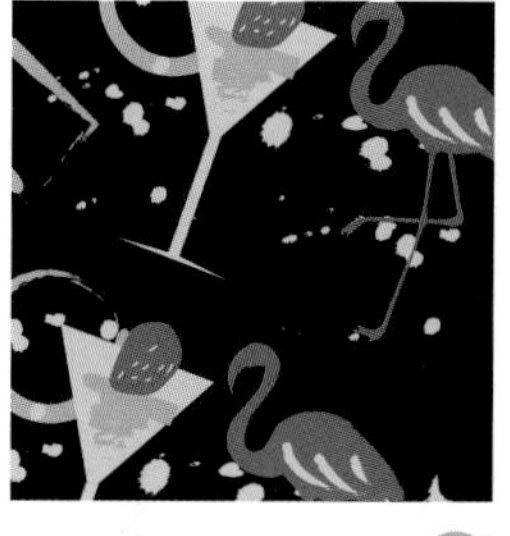

1 3 4 7 color 4

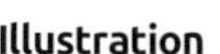

Illustration

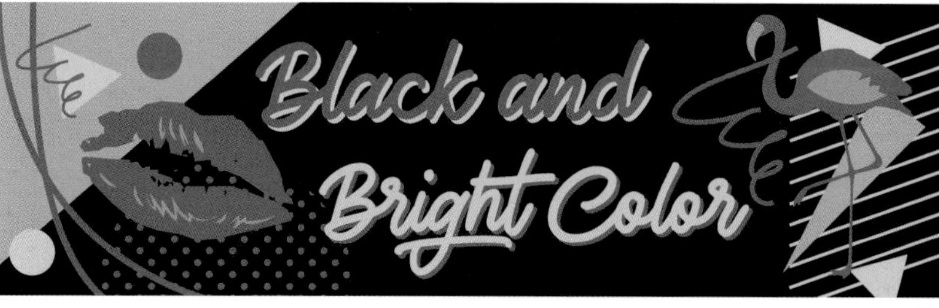

1 2 3 4 7 color 5

Recipe
106

Duo Tones

This color scheme became popular in the web design industry around 2016. Monotone indicates achromatic colors, while duotone of course means having two tones. This is achieved by combining a highlight color with a base tone. Using complementary colors creates the greatest impact and visual appeal.

- **FEELING** Pop, contemporary, impactful.
- **COMBINATIONS** Use two tones to create contrast.
- **TIPS** Use whatever hues you like; complementary or contrasting colors are recommended.

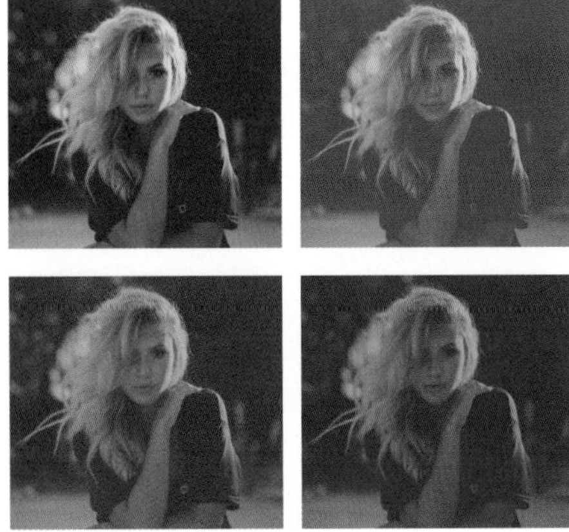

This color scheme is suitable for digital formats such as web design and image processing.

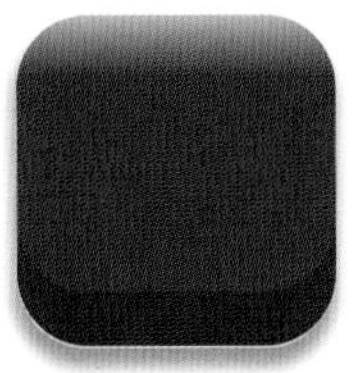

❶ Sea Cave
A dark blue that suggests a cave on the ocean floor.

❷ Neo Yellow
A yellow with a sophisticated, stylish air.

❸ Inspire Green
A deep green that helps spark inspiration and ideas.

❹ Strong Purple
A deep purple with powerful impact.

❺ Future Pink
A color expressing hopes and slight uncertainty about the future.

❻ Spiritual Blue
A translucent blue that symbolizes spirituality.

❼ Electric Red
A splendid red that seems to gleam with light.

❽ Striking Pink
A purplish pink with powerful impact.

❾ Green Flash
The green flash of light seen at the moment the sun sets.

1 C75 M70 Y0 K35
R63 G60 B124
#3F3C7C

2 C20 M3 Y65 K0
R217 G224 B115
#D8E072

3 C80 M0 Y65 K0
R0 G170 B123
#00AA7A

4 C50 M77 Y0 K50
R92 G42 B99
#5B2962

5 C10 M43 Y0 K0
R226 G167 B202
#E1A7CA

6 C50 M30 Y0 K13
R126 G150 B195
#7E95C2

7 C30 M95 Y55 K0
R184 G41 B81
#B82850

8 C3 M75 Y0 K30
R182 G74 B126
#B6497E

9 C30 M4 Y40 K0
R191 G217 B171
#BFD9AB

Two-color combinations

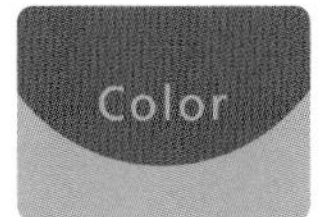
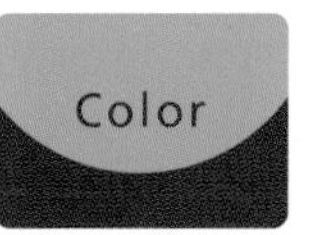
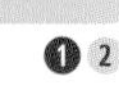
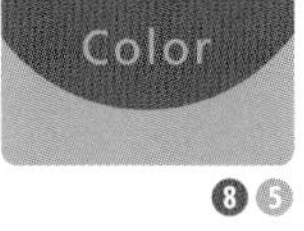
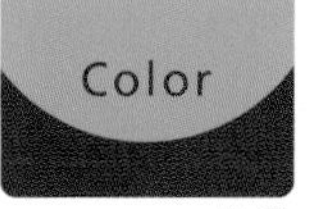

1 2 · 8 5 · 3 4

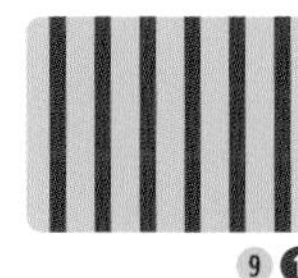
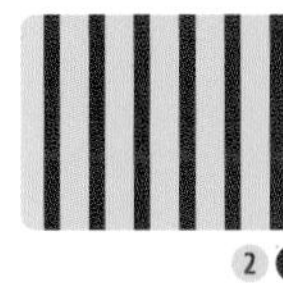

7 5 · 9 1 · 2 4

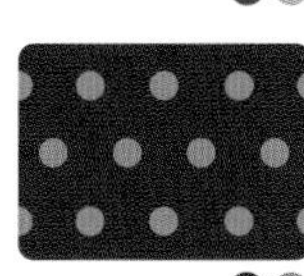
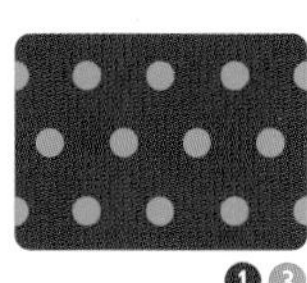
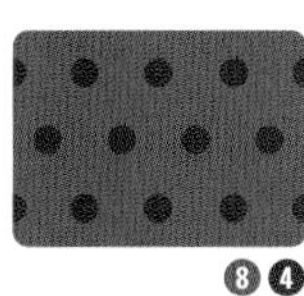

4 6 · 1 3 · 8 4

Three-color combinations

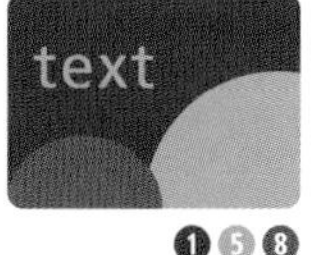
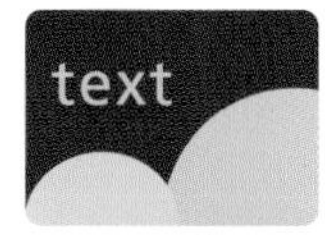
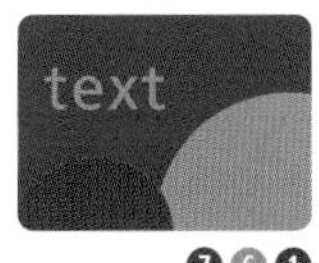

1 5 8 · 4 9 2 · 7 6 1

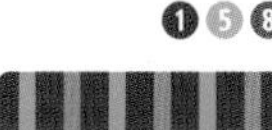
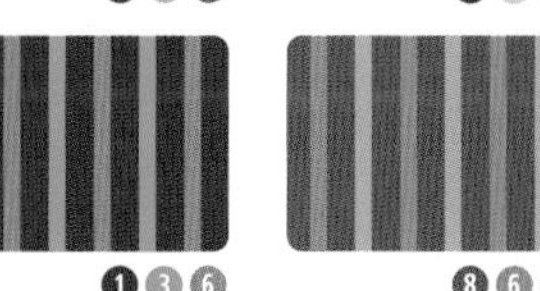
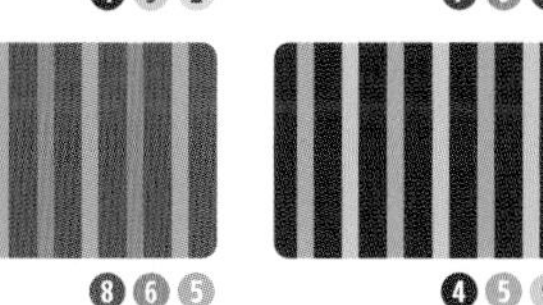

1 3 6 · 8 6 5 · 4 5 9

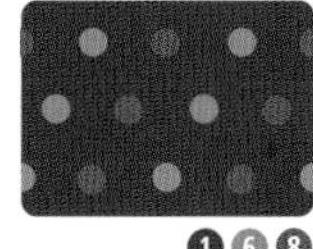
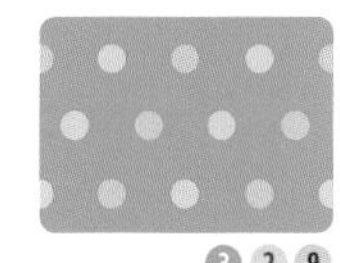
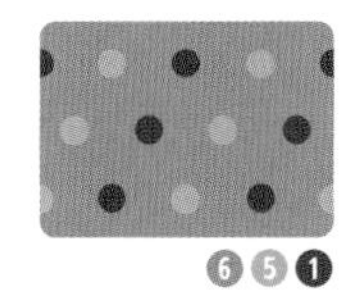

1 6 8 · 3 2 9 · 6 5 1

Designs

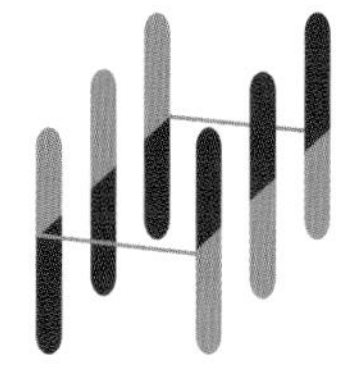

4 6 color 2

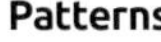

5 8 color 2

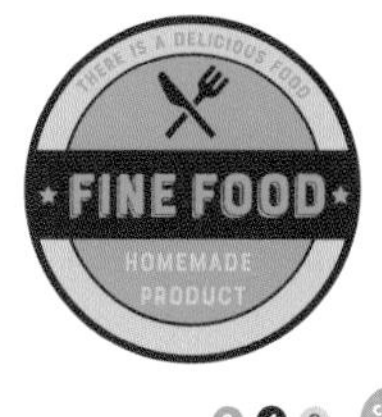

3 4 9 color 3

Patterns

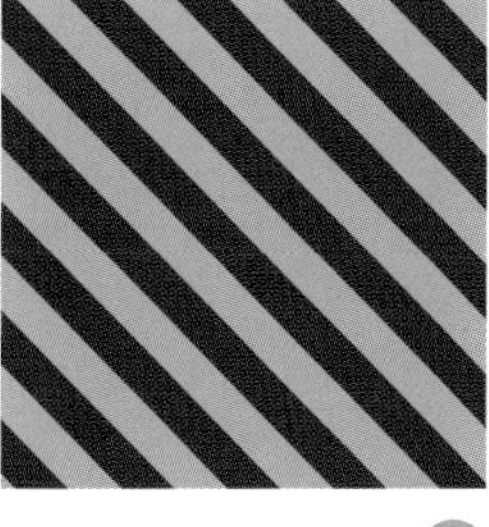

4 5 color 2

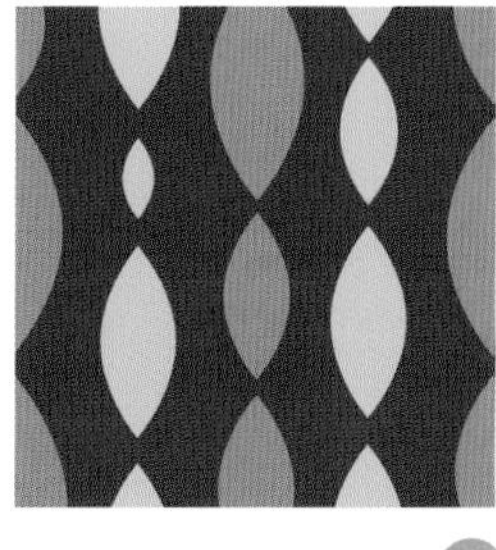

1 6 9 color 3

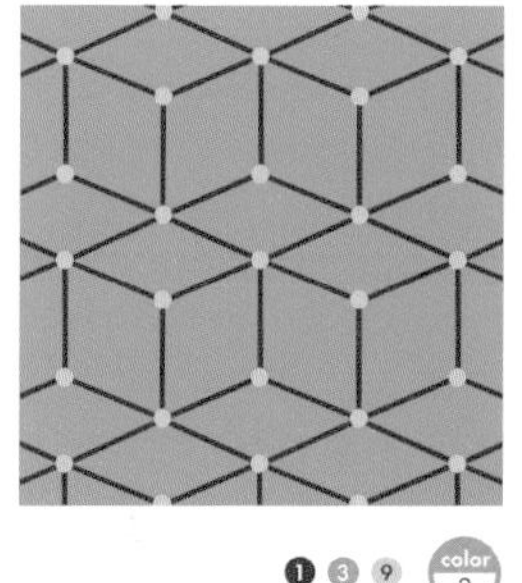

1 3 9 color 3

Illustration

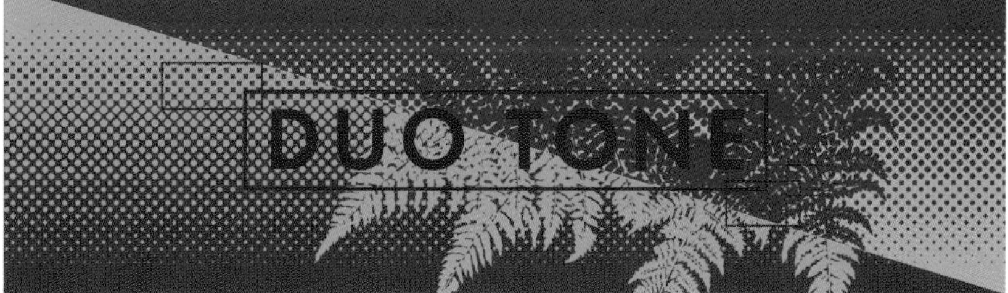

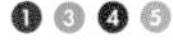

1 3 4 5 7 color 5

Recipe
107

South Wind, Clear Sky

Along with *The Great Wave off Kanagawa*, this is one of Hokusai's masterpieces. The indigo sky and the red Fuji create a powerful contrast. In the word *ukiyo-e*, ukiyo means "contemporary, of this world" and due to the wood-block prints lending themselves to mass production, this was a genre for ordinary people. While the color scheme derived from the colors in this work is novel, there is also an air of nostalgia about it.

- **FEELING** Bold, lucid, clear.
- **COMBINATIONS** Contrast hues and keep brightness levels in check.
- **TIPS** Create a color scheme that uses indigo blue to effect.

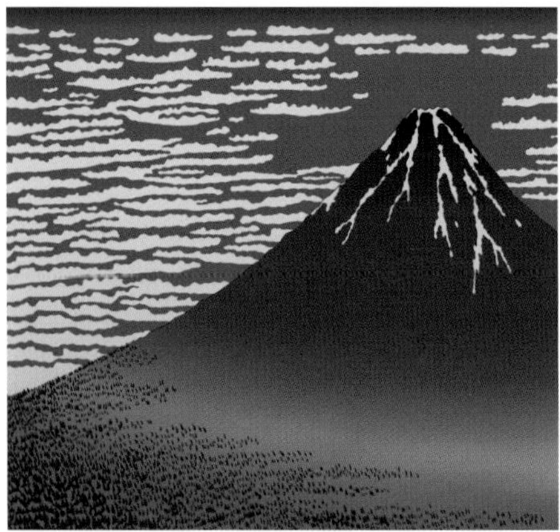

One of the standout works from the series *36 Views of Mt Fuji*.

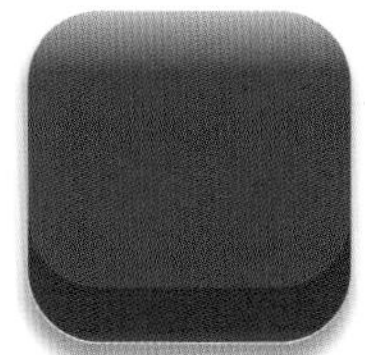

❶ Red Fuji
The mountain colored by the morning light from late summer to early fall.

❷ Berlin Blue
A blue achieved using foreign pigments is featured in the series.

❸ Foot of the Mountain
The green-tinged gray used for the areas around the base of Mount Fuji.

❹ Fifth Station
The dull red used for the central area of Mount Fuji.

❺ Woodblock Paper
The plain sections of paper that aren't printed in a multicolored woodblock print.

❻ Publisher
The main figure behind the production of *ukiyo-e*; the publishers of the day.

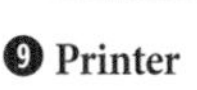

❼ Eshi
Both Hokusai and Hiroshige were painters active during the last half of the Edo period.

❽ Engraver
An artisan who engraves the image created by a painter onto a woodblock.

❾ Printer
An artisan who prints *ukiyo-e*, following the directions of the painter and engraver.

	CMYK	RGB	Hex
1	C5 M90 Y85 K30	R178 G41 B28	#B2291C
2	C77 M45 Y0 K40	R35 G86 B138	#22558A
3	C50 M0 Y40 K55	R74 G119 B101	#4A7664
4	C0 M55 Y45 K25	R199 G119 B101	#C77665
5	C9 M10 Y20 K5	R229 G222 B203	#E5DECA
6	C30 M2 Y40 K45	R126 G148 B116	#7E9374
7	C10 M85 Y80 K83	R72 G0 B0	#470000
8	C60 M0 Y50 K83	R13 G60 B43	#0D3B2B
9	C70 M27 Y0 K75	R4 G57 B87	#043956

Two-color combinations

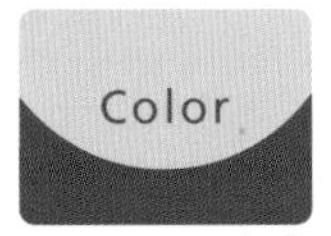
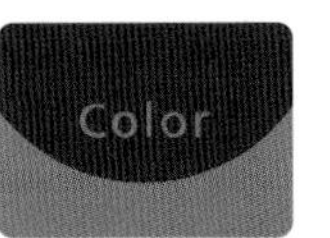
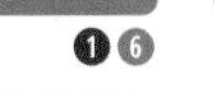
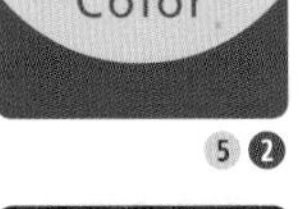

1 6 · 5 2 · 8 4

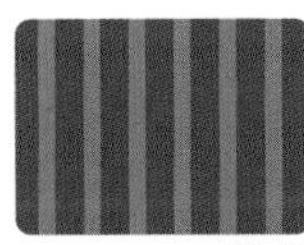
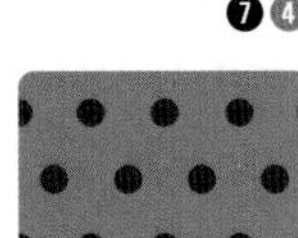

7 4 · 9 1 · 2 6

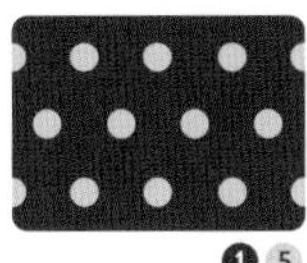
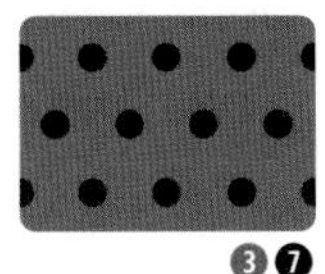

6 8 · 1 5 · 3 7

Three-color combinations

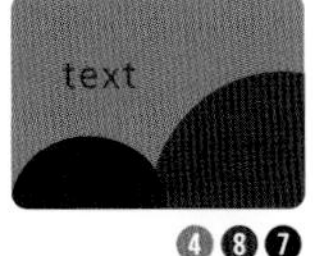
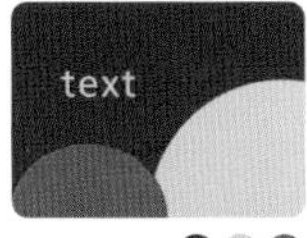
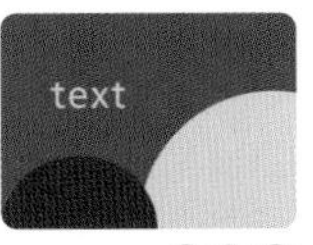

4 8 7 · 1 5 3 · 2 5 9

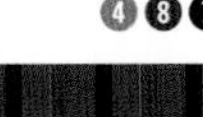

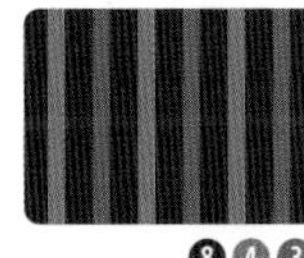

1 9 7 · 8 4 3 · 4 7 5

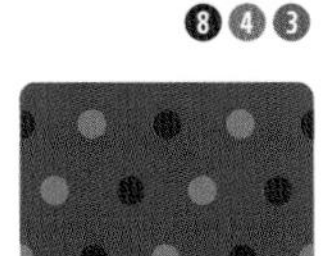
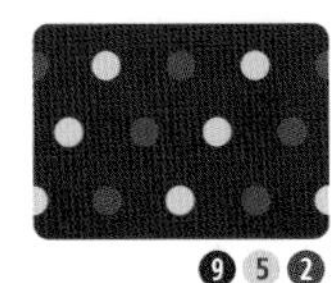

5 1 2 · 2 6 9 · 9 5 2

Designs

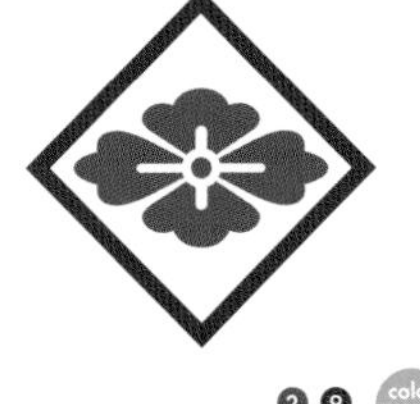

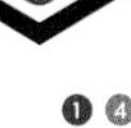
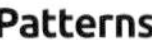

2 9 color 2 · 3 8 color 2 · 1 4 7 color 3

Patterns

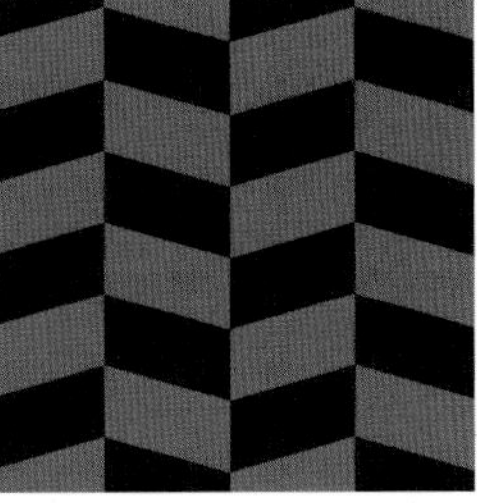
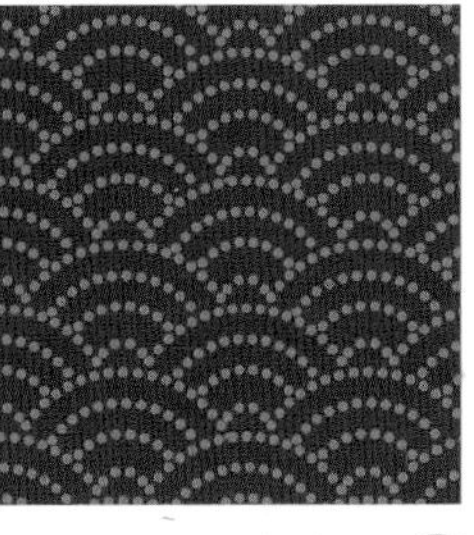
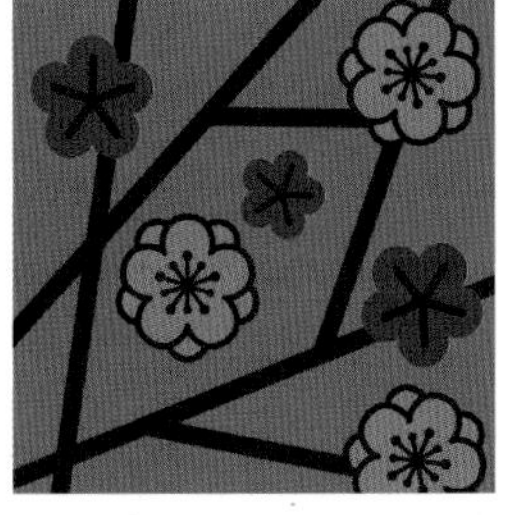
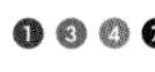
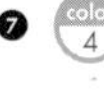

3 7 color 2 · 1 6 color 2 · 1 3 4 7 color 4

Illustration

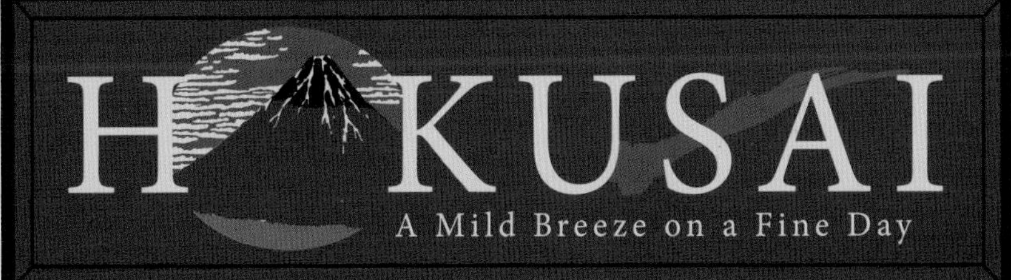

1 2 3 5 7 color 5

Recipe
108

Woman with a Parasol

Waterlilies is a masterpiece by Monet. The artist purchased his neighbor's land and in 1893 began drawing water from the river to create a pond for waterlilies. The work here was painted in 1875 and was entered in the Second Impressionist Exhibition, but the use of translucent blues and grayish greens carries through to *Waterlilies*.

- **FEELING** Invigorating, clear, pure.
- **COMBINATIONS** Focus on blue gray and add a little green.
- **TIPS** Use light grayish tones as the main colors.

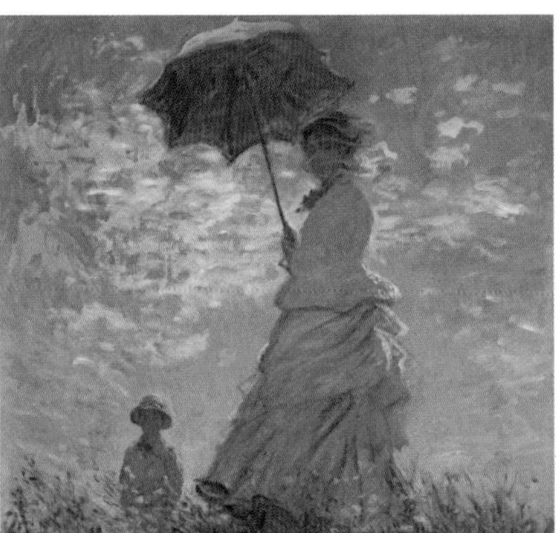

Monet's underappreciated *Woman with a Parasol*.

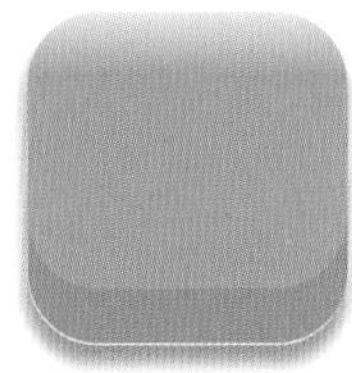

❶ Bleu Ciel

Ciel means "sky" in French, the color of blue sky.

❷ Vert d'herbe

Herbe means "grass." This is one of the oldest color names.

③ Faux Blanc

Meaning "fake white," in English this color would be called off-white.

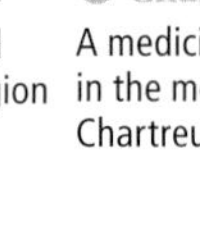

❹ Bleu de Provence

The blue of the sky and sea in the Provence region of southern France.

❺ Chartreuse

A medicinal liqueur made in the monasteries of the Chartreuse region.

❻ Versailles

A deep blue originating at the Palace of Versailles.

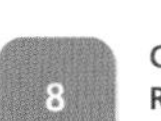

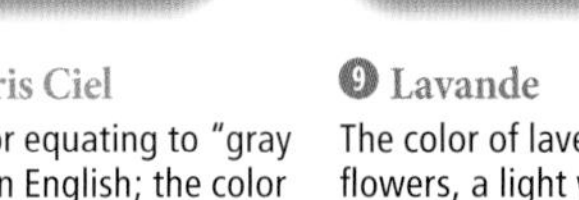

❼ Bleu Bébé

The custom of dressing baby boys in blue started at the end of the 19th century.

❽ Gris Ciel

A color equating to "gray sky" in English; the color of a cloudy day.

❾ Lavande

The color of lavender flowers, a light wash of purple.

No.	CMYK	RGB	Hex
1	C50 M20 Y0 K5	R130 G173 B217	#82ADD9
2	C50 M10 Y65 K25	R117 G155 B96	#749B5F
3	C0 M2 Y10 K10	R239 G236 B222	#EFEBDD
4	C50 M23 Y0 K40	R95 G124 B158	#5F7C9E
5	C20 M10 Y60 K8	R205 G204 B118	#CCCB75
6	C95 M60 Y30 K30	R0 G74 B112	#004970
7	C35 M15 Y0 K33	R134 G154 B179	#8599B3
8	C17 M20 Y0 K33	R166 G159 B177	#A59EB1
9	C40 M50 Y3 K15	R150 G122 B168	#967AA8

Two-color combinations

Color — 1 4

Color — 8 3

Color — 5 6

7 8

9 1

2 4

6 9

1 5

8 4

Three-color combinations

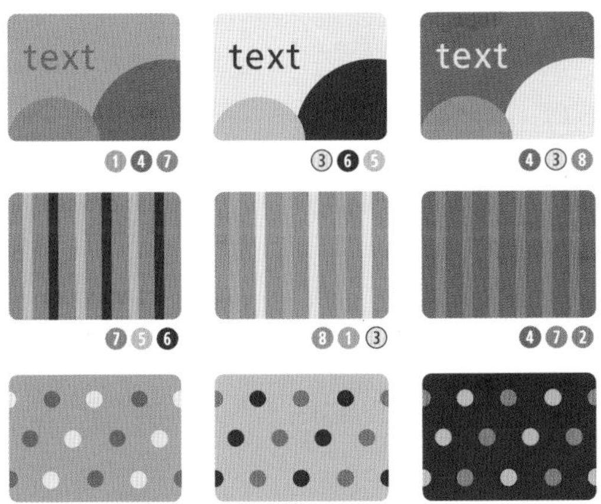

Designs

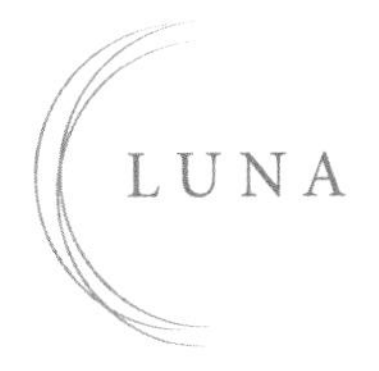

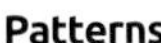

8 9 color 2

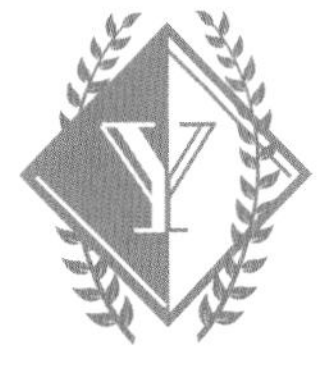

2 7 color 2

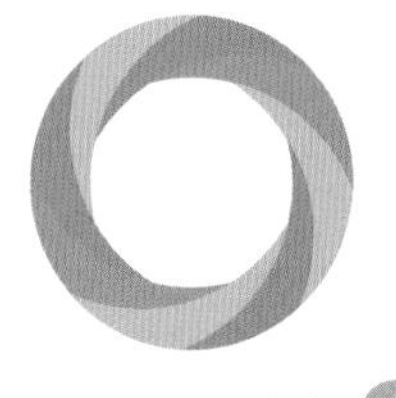

5 7 8 color 3

Patterns

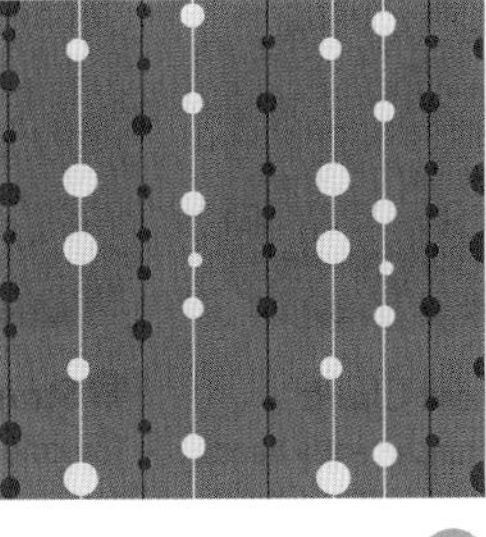

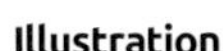

3 4 6 color 3

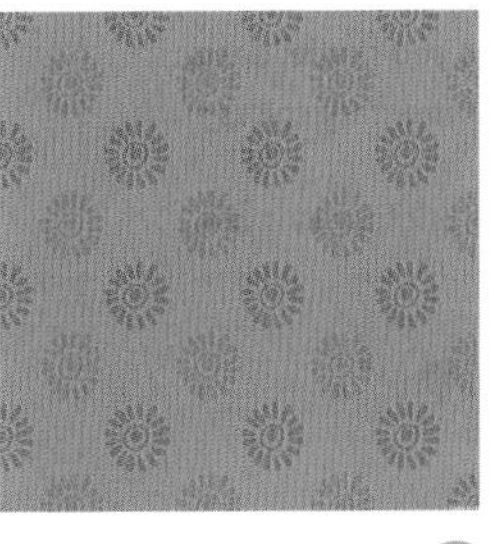

2 8 9 color 3

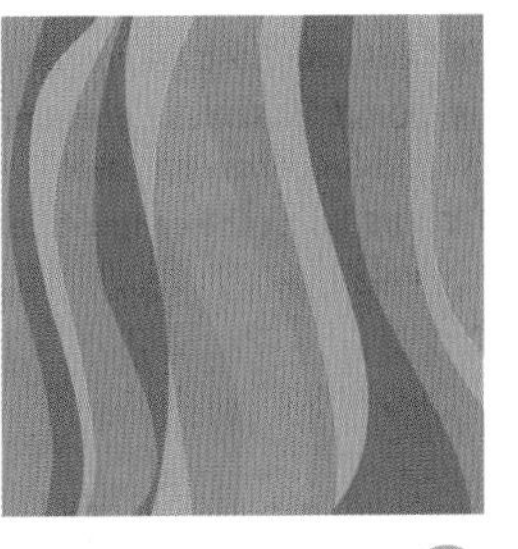

1 4 7 8 color 4

Illustration

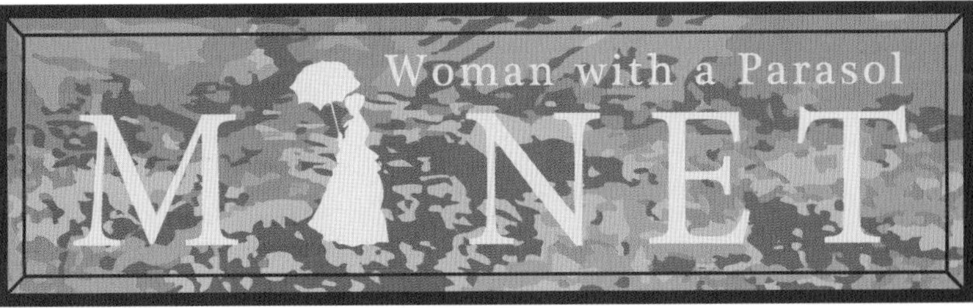

1 3 4 5 6 8 color 6

Recipe
109

Girl with a Pearl Earring

In Vermeer's work, every single color appears to stand out conspicuously. The blue of the turban wrapped around the girl's head is painted using lapis lazuli pigment, which at the time was more costly than pure gold. As the girl appears to be smiling, the painting is also referred to as the Mona Lisa of the Netherlands or the Northern Mona Lisa.

- **FEELING** Effective contrasts, light and shade, deep.
- **COMBINATIONS** Combine complementary colors such as yellow and blue.
- **TIPS** Boost the contrast between brightness levels and hues.

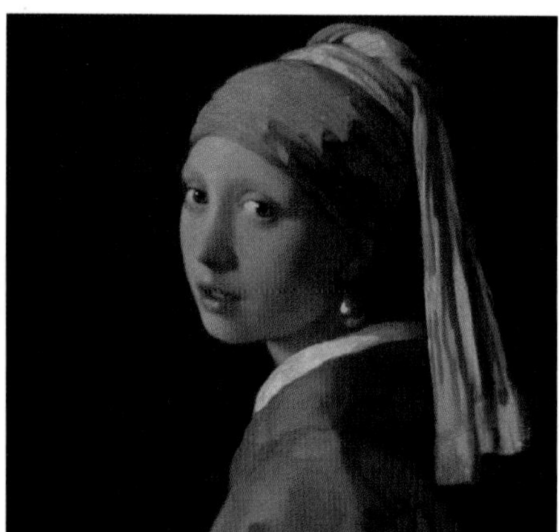

Vermeer's *Girl with a Pearl Earring*. ©Mauritshuis, The Hague

❶ Vermeer Blue
This blue is often used in Vermeer's works.

❷ Deep Yellow
A yellow with depth as if black has been mixed into it.

❸ Midnight Sky
A deep black like that of a moonless sky at midnight.

❹ Rose Cheek
The translucently healthy rose-like hue of cheeks.

❺ Straw
The color of straw.

❻ Lapis Blue
The light blue of finely powdered lapis lazuli.

❼ Dusty Brown
A brown that calls to mind a dusty storeroom.

❽ Fragment of the Sky
A color suggesting a "fragment of the sky," another name for lapis lazuli.

⑨ Cotton Shirt
A simple white like that of a cotton shirt.

1 C75 M53 Y20 K0 R76 G112 B159 #4C6F9E

2 C7 M30 Y75 K15 R214 G170 B70 #D5A945

3 C20 M20 Y20 K93 R42 G33 B32 #29211F

4 C0 M15 Y17 K7 R241 G218 B202 #F1D9C9

5 C10 M7 Y60 K27 R192 G185 B101 #BFB865

6 C35 M10 Y8 K20 R152 G180 B196 #97B3C3

7 C35 M30 Y70 K65 R87 G82 B39 #575127

8 C45 M15 Y0 K77 R50 G70 B88 #324658

9 C2 M2 Y7 K0 R252 G250 B242 #FBFAF1

Two-color combinations

Color
2 1

Color
4 3

Color
8 6

4 1

1 5

2 7

2 3

7 9

8 4

Three-color combinations

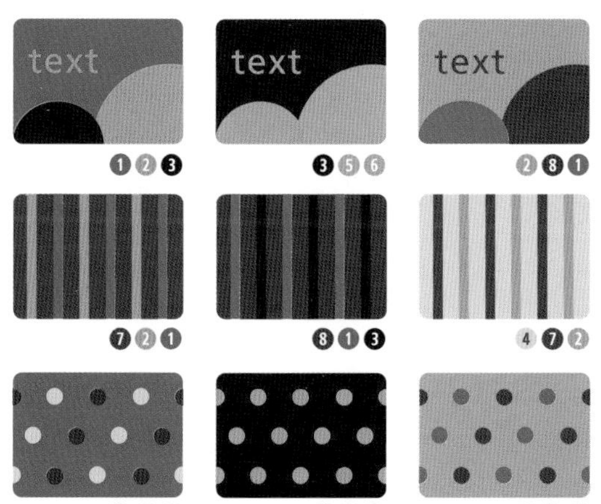

1 2 3

3 5 6

2 8 1

7 2 1

8 1 3

4 7 2

1 4 8

3 6 2

6 1 7

Designs

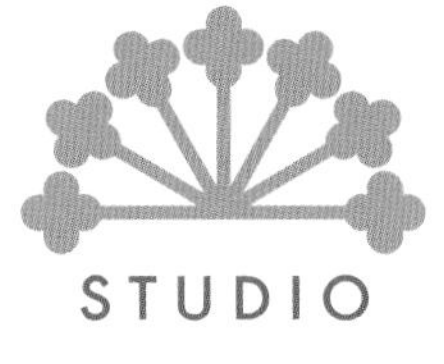

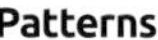

1 2 color 2

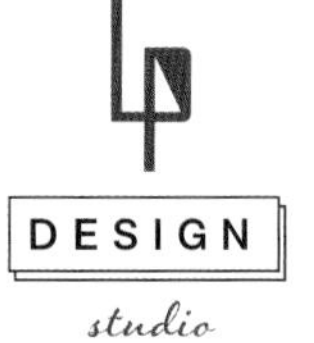

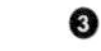

3 7 color 2

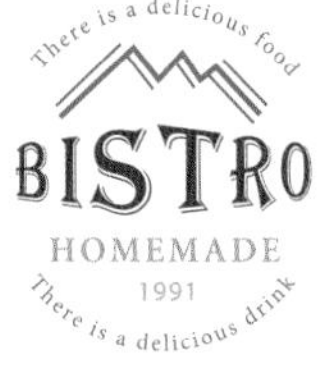

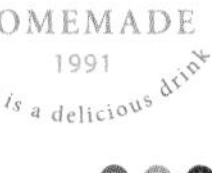

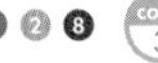

1 2 8 color 3

Patterns

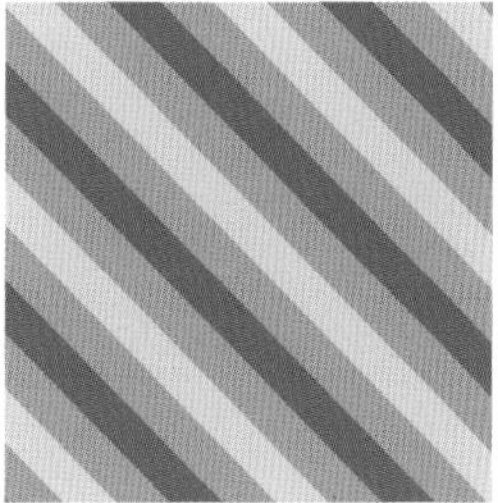

1 2 4 color 3

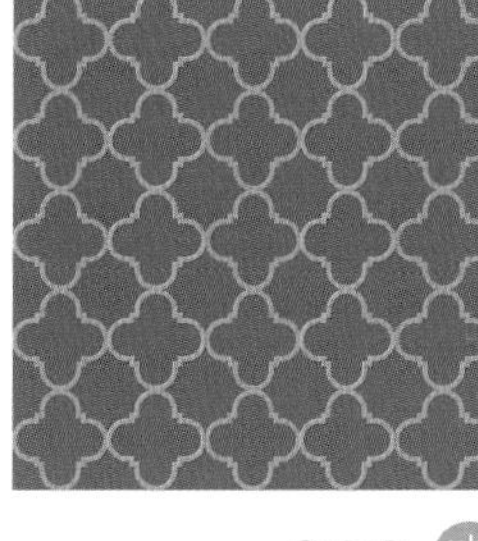

1 5 6 color 3

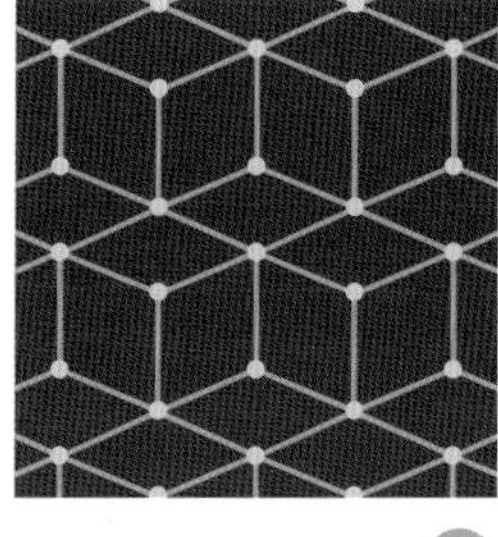

4 5 8 color 3

Illustration

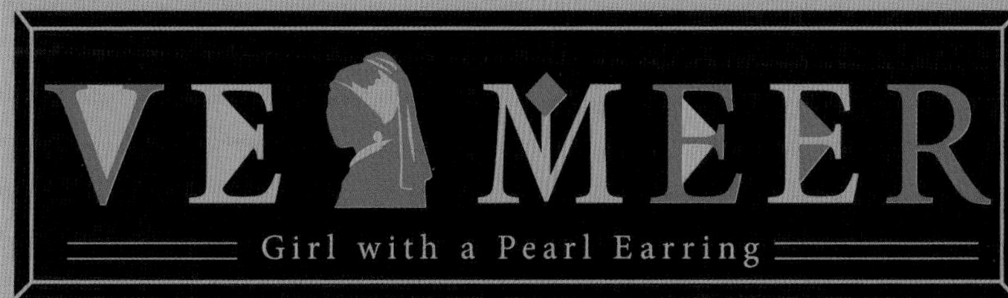

1 2 3 5 6 color 5

Recipe
110

The Dance Lesson

Degas has left us with many works where ballet is the main theme, in particular scenes of day-to-day rehearsals and backstage antics. Born to a wealthy family, Degas was a regular at the opera and was able to freely enter dressing rooms and rehearsal halls. This palette has been developed by carefully drawing on the colors used in his paintings, with Colors 7 and 8 as gentle accents.

- **FEELING** Calm, tranquil, Parisian.
- **COMBINATIONS** Add pinks and reds to gray beige.
- **TIPS** Aim for a grayish, elegant finish.

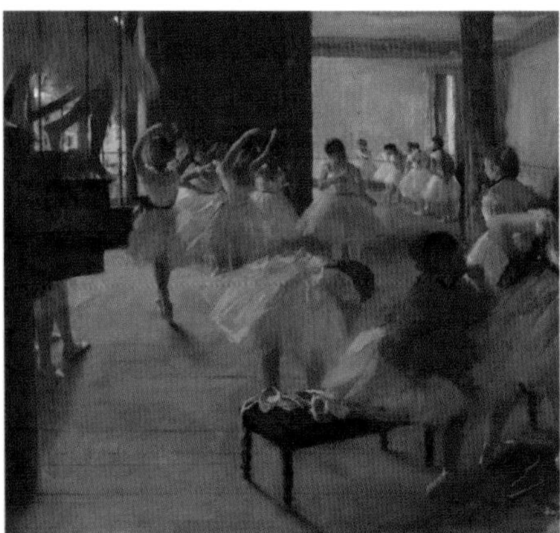

Degas's *The Dance Lesson.*

1 Cendre
This word means "ash," the color of cinders.

2 Gris Perle
Perle is French for "pearl." This is a pearl gray.

3 Taupe
Taupe means "mole" in French.

4 Sable
The equivalent of sand, a common shade of brown.

5 Blanc de Roi
The white of the king. In portraits Louis the 14th is wearing white fur.

6 Ardoise
The gray of slate, roofing tiles or a stone slab.

7 Framboise
The red purple of ripe raspberries.

8 Rose de Malmaison
The roses that bloomed at the chateau of Napoleon and Josephine.

9 Petrole
The blue of petroleum or oil, this color name is unique to France.

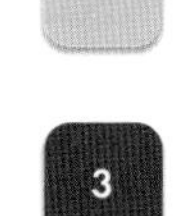

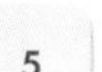

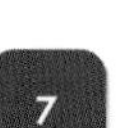

No.	CMYK	RGB	Hex
1	C25 M20 Y40 K15	R182 G177 B145	#B5B190
2	C12 M0 Y5 K20	R199 G211 B212	#C7D3D4
3	C10 M35 Y35 K75	R92 G68 B58	#5C4339
4	C25 M30 Y60 K5	R196 G173 B111	#C4AC6E
5	C12 M0 Y3 K0	R230 G244 B249	#E6F4F8
6	C15 M10 Y25 K75	R88 G87 B76	#58574C
7	C25 M85 Y70 K20	R168 G59 B58	#A83A39
8	C0 M55 Y45 K10	R225 G135 B115	#E18672
9	C85 M40 Y55 K55	R0 G71 B70	#004745

Two-color combinations

Color — 1 5

Color — 2 3

Color — 4 6

7 4

1 9

5 3

6 9

1 5

2 8

Three-color combinations

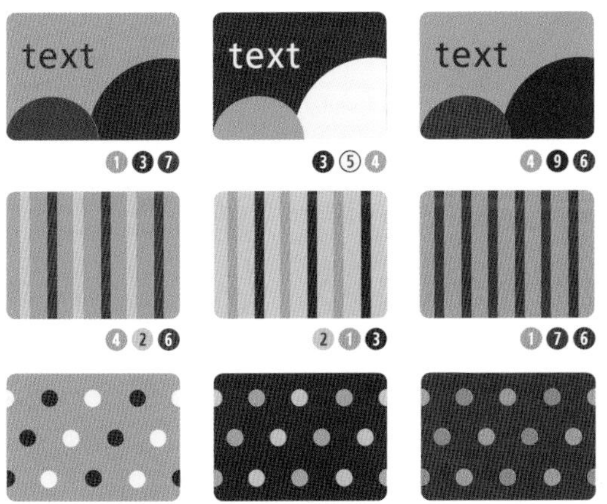

1 3 7 | 3 5 4 | 4 9 6

4 2 6 | 2 1 3 | 1 7 6

1 3 5 | 3 4 2 | 6 8 1

Designs

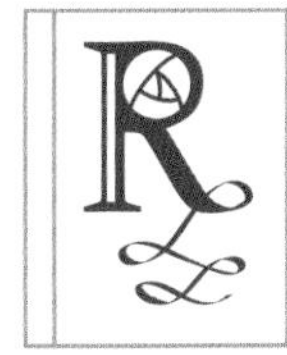

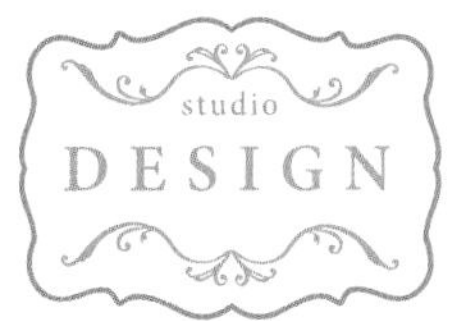

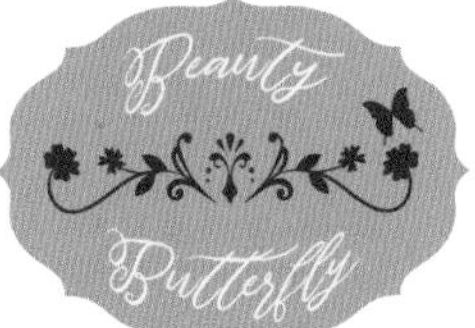

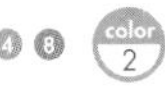

1 7 — color 2 | 4 8 — color 2 | 1 5 9 — color 3

Patterns

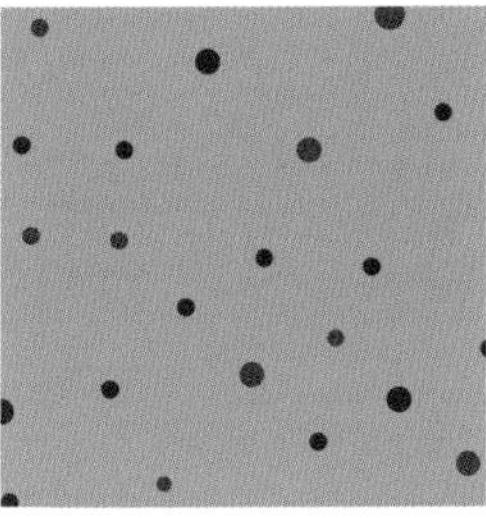

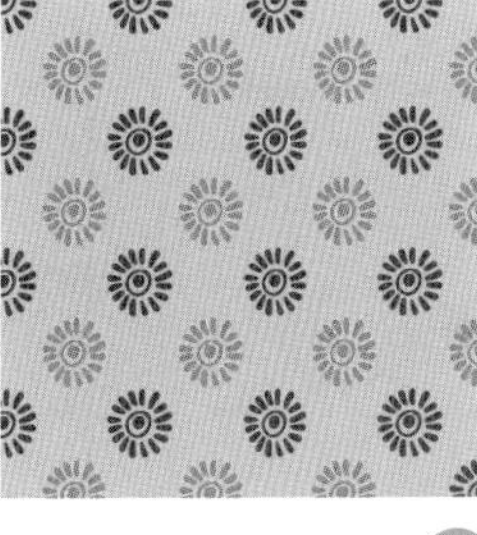

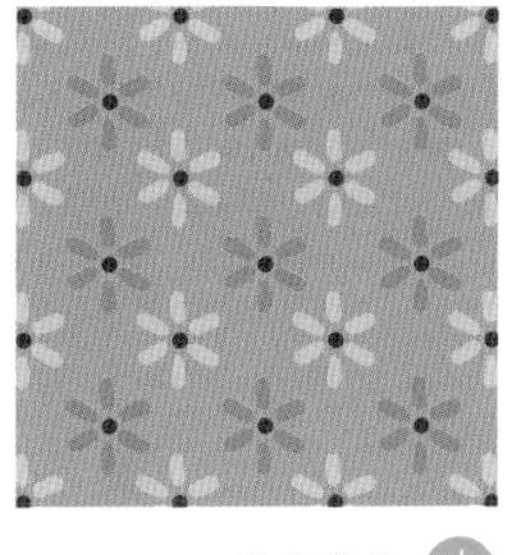

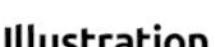

4 7 9 — color 3 | 2 6 8 — color 3 | 1 2 3 8 — color 4

Illustration

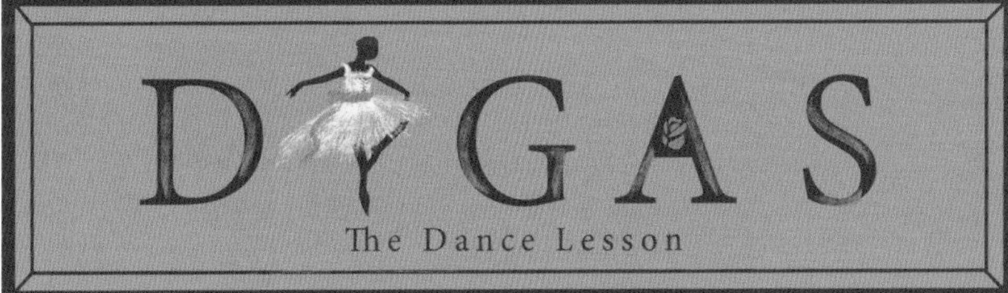

1 2 4 5 7 8 — color 6

Recipe
111

Night Watch

Along with Vermeer, Rembrandt is a Dutch painter representative of the Baroque period. Using the chiaroscuro technique, he dramatically expressed light and shadow, becoming known as "the magician of light and shadow" or "the master of shading." The bright sections of the picture stand out as if lit by a spotlight, while the dark sections create a sense of depth.

- **FEELING** Dignified, calm, serene.
- **COMBINATIONS** Use solemn colors with low levels of brightness across large surface areas.
- **TIPS** Use light colors as accents.

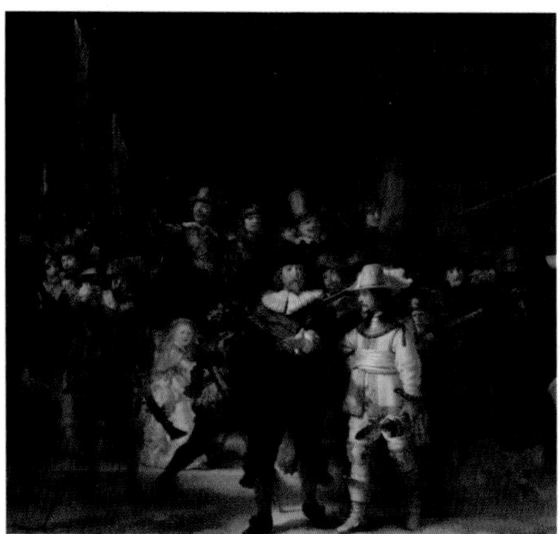

Rembrandt's *The Night Watch.*

❶ Baroque Art
In Baroque art of the 17th century, shadow played a key role.

❷ Velvet
A deep, lustrous red like that of velvet.

③ Silk
A color like silk fabric with an elegant gloss.

❹ Moderate Gold
A gold with a dull burnished hue to it.

❺ Brunette
An extremely common hair color among Europeans.

❻ Burgundy
The deep red of the red wine of the Bourgogne region.

❼ Smoke Gray
The gray of smoke produced from burning something.

❽ Blue Black
Black with the merest hint of blue.

❾ Dove Gray
The color of dove's wings, similar to dove-wing gray.

1 C10 M30 Y40 K98
R34 G13 B1
#220C00

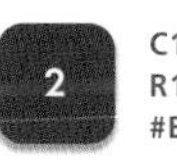

2 C10 M85 Y80 K25
R181 G57 B40
#B53827

3 C2 M5 Y20 K5
R244 G236 B208
#F4ECD0

4 C0 M15 Y55 K35
R189 G166 B99
#BDA662

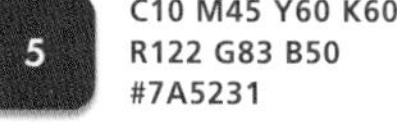

5 C10 M45 Y60 K60
R122 G83 B50
#7A5231

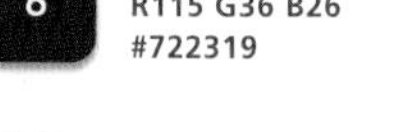

6 C15 M80 Y70 K60
R115 G36 B26
#722319

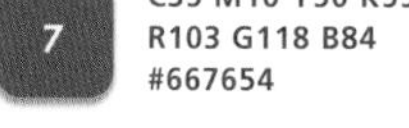

7 C35 M10 Y50 K55
R103 G118 B84
#667654

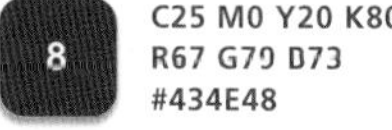

8 C25 M0 Y20 K80
R67 G79 B73
#434E48

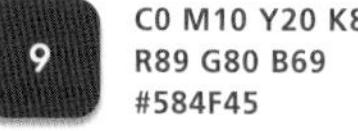

9 C0 M10 Y20 K80
R89 G80 B69
#584F45

Two-color combinations

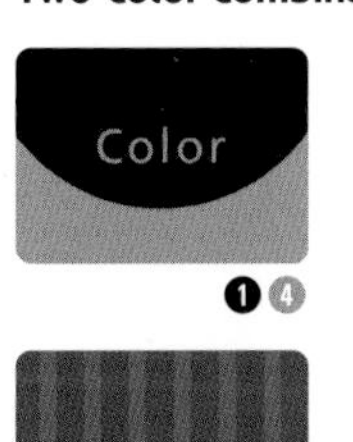

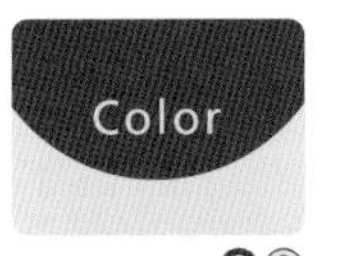

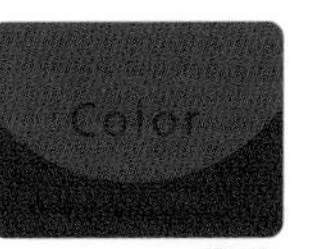
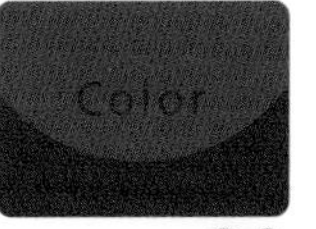

1 4 | 8 3 | 2 6

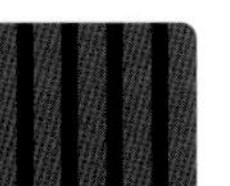
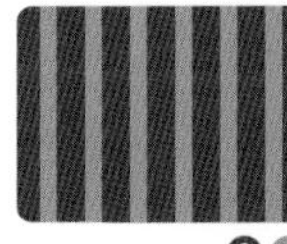

5 7 | 9 1 | 8 4

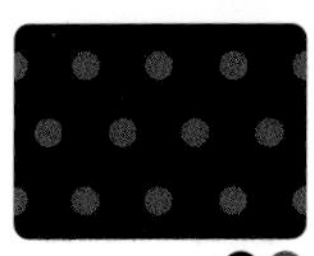
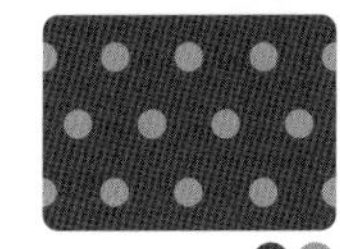

6 1 | 1 5 | 9 4

Three-color combinations

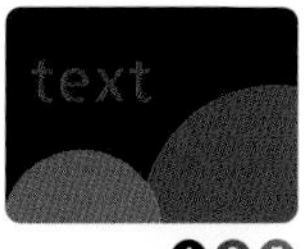

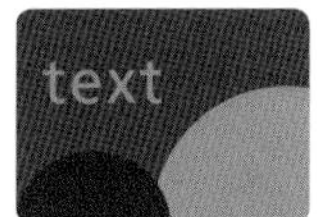

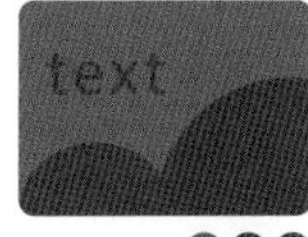

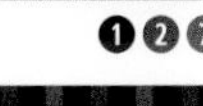

1 2 7 | 9 4 6 | 7 8 9

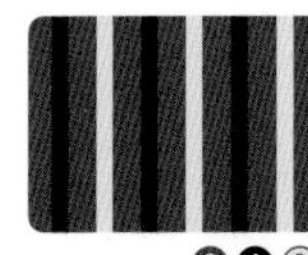

1 2 6 | 8 1 3 | 6 7 2

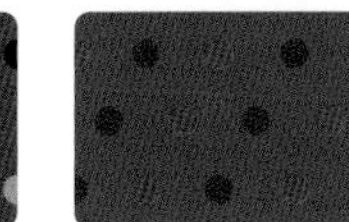
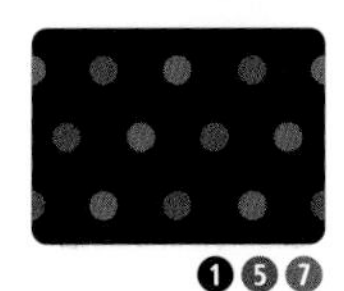

9 4 1 | 2 6 9 | 1 5 7

Designs

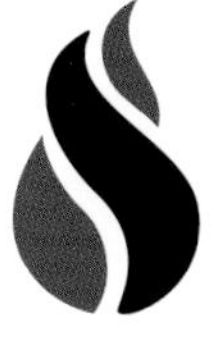

1 5 color 2

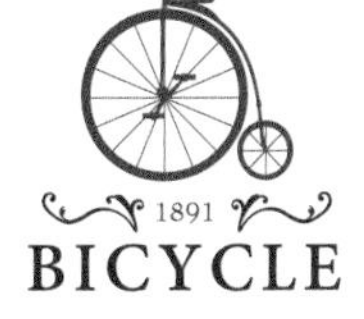

2 6 color 2

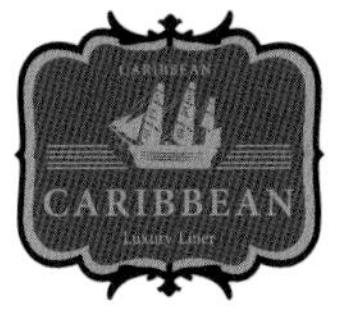

1 4 8 color 3

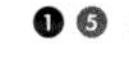

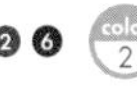
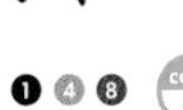
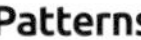

Patterns

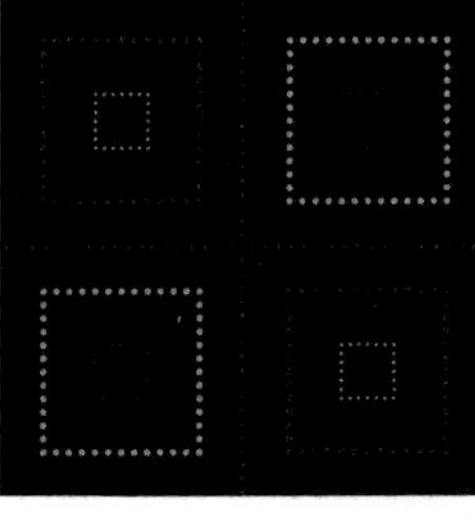

1 4 6 color 3

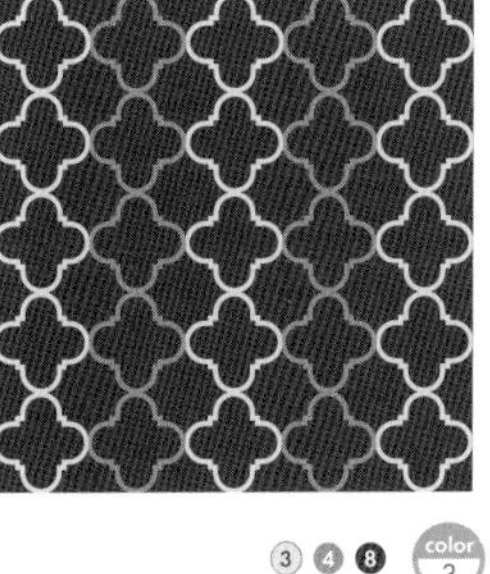

3 4 8 color 3

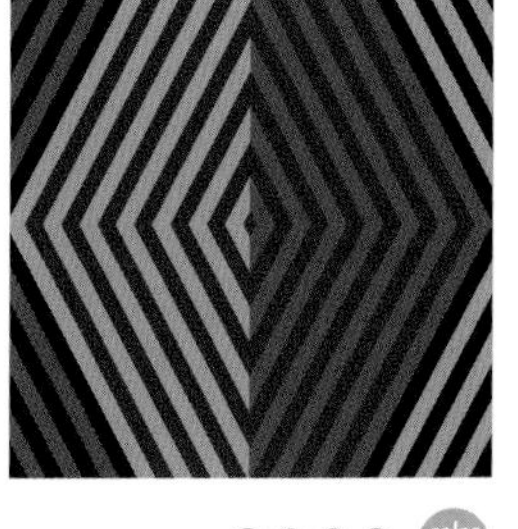

1 4 5 6 color 4

Illustration

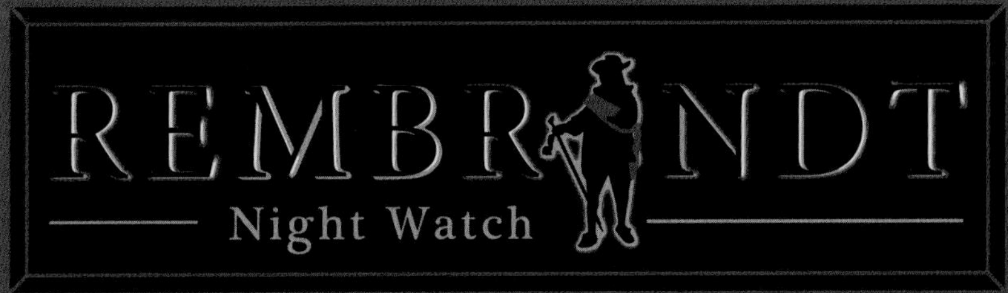

1 2 3 4 8 color 5

Part

13

Rainbow Palettes

In this chapter, we head to the end of the rainbow, and beyond. The exclusively red color scheme has a powerful, positive air, while blue evokes calm and a sense of trust. Green suggests serenity. What are some of the other associations? Let's look!

Color Schemes Grouped by Color

Recipe
112

Red

This color has traditionally been seen as a sacred color and has also been used to ward off evil. At Kyoto's Fushimi Inari-taisha Shrine, 1,000 torii gateways form a spectacular sight, but the red used in that instance signifies abundance. There are many Japanese characters that mean "red," indicating the significant role it plays both culturally and socially.

- **FEELING** Active, passionate, powerful, exciting.
- **COMBINATIONS** Fire, blood, the sun, apples, tomatoes, roses, torii gateways.
- **TIPS** Use a dash of red on areas you want to make stand out.

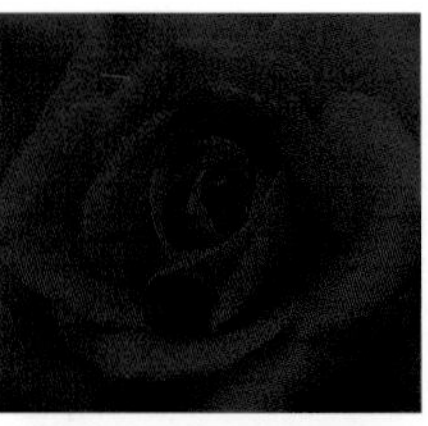
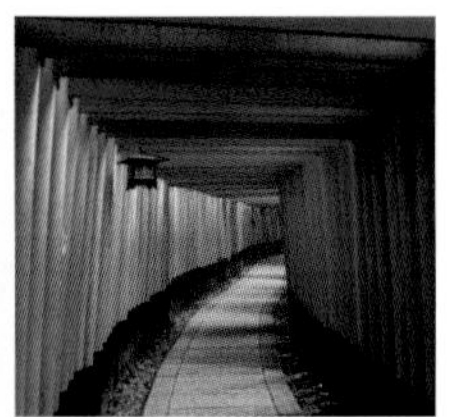
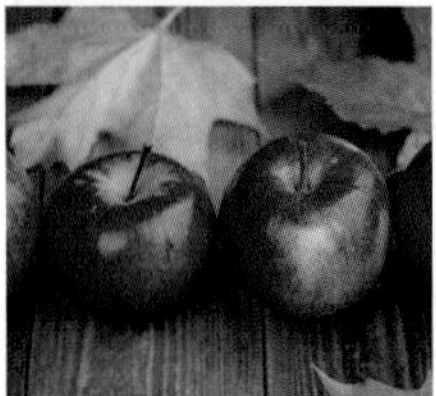
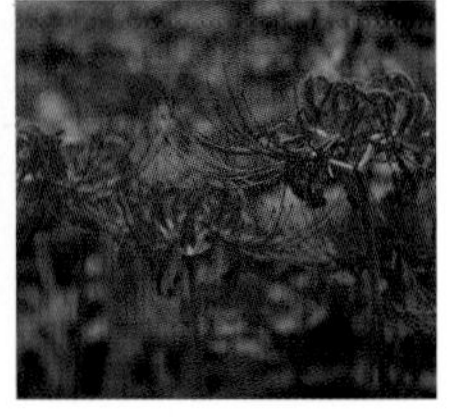

Red is a color that constantly stands out and attracts attention.

❶ Crimson
A color created with the pigment of the saffron flower.

❷ Korean Red
An imported red, a neighboring nation's take on the color

❸ Madder
A color created with the pigment made from the roots of the madder.

❹ Vermilion
A color with mercury sulphide as its main component.

❺ Cochineal Red
A color created from the insects that feed on cactuses in Latin America.

❻ Rose
A color like that of a red rose. In Japanese it's *bara-iro* (rose color).

❼ Wine Red
A deep, reddish purple color like that of red wine.

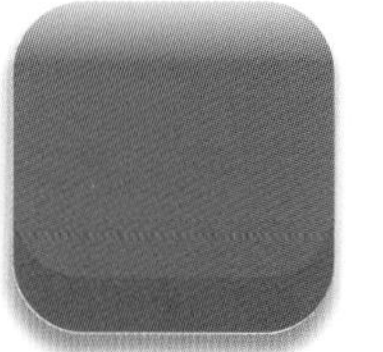

❽ Tomato Red
A red that is slightly closer to yellow than that of an actual tomato.

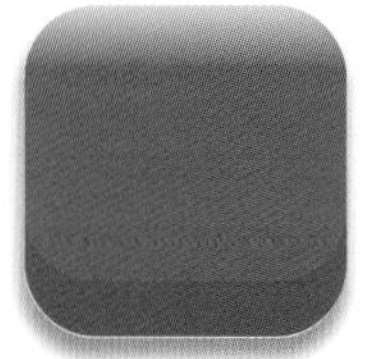

❾ Poppy Red
The color of the peel of the *daidai* fruit (in the citrus family).

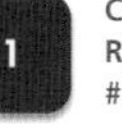
1 C0 M100 Y65 K10
R215 G0 B58
#D7003A

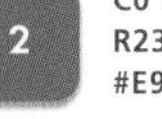
2 C0 M80 Y45 K0
R233 G84 B100
#E95464

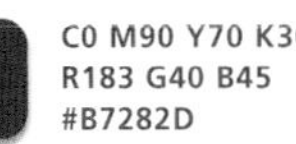
3 C0 M90 Y70 K30
R183 G40 B45
#B7282D

4 C0 M85 Y100 K0
R233 G71 B9
#E94709

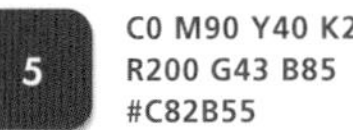
5 C0 M90 Y40 K20
R200 G43 B85
#C82B55

6 C0 M87 Y45 K0
R232 G63 B95
#E83F5F

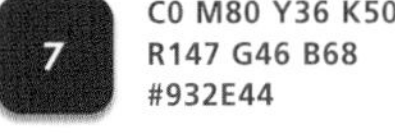
7 C0 M80 Y36 K50
R147 G46 B68
#932E44

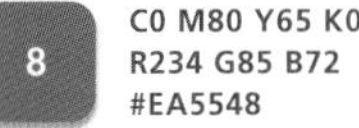
8 C0 M80 Y65 K0
R234 G85 B72
#EA5548

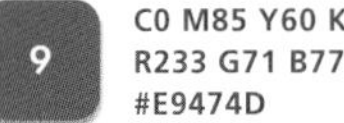
9 C0 M85 Y60 K0
R233 G71 B77
#E9474D

Two-color combinations

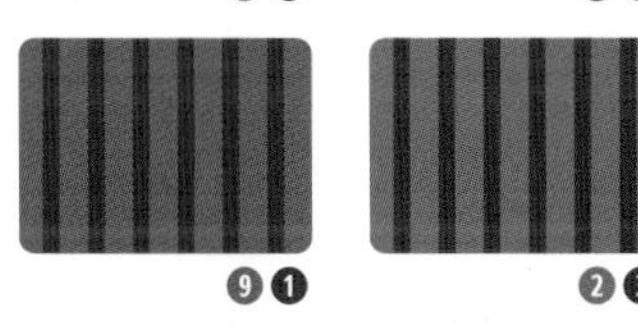

1 2 | 4 7 | 5 6

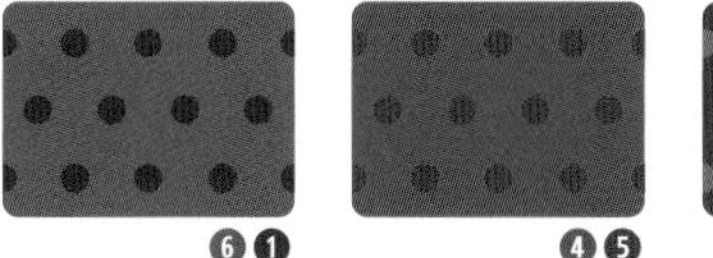

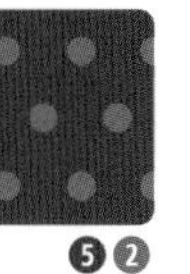

7 8 | 9 1 | 2 3

6 1 | 4 5 | 5 2

Three-color combinations

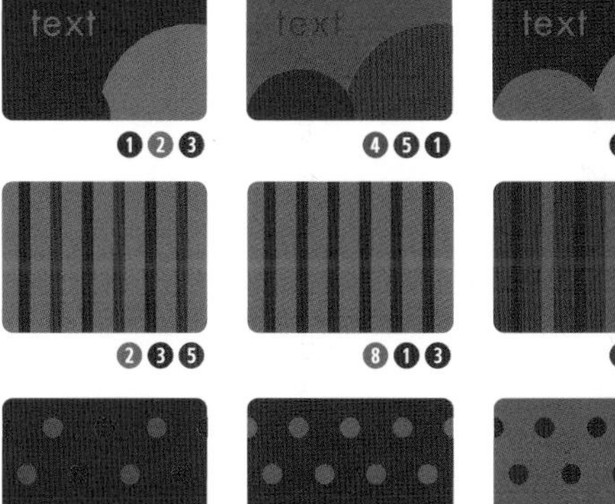

1 2 3 | 4 5 1 | 7 8 9

2 3 5 | 8 1 3 | 5 7 9

1 4 7 | 3 6 9 | 6 1 7

Designs

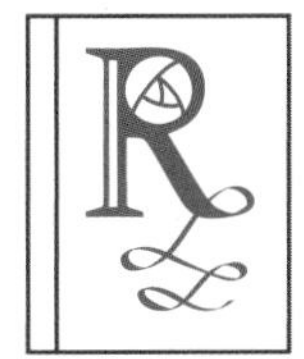

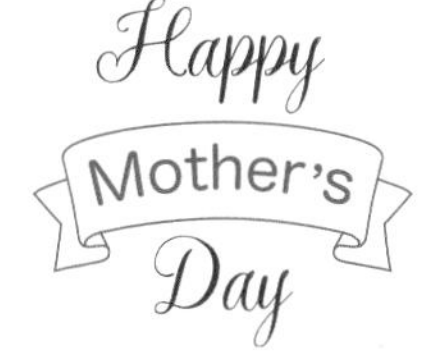

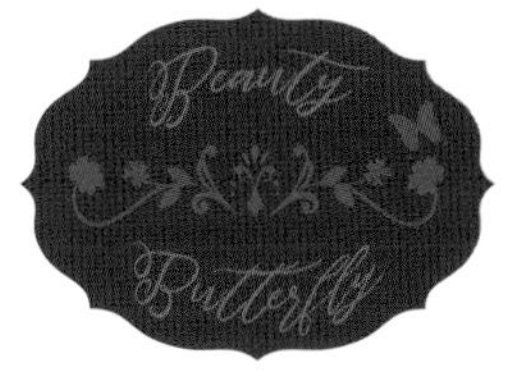

6 7 color 2 | 1 9 color 2 | 2 3 4 color 3

Patterns

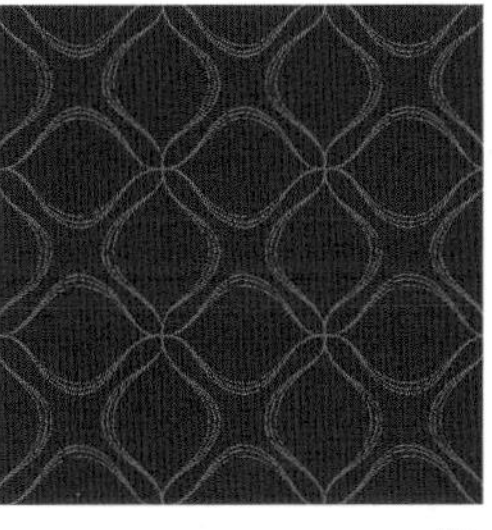

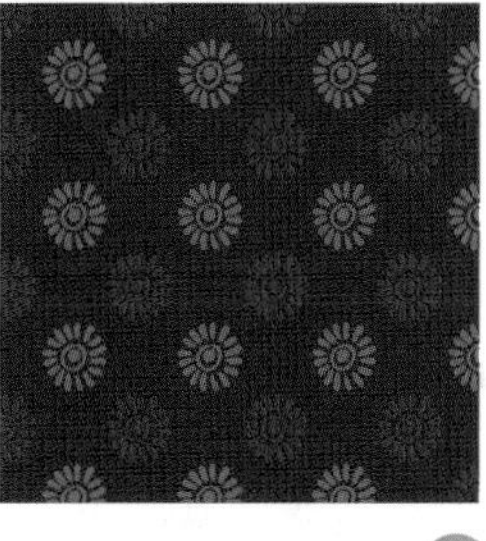

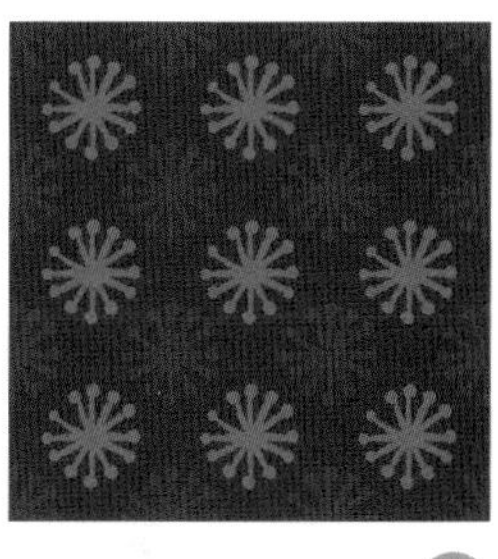

1 2 color 2 | 2 5 7 color 3 | 2 3 5 color 3

Illustration

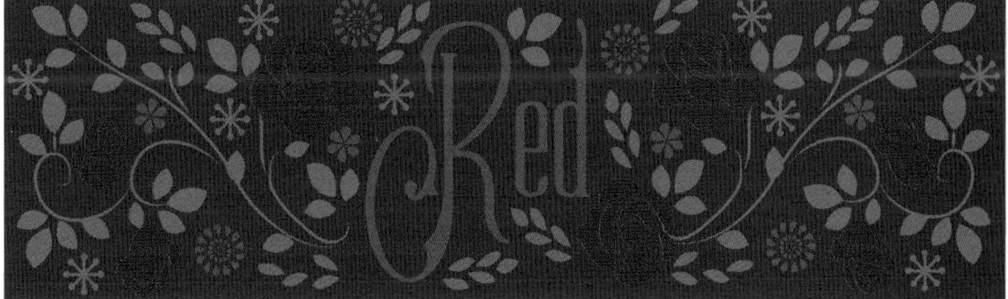

1 2 4 7 8 color 5

Recipe
113

Orange

Orange is a "tasty color" that stimulates the appetite. It has a healthy, fun air. Historically, it was an undefined color as it falls between the intensely individualistic colors of red and yellow, with orange sometimes judged to be a red and sometimes a yellow. This color's Japanese name of *daidai* (a bitter orange) is borrowed from fruit.

- **FEELING** Sprightly, serene, full of vitality, casual.
- **COMBINATIONS** Mandarins, carrots, pumpkins, sunsets.
- **TIPS** Orange can create a casual, warm air.

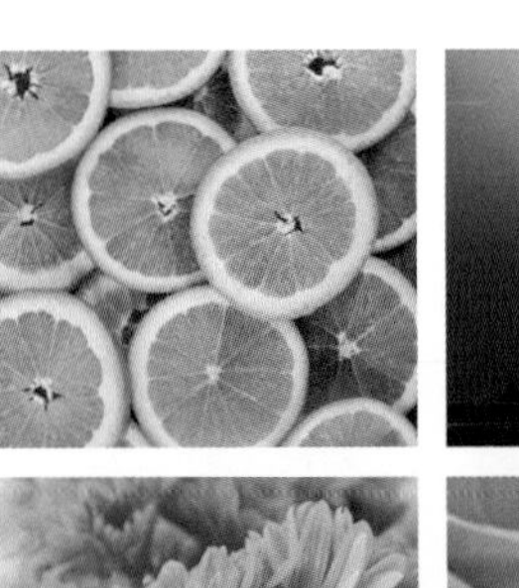

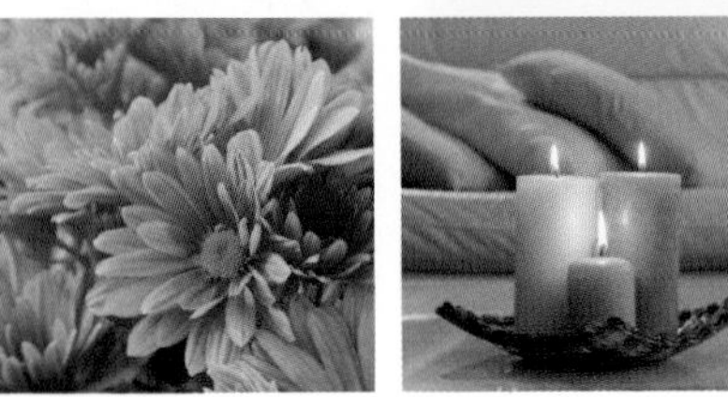

Orange is a warm, social color that makes people feel energetic.

❶ **Daidai**
The color of the peel of the *daidai* fruit (in the citrus family).

❷ **Persimmon**
The color of the fruit or the reddish brown of persimmon tannin.

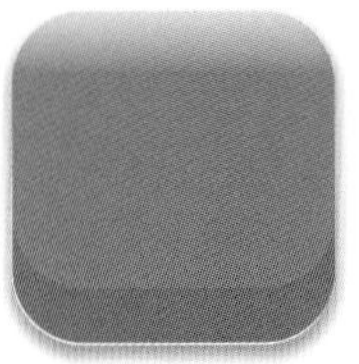

❸ **Ouni**
Safflower and gardenia dyes used for robes worn by the Crown Prince.

❹ **Kouji**
A color like that of the kouji citrus fruit.

❺ **Apricot**
A color like that of ripe apricots.

❻ **Mandarin Orange**
The color of mandarin, orange suffused with yellow tones.

❼ **Marigold**
The color of marigold flowers, originally from Mexico.

❽ **Peach**
A color like that of peach flesh but also suggesting the blossoms.

❾ **Carrot Orange**
A traditional deep orange like that of carrots.

1	C0 M60 Y100 K0 R240 G131 B0 #F08300
2	C0 M70 Y75 K0 R237 G109 B61 #ED6D3D
3	C0 M65 Y70 K0 R238 G121 B72 #EE7948
4	C0 M40 Y75 K0 R246 G173 B72 #F6AD48
5	C0 M35 Y55 K0 R247 G185 B119 #F7B977
6	C0 M40 Y90 K5 R239 G167 B24 #EFA718
7	C0 M50 Y95 K0 R243 G152 B0 #F39800
8	C0 M20 Y30 K0 R251 G216 B181 #FBD8B5
9	C0 M67 Y80 K10 R223 G108 B49 #DF6C31

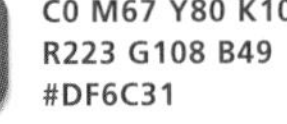

Two-color combinations

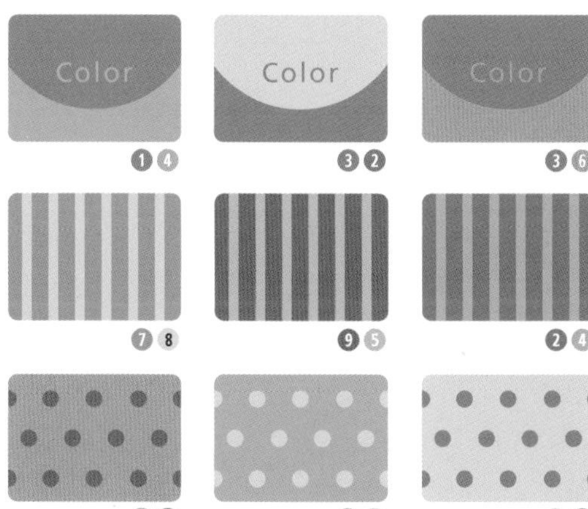

Three-color combinations

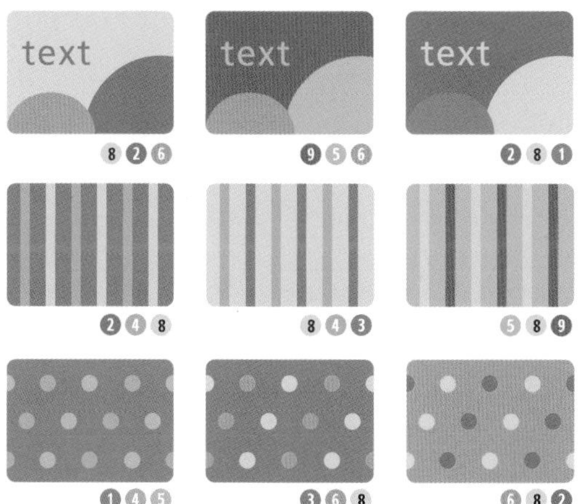

Designs

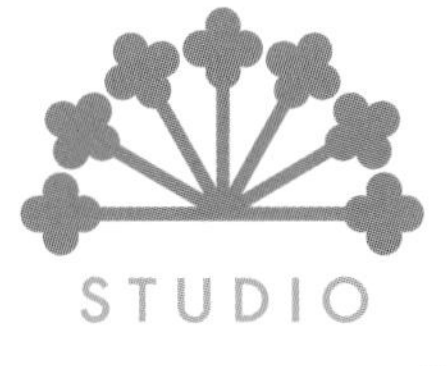

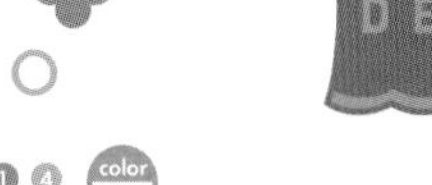

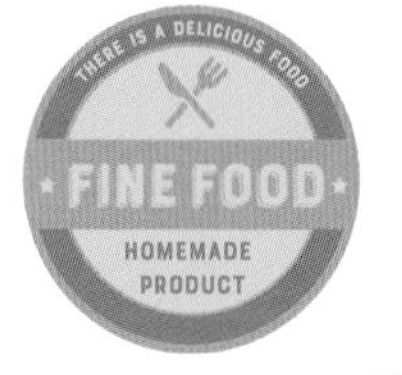

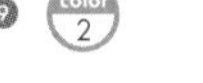

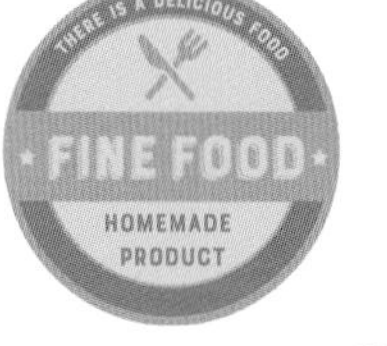

Patterns

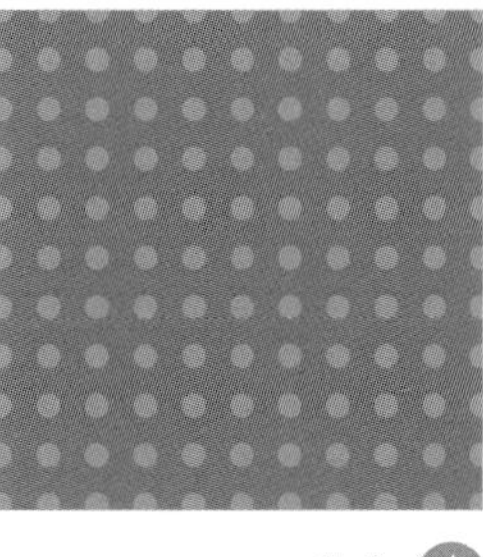

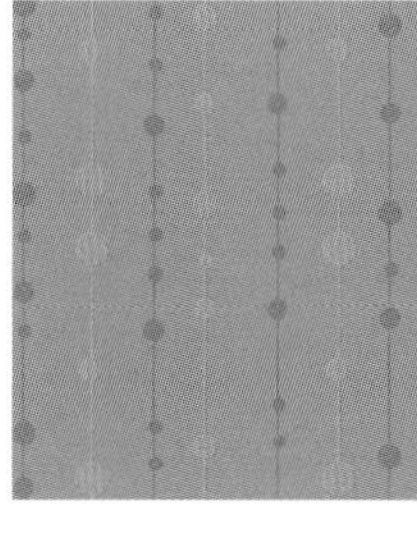

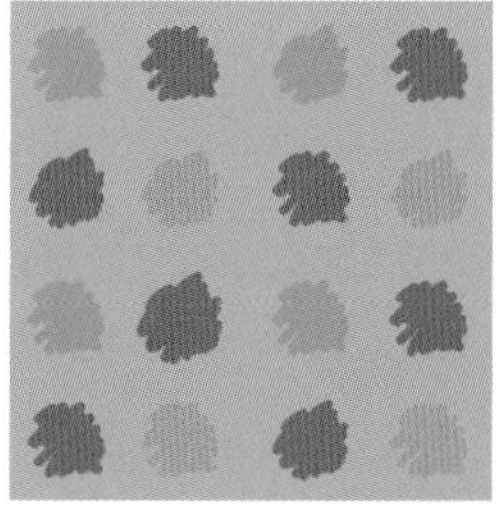

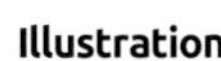

Illustration

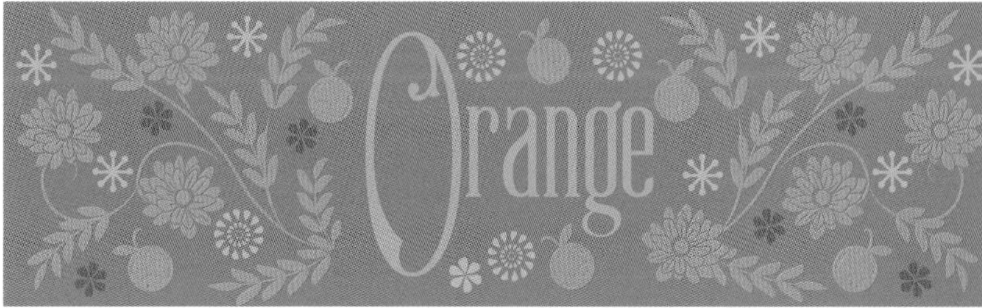

Recipe

114

Yellow

Viewed as a single color, red stands out the most, but when combined with black, yellow is more attention grabbing. Yellow and black is also a color scheme for alerts or warnings. In Japan, many people associate the moon with yellow and the sun with red, but in most countries, yellow symbolizes the sun.

- **FEELING Bright, positive, lighthearted, happy, not yet mature.**
- **COMBINATIONS Bananas, lemons, rapeseed flowers, sunflowers, light.**
- **TIPS This color has a childlike innocence to it.**

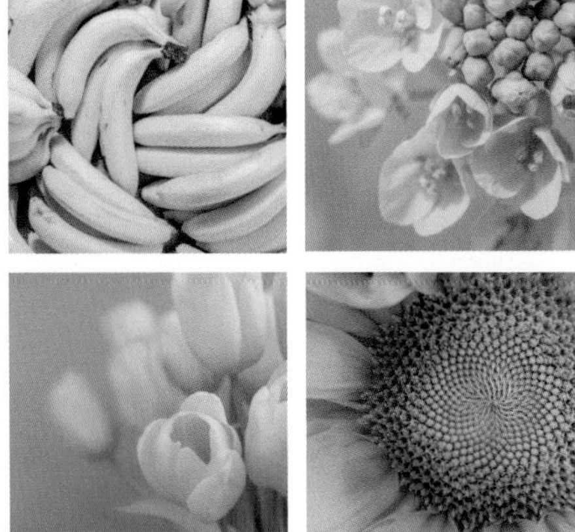

Yellow is the brightest of all colors and symbolizes light.

1 Dandelion

A vibrant yellow like that of a dandelion flower.

2 Sunflower

The color of sunflowers, a hint of orange suffuses this hue.

3 Kariyasu

A color created with the dye from *kariyasu*, a tall grass.

4 Mustard

The color of mustard made by crushing the seeds into a powder.

5 Japanese Globeflower

A color like that of Japanese globeflowers, which bloom in the spring.

6 Lemon Yellow

A vibrant yellow like that of the skin of ripe lemons.

7 Cream Yellow

A soft color like that of custard cream.

8 Jaune Brillant

In French, this color signifies a yellow that seems to sparkle.

9 Canary

A light yellow like that of a canary's feathers.

1 C0 M15 Y100 K0 R255 G217 B0 #FFD900

2 C0 M25 Y100 K0 R252 G200 B0 #FCC800

3 C0 M3 Y65 K8 R245 G229 B107 #F5E56B

4 C0 M14 Y70 K25 R210 G183 B78 #D2B74E

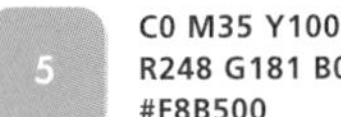

5 C0 M35 Y100 K0 R248 G181 B0 #F8B500

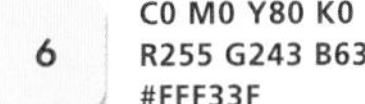

6 C0 M0 Y80 K0 R255 G243 B63 #FFF33F

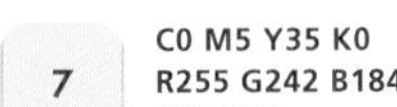

7 C0 M5 Y35 K0 R255 G242 B184 #FFF2B8

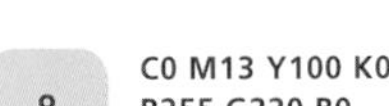

8 C0 M13 Y100 K0 R255 G220 B0 #FFDC00

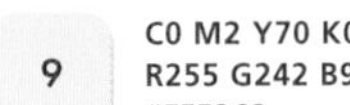

9 C0 M2 Y70 K0 R255 G242 B98 #FFF262

Two-color combinations

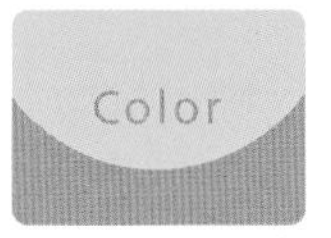

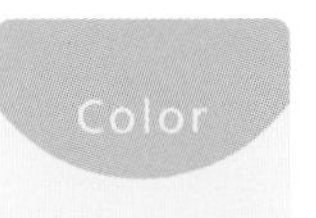

1 5 · 3 4 · 2 6

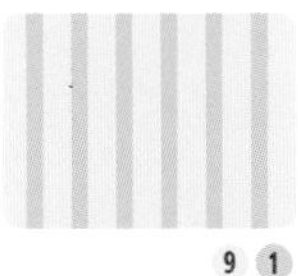

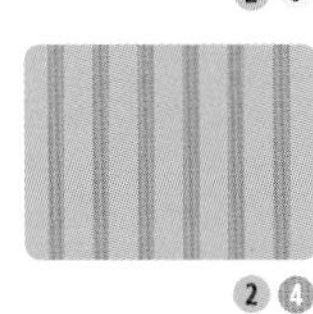

7 8 · 9 1 · 2 4

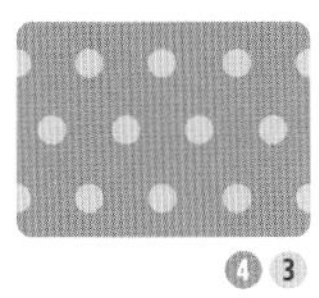

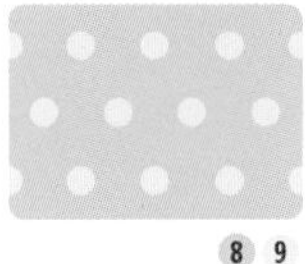

6 2 · 4 3 · 8 9

Three-color combinations

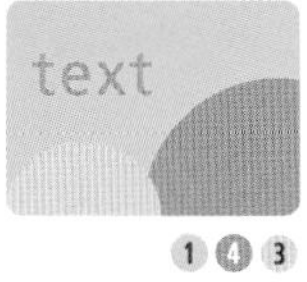

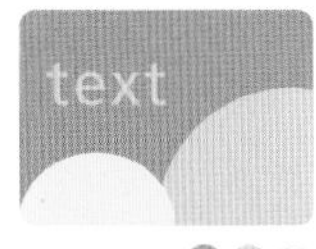

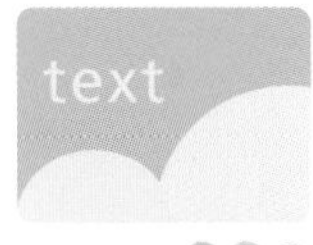

1 4 3 · 4 3 6 · 2 8 7

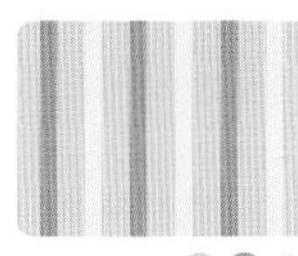

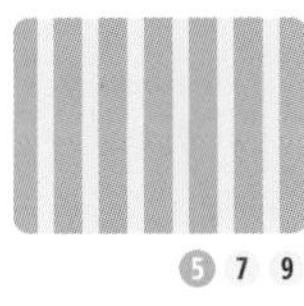

3 4 7 · 8 5 2 · 5 7 9

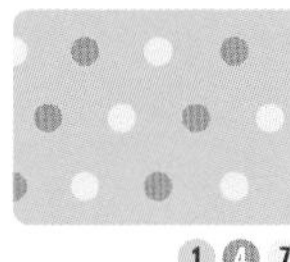

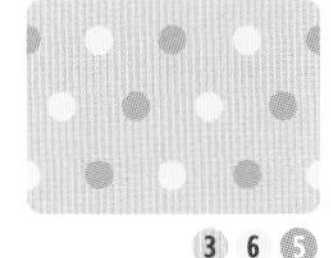

1 4 7 · 3 6 5 · 6 8 2

Designs

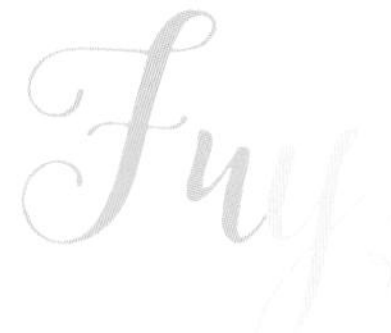

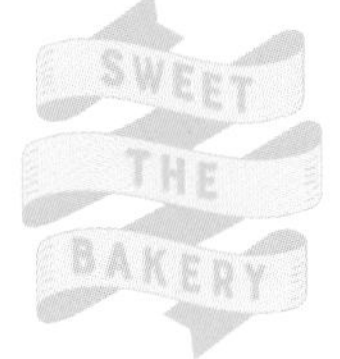

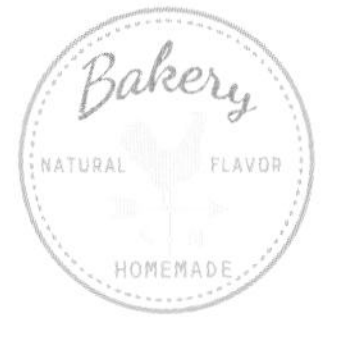

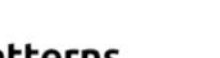

5 9 color 2 · 7 8 color 2 · 2 4 6 color 3

Patterns

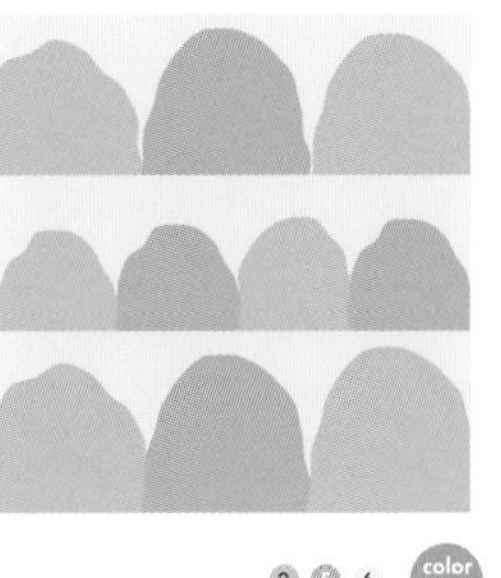

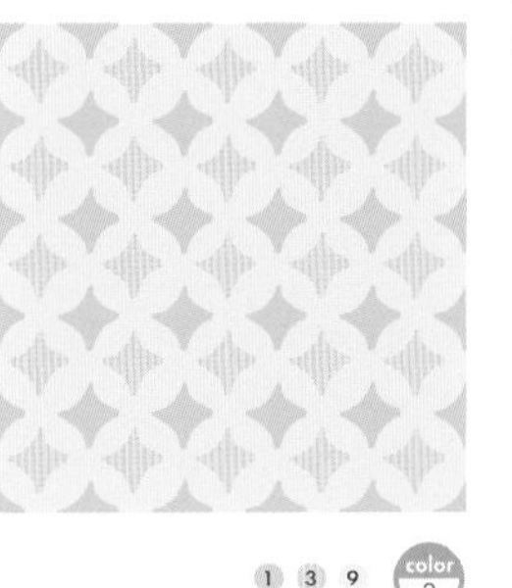

2 3 6 color 3 · 2 5 6 color 3 · 1 3 9 color 3

Illustration

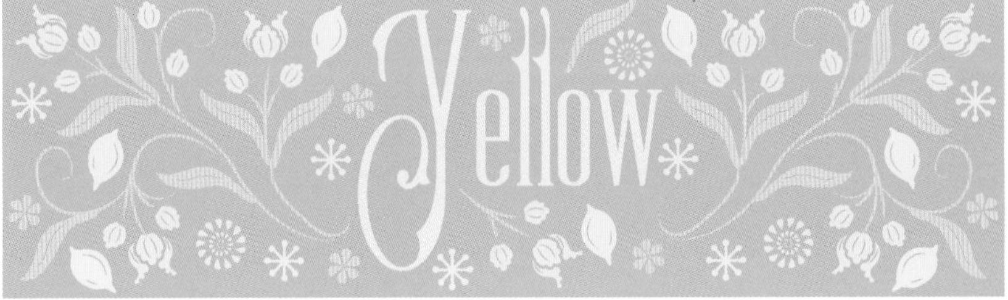

2 3 6 7 9 color 5

Recipe

115

Lime

Lime, or yellow green, is the color of spring, summoning the feeling that something new is about to begin. In the Heian era, among the nobility, it was a color worn by the young. The deep color created by mixing black into yellow green is called matcha. Yellow green is also a color that brings together the cheerfulness of yellow and the feeling of growth and stability suggested by green.

- **FEELING** New, innocent, fresh, having potential.
- **COMBINATIONS** Sprouts, new greenery, young leaves, moss, matcha.
- **TIPS** This color has a fresh, positive feel to it.

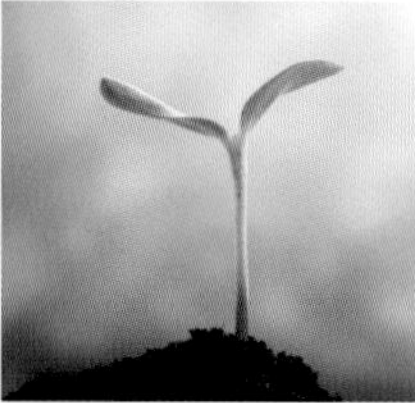

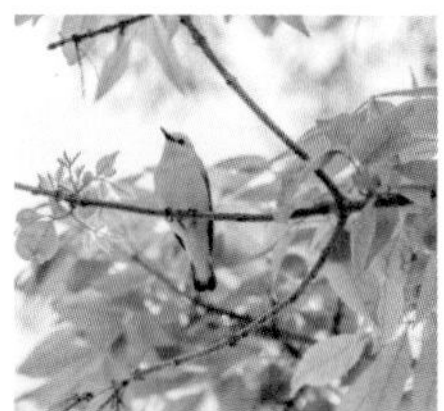

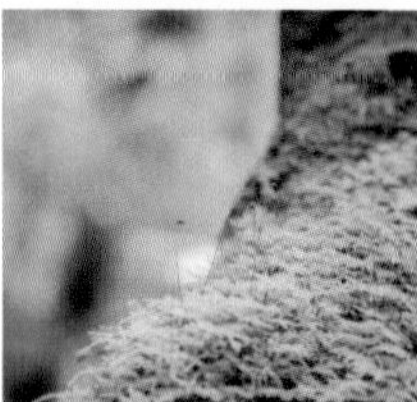

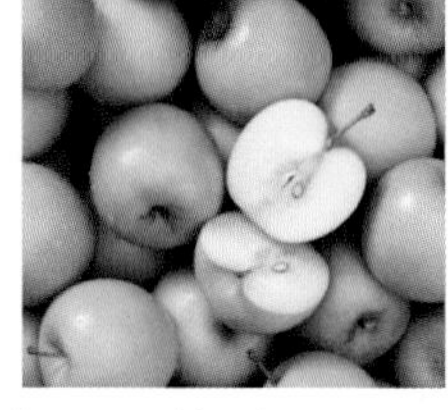

Yellow green evokes the sense of a new world and new beginnings.

1 Young Grass
A color like that of young grass shoots at the start of spring.

2 Matcha
Tea that's steamed and stone ground into powder.

3 Bud Green
The color of new shoots of grass and budding flowers and trees.

4 Greenfinch
A color calling to mind the feathers of a greenfinch.

5 Nightingale
A dull color like that of nightingale feathers.

6 Young Leaf
The color of leaves that have only just unfurled.

7 Leaf Green
This term indicates a wide range of yellow-green shades.

8 Apple Green
In Europe, green is seen as the typical color for apples.

9 Chartreuse Green
A color like the green of Chartreuse liqueur.

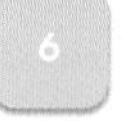

No.	CMYK	RGB	Hex
1	C28 M0 Y92 K0	R200 G217 B33	#C8D921
2	C10 M0 Y60 K25	R196 G196 B106	#C4C46A
3	C38 M0 Y84 K0	R175 G209 B71	#AFD147
4	C5 M0 Y80 K20	R215 G207 B58	#D7CF3A
5	C3 M0 Y70 K50	R157 G151 B59	#9D973B
6	C28 M0 Y52 K10	R197 G222 B147	#C5DE93
7	C40 M0 Y80 K12	R157 G192 B76	#9DC04C
8	C40 M0 Y55 K0	R167 G210 B141	#A7D28D
9	C20 M0 Y70 K0	R217 G227 B103	#D9E367

Two-color combinations

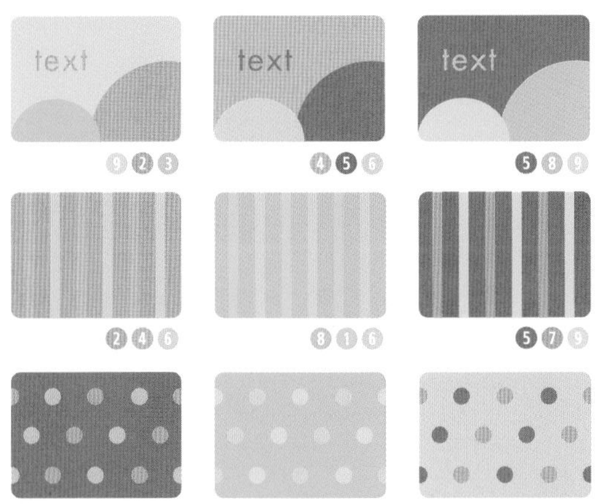

Three-color combinations

Designs

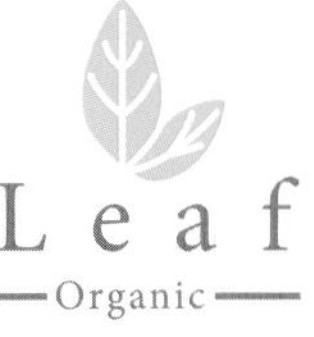

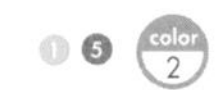

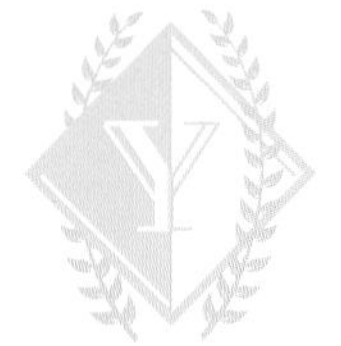

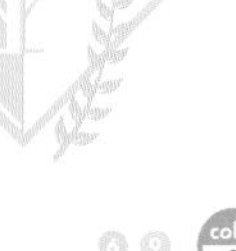

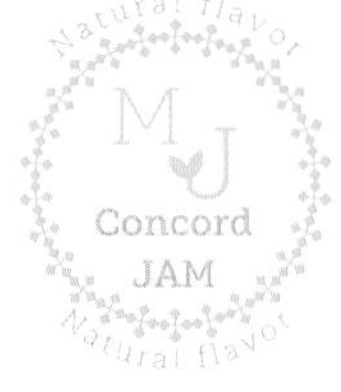

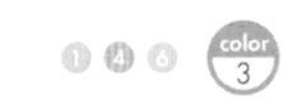

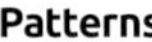

Patterns

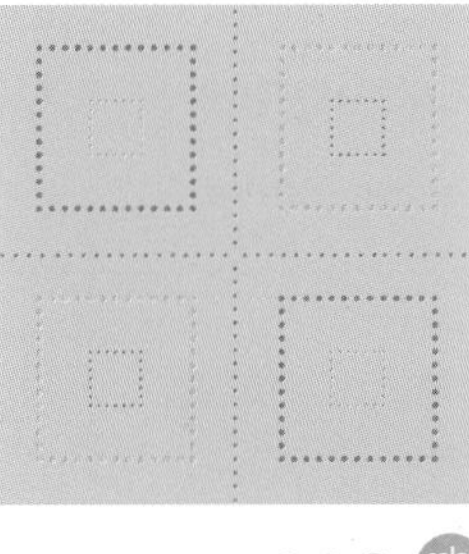

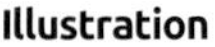

Illustration

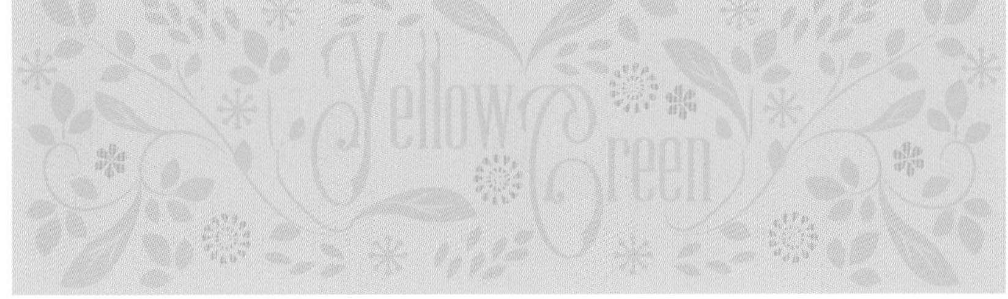

Recipe
116

Green

Green is a color that suggests nature, health and repose, much less fertility and the growth of the new. It's one of the three primary colors in light. The various colors seen on the screens of computers and smartphones are created by mixing red, green and blue. Who knew you'd be seeing green while texting or checking your email?

- **FEELING** Natural, harmonious, secure, healthy, restful, renewed.
- **COMBINATIONS** Forests, emeralds, green bamboo, vegetables.
- **TIPS** Green is neither warm nor cool, but rather an intermediate color.

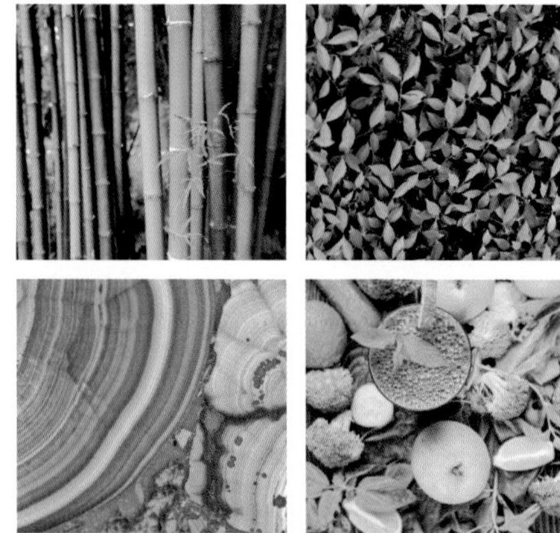

Green is a color that symbolizes growth, fecundity, the health and abundance of nature.

❶ Evergreen
The color of pine needles and boughs.

❷ Peacock Blue
The color of malachite, long used as a pigment.

❸ Deep Green
A deep hue highlighting the color's darker side.

❹ Young Bamboo
The color of new shoots of bamboo.

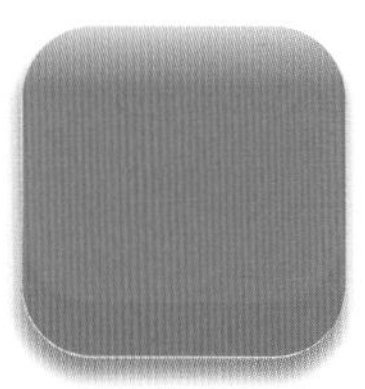

❺ Malachite Green
Malachite is also known as peacock stone.

❻ Emerald Green
A strong green like that of an emerald.

❼ Mint Green
A color like that of liqueur with peppermint oil as an ingredient.

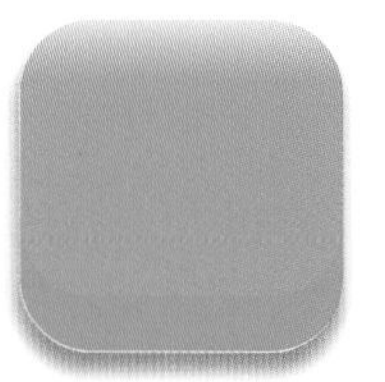

❽ Cobalt Green
A green pigment used in paints.

❾ Forest Green
The deep green of the woods.

1	C82 M0 Y80 K38 R0 G124 B69 #007C45
2	C57 M0 Y60 K40 R79 G138 B93 #4F8A5D
3	C95 M0 Y65 K60 R0 G88 B66 #005842
4	C60 M0 Y55 K0 R103 G190 B141 #67BE8D
5	C90 M0 Y85 K10 R0 G152 B84 #009854
6	C80 M0 Y72 K0 R0 G170 B110 #00AA6E
7	C45 M0 Y50 K0 R152 G206 B151 #98CE97
8	C70 M0 Y60 K0 R58 G180 B131 #3AB483
9	C70 M0 Y55 K33 R37 G140 B109 #258C6D

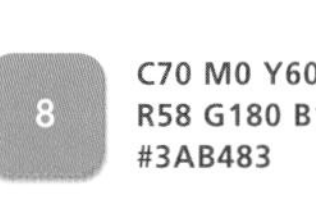
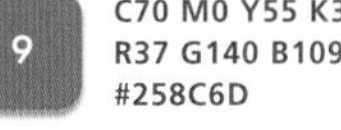

Two-color combinations

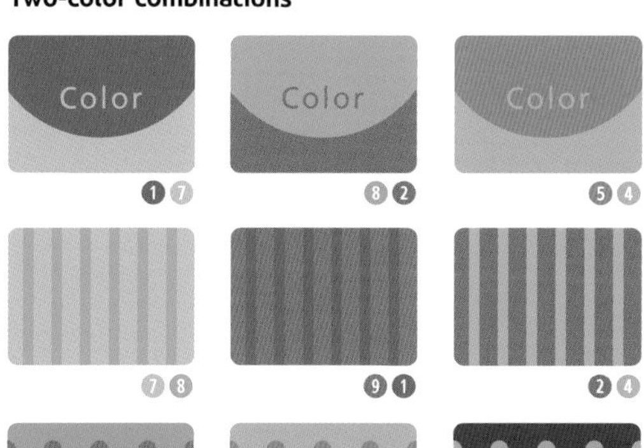

Three-color combinations

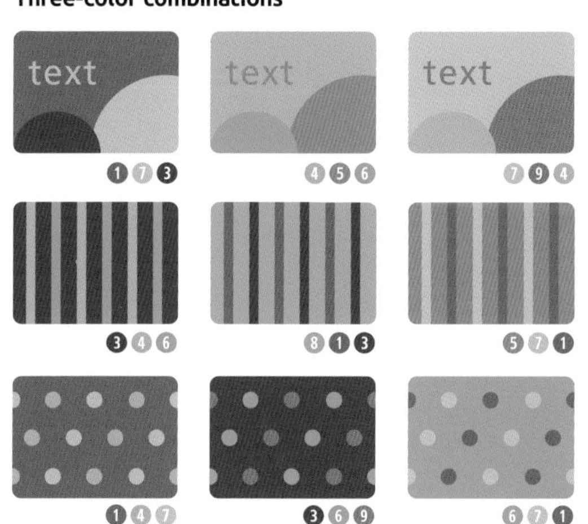

Designs

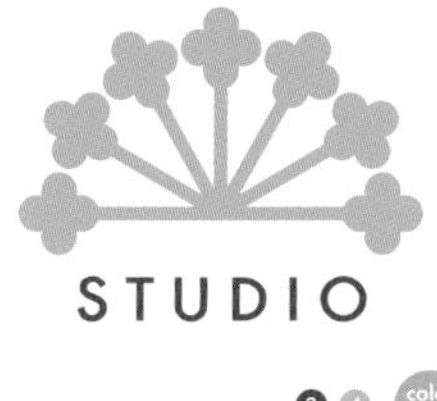

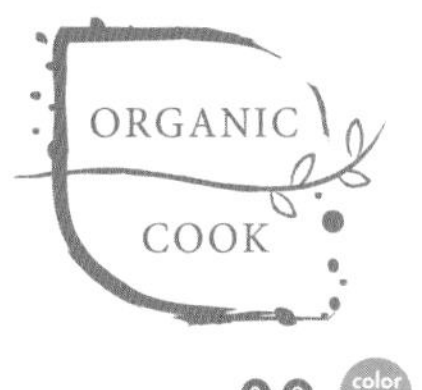

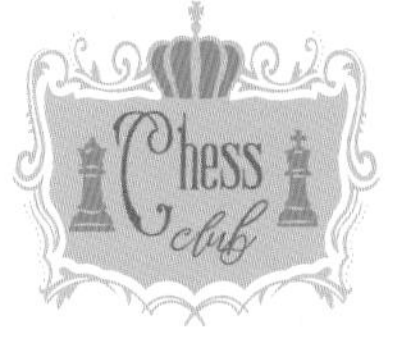

Patterns

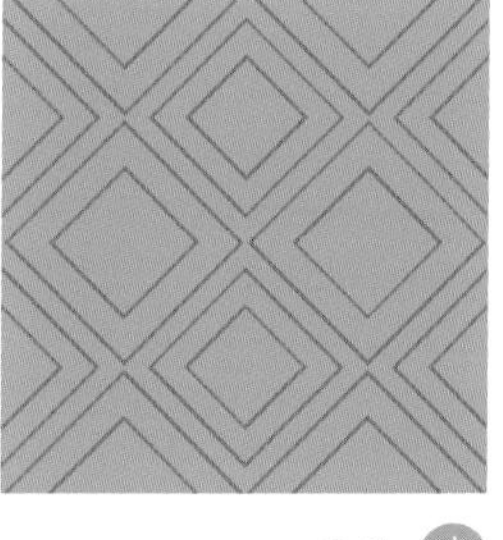

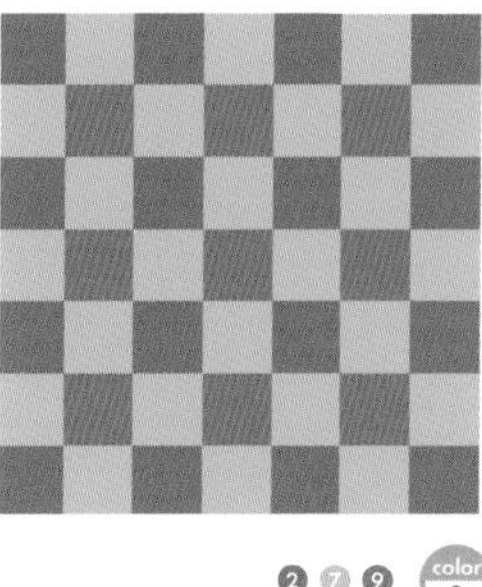

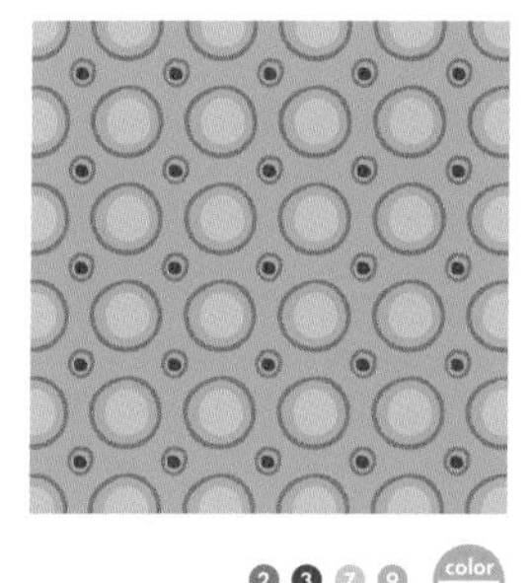

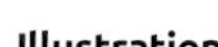

Illustration

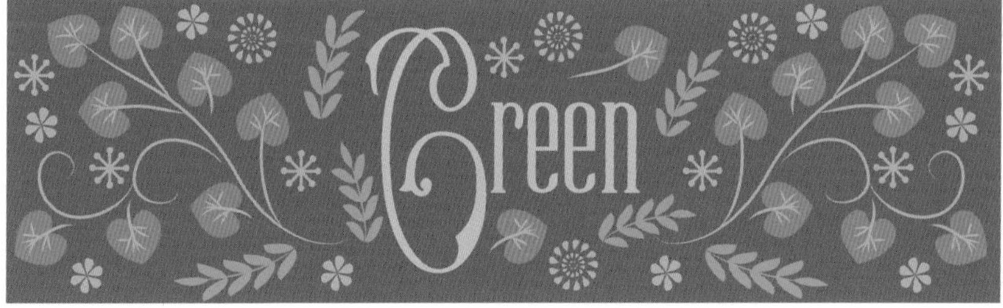

1 4 5 6 7 color 5

Recipe
117

Turquoise

With its cool, intellectual, near-futuristic air, blue green is a hybrid hue that bears both heavy and light loads. The ornamental feathers of a male peacock change color depending on the angle that the light hits them or the angle on which they're viewed; this is called iridescent color.

- **FEELING** Cool, near futuristic, mysterious, out of the ordinary.
- **COMBINATIONS** Peacocks, the aurora, mint.
- **TIPS** The appeal of blue green is its elusiveness.

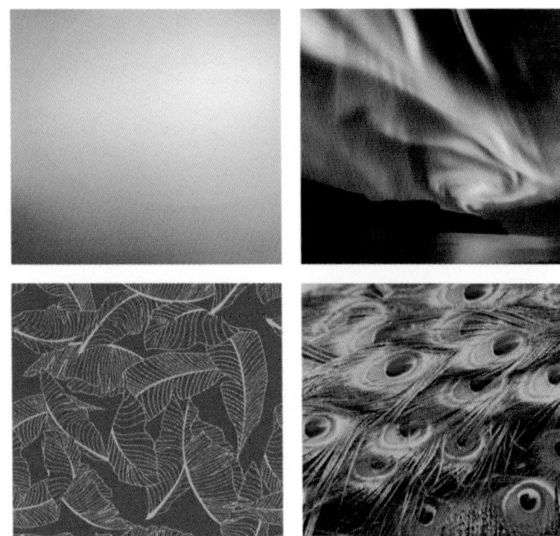

Blue green is a color not commonly seen in the everyday, thus its associations with ornamental plumage and natural phenomena.

❶ Celadon
Porcelain with only a tiny amount of iron in the clay or glaze.

❷ Green Bamboo
The color of fresh green bamboo entering its next stage of growth.

❸ St. Patrick's Day
March 17 marks this day celebrated by the "wear-ing of the green."

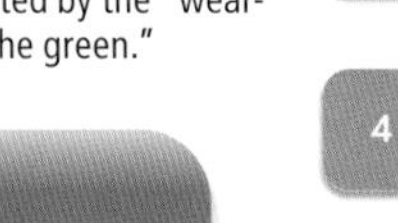

❹ Turquoise Green
Pale blue green is one of the blues achieved by indigo dyeing.

❺ Nile Blue
The color of the Nile River as rendered in ancient Egyptian mythology.

❻ Viridian
Refers to a highly durable blue-green pigment or the color it produces.

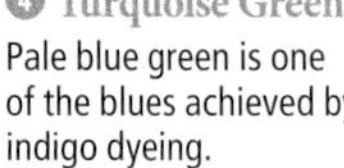

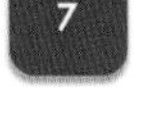

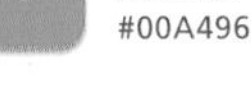

❼ Billiard Green
A color associated with the deep green of a billiard table.

❽ Peacock Green
The strong green seen in peacock feathers.

❾ Peacock Blue
The blue green seen in peacock feathers.

1	C57 M0 Y40 K10 R104 G183 B161 #68B7A1
2	C50 M0 Y35 K10 R126 G190 B171 #7EBEAB
3	C70 M0 Y50 K70 R0 G82 B67 #005243
4	C40 M0 Y20 K30 R127 G171 B169 #7FABA9
5	C70 M0 Y40 K20 R37 G159 B148 #259F94
6	C80 M0 Y60 K30 R0 G137 B105 #008969
7	C85 M0 Y55 K60 R0 G92 B76 #005C4C
8	C90 M0 Y50 K0 R0 G164 B150 #00A496
9	C100 M0 Y40 K5 R0 G154 B163 #009AA3

Two-color combinations

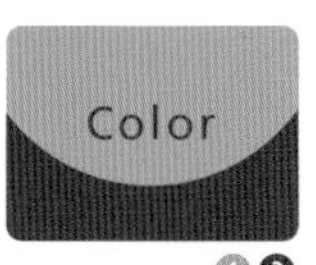

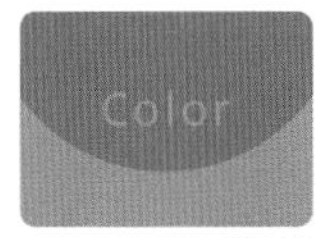

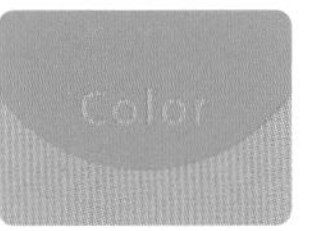

1 3 | 6 4 | 8 2

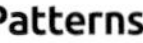
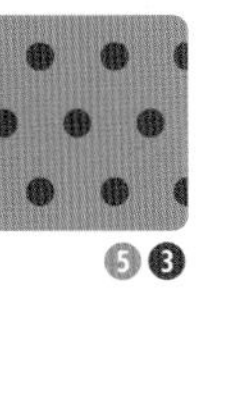

7 5 | 9 1 | 2 6

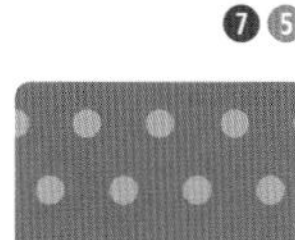

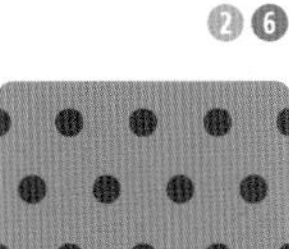

6 2 | 4 9 | 5 3

Three-color combinations

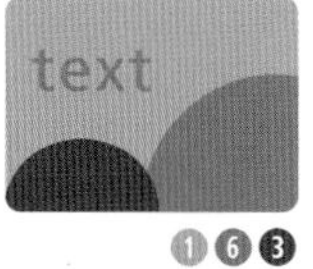

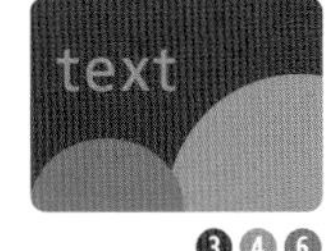

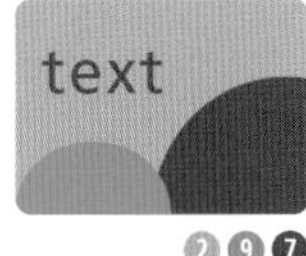

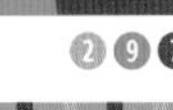
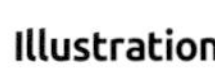

1 6 3 | 3 4 6 | 2 9 7

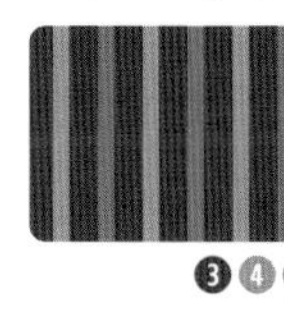

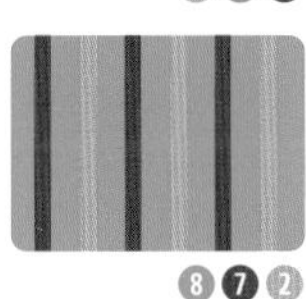

3 4 6 | 5 1 2 | 8 7 2

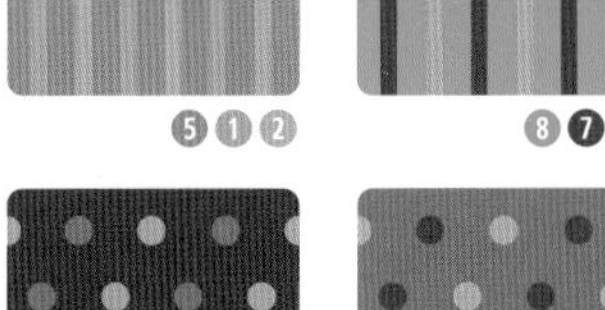
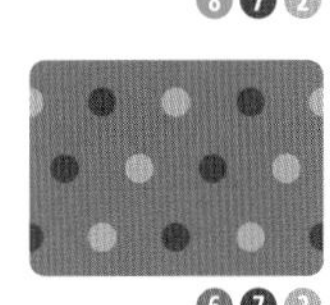

1 8 7 | 3 6 1 | 6 7 2

Designs

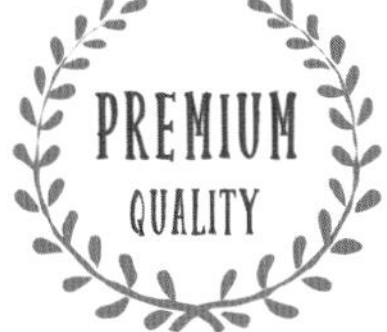

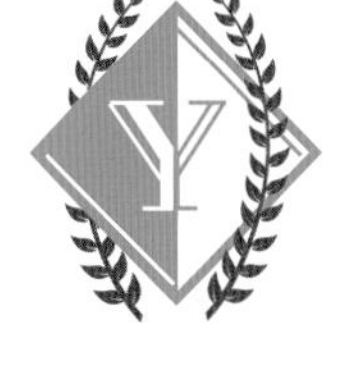

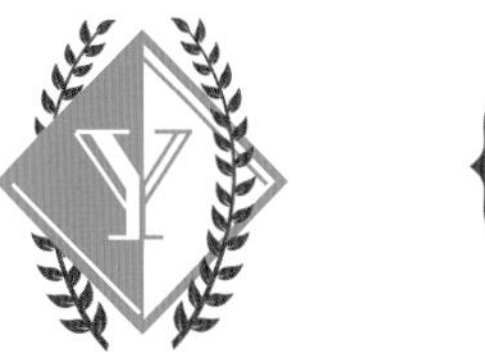
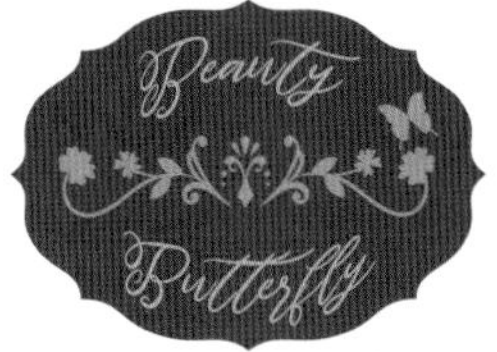

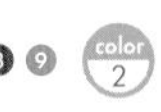
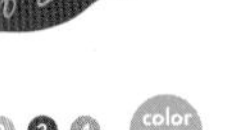

6 7 color 2 | 3 9 color 2 | 2 3 4 color 3

Patterns

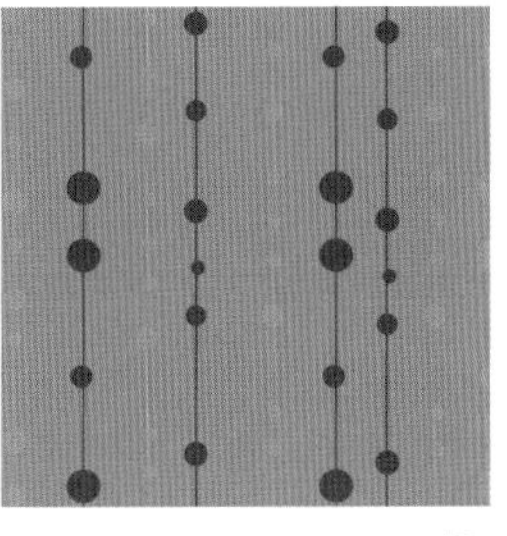
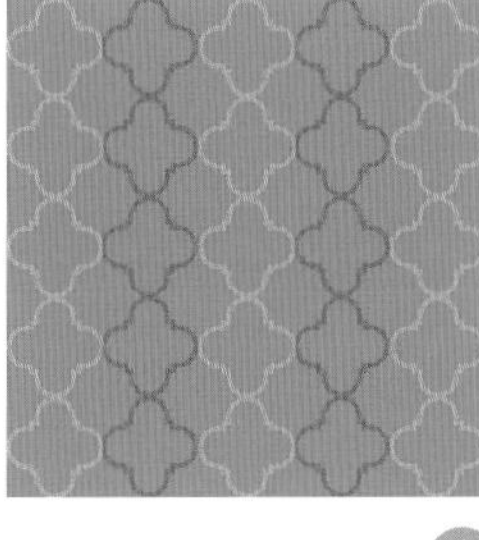
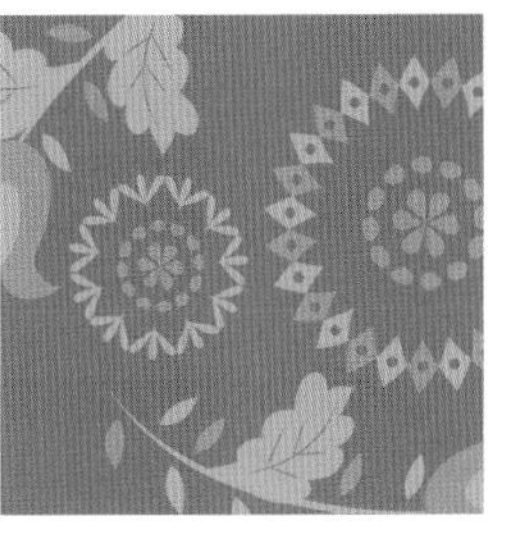

4 5 7 color 3 | 1 6 9 color 3 | 2 4 6 color 3

Illustration

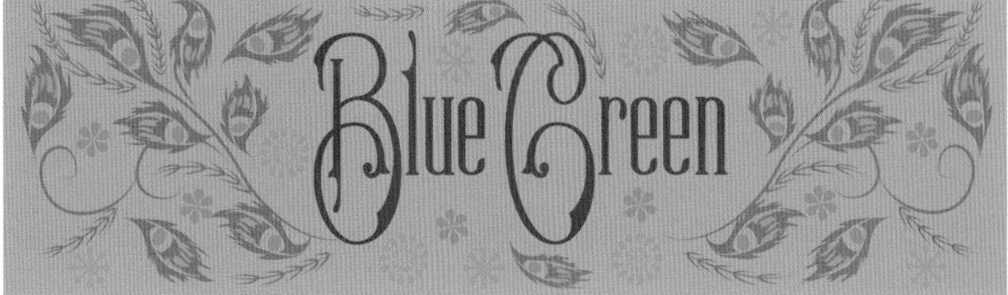

1 6 7 8 9 color 5

Recipe
118

Aqua and Sky Blue

Among shades of blue, those with a high level of brightness and low level of saturation are called aqua and sky. They're colors with a sense of translucency. Blue is a color that we are used to seeing as part of scenery, but when it comes to food it's highly unusual. Blue flowers aren't so common either, the Himalayan blue poppy, the bluebonnet and the bluebell being a few examples.

- **FEELING** Pure, bracing, clear, translucent.
- **COMBINATIONS** Water, sky, glass, air, morning.
- **TIPS** This color expresses invigoration.

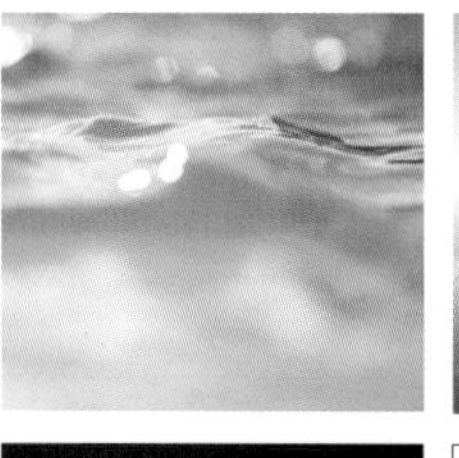

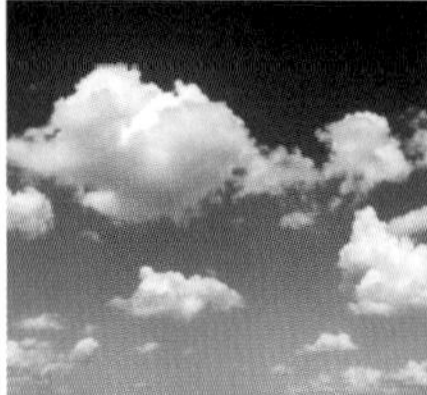
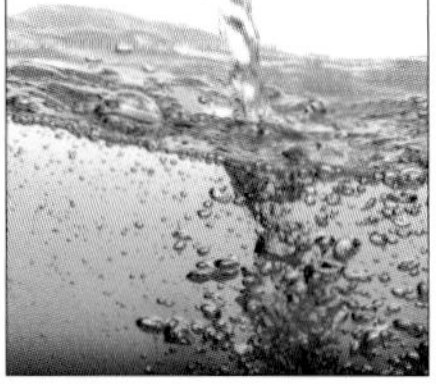

These colors alter in expression easily, having subtle gradations and layers not readily noticed.

1 Aqua
The color of clear, clean water.

2 Sky
The color of the sky is faint close to the horizon and deeper higher up.

3 Glimpse of the Pot
A pale indigo made by only the slightest dip into the indigo vat.

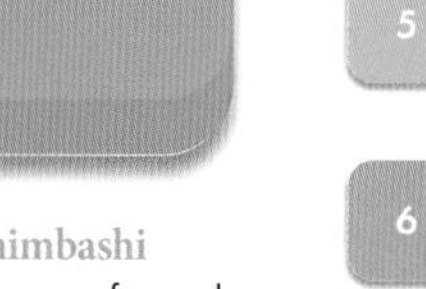

4 Forget-me-not
A blue like that of forget-me-nots.

5 Pastel Blue
Of all the ultramarine mineral pigments, this has the finest particles.

6 Shimbashi
A color once favored by geisha in Tokyo's Shimbashi area.

7 Turquoise Blue
Signifying the gemstone called turquoise, this is a greenish blue.

8 Horizon Blue
The blue seen in the sky close to the horizon line.

9 Hyacinth
The blue of the hyacinth flower.

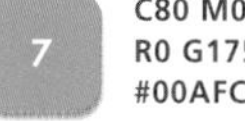
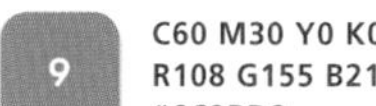

	CMYK	RGB	Hex
1	C30 M0 Y10 K0	R188 G226 B232	#BCE2E8
2	C40 M0 Y5 K0	R160 G216 B239	#A0D8EF
3	C40 M0 Y15 K0	R162 G215 B221	#A2D7DD
4	C48 M10 Y0 K0	R137 G195 B235	#89C3EB
5	C50 M0 Y20 K0	R131 G204 B210	#83CCD2
6	C57 M0 Y20 K8	R100 G188 B199	#64BCC7
7	C80 M0 Y20 K0	R0 G175 B204	#00AFCC
8	C40 M0 Y8 K0	R160 G216 B234	#A0D8EA
9	C60 M30 Y0 K0	R108 G155 B210	#6C9BD2

Two-color combinations

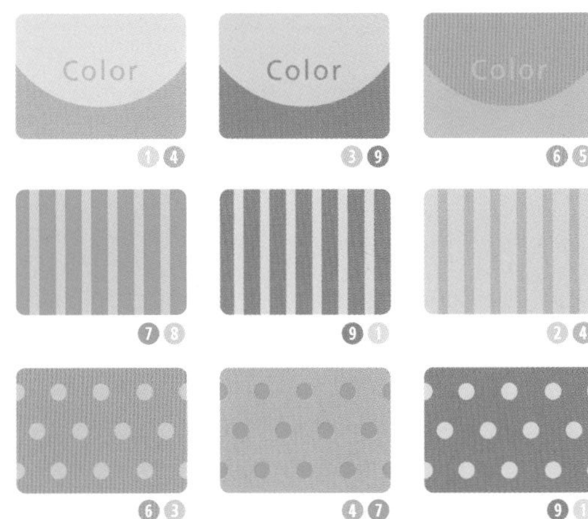

Three-color combinations

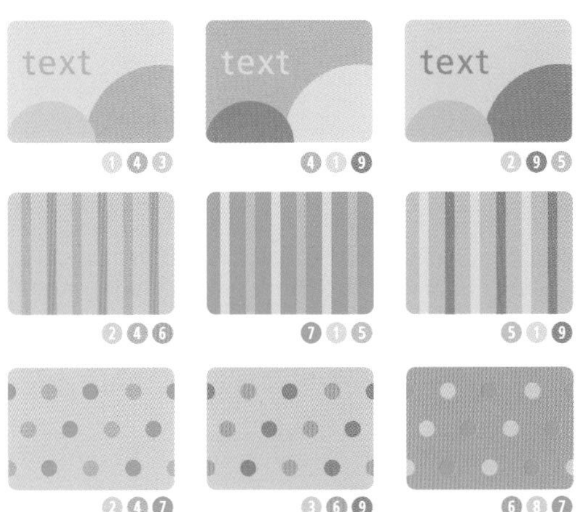

Designs

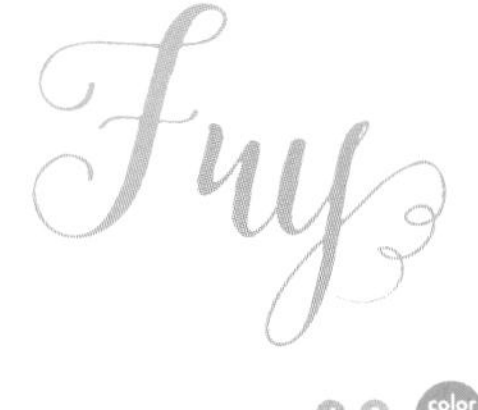
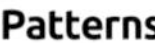
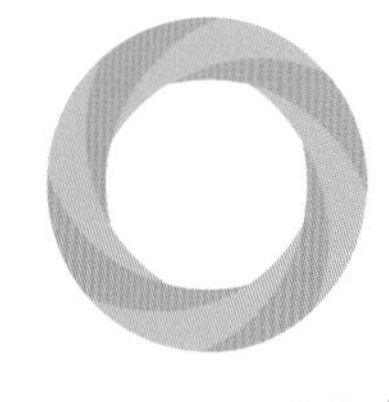
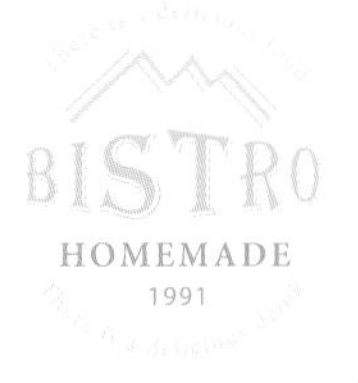

Patterns

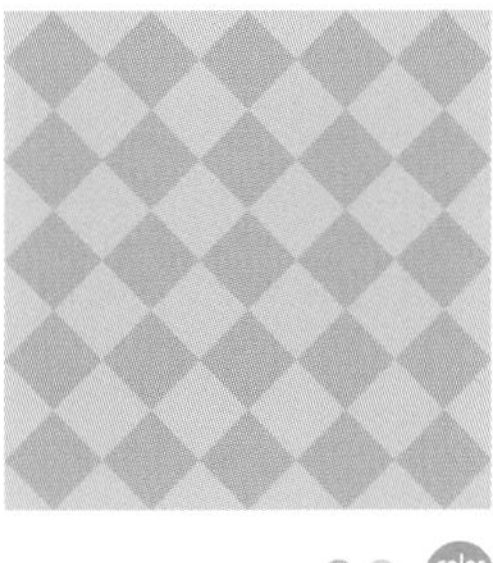
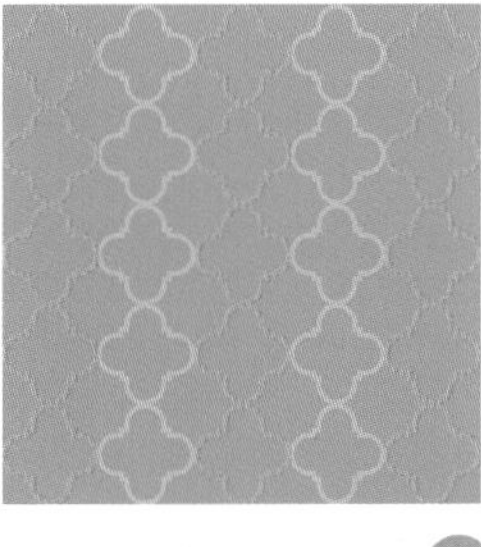
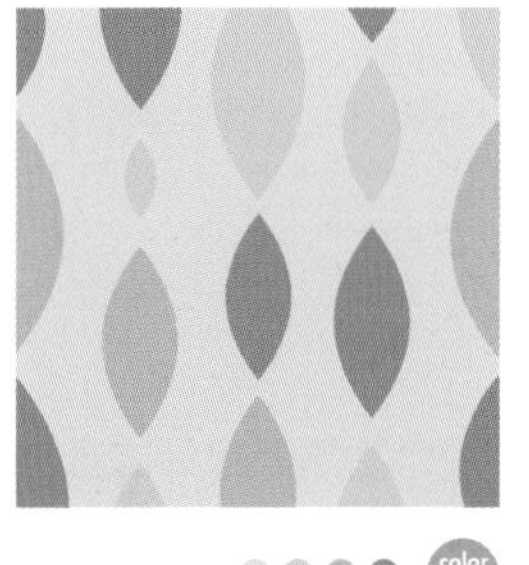

Illustration

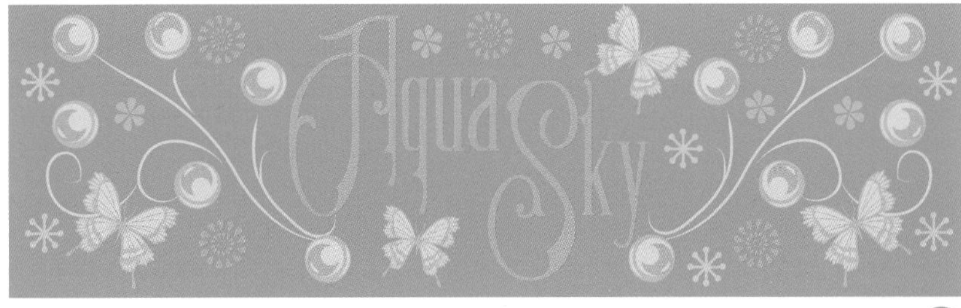

Recipe
119

Blue

It has long been a custom for brides to wear "something blue" on their wedding day as a way to assure happiness. This blue garment is also symbolic of the Virgin Mary and signifies chastity. Blue takes on a range of meanings, from bright, hopeful overtones to dark, murky hues that symbolize melancholy emotions.

- **FEELING** **Logical, quiet, mature, cerebral, melancholy.**
- **COMBINATIONS** **Sky, sea, bluebirds, sports drinks.**
- **TIPS** **This is a popular, unifying family of hues.**

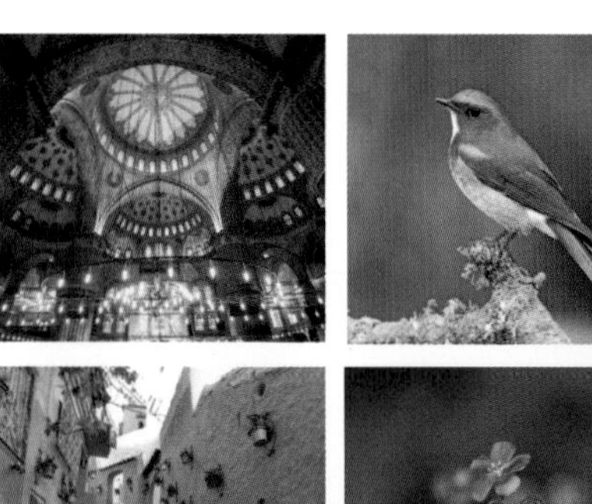

Blue is a calm, deep color that soothes and softens.

❶ Dayflower
A color achieved with the dye from dayflowers.

❷ Light Indigo
A color that is more intense than pale blue but lighter than indigo.

❸ Lapis Lazuli
A color like that of lapis lazuli, one of the seven treasures in Buddhism.

❹ Grayish Blue
One of the colors made with indigo dye, popular in the Edo period.

❺ Cobalt Blue
A blue used to paint porcelain and create synthetic resins.

❻ Cerulean Blue
More vivid than sky blue, this color has a greenish tinge.

❼ Cyan
One of the three primary colors used in paint and ink.

❽ Sax Blue
The English name for the Sachsen region of Germany is Saxony.

❾ Oriental Blue
This refers to the blue of gosu porcelain in China; an Eastern hue.

1 C73 M21 Y0 K0 R35 G157 B218 #239DDA

2 C70 M20 Y0 K30 R41 G128 B175 #2980AF

3 C90 M70 Y0 K0 R29 G80 B162 #1D50A2

4 C82 M0 Y25 K40 R0 G125 B142 #007D8E

5 C100 M50 Y0 K0 R0 G104 B183 #0068B7

6 C80 M0 Y5 K30 R0 G141 B183 #008DB7

7 C100 M0 Y0 K0 R0 G160 B233 #00A0E9

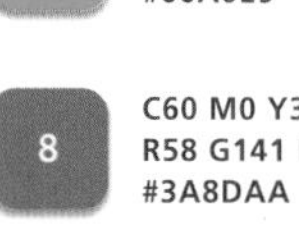

8 C60 M0 Y3 K40 R58 G141 B170 #3A8DAA

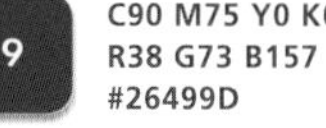

9 C90 M75 Y0 K0 R38 G73 B157 #26499D

Two-color combinations

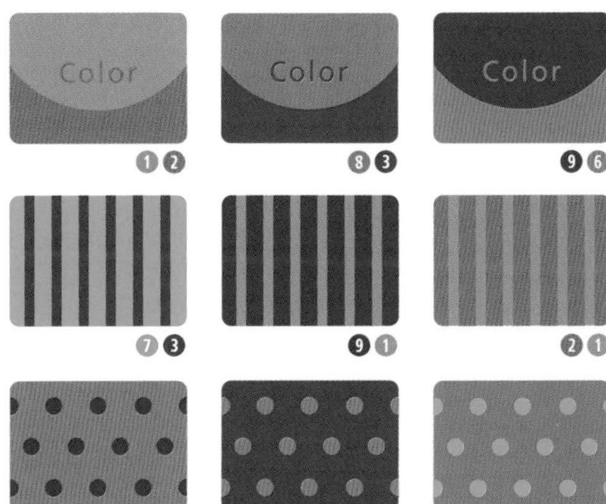

Three-color combinations

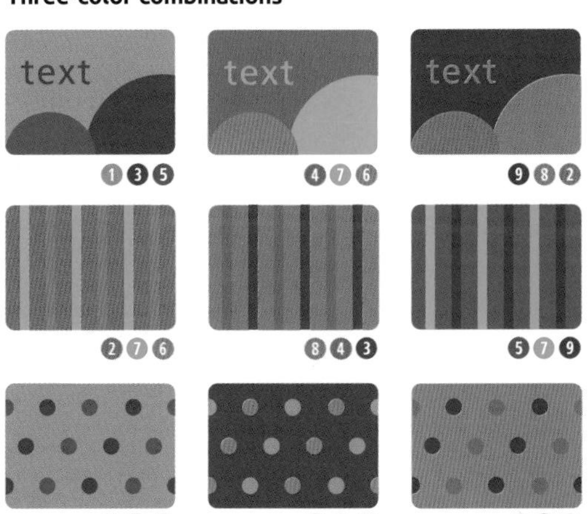

Designs

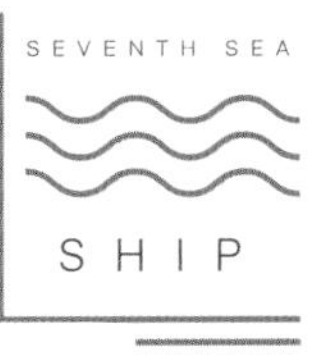

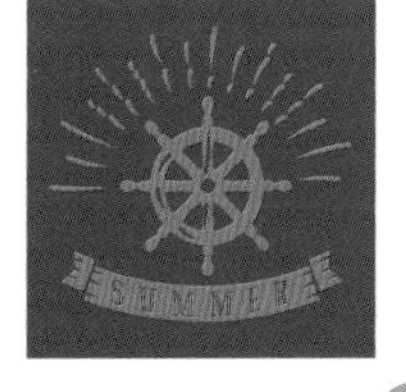

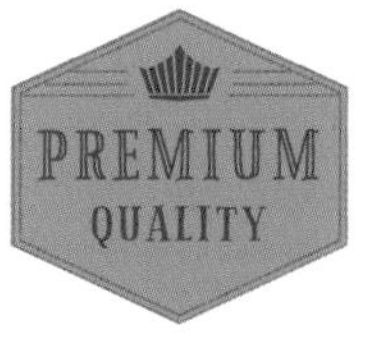

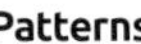

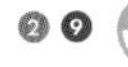

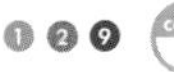

Patterns

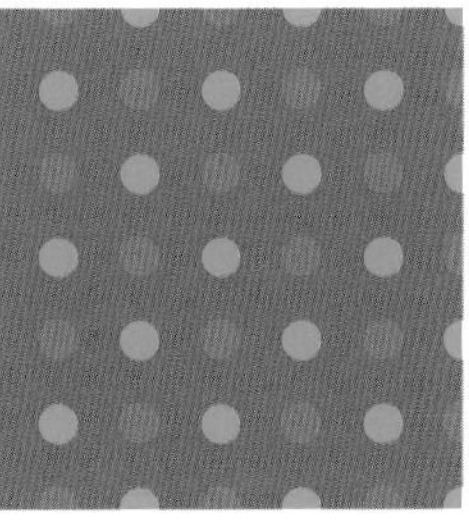

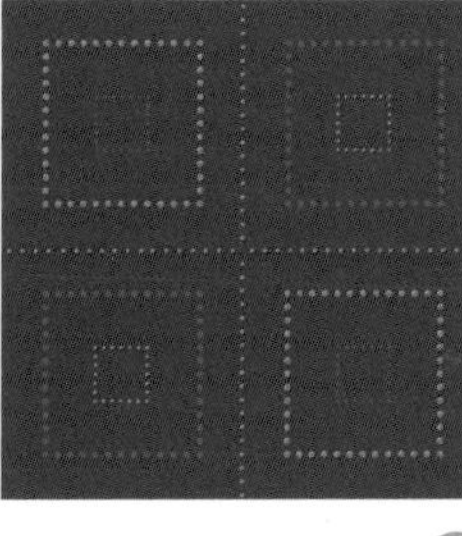

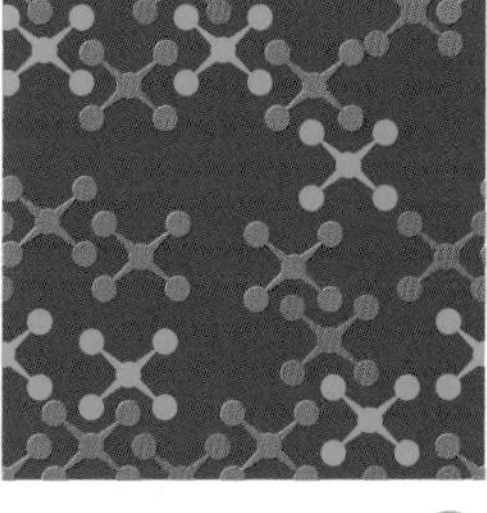

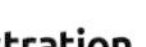

Illustration

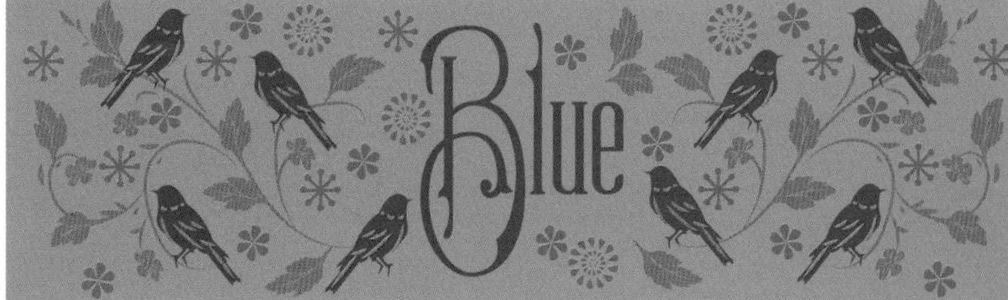

Recipe
120

Indigo

Arriving in Japan from England during the Meiji period, chemist Robert William Atkinson praised the indigo-dyed blue so often used for kimonos and noren curtains, calling it Japan blue. Many colors derived from indigo dyeing remain among the Japanese traditional colors, and the ubiquity of jeans keeps shades of indigo alive.

- **FEELING** Mysterious, profound, deep, orderly.
- **COMBINATIONS** Starry skies, outer space, jeans, uniforms.
- **TIPS** This color is also said to be the "soul color" for the Japanese people.

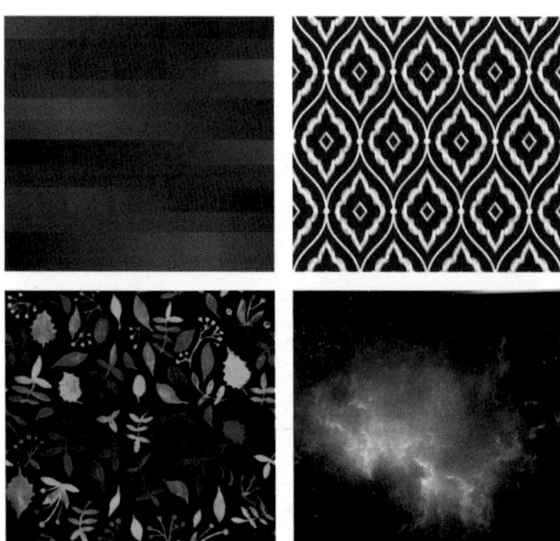

Indigo is a quiet color with a sense of depth and expanse.

❶ Indigo
An intense blue achieved from the dye of Persicaria tinctoria.

❷ Navy
The deepest blue that can be achieved by indigo dyeing.

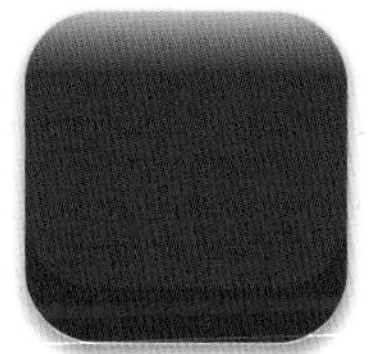

❸ Lapis Lazuli Navy
A color close to navy and darker than lapis lazuli.

❹ Kachi-iro
As *kachi* means "to win," this was a color popular among samurai.

❺ Deep Indigo
An even more deeply dyed blue than that of the indigo of Color 1.

❻ Navy Blue
A color associated with the uniform of the English Navy.

❼ Marine Blue
A blue that calls to mind the blue-green of seawater.

❽ Prussian Blue
Invented at the start of the 18th century, also known as Berlin blue.

❾ Mid-century Blue
A blue close to black that recalls the depths of night.

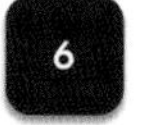

No.	CMYK	RGB	Hex
1	C70 M20 Y0 K60	R15 G87 B121	#0F5779
2	C80 M60 Y0 K50	R33 G58 B112	#213A70
3	C90 M70 Y0 K20	R24 G68 B142	#18448E
4	C35 M27 Y0 K65	R85 G87 B108	#55576C
5	C80 M55 Y0 K70	R8 G39 B82	#082752
6	C70 M50 Y0 K70	R31 G46 B85	#1F2E55
7	C100 M0 Y15 K50	R0 G103 B136	#006788
8	C80 M50 Y0 K50	R21 G69 B119	#154577
9	C80 M50 Y0 K80	R0 G29 B66	#001D42

Two-color combinations

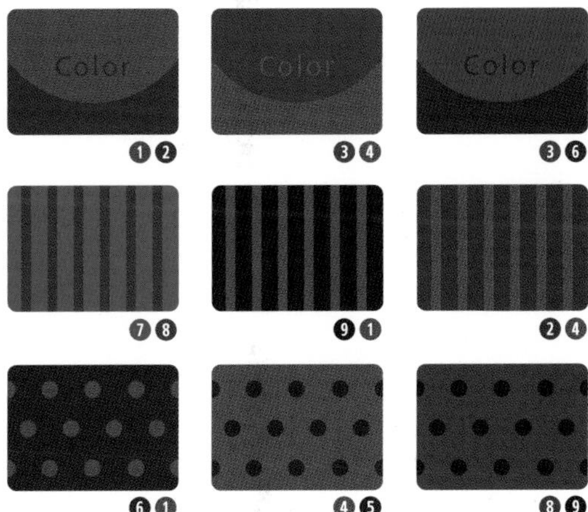

Three-color combinations

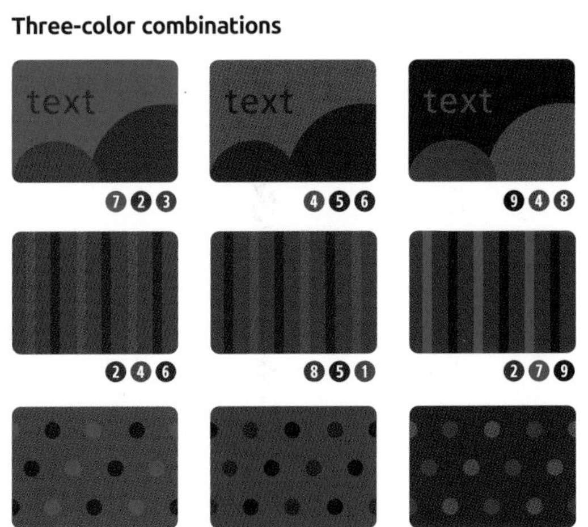

Designs

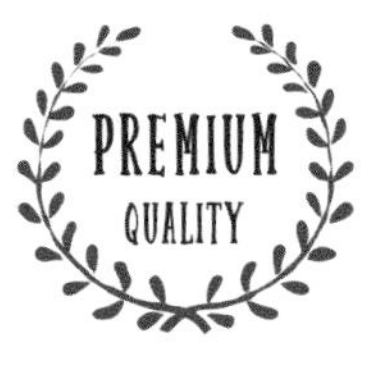

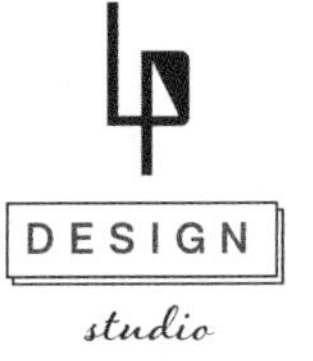

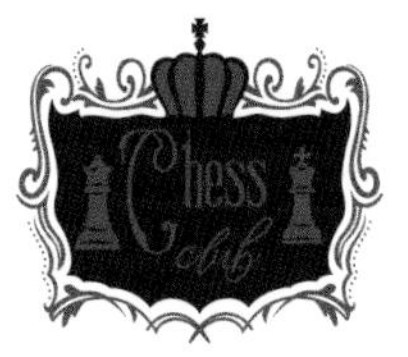

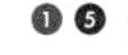

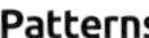
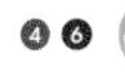

Patterns

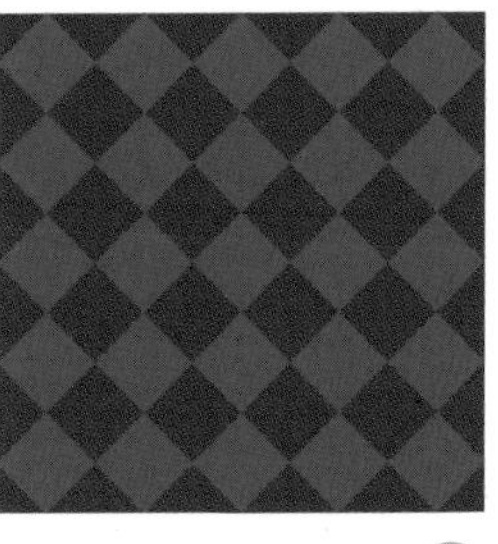
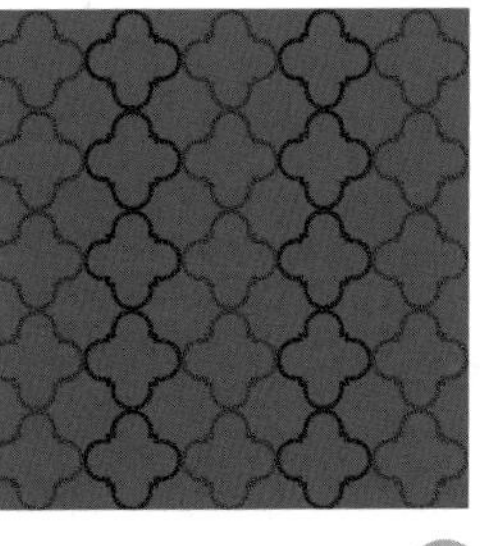
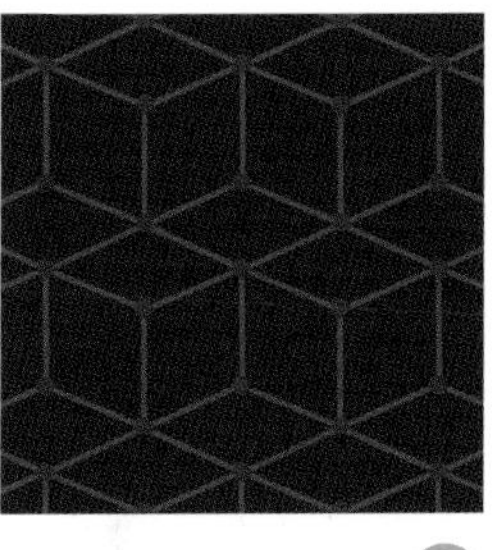
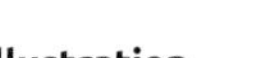

Illustration

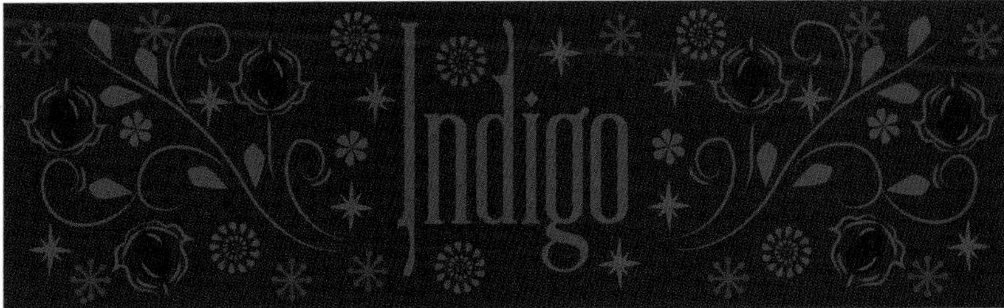

PART 13

RAINBOW PALETTES

Recipe
121

Violet

In the visible light spectrum, violet has the shortest wavelength. Once wavelengths become any shorter, they fail to be perceived as colors and are ultraviolet rays. Violet was the color reserved for the highest-ranking officials in the Twelve Level Cap and Ranking System, and was popular among aristocratic families in the Heian period and a chic color in the Edo period.

- **FEELING** Traditional, mysterious, deep, serene.
- **COMBINATIONS** Violets, grapes, eggplants, blueberries.
- **TIPS** This color has a deeply calm, tranquil air.

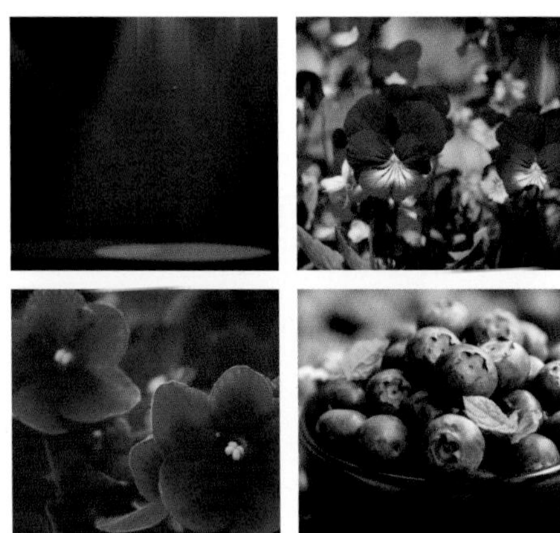

Violet is a deeply calm, healing hue.

❶ Ultramarine
Ultramarine is a natural mineral pigment.

❷ Bellflower
A color like that of bellflowers.

❸ Wisteria 1
In the range of grayish blues, this one tends toward purple.

❹ Wisteria 2
The color of wisteria, as is 9 but a slightly lighter shade.

❺ Pansy
A color like that of pansies.

❻ Ultramarine Blue
Pigment made from lapis lazuli.

❼ Violet
The color of the flowers most commonly associated with purple.

❽ Lavender
The color of lavender flowers, a common ingredient in perfume.

❾ Wisteria 3
A color like that of wisteria flowers.

No.	CMYK	RGB	Hex
1	C75 M58 Y0 K0	R78 G103 B176	#4E67B0
2	C75 M70 Y0 K0	R86 G84 B162	#5654A2
3	C60 M55 Y0 K10	R112 G108 B170	#706CAA
4	C30 M25 Y0 K0	R187 G188 B222	#BBBCDE
5	C80 M90 Y0 K0	R81 G49 B143	#51318F
6	C82 M70 Y0 K0	R64 G82 B162	#4052A2
7	C65 M75 Y0 K0	R113 G79 B157	#714F9D
8	C23 M30 Y0 K5	R197 G179 B211	#C5B3D3
9	C50 M45 Y0 K0	R142 G139 B194	#8E8BC2

Two-color combinations

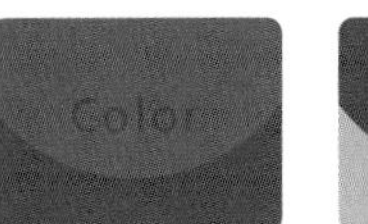

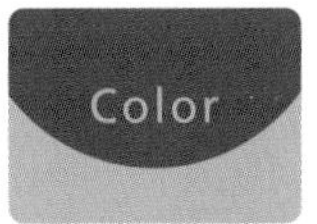

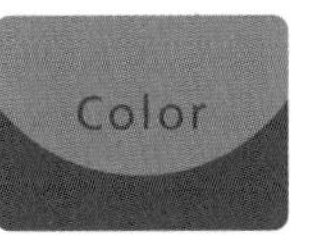

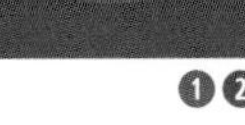

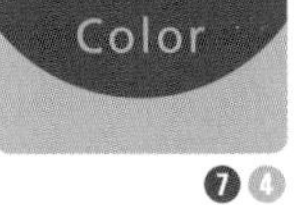

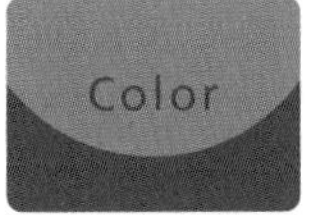

1 2 · 7 4 · 9 6

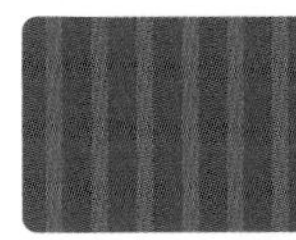

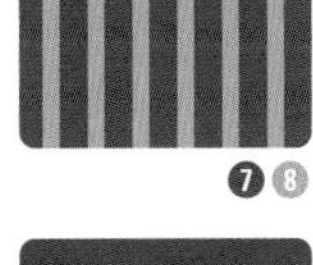

7 8 · 9 1 · 2 3

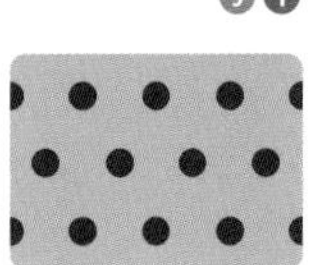

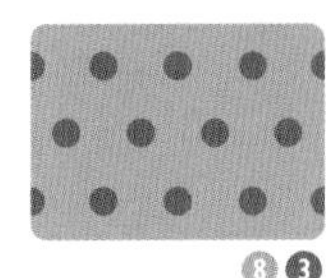

6 9 · 4 5 · 8 3

Three-color combinations

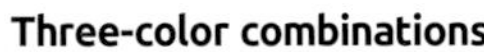

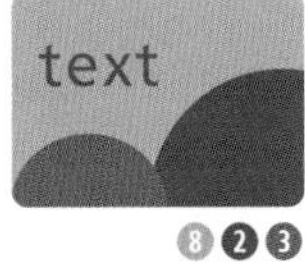

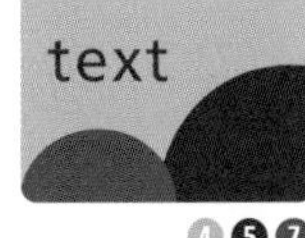

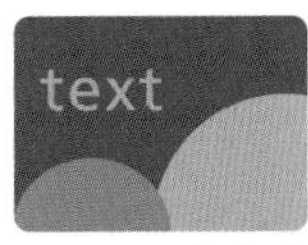

8 2 3 · 4 5 7 · 2 8 9

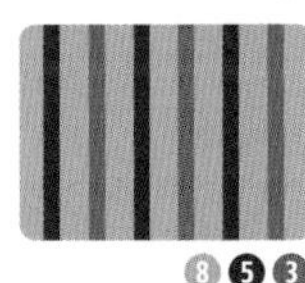

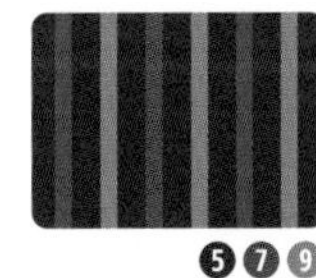

2 4 6 · 8 5 3 · 5 7 9

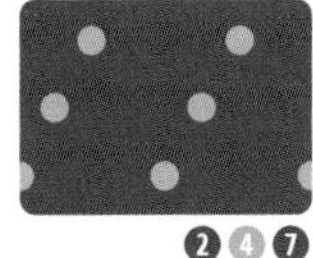

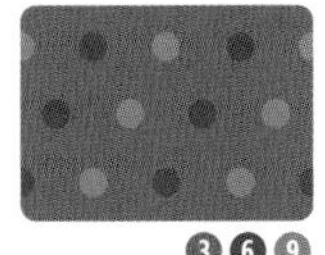

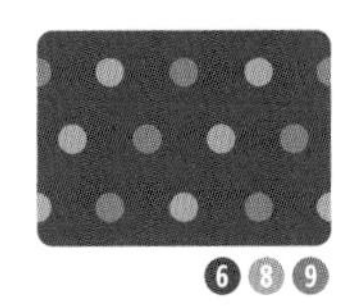

2 4 7 · 3 6 9 · 6 8 9

Designs

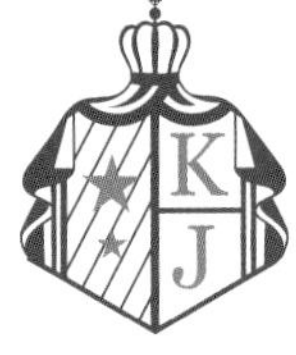

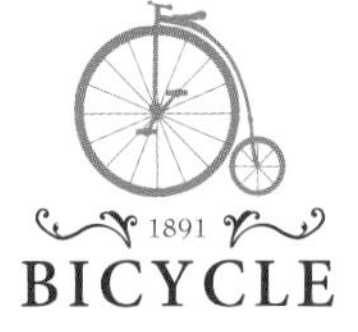

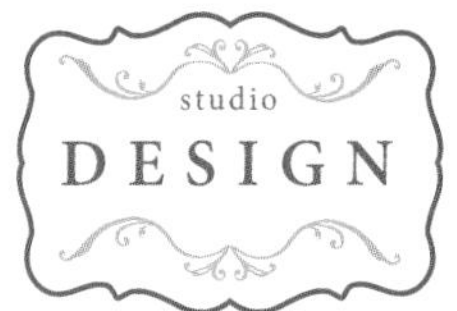

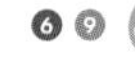

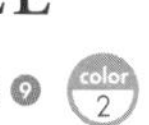

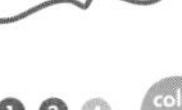

6 9 color 2 · 5 9 color 2 · 1 3 4 color 3

Patterns

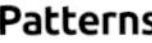

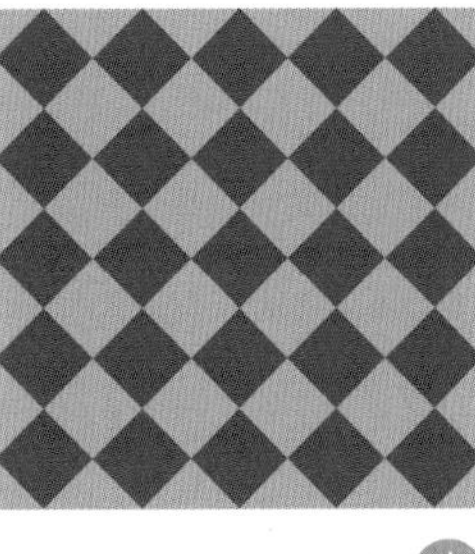

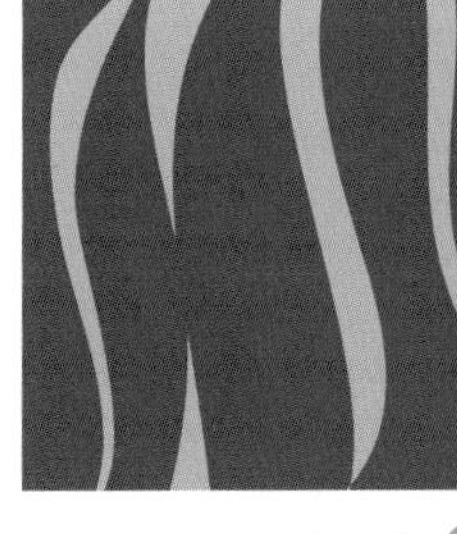

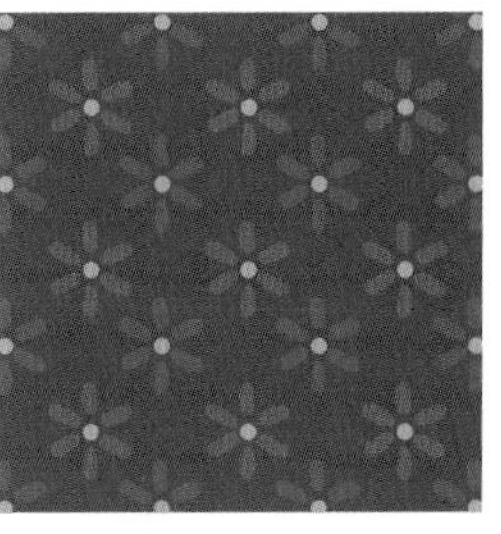

7 8 color 2 · 2 4 7 color 3 · 1 2 3 8 color 4

Illustration

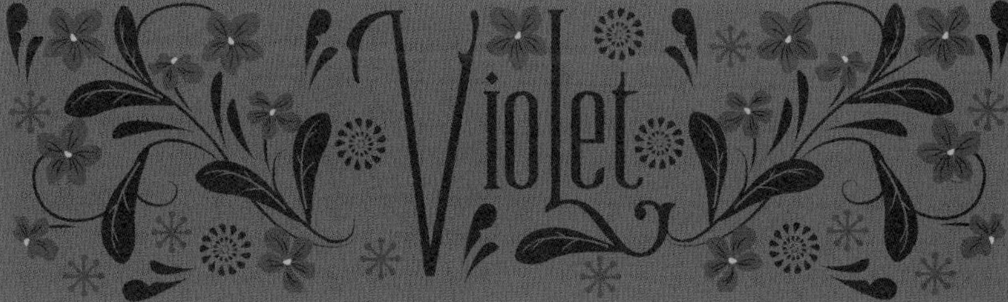

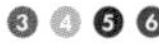

3 4 5 6 7 color 5

Recipe
122

Purple and Magenta

Purple is seen as a noble color as the dye once used to create it was extremely precious. In Japan, dyes made from the roots of gromwell were used, while in the West, the mollusc known as Bolinus brandaris was the source. To create just one gram of the dye, 2,000 Bolinus brandaris snails were needed.

- **FEELING** Graceful, elegant, feminine.
- **COMBINATIONS** Hydrangeas, kimono, orchids, morning glories.
- **TIPS** These colors can also be used to create an air of mystery.

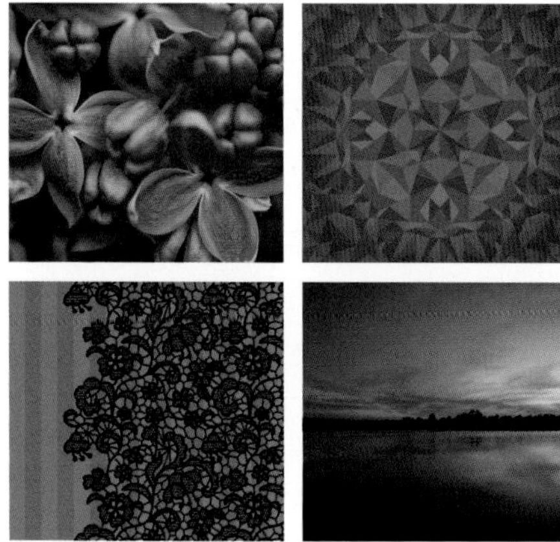

These colors are flexible, offering pop and contrast or softness and layering.

❶ Tyrian Purple
A darker, duller purple than Edo purple or Kyoto purple.

❷ Iris
A color like that of an iris flower.

❸ Azalea
A vivid color like that of an azalea.

❹ Blueish Purple
A color like that of gromwell root, an ingredient in dyeing.

❺ Peony
A purplish crimson like that of peony flowers.

❻ Lilac
An evergreen in the Oleaceae family, lilacs have fragrant flowers.

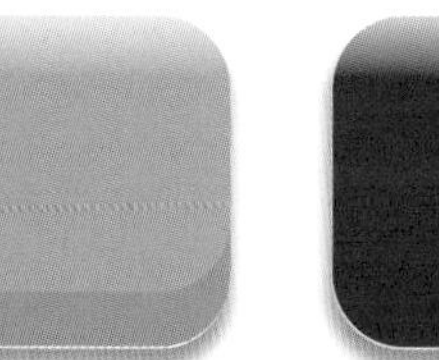

❼ Orchid
A soft, light purple like that of an orchid.

❽ Magenta
Along with cyan and yellow, magenta is one of the primary colors.

❾ Cherry Pink
While not the color of actual cherries, the name is commonly used.

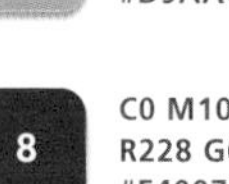
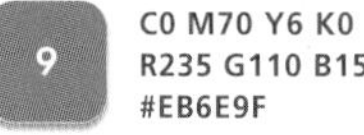

1	C35 M63 Y0 K32	R137 G86 B135	#895687
2	C20 M60 Y0 K0	R204 G125 B177	#CC7DB1
3	C0 M80 Y3 K0	R233 G82 B149	#E95295
4	C45 M80 Y0 K70	R70 G13 B67	#460D43
5	C3 M77 Y0 K0	R229 G90 B155	#E55A9B
6	C20 M30 Y0 K0	R209 G186 B218	#D1BADA
7	C15 M40 Y0 K0	R217 G170 B205	#D9AACD
8	C0 M100 Y0 K0	R228 G0 B127	#E4007F
9	C0 M70 Y6 K0	R235 G110 B159	#EB6E9F

Two-color combinations

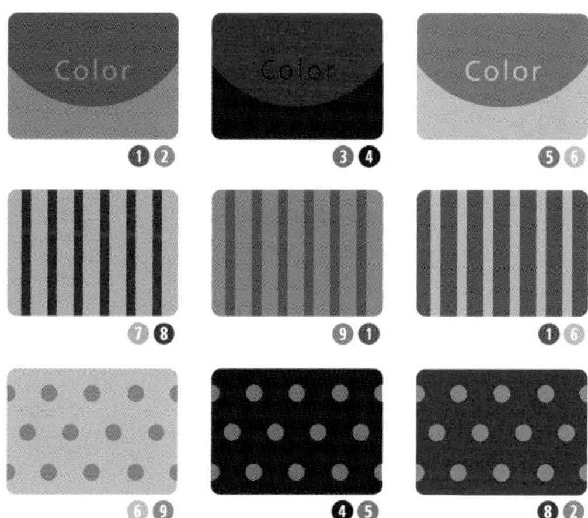

Three-color combinations

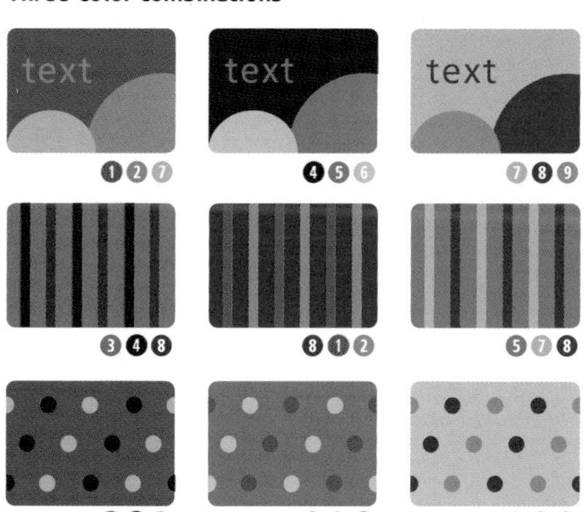

Designs

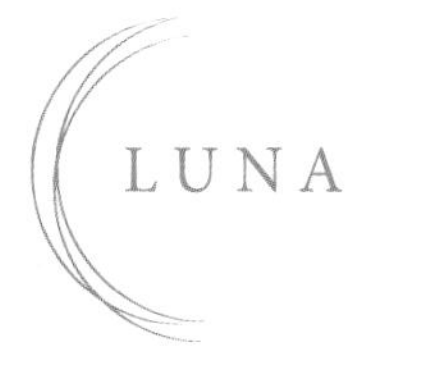

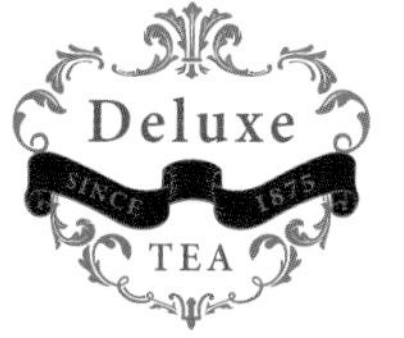

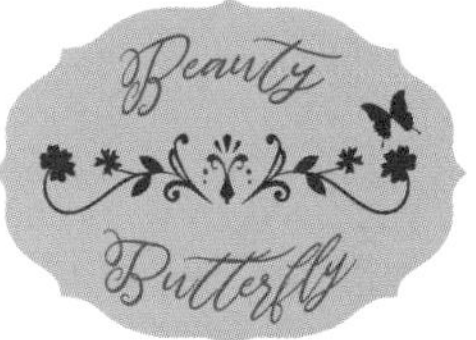

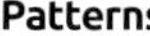

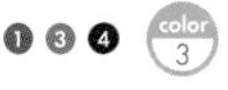

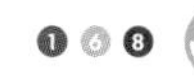

Patterns

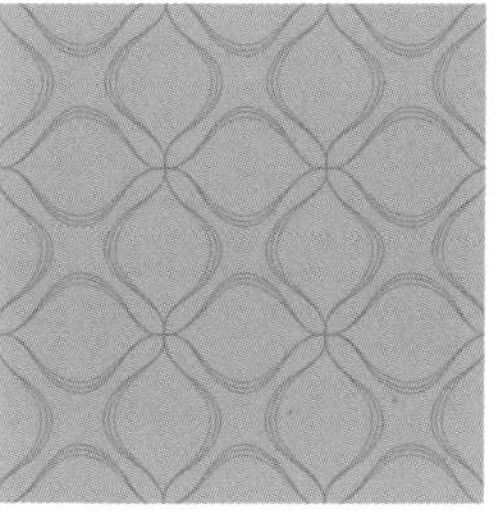

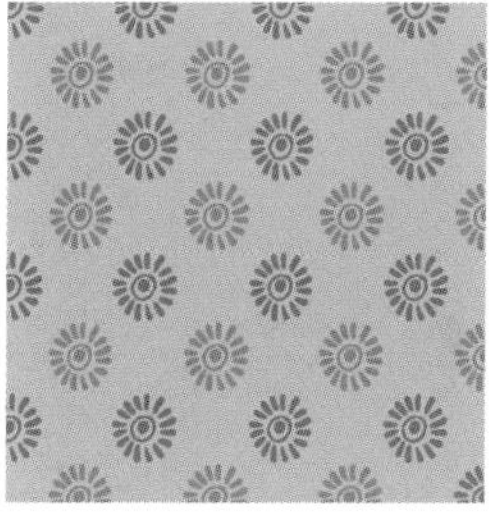

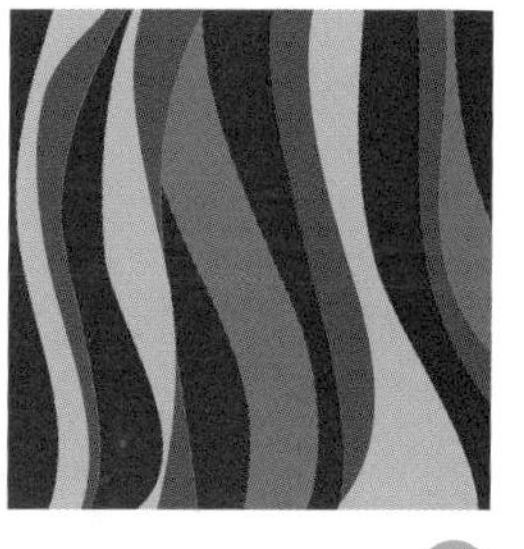

Illustration

Recipe
123

Pink

Pink is said to be the color of love and romance. Lacking the fierceness of red, it has a gently embracing energy. Pink is also a color that symbolizes the bond between people. Once aligned with the feminine, its repertoire of meanings has now expanded to embrace new moods and associations.

- **FEELING** Gentle, happy, in love, adorable.
- **COMBINATIONS** Cherry blossoms, peach blossoms, strawberry ice cream, anime.
- **TIPS** Deep pink is energetic while pale pink is gentle.

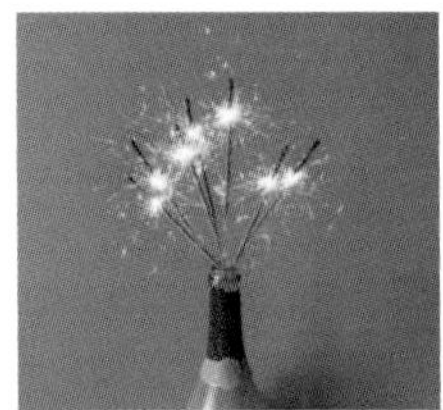
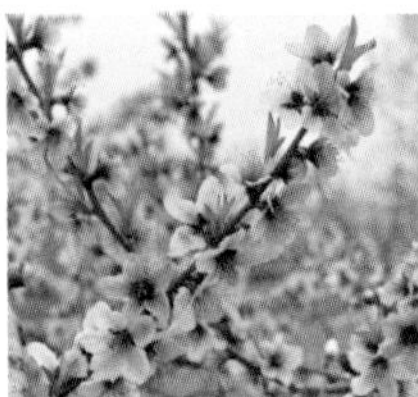
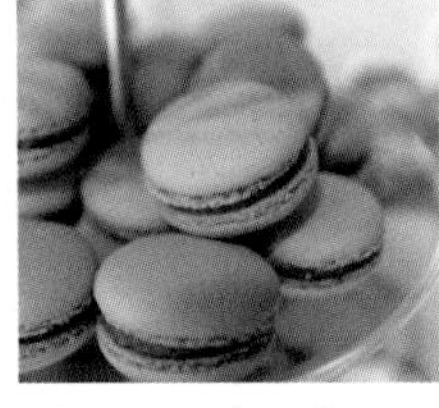
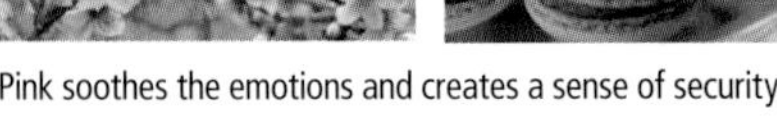

Pink soothes the emotions and creates a sense of security.

❶ Peach
A color like that of a peach blossom or the fruit iself.

❷ Crested Ibis
The color of the flight feathers of crested ibis, once ubiquitous in Japan.

③ Cherry blossom
An extremely faint crimson like that of cherry blossom petals.

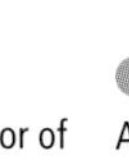

❹ Rose
This refers to the color of red roses.

❺ Rose Pink
A color associated with pink rose petals.

❻ Coral Red
The color of red coral.

⑦ Baby Pink
A color used for infants' clothing, especially baby girls.

❽ Old Rose
A dusty rose, a tone of long ago, faded with age.

❾ Salmon Pink
A soft pink like that of salmon.

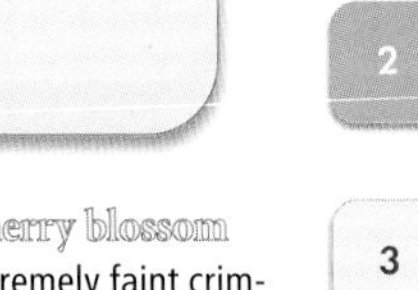

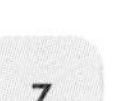

1 C0 M55 Y25 K0 R240 G145 B153 #F09199

2 C0 M40 Y10 K0 R238 G176 B185 #E7ACB9

3 C0 M7 Y3 K0 R254 G244 B244 #FEF4F4

4 C0 M82 Y42 K0 R233 G78 B102 #E94E66

5 C0 M50 Y25 K0 R242 G156 B159 #F29C9F

6 C0 M42 Y28 K0 R244 G173 B163 #F4ADA3

7 C0 M12 Y12 K0 R253 G234 B223 #FDEADF

8 C0 M50 Y23 K15 R218 G141 B147 #DA8D93

9 C0 M40 Y40 K0 R245 G176 B144 #F5B090

Two-color combinations

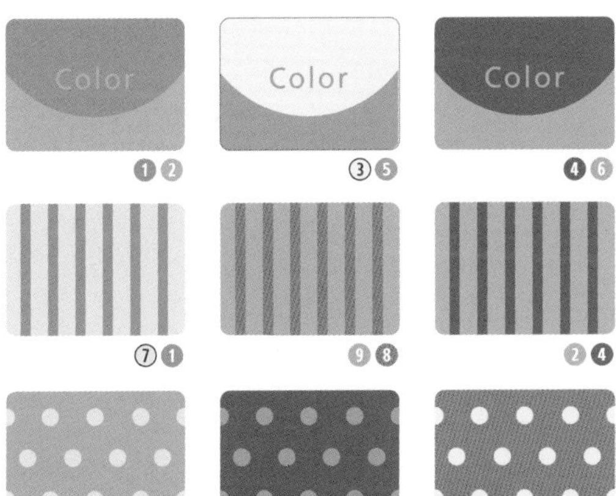

Three-color combinations

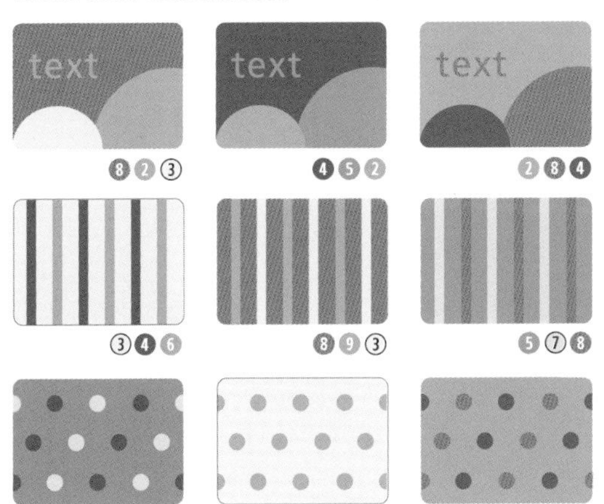

Designs

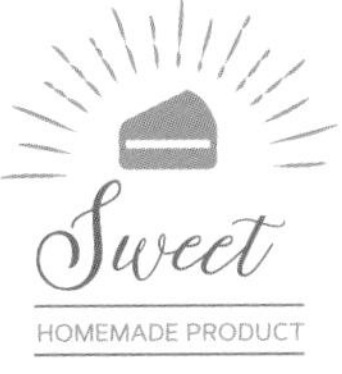

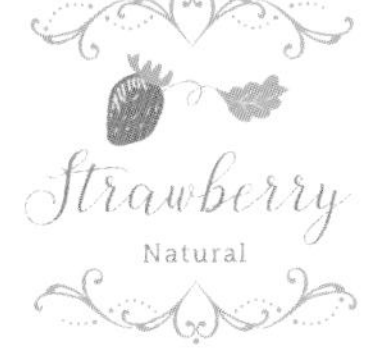

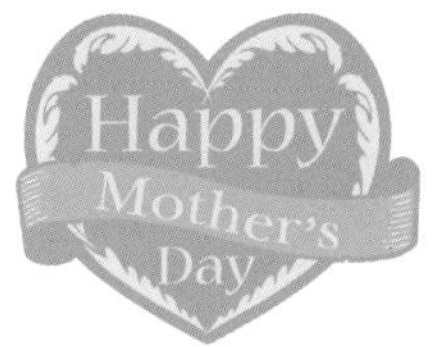

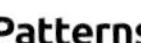
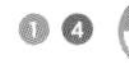
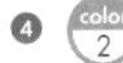
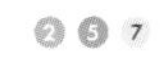

Patterns

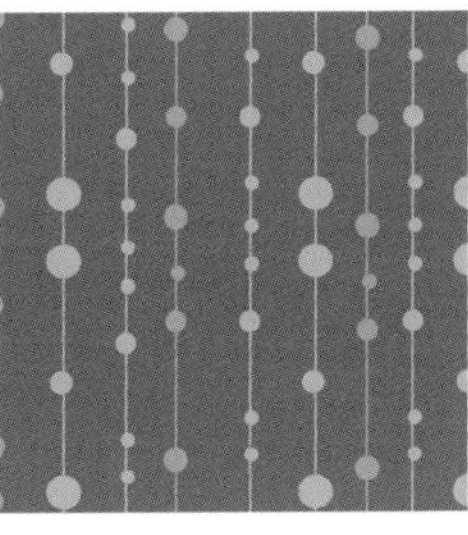

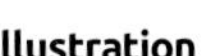

Illustration

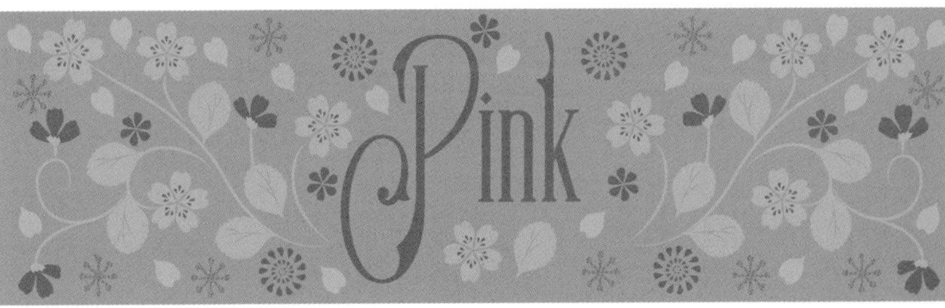

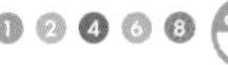

Recipe
124

Brown

The Japanese name for brown translates as "tea color" and derives from the color of fabric dyed in tea leaves. Since then, the palette has evolved. The world went brown after the global oil crisis of 1973. Earth tones and natural hues proliferated (see page 254). Since 1990s, browns have been a fashion staple.

- **FEELING** Composed, secure, natural, unadorned.
- **COMBINATIONS** Earth, tree bark, animal fur, chocolate.
- **TIPS** Brown is often used as a color for materials used in interiors.

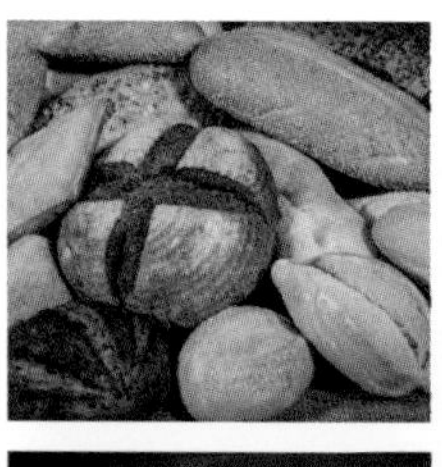
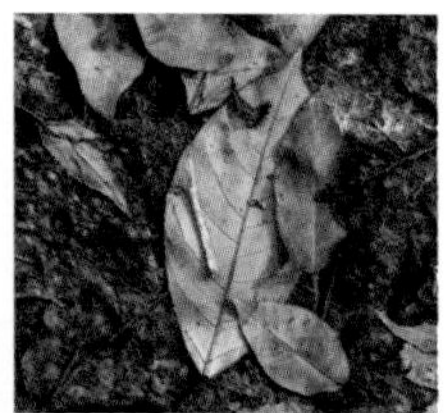
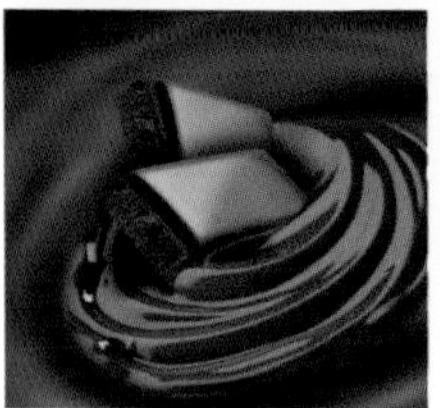
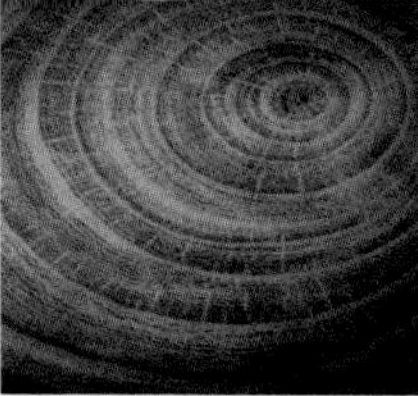

Brown is a color that creates a sense of security and calm.

❶ Amber
Amber is the fossilized resin of ancient trees.

❷ Maroon
A color for uniforms at aristocratic girls' schools in the Meiji period.

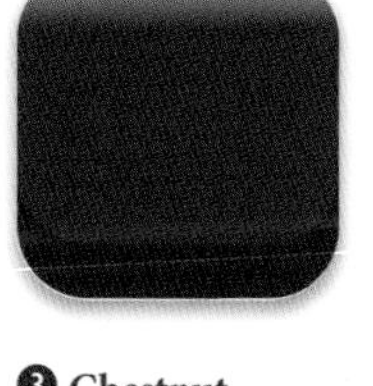

❸ Chestnut
A color like that of a chestnut; the skins are used as dyes.

❹ Burnt Tea
A color like that of something that has burnt; a blackish brown.

❺ Cypress Bark
The color of the bark from Japanese cypresses and cedars.

❻ Sepia
A paint color made from squid ink.

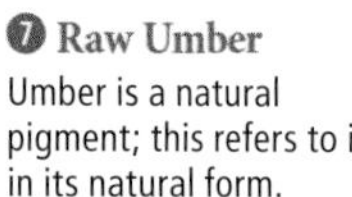

❼ Raw Umber
Umber is a natural pigment; this refers to it in its natural form.

❽ Cocoa Brown
A beverage made from the powder of roasted cacao beans.

❾ Chocolate
The color of chocolate, also made from cacao.

1 C0 M50 Y75 K30 R191 G120 B52 #BF7834

2 C0 M60 Y50 K60 R129 G67 B54 #814336

3 C0 M70 Y80 K65 R118 G46 B5 #762E05

4 C0 M38 Y38 K70 R111 G77 B62 #6F4D3E

5 C0 M60 Y60 K50 R150 G80 B54 #965036

6 C0 M36 Y60 K70 R111 G78 B39 #6F4E27

7 C0 M30 Y75 K55 R145 G111 B36 #916F24

8 C0 M45 Y45 K55 R142 G94 B74 #8E5E4A

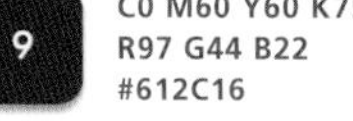

9 C0 M60 Y60 K75 R97 G44 B22 #612C16

Two-color combinations

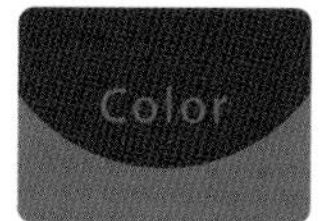

1 2

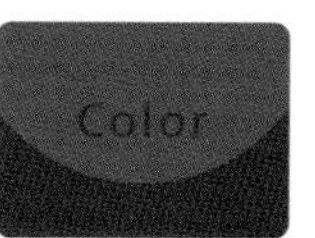

9 7

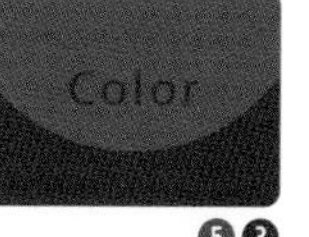

5 3

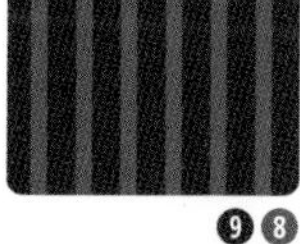

9 8

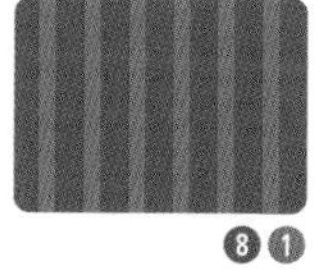

8 1

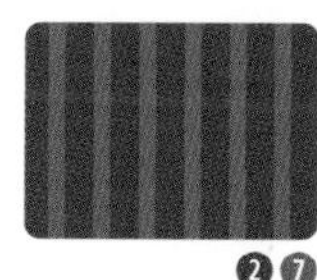

2 7

6 9

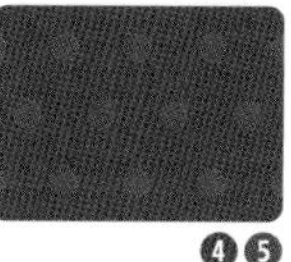

4 5

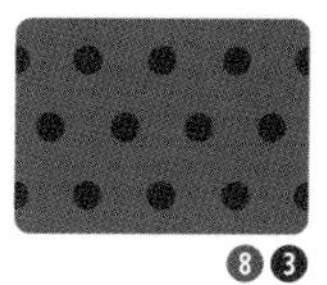

8 3

Three-color combinations

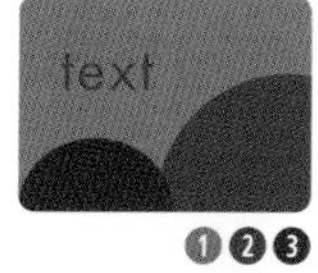

1 2 3

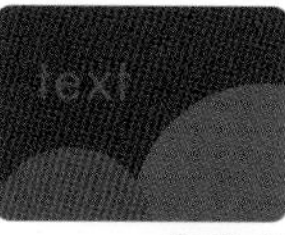

9 5 6

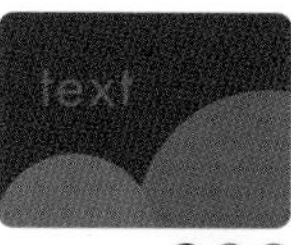

3 8 7

3 4 8

8 1 3

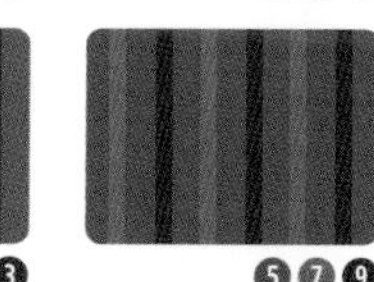

5 7 9

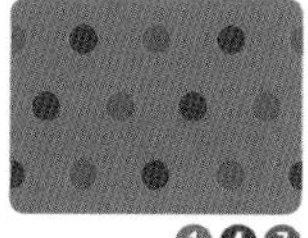

1 4 7

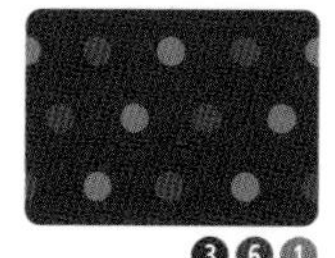

3 6 1

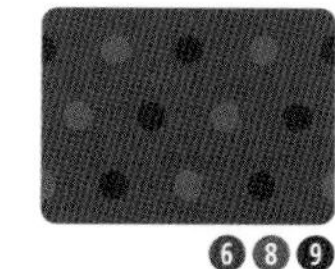

6 8 9

Designs

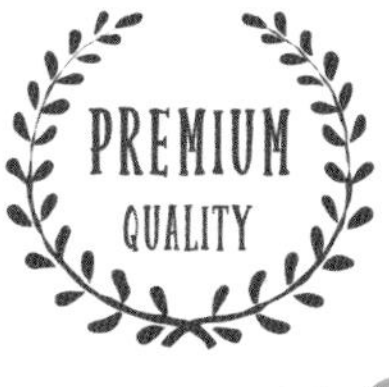

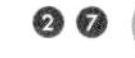

2 7 color 2

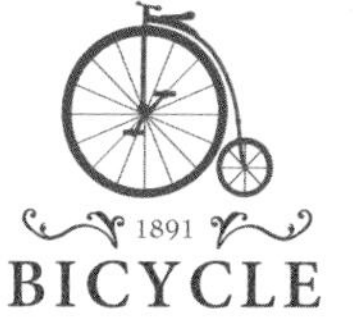

4 5 color 2

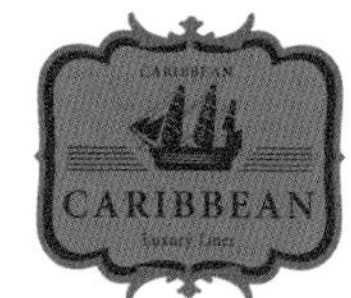

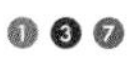

1 3 7 color 3

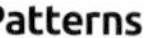

Patterns

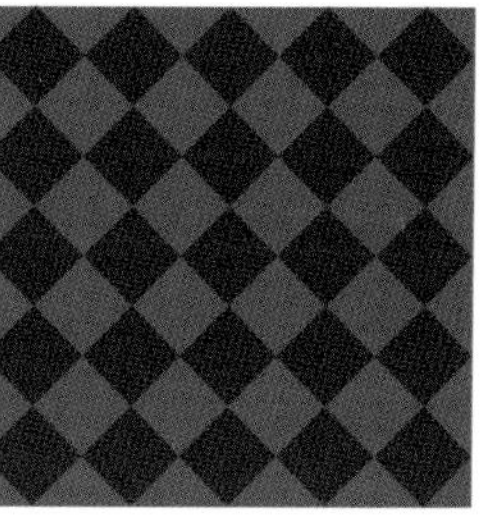

3 8 color 2

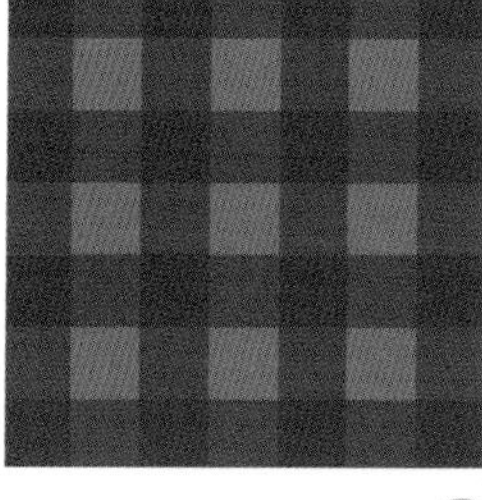

1 2 5 color 3

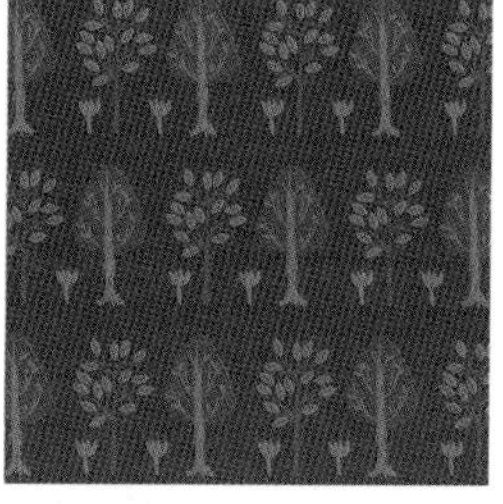

1 4 5 8 color 4

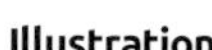

Illustration

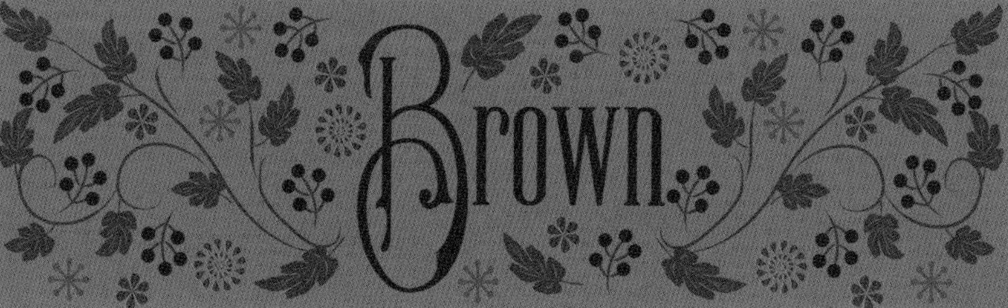

1 2 3 4 8 color 5

Recipe
125

Black and White

Black is associated with a complete lack of light or with all light being absorbed on an object's surface. White is of course aligned with the opposite effects. In package design, black or a color close to it works to create a sense of high quality, as darker colors suggest dignity and depth.

- **FEELING** Genuine, innocent, chic, honest, feelings of fear.
- **COMBINATIONS** Snow, white robes, wedding dresses, night, dark, mourning attire.
- **TIPS** Use as base or accent colors.

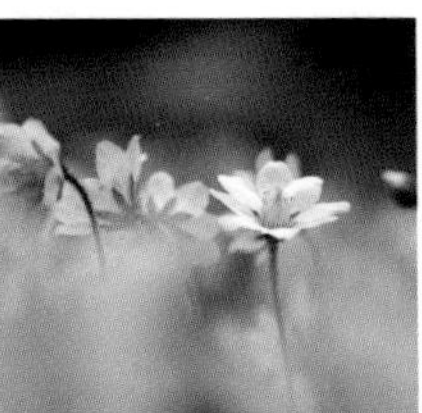
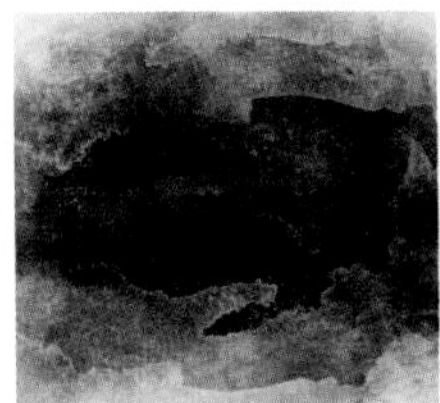
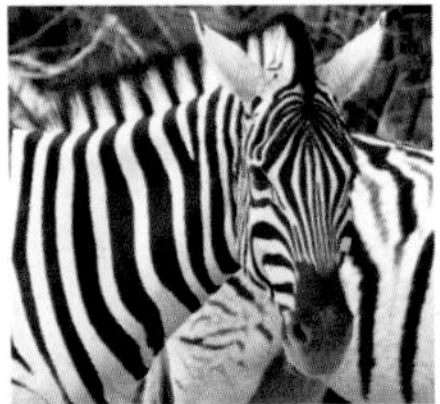
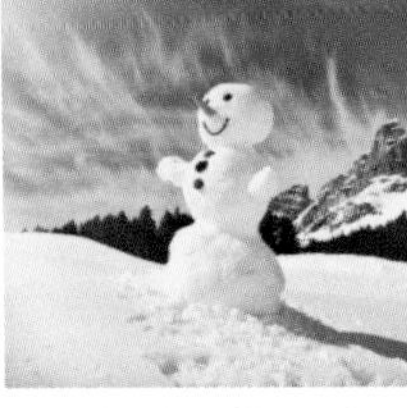

White is effective as a "noncolor," while black is effective for creating a poweful, bold look.

❶ Japanese Ink
Japanese ink is made from soot, glue and fragrance.

❷ Iron Black
A color name associated with the inorganic pigment of iron compound.

❸ Black Brown
A brown extremely close to black.

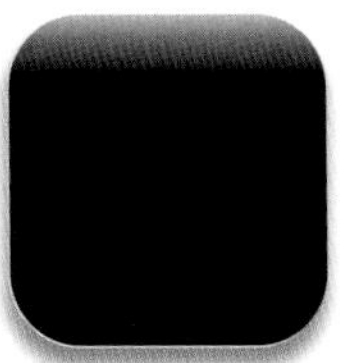

❹ Lamp Black
The color of black paint made from soot.

❺ Charcoal Gray
A gray that is nearly black.

⑥ Unbleached
Yarn or fabric that has not been scoured, dyed or treated.

⑦ Ivory
A color like an elephant's tusks. A light gray with a touch of yellow.

⑧ Paris White
Paris White or whitewash is made from crushed oyster shells.

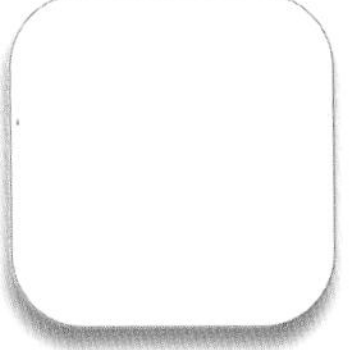

⑨ Snow White
A white like that of snow. In Japanese it's equivalent to pure white.

No.	CMYK	RGB	Hex
1	C0 M0 Y0 K95	R47 G39 B37	#2F2725
2	C0 M20 Y20 K98	R39 G18 B10	#27120A
3	C0 M40 Y50 K85	R75 G45 B22	#4B2D16
4	C0 M10 Y10 K100	R36 G19 B13	#24130D
5	C5 M15 Y0 K83	R78 G68 B73	#4E4449
6	C0 M0 Y5 K3	R251 G250 B243	#FBFAF3
7	C0 M1 Y12 K5	R248 G245 B227	#F8F5E3
8	C0 M0 Y2 K0	R255 G255 B252	#FFFFFC
9	C3 M0 Y0 K0	R250 G253 B255	#FBFDFF

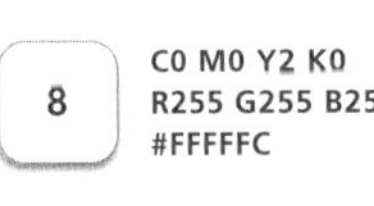
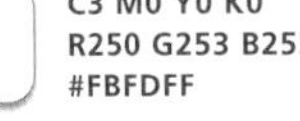

Two-color combinations

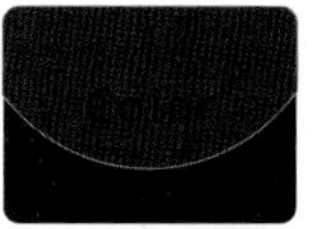

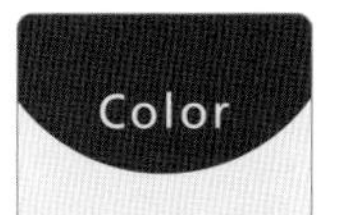
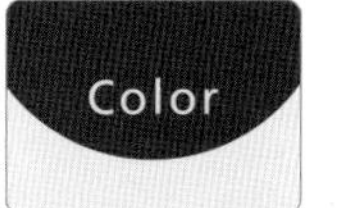

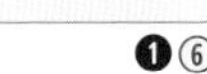

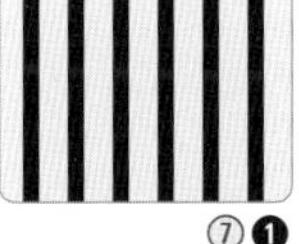

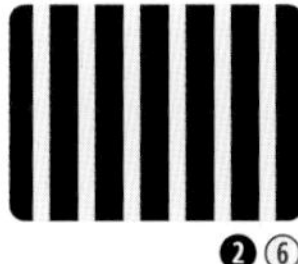
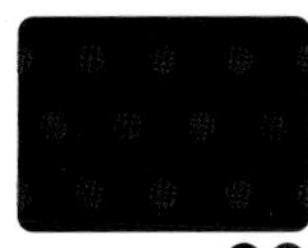
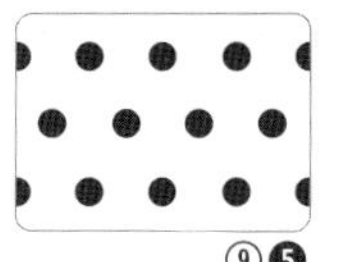
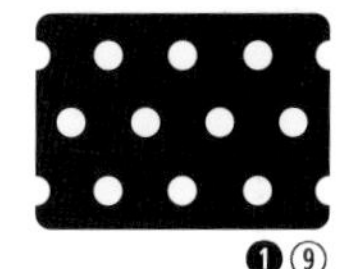

Three-color combinations

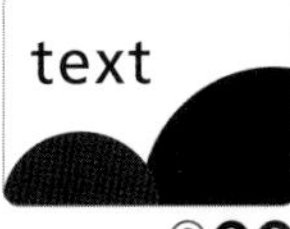

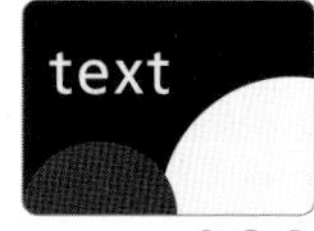

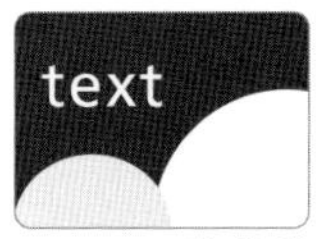

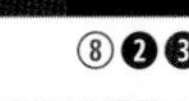

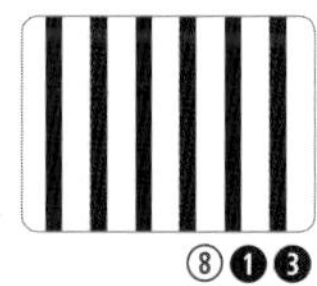
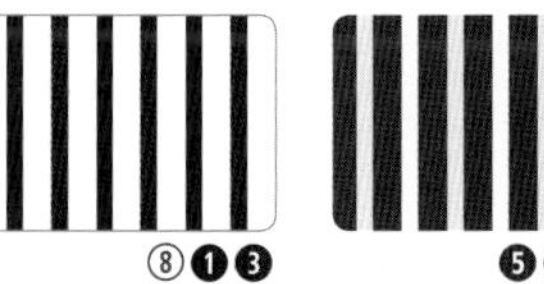
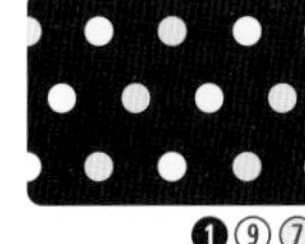
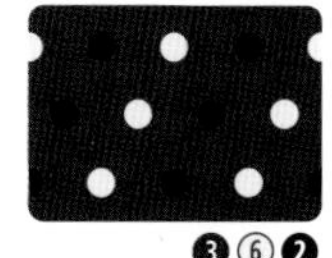
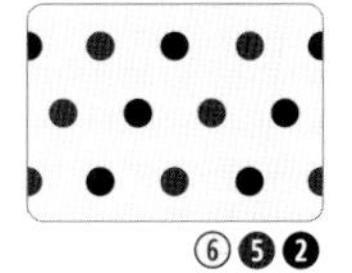

Designs

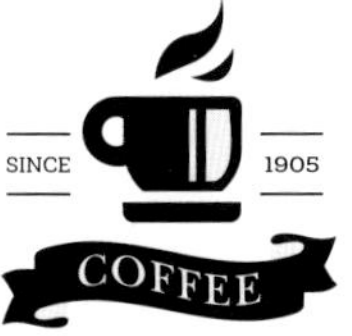

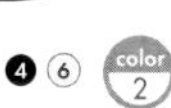
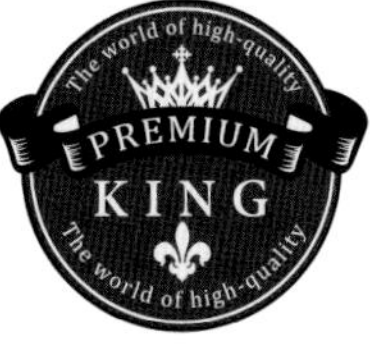

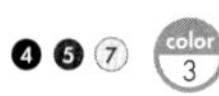
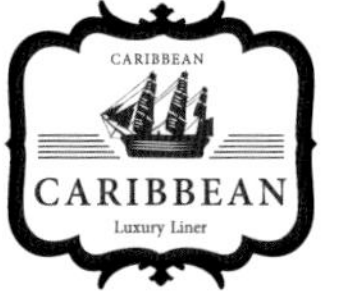

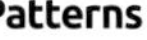

Patterns

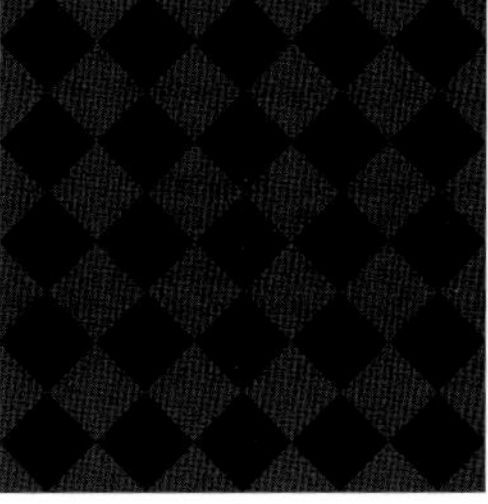
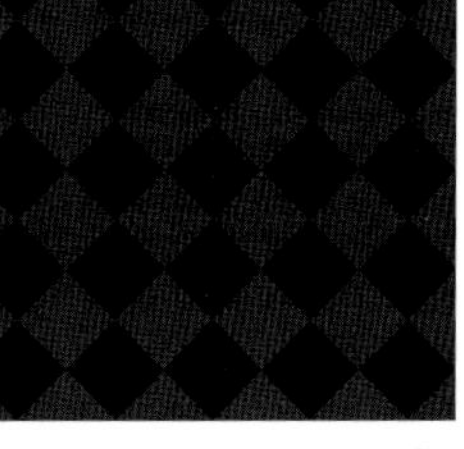
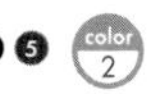
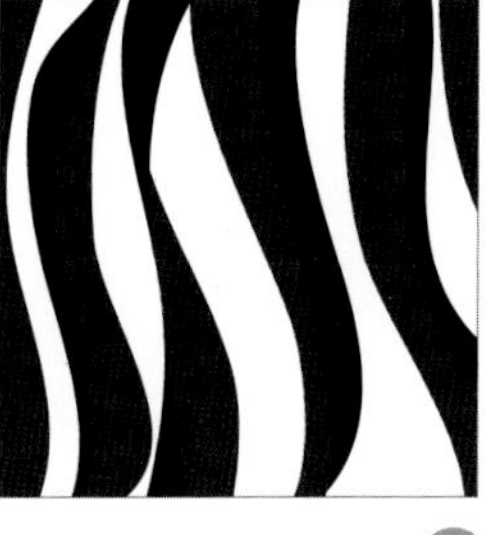
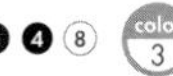
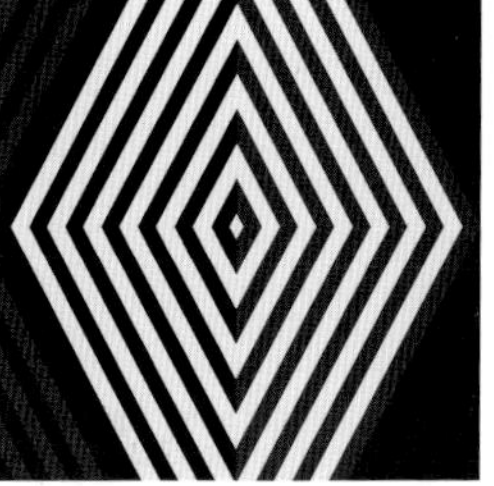

Illustration

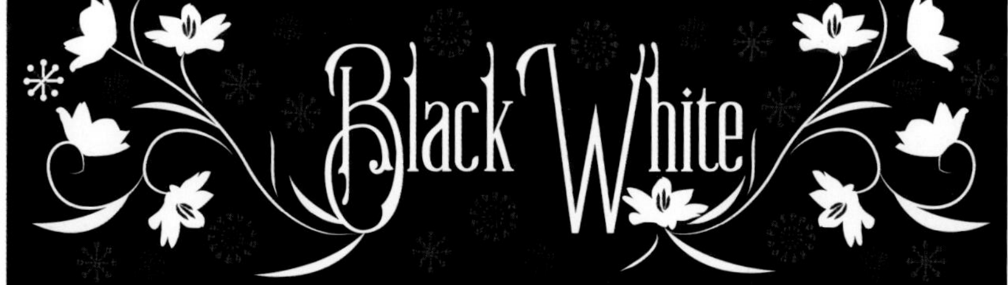

Recipe
126

Gold

This color has captured imaginations as it's associated with treasure, items of value and objects worth coveting. It has also been used by as a sign of power by rulers of the past, from ancient Egyptian pharaohs' tombs to Japanese regent Hideyoshi's gilded tea room as just two examples.

- **FEELING** Glorious, abundant, elite, fulfilled, mellow.
- **COMBINATIONS** Gold leaf, gold medal, ears of rice, festivals, champagne.
- **TIPS** Use gold to create the sense of something special or high quality.

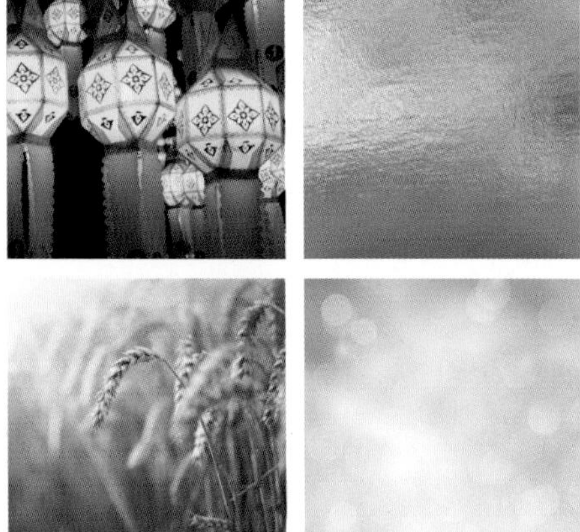

Gold is a symbol of both social status and material wealth.

❶ Golden Brown
The name for a brown with hints of gold.

❷ Turmeric
A clear yellow made with the dye from turmeric roots.

❸ Blonde
A color of flaxen hair. The word can also indicate a blonde-haired person.

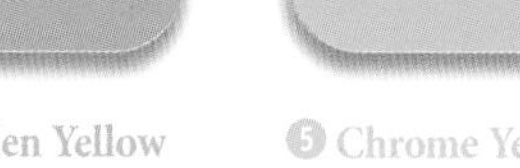

❹ Golden Yellow
Golden as in shining, glittering, having value.

❺ Chrome Yellow
As it contains lead, this color stopped being used in paints and varnishes.

❻ Bronze
The Japanese 10-yen coin is made of bronze.

❼ Raw Sienna
The color of earth from Italy's Sienna region.

❽ Yellow Ochre
This refers to ochre or loess.

❾ Naples Yellow
This refers to the Neapolitan shade.

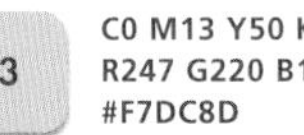
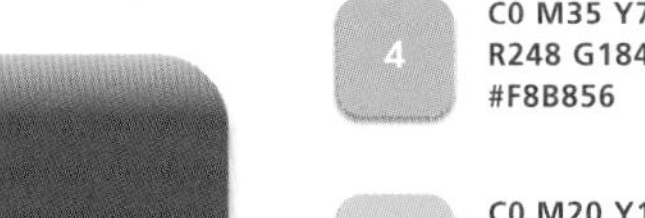
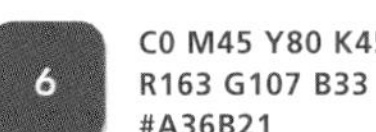

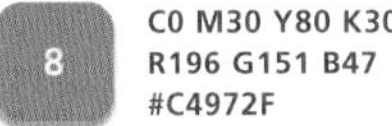

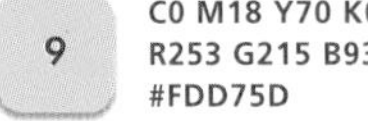

1 C0 M50 Y100 K10 R228 G142 B0 #E48E00

2 C0 M30 Y90 K0 R250 G191 B19 #FABF13

3 C0 M13 Y50 K5 R247 G220 B141 #F7DC8D

4 C0 M35 Y70 K0 R248 G184 B86 #F8B856

5 C0 M20 Y100 K0 R253 G208 B0 #FDD000

6 C0 M45 Y80 K45 R163 G107 B33 #A36B21

7 C0 M55 Y80 K15 R217 G128 B50 #D98032

8 C0 M30 Y80 K30 R196 G151 B47 #C4972F

9 C0 M18 Y70 K0 R253 G215 B93 #FDD75D

Two-color combinations

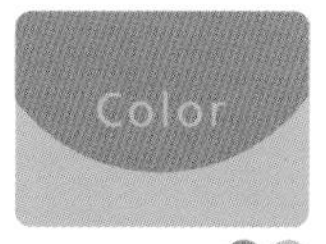

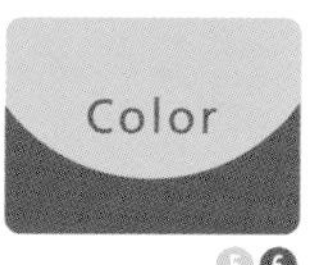

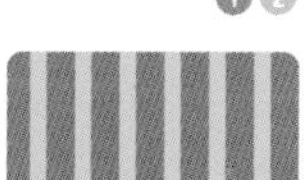

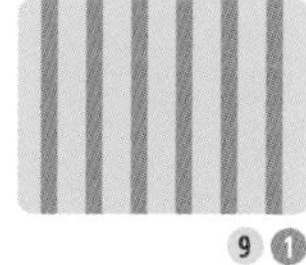

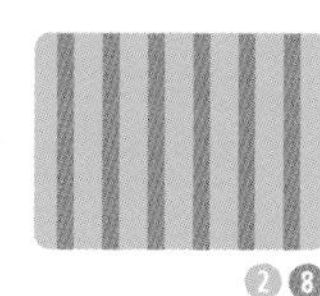

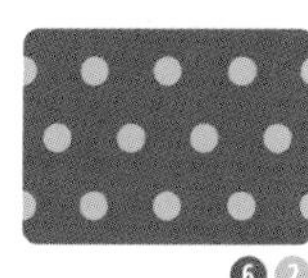

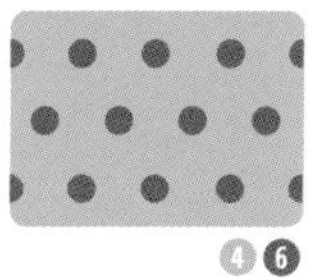

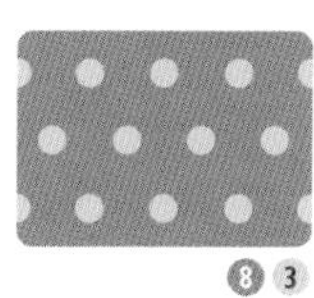

Three-color combinations

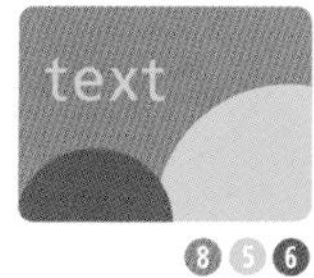

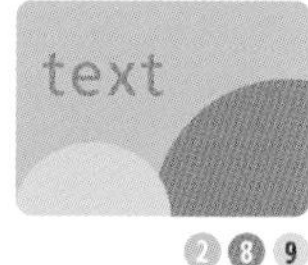

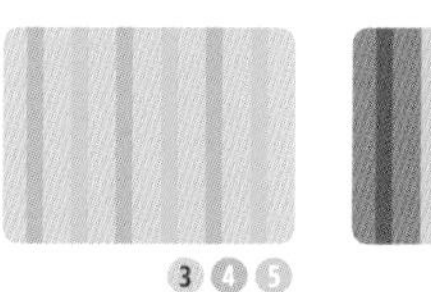

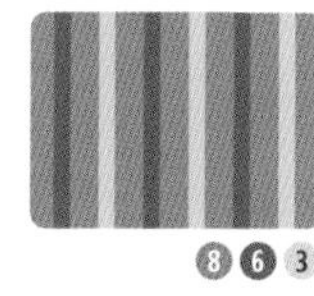

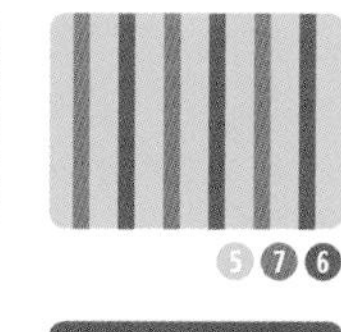

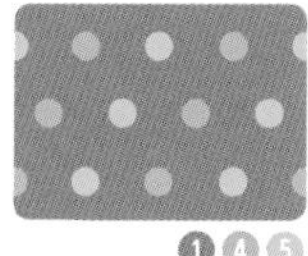

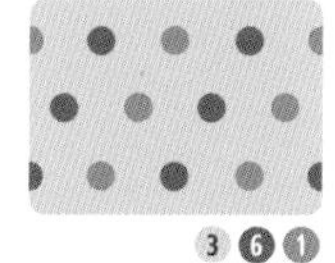

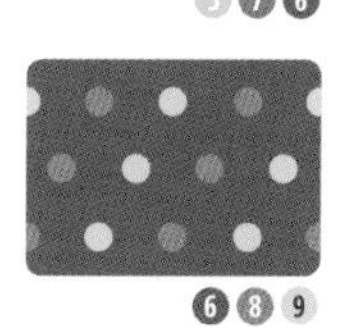

Designs

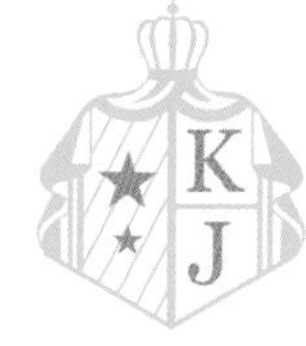

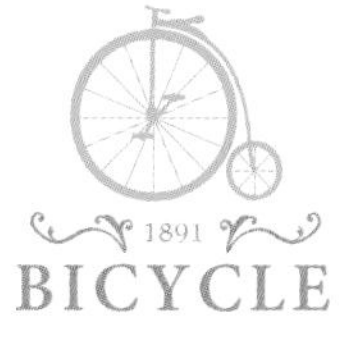

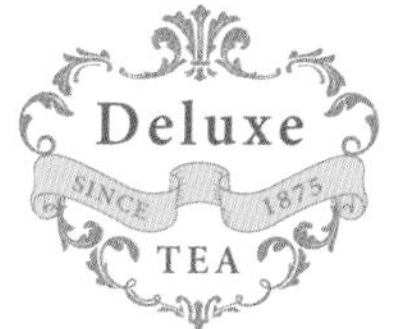

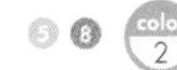

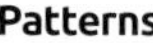

Patterns

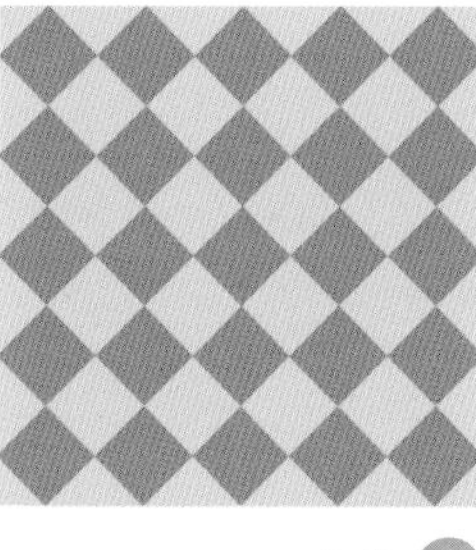

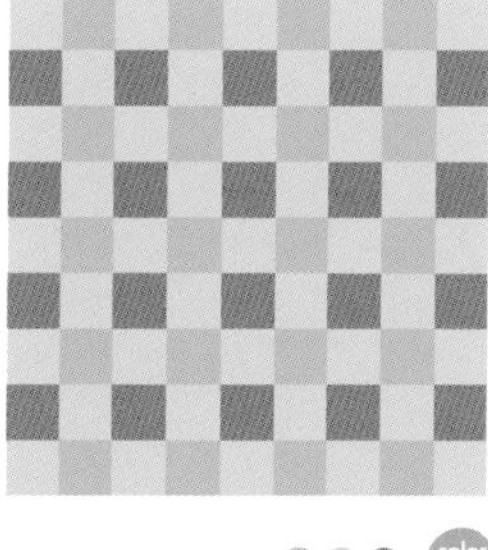

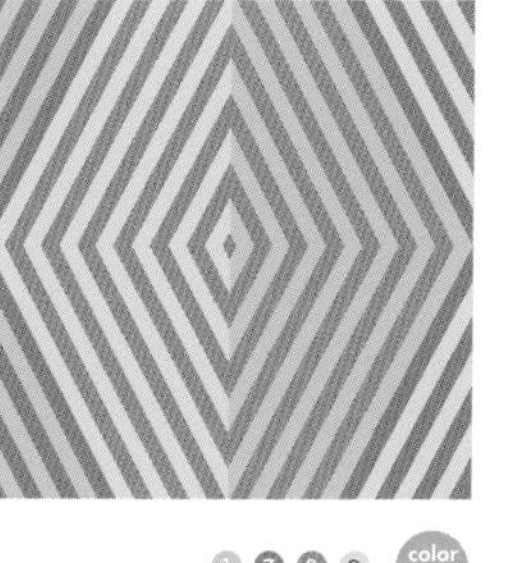

Illustration

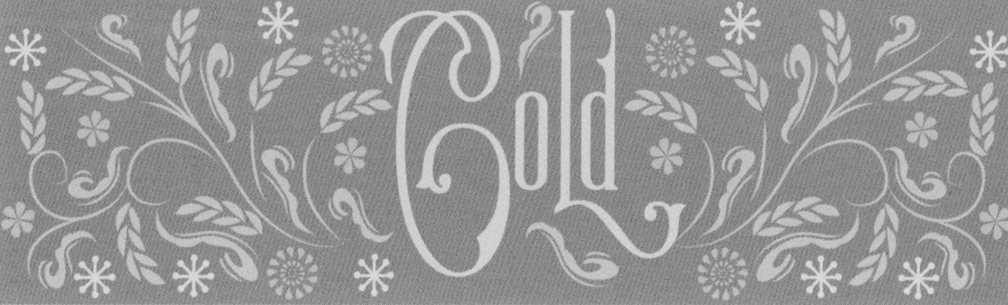

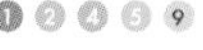

Recipe
127

Gray and Silver

Silver is often used to describe things relating to an advanced age, as is the color gray. That hue is created by mixing black and white, with light gray symbolically close to white and dark gray symbolically close to black. With a foot in both worlds, the range of possible grays and their attendant associations seem limitless.

- **FEELING** Moderate, refined, neutral, acceptable, uneasy.
- **COMBINATIONS** Clouded sky, concrete, mice, silver coins.
- **TIPS** Plays a side role to set off colors around it.

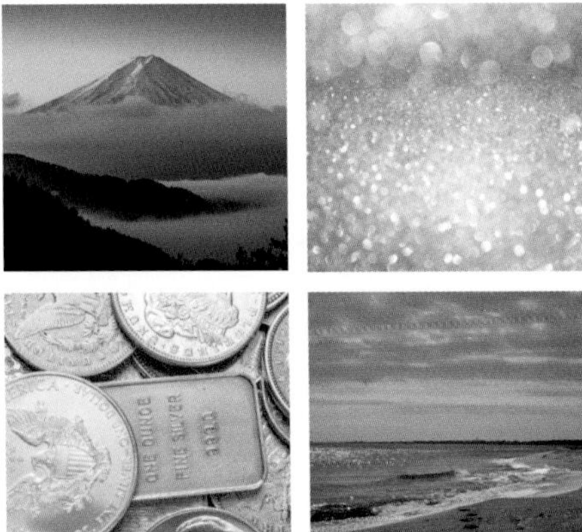

Sometimes an indistinct or hybrid color strikes the ideal balance in its blending of contrasting hues and effects.

❶ Mouse
A color like that of a rodent, used since olden times to indicate gray.

❷ Ash
The gray of ashes, a symbol of impurity or transformation.

❸ Rikyu Mouse
A color associated with Senno Rikyu to which gray has been added.

❹ Lead
A bluish gray like that of lead.

❺ Silver Mouse
Silvery in tone, this is a light gray.

❻ Brown Mouse
Close to brown, this is a gray with a sense of warmth.

❼ Sky Gray
A light bluish gray as seen in a sky with light cloud cover.

❽ Pearl Gray
A gray with a sense of luster like that of a pearl.

❾ Slate Gray
The color of slate shingles used on roofs.

No.	CMYK	RGB	Hex
1	C0 M0 Y0 K55	R148 G148 B149	#949495
2	C0 M0 Y0 K68	R118 G118 B118	#767676
3	C12 M0 Y20 K60	R123 G129 B116	#7B8174
4	C3 M0 Y0 K65	R122 G124 B125	#7A7C7D
5	C0 M0 Y0 K43	R175 G175 B176	#AFAFB0
6	C0 M10 Y15 K45	R169 G158 B147	#A99E93
7	C3 M0 Y0 K25	R206 G209 B211	#CED1D3
8	C0 M0 Y5 K30	R201 G201 B196	#C9C9C4
9	C5 M5 Y0 K75	R97 G95 B98	#615F62

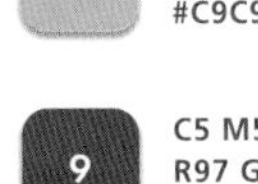
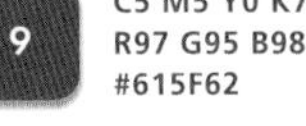

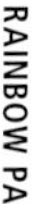

Two-color combinations

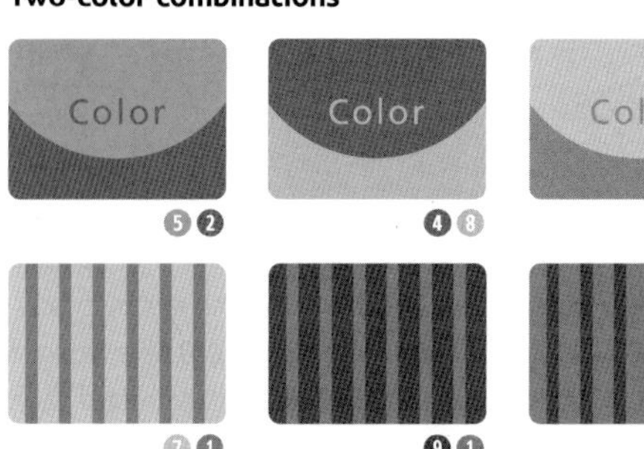

Three-color combinations

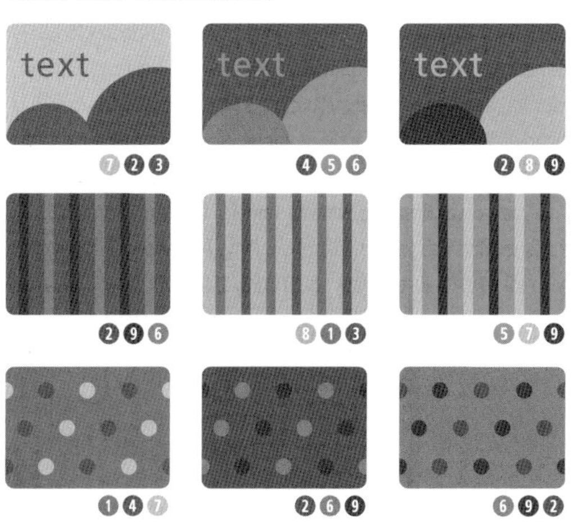

Designs

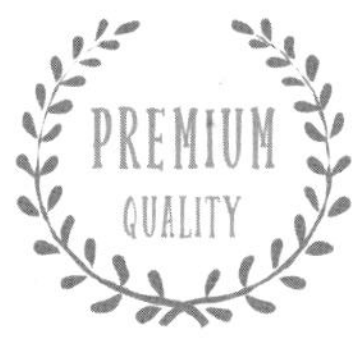

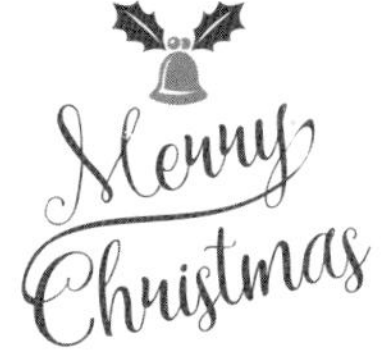

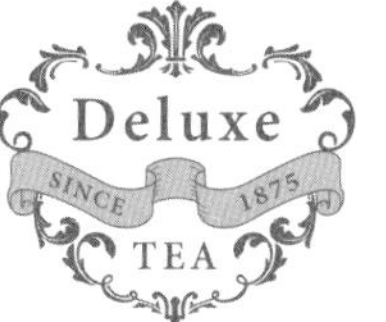

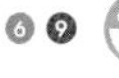

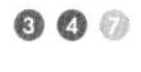

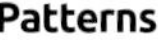

Patterns

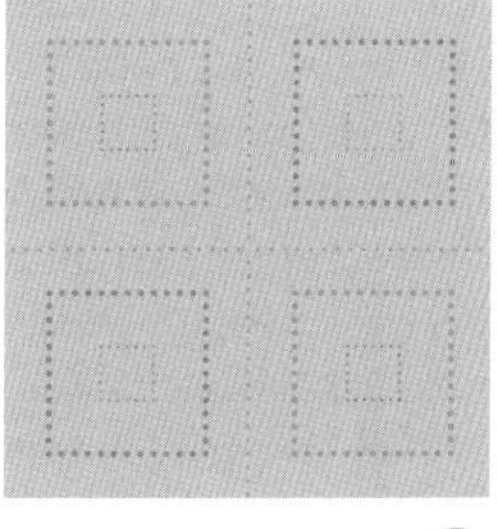

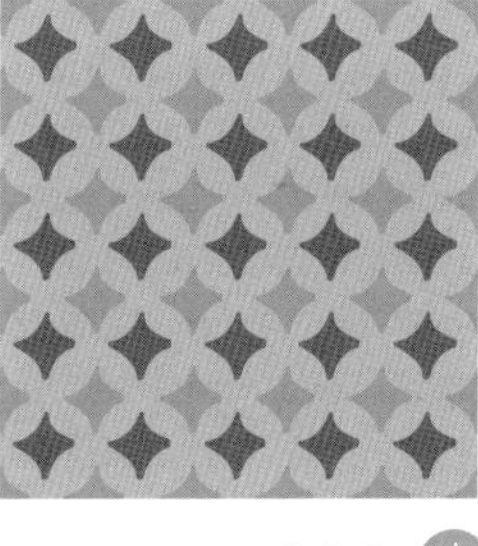

Illustration

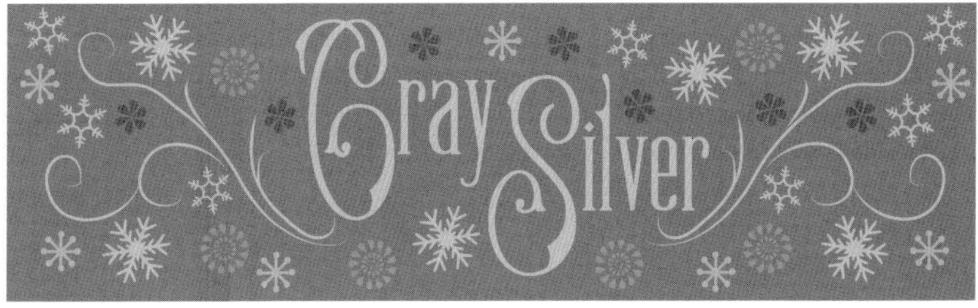

Photo Credits

Credit (URL: Shutterstock: https://www.shutterstock.com/ja PIXTA: https://pixta.jp)

P.15 djgis / **Part 01** Anna_Pustynnikova / **Part 02** KPG Payless2 / **Part 03** Dionisvera / **Part 04** canadastock / **Part 05** TatyanaMH / **Part 06** J. Palys / **Part 07** pondpony / **Part 08** Subbotina Anna / **Part 09** LedyX / **Part 10** Luciano Mortula – LGM / **Part 11** NOBUHIRO ASADA / **Part 12** optimarc / **Part 13** MemoriesStocker / **001** Login / **002** Teresa Kasprzycka / **003** Anna_Pustynnikova / **004** Vlad61 / **Front cover, 006** Meg Wallace Photography / **007** Kostikova Natalia, Leigh Prather / **008** JeJai Images / **009** Africa Studio / **010** Mike Richter / **011** Africa Studio, JeniFoto / **012** Oksana Alekseeva / **013** Tappasan Phurisamrit / **014** narinbg / **015** Ruth Black / **016** iravgustin / **017** Africa Studio / **018** Shebeko / **019** enchanted_fairy / **020** Johann Knox / **021** Tupungato / **022** Uximetc pavel / **023** 00coffeecat00 / **024** yuda chen, NoirChocolate / **025** Brian A Jackson / **026** aboikis, JurateBuiviene / **027** Creative Travel Projects / **028** SAPhotog / **029** mihaiulia / **030** Creative Travel Projects / **Front cover, 031** Pongpet Sodchern / **032** wada / **033** Triff / **034** Stockforlife / **035** JC Photo / **036** Forrest9 / **037** Scorpp / **038** OHishiapply / **039** Shulevskyy Volodymyr / **040** d_odin / **041** Seqoya / **042** matka_Wariatka, kubais / **043** Anna Leschenko / **044** MorganStudio, elgreko / **045** Tamara83 / **046** airdynamic / **047** Yuganov Konstantin / **048** Africa Studio / **049** Serhiy Shullye / **050** aaltair / **051** My Good Images / **052** LANBO / **053** Viktoriia Hnativ / **054** Tatiana Popova / **055** Olga Vasilyeva / **056** Keymetric / **057** IVANCHINA ANNA / **058** The Orange Turtle / **059** Pearl-diver / **060** Neale Cousland / **061** Andrey Armyagov / **062** Sandratsky Dmitriy / **063** Tomislav Pinter / **064** milka3, Chursina Viktoriia / **065** I. Pilon / **066** Naddya / **067** FamVeld / **068** Ori Artiste / **069** Shaiith / **070** Oktora, Ilkin Zeferli / **071** zhangyang13576997233 / **072** Triff / **073** Roman King / **074** littlenySTOCK / **075** silm, Mikhaylova Liubov / **Front cover, 076** Norikazu / **Front cover, 077** Sann von Mai, ziggy_mars / **078** zippig / **079** Sunny studio, m161m161 / **080** Patrick Foto / **081** aabeele, Artens / **082** Auttapon Nunti / **083** fotohunter, norikko / **084** alphabe / **085** AleksandraV / **086** Richard Yoshida / **087** TT69 / **088** Tsuguliev / **089** Nakcrub / **090** Krzyzak / **091** Efired / **092** Vaclav Volrab / **093** Stefano Termanini / **094** Martin M303 / **095** Gold Stock Images / **096** YaromirM / **098** Luciano Mortula – LGM / **099** standa_art / **100** EE SPACE, Marochkina Anastasiia / **101** Martyshova Maria / **102** gigirosado / **103** Andrei Verner / **104** Minii Ho / **105** melis / **108** Everett – Art / **110** Everett – Art / **111** Everett – Art / **P.15, 112** Kella Carlton, Blanscape, Room 76, Taku / **113** Alexandra Lande, Sakarin Sawasdinaka, Kanjanee Chaisin, villorejo / **114** Hanna_photo, Zhao jian kang, Shyvoronkova Kateryna, Still Life Photography / **115** Triff, Mark C. Morris, Kris Tan, Daxiao Productions / **116** khlongwangchao, Arayabandit, Potapov Alexander, Malyugin / **117** Lenka_X, MikeDrago.cz, MattheW-RK, fotohunter / **118** Only background, Evgeny Karandaev, Pakhnyushchy, pinkomelet / **119** Yarygin, Panu Ruangjan, Visual Intermezzo, ZoranKrstic / **120** creativenv, Picksell,Akita, nienora / **121** Yongcharoen_kittiyaporn, Dmitry Flasher, Nella, Brian A Jackson / **122** Roxana Bashyrova, Oksancia, Baleika Tamara, Thanayut Polyiem / **123** JBOY, Zamurovic Photography, pan demin, Petrut Romeo Paul / **124** Andrey Armyagov, patpitchaya, tgavrano, Triff / **125** Peter Radacsi, vector illustration, Pyty, Alexander Chaikin / **126** foxaon1987, letovsegda, Subbotina Anna, Iuliia Syrotina / **127** WorldWide, tomertu, Aleksandar Mijatovic, sebastianosecondi / **P240** Justin Black, BESTWEB, Jiffy Avri, Lisa S, sasaken, Darkkong, Tataya Kudo / Shutterstock.com, **107** J Williams / PIXTA (ピクスタ)